DEMOCRACY
AND
ACTION

This page left blank intentionally.

DEMOCRACY AND ACTION

Michael C. Petri

KENDALL/HUNT PUBLISHING COMPANY
4050 Westmark Drive   Dubuque, Iowa 52002

Contributors:
Dr. Christian Søe
Cynthia A.V. Azarcon
Noelle Seguin

Co-Contributors:
John E. Wills, MPA
Ali B. Taghavi, MA
Maura Priest

Editorial Staff:
Lead Editor: Cynthia A.V. Azarcon
Content Editor: John E. Wills, MPA

Design and Layout:
Initial Design: Cynthia A.V. Azarcon
Graphic Design and Layout: Mercedita V. Azarcon

Cover image (c) 2007 Jupiter Images Corporation
Inside cover map courtesy Central Intelligence Agency

Copyright © 2007 by Michael C. Petri

ISBN 13: 978-0-7575-4206-0
ISBN 10: 0-7575-4206-9

Printed in the United States of America
10 9 8 7 6 5 4 3 2 1

For Cynthia and Sarah whom I love very much.

This page left blank intentionally.

DEMOCRACY AND ACTION

Brief Table of Contents

Preface

In his book, *Corrupting Youth*, J. Peter Euben asks the question, "How do we 'make' someone better; 'make' them into good citizens?" This is a question that has been asked since the concept of government was developed. In democratic terms it means that we must find a way to keep the citizenry involved by instilling a sense of civic duty. If you haven't guessed by the title, the book is a call to action. Not one of violence but the power of the pen - or in techno-speak - the computer or PDA. The power of information is invaluable. The more informed you are the more power you have. My hope for this book is that it provides you with information and a unique perspective on models of democracy, both in the U.S. and abroad. It is up to you whether to use the information and put it into action or not.

For years we have heard political pundits talk about voter apathy. There are numerous explanations as to why people don't vote, ranging from lack of confidence in the system to a general malaise for politics all together. I do not subscribe to either of these defeatist attitudes. My position is if the system doesn't work, it's because we have failed in our duties to change it. If your vote doesn't count, then do something to make it count. If you don't care, think about your paycheck, gas prices, the wars in Iraq and Afghanistan, and maybe you will realize why you should care. It should be noted that this book was not written to attack anyone's political beliefs. It is meant to encourage deliberation and action.

Democracy & Action is designed to be an intelligent and thoughtful American Government textbook with a few surprises thrown in. The ironic thing about this project is that I never saw myself writing a textbook, let alone about American Government. My areas of expertise include Comparative Politics, Political Theory, Gender Studies, and Public Policy. But, the more I tried to develop my classes with these disciplines in mind, the longer the list of required books. As the prices of all these books skyrocketed, I felt frustrated and found the situation to be unacceptable. I am hoping that students and professors alike will see that this is really three books in one and that the content, as well as the price, are satisfactory.

Practical Application

The text begins by examining the general concepts of American Government and with each chapter, gradually moves into the specifics and develops the over-arching theme of Deliberative Democracy. Each chapter opens with a "vignette" or brief description of specific current events and how they relate to the theme of America's ongoing quest for Democracy. Then it moves in to the main focus of the chapter. Throughout each chapter there are "Profiles in Politics" to help inspire students with examples of extraordinary figures throughout history. In addition there are featured articles called "For Your Consideration" which help the student understand principles of democracy in practical terms. Throughout the book you will find side-bar questions called "Issues for You", which guide students' to a higher level of critical thinking. The questions are useful for ice-breakers or when breaking the class into discussion groups.

Issues in State & Local Government

I am very excited to present a California section in each chapter. After reading about the federal government, students will find that the California sections serve as a roadmap as to how the federal and state governments differ and how they are alike. This will help students apply lessons in democracy to local government issues. This reinforces key concepts and themes that were initially discussed in regards to the federal government.

Comparative Politics & Political Theory

I included a comparative section in each chapter to open up a forum for the students to use their analytical skills. Discussing foreign governments can be a daunting task for students and even professors sometimes, so I believe these sections are rich with possibilities. With some countries, the comparisons between the United States and the featured country are quite striking. For other countries, the political events were so dense that it was simpler to just focus on overarching themes in their development rather than compare and contrast in a more traditional back and forth manner. Either way, I believe the comparative country sections will provide students with a deeper insight to the many different cultures, values, and political institutions around them.

Companion Website & Technology

In addition to all of the above, the book comes with a companion website that was developed specifically for this text. It is easily adaptable for in class or online use as the website is set up for accessibility that is as effortless as possible. The companion website is designed for the modern student with interactive exercises, step-by-step study guides, reading and writing exercises, eBook, pre-/post-tests, and access to an online library for more in-depth research. Each companion chapter is designed to accommodate PowerPoint presentations, instructor's manual with suggested assignments, test banks, research aids, and simulations.

One of the questions that I constantly hear from students is how can one person make a difference? To answer this question, I challenge the students to first think of the changes they'd like to see around them and then think about the smallest easiest step they could take to make them happen. Invariably, the student realizes of their own accord that taking action is easy and that standing idly by certainly doesn't accomplish anything at all. I also remind them that change comes slowly, but if we persevere, we always have options. If you look throughout history, you'll see how one person can and has made a difference. Whether it is Alice Stone Blackwell, who championed universal suffrage; Rosa Parks, who refused to give up her seat on a bus; Caesar Chavez, who lead the farm labor movement; or Earl Warren, who ended segregation in California and later in schools throughout the nation; each of these individuals and many others made a difference by taking a stand.

Acknowledgements

Why did I write this textbook? Well, there is the obvious answer - the books that I have used in the past were, in their own right, very good; however, I often found them lacking in certain areas. I didn't feel that they were in line with the direction I wanted to go, so here we are. The less obvious reasons that I jumped at the opportunity to write a textbook are personal in nature. In high school, my guidance counselor looked me in the eye and said that the best thing for me to do was to join the Marine Corps and become 'cannon fodder'. Conversely, another teacher, who saw potential in me that I didn't even see, took me aside and said that if I took one class with him every semester (Shakespeare, more Shakespeare, and modern literature!), he would work with me to make sure I graduated. This book is not only a triumph for me personally but a symbol of gratitude for all the teachers who have supported me along the way.

On to my acknowledgments. I would like to first acknowledge the following authors who have provided me with insight on how to structure my book: Michael Parenti, Edward Greenberg, Benjamin Page, John J. Harrigan, Thomas Dye, Michael Roskin, and Christian Søe. I would also like to thank all of the book and technical representatives from *other* publishers – you know who you are. They have provided much needed guidance and assistance over the years. To the good folks at Kendall/Hunt Publishing: Patti Deutmeyer, Billie Jo Hefel, Karen Hoffman, Renae Horstman, Janice Samuells, and Michael Volk and all other staff diligently working behind the scenes – thank you all very much.

I would like to thank all of my instructors, colleagues, associates, friends, and the department/division secretaries and assistants who have kept me in touch with "reality" as I've ventured along my path. To all of them, a heartfelt thanks: Barry Grimes, Gerry Riposa, Mary Caputi, Barry Steiner, Chris Dennis, Charles Noble, John Ostroski, Bill Moore, Peter Mathews, Kevin Eperjesi, Amy Pritchett, Danny Lind, Mike Flores, Fola Odebunmi, Betty Disney, Nina DeMarkey, Cameron Hastings, Narges Niedzwiecki, Lee Haggerty, Alannah Rosenberg, Ina Hutchison, Heidi Berry, Kristine and Steve West, Ellen Teneriello, Michele Mumm, LeAndre Turner, Judith Barthell, Nancy St. Martin, Robin Quark, Shawn Bauer, Deborah Chennault, Cynthia Roberts, Sue Brown, Michelle Lucus, Nancy Pound, and Pam Bettendorf. A special note of thanks to Edwin Roberts and Frank Baber who peaked my interest in and kept me focused on the theories of deliberative democracy; Patricia Flannigan, who allowed and encouraged me to develop and teach a variety of political science courses; and David Phillips, Ken Graham and Larry Twicken, who took me under their wings and helped me develop as an instructor, met with me throughout my formidable years, and imparted their wisdom and insight upon me.

To Ashraf Elgohary and the crew at Computech, thank you for keeping the computers running and for reviving our challenged network system during "crunch time"! Also, my family and I would like to send out a big thank you to all those who contributed to the book and supported this project in a variety of ways: Noelle Seguin, John Wills, Lloyd and Claudia Hastings, Jennifer Navarro, Bruce Ladd, Steve Carne, Sander R. Wolff, Tony King, MaryLou Hein, Chelsea and David Isaacs, Martee and Steve Nott, Lurene Witten, Rick Uhls, Suzanne Barron, all of our friends at BHUMC, and other friends and family members too numerous to mention, thank you all for your unwavering support and love.

Thanks to Ali B. Taghavi who spent countless hours over the years listening to my rants and sharing my joys during graduate school, research, relationships, the birth of my daughter, my wedding to Cynthia, and now with this book – we made it! To Mercy Azarcon, thank you for shouldering the heavy load of graphic design and layout beneath crushing deadlines. Despite all the madness – it's beautiful.

I owe a great debt of gratitude to Dr. Christian Søe who mentored me in comparative politics as well as shared invaluable research methods in the field with me. Dr. Søe provided exceptional support and input on the comparative sections, which are sprinkled with clever anecdotes, some of which have been incorporated into the text.

To the students and professors who will be using this book in their studies – may you find it resourceful and insightful.

I thank my enduring family who have not only developed my political and rhetorical skills but who have been there in the good and not so good times. I grew up in a military family, with generations of my family serving our country from the beginning to the present day. I credit my family for my strong sense of civic duty and honor, especially to my mother who made us idealists and my father who kept us firmly rooted in the ground. I also thank all of my siblings, Cecilia, Barbara, Alma, Lawren, Larry Jr., Albert, James, Erin, Harold, Mary, and Marian (yes, it's true, all from the same parents), and all of my nieces and nephews who have carried on the family tradition of free speech and political discourse.

And of course, last but not least, to Cynthia and Sarah who tried hard to allow me my solitude, endured me taking the laptop to family events, put up with me missing family outings all together, and helping me produce a quality book – thank you for giving me strength and love when I needed it and a kick in the butt when it was warranted.

Michael C. Petri

About the Author

MICHAEL C. PETRI is a passionate advocate for deliberative democracy. His conversational teaching style, ability to illustrate complex concepts to students of all levels and ages, and use of the Socratic Method in the classroom are received by students and faculty with enthusiasm and intrigue. For his relentless dedication to the teaching profession and to the improvement of his department, he received an Academic Leadership Award from the Social and Behavioral Sciences department at Saddleback College in Mission Viejo, California.

Mr. Petri's participation in local politics has made him well-versed in California government. At the California State University, Long Beach, he received degrees in the following programs: a Bachelor of Arts in Political Science emphasizing Political Theory, Comparative Politics, and International Relations and a Master of Arts in Political Science with emphases in Political Theory, American Government, and International Relations and a Certificate in Peace Studies. After receiving his MA, he went on to obtain a Master in Public Administration, in which he focused on Information Technology Systems (ITS) and Geographic Information Systems (GIS). This experience is now used in support of his lectures and research on redistricting, voting behaviors, and deliberative democracy models. At the behest of the Dean of the Social & Behavioral Sciences division at Saddleback, he created online courses that meet UC and CSU articulation requirements. Since working closely with deans and fellow colleagues, Mr. Petri's expertise in the area of technology in the classroom, both traditional and on-line, is in high demand.

His teaching experience covers many fields in political science. At Cypress College in Cypress, California, he teaches Introduction to Political Theory and American Government. At Saddleback College, he teaches the aforementioned courses and also Comparative Politics, Gender and Politics, Middle Eastern Politics, and introductory classes in Political Science, Public Administration, and Honor's Political Theory. Due to Mr. Petri's fervor for the life of academia, he continually seeks to study many varied subjects and communities that make up our democracy. Under the tutelage of Dr. Mary Caputi, he studied Political Theory and Gender and Politics. Subsequently, he appeared as a guest lecturer, speaking on "Empowerment of Women in Politics, based on European Models," for former professor and leading scholar in Women's Studies, Dr. Betty Brooks. These valuable experiences brought him to develop an unprecedented course devoted entirely to Gender and Politics. It will be offered for the first time at Cypress College in the fall of 2007.

When it appeared that an "outbreak of peace" between Israel and the Palestinians in the early 1990's was on the horizon, there was a glimmer of hope for amicable resolutions and, as Samuel Huntington might say, a "third wave" of democratization, among many Arab nations and former Soviet republics. It was at this time that Mr. Petri developed an interest in Middle Eastern Politics, and less than a decade later, the tragedy of 9/11 struck. After hearing students express many concerns and questions about the tragedy, Mr. Petri began developing a course on Middle Eastern Politics. Seeing that Cypress College could benefit from such a course, he proposed that the class be incorporated into the Political Science curriculum. The course was approved in 2007 and its projected launch date is fall 2008 at Cypress College.

Past partnerships in collaborating have included his work as a research aide for *Annual Editions: Comparative Politics* (Dubuque: McGraw-Hill) with the editor, his mentor, Dr. Christian Søe. After the launch of *Democracy and Action*, his first textbook, Mr. Petri is setting his sights on writing textbooks on California Politics, Introduction to Political Science, and Comparative Politics.

This page left blank intentionally.

New York City, 1909
Two young girls stand out in a crowd of protesters.
Their banners read "ABOLISH CHILD SLAVERY!!" in both Yiddish and English.
Courtesy of the Library of Congress

CHAPTER 1

THE CITIZEN AND GOVERNMENT

CHAPTER OUTLINE

- THE RIGHT TO VOTE AND ELECTRONIC VOTING
- WHY DO WE NEED GOVERNMENT?
- INTRODUCTION TO DEMOCRACY
- TYPES OF DEMOCRATIC GOVERNMENTS
- HOW DO WE COMPARE?
  AN INTRODUCTION TO COMPARATIVE POLITICS

The Right to Vote and Electronic Voting

The right to vote is taken for granted by many people in the United States nowadays. However, the right to vote, or **universal suffrage**, is one of the minimum requirements needed by citizens in order to control their government in a democracy. Many groups had to fight long and hard to receive the right to vote, and with each advancement of technology, there is worry that we are perhaps increasingly disenfranchising voters.

Our founding fathers at first did not offer the right to vote to all citizens of their new union - only white male landowners were given that privilege. However, the founders did relinquish to the individual states the right to decide who is allowed to vote. During the first half of the 19th century, there was much political infighting regarding the removal of property requirements for white males. This was finally realized in the 1850s, prior to the Civil War.

Following the Civil War and the technical end of slavery, the Fifteenth Amendment was ratified. The Amendment afforded all males over the age of 21 the right to vote, "regardless of race, color, or previous condition of servitude." This was the first time the Constitution set a determining measure on suffrage, instead of deferring to the states. This upset many southern states, and, in retaliation, implemented laws which have become known as **Jim Crow laws** in an attempt to prevent black men from exercising their right to vote. These laws included intimidation tactics such as a **poll tax** required of all voters. Newly freed slaves were unable to pay such a tax and were therefore denied the right to vote. Another popular tactic was a voter literacy test, which is a test administered by local officials. These officials rarely allowed blacks to pass, regardless of their level of education. However, if a white man failed, that man could still vote under the **grandfather clause**, which provided that all men whose ancestors had voted prior to 1867 would be able to vote as well. In addition to these laws and intimidation by the Ku Klux Klan, many black voters were disenfranchised for approximately the next 100 years. This disenfranchisement was not remedied until the Civil Rights Act, the Voting Rights Act, and the 24th Amendment, all passed between 1964 and 1965.

Officially, women were not allowed to vote (with very little and short-lived exceptions) until the early 20th century. When the Constitution was being drafted, Abigail Adams wrote several letters to her husband, John Adams, who was one of the Framers. In these letters she reminded him of the role women played during the Revolution. Abigail reminded him that "the ladies" should not be forgotten when it was decided who should have the right to vote in the fledgling nation. She also gently asserted that decisions should not be left in the hands of men alone because by their "sex [they] are naturally tyrannical." As history shows, her plea fell on deaf ears. However, in the 19th century, women became outspoken visible leaders in many political movements, including the abolition movement, the temperance movement, and of course, the women's suffrage movement. In 1869, Wyoming Territory became the first to allow women the right to vote, shortly followed by Utah, Colorado, and Idaho. The women's suffrage movement fought hard for more than 150 years and finally gained the full-fledged right to vote across the nation with the passages of the Nineteenth Amendment in 1920.

Courtesy of the Library of Congress

Universal Suffrage – That everyone must have the right to vote.

Jim Crow Laws – Laws passed by southern states that separated the races in public places such as railroads, streetcars, schools, and cemeteries.

Poll Tax – A fee that had to be paid before one could vote; used to prevent African Americans from voting; now unconstitutional.

Literacy Test – A test that required voting applicants to demonstrate an understanding of national and state constitutions. Primarily used to prevent African Americans from voting in the South.

Grandfather Clause – A device that allowed whites who had failed the literacy test to vote anyway by extending the franchise to anyone whose ancestors voted prior to 1867.

Lastly, the 26th Amendment was ratified in 1971. This lowered the voting age from 21 years to 18, the age at which one reaches adulthood.

With all the strife that Americans have endured to guarantee any person of adult age the right to vote, one would think that this right is a fairly secure one. Unfortunately, with the advancement of technology, new voting machines have once again brought the fear of **disenfranchisement** to the forefront of voting.

Since the 2000 election, most states have implemented use of at least some direct-recording electronic voting systems. These appropriately named systems directly record each vote as it is cast into their servers, most leaving no paper trail behind for verification. This has caused much controversy, because, as seen in many computer-based machines, there is always the possibility of 'bugs' affecting the data. In a democracy, where one of the

Courtesy of the Library of Congress

Disenfranchisement – Preventing the right to vote to a person or group of people. It may occur explicitly through law, or implicitly through means such as intimidation.

most treasured rights is exercising the right to vote, the integrity of the electronic ballot poses a myriad of questions about the accuracy of the vote count. Without a paper trail to confirm the count, there is no guarantee that a true count has been tabulated - how many votes may have been lost due to malfunction? Has each vote been correctly logged into the proper category according to the voter's intention? Can these machines be easily manipulated?

The main question becomes, how can we make sure that each vote is secure, private, and counted correctly? Some states have addressed this problem by including some form of paper audit trail that works in conjunction with the machines. These paper trails are not traceable back to the individual voter, thus protecting the privacy of the ballot. Additionally, they provide a secure compartment where the voter can actually verify their vote on the paper log in addition to digitally confirming their choice. This remedy is, at the present time, the most logical and accurate one; however, in a world of rapidly changing technology, there may yet be a better way for the citizens of a democracy to exercise their right to vote.

Why Do We Need Government?

No one pretends that democracy is perfect or all wise.
Indeed, it has been said that democracy is the worst form of Government
except all those other forms that have been tried from time to time.
~ Winston Churchill

Preamble to the Constitution of the United States of America

We the people of the United States, in Order to form a more perfect Union, establish Justice, insure domestic Tranquility, provide for the common defense, promote the general Welfare and secure the Blessing of Liberty to ourselves and our Posterity, do ordain and establish this Constitution of the United States of America.

Natural Rights –
A right that everyone has by way of being human - they cannot be granted or taken away by anyone or any political authority.

As you will see in various examples throughout the book, all governments perform the same tasks. For example, some of these tasks are national defense (both foreign and domestic) and social welfare policies. In order to pay for these programs, governments must collect taxes. The United States government is no different than other governments with regards to these tasks. What set the United States apart from other countries in the late 1700's was our belief that government is meant to serve the people, deriving its power from the consent of the people. The preamble is the peoples' contract with the government. We the people, consent to be governed as long as government fulfills their part of the contract. To fully understand this, one must examine the components in greater detail. To further elaborate, the purpose of government as identified in the Preamble to the Constitution of the United States is to:

Establish Justice and Insure Domestic Tranquility

Some of the government's responsibilities are to maintain order and security. Because of this, the Constitution may be seen as a social contract, in which people allow themselves to be ruled in exchange for protection of their property and lives. No civil society can allow the vigilante justice that arises as a result of the "state of nature," as described by philosopher Thomas Hobbes. For Hobbes the current state of civil society was intolerable. After many bloody years of English civil wars, he wanted to clarify the political authority figurehead and how they came to obtain their power. In Hobbes' book, the *Leviathan* (1651), Hobbes wrote that in the state of nature, man is in a constant state of war of all against all. In the state of nature, man has **natural rights** and these rights equate to doing whatever he wishes. Because of this combative state of being, life is nothing but "solitary, poorer nasty, brutish, and short."[1] In order for man to gain safety from these evils in the state of nature, he entered into a social contract with the government - he surrendered to the king, all of his rights except for one - the right to defend himself in order to gain security. Thus, government is founded on the consent of the people. Government will remain in power as long as it protects the individual. In exchange, the sovereign will do whatever it takes to provide security and in return, the people will do as the sovereign commands, including worshiping they way the king desires. For Hobbes, religious difference was one of the major sources of conflict; therefore, it should be removed from the equation.

Profiles in Politics
Socrates (470-399 BCE)

"El Socrates," by A. Bijur. Entered into the Library of Congress in 1859

What might happen to you if you are a man living during the time of Ancient Greece who says that rain comes from precipitation instead of the gods, humans can become god-like, and that your mission in life is to expose the ignorance of those who think themselves wise? 6-feet-under, you say? Exactly. The engaging and influential thinker, Socrates, lived in ancient Athens during the fifth century BCE. What we have come to know about Socrates is based on the writings of Xenophon and Plato. During his early schooling as a pupil of Archelaus, Socrates had a great interest in the scientific theories of Anaximenes, who, it is believed, was the first to state that condensation or mist was a product of the natural world, rather than a mystical deity-inspired phenomenon. Socrates' interest in the natural sciences was futher incited by his grueling experiences as a soldier during the Peloponnesian War.   Years later, Socrates would abandon this research to pursue answers to his deepening queries of morality.

Socrates is known for his critical evaluation of truth. The need for higher education for the male citizenry came with the development of an Athenian democracy. To fill this void, traveling teachers called Sophists emerged to teach the fine art of glib speech and rhetoric. The goal was to teach the men to win arguments during assemblies and courts, regardless of whether their arguments were based on truth or not. Socrates challenged this practice by pointing out that every man should be responsible for their own moral code. He separated himself from the pragmatic Sophists by saying that it was the pursuit of understanding and knowledge that was, in itself, a moral, intellectual, and virtuous quest.

His method of public speaking and unique teaching style have become known as the "Socratic method." The Socratic method is learner-centered, rather than a straight lecture style of teaching. For example, with instructor-centered teaching, the instructor simply presents the subject matter and dominates the entire discussion. With the Socratic method, the teacher initiates discussion by asking students to ponder a series of questions or hypotheses, thereby skillfully guiding the students to acquire knowledge using their own critical and analytical thinking. All the while, the student may be unaware that the instructor is navigating the whole discussion with questions until the student comes upon that 'eureka' moment themselves.

Socrates spent his time discussing with the youth of Athens the conventional wisdom of the times, mainly focusing on developing democratic style of government and the chaos that ensued after the war. Due to his loathing of material successes, he offered his teaching services free of charge, despite his dire financial situation. As Socrates' following increased and his controversial ideas became widespread, this greatly confounded the existing leadership. They became so enraged with Socrates that they wanted to silence him. However, they were prevented from doing so due to an amnesty in 405 BCE, which prevented the direct prosecution of political activities. Therefore, the leadership found a way to bring him to trial by charging him with corrupting the youth and introducing strange gods through his theories on natural sciences. During his trial, Socrates challenged his accusers by using their arguments against them. When charged with introducing strange gods, Socrates responded by telling them that there was no need for the disturbance. He continued by saying that a reputable friend of his and of the court had approached the oracle at Delphi and was told that there was no man wiser than [Socrates]. Socrates told the court that he could not believe this to be true, so he set out on an "investigation" searching for someone wiser. After speaking with a variety of people, Socrates came to "ask himself, on behalf of the oracle, whether I should prefer to be as I am…The answer I gave myself and the oracle was that it was to my advantage to be as I am." It was sarcastic comments like these that seemed to get Socrates into trouble. After the trial concluded, he was convicted by a jury of 501 members to be sentenced to death in 399 BCE. Gracefully accepting his sentence, Socrates drank a cup of hemlock while surrounded by his family, friends, and students.

To provide for common defense

As we have experienced for the last two hundred years, government from time to time must go to war or engage in some form of conflict in order to protect the nation. In order for government to insure a swift response to threats, it must provide for a standing military. A standing military is one in which men and women are on active duty and reserve duty; they are prepared to deploy at any time. Today, the federal (national) government is responsible for providing protection against threats to our nation. The cost of defending the nation is always expensive. In 2006, according to the Office of Management and Budget (OMB), the government spent approximately 410.8 billion dollars on defense and has requested 439.3 billion dollars for the Department of Defense for the 2007 Fiscal Year. This is a 6.9% increase in spending as compared to the 2006 Fiscal Year.[2]

To promote the general welfare

The government promotes the general welfare by providing for public goods and services. These goods and services could not profitably be provided by the private sector, such as roads/highways, clean air/water, and public schools. Although we live in a free market economy, the market does not meet the needs of the public because of lack of profit. Herein lies the difference between the private sector (business) and the public sector (government agencies). The private sector must maintain profits for the shareholders. If a company is not profitable, they will lose investors and eventually be out of business. In contrast, the government is in charge of providing for the public good, regardless of the cost. These costs are covered through various taxes. For example, when you fill up your car's gas tank, you pay both a federal tax and a state tax. These taxes are applied toward maintaining roads, highways, bridges, and other infrastructure projects.

In addition, the government uses taxes to redistribute wealth. Income tax is a progressive tax, which means it takes money from the wealthy and redistributes it to social programs for groups of people who qualify for these programs. Examples of this would be Social Security and Medicare, which are paid to the elderly regardless of their personal wealth. Some may call this transfer unfair to those who earn it. How can we justify taxing a physician who makes mid-six figures when she had to go to expensive medical schools and has rightfully earned her money? The answer is found in a theory by John Rawls called the "veil of ignorance."

In his book, *Theory of Justice,* Rawls states that in the veil of ignorance, a person does not know what they will be born into or what attributes they will have: class position, social status, natural talents and abilities, intelligence, strength, and so on. The individual's success is based on society's designs at large. It is out of these designs that programs for the greater good emerge - such as, better education, health care, social welfare, and career placement assistance. Rawls continues with the idea that because people are under a veil of ignorance, they will end up designing a society that will be fair to all for fear of ending up in an intolerable position themselves.[3]

In summation, one can see why we need government and why we need to develop a better understanding of its inner workings. To do this, we will need to cover a few more concepts before moving on to the rest of the foundations.

Issues For You

Do you think John Rawls's veil of ignorance theory is a good justification for the upper class paying more taxes?

Introduction to Democracy

The Democratic Ideal

The word **democracy** breaks down as demos meaning "the people" and kratein meaning "to rule." Thus the main idea of democracy is rule by the people, or self-government by the many. This is in contrast with other forms of government, such as an aristocracy (rule by a few) or a monarchy (rule by one). The main idea of democracy requires that the citizenry remain informed so that they can make wise decisions.

Democracy requires that people not look after their own interests but rather the good of society. It is from this philosophy that the idea of civic duty emerges. As history has shown, a government, whether democratic or republican, has the potential of being converted into a tyranny, as in the case of Rome under Caesar or, more recently, Augusto Pinochet of Chile. A tyrannical form of government may emerge when power shifts from the people to a handful of elites, which eventually falls into the hands of one dictator.

Direct Versus Indirect Democracy

The concept of democracy as we know it originated in Greece - more specifically Athens. The people ruled through open assemblies or forums, as in the case of the Athenian democracy. Today, we would call these forums an exercise in **direct democracy**. While the Athenian form of government involved engaging citizens to reach a consensus, it too had the problem of disenfranchising parts of the population. Only free male citizens were allowed to participate - slaves and women were excluded from the deliberative process. In addition, before Socrates drank the hemlock, he warned of one of the great dangers of a democracy: **majority tyranny**. Socrates argued that in a democracy, one should to be careful to protect the rights of minorities.

Here in the United States, direct democracy does not exist at the national level. We can see direct democracy applied at the state and local levels. Today, some states have party caucuses where the deliberative issues are discussed and candidates are chosen. Other states have **initiatives** or propositions that require voters to sign a petition for the proposition to be placed on the ballot. Another form of direct democracy is the **recall**, which allows the voters to remove an elected official from office before the end of their term. As in the case of California, Governor Gray Davis was voted out of office in October 2003 and replaced by actor and body builder, Arnold Schwarzenegger.

Most democracies today have a **representative democracy**, also known as indirect democracy. A representative democracy is one in which the people rule indirectly through representatives who they elected to govern in their stead. There are two main forms of representative democracy. The first is the **steward or delegate theory**, in which the elected representative votes the way the constituency would like. The second theory is the **trustee theory**, in which the representative votes the way they feel is best. In the United States, representatives often carry out the latter of the two theories. Edmund Burke, British parliamentarian and political philosopher, described these theories in a letter to his constituents, written in 1774.

Democracy – A system of government in which the people rule, either directly or through elected representatives.

Direct Democracy – A type of government in which people govern themselves, vote on policies and laws, and live by majority rule.

Majority Tyranny – Suppression of the rights and liberties of the political minority by the majority.

Initiative – A proposal submitted by the public and voted upon during elections.

Recall – Progressive reform allowing voters to remove elected officials by petition and majority vote.

Representative Democracy – A system of government in which the voters select representatives to make decisions for them; sometimes called an indirect democracy.

Steward or Delegate theory - An elected representative acts on the wishes of their constituents.

Trustee Theory – Based on Edmund Burke's philosophy that an elected representative acts under the own volition and takes the constituents input under advisement.

Key Concepts of Representative Democracy

It is what men think that determines how they act.
John Stuart Mill, Representative Government

There are three main concepts that are associated with representative democracy. They are **popular sovereignty**, **political liberty**, and **political equality**. In popular sovereignty, the citizens hold the power and therefore, the government is responsive to the citizens' needs. It also requires the citizenry to make informed decisions and to participate in the democratic process via deliberation, voting, and keeping a check on government.

In order for popular sovereignty to exist the following functions and actions of government must prevail:

Government must implement the will of the people. Is it possible for the government to accomplish this task in a timely manner? If the answer is no, then what happens to the contract between the elected representatives and the electorate? Representatives at all levels of government look at opinion polls and monitor communications with constituents to discuss local issues to determine what it is that people want. This enables them to keep fingers "on the pulse of the people." If an important issue emerges, the government will not waste time in order to show the voters that they are responding to their wants and needs. An example of this would be the attacks on September 11, 2001. Within days of the attacks on the World Trade Center and the Pentagon, elected officials, from the President down to state and local leaders, began implementing 'home security' policies in an attempt to reassure the American people that they were safe and something like this would not happen again.

Government policies should reflect the wishes of the people. The most obvious sign of popular sovereignty is the existence of a close correspondence between what government does and what the people want it to do. It is not hard to imagine a situation in which the people rule but government officials make policies contrary to the people's wishes. However, government must be responsive to the deliberations of the people. This concept is called **deliberative democracy**. It requires that the constituency be informed of the actions of government and that they deliberate (discuss or debate) throughout the process of governing, from beginning to end, including evaluation of actions taken. The framers had a different opinion of how much the people should be involved. They worried that the common folk would have too much influence and that the "passions of the people" would overcome their government ideal with their simplistic whims or passing fancies.

Citizens must have access to accurate information. If the people are responsible for making rational decisions, they must have access to quality information. In order for the people to deliberate on issues, qualifications of elected officials, and other important matters, it is the responsibility of the government to insure that the media is providing accurate information to the public. If media is not, the government should institute and enforce a "fairness doctrine" insuring that media upholds its duty to the general public. If the public receives false or corrupted information, they cannot deliberate effectively, nor can they make rational decisions, thus undermining popular sovereignty.

Issues For You

The chapter raises major objections to majoritarian democracy.

Do you have any other objections that you think should be discussed on this issue?

People must be part of the political process. It has been said that those who show up, govern. Once the people have received accurate information, they must deliberate on the issues and act on their conclusions. These actions can take the form of voting, contacting government representatives, working on political campaigns, or encouraging others to stay informed. In recent years, we have heard how those who are eligible to vote usually don't. "Voter apathy" as it's called, is an issue that works against popular sovereignty and the very concept of democracy. If the people refuse to participate, they are entrusting their future to the hands of the few who understand the value of being politically active. An example is the difference between voters 18-25 years of age and voters in the 55 and older age group. On average, the older group is more active, thus getting the lion's share of the benefits. For example, in 2003, politically active 'senior citizens,' were successful in lobbying for prescription drug benefits for Medicare. At the same time, funding for federal scholarships and student loans decreased, due to lack of participation amongst young adults. One of the main purposes of this book is to show you how to become active in democracy via the use of technology. This will be covered in following chapters as well as on the companion website.

Representatives are elected. In order to insure that people are sovereign, they must have elections thus allowing for them to remove those who do not do the people's bidding and reward those who do, by reelecting them to office. While some countries have elections, they do not always guarantee that a democratic government exists, as in the case of Iran, for example. In Iran, in order to be placed on the ballot, the candidate must be approved by religious clerics, called mullahs. Candidates' religious convictions are scrutinized very closely and if they do not measure up, they are not placed on the ballot.

Free and Fair Elections are held. Despite the controversy that has arisen with the dawn of electronic voting, elections are still the most tangible reflection of the people's will.[4] In order for elections to be free and fair, there must be no voter intimidation by outside forces or political organizations. Furthermore, any citizen that desires to run for office must have access to do so. In order to be fair, election rules must not be skewed in favor of one party or person, and all votes must be accurately counted. As we've seen from the opening vignette, it has been a very long struggle for some groups to gain the right to vote. Recently, we have seen a push for the use of computers at polling places in lieu of the older punch-card method. However, election officials and voters are still debating on the validity of computer technology. Some people do not feel assured that their vote will be accurately recorded simply because the system is not transparent. Computer software companies that develop the programs are privately owned and election officials do not have access to the software codes. Therefore, how can they be completely secured against hackers and software errors? In addition, if a technical error arises, election officials must rely on the software company to remedy the problem, rather than correcting the problem themselves. Nevertheless, technology in voting provides enormous potential in the way of accessibility for all voters.

The Majority Rules. In a democracy, the issue or candidate with the most votes wins. Theoretically, this means that the majority of voters have reached the same conclusions about issues that impact their lives. Hobbes wrote that government acquires its power from the consent of the governed. In order to implement their agenda, the people vote on said issues, thereby giving their consent to public officials to govern. The ideal situation for majority rule is that the voters continue to stay apprised of the issues and persist in debating them. If any part of these elements does not work, the system doesn't work and we will have minority rule. If the minority rule governs, it means that the will of the majority is ignored promoting an agenda that doesn't truly represent the populous. Again, this defeats the concept of popular sovereignty.

Political Equality is the second component for a representative democracy to exist. The concepts of political equality date back to the Declaration of Independence, that "all men are created equal."[5] This is to say that all citizens are not only equal in the eyes of the law and but also in their political standing as well. It is reinforced again with the Fourteenth Amendment that calls for all citizens to have "equal protection" under the law. Government must provide the same privileges and benefits to all. Simply put, government cannot discriminate against any class or group of people nor can it promote one group over another.

In a democracy, what could be considered more fundamental to expression of personal will besides the right to vote? This is why we have seen so many disenfranchised groups fight to gain this right. Even today, the struggle continues for specific groups who are still prevented from voting for various reasons. For example, groups such as the homeless, convicted felons, and permanent residents (foreign nationals) have difficult obstacles that keep from voting. In terms of political equality, regardless of one's socioeconomic standing, one's vote carries the same weight as everyone else's. Just because Bill Clinton was President of the United States does not mean he is entitled to 100 votes to everyone else's one vote. Likewise, Arnold Schwarzenegger's vote does not carry more political weight because he is an actor and Governor of California compared to the former child actor, Gary Coleman, who ran but didn't win the office of Governor.

Political Liberty is the third component of democracy. Political liberty is not a new concept. It roots can be traced back to thinkers such as Adam Smith, Jean Jacques Rousseau, and John Locke who discussed various concepts of liberty and influenced Thomas Jefferson's writing of the Declaration of Independence. The framers were more apprehensive when promoting political liberties because they feared the concept of democracy. Alexander Hamilton firmly believed that the passions of the people should be kept in check by a strong central government. In order to ratify the Constitution, the federalists, i.e., Madison, Hamilton, Washington, and so on, made a concession to the anti-federalists, i.e., Thomas Jefferson, by agreeing to add the Bill of Rights.

The Bill of Rights was enacted to insure that the people's liberties were secured from government. The main focus of political liberties can be found in the First Amendment to the Constitution, which ensures the freedom of speech, press, religion, assembly, and association. Without these liberties, how can the people rule? If we are to maintain popular sovereignty, we must be granted these liberties in order to insure that democracy can flourish.

Profiles in Politics
Alice Stone Blackwell (1857 - 1950)

Courtesy of the Library of Congress

Alice Stone Blackwell was born September 14, 1857 in Orange, New Jersey. She was the only child of Henry Browne Blackwell and Lucy Stone. Alice was born into a family of strong, independent-minded, pioneering women. Her mother, Lucy Stone, was the first woman to earn a college degree in Massachusetts, the first woman to speak full-time on women's rights, and the first woman to keep her maiden name when she married. Even in death, the matriarch Lucy Stone was a leader, being that she was the first New England resident to be cremated. Alice's aunt, Elizabeth Blackwell, was the first woman to graduate from medical school in the United States and she subsequently founded The Women's Medical College.[6] In 1881, Alice graduated from Boston University, Phi Beta Kappa. She then went to work as an assistant editor for her parents who founded the Woman's Journal, the official magazine for the American Woman Suffrage Association (AWSA). In 1890, Alice led the movement to reconcile the two competing factions of the suffrage movement - the American Woman Suffrage Association and the National Woman Suffrage Association - into the National American Woman Suffrage Association (NAWSA) where she served as the recording secretary until 1918. Alice remained the editor in chief of the Woman's Journal for thirty-five years. She "..urged women to remain an autonomous moral force in politics."[7]

1893 proved to be an eventful year for Ms. Blackwell. In the fall of 1893, after her mother died, she became editor-in-chief of the Woman's Journal. It was also "the moment she found herself engaged in the Armenian Question," when she met Ohannes Chatschumian, a theology student, from whom she learned, in great detail, about the worsening plights of the Armenians.[8] Together they began to work translating some of Armenia's poetry into English verse. They created a society known as "Friends of Armenia," which provided information about the Armenians and the Armenian Question to the American media. This society expanded and became central to launching America's first international human rights movement.[9]

For Alice, equal rights for women were the bedrock on which her life rested, and her passion for Armenian human rights had its origin there.[10] In 1896, Armenian Poems was published. Subjects consisted of Armenian history, the recent massacres, the Armenian Church, and the advanced status of Armenian women.13 In addition to the Armenian Poems, Alice also translated several other volumes of poetry into English, including publications in Russian, Yiddish, Spanish, Hungarian, and French.

Following in the great tradition of high achieving women, Alice received an L.H.D. degree (Doctorate of Humanities) in 1945 from Boston University in recognition of her work. Like her mother, she too was cremated when she died on March 15, 1950, at the age of ninety-two.

The First Amendment guarantees individuals the freedom to communicate with one another. Communication takes place through all types of venues. Below these liberties are summarized - we will discuss them in greater detail in chapter 13.

Issues For You
The separation of church and state has become a widely debated issue. One part of this is when church officials want to "pray" that one person is elected to an office over another.

Do you think they should be allowed to do this and if so, should they keep their tax except status?

Courtesy of the Library of Congress

Freedom of Speech. In a democracy where the citizens have popular sovereignty, they need to deliberate the issues in order to insure that they make the best decisions. This freedom includes not only the spoken and written word but symbolic speech as well. An example of this would be in the case of Cohen v. California (1971) when an individual was convicted of disturbing the peace because he entered a courtroom wearing a jacket that said, "Fuck the Draft" on the back. A state, according to the Supreme Court decision, may not "forbid particular words without also running a substantial risk of suppressing ideas…"

Freedom of the Press. The role of the press is to act as the "watch dog" by informing the voters on the daily workings of the government. The press must also provide clear and accurate information so the voters can make informed decisions.

Freedom of Assembly and Association. Voters need to be able to assemble in order to deliberate on the issues. They also have this liberty so they can show mass support or mass disapproval for the government via rallies and other forms of protest. We live in a pluralistic society and we may or may not always agree on the best course of action; therefore we must be able to come together and associate with those who share our political views as well as discuss our differences with those who don't. In addition, we need to be able to meet in assemblies and discuss the candidates, issues, and other party business.

Freedom of Religion. Originally, freedom of religion meant that government should not promote, show preference to, nor inhibit religion. But there is another way to look at it. As discussed earlier, all governments have similar functions but it should also be noted that some philosophers have contrasting views of human nature, which in itself dictates the role of government. With that in mind, we should examine these viewpoints.

Christians believe that humans are born with 'original sin' and thus require the government to protect them from harming themselves and others, which falls in line with Hobbes' philosophy of the role of government. If one subscribes to this view, they would see the need for a strong state with broad police powers and a court system that focuses more on criminal laws over justice and equality.[11]

In contrast, Buddhists believe that humans are inherently good, thus making the role of government one of assisting individuals along their journey through this life. While there is still a need for protection from harm, government should focus more on social programs to help those less fortunate. The police powers would be limited and the court system should focus more on the concepts of justice and equality.[12]

FOR YOUR CONSIDERATION
INCREASING ACCESS – THE MOTOR VOTER LAW

As you have already learned, the right to vote is key in a democracy. In 1996, the National Voter Registration Act (NVRA), known as the Motor-Voter Law, was designed to encourage voter registration by simplifying the process. The law required states to provide registration services through driver's license agencies, public assistance agencies, disability offices, and mail-in registration. The bill was made a priority of the Clinton Administration after President George H. Bush vetoed a similar bill in 1992. The NVRA bill passed in the House of Representatives within weeks of Clinton taking office, but soon ran into stiff opposition in the U.S. Senate, where the Republicans threatened to filibuster. The opponents claimed that the NVRA would impose excessive costs on States as well as increase voter fraud. There was a belief that the law would benefit Democrats more than Republicans by making it easier for more inner-city and lower-income people to register. After a compromise was reached in the Senate, President Bill Clinton signed the bill into law in 1993. It went into effect on January 1, 1995.

After the law passed, Governor Pete Wilson of California refused to implement the act, claiming that it would cost more than $35 million as well as increase voter fraud. The justice department filed lawsuits against California and two other states in order to enforce compliance of the law. The U.S. Supreme Court ruled that the Motor-Voter Law was not an infringement on the states' rights to govern because it was not an unfunded mandate, and not a tool for increasing voter fraud.

Did the Motor-Voter Law achieve what it set out to achieve? While there was an increase in voter registration after the law was enacted, voter turnout in the 1996 presidential election was less than 50%, the lowest since 1924. In November 2000, more than 105 million people voted in the presidential election, an increase of 9.5 million more than the 1996 election (from 49% to 51%). The U.S. Census Bureau reported that in the 2000 presidential election, 7.4 % of registered voters who did not vote (3 million people) identified trouble with their registration as the main reason they did not vote. In the 2004 and again in 2006 elections, both the republican and democratic parties organized massive voter registration drives.

For additional information on the Motor-Voter Law, you can access it on the web at: http://www.usdoj.gov/crt/voting/nvra/activ_nvra.htm#1993#1993

Concerns about Representative Democracy

As quoted at the beginning of the chapter, Churchill said that democracy is the worst form of government except for all of those that came before it. No one argues that democracy is perfect – in fact, it's far from it. In actuality, democracy is a continual work in progress. It is our responsibility as citizens to stay informed and hold government accountable. For if we don't, a misinformed electorate can make bad decisions, creating an ineffective government, which in turn leads to poor policies and resentment from the people. In all, if the main components of popular sovereignty, political equality, and political liberty fail to work, we would potentially follow the same course as Rome and Chile. In addition to this, there are other concerns regarding representative democracy.

Majority Tyranny. If representative democracy is to work, majority rule must be accepted. However, we must be cautious of majority rule turning into majority tyranny. In order for the system to work, the majority must respect the opinions of the minority as well as protect them from political harassment.

The idea of protecting the minority opinion dates back to Ancient Athens. The Greek philosopher Plato wrote about majority tyranny because of the events surrounding his mentor, Socrates. Socrates was charged with the crimes of corrupting the youth of Athens and not believing in the Athenian gods. During his trial, Socrates used logic and reason to illustrate the potential misuse of power by the majority rule, and warned that minority rights must be safeguarded. Socrates was found guilty and was sentenced to death by drinking hemlock. His experiences serve as a cautionary tale of how the majority can oppress dissenting views, going as far as execution to silence any alternative thought.

Oppression American Style. The source of all oppression is fundamentally rooted in fear. In turn, fear is based on the unknown, unfamiliarity of other cultures, and uncertainty of future events. Much like Athens in the time of Socrates, modern America has seen many periods in which fears of the majority led to the oppression of many minority groups. Early examples of oppression against minority groups were those of slavery, treatment of Native Americans, Asian Americans, and religious groups such as Irish Catholics. During World War II, the internment of Japanese Americans, who were forcibly removed from their homes along the west coast and displaced to camps throughout the Midwest, was a reaction to Japan's attack on Pearl Harbor on December 7, 1941. There was a nation-wide fear that these Japanese Americans, most all of whom were American-born, would somehow be a threat to national security. Another example occurred at the beginning of the Cold War in the 1950's. Dubbed the 'McCarthy era,' anti-communist movements limited freedom of speech amongst high profile celebrities, due to the fear that these liberal individuals were part of the communist party. And, most recently, directly after the attacks on the Twin Towers in New York and the Pentagon on September 11, 2001, American Muslims experienced political harassment, such as lengthy detentions without legal representation, mass indiscriminate deportations of immigrants, and, in some cases, American citizens because of their religious and cultural beliefs.

Robert Dahl in his books, *Democracy and Its Critics* argues, there is no evidence to support the belief that the rights of minorities are better protected under alternative forms of political government, such as fascism, communism, authoritarian dictatorship, theocracy, and others. Dahl contends that given the other benefits of majority rule, democracy is still preferred over all other forms of government.[13]

People can be irrational and ignorant of the issues and facts. For decades political scientists have examined the attitudes and behaviors of American citizens, and some of the conclusions made do not bode well for popular sovereignty. Evidence suggests that individuals do not care a great deal about politics, they are ignorant of the issues and facts, and they can be fickle when it comes to making political decisions. Some political scientists assert that these findings support Hamilton's believe that "the masses are asses" and are ill equipped for the responsibility of self-governance. There are those that believe these ideas hold some validity but for the most part, American citizens are being misinterpreted. However, another viewpoint is that the American public, taken as a whole, is more informed than generally believed. Technology today provides more information at a moment's notice and from multiple sources. It enables the public to make more educated and rational decisions. The priority should be for citizens to take the information and encourage the public to take part in the democratic process and take some form of political action.

Types of Democratic Governments

When looking at the globe and examining each country's political institutions, one can see a pattern emerge. There are three main types of democratic governments and they are the parliamentary system, the presidential system, and the semi-presidential system - found within these types of governments are various hybrids.[14] Please note that this is a brief overview to give you an idea of the main structures of democratic governments. Throughout the text, we will examine key concepts comparing the United States with other nations. Another thing to note is that all of these systems begin with the concept of popular sovereignty. The first of these structures begins with the voter in conjunction with free and fair elections.

Issues For You
What do you think are some of the advantages and disadvantages to a Parliamentary structure of government?

Parliamentary system. The parliamentary system is the most commonly used of the three. Most of the governments who use the parliamentary system base their designs on the Westminster model created in the United Kingdom.

In the parliamentary system, the voters elect representatives to the legislature. The party that wins the most seats in the legislature becomes the ruling party. If neither party has a clear majority, they can form a coalition with a minor party in order to proceed with establishing a government. Once there is a ruling government, a prime minister is selected by the ruling party to lead the government. The prime minister fills the cabinet positions with senior party members. The cabinet then oversees the various ministries to insure that the government's policies are being implemented.

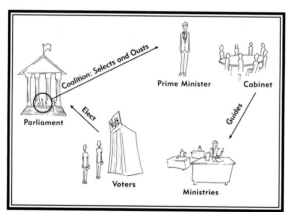

As one can see, there is no real separation of powers between the parliament and the prime minister. If the government loses the support of the people because of the prime minister's policies, the parliament can call for a "vote of no confidence" in which the prime minister is forced to step down. In addition, Britain does not have an implicit codified constitution. Instead their constitution is derived on their history of common laws, traditions, and acts by parliament. Because the constitution is so fluid, very few actions taken by the prime minister can be ruled unconstitutional. The prime minister can call for elections at any time as long as they are within five years of the previous elections. Usually, the prime minister will call for elections when there is stronger public support for their policies, thus enabling their party to gain more seats in parliament.

Presidential system. As you will be reading throughout the rest of the text, the presidential system here in the United States is based on three main concepts – separation of powers between the branches, each branch of government is sovereign within it's sphere of influence, and each branch has checks and balances on the others.

In the presidential system, the voters elect the legislature separate from the president. In some systems, the president is popularly elected, while here in the United States, the Electoral College elects the president. The president selects the cabinet and the cabinet oversees the ministries or agencies.

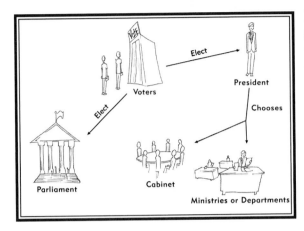

In contrast to the parliamentary system found in Britain, the president and the legislature have explicit guidelines in the constitution. If the president is implicated in illegal actions to the level of high crimes or treason, then the president can be impeached by the lower house and removed from office by the upper house. If the legislature does not like the policies of the president, they do not have the option of voting for a no-vote of confidence if they do not like the president's policies. The president cannot call for early elections to help his party gain more seats in the legislature - the Constitution spells out when elections are to be held. In order for this to change, the Constitution would need to be amended.

Semi-Presidential System. The semi-presidential system, also known as the French system, is a combination of the parliamentary system and the presidential system. President Charles de Gaulle created the semi-presidential system (see his profile in chapter 10) after the fourth republic was no longer functioning.

For the semi-presidential system, the voters elect the legislature and president separately. The president selects the premier and the cabinet. The premier and cabinet guide the ministers in implementing of the president's policies. If the government's policies are at odds with each other and are in a deadlock, the premier can be censured by the parliament and be forced to resign. If this occurs, the president can dissolve the parliament and call for new elections.

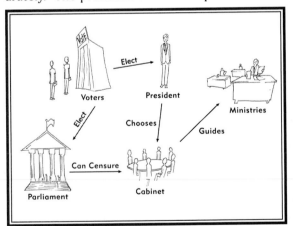

Unlike the president and the parliamentary systems, the semi-presidential system gives more power to the president than the legislature. It has some checks and balances between the branches but not as much as the presidential system. Because the executive has more power than the other two systems, the governments of Russia and China have elected to use this as a guide for their structures of governments.

FOR YOUR CONSIDERATION
A PAUSE IN DEMOCRACY'S MARCH

By Laza Kekic

The global spread of democracy since the 1970s, especially after the collapse of communism, has been impressive. According to Freedom House, an American organization that tracks global trends in political freedom, at the end of 2005 there were 122 "electoral democracies" (64% of the world's states, compared with 40% in the mid-1980s). On a more stringent criterion, 89 of these were rated as "politically free"—46% of all states, compared with only 25% in 1975. However, the spread of democracy appears to be coming to a halt.

Negative examples abound. The weak response in the Middle East to pressures for democratization, as well as the experience with imported political change in Iraq, is making a mockery of George Bush's "freedom" agenda. In Asia, the coup in Thailand was a reminder of democracy's fragility. The promise of the multi-coloured revolutions around the former Soviet Union remains unfulfilled, and a slide into authoritarian ways in Vladimir Putin's Russia continues. Political crises in central Europe have raised questions about the strength of the region's democratic transition. In Latin America populist forces with dubious democratic credentials have come to the fore, in Venezuela and elsewhere. Even in the developed West, a lack of interest in politics and security-related curbs on civil liberties are having a corrosive effect on some long-established democracies.

A new democracy index devised by the Economist Intelligence Unit illustrates some of these trends. Compared with Freedom House's measure, it delves "deeper" into the texture of democracy, looking at 60 indicators across five broad categories: free elections, civil liberties, functioning government, political participation and political culture. Free elections and civil liberties are necessary conditions for democracy, but they are unlikely to be sufficient for a robust democracy if unaccompanied by transparent and at least minimally efficient government, adequate participation in politics and a supportive culture. It is not easy to build a sturdy democracy. Even in long-established ones, if not nurtured and protected democracy can corrode surprisingly quickly.

The index provides a snapshot of the current state of democracy for 165 independent states and two territories. Although almost half of the world's countries can be classified as democracies, the number of "full democracies" is low (only 28). Almost twice as many (54) are rated as "flawed democracies." Even a flawed democracy is better than no democracy at all; of the remaining 85 states, 30 are considered to be "hybrid regimes" and 55 are authoritarian. As could be expected, developed OECD countries (with the notable exception of Italy) dominate among the full democracies, although there are also two Latin American countries, two from central Europe and one African country.

FOR YOUR CONSIDERATION
A PAUSE IN DEMOCRACY'S MARCH

Sweden, a near-perfect democracy, comes top, followed by a bevy of similarly virtuous northern European countries. More surprising are the relatively modest scores for two traditional bastions of democracy—Britain and the United States. In America there has been a perceptible erosion of civil liberties related to the fight against terrorism. Long-standing problems in the functioning of government have also become more prominent. In Britain, too, there has been some erosion of civil liberties but also a shocking decline in political participation. Britain's score in this area is the lowest in the West and is reflected across all dimensions—voter turnout, membership of political parties, willingness to engage in politics and attitudes towards it.

Why the setbacks in democracy's spread and quality? The pace of democratization was bound to slow after the easy gains that followed the fall of the Berlin Wall. China and Middle Eastern autocracies were always going to be a more difficult proposition. Many autocrats preside over energy-rich states and have been strengthened by high oil prices. And America, which should be a shining example, has damaged its liberty-enlarging cause: its military intervention in Iraq is deeply unpopular around the world, Mr Bush is widely loathed and Guantánamo and other cases of prisoner-abuse have led to charges of hypocrisy against the United States.

There have been reversals before—a wave of democratization after 1945 ended with more than 20 countries sliding back into authoritarianism. We are not witnessing that sort of regression, but in 2007 the threat of backsliding outweighs the likelihood of further gains. Accompanying our new index is a watchlist of significant changes in 2007: nine countries are on negative watch and only one (Hong Kong) on positive watch.

Nevertheless, it would be wrong to be too pessimistic. Democracy as a value retains strong universal appeal. Creating democracy by external intervention has not gone smoothly. But trends such as globalization, increasing education and expanding middle classes favour its organic development. These underlying forces suggest that any retreat from democracy will be temporary.[15]

How Do We Compare?

This section will introduce a basic overview of comparative politics. In the following chapters, the methods used here will be applied to comparing the United States to other countries. These sections will focus on the chapter topic and will discuss how other countries use the same topic.

Issues For You

Do you find using comparative politics as a method of learning about the United States helpful?

What do you think Aristotle would say if he were here today?

RThe republican policy of balancing rule by one,by the few, and by the many in to a single government. This creates a system of checks and balances preventing on branch of government or group of people from gaining control over the others, according to Aristotle.

Introduction to Comparative Politics

In comparative politics, political scientists study the nations (the people) and the states (the territory). There are thousands of nations around the world but only a small fraction controls their own territory. A country encompasses territory, population, sovereignty, and government. When we hear people refer to the "nation-state," they are actually referring to a country. The modern state is only about five centuries old and is the result of absolutism, economic and territorial expansion, secularization, and improved administration.[16] A 'comparativist,' looks at all of these factors to gain a greater understanding of how humans interact with each other and to see if patterns begin to emerge. Comparative politics is not a new subject. In fact, it can be traced back for thousands of years.

Within this section, we will examine some comparativists and how they have contributed to the field. The following three individuals were selected because of their influence on the field of comparative politics, how they viewed democracy, and how they used comparison in their theories.

Important Thinkers

Aristotle (384-322 B.C.). Aristotle was a pupil of Plato. If you remember from earlier, Plato's teacher, Socrates was put to death by the Athenian democracy. This incident left Plato extremely skeptical of democratic rule. In his book Politics, Aristotle described the governing power to be in the hands of one, few or many and used for the good of the community (positive) or for the good of the rulers.[17]

According to Aristotle, types of governments reflect a tyranny (ruled by one but serves their own interests), a monarchy (rule by the one but serves in the public's interest), an oligarchy (rule by the few but serves their own interests), an aristocracy (rule by the few but serves the public's interests), a democracy (rule by the many but serves their own interests), and a polity (rule by the many but serves the public's interests). For Aristotle, the most desirable would be a polity, or what we refer to as a republic or a republican form of government. In a polity, there exist organic checks and balances in so far as the rule of the few is checked by the many. Likewise, the many are kept accountable by the few. Therefore, a balance is maintained because neither side can serve their own interests. This environment of selflessness is the virtue of this **mixed constitution**, according to Aristotle's beliefs.

Aristotle focused on two distinct features of democracy. In his definition, democracy was the most corrupt and vile form of rule. His rationale for this was that the "demos" are shortsighted and selfish by pursuing wealth, power, and property. Therefore, they had little or no regard to the polis altogether, which could bring chaos and despotism as a whole. This is why Aristotle believed polity to be the best option of the six regimes and democracy to be weak but yet better than tyranny or oligarchy.

Alexis de Tocqueville (1805-1859). Alexis de Tocqueville was a French aristocrat who traveled to the United States in the 1830's. During his travels, Tocqueville observed that the United States, over a span of about 40 years, established a democracy that was still expanding and flourishing. In contrast, France's democracy only lasted about ten years before giving way to Napoleon. From 1814-1830 the Bourbon Restoration emerged to restore the monarchy but failed.[18]

Upon returning home to France, Tocqueville wrote a book titled, *Democracy in America*. The two-volume work analyzed the fledgling United States democracy in the hopes of predicting the implications of democracy for France and Europe.

Tocqueville's premise was simple. Since democracy emphasizes equality, it could have a negative impact by producing a society of under-achieving clones. The *Tyranny of the Majority*, according to Tocqueville, will take root because in democracy, the pressures of conformity will occur when everyone is pressured into blending in by acting and thinking just like everyone else, in an attempt to maintain equality. Like Plato and Aristotle, Tocqueville warned that demagogues who use the peoples' weaknesses in order to gain power, thus turning the democracy into a despotism, will eventually manipulate the common people.

Although Tocqueville was concerned about the rise of despotism, he did see promise in the usefulness of merging a republican form of government with those positive attributes found in a democracy. When people work together to settle problems, it teaches them to learn to cooperate with each other; thus building a stronger community and a sense of civic pride. This encourages a network of people who strive to serve the greater good, rather than their own self-interests, much like the polity that Aristotle sought. He based his theory on the exercises of democracy in the U.S. that existed at New England town meetings, where citizens were encouraged to deliberate and participate in a form of direct democracy. Jury duty, also well established by the 6th and 7th amendment[19] Amendment VI: right to a speedy and public trial before an impartial jury, to cross-examine witnesses, and to have counsel; Amendment VII: Right to a trial by jury in civil suits. of the U.S. constitution, was another example where citizens actively participated in the judicial process.[20]

Seymour Martin Lipset. Like Tocqueville, Lipset was an outsider looking in. Being the child of immigrants and not at all like typical a American WASP, his perspective allowed him to hypothesize about America, as only an outsider can. Lipset came from a working-class, liberal, Jewish upbringing. While most of America saw socialism as a strange even fearful concept, Lipset, as a young college student at City College of New York, became national chairman of the Young People's Socialist League. Lipset later became a political scholar who was a senior fellow at the Hoover Institute and a Professor of Public Policy at George Mason University.

In analyzing America's "exceptionalism", Lipset came up with many theories. Initially in his political career, he tried to explain why America, being an industrial super-power, does not have a major socialist party. As America struggles to "come of age", and define itself as a nation, it's persona is encompassed by inner conflicts - when in truth, the contradiction of individualism versus covert socialism is the essence of its identity. Furthermore, America's persistent emphasis on equal opportunity and equal status differs greatly from Europe's fixation on status differences, much more than most Europeans would like to admit. However, with such a strong history in volunteerism and religiosity, one might expect America's voter turnout rates to be higher and the desire to go to war as a first option to be lower. America is in fact, behind many countries in voter turnout statistics[21] and at the height of Bush's "war on terror", civil liberties of American Muslim citizens were being forcefully usurped in airports all over the country. Lipset is considered to be an expert on political issues such as these as well as trade union organization, social stratification, public opinion, and democracy in comparative perspectives. Lipset researched all characteristics of America's exceptionalism, including America's background in assimilation, which gave rise to the description of America as a "melting pot". In 1996, he pointed out that America was "melting as never before" due to the relatively high statistics of inter-religious marriages between Jews, gentiles, and other religious organizations, when only 40 years ago, whites and non-whites were not permitted to marry.[22]

As one of America's foremost comparitivists, Lipset wrote a highly lauded book comparing Canada and the United States called *Continental Divide*. In it, Lipset argues that Canada has a more conservative and statist political tradition as well as a less individualistic culture than the United States. These special traits are exemplified in the stronger presence of government interventions and controls in public life in Canada. This includes the extensive regulation of firearms, a comprehensive national health insurance system, some publicly owned corporations (federal and provincial), and so on. One definition of a Canadian could be: "A Canadian is a North American who is covered by a national health plan and who is not likely to have an unregistered firearm."

Lipset's recent death (January 2007) seems to come at an interesting period in America's history, in light of the Democrats' taking control of Congress, boasting the first female Speaker in Nancy Pelosi, and the approaching 2008 Presidential elections, with the first substantial female Presidential candidate (Sen. Hillary Clinton (D-NY)) and the first Muslim (Keith Ellison (DMN) to be elected to the House of Representatives. If Lipset had a legitimate successor, s/he would endeavor to observe and analyze the anticipated unity of America and Europe in this apparent changing of the guard. It is trailblazers and events like the aforementioned that cause the rest of the world to prick up their ears. Lipset was a formidable scholar who spent his life doing exactly that - pricking up his ears and listening to what makes America so uniquely complex, troubled, and exceptional.

Chapter Summary

In this chapter we have examined the role of and need for government and the democratic ideal that outlines the two types of democracy, direct and representative. Building on this, we have examined the main components of representative democracy, which are popular sovereignty, political equality, and political liberty. While all three components are considered to be a prerequisite for a democratic government to flourish, they leave a republic susceptible to majority tyranny. In theory, the above concepts were further illustrated through the three most commonly found structures of democratic governments: the parliamentary system used in the United Kingdom, the presidential system used in the United States, and the semi-presidential system created in France but also used in Russia and China. Analyzing these diverse forms of government in the model of Aristotle, Tocqueville, and Lipset, provides additional skills when examining the American Government. In chapter two, we will study the Constitution in depth and gain insight as to how this living, breathing document is still evolving over 200 years later.

Key Terms:

Universal Suffrage

Jim Crow Laws

Poll Tax

Literacy Test

Grandfather Clause

Disenfranchisement

Natural Right

Democracy

Direct Democracy

Majority Tyranny

Initiative

Recall

Representative Democracy

Steward or Delegate Theory

Trustee Theory

Deliberative Democracy

Bill of Rights

Parliamentary System

Presidential System

Semi-Presidential System

Mixed Constitution

This page left blank intentionally.

THE DECLARATION OF INDEPENDENCE.

The Signing of the Declaration of Independence, 1776
The formal proclamation declaring independence for the thirteen colonies
of England in North America, approved and signed on July 4, 1776.

Courtesy of the Library of Congress

CHAPTER 2

DEMOCRACY AND ACTION

CHAPTER OUTLINE

Democracy and Action

Signing Statements

When our Founding Fathers set up the government, they set up a **Separation of Powers**. The three separate and independent branches of government are: a legislative branch to make the law; an executivebranch to enforce the law; and a judicial branch to clarify the law. These branches were given certain powers through the Constitution in order to keep a check on

© Reuters/Jim Young

the other branches and prevent any one of them from garnering too much power. The Framers wanted balance to prevent tyranny.

The Constitution assigns the role of lawmaking to the Congress, and in Article 1, Section 7, the Constitution specifies that each bill, after passage by both houses, be sent to the President for his approval. It states that the President may either approve and sign the bill or return it to Congress with his objections; this has always been construed as the **veto power**, though the word "veto" does not appear in the Constitution. Article 2, Section 3 of the Constitution further charges the President with the task of making sure that the law is faithfully executed.

When the President signs a bill into law, occasionally he has issued what is called a **signing statement**, which is an official legal document that gets recorded in the federal register. These statements have been used by presidents as a way of explaining the particular significance or effects of the bill or act he is signing into law. It can also act as a guiding directive to others in the executive branch on how to interpret and administer the law. Lastly, it can express opposition to perceived areas in the bill, which the president considers to be unconstitutional.[1]

Signing statements have been sparingly used throughout American history, but have become commonplace during the past 25 years. This practice appears to be contrary to what the Framers had in mind when they wrote the Constitution; it has subsequently generated much controversy.

Until 1981, when Ronald Reagan became President, only 75 signing statements had ever been issued. During his eight years of presidency, Reagan issued 72 signing statements, under the advice of Attorney General Edward Meese. Meese and his Justice Department staff advocated that these statements could be used to enhance the power of the Executive Branch to shape the law. George H. Bush followed suit and issued 232 statements during his four years as president. President Bill Clinton, during his eight years in office issued 140 statements. Most of the statements made by these latter two Presidents were regarding foreign policy objections.[2]

Since taking office in 2001, George W. Bush issued more than 807 signing statements in a mere six years. Bush's signing statements have taken on a different tone than those of past Presidents, prompting concern from the American Bar Association (ABA) as well as Congress. The ABA went so far as to issue a bipartisan report stating that

Separation of Powers– State in which the powers of the government are divided among the three branches: executive, legislative, and judicial.

Veto Power – Presidential power that can stop a bill, which was passed by both houses, from becoming a law.

Issues For You

Do you think the President's "power" is unconstitutional?

such signing statements appear to be in violation of the Constitution's Separation of Powers. This prompted the ABA to urge Congress to pass legislation in order to have the Supreme Court review such statements. Congress responded with a bill to curb the effect of signing statements, directing lower courts, both state and federal, to ignore the statements. This allowed either house of congress to file lawsuits in the Supreme Court rather than the lower courts, to determine the constitutionality of the signing statements at a much more expedient rate; however, the 109th Congress, which was controlled by the Republicans (same party as the President), prevented the bill from going to the floor for a vote. So, whether or not these latest signing statements are in violation of our Constitution remains to be seen.[3]

Political Theories of the Time

Over himself, over his own body and mind, the individual is sovereign.
John Stuart Mill, On Liberty

As noted in chapter one, the democratic and republican theories emerged in ancient Athens and Rome. With the dawning of Christianity as a major force in Europe, democratic ideals were ignored by the political and religious powers of the time, which preferred to maintain feudalism as the main social and economic system. Feudalism, which began in the 9th century, was also widely supported by the Catholic church. The two main ideas that were emphasized at this time were the "divine rights of kings"[4] and the afterlife.

Under feudalism, the monarch was "anointed by God" and was therefore sovereign - to question the monarch's authority was to question God. Any individual who questioned the authority of the monarch was ostracized by the church and was sometimes condemned to death for heresy. In addition, Christians were told not to seek their rewards here on earth but to seek them in the afterlife in heaven.[5]

It wasn't until the Italian Renaissance and the Protestant Reformation that democratic principles begin to emerge after a long absence from politics, replacing feudalism. Thinkers like Niccolo Machiavelli (1469-1527) began to promote the value of civic participation. When the Medici family of Florence overthrew the republic in 1512, there was a plot to remove them from power and it failed. Machiavelli was implicated as one of the conspirators. The Medici's had him arrested, tortured, and exiled to his family estate in a remote part of the country. Based on his experiences, Machiavelli wrote his first and best-known cynical commentary, *The Prince*.[6] Later, he made his deepening distrust of the monarch known in his second work called *Discourses*. In it Machiavelli, like the ancients before him, warned the people about the dangers of power being concentrated in the hands of the few. His idea of a republic was that all classes should share the power and place checks on each other, ensuring that no one class could gain too much power. Therefore, if citizens were vigilant enough, they could protect their liberties.

In 1517, Martin Luther, in a fit of passion, nailed a list of 95 theses on a church door in Wittenberg, calling for the Catholic Church to reform some of its practices. While these charges did not call for democracy, it was a catalyst for greater challenges to come for the church authority and parts of its doctrines. The challenges first emerged in Germany, when Luther and some of his followers translated the bible from Latin to German. This allowed individuals to interpret the passages themselves, thus promoting free thought. The second example occurred in England when King Henry VIII established his own national church. This act sparked many years of civil wars and fervent ongoing intellectual debate amongst authors such as Thomas Hobbes (see chapter one) and John Locke. Hobbes argued that absolute power

Courtesy of the Library of Congress

Issues For You
What influence
do you think
John Locke's
political
philosophies had
on the framers?

Factoid:
Several times over
the last 30 years, the
U.S. Treasury has tried
to introduce coined
dollars as a way of
saving money. A paper
dollar lasts 3 – 5 years,
whereas the average
life cycle of a coin
is 30 years.

should rest with the monarch. Countering this, Locke believed that the power should rest with the people. Locke's writings had tremendous influence on the American colonists who were eager to embrace a more balanced government.

John Locke wrote his books, *Two Treatises on Government and Letters Concerning Toleration*, while in exile in Holland. Like Hobbes, the main premise was to establish who had the political authority and how it was obtained. Locke was pleased with England's new constitutional monarchy and the Toleration Act of 1689.[7] The fact that these civil wars were based on religious intolerance concerned Locke. He wrote that religious beliefs should primarily be a private concern and that government should not interfere. Locke's writings imply that the seeds of separation of church and state had been sown. In addition, he also used Hobbes' concepts of the state of nature and natural rights, which Locke commonly referred to as life, liberty, and property. Unlike Hobbes, however, he said that in the state of nature, people were not at their worst but rather that they were in a natural state of freedom.

According to Locke, the theory of the state of nature in which society is in a war of "all against all" as Hobbes describes it, is false. Rather, Locke argued that people are equal and are endowed with natural rights and live free without any overarching power. In Locke's state of nature, everyone could live by God's grace and abundant earth. People could take as they needed and if there was excess, they could use it for trade. In this way, one could not charge another person for a "gift from God." They can, however, charge for the added value of labor. They can profit off of the labor but not for the actual fruit. For example, if God provides an apple tree then a person can pick from it what s/he needs. Any extra fruit that is picked but not needed can be taken to market or shared freely. Furthermore, if a person hordes large quantities of fruit and allows it to spoil without giving others the opportunity to consume it, this is considered a sin. To avoid the sin of spoilage, the goods were used as a symbolic precursor to currency, thus creating a system of economic exchange. It allowed the community to acquire wealth, which then lead to the purchase of more goods and land, free from sin or spoilage, since money's freshness lasts years and years, versus the short shelf-life of fruit.

As people accumulated more wealth, they required assistance to protect their estates and families. People agreed to sacrifice some of their rights in order to create a society. This society is governed by common laws and a structure of government to enforce the laws. Locke stated that people create government for one purpose: to protect natural rights. These common laws govern human behavior and if one party infringes upon another, then it is the responsibility of the government to enforce the law against that perpetrator. The government's power over the people should extend only as far as necessary to protect the people's life, liberty, and property. If government fails, however, the people have a right and responsibility to overthrow it and establish a new one in its place. This concept is called a right to revolution. In the next century, Locke's theories were put to the test when Thomas Paine wrote *Common Sense* and Thomas Jefferson incorporated these principles into the Declaration of Independence.

Precursor to Independence

Issues leading up to the Declaration of Independence

The issues leading up to the Declaration of Independence mainly revolved around the unchecked power of the monarchy that the colonist view as tyrannical. After many years of costly wars with the French, the British monarch found themselves heavily in debt. Resentment toward the cost of protecting the colonies began to intensify in England. After the French withdrawal there were 17 British colonies; it was only the lower 13 that wanted to separate. The four northern colonies, now known as the country of Canada, remained loyal to the Crown, making Canada and the U.S. sister countries.[8] To generate revenue, George Grenville, the "first lord of the Treasury," was elected to raise taxes on the colonists. As a result, Parliament imposed three main acts. The American colonists saw this as taxation without representation.

Factoid:
The four northern colonies that remained loyal to the monarch were Newfoundland, Nova Scotia, Prince Edward Island, and Québec.

The first act was the Sugar Act imposed in 1764. It was a tax on sugar, molasses, and other goods imported into the colonies. The second act was the Stamp Act of 1765, which required revenue stamps be placed on all printed materials and legal documents. This impacted all commercial life in the colonies. The third act, passed by Parliament in 1767, was the Townshend Revenue Act. This act taxed all glass, lead, tea, and paper brought into the colonies. The revenue generated from this act would be used to support civil government in the colonies, including the salaries of the governor and other high officials. Since the colonial assemblies originally paid the governors' salaries, Parliament's passage of the Townshend Revenue Act weakened the colonial assemblies' influence over the governor.

In an atmosphere of increasing frustration and deteriorating tolerance for English rule, colonists had begun to heckle and verbally harass British troops and citizens. As tensions mounted, harassment became more volatile, and taunting turned into brawls, which continued over a period of more than eighteen months. On March 5, 1770, in front of the British Customs House, the Twenty-Ninth Regiment led by Captain Thomas Preston, was met by a large hostile crowd who refused to disperse when ordered. As the crowd became more hostile and commotion erupted, the captain ordered his troops, "Don't Fire!" But, in the melee he was apparently not heard. His troops opened fire on the crowd, killing five men. Following this horrific event, Governor Hutchinson immediately ordered all Redcoats out of the city and arrested the officer and soldiers involved. In the ensuing trial seven months later in Boston, Captain Preston was charged with murder but was later acquitted. He was defended by John Adams and Josiah Quincy Jr., who also later defended the soldiers in their separate trial. Although the incident subdued tensions, it did not defuse the spark of revolution that was igniting throughout the colonies.[9]

Enraged by the massacre, the American colonists forced Parliament to repeal all the Townshend duties except for the tax on tea. The intense events that occurred at the massacre reinforced the importance of freedom of assembly found in the first amendment that citizens should be able to protest the actions of the government without fear of reprisal. With the levying of taxes on tea via the Townshend act, the colonists began smuggling it from the Netherlands. In May of 1773, The East India Trading Company was having financial difficulties and so requested assistance from Parliament. Parliament passed the Tea Act, which allowed the East India Trading Company to sell their tea below market value, thus undermining the colonies' tea merchants. This stoked the rage of the colonists because they remembered the previous Acts and the damage they inflicted on their livelihood. At midnight on

December 16, 1773, Samuel Adams led a group of colonists, dressed like Mohawk Indians, to ransack ships in the Boston Harbor and dumped 342 crates of tea into the water. This has become known as the Boston Tea Party. The King and Parliament responded by passing the Coercive Acts (colonists refer to them as the Intolerable Acts) in the spring of 1774. The Acts forced civilians, upon demand, to quarter British troops without compensation. Parliament also closed the Boston Harbor until the tea was paid. They also established a military governor, General Thomas Gage, to enforce these Acts.

Red Coats –
The British troops came to be called derogatory names like "red coats" and "lobster backs" by the colonists.

Minutemen –
American militia called as such because they were ready to fight at a moment's notice.

Gage's rule over the colonies had the strength of the monarchy – in fact, the only person above his authority was the King himself. Any town meetings the colonists called had to be approved by the General. He also had the authority to issue "writs of assistance," which was a general search warrant, allowing the British officials to forcibly collect taxes and to search for evidence of criminal activity, whether real or staged. There was no privacy for the colonists since the **red coats** could search any part of their property at any time of the day or night.

On September 5, 1774, fifty-six elected delegates from twelve of the thirteen colonies met in the First Continental Congress at Philadelphia's Carpenters Hall. The intent was to reestablish pleasant relations with the Crown and Parliament while also insisting on their rights as English citizens. Washington wrote to a colleague about how the delegates felt that they were being treated as poorly as the slaves they owned.

The First Continental Congress wrote the Declaration of American Rights, maintaining that they alone held power over taxation and "all the rights, liberties, and communities of free and natural-born subjects within the realm of England." By the end of the Congress, it was agreed by most that war with England was not realistic. However, there were a few delegates like George Galloway, who expressed the desire to form a new nation.[10]

The Second Continental Congress was convened after the "shot heard 'round the world." The phrase refers to the events surrounding General Gage and the colonial militia outside Concord and Lexington. The groundwork for this conflict began to unfold when Parliament declared Massachusetts to be in an open state of rebellion. Parliament's response to this threat was to increase British troops within the Massachusetts colony, further escalating tensions. This came to a head on the night of April 18, 1775, when General Gage marched west of Concord to destroy ammunition and gunpowder that was stored there. Paul Revere and others rode out to notify the local militia that "the British are coming!" As morning approached, the British reached Lexington where they were met by 70 **minutemen**. Gage ordered the militia to disperse but a stray shot was fired and the British responded by opening fire, killing eight Americans. The British continued on their march to Concord where they clashed with more minutemen at the north bridge. By the end of the day, 250 British troops and 90 Americans were dead or wounded. This conflict is what Henry Wordsworth Longfellow called, "the shot heard 'round the world." The colonies were now at war with Britain, beginning their struggle toward independence.

On May 10, 1775, all thirteen colonies met to deliberate whether or not to declare their independence from England. The Continental Congress was the only institution that represented all of the colonies and therefore assumed the leadership role. It took control of the militia outside of Boston and placed them under the command of newly commissioned General George Washington. On June 17, 1775, Washington had his first of many conflicts with the British at the Battle of Bunker Hill. The delegates still hoped to resolve their differences with the Crown. After both King

George III and Parliament rejected the peace proposal, the colonists came to the realization that they were now on their own. They resolved to declare themselves separate from England in the hopes of gaining military and economic support from France, England's old rival.

Around the same time, Thomas Paine wrote his infamous pamphlet, *Common Sense* in January of 1776. The pamphlet, which was published anonymously to avoid charges of treason, helped the idea of revolution come to fruition for the colonists. Paine questioned not just the power of Parliament over the colonies but also the structure of the monarchy. He advocated that the colonies needed to dissolve their ties with England and embrace Locke's notion of a sovereign government that protects the natural rights of its citizens: "and when a man seriously reflects on the precariousness of human affairs, he will become convinced, that it is infinitely wiser and safer to form a constitution of our own in a cool, deliberate manner, while we have it in

Courtesy of the Library of Congress

our power, than to trust such an interesting event to time and chance…Ye that tell us of harmony and reconciliation, can ye restore to us the time that is passed? Can ye give to prostitution its former innocence? Neither can ye reconcile Britain and America. The last cord now is broken."

Paine further advocated the advantages of a republican form of government over a monarchy by claiming that an American republic would be a worthy political experiment in which citizens could enjoy full representation and equality of rights. Selling over 150,000 copies within the first three months of being published, Common Sense hit a chord with the colonists. As the pamphlet's popularity increased, so did the demand for independence.

The Declaration of Independence

Courtesy of Corel

After coming to the conclusion that independence was necessary, the Second Continental Congress selected a committee that consisted of primary author Thomas Jefferson, John Adams, and Benjamin Franklin. Jefferson's Declaration of Independence was based on John Locke's ideas in *The Second Treatise on Government*. Kings ruled most governments in Europe and around the world at the time Jefferson wrote the Declaration. As stated in chapter one, the monarch ruled with authority derived from God. The subjects could not question the authority of the King because to do so was essentially to question God. Jefferson's argument that legitimate government can be established only by the consent of the people was a revolutionary notion. The justification for independence from England was based on the following points:

Courtesy of the Library of Congress

1. "We hold these truths to be self-evident, that all men are created equal, that they are endowed by their Creator with certain unalienable Rights, that among these are Life, Liberty, and the Pursuit of Happiness." Humans have inherent natural rights and liberties that cannot be taken away from them.

2. "That to secure these rights, Governments are instituted among Men, deriving their just powers from the consent of the governed." Citizens consent to be ruled by a government solely have these rights protected.

3. "That whenever any Form of Government becomes destructive of these ends, it is the Right of the People to alter or to abolish it, and to institute new Government, laying its foundation on such principles, and organizing its powers in such form, as to them shall seem most likely to affect their Safety and Happiness." If government does not adhere to this social contract (see chapter one), the citizens have the right to remove their consent and create a new government – basically summarizing Locke's right to revolution.

Declaration of Silence

In order to reach a consensus for approval, divisive issues were avoided so that all delegates could agree. One of the issues not included into the final draft of the Declaration of Independence was the problem of slavery. While Jefferson's first versions of the Declaration reprimanded the Crown for "captivating and carrying Africans into slavery," it was dropped from later revisions to appease the southern colonies. The apparent hypocrisy of the legality of slavery as compared to the grandiose language of "all men are created equal," was and still is an egregious contradiction.

Other groups excluded from the Declaration were women, Native Americans, and free African Americans. There is no indication that these groups were even considered in the deliberation process, despite the fact that they were actively involved in the revolutionary effort against England.[11]

Issues For You

What do you think some of the difficulties the central government encountered under the Articles of Confederation?

FOR YOUR CONSIDERATION
THE ROLE OF AFRICAN-AMERICANS

African-Americans and the Revolutionary War

Rarely rewarded or appreciated for their participation, African-Americans played an important part in America's struggle for freedom. With an estimated 360,000 Africans forcibly immigrated into the colonies over the 17th and 18th centuries, slaves provided an important labor force during the Revolution.

The English, recognizing a dual advantage of gains soldiers and weakening the southern economy by luring slaves away from their colonist masters, made promises of freedom in return for service in the English armies. In November 1775, Britain's Lord Dunmore proclaimed that freedom awaited all slaves who enlisted and were "able and willing to bear arms." While listening to their masters discuss the merits of liberty and inalienable rights, many slaves were already questioning their own oppression. England's offer of freedom appealed to these slaves who fled their masters to become soldiers under English rule. The Black Pioneers, an English Black-officered regiment[12], and the Ethiopian Regiment[13], were two of several regiments comprised of slaves who had fled to England's side. Besides empowering their armies, the economic loss experienced by Southerners who lost valuable slave-labor was another advantage the English thought would help win them the war. Although there was some impact, it was not as successful as they had hoped.

On April 19, 1775 the first armed skirmish involving Black colonist forces occurred while they were defending the Concord Bridge. Salem Poor was the first Black soldier to win a battle commendation for wounding a British soldier at the battle of Bunker Hill. Although few fought in the beginning years of the war, the slave-owning colonists began using slaves in militias as forces depleted over time. The colonists sometimes made promises of freedom in the same way that England had been. Eventually, the slaves made up one third of Washington's army. The only all-Black regiment in the army, the First Rhode Island Regiment is credited with making three successful stands against the British, enabling the remainder of the American Army to safely retreat at the Battle of Rhode Island. Unfortunately, while many slaves were granted freedom following their service, many more were not, either being returned to their slave owners or fleeing to the North, to freedom.

Courtesy of the Library of Congress

FOR YOUR CONSIDERATION
WOMEN IN THE COLONIAL STRUGGLE

The Woman's Role in Colonial America

Colonial women played a two-part role in the struggle for independence. While husbands, fathers, and brothers fought for freedom from tyranny and oppression in combat, women worked to undermine the English in the political forum at home. Some tactics they used included harassing non-complying merchants and organizing "fast days" to pray for deliverance from oppression. Their most important and influential act was the boycotting of English goods, especially tea.

The sale of tea and textiles was dramatically impacted by women who chose to spin their own textiles and forego tea altogether. Non-consumption pacts were signed across the colonies, and women and girls began spinning their own textiles, even holding spinning contests to publicize their loyalty and dedication. Realizing the potential depth of economic devastation brought on by boycotting tea, the women were committed in their abstinence of their favorite refreshment. In Wilmington, North Carolina, a parade of women burned their imported tea in a symbolic fire of protest and solidarity. These simple acts of protest caused sales to decline dramatically, devastating English commerce. Their efforts laid the foundation for women's rights, suffrage, and political activism.[14]

FOR YOUR CONSIDERATION
THE ROLE OF NATIVE-AMERICANS

Intrinsically intertwined with the British and the colonists, the war drew numerous Native-Americans into the fighting and struggle for independence. Although most of the coastal tribes were gone at the time of the war, other powerful tribes remained, and became enmeshed in the skirmishes and politics of the war.

The Iroquois Six Nations, numbering over 15,000 people, controlled much of the North-Eastern region, and the interior region held a large population of Choctaw, Chickasaw, Seminole, Creek, and Cherokee, numbering another 60,000 people. With such large numbers at stake, both the Americans and the British urged neutrality from tribal leaders, yet these tribes were also too important to ignore seeking alliance with. By spring of 1776, both sides sought alliances with the tribes; crucial to both sides was the regional familiarity and warfare knowledge the tribes possessed, as well as manpower for fighting. A number chose to remain neutral, while others agreed to either fight, provide supplies, or simply allow safe passage through territory.

A few tribes, such as the Cherokees, chose to take their own action against both the American colonists and the British forces by conducting raids, but retaliation was swift and harsh against those who did so. Retaliation set an example that other tribes preferred not to endure, who chose, rather, to remain neutral.

The Iroquois, however, did not ultimately choose neutrality. In late 1776 they became allies to the British, much to their later demise. Although the Iroquois and British were a strong force to be reckoned with, terrorizing and viciously attacking American townships and villages. But the Iroquois people would feel Americans vengeance much more deeply and swiftly. Whole villages, families, crops, and populations were destroyed in return for their loyalty to the British. By the end of the Revolutionary War, the Iroquois had lost over a third of their people; many towns and entire families were permanently destroyed.

Although other tribes, the Oneida and Tuscarora for instance, had sided with the Americans, they received little reward for their loyalties. As was the practice during the 18th century, Native-Americans were used and discarded, often their loyalty only rewarded at a later time by other acts of unfairness or malice.[15]

Articles of Confederation

Problems with Initiation

Courtesy of the Library of Congress

Given the diversity of the population and regional differences, the state delegates elected to create a confederation. Each state would be independent from the others but would work collectively on the issues that impacted them as a whole.

The Second Continental Congress wrote the Articles of Confederation in 1777 but the Articles were not ratified until 1781 because of the Revolutionary War. The loose confederation of states wanted a weak central government with very limited powers. The states controlled the majority of power by way of their legislatures. The main power the central government had was the ability to declare war. However, it could not raise taxes to fund war – it had to rely on each state to contribute their share. In addition, the central government had no jurisdiction over State relationships, nor could it regulate foreign commerce between them. Furthermore, it didn't have a chief executive or a court system to enforce any of the laws passed by Congress. Each state had its own currency system, which further complicated interstate trade. The Articles of Confederation also required that any laws passed by Congress had to be approved by 9 of the 13 states, making codification nearly impossible; it also required that any amendments made to the articles had to be approved by all 13 states. The Articles of Confederation did exactly what they were intended to do: prevent the national government from obtaining too much power.

The main function of the national government was to provide protection as the settlers moved west. As they occupied land that was already populated by Native American Indians, agitation among the groups was amplified. The militia proved ineffective in protecting American citizens from being displaced, due to poor training and inadequate equipment. Because of this, commoners fought for the right to have more influence over government as well as to improve their standings in life.[16] Likewise, the elite became worried about the commoners gaining too much political influence stemming from a different view of the purpose of the revolutionary war. For the elite, the war wasn't fought to separate from England but to regain the powers taken away by Parliament. The true degree of fear and animosity that the elite felt is often understated in America's history. In reality, the interests of the elite and the commoners were on a collision course, the effects of which are still felt today.

Issues For You

Can you think of any examples in which the "commoners" of today (middle and lower class), are undermined by the rich when it comes to policy-making?

What were they scared of?

Early Movement Toward Democracy

After the war, democracy began to emerge in all areas of economics and politics. Some states, such as Pennsylvania, expanded the voting rights to landless white males. Pennsylvania's constitution was considered to be the most radical of all the states. Thomas Paine and Benjamin Franklin praised it for being so progressive and others feared its impact on the current political order.[17] In other states, direct democracy began to take root as citizen commissions, otherwise known as conventions, were established to monitor state legislatures and when needed, issue instructions on how they should vote.[18]

After the revolutionary war ended, many people pursued their goals of living a better life. Unfortunately, the colonies' largest trading partner prior to the war was England. Now that the war was over, England placed strict regulations limiting the amount of goods the state could export to the Kingdom. Low-income levels of society felt the brunt of the economic situation as it moved from bad to worse.

Those who had purchased war bonds (primarily soldiers, war contractors, wealthy individuals, and France)[19] were not being paid. Most of the soldiers had been **tenant farmers** before the war and upon their return they were faced with economic hardship. Most states were not sympathetic to those with debts, forcing those with little or no income to pay what they owed, regardless of more pressing needs. Those who held the bonds sold them for pennies on the dollars, thus losing what little savings they may have had. The banks and creditors began to accumulate large amounts of war bonds, only to be told they could not collect on them. Most states during the war issued paper money but later returned to the gold standard after the war. In states like Rhode Island, where citizens became politically active, they returned to issuing paper money to help the farmers and small businesses, an action that harmed creditors. Still other states went as far as to pass "stay laws" forbidding foreclosure for non-payments on a person's residence.[20] In contrast, states like Massachusetts increased taxes on the farmer in the western part of the state. If farmers could not pay their taxes, the state ordered their property to be seized and sold. All of these events culminated into one conflict that changed the course of American History - Shays' Rebellion (see profile). When Hamilton heard of the rebellion and how public opinion supported Shays' cause, he called for the convening of another Constitutional Convention.

Tenant farmers – Farmers who farmed the land of another and paid rent with cash or with a portion of the produce.

Profiles in Politics
Daniel Shays (1747-1825)

Prior to the momentous rebellion, very little is known of Daniel Shays except that he was born in Hopkinton, Massachusetts circa 1747, married Abigail Gilbert in July of 1772, and died in Sparta, New York on September 29, 1825. During his military service during the Revolutionary War, he reached the rank of captain in the Continental Army. After the war, he settled in Pelham (now Prescott), Massachusetts. By the age of 39, Shays had been in the Battles of Lexington, Bunker Hill, Saratoga, and Stony Point, and was now ready to settle into a humble living as a farmer. Despite the call of the simple life, his truer spirit won out. Shays became the protagonist of a popular movement, leading outraged farmers into taking action in Springfield, MA. It wasn't long before Captain Shays' name became synonymous with rebellion for the common man, including over nine thousand farmers throughout the New England states.

Issues For You
What were the concerns Daniel Shays had that led to the rebellion?

The weak economy of the post Revolutionary war years had many negative impacts on the farmers, most of who were veterans of the Revolutionary war. The farmers' returned to a dismal situation – no compensation from the Continental Congress for their efforts. Furthermore, the farmers' situation was made worse by unjust land taxes that forced the farming communities to sell off furniture, grain, and livestock for cents on the dollar. Some were even forced into court, adding legal fees to their debt; and if they couldn't pay, the possibility of being thrown into jail increased. With the added burden of taxes, the farmers of western and central Massachusetts felt as if they would become tenant farmers. The farmers' complaints ranged from that the excessive governor's salary, the aristocracy of the senate, inflated attorney's fees, extreme taxes, and using courts of law to act as tyrants.

During the fall of 1786, Daniel Shays, along with fellow veterans, gathered in solidarity into organized units with the intent of preventing debtors' courts from continuing foreclosures. They were successful in terms of provoking fear in the hearts of Boston merchants and legislators, who equated their actions as an attack on the state. The Governor ordered the Boston troops to respond to the uprising. However, the national Congress could not raise the money necessary to finance troops to fight the rebellion. Furthermore, the militia was often powerless to do anything, due to its members largely sympathizing with the mobs. This event made it all too clear that the national government had no control over taxation, which contributed to problems that originated with the Articles of Confederation.

Shays and the other rebels never imagined that they would be charged with treason. One fellow fighter said, "I earnestly stepped forth in defense of this country, and liberty is still the object I have in view." However, by December, Shays admitted to antihero sentiments, seemingly regretting his part in the uprising. He expressed to a confidante a desire to desert his followers and receive a pardon. Nevertheless, in January of 1787, three groups of insurgents concentrated on Springfield, where they hoped to capture the Continental arsenal. The largest body, under Shays, numbered 1,100 men attacked the arsenal and after repeated warnings, the militia from Boston fired directly into their ranks, killing three men and wounding one. Shays attempted to rally his men, but they retreated through South Hadley to Amherst where he was pursued by the state troops. Shays's duties as rebellion leader ended when the insurgents were overtaken. After living in the Vermont Republic for approximately one year, Shays asked for and received a pardon. Now an old hero whose eyes had seen much and whose shoulders bore the pain of many, Shays finally retired to Sparta, New York.[22]

FOR YOUR CONSIDERATION
CHARACTERISTICS OF THE FRAMERS

The Federal Convention convened May 14, 1787 in Philadelphia with the purpose of rewriting the Articles of Confederation. By mid-June it was clear to the members that, rather than amending the Articles of Confederation, it would be wiser to create a new government entirely. The document that ultimately embodied this endeavor, the United States Constitution, has served as the cornerstone of our nation's government since then, and the credit for its structural integrity and continuity goes to the 55 men who drafted it.

Of the 55 members, now referred to as the Framers, all were men, and all were white, of Anglo-European descent. Age was not a significant factor, the youngest member was 26 years old, and the oldest, Benjamin Franklin, was 81. Nearly every member had participated in the Revolution, and at least 29 were known to have served in the Continental Army as commanders.

Overall, the delegate members were well-educated, with a diverse range of educational and professional backgrounds, as well as extensive political experience. Most had held either local or state political office, and eighty percent were members of the earlier Continental Congress. Quite a number held degrees of varying advancement, while several were self-taught. Those who were formally trained had attended a variety of schools, ranging from private academies and tutors, to elite colleges and universities. Lawyers dominated the group with 35 members practicing law. But nearly all were involved in more than one occupation or enterprise, such as trade, commerce, shipping, ministry, medicine, and academics. A number were born into affluent, esteemed families, others were self-made men from more humble backgrounds. Nearly all were landowners, 12 owning large, slave-operated plantations or farms. Reflecting the 18th century American religious atmosphere, nearly all the men, 53 to be exact, were practicing Protestants of varying denominations; only 2 were Roman Catholics.

As representatives of the states, these men were considered a cross-section of America's leadership. America's leadership in the 18th century was primarily made up of wealthy, white, landowning Christian males, with the rare exception. Women and other minorities, the poor, and non-landowning citizens were rarely, if ever, allowed to participate in political processes, and the framing of our government and its Constitution would certainly not prove to be an exception.[23]

The Constitutional Convention

In 1787 the elite of the nation no longer had faith that the Articles of Confederation would work. The state selected 73 delegates to attend the Philadelphia Convention and deliberate on how to fix the problems with the Articles - only 55 delegates showed up. On May 25, 1787, the convention officially convened with George Washington presiding. Shortly after the convention opened, the plan changed directions - no longer were they going to fix the problems with the Articles. Instead, they planned to create an entirely new structure of government - one that put greater power in the hands of the national government while simultaneously placing a check on the "passions of the people." For the next four months, the delegates met in secret. Every night, any notes written down were collected to insure that their deliberations remained secure. The only fairly accurate account of the Convention was a journal kept James Madison.[21] At the end of the deliberation, they emerged with an entirely new document, the Constitution of the United States. This document has been our "rule book" on how the game of American Government is played. In over two hundred years, it has only been amended 27 times.

Who Were the Founders?

Most of the delegates came from a privileged background and they were all rich white men (see For Your Consideration, this chapter). Excluded from the convention were women, small farmers, Native Americans, African Americans, skilled artisans, or any commoners. Some historians and political scientists see this as an insignificant issue, while others point out that these exclusions created a flawed document.

Developing a New Government

The 55 delegates agreed on the following points: the Articles of Confederation created too much chaos and needed to be discarded; and the national government needed to be strengthened to provide security and regulate interstate and international trade. Additionally, Alexander Hamilton argued that a strong centralized government was needed, a concept he had defended for many years. Those who opposed this idea, such as James Madison, agreed that it was a necessary step despite the dangers of tyranny. The delegates needed to find a balance by way of a republican form of government which was founded on popular consent but that also placed checks on the democratic fever that had spread throughout some of the states.

Issues For You
Examine the major points of difference between the Virginia Plan and the New Jersey Plan. Which plan do you think is better? What would you add to the discussions?

The Great Compromise
Size Doesn't Matter...or does it?

From the beginning, there was tension between the states. Large states pushed an agenda that favored populous-based representation, while smaller states wanted equal representation regardless of size. There were five different plans proposed to the delegates but most of the debate focused on two of them. The Virginia plan drafted by James Madison, called for the government to be dominated by a powerful Congress based on the most populous states. This plan would favor Virginia, Massachusetts, and Pennsylvania. The smaller states liked the New Jersey plan, which promoted revising the Articles of Confederation, rather than replacing them. Alexander Hamilton sent a letter to Thomas Jefferson, who at the time was the ambassador to France. The letter explained the delegates' intent to discard the Articles and create a new document with a strong central government. Hamilton impressed upon Jefferson that his support was needed because he was the architect of the Declaration of Independence. Jefferson's response to Hamilton was to remind him that the whole point of the Convention was to "amend" the Articles, not throw them out. Jefferson added that Hamilton should dissolve the Convention and request that new delegates be sent. Jefferson's reprimands fell on deaf ears. Hamilton and the other delegates continued the Convention in secret.

The Virginia Plan proposed the following solutions for the assumed defects of the Articles:

1. Madison's plan called for three branches of government: a **legislative branch** that makes laws, an **executive branch** that executes the laws, and a **judiciary** that interprets the laws. To ease the concerns of tyranny, Madison introduced a system of **checks and balances**. For each branch, an equal and opposite force in a separate branch would tame its power within its sphere of influence. This brought the idea of separation of powers to the forefront.

2. The plan also included the belief that the ultimate power to govern resides with the people. Therefore, it proposed a system of **proportional representation**, meaning that the number of delegates from each state is based on the state's population for both houses of Congress, instead of the one-state, one-vote rule in the Articles of Confederation. This would give Virginia more than ten times as many members in Congress as Delaware.

3. Congress would be a **bicameral legislature**. The people would directly elect members in the lower house. The lower house, in turn, would elect the members in the upper house from a list of nominees provided by the state legislatures.

4. Congress would elect the single executive for a maximum of one term.

5. The judiciary would serve for life and would consist of one or more supreme courts and other lower national courts.

6. There would be a **council of revision**, which was a combination of judges and members of the executive branch who would have limited veto power over national legislation and an unlimited veto power over state legislation.

7. The legislature would have the power to override state laws.

As one can see, the Virginia Plan gave an enormous amount of power to the national government. In addition, by allowing the legislature to be chosen by proportional representation, populous states dominate. With the legislature having appointment powers over the judiciary and the executive branch, the large states could wield expansive powers there as well, effectively giving large states virtually total control over the central government.

The New Jersey Plan

Smaller states led by the New Jersey delegation found Madison's proposal reprehensible. The Virginia Plan gave a disproportionate amount of power to the majority, creating a threat of tyranny over the minority. In response to this, William

Virginia Plan – Plan presented at the Constitutional Convention; favored by delegates from bigger states.

Legislative Branch – The branch of government that makes laws.

Executive Branch – The branch of government that executes laws.

Judiciary – The branch of government that interprets laws.

Checks and Balances – Systems that ensure that every branch in government has an equal and opposite powers in a separate branch to restrain that force.

Proportional Representation – A system of representation popular in Europe whereby the number of seats in the legislature is based on the proportion of the vote received in the election.

Bicameral Legislation – Legislative system with two houses or chambers

Council of Revision – A combined body of judges and members of the executive branch having a limited veto over national legislation and an absolute veto over state legislation.

New Jersey Plan – A plan presented to the Constitutional Convention of 1787 designed to create a unicameral legislature with equal representation for all states. Its goal was to protect the interests of the smaller, less populous states.

Paterson proposed the New Jersey Plan, which was comprised of the following:

1.   Reinforcing the concepts in the Articles of Confederation, there would be a **unicameral legislature** and each state would have one vote.

2.   The legislature would select an executive committee that would serve for one term and they would be allowed to enforce the law, even if it countered state legislation. To reinforce state powers over the national government, the governors could collectively remove an executive member from the board.

3.   The issues that plagued the Articles, such as foreign and domestic policies and tax and trade concerns, were given to a supreme court that was chosen by the executive board.

4.   Tariffs would be regulated by the national government instead of the states. Moreover, the legislature would be able to impose upon the states' taxes based on population.

5.   All legislative acts would become the supreme law of the land and enforced by the executive board.

The New Jersey plan increased the powers of the national government while maintaining the majority of the power within the states. Obviously, the New Jersey Plan met with the requirements of the original Convention. Given the resolve to maintain the Articles, this plan offered the idea of legislative laws act as the dominant law of the land. This concept was implemented as its own article in the final draft of the Constitution and is known as the **supremacy clause**.

While the differences between the Virginia and New Jersey plans seemed great, it laid the groundwork for the "**great compromise.**"

Debate was intense and no decision could be reached at the Convention. In order to resolve the impasse, a "Committee of Eleven" convened during the Fourth of July holiday while the rest of the convention adjourned. On July 5, 1787, the Committee produced what has become known as the Connecticut Compromise or the Great Compromise. The agreement included the following features:

1. It established a bicameral (two-house) legislature. To appease the large and small states, representation in the House of Representatives was to be based on population and representation in the Senate would have two representatives from each state, thus creating an equal balance.

2.   The compromise was adopted by the Convention on July 16, 1787. With the compromise in place, the delegates could now begin work on the other issues that needed to be addressed by the convention.

Issues To Be Addressed by the Convention

The Issue of Slavery

The word slavery is not mentioned in the Constitution. This was a very contentious issue for many of the delegates. For those delegates who lived in the southern states, it was a way of life that had existed since the 1600s. Africans had been captured and sold as slaves in the colonies. Southern plantations needed cheap slave labor to work the fields and other manual labor jobs. Although delegates like Benjamin Franklin wanted to write provisions into the Constitution condemning slavery and the slave trade, they were eventually convinced that the southern states would not accept any such language and that this was an issue that would divide the Convention. In order for the Convention to move forward, slavery was discussed

Unicameral Legislature –
A legislative system consisting of one chamber.

Supremacy Clause –
A clause in Article IV of the Constitution holding that in the case of conflict between federal laws and treaties and state laws, the will of the national government always has the last word.

The Great Compromise –
Also called the Connecticut Compromise, was a plan presented at the Constitutional Convention that upheld the large-state position for the House, its membership based on proportional representation.

Issues For You
What was the rationale behind the three-fifths compromise? Do you agree with the solution?

indirectly as "involuntary servitude." Being that the lower house was based on population, southern states wanted to increase their representation, arguing that slaves should count as a whole person. This would increase their number of house seats from 41 to 50. Some northern delegates refused to allow this hypocrisy. After much debate, an agreement was reached known as the **three-fifths compromise**. The compromise referred back to the Articles, which stated the apportionment of taxes and representatives for each state should be determined "by adding to the whole Number of free Persons . . . three fifths of all other Persons" (Article I, Section 2). This meant it took five "other Persons" to equal three "free persons." The accepted rationale for this was that slaves were not as productive as free men and were therefore worth less. In reality, slavery is what kept the southern economy alive for over 200 years. The damage created by this compromise had far reaching implications. In addition to giving southern states more representation in the house, it also increased the number of electoral college votes held for presidential elections. There were other compromises reached as well. They were:

Three-fifths compromise – From Article I, Section 2; 5 slaves are equal to 3 free people when counting the population for representation and taxation purposes.

Courtesy of Corel

- Article I, Section 9 allowed for the slave trade (brought in from Africa) to continue until 1808.

- Article IV, Section 2, paragraph 3 required non-slave states to return all runaway slaves to their original owners.

These items would remain the "Law of the Land" until the end of the Civil war in 1865 when the passage of the Thirteenth Amendment officially ended slavery in the United States.

The Issue of the Executive Branch

In the Virginia Plan created by James Madison, there would only be one executive. In contrast, the New Jersey Plan proposed by William Paterson called for an executive committee. The delegates finally agreed that there would be one president (executive) and one vice president. The issue of how the president would be elected still remained. Both sides agreed that direct election by the commoners would create too much democracy and they would have the same problems they had under the Articles. The solution came in the form of an electoral college. A state's votes would be equal to the number of representatives and senators of that state. The electoral college delegates would meet in their home states and cast their votes for president. If they did not yield a majority for any one candidate, Article II, Section 1, paragraphs 2-3 states that the House of Representatives would choose the president, each state casting one vote for president.

The Final Product

The final product from the Constitutional Convention was the Constitution. The Constitution uses a republican form of government. Although it is based on popular consent and civic participation, it keeps a watchful eye on the passions of the people - in other words, it prevents a majoritarian democracy. To summarize, the Constitution ensured that the actions of the government were limited enough to prevent tyranny but vigilant enough to control the spread of direct democracy. The following sections outline how the structure created by the framers achieved the above goals.

Free and Fair Elections

The idea behind a representative government is that elected representatives implement policies that benefit the people. Each district elected representatives who acted on the constituents' behalf. State assemblies elected the upper house or Senate, thus holding the Senate accountable for their state needs. Being that the state assemblies were "popularly elected," the voters would have indirectly elected

IX Amendment –
IX Amendment states that all traditional rights are retained by the people and the X Amendment gives all non-enumerated powers to the States.

Federalism –
The relationship between the centralized national government and the state governments

Courtesy of the Library of Congress

the Senate. The President is elected by the electoral college, making him accountable to the nation, and therefore responsible for protecting national interests. With the passage of the XVII Amendment to the Constitution in 1913, Senators became popularly elected. All of these avenues legitimized the national government through popular consent and by preventing a tyrannical government from emerging.

Federalism

It is important to understand that **federalism** is a division of powers between the states and the national government. Each one is sovereign within its own sphere of influence. When a conflict arose between state and federal law, the framers would refer to Article VI, Section 2, known as the supremacy clause:

> *This Constitution and the Laws of the United States, which shall be*
> *made in Pursuance thereof; and all Treaties made, or which shall*
> *be made, under the Authority of the United States, shall be the supreme*
> *Law of the Land; and the Judges in every State shall be bound thereby, any Thing*
> *in the Constitution or Laws of any State to the Contrary notwithstanding.*

While we would like to think of the Constitution as providing a balance between the state and national governments, in reality it tends to favor the federal government. Most of the responsibilities that were assigned under the Articles to the states were placed squarely under the jurisdiction of the national or Federal government. The national government was now responsible for regulating commerce, creating a common currency, developing national laws on bankruptcy, collecting taxes and customs duties, declaring war, and providing for the common defense of the country. The key to executing these powers is found in Article I, Section 8. The focus of this section is the "elastic clause", which mandates Congress' power to "make all laws which shall be necessary and proper" in carrying out its duties.

Issues For You
Examine the points made by progressives and Charles Beard. Do you think these are valid criticisms of the framers and the Constitution?

All that was left for the states to determine were voting qualifications. Most of the delegates wanted some type of property requirement but they could not reach an agreement on what the requirement should be. In the end, the delegates agreed to allow each state to decide. At that time most states did have property requirements as well as restrictions that denied women, slaves, and Native Americans the right to vote. By the 1830's, most states had removed property qualifications, establishing white male suffrage. This concept will be explored in greater detail in chapter 3.

Limited Government

The basic purpose that drives the Constitution is to define the role and power of the national and state governments. Most of the powers of the federal government are defined in Article I, Section 8 (coin money, declare war, etc), while restrictions on the federal government are found in Article I, Section 9. For example, Congress cannot suspend the Writ of Habeas Corpus, pass a bill of attainder, or impose ex post facto Laws. Other restrictions are also found in the first ten amendments, otherwise known as the Bill of Rights.

Separation of Powers and Checks and Balances

Although the framers were concerned about the power of the executive and judicial branches, they were more worried about the legislature and its ability to be influenced by public opinion. To deal with this, they turned to the theories of French philosopher Charles de Secondat, Baron de la Brède et de Montesquieu (1689-1755) (Montesquieu for short), as explained in his book The Spirit of Laws (1748). As a way to prevent tyranny, the power of the government should be fragmented or separated. The powers would be split between the executive, legislative, and judicial branches of government. All three branches would have their own powers and would be sovereign within their own sphere. The Constitution divides the power in the following manner:

TABLE 2.1 - The Constitution of the United States of America Quick Guide	
Preamble:	Establish Justice, domestic Tranquility, common defense, and general welfare
Article I:	Establishes the Legislative Branch
Article II:	Establishes the Executive Branch
Article III:	Establishes the Judicial Branch
Article IV:	Full faith and credit clause; judicial proceedings; privileges and immunities of citizens of several states; rendition of fugitives (slaves); control of territories by Congress
Article V:	Methods of amending the Constitution
Article VI:	Supremacy of the Constitution, laws, and treaties of the United States; oath of office - prohibition against religious tests
Article VII:	Method of ratification of the Constitution

Article I - legislative branch

Article II - executive branch

Article III - judicial branch

For example, Congress is charged with creating bills. A bill is introduced to the House of Representatives (the people's branch) and a companion bill is introduced to the Senate (state's branch). After going through a lengthy process, each house votes on their own version of the bill. If the two bills differ from one another, joint committees from both chambers scrutinize the bills and try to resolve the discrepancies found. The amended bill is sent back to both houses for another vote. This process places a check on both the people and the states. The approved bill then goes to the president. The president can sign the bill into law or veto it. If the president vetoes the bill, Congress can override it. If the president signs the bill into law, and a conflict arises between the Constitution and the law, the Supreme Court has the power to rule the law as unconstitutional through judicial review, which is an implied power.

Property Rights and Economic Policies

In response to all of the economic chaos under the Articles of Confederation, the framers wanted to insure that property rights were protected and free trade was allowed to flourish. In order to do this, they drafted into the Constitution new articles, such as Article I, Section 10, which prevents states from making paper currency. Article IV, Section 1 requires states to guarantee the enforcement of contracts by establishing the "full faith and credit" clause on all public contracts and records and judicial orders of all states. Lastly, Article VI, Section 1 of the Constitution guarantees that the U.S. government would pay all debts contracted under the Articles of Confederation, insuring that investors would receive full payment of war bonds.

The framers took additional steps to nurture economic development by removing the barriers that were created by the Articles. Article I, Section 8, gives Congress the power to monitor interstate commerce; coin money and regulate its value; regulate bankruptcy; and establish patent and copyright laws. Article I, Sections 9 and 10 removed these powers from the states, thereby creating a mechanism for free trade and economic development to prosper.

Checks on Majority Rule

To reiterate, the framers were fearful of a majoritarian democracy, which they defined as the "irresponsible" governing by the masses. To deal with these fears, they created a number of obstacles to prevent this type of government from developing. Some of the obstacles were already discussed above under the free and fair elections section. Other issues that haven't been examined yet are the appointment of judges, terms for the elected representative, and amendments to the Constitution.

Article 2, Section 2, paragraph 2 gives the president the authority to nominate judges to the Supreme Court "...with the Advice and Consent of the Senate." As stated above, the president is elected by the electoral college and the Senate is selected by the state legislatures, two branches of the national government that are indirectly put into office by the people. Having the judges appointed to the bench allows them to remain insulated from political debates and public opinion.

Articles 1, Sections 2 and 3 establishes the framework as to how Congress will be elected and the length of the term served. In the lower-chamber, all members of the House are elected every two years and each term lasts two years, without term limits. The upper-chamber or Senators are elected for six-year terms. The elections for the senate are staggered. Every two years, one-third of the senate is up for election. In Article 2, Section 1, the President and Vice President serve a four-year term and will have to run for office every four years. The above specifications were put into place so that no one branch of government would be able to acquire excessive powers. This distribution of power, sometimes referred to as fragmentation, protects the federal government from becoming tyrannical. It also provides a system in which public opinion could be observed but not always acted upon given the brevity of the elected terms.

The last check on majority rule is creating a structure in which the Constitution could not easily be amended. Thomas Jefferson argued that the Constitution should allow for fluidity within each generation thus reflecting their values and needs. The framers wanted a system that provided stability and the strength to withstand the whims of public opinion. The end result was Article V, which created a cumbersome and dense maze to navigate in order for the Constitution to be amended. Most of the time, this maze prevented proposed amendments from passing, such as the proposed flag burning amendment and the equal rights amendments. In other instances, it hasn't always worked, as in the case of the Eighteenth Amendment which prohibited "the manufacture, sale, or transportation of intoxicating liquors within…the United States and all territory" in 1919, only to be repealed in 1933 by the Twenty-first Amendment. It should be noted that in over two hundred years, the Constitution has only been amended 27 times, 10 of which were the Bill of Rights in order for the Constitution to be ratified.

The Contest of Ratifying the Constitution

Congress instructed the delegates to attend the Convention to suggest revisions to the Articles of Confederation. Under the Articles, any modifications would require the unanimous consent of the 13 states. To avoid this process, the framers elected to have the new document approved under it's own Article VII, which required the approval of only 9 of the 13 states. If they would have submitted the document to be approved under the Articles, Rhode Island and one or two other states may well have rejected it. Congress agreed to this procedure, voting on September 28, 1787, and sent copies of the Constitution to the states for their consideration. There were two main groups that developed during the ratification process. The Federalists, who were thought to be in the minority, had the advantage of unity and incentive for the Constitution to be ratified. The other camp was the Anti-Federalists. They were the majority but they were divided amongst themselves and were unorganized. The stage was set for the battle to begin.

Discussion in the Press

The text of the Constitution and the argument surrounding its ratification occupied much more space in U.S. newspapers in the ensuing months, than any other story. The Federalist supporters wrote 85 noteworthy articles in support of the adoption of the Constitution. While the articles for the New York papers were published under the name "Publius," the real authors were Alexander Hamilton, James Madison, and John Jay. Their essays formulated a theory of maximum liberty and governmental effectiveness through federalism while refuting the arguments of the Anti-Federalist on theoretical and practical grounds. Of the three authors, Madison's writings were the most persuasive.[24] Hamilton wrote most of the articles while Jay only wrote three. The articles were later collected and published under the title, *The Federalist Papers*. Even today, these articles remain the best theoretical justification of the U.S. Constitutional system.

The best-known author for the Anti-Federalists was Richard Henry Lee. In his series of essays titled, *Letters of the Federal Farmer*, Lee stated that the new system of government was "calculated ultimately to make the states one consolidated government." Lee focused on concerns about preserving individual states' customs, laws and constitutions. He also pointed out that the House of Representatives would not be able to respond to the wishes of the people and that there were no protections offered in the Constitution to protect individual liberties, which is what the Bill of Rights came to do. Other Anti-Federalists took a more legalistic view of the proposed document. First they pointed out that the Convention was called to discuss modifications to the Articles, not create a new government. They demanded to know by whose authority the Convention could use the phrase,

"We the People," since it was the states who were the agreed upon power under the Articles of Confederation.

Ratification of the Constitution

Copies of the Constitution were sent to each state's assemblies for ratification. By January 1788, only Delaware, New Jersey, Georgia, Connecticut, and Pennsylvania had ratified the Constitution. In the remaining states, the Anti-Federalists put up an intense opposition. Massachusetts had long and heated discussions and it was only after the Federalists agreed to allow the Anti-Federalist amendments to the Constitution was it ratified on February 6th. Maryland ratified it on April 28th and South Carolina on May 23rd, leaving only one state outstanding for the Constitution to be adopted. On June 21st, New Hampshire became the ninth state to ratify the Constitution. Four days later, New York and Virginia approved it. The Constitution would become the supreme law of the land on April 30, 1789. North Carolina entered the Union the following November and Rhode Island joined more than a year later.

TABLE 2.2 - The Bill of Rights (the first ten amendments to the Constitution, which went into effect in 1791)	
Amendment I:	Freedom of religion, speech, press, assembly, and association
Amendment II:	A well regulated militia and the right to bear arms
Amendment III:	Prohibition against quartering of troops in private homes
Amendment IV:	Prohibition against unreasonable searches and seizures
Amendment V:	Protections against double jeopardy and self-incrimination; guarantee of due process
Amendment VI:	Right to: a speedy and public trial before an impartial jury; cross examine witnesses; counsel
Amendment VII:	Right to a trial by jury in civil suits
Amendment VIII:	Prohibition against excessive bail and fines; protections against cruel and unusual punishment
Amendment IX:	Traditional rights not listed in the Constitution are retained by the people
Amendment X:	Powers not denied to them by the Constitution or given solely to the national government are reserved by the states

It is widely accepted that without agreeing to a Bill of Rights, the Federalists would have lost the debate on the Constitution. During the first session of Congress the Bill of Rights was passed and by 1791, the required number of states eventually ratified the amendments. In analyzing where each group received its support, the Federalists had most of the support along the coast (ship builders, merchants, and artisans) and the border areas along the frontier. Both of these areas saw the need for a strong central government that could provide a well-trained military for protection against foreign aggression. The Anti-Federalists found the majority of their support in the countryside, with farmers who needed infrastructure projects and held the view that local and state governments could do a better job at providing for them than a national government could.

Truth Behind Agendas

Charles Beard and Other Progressives

Since it's inception, every aspect of the Constitution has been analyzed. Most of the criticism of the Constitution has come from the progressive movements. Some of their concerns are as follows:

– The constitution did not establish a democracy, instead the structure was intentionally designed to dilute and limit the popular will.

– The framers were men of wealth and thought that the common man could not be trusted.

– Article I, Section 10 prohibited states from inflating their currencies or forgiving debts.

– Article I, Section 8 and Article IV, Section 3 allowed the Federal government the authority to suppress social or political movements like Shays' Rebellion, which threatened to destabilize the government.

– Article IV, Section 2, paragraph 3 guaranteed that runaway slaves be returned to owners.

– Article VI, Section 1, had the Federal government accept financial obligations under the Articles of Confederation.

Most methods of analysis were usually in historical or political perspectives. Despite the obvious connection of the framers to their economic interests, very few individuals dared to attempt any economic analysis. The best-known author who ventured down that road was historian, Charles Beard. In as many years, Charles Beard published two books. The first book was *The Supreme Court and the Constitution* (1912) and the second book titled, *An Economic Interpretation of the Constitution* (1913). Both examined the relationship between the drafting and adoption of the Constitution and the men who wrote it.

In *The Supreme Court and the Constitution* (1912), Beard wrote, "The men who were principally concerned in this work of peaceful enterprise were not the philosophers, but men of business and property and the holders of public securities…The radicals… like Patrick Henry, Jefferson, and Samuel Adams, were conspicuous by their absence from the Convention." Perhaps some of the men were men of virtue and truly selfless in their actions. However, as one can see, Beard points out that most all of the framers were, in fact, creating a system that guaranteed their wealth and privileged status. Those who criticized what the framers were doing in Philadelphia were excluded from participating in the debates until after the document was completed.

TABLE 2.3 - Legislative Representation – As the representation of small farmers increased in state legislatures, representation of wealthy men decreased.				
State	% of Farmers Before the War	% of Farmers Before the War	Wealthy Before the War	Wealthy After the War
New York	23%	55%	36%	12%
New Jersey				
New Hampshire				
Maryland	12%	26%	52%	23%
Virginia				
South Carolina				

An Economic Perspective

In his pioneering book, *An Economic Interpretation of the Constitution*, Charles Beard identified five economic groups of people in 1787 - four of which had no representation at the Constitutional Convention. These unfortunate groups were among the poorest, both in representation and in wealth: women, slaves, indentured servants, and property-less white men. In stark contrast, the delegates were all white men who owned enough property to earn them the right to vote. However, even in this group there were some small farmers but no urban tradesmen.

Beard revealed the truth behind the 55 delegates' personal agendas: 38 owned government bonds that they wanted to protect; 24 were bankers and/or investors with private investments they needed to stabilize; 15 owned slaves; and 14 had business transactions in western lands that they wanted to safeguard. It was Beard's keen observation skills that exposed that the aim of the elite delegates was to insure the divisions within society – controlled at the state level and out of their new national government. These men of so-called substance felt threatened by the growing outspoken voices of the common man, and rightly so. He wrote this on the constitutional debate: "every page of the laconic record of the proceedings of the convention…shows conclusively that the members of that assembly were not seeking to realize any fine notions about democracy and equality, but were striving…to set up a system of government that would be…safeguarded on the one hand against the possibilities of despotism and on the other against the onslaught of majorities."

Following the Revolutionary War, small farmers and families of moderate income increased their representation in the state legislatures.

With these gains for the "working-class," it behooved the legislatures to become more attentive to the needs of the people. Pennsylvania was quite the trailblazer, coming as close to direct democracy as could be expected during that time. Among the many revolutionary acts they carried out was placing the executive power in a twelve-member committee with three-year overlapping terms. They held annual elections and prohibited anyone from serving more than four years in any seven-year term. In addition to this, all legislative votes and proceedings were made public. Along the same lines, no bill could become law until it had been properly publicized throughout the state and then a second vote held at the next legislative election. Pennsylvania was one of the first states to do away with property requirements for office officials and one of the first to extend the right to vote to all taxpayers.

Following the example of Pennsylvania, Rhode Island, in the interest of supporting the small farmers over the wealthy, issued an inflated currency. The state subsequently passed the Force Act, which required the wealthy to accept payment in the form of this devalued currency. The elite merchants perceived the Force Act as a violation of the economic freedoms; this lead to the beginning of a rift between the 'haves' and the 'have-nots.' Needless to say, the 55 delegates were strongly motivated to tame this wild democracy beast that had broken free from their control. Some of their recorded comments were as follows:

– Elbridge Gerry (MA): the problems under the Articles flowed "from the excess of democracy." History had taught him "by experience the danger of the leveling spirit."

FOR YOUR CONSIDERATION
ATTIRE, HYGIENE, AND THE WEATHER OF THE DAY

Constitution Hall, 1787. Wool underwear. Long wool underwear. Wool pants, cotton shirt (called a sleeved waistcoat), wigs on heads - usually bald or shaven due to lice (no all-in-one shampoo & conditioners back then). Jackets - usually linen, sometimes silk or wool. Pants were called "breeches" (rhymes with "witches") and they only came down to just below the knee. So, underneath the breeches - you guessed it - men in tights, which can be quite constricting. On to personal hygiene … not so much. Maybe bathed once a week, if that. As for dental hygiene – practically nonexistent. There were no whitening toothpastes, no breath freshening mouthwash; perhaps just a primitive stick with mystery bristles used for scraping. Deodorant? Same as the toothpaste. Clothes were not washed regularly and soap took on a different substance (sometimes made from animal fats) that seemed to defeat the whole purpose of "cleaning". To "cover up" the aromas that were no doubt emanating forth, they were as liberal with their cologne as they were with their politics (classical liberal, that is). Now add to that mix the climate. First, throw in their only sources of light - whale oil lamps, candles, and a fire in the fireplace (for light and food, not necessarily for warmth) which produced even more heat. Imagine wearing all of the above from May 14 to September 17, in the humid (75% to 83%), hot weather (around 75o and rainy) of Philadelphia, around 55 other guys, all expounding, pontificating, and expelling a lot more hot air. Keep in mind that they were supposed to be revising the Articles of Confederation when in reality, they were drafting a new government, which could be construed as a coup. Due to the secretive nature of what was taking place, they kept all the windows and doors shut and covered, so there was little circulation of fresh air. The fear was that if any commoners found out, then those responsible would be hung for treason. George Washington himself collected all the loose notes that the men made so that no one would accidentally discover their plans. Nevertheless, with temperatures rising both in climate and in excitement, they pressed on, focused and determined to carry out their mission.

Issues For You

Put yourself in Constitution Hall in 1787. How long would you last without air conditioning and other modern conveniences we have today, like pizza delivery and convenience stores?

- Edmund Randolph (VA): "the general object (of the constitution) was to provide a cure for the evils under which the United States labored; that, in tracing these evils to their origin, every man had found it in the turbulence and follies of democracy…"

- Alexander Hamilton (NY) (when making the case for a life term for Senators): "all communities divide themselves into the few and the many. The first are the rich and well born and the other the mass of the people who seldom judge or determine right."

- Gouverneur Morris (PA): It was necessary to check the "precipitancy, changeableness, and excess" of the representatives of the people by the ability and virtue of men "of great and established property – aristocracy… Such an aristocratic body will keep down the turbulence of democracy."

- Benjamin Franklin (PA): "We have been guarding against an evil that old states are most liable to, excess of power in rulers but our present danger seems to be a defect of obedience in the subjects."

These comments were indicative of most of the framers' views on the common people as well as the concept of democracy. While Beard's books have received much criticism from a variety of academics, his analysis does allow for a different perspective for deliberation. Even though his work was written almost a century ago, there are still scholars who express some of the concerns that Beard put forth. One such scholar is historian Howard Zinn. In an article entitled *Big Government for Whom?*, Zinn writes, "The Constitution set up big government, big enough to protect slave-holders against slave rebellion, to catch runaway slaves if they went from one state to another, to pay off bondholders, to pass tariffs on behalf of manufacturers, to tax poor farmers to pay for armies that would then attack the farmers if they resisted payment."[25]

Does it Still Apply Today?

The Constitution can be thought of as the rulebook for one of America's favorite pastimes - politics. Constitutional rules outline the responsibilities and powers among the national and state governments. They define relationships between governmental institutions. More specifically, they determine how candidates are selected and they explain how to modify the rules of the game as time progresses. Every aspiring politician who wants to attain office, every citizen who wants to influence what government does, and every group that wants to advance its interests in the political arena must know the rules and how to use them to their best advantage. Because the Constitution has this character, we understand it to be a fundamental structural factor influencing all of American political life. As with most games, the rules may change over time. The Constitution is no different. It is for this reason that the Constitution is sometimes referred to as a "Living Constitution."

The Constitution can be changed in three ways: the first is a formal amendment to the Constitution. The second and most common way is through judicial interpretation of the Constitution. The third way is through the political process. The Constitution may be formally amended by use of the procedures outlined in Article V of the Constitution (again, refer to Figure 2.3). This method engendered 27 amendments to the Constitution. Since its adoption, the first ten amendments added to the Constitution, also called the Bill of Rights, were added within three years of the Constitution being ratified. The fact that only 17 have been added in roughly 200 years suggests that this method of changing the Constitution is extremely difficult. Nevertheless, the formal amendments process is an important part of expanding democracy in the United States. Additional amendments have ended slavery, extended voting rights to African Americans, women, and people between the ages 18 to 20, and made the Senate subject to popular vote instead of by the state assemblies.

The Constitution is also changed by how it is interpreted by the courts – more precisely - the U.S. Supreme Court. Take for instance, in Marbury v. Madison (1803), the Court, led by John Marshall, claimed the power of **judicial review**, even though such a power is not specifically spelled out in the Constitution. This can be thought of as implied power. In Griswold v. Connecticut (1965), and also in Roe v. Wade (1973), the Supreme Court supported the claim for the fundamental right of privacy, even though again, such a right is not stated in the Constitution.

The meaning of the Constitution has also been changed through political processes, which act as guidelines for politicians and professional political operatives. Neither political parties nor their conventions are mentioned in the Constitution, but they have become an accepted and expected part of the beauty of the democratic political process. It is also fair to say that the framers would not recognize the modern presidency, which is now a far more important office than they envisioned, a change that has been brought about largely by the political and military involvement of the United States in world affairs.

Courtesy of the Library of Congress

The story of how formal amendment, judicial interpretations, and political practices have changed the constitutional rules in the United States will be told in more detail throughout this text.

Judicial Review – The right to call the actions of the other government branches null and void if they contradict the Constitution.

Mission – Spanish style adobe building with high arches and long corridors with a courtyard.

Presidios – Spanish forts along the frontier.

Pueblos – A group of adobe homes, a church, and small business that created a small town.

Ranchos – Large parcels of land given to influential families to raise cattle.

Welcome to California – History & Government

Approximately 300,000 Native Americans resided in the area we now call California. In 1542, Juan Rodriquez Cabrillo sailed into the natural harbor and named the area "San Miguel." San Miguel is now San Diego, the first European settlement along the California coast. All of the settlements would be linked by a mission system that was created by Fray Junipero Serra. Father Serra established the first **mission** in San Diego in 1769 and the second in Monterey. Before Father Serra died, he established 7 more missions along the California coast. Spain colonized California by establishing four types of settlements, the mission, **presidios**, **pueblos** and **ranchos**. Out of these four, the mission system was the most effective.

Missions were used for more than just religion. They were used as trading centers, provided educational services, and a small farm if they were they were not close to a port or pueblos. The missions were designed to be no more than a days horse ride from each other. The route used to be the main through way between missions and it became known as El Camino Real or "the King's Highway." The missions provided access to trade network that inspired larger settlements, such as San Jose (1777) and

Los Angeles (1781). Before Spain's rule came to an end, it had established 21 missions throughout California. Many of these are still in existence today. Some as functions churches while others are museums and tourist attractions.

Mexico won its independence from Spain in 1821 and gained control over all of the vast resources and lands. By 1833, Mexico seized the missions and their lands via the Mexican Secularization Act. The Mexican government converted the missions

Eureka -
"I have found it!"

Issues For You
Discuss some of the issues that had an impacted California's history but still impact the state today?

Courtesy of the Library of Congress

into parish churches and proceeded to give the Native Americans half of the land. This action increased their influence by expanding the ranchos. Within 15 years from 1830 to 1845, the number of private land grants to establish ranchos increased from 50 to 1,045. As all of this was taking place, American settlers from the east began to arrive and as time progressed so did the number of foreigners living in Mexican territory.

The 31st State

On June 14, 1846, American settlers in California started the **Bear Flag Revolt**. The revolt began in Sonoma when they placed General Marino Guadalupe Vallejo under house arrest and then declared an independent "Republic of California." The new Republic's flag had a bear and a single red star with the motto: "A bear stands his ground always and as long as the stars shine we stand for the cause." The revolt lasted for 22-days. Just as the revolt began, the United States declared war on Mexico. The Bear Flag Revolt ended when Mexico surrendered Monterey to the United States.

Prior to the Mexican American War, the United States attempted to purchase California and other western territories from Mexico but failed. Under the guise of a dispute over the Texas border, the United States used this to go to war. On May 13, 1846, President Polk asked for a declaration of war against Mexico. By 1847, the United States had seized the northern territory of Mexico or over half of Mexico's total land. The land included Texas, New Mexico, Arizona, and California. On February 2, 1848, Mexico and the United States ended hostilities by signing the Treaty of Guadalupe Hidalgo. The treaty established a new border between the United States and Mexico as well as recognized the existing Spanish and Mexican land grants.

On January 24, 1848, James Marshall discovered gold at Sutter's mill. No sooner had the discovery been made than "**Eureka**" was heard around the globe. By 1849, people began to come to the "golden state" from all corners of the earth. The gold rush increased California's population by astronomical rates. According to the U.S. Census, in 1848 there were 15,000 people who lived in California. By 1850, there were 92,000 and by 1860 there was 380,000. This trend continues today. In 1990, the U.S. Census reported 30 million people living in California. The 2000 Census report approximately 34 million residents, and the projection for 2010 is approximately 39 million. In order to move people and goods more efficiently, greater emphasis was put on developing a transnational railroad.

In the fall of 1849, Californian overwhelmingly ratified the first California Constitution. The Constitution created a republican form of government that is very similar to the one that exists today. The Constitution included:

Bill of Rights

Plural executive branch (Governor and Lt. Governor)

Legislature (Senate and Assembly)

Elected judicial branch (four levels to the state courts)

Voting was limited to White males over the age of 21

Both English and Spanish were recognized as the state languages.

On September 9, 1850, California became the 31st state admitted to the Union. Shortly thereafter, Congress quickly moved to make California a non-slave state. What should be especially noted is that California was not required to be a territory as other states were and it was the first state to not share a common border with another state. The most powerful group of individuals in the state were the Central Pacific Railroad founders, also called the "Big Four": Leland Stanford, Collis P. Huntington, Mark Hopkins, and Charles Crocker. In 1862, President Lincoln signed into law the Pacific Railroad Bill. The creation of the Pacific Railroad added tremendous wealth and power to the "Big Four." The railroads were the main economic power brokers in California. No one could successfully run for state of local office without their approval. Because of the control over the state political machines, the railroad companies were able to bring in thousands of Chinese to work in slave-like conditions to help build the rail infrastructure. When the rails connected in Promontory, Utah in 1869, completing the transcontinental railroad, many of the Chinese workers were left to fend for themselves. Having limited skills and even less knowledge of English, most of the workers experienced great difficulties trying to gain employment. In addition, hostility towards them began to grow.

As a reaction to the large number of unemployed Chinese people abandoned by railroad companies, the Workingmen's Party formed. The party consisted of disgruntled white workers who were unhappy with the situation. Several measures were passed: a public school system, an eight-hour workday, and land monopoly laws. In addition, they passed anti-immigrant measures that placed restrictions on Chinese labor. It was from the strength of this movement that a Second California State Constitution (1879) came to be adopted and ratified by voters. After the State Constitution was ratified, the United States Supreme Court declared anti-immigrant measures unconstitutional. Today, immigration remains a divisive issue amongst Californians and

Courtesy of the Library of Congress

the country at large. In the 1990's, proposition 187 prevented illegal Mexican immigrants from receiving such services as medical treatment or access to education for their children; it also eliminated affirmative action in public education. Even in 2007, the U.S. Congress and President Bush have debated how best to "secure" our borders. Private citizen groups, such as the "Minute Men" have created vigilante organizations that patrol the southern border to stop the "invasion" of foreigners.

The California Progressives

At the turn of the 20th century, the Southern Pacific Railroad, which owned one-fifth of all non-public land in the state, dominated state politics and controlled California politicians. The progressive wing of the state Republican Party championed such issues as reforming politics, weakening political parties, enacting child labor laws, and conservation policies led by Governor Hiram Johnson. William Randolph Hearst, who published critical articles and political cartoons in his San Francisco Examiner, aided the progressives in diluting the power of the railroads.

In addition to ending the power of the "Big Four" over state and local politics, the most important legacy the Progressives left behind in California was the implementation of direct democracy (see chapter one). Power was placed in the hands of the voters to pass laws or amend the state constitution through the electoral process. In addition, the recall was put into effect to remove corrupt politicians from state and local offices. In 1911, the Progressives brought suffrage on state issues to California women nine years before they had the right to vote in federal elections.

Issues For You
What is the legacy of the Progressive movement in California?

How Do We Compare?

Constitutions

The United Kingdom and The United States[26]

When we make a simple institutional and political comparison between the United States and Britain, the following are among the most striking differences. Throughout this section, notice how Britain's constitution evolved in comparison to the United States' Constitution. For example, Britain's constitution does not consist of just one document. Their constitution is encompassed by British traditions, laws, and Parliamentary acts, whereas the U.S. has one main document that embodies the law of the land, which is not easily amended, as you read earlier in this chapter.

Unlike the U.S. and almost all other modern nation states, Britain has no codified constitution. But, the United Kingdom does have a constitution in the sense

Factoid:
In the movie, *V for Vendetta*, the British Parliament building played a leading role. The historical basis of the movie recounts the opening of Parliament on November 5, 1605, when 13 disaffected Catholics tried to assassinate King James I (Protestant) by blowing up the building; this daring act became known as the "gun powder plot."

of basic rules of the game that are generally recognized, internalized and observed by the political class, and guarded over by a number of "watchdogs".[27]

Briefly retracing the manner of Britain's constitutional development, we begin with the Magna Carta (1215),[28] which established the principle of limited government and rule of law, but not a democracy. English nobles prevented the

Courtesy of Corel

Profiles in Politics
Tony Blair (1953 -   )

Borne to a **barrister** and lecturer, Tony Charles Lynton Blair has continued to build upon expanding the power of prime minister, making the position more akin to a presidency than a "first among equals." Long before he became **prime minister**, Blair had ideas about how he would move the Labour Party from left to center. During one of the Labour Party's conventions, Clause IV of the party's constitution provoked much discussion. The clause referred to the means of production being commonly owned, Blair urged the conventioneers to modify the Clause. Strong opposition from the old Labour members emerged but was ineffective. His success in modifying Clause IV allowed him to call the Labour Party the New Labour Party. In May 1997, Mr. Blair led his party to huge success at the general election. With that victory, the New Labour Party increased its majority. As a result, Blair was appointed prime minister, the youngest since 1812.

Blair's ideology, sometimes called the "third way" between capitalism and socialism, appeared to be **zeitgeist**, or the spirit of the time. As Blair progressively moved his party toward the center, so did President Bill Clinton for the democrats and Gerhard Schroeder for the Sozialdemokratische Partie Deutschlands (SPD) or the Social Democratic Party of Germany. Within the first two years of his term, Blair removed from the House of Lords, 92 hereditary peers. He increased funding for health and education programs. In June 2001, Blair again led his party to another victory. The next day, Blair described his party's victory as "a mandate for investment and reform."

With the War on Terror launched in September 2001, Blair's second term focused on foreign policy issues. While his domestic policies remained unaffected, it was his foreign policies that became troublesome for him. His "canine-like loyalty" to Bush's "cowboy military tactics" have been both praised and criticized by Americans and Britons alike. As the "sectarian violence"[29] continued, Blair and his New Labour Party won a third term in May 2005, but its majority control narrowed. Acquiescing to public opinion, Blair shifted his attention back to domestic policies. Plagued with criticism over his foreign policies, Blair said that "respect" would be the focus of his third term, which he describes as "A proper sense of respect in our schools, in our communities, in our towns and our villages." After ten years as Prime Minister, Tony Blair submitted his resignation to Queen Elizabeth on June 27, 2007.

Barrister -
A barrister a lawyer who is a member of one of the Inns of Court; s/he has the honor of making appeals in the higher courts.

Minister -
head of a major department as in a "ministry of government.'

Prime Minister -
chief of government in Parliamentary systems.

Zeitgeist –
Spirit of the Time

King from carrying out tax increases without their input, creating a mixed monarchy (see chapter one). Parliament was originally created to raise funds for the wars with France but eventually became its own entity, preventing the king from obtaining absolute power. In medieval England, a semi-independent judiciary began to make laws, based on prior rulings. This is now known as the Common Law system, which is also practiced in America.

Institutional Pluralism -
Refers to the creation of a monarchy, two legislative houses, civic governments in the cities and courts.

Following the Magna Carta was the growth of **institutional pluralism** and later a sporadic series of power shifts from the monarchy to Parliament - more specifically, the House of Commons. Parliament's victory over the King during the English civil wars (1643 - 1648) further encouraged their quest for power. After the wars, Parliament began to feel on par with the King. Primarily through the House of Commons, Parliament began to impose its rule over the monarchy. Nevertheless, democratic principles were beginning to take shape. For example, the call for "one man, one vote," came about. This principle was based on the Puritan belief that all men are created equal in the eyes of God. These were anti-loyalist sentiments, which took on the shape of republican values. Soldiers, tradesmen, artisans, and farmers argued that they were equal to the nobles and should have the right to vote. Out of this group came the "levelers," who were called this because they desired to level out society. They advocated the radical idea of one man, one vote, which was two centuries ahead of its time. However, the more powerful and conservative population of England, including Oliver Cromwell, won out. In spite of this, the levelers' place in history was secured by their introduction of universal franchise (giving everyone the right to vote) into the collective mind.

As a result of the civil wars, Parliament captured Charles I, put him on trial, and found him guilty. Parliament secured their superiority over the monarchy with the execution of Charles I in 1649. During the years 1649 - 1660, England had no reigning monarch. Since there was no one to lead, England turned to the only power structure left - the army, led by Oliver Cromwell. He formed a republic called a Commonwealth. Once the republic was set up, he relinquished complete control to Parliament. Infighting and power struggles ensued. In 1653, the aid of Cromwell was sought once again by his followers in Parliament, who designated him Lord Protector - a kind of king without a crown. He declared a military dictatorship to try to provide some stability. By the time Cromwell died in 1658, the British subjects had had enough of the chaotic republic.

Parliament renewed the monarchy by installing Charles II in 1660. Charles II, who was deeply loyal to the Pope and Catholicism, removed laws that discriminated against Catholics and non-Anglican Protestants. This alarmed the people because they just endured decades of religious conflict between the Protestant and Catholic monarchs. Their worries continued after Charles II died in 1685 and his brother James II ascended to the throne. James, being openly Catholic, continued carrying out his brother's legacy. Parliament saw this as the return to a Catholic state and absolutism. Seeing the errors of their ways, Parliament took advantage of the people's disdain for James II and had him exiled in 1688. Parliament invited James II's daughter, Mary, and her husband, William, to rule as England's new King and Queen. This new dawn was called a "glorious revolution" and was truly so, since this new peaceful leadership was set up by contract rather than with war and bloodshed. This contract was called a "Bill of Rights" (not the same as the U.S.'s Bill of Rights), which, in 1689, outlined Parliament's relationship with the Crown. They would do this again by contract with George I of Hanover in 1714.

George I gave the House of Commons its executive power, which was composed of ministers and presided over by a first or a prime minister. This system is similar to what it is today, except at that time, the monarch picked the ministers; today, the prime minister makes the selections. Furthermore, the cabinet answered to the King instead of Parliament, which is also the practice now. By the time of the American Revolution in 1776, George III temporarily took over the House of Commons by packing it with his supporters. After the British defeat in the colonies, power over the cabinet and prime minister was made responsible only to Commons and not the King. Since that time, the prime minister has been the focus of political power in Britain, making the monarch a figurehead - one who reigns but does not rule. Later on in the 19th century, a system of political parties, the Tories and Whigs, emerged. The parties were identified by their degree of support for the King. Out of the Tories came the conservative party and from the Whigs, the liberal party – similar to the way that the Federalists and the Democratic Republicans evolved as the first official political parties in the United States.

Issues For You
Compare and contrast the American Presidential system and the British Parliamentary system.

With the cabinet and prime minister's new roles, a tradition began that the government should be made up of the largest (numerically superior) party. This specification has never been written into British law. This can be thought of as the principle of parliamentary confidence. In other words, a government stays in office only as long as it has a sustained flow of political support from a majority in the House of Commons. This is the approximate point at which Walter Bagehot described what he called "the English Constitution" in 1867. Similar to Britain, the United States' Constitution does not mention parties. However, Madison did point out in the Federalist papers that "factions" are a necessary evil.

In addition to this, a series of electoral reforms beginning in 1832 led to the rise of the modern party system.[30] At this time, very few Britons were allowed to vote. This occurred at approximately the same time that white males gained the right to vote in the United States. The Reform Acts of 1832, 1860s, 1880s, 1918, and 1928 expanded the right to vote to the majority of Britons. As the voting franchised expanded, both the Conservative and Liberal parties turned their focus to the citizens and some of the principals of democracy with rival parties organized outside Parliament as competitive electoral organizations. During this time, the Labour party surpassed the Liberal party. The support for Labour primarily came from labor unions and other workers' organizations based on Labour's promise to focus on welfare measures. In 1945, Labour victory came to power and established a welfare state, which is a system that redistributes wealth from the rich to the poor through health care, financial assistance, retirement plans, and so on. The welfare state receives constant criticism. Conservatives and "New Labour" Party leader, Tony Blair, are persistent in their efforts to undercut the system. Once again, we see the same issues arise with Britain as did in the U.S. with the New Deal of the 1930's and the Great Society of the 1960's - both instances where conservatives and "New Democrats" proceeded to dismantle components of our welfare state.

Since Britain's constitution is unwritten, very few acts can be ruled unconstitutional. Case in point, nowhere does it specifically grant power to a bicameral legislature such as the House of Commons and the House of Lords. The House of Commons can legally restructure the House of Lords. For example, Lloyd George passed the Parliamentary Act of 1911, which prevents Lords from delaying financial legislation (taxes, appropriations) for more than 30 days and all other legislation for more than two years. Lords can amend legislation and send it back to the House of Commons, where a simple majority deletes the recommendations. The House of Lords is the only check on the House of Commons. The more power that is gained by one House over the other, the further weakened the concept of checks and balances and separation of powers becomes.

Since 1958, the upper chamber has benefited from having many accomplished "life peers" added to its ranks. Life peers are distinguished Britons who excel in science, literature, politics, military service, business, and the arts. A life peer title cannot be passed on to the next generation like previous hereditary titles. The hereditary titles made the House of Lords retain much of its original "feudal" image. It had become a kind of pre-democratic relic in a democratic age. Many Britons agreed that Lords needed reform, but were uncertain as to how to accomplish this. In 1999, Tony Blair removed most hereditary lords from their positions while allowing the life peers to retain their votes. Without a codified constitution, prime ministers and the ruling party can alter the political process with a simple plurality in the House of Commons.

However well the British constitutional system may have worked in the past, it has become increasingly difficult to maintain the credibility and legitimacy of such potentially ambiguous traditional conventions and "understandings." Today the House of Lords is close to being powerless, but it is not entirely functionless. The famous musical writing team of the Victorian era, Gilbert and Sullivan summed it up nicely – "The House of Peers, throughout the war, did nothing in particular, and did it very well"[31]

Given the complexity of the British constitution as compared to the United States, one can hopefully see the need not only for enforcement but also for respecting the supreme law of the land. Without both elements of enforcement and respect for the rulebook, the game would simply need to be called off. If you have had the experience of siblings or bigger stronger friends altering and making up rules to benefit them during play, then you are well familiar with the countless quarrels and time-outs that ended ultimately in everyone being sent home.

Chapter Summary

During this chapter, we looked at a number of issues surrounding the Constitution of the United States. While it is not perfect, it is what we have and we must try to understand its complex origins. A document like the Constitution that has lasted over 200 years with only 27 amendments is proof that the framers created an amendment process that was so complex it insured the Constitution's survival well beyond the authors' lifetimes. The framers were just human like the rest of us, full of contradictions, prejudices, emotional outbursts, and profound realizations. What their true motivations were we may never truly know; but what we do know is this - they produced an end product. The Constitution is widely viewed as a living, breathing document that was meant to provide stability for all times. If this is true, we, as citizens, must make sure we keep a constant vigil to insure that it does not die or even be put on life support. It is our civic duty to hold the elected officials responsible for their actions and when they fail to do their job, we must take action - not through violence but through the power of the pen, or in today's world, the computer. In adding some information on California, we are able to see how a state constitution is able to change more quickly and be more responsive to the events of the time. This is what Thomas Jefferson had in mind when he said a constitution should reflect the ideals of the people at that time. We have also seen the result of when a state's desires come into conflict with the U.S. Constitution, Article VI's "Supremacy Clause" rules it "unconstitutional", forcing the voters of the state to seek alternative remedies to their problems. To gain an aerial view perspective of our Constitutional process, we surveyed and compared the United Kingdom's version of the constitution to ours. As is the case for many countries, events dictate the course of politics - for America, it was the Revolutionary War, the chaos that ensued, and 55 rich white guys meeting in secret. For the U.K., it was religious clashes, civil wars, and the evolution from a feudal past to a modern democracy. After 200 years, the Constitution is still the Supreme Law of the Land, making us a nation of laws, and not just people. Simply put, no one, regardless of socioeconomic status, is above the law. We must all play by the rules of the game or else democracy will not succeed.

Key Terms:

Separation of Powers

Veto Power

Signing Statement

Red Coats

Minutemen

Tenant Farmers

The Virginia Plan

Legislative Branch

Executive Branch

Judiciary

Checks and Balances

Proportional Representation

Council of Revision

The New Jersey Plan

Unicameral/Bicameral Legislature

Supremacy Clause

The "Great Compromise" or Connecticut Plan

Three-fifths Compromise

Federalism

IX Amendment

Judicial Review

Mission

Presidios

Pueblos

Ranchos

Eureka

Institutional Pluralism

Barrister

Minister

Prime Minister

Zeitgeist

Websites:

Federal Sites:

www.archives.gov/national_archives_experience/constitution_founding_fathers.html

http://www.archives.gov/national-archives-experience/charters/constitution.html

www.usconstitution.net

www.house.gov

www.senate.gov

www.whitehouse.gov

http://www.supremecourtus.gov/

California Sites:

http://www.ca.gov/

http://www.leginfo.ca.gov/const-toc.html

http://www.ss.ca.gov/archives/level3_const1849.html

Boulder Dam, 1940
Dams like the Boulder Dam, also known as the
Hoover Dam, are examples of cooperative Federalism.
Courtesy of the Library of Congress

CHAPTER 3

FEDERALISM

CHAPTER OUTLINE

- DEMOCRACY AND ACTION –
  PUBLIC SCHOOLS: "NO CHILD LEFT BEHIND"

- WHAT IS FEDERALISM?

- EVOLUTION OF FEDERALISM
  EXPANDING THE NATIONAL GOVERNMENT

- DEVOLUTION: THE NEXT PHASE?

- THE "GOLDEN STATE"
  AND THE FEDERAL GOVERNMENT

- HOW DO WE COMPARE?
  GERMANY AND THE UNITED STATES

Democracy and Action - Public Schools: No Child Left Behind?

In the presidential election year of 2000, one of the prime issues was education – more specifically, the ailing condition of public education. What could be done to remedy such a complicated issue? The people wanted to know and they looked to future presidential candidates for answers. At that time, each state received federal funding for education and in addition, could spend that money the way they saw fit.

Courtesy of Jupiter Images

Furthermore, they had the authority to set their own curriculum. Recognizing the opportunity of this situation, republican candidate George W. Bush made education one of the signature issues of his entire presidential campaign. One of the first pieces of legislation the Bush Administration pushed through was called the No Child Left Behind Act. The White House had strong bipartisan support from Democratic Senator Ted Kennedy (D-MA) and, at the time, it was hailed by members of both Democrat and Republican alike as a giant step forward in education. It was signed into law in early 2002.

The No Child Left Behind Act requires that all states provide formal outlines that show how students will achieve academic proficiency. Schools are also accountable for producing state and school district report cards annually, based upon **standardized test** scores. Schools that are not showing tangible progress must alter their strategies; if the school is still failing after five years, the Act stipulates that the school will be subject to major changes, which may include staff replacement, management changes, and/or state takeover. Obviously, this law makes it very easy for the federal government, instead of teachers and parents, to have more control over educational funds and essentially, school curriculum. Because states have to show tangible improvement or risk having their federal funding cut, many schools implement test preparation programs consisting of intensive math and reading. Needless to say, the consequence of replacing traditional creative curriculum with mostly test preparation exercises is that other much-needed subjects such as science, history, art, and music, are deemed less crucial. Physical education is usually spared because obesity among children is also considered a major public health issue. Students with economical or social disadvantages are allotted even more time for test preparation, virtually cutting out all other subjects. Those students who are learning English as a Second Language are in even more of a quandary because not only are they negotiating acquiring language just as all children do in early grades, but they also have to adapt to American culture, something that is often a point of contention in standardized test language. This essentially puts the focus on teaching children how to test well rather than teaching any real curriculum.

In the five years since the law went into effect, it has become clear to many states and educators that the No Child Left Behind Act has shown evidence of being more detrimental to children than helpful. In an exercise of state power, many states have begun the process of passing legislation to either amend the Act or seek waivers excepting them from having to enforce the Act. At of the end of 2006, the positive implications of the No Child Left Behind Act remains to be seen.[1] Within this chapter, you will read about some of the major points of federalism that began to take shape in the Constitution. In addition, we will compare federalism between the United States and Germany.

What is Federalism?

"All communities divide themselves into the few and the many. The first are the rich and the well-born; the other the mass of the people ... turbulent and changing, they seldom judge or determine right. Give therefore to the first class a distinct, permanent share in the Government ...Nothing but a permanent body can check the imprudence of democracy."

~ Alexander Hamilton (1757-1804) [2]

A federal system of government is one in which powers are divided between a national government and smaller governments, such as a state, or provinces. Each unit of government is sovereign within its own sphere of influence. As discussed in chapters one and two, there are many different structures of democratic governments – two of which are the **unitary system** and a **confederation**. For example, the British use a unitary system in which all authority rests with the national government. The confederate style can be seen in the United States under the Articles of Confederation and more recently, in the European Union, where each state or country has the ultimate authority.

The Constitution and Federalism

As it appears with the Constitution, historical concepts may appear to be simple and straightforward, but in actuality, they are extremely complex. Federalism is no different. Before moving ahead, let's do a quick review of chapters one and two. In chapter one, you learned about the major points that encompass democracy. In chapter two, you read how the country was in a terrible state under the Articles of Confederation. The framers specifically rejected a government based on a confederation, in which power is decentralized among sovereign states, and the national government has limited powers to the degree that it must acquiesce to the states' wishes. In the end, the framers selected a republican form of government - it is from this structure that our style of federalism has developed into what it is today.

Theories of Federalism

Two types of federalism can be described as dual and cooperative. Since its inception in 1787, the concept of federalism has evolved. The framers who advocated a strong central government would be in awe of what it is today - the national government is involved in education, public transportation, public health, and welfare programs. Remember that the Constitution is the supreme law of the land and it divides powers between the national and state governments. A clear distribution of powers between the national government and several smaller state-run governments is precisely what the framers had in mind when the Constitution was drafted. This is known as dual federalism. From economic necessity emerged cooperative federalism, which may at first appear chaotic in terms of determining which branch of government has jurisdiction over each issue and concern. But as the name suggests, cooperative federalism brings the federal and state governments together to work in tandem to insure that citizens' needs are being met.

Federalism –
The distribution of power in a government between a central authority and individual state governments

Unitary Government or System –
Locus of power is given to centralized government

Confederation –
An association of sovereign states or communities

Dual Federalism –
A system in which each level of power remains supreme in its own jurisdiction, keeping the states separate and distinct from the national government

Cooperative Federalism –
Federal and state governments work in tandem to insure that the general welfare of the people is taken care of.

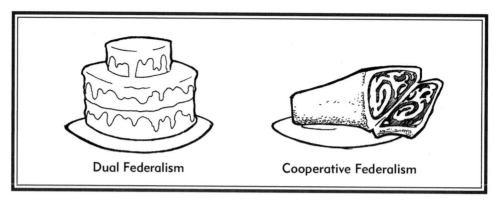

Dual Federalism   Cooperative Federalism

Dual Federalism

Although the Constitution does not specifically use the term "federalism", it does explain which government possesses which specific power. For example, the Constitution states that the national or federal government has delegated or enumerated powers. These powers include coining of money, providing for the military, making treaties with foreign governments, and declaring war to reiterate from chapter two. All powers not specifically stated in the Constitution are given to the states or are placed under the reserve clause in the Tenth Amendment. These powers include conducting elections, establishing local governments, and developing and maintaining intrastate public works. Common powers that both the federal and state governments hold are known as **concurrent powers**. These concurrent powers allow both the federal government and the states to collect taxes, borrow money, create laws, and use eminent domain to name a few shared governances.

Since the Constitution wasn't ratified until the 1930's, the country has been under a system of dual federalism. One way to view dual federalism is by looking at it as if it was a cake - a layer-cake to be exact.[3] You'll notice that the layer cake has one layer on top of the other with a clear division between the two by some type of cream or frosting. In this analogy, the top layer is the federal government and the bottom layer is state government. The cream frosting in the middle is the Supreme Court keeping the system in balance. The third layer of the cake is the states, which are directly in charge of the day-to-day operations of maintaining peoples' lives. If someone is in need of welfare assistance for example, they turn to the state or local government, not the federal government. However, most state and local government policies were enacted by many social and church organizations such as the National Congress of Mothers, the General Federation of Women's Clubs, and the National Association of Colored Women.[4]

Migrant Mother, Nipoma, California, 1936
Courtesy of the Library of Congress

Due to the crash of the stock market in 1929, companies lost millions of dollars, forcing workers to be laid off. This set off a chain reaction. Dual federalism effectively succumbed to its ailing health with the onslaught of the Great Depression in the 1930s after being on life-support since 1865. Most states could not deal with the sudden economic vacuum. With unemployment rates reaching 25% in 1932, the general public could not support itself or make mortgage payments, requiring banks and other financial institutions to foreclose on properties. Because of the shortage of jobs, very few buyers were available who could purchase the foreclosed properties and as a result, banks suffered huge losses. The downward spiral continued as banks ceased operations and closed their doors. The entire economic system was on the verge of collapse and people began to think Karl Marx was right about capitalism. As fear set in at all levels of society, states realized they could not adequately deal with their problems or the needs of the people. Everyone turned to the federal government for assistance.

To address the problems facing the nation, under the leadership of President Franklin Delano Roosevelt, the federal government implemented the New Deal. The New Deal consisted of programs that were carried out under the umbrella of the state governments. Some of these programs included unemployment benefits, welfare for families in need, and employment programs. To help reinstate trust in the banks, the federal government created federal deposit insurance, which guaranteed deposits. In addition, the Federal Reserve Board was given more power to regulate the banks. The Federal Housing Administration (FHA) was created to aid home buyers. The FHA developed the federal guaranteed home loan with little money down, long-term home loans. This was the beginning of what has been termed Cooperative Federalism.

Cooperative Federalism

Unlike dual federalism, cooperative federalism is always adapting to the needs of the country. The federal and state governments work in tandem to insure that the general welfare of the people is taken care of. The concept of an unmistakable division of powers between the states and the national government was replaced with the idea that all branches of government should and can work together. Returning to the cake analogy, cooperative federalism can be viewed as a marble cake. When viewed as a marble cake, one cannot see a clear separation between the flavors – the flavors represent powers and they are all intertwined.

Within cooperative federalism, we have seen several trends evolve over the years. The first trend of cooperative federalism, which was in place during the 1930s and 1940s, was discussed above. The next trend developed in the 1960s with President Lyndon Johnson's "War on Poverty." This period has been called creative federalism. The last program was a reverse trend, shifting powers back to the states. This started under President Nixon but didn't take off until the 1980s under President Reagan - it seems to be continuing through to today. This period was coined "New Federalism". During this time, one of the most effective tools the federal government had to disburse funding was through federal grants.

Federal Grants

Since the Great Depression the federal government has gradually increased federal spending in order to aid the state. In doing so, it also increased its power over the states. The funding usually comes in federal grants. This is known as grant-in-aid system.

Grant-in-Aid.

The main device for employing cooperative federalism is the grant-in-aid system. A grant-in-aid is a federal payment to a state or local government for a specific item. This can include building or maintaining infrastructure such as highways, bridges, and aquifers, to name a few. Grant-in-aid comes in two specific types. The first is a categorical grant, which is given on condition that the state or local government completes a specific activity. The second is a block grant, which means the federal government provides funding with very little oversight or instruction on how the state should run the program.

Categorical Grants

Matching Funds –
Federal funds given to the state or local governments that must be matched, dollar for dollar by the receiving agency, or they will not be granted.

As stated above, these funds are set aside for a specific program and cannot be used for anything that is not specifically stated in that program. The grants have detailed guidelines on how the programs are to be administered. In addition many of these programs require **matching funds**.

There are three types of categorical grants. They are project grants, formula grants, and open-ended reimbursements. In order for a state or local government to receive funds, the agency must submit an application to the federal government who decides who receives the money. With a formula grant, the funds are automatically distributed according to a calculation derived by Congress. Lastly, with open-ended reimbursements, state and local governments are reimbursed for the funds they distribute on behalf of the federal government. They are open-ended because the funding varies with the economic time. The federal government must reimburse states and local agencies for unemployment compensation and welfare programs, more so during times of economic recession than when the economy is booming. The majority of federal aid is categorized as open-ended reimbursements.

It is important to note the differences between the programs since specific groups favor specific types of grants. Federal agencies prefer the project grants because they have control over who gets the funding. Similarly, Congress prefers the formula grants because they determine who gets what. A thrifty Representative could work the formula to benefit their district over others. State and local officials prefer the open-ended grants because they are based on the economy and they automatically adjust when needed. All three types serve the nation's needs but they all shift power from the states to the federal government - or simply put, whoever does the paying does the saying.

Block Grants

Block grants are tools that are favored by Republicans because they are extremely flexible for states to administer with very little limitations from Washington. Most of the block grants are used on issues that those on the political right feel the federal government should not be involved. These include funding education and welfare programs. As an additional feature, most block grants require matching features so if states and local governments cannot meet their part of the financial obligation, the federal government can cut funding in following years, thus effectively cutting aid to programs without having to rewrite the legislation or face criticism in the media or in their home states. Lastly, block grants are a way to shift power back to the states from the federal government. This method of grants was the method in which conservatives who wanted to cut federal programs were able to shift the responsibilities to the states. This trend has become known as devolution.

Evolution of Federalism

Expanding the National Government

The Early Years

Despite the delegated powers in the Constitution, there were many issues that were left unresolved. Some of these problems emerged right away and the need for additional powers was realized – however, this unto itself was a problem. In the debate between which level of government had the power, the courts have often been the final arbitrators.

Writ of Mandamus – A court order that forces an official to act

Hamilton v. Jefferson

The first arguments over the powers of the federal government began during President Washington's first term. The issue was the creation of a national bank. The elastic clause in Article I, Section 8, Clause 18, gives the power to Congress "to make all Laws which shall be necessary and proper for carrying into Execution" its delegated powers. In 1791, Secretary of the Treasury, Alexander Hamilton, argued that Congress now possessed the power to create a national bank because it was charged with the power to coin money, maintain a uniform monetary system, and regulate commerce. The Secretary of State, Thomas Jefferson, argued that the states had power of the banking system. The Constitution did not give that power exclusively to the federal government - with the Tenth Amendment in place, it defaulted to the states.

These arguments go back to the disagreements between the federalists and anti-federalists (see chapter two). Hamilton was promoting a new type of powers called implied powers. Jefferson opposed these powers for fear that Congress would usurp any powers it desired. In the end, President Washington authorized a national bank. A larger issue loomed, however - was the bank unconstitutional?

Marbury v. Madison (1803)

The issue of implied powers emerged again in 1803. This decision was the Court's first exercise of the judicial review. William Marbury had been named Washington D.C.'s justice of the peace by President John Adams and confirmed by the Senate in 1801 just before Thomas Jefferson took office. At the time of the appointment, John Marshall, Adam's Secretary of State, was chosen to serve as Chief Justice to the United States Supreme Courts. It was Marshall's responsibility to convey Marbury's commission. Marshall did not deliver it before turning the position over to Jefferson's secretary of state, James Madison. Marbury, having not received his commission, requested Madison to turn it over to him. Madison refused the demand. Marbury asked the Supreme Court for a **writ of mandamus** via a provision in the Judiciary Act of 1789. Chief Justice Marshall, when writing the Court's majority opinion, stated that Article III, Section 2, in the Constitution, which allows the Court to issue a writ of mandamus only under its jurisdiction as an appellate court. Therefore, that section of the Judiciary Act of 1789 that allowed for such requests to be fast tracked to the Supreme Court was void. In a case where there is conflict between legislation and the Constitution, the legislation is found to be unconstitutional, based on Articles III and VI's supremacy clause of the Constitution. This case codified the court's power for judicial review and implied powers. Despite this ruling, other challenges to the expansion of national government powers continued to emerge.

Issues For You
Which social problems do you think should be handled by the federal government and which should be handled by the states?

McCulloch v. Maryland (1819)

The issue of implied powers emerged again with the charter of the second national bank in 1816. The case came about due to the bank's refusal to pay a tax levied by Maryland on notes issued by the bank. Chief Justice Marshall ruled that the last clause of Article I, Section 8, gives Congress the power to carry out its expressly granted powers, and that it was "necessary and proper" for the bank officials to impose taxation, borrowing, and dispatching of funds for the support of its military. "Let the end be legitimate, let it be within the scope of the Constitution, and all means which are appropriate, which are plainly adapted to that end, which are not prohibited, but consistent with the letter and spirit of the Constitution, are constitutional."

Marshall continued that Maryland could not hold the bank responsible for taxes because states' that exercised their powers to state tax threatened the supremacy of the federal government within its own sphere of influence. "The States have no power, by taxation or otherwise, to retard, impede, or in any manner control, the operation of the constitutional laws enacted by Congress to carry into execution the powers vested in the general government."

Creative Federalism –
An Initiative begun in the 1960's under President Johnson that augmented the idea of a partnership between the national government and the states.

The Power to Control Commerce

Gibbons v. Ogden (1824)

In a classic opinion, Chief Justice Marshall again defines the powers of the federal government quite broadly. According to the Chief Justice, Congress's power was defined to include regulating foreign and interstate commerce, including navigation between the United States and foreign nations, as well as every commercial transaction that occurs between two or more states. This meant that the interstate commerce could regulate intrastate commerce as well - thus effectively expanding the powers of the federal government over state governments.

Federalism in the Twentieth Century –
The Rise and Fall of Cooperative Federalism

Cooperative Federalism 1930-1960

As you have already read, cooperative federalism began as a result of the Great Depression during the 1930s and 1940s. During this time Congress created many new federal programs to assist state and local agencies with the economic disaster. With the success of the New Deal, President Truman continued using grant-in-aid for education, transportation, and health programs. These were further expanded under President Eisenhower's administration. By 1960, the federal government was spending close to $7 billion a year on 132 grants. As the federal governments spending grew, so did the conditions and regulations.[5]

Creative Federalism 1963-1968

In 1963, President Johnson launched his attack on poverty by declaring war on it and in the end, using his Great Society program, which included federal programs to make a social welfare system that operated more efficiently. Johnson used **creative federalism**, a tool to further develop the relationship between the national government and the states. In theory, the national government works directly with cities, counties, and school districts, in order to provide social services. In addition, he extended funding to nonprofit organizations and extended existing programs to reach rural and poor communities. President Johnson's "war on poverty" promoted equal opportunity in education, solved urban problems by providing direct aid to the cities, and guaranteed equal rights for all minority groups. Most of the increase in funding went to new programs, such as Medicare and Medicaid. These programs provided national health care for the elderly and poor, and the Elementary and Secondary Education Act (ESEA) that gave national funding for public education. Johnson plan was to provide the funding and direction and the states and local government would administer them. But with all well-intentioned plans, problems began to overtake the systems. Bureaucracies at all levels of government began to become large and inefficient. Individuals became dependent on the government to provide for them.

Johnson's focus on education was far reaching. Programs like Head Start and Public Broadcasting System (PBS) helped children from all walks of life. Those who attended Head Start were introduced to a,b,cs and 1,2,3s earlier in life, laying the foundation for their primary education. Those who could not attend school could watch educational programs on PBS such as Sesame Street and Mr. Roger's Neighborhood. Hot breakfast and lunch programs were put in place to provide nutritious meals. Statistical evidence suggests that Johnson was on the right track because retention and graduation rates amongst lower-income families increased between the 1970s and 1980s.[6]

The Great Society programs provided positive results as well. Minority groups that were marginalized before became empowered and active in the democratic process. The funding aimed at improving quality of life for the disabled, migrant workers, and neglected children was effective. Other programs that promoted bilingual education and desegregation were successful as well. By 1968 when President Johnson left office, his programs were a great success and they helped empower those whom society had forgotten along the way. While critics of these programs have said there is little evidence to show that Head Start helps children beyond fourth grade, it begs the question - is this because Head Start wasn't effective or is it because of cuts in funding to the program over the last few decades?

New Federalism –
A program that shifted power away from the federal government to the state governments.

General Revenue Sharing (GRS) –
A function from the New Federalism program in which funds were given to the states, free of any restrictions on how it could be spent.

Special Revenue Sharing (SRS) –
Another facet of the New Federalism program in which clusters of categorical grants-in-aid in like policy areas, such as crime management or health care, were joined into a single block grant.

The Birth of New Federalism 1969-1974

President Nixom at a Press Conference
Courtesy of the Library of Congress

President Nixon's **New Federalism** program was created to rollback many of the programs created under the New Deal and President Johnson's creative federalism. The ultimate desire was to remove power from the national government and return it to the state. In 1972, President Nixon used **general revenue sharing (GRS)**, which distributed money to the states with no restrictions, and **special revenue sharing (SRS)**, which grouped grants-in-aid in other similar policy areas and turned them into a single block grant. These programs were not successful. The formulas over compensated some cities and states while under funding others. In addition, while the programs were thought to give power back to the states, they actually had the adverse effect. The GRS extended the national government's influence over states and local governments. Funds were placed in each jurisdiction's general treasury thus placing states under national regulations in areas like civil rights, affirmative action, and fair wages; meanwhile, in the SRS, funding actually increased with several block grants. Trying to gain support for his New Federalism programs, Nixon promised to increase funds to state and local officials' pet projects. All of President Nixon's efforts to rollback the social welfare state ended when Watergate came to light.

The Return of Creative Federalism 1977-1980

When President Carter took office in 1977, he tried to reinstate some of the programs that were created under the Great Society. In order to do this, President Carter tried to combine the best parts of creative federalism with new federalism to more precisely channel federal aid to the communities most in need. In addition, he tried to use public funds to encourage private investment for specific problem areas that the government could not administer effectively. In order to accomplish these goals, President Carter began to reduce the amount of governmental red tape in order to see immediate results. Although positive results began to appear, President Carter did was not reelected and so, his plans were not continued under his successor.

Return to New Federalism 1981-1992

While running for president in 1980, Ronald Reagan vowed to reestablish the strength and command of state governments. In his first inaugural address, Reagan said he would restrict the size of the federal government and return the power to the people. His strategy included reducing taxes, federal regulation and bureaucracy, and cutting federal funding on unwanted programs. From the beginning, he faced harsh criticism and opposition from state governors, special interest groups, and Congress. In the end, Congress consolidated over seventy categorical programs into nine block grants. In January 1982, President Reagan proposed a complete overhaul of the nation's spending priorities. The federal government would use a "swap and turn back program". It would take control over Medicaid, and in return the states would take on sixty programs, such as food stamps and the welfare program called Aid to Families with Dependent Children (AFDC). These reforms met with resistance as well. States wanted a guarantee that funding would continue and not turn into unfunded mandates. This became a problem for the administration because they wanted to reduce spending levels. As a result, Reagan's programs achieved mixed results and faced the same problems as President Nixon. Funding for the block grants lost value as inflation increased. This created real challenges for states now expected to do more with less money. Despite these issues, some of President Reagan's policies did start to show promise by the time he left office in 1988. The continuation of these policies would be passed on to his former vice president George H. W. Bush.

President George H. W. Bush sought to continue downsizing the federal government. In one speech he declared that personal volunteerism, not the federal government, could address social problems; he encouraged states to cover the costs of national programs, such as mass transit and wastewater treatment plants. By 1992, President Bush's plans to reduce dependency on the federal government experienced the same problems as his predecessor. Rising budget deficits, increased demand for public services and lower taxes, and financial problems with states made reforms next to impossible.

Devolution: The Next Phase?

Devolution 1993-2001

In the spring of 1993, Bill Clinton took over the office of President of the United States. Some of the problems he faced upon moving in were a budget deficit, soaring national debt, and the unwillingness of Americans to pay more in taxes for the programs they were receiving. By far the largest expense for the federal government was Medicaid or Medicare. President Clinton was elected based on his "New Democrat" ideology. A New Democrat is a conservative, usually from the south or Midwest, who supports states' and individuals' rights over the national government. But when Clinton came to power, he had to appease the liberal wing of his party. Their focus was maintaining the safety net and rebuilding some of the programs lost to the prior Republican Presidents. This meant that grant funding rose during his first two years in office.

Issues For You
What political party do you see yourself belonging to and how would this affect your views on federalism?

As resentment by upper middle class white males grew so did support for conservative republicans. After the midterm elections in 1994, President Clinton faced new challenges from the other side of the aisle. For the first time in over forty years, Republicans controlled both houses of Congress and most state governorships. During the election, the Republicans promised "A Contract for America" if they were elected. With support in most states, the devolution revolution began. Devolution is a shift of policy-making responsibility to the states away from federal government. The federal government would continue to fund programs through block grants, thus giving states the flexibility to administer the programs how they saw fit.

The important thing to note is the controversy the Republican victory brought to the issue of federalism. Speaker of the House, Newt Gingrich (R-Georgia), led the charge. Representative Gingrich was a professor of history before winning his seat in 1978. As a historian, Gingrich was knowledgeable about the ongoing debate surrounding federalism. At the core of the issue was nothing less than the division of power between the federal and state governments as they have evolved over the previous sixty years. Congressional Republicans sought to strip the national government of its vast domestic policy programs and turn them over to the states. Some of these programs included welfare, environmental protection, civil rights, and regulation of abortion. Within the next two years, some of the provisions in the Contract had succeeded and others were negotiated. For example, in 1996 President Clinton signed into law a welfare bill that gave the states much more control over welfare and forced recipients back to work after a two-year period of assistance. In addition, the legislation placed an overall limit of five years of support in one's lifetime. The end result of these compromises was that the amount and type of welfare assistance varied from state to state, leading to millions of people being dropped from the welfare rolls or people moving to states that offered more welfare benefits than others, thus straining their budgets. This weakened the system, which made it easy for some desperate and unscrupulous individuals to commit fraud by cheating the system, filing for welfare in several states.

On May 1, 1998, President Clinton began to push these changes back by altering a 1987 Reagan executive order designed to prevent federal interference in state and local government. Clinton laid the groundwork for increasing federal power over states by signing Executive Order 13803, which allowed federal agencies to "consult" with state and local officials on policy matters. Conservative members of Congress immediately charged that this order seriously eroded federalism, leading the president to suspend the order pending further review. In the end, the battle over devolution between President Clinton and Congress created turmoil at all levels of government. This perpetuated the image that the federal government was incompetent and self-serving when dealing with the needs of the people.

2001-Present

President George W. Bush's big push for a change in domestic policy came to an end on the morning of September 11, 2001. Prior to the attacks on the Twin Towers in New York City and the Pentagon in Washington D.C., Bush was pushing his major domestic initiative, the No Child Left Behind Act. Although this act allowed states broad control over how to spend the federal funds targeted for low-income students, they still felt it was not enough control. As the cost of the war in Afghanistan and Iraq increased, funding for domestic programs was cut; as a result, states and school districts began to complain about insufficient funds and a need for more spending power.

Since 2003, the administration's preoccupation with the war at a cost of over $6 billion a month, there has been very little focus paid to domestic issues aside from homeland security. In addition, the bumbling of Hurricane Katrina and the devastation that followed showed Americans the urgent need for the federal government to oversee disaster relief. As a result, the Republicans lost control of both Houses of Congress to the democrats in the 2006 mid-term elections. Now with new leadership in the House and Senate, the President may have to acquiesce to their demands to strengthen the federal government's control over states on specific issues.

Advantages and Disadvantages of Federalism

During President George W. Bush's second term, a new Secretary of Education took over. The main focus of Sec. Margaret Spelling's job was to enforce the "no child left behind" policy that was enacted in President Bush's first term. As indicated from the opening vignette, this program has both positive and negative impacts. What follows here is a description of how the federal government can institute a national policy while only contributing approximately eight percent of the funds for public education. With this program along with thousands of others, one can see how the concept has many advantages and disadvantages. In deciding what these advantages and disadvantages are, one needs to ask what kind of relationship should exist between the national and provincial authorities. After we examine this, we will survey how Germany's federal structure differs from ours.

Advantages of Federalism

While there are numerous advantages that can be found with federalism, here are three of the most important in relation to the focus of this book. They are checks on power, flexibility, and citizen participation.

Checks on Power. The first advantage of federalism is that it provides a system of checks and balances not only between branches of governments, but also between jurisdictions. Refer back to the beginning of the chapter where it was discussed that the Constitution gives the federal government enumerated powers (coin money, declare war, etc) and all other powers not declared are given to the states by way of the Tenth Amendment.

Flexibility. Federalism allows for the national government to provide funding through grants; depending on the type of grant, the states have the flexibility to use it on what best suits their needs. For example, mass transportation on the west coast has more freeways and highways than light rail systems (subways). In contrast, the east coast depends more on light rail systems, especially when commuting between "Bonywash" (Boston, New York, and Washington D.C.).

Citizen Participation. By having power diluted among the federal, state, and local governments, citizens have greater access to influence policy decisions. For example, in 2004, through the initiative process, California communities prevented the creation of Wal-Mart superstores that tried to circumvent the normal review process.[7] These communities felt that holding Wal-mart accountable was important because of the negative impact large corporations like this had on the environment, traffic congestion, and local small businesses. Around the same time, Massachusetts passed legislation trying to force Wal-mart to pay some form of compensation to their employees for health insurance. The motivation for this action was spurred on by the fact that Wal-Mart is the second largest user of the public healthcare program in Massachusetts. Of its 11,625 employees in the state, 2,081 of them with their children are enrolled in MassHealth and Uncompensated Care Pool. [8]

Disadvantages of Federalism

Although there are many disadvantages to discuss, the two that follow clearly illustrate how government can be inefficient despite all attempts of evaluation and self-examination.

It's Obstructive and Inefficient. If you pay close attention, you may observe that there are more agencies governing over you than just the obvious ones, such as the national, state, county, and city governments. In fact, there are over 95,000 types of government agencies that are intricately woven to form a network of bureaucratic structures that impact your life on a daily basis. Given the size and complexity of the system, it's hard to know where to go to resolve an issue. There are numerous procedures that need to be followed (aka "red tape") and that alone can prevent someone from finding the resolution they seek. In addition, there are no clear lines of communication. Think again about Hurricane Katrina and the local, state, and federal agencies that couldn't coordinate relief for thousands of people until many days after the hurricane hit. To put it on a more personal level, most of you reading this book are enrolled in college courses. Think about all of the obstacles you had to overcome in order to take this class. You had to apply to the school, pay fees, meet with an advisor on what classes to take, coordinate the location of your classes to get to each in time, and perhaps fit your class schedule around your work and/or your family's work and school schedule. Now let's put this on a larger scale - think about all of the organizational structures that exist behind the scenes. There are all kinds of departments that must interact with each other to insure that you get every thing you need: books, notices of deadlines, financial aid paperwork, and the like. If any part of the system fails, you will have a problem or at the very least, you may not get confirmation that you are enrolled in that class for several weeks. The same applies to the government. With thousands of departments interacting with each other, there are bound to be communication problems. If paperwork isn't delivered or completed in time, entire projects can fail. In addition, given the number of different agencies, time and money will seemingly be wasted or spent on unnecessary items. Case in point, in order to cut down on costs and for expediency's sake, FEMA waived flood safety regulations to mobile home manufacturers who were being hired to build mobile homes for New Orleans and surrounding areas,

Issues For You
After reading this section on disadvantages of Federalism, how did your views change or become more certain as to how much the federal government should be held responsible for areas in the U.S. hit with hurricane disaster?

post Hurricane Katrina.   Unfortunately, because New Orleans and areas of Mississippi are below sea level, thousands of mobile homes stand empty in neighboring states, translating to millions of dollars being squandered. In his feature length documentary film, When the Levees Broke: A Requiem in Four Acts (aired on HBO), Spike Lee reveals an intimate and disturbing look at the devastation and personal stories of people that lived through Hurricane Katrina. Lee exposes preexisting problems with the decrepit and worn down levees. The film implies that if a number of key bureaucratic agencies (listed below) had agreed upon the importance of maintaining the levees in an area often stricken by hurricanes, perhaps the domino effect of disaster would have been slowed.

Lack of Accountability. As you can see from the above disadvantage of federalism, when problems occur, who is to be held accountable? Again, let us look at Katrina. Before the wind and rain stopped, people were asking who was responsible for all of the problems. Was it the Mayor of New Orleans, the Governor of Louisiana, the Army Corp of Engineers, the director of FEMA, the head of Homeland Security who oversaw FEMA, the President, previous administrations, or the people for not getting out? No one wanted to accept responsibility for the chaos; every level of government blamed another. In the end Michael Brown, director of FEMA, was the unfortunate scapegoat and recipient of criticism when in reality, everyone was to blame.

Federalism is still a widely contested issue today. Who should have the power - the national government or the states? Clearly, there are pros and cons on both sides of the issue but what we can say is, federalism is part of the American political structure and we must continue to work within the confines of it.

The "Golden State" and the Federal Government

California is an excellent case study when examining the relationship between states and federal governments. California is the most populous state in the union with over 38 million residents from a variety of ethic and cultural backgrounds, it is the world's sixth largest economy, it has vast natural resources and ports, and it is in a central location in relation to Asia and

Golden Gate Bridge
Courtesy of Jupiter Images

Central and South America for commerce. Being the most populous state in the union also means that the Golden State has large issues it needs to deal with. California is the twelfth largest producer of greenhouse gases in the world because of its industrial base, the number of cars on the road, and the ships emitting pollution while they idle waiting to go into port. California's diverse culture also creates tensions between groups when competing for jobs. Due to California's location along the Pacific Ocean and the common border with Mexico, it has served as a causeway for immigrants (both legal and illegal) from Central and South America and others from around the world.

It has been said that the rest of the country watches what California does in much the same way a younger sibling mimics an older sibling, sometimes to see what the latest fashion or music trends are or simply to just observe how things are done. For these and other reasons, the relationship between the state and the federal governments is the subject of analysis in this section.

As you learned in the previous chapter, representation in the House of Representatives is based on population. Given the size of California's population, the state has the largest caucus with 53 Representatives, whose political views tend to reflect the parts of the state from which they originate. These members of the House represent their districts' interests and the two Senators represent the state's interests. With regards to the federal executive branch, California has 55 electoral college votes. In addition to this large number of votes, California's wealth has an enormous amount of influence on the Presidency. In this manner, we will examine the role that California plays in national politics and how the aid the state receives from the federal government is utilized.

Reserved Powers for the State

The U.S. Constitution is the highest law in the nation. Within the Amendments, the 10th Amendment reads:

"The powers not delegated to the
United States by the Constitution, nor prohibited by it to the States,
are reserved to the States respectively, or to the people."

Police Powers –
These powers permit all the stats to protect citizens' health, safety, and welfare.

The powers reserved to the states are: create and control county and local governments, hold "free and fair" elections, **police powers**, and establish criminal and civil laws. The states also possess concurrent powers such as collecting taxes and borrowing money.

Funds from Washington

As you read above, over the last few decades the federal government has been shifting funds and responsibility to state by way of devolution. The monies received

Funds from Washington built this school in El Monte, CA.
Courtesy of the Library of Congress

are used to pay for federal programs and it comes in the form of grants-in-aid (categorical or block). Money or the promise of money can be used as a method of coercion. As the states become more dependent on federal funds, the federal government can add conditions that must be met before dispersing the funds. In the 1960's under creative federalism, the federal government began devoting approximately 15% of the nation's budgets to the states; by the 1980's the funds increased to 23%.[9]

Grants-In-Aid

California and other states usually have Congressional requirements associated with them. Most of these grants come with the requirement of matching funds. Grant-in-aid is usually distributed as categorical grants and block grants, which were briefly described earlier in the chapter. The Head Start program, which helps children from low income families go to preschool, is an example of a recipient of categorical grants. In contrast, block grants are funds where the state can allocate the money to projects within the individual programs. For example, if the grant is designated for mass transit projects, the state can specify the funds to build or improve bridges, buses, trains, and railways.

Welfare is another example of a block grant. In 1996, the federal government gave the responsibility of overseeing the program to the states while the federal government supplied the money. By having the funds disbursed as block grants, each state was able to apply the funds as they saw fit. As a result, each state's welfare is unique unto itself. California's program was more liberal than other states. In some cases, it provided money for job training, living assistance, and day care to name a few services under their welfare umbrella. As a result, people from other states began to move to California because they preferred the benefits. This population shift caused a strain on California's ability to offer welfare aid to all that needed it. When it requested additional funds from the federal government, they were denied, forcing California to remove some of the benefits it offered.

California Federal and State Structures

The structures of the federal and state governments are almost identical or a mirror image of each other. At the national level there is a bicameral legislature consisting of the United States Senate and the House of Representatives. Within California, there is a bicameral legislature with an upper house, the state Senate and the lower house, the state Assembly.

Men's work camp funded with Federal money.
Courtesy of the Library of Congress

Anyone studying this process should pay special attention to the subtle differences because they are often confused. At the federal level, there is a President and Vice President. At the state level, there is a Governor and Lieutenant Governor. Both have cabinets and other executive offices.

The judiciaries of federal and state governments share similar structures. The federal judiciary consists of the United States Supreme Court (the highest court in the land), the Federal Court of Appeals (aka the Circuit Court), and the Federal District Courts. In California, there is also a State Supreme Court (the highest court in the state), the California Court of Appeals, and Superior Courts. All three branches will be explored further in following chapters.

State Redistricting and Federal Representation

Article I Section 2 states, *"Representation and direct Taxes shall be apportioned among the several States which may be included within this Union, according to their respective Numbers ... The actual Enumeration shall be made within three Years after the first Meeting of the Congress of the United States, and within every subsequent Term of ten Years, in such Manner as they shall by Law direct."* Reapportionment occurs every ten years after the U.S. Census is completed. The controlling political party in California's State Legislature has the power to redraw the boundaries for the congressional districts as well as their own legislative districts. However, there are specific federal laws that prohibit legislatures from abusing this power, for example, they can not create nor can they break a majority-minority district. But, as we saw in Texas in 2003, the Republicans were able to gain 6 additional seats in the House of Representatives by pulling off some very creative **redistricting** to their party's advantage. In this unique case of "partisan **gerrymandering**", it included "3 bacon-strip thin districts that are over 300 miles long."[10] Currently, both the State Senate and State Assembly are controlled by the Democratic Party and the Governorship is controlled by Republican Arnold Schwarzenegger who has the power to veto the legislature's redistricting plan. This check on the legislature prevents them from overly gerrymandering the districts. If the legislature and governor cannot agree, the California Supreme Court has the power to determine the districts.

Redistricting – Also know as reapportionment. The process by which the state legislature redraws the district lines for its members of the U.S. House of Representatives, and at the same time, redraws district lines for its own state legislature.

Gerrymander – An attempt to create a safe seat for one party during state redistricting of congressional voting boundaries.

Nonpartisan Elections – Elections where the party identity of the candidate is not disclosed to the public. This was done to weaken the party system in California.

California's
58 Counties

Creatures of the State – Local Government

Jurisdiction over county and city governments is given to the states. Currently, California's local governments are struggling from decades of neglect by the state. The counties and cities were intentionally designed to be weak with very little political power. Most cities have a "weak mayor" system, which means that the mayor does not have power to govern directly and the power at the county level is heavily diluted by boards of supervisors who tend to push their own agendas (see section on City Administration, later on in this chapter). The structure of local government, which consists of counties, cities, districts and regions, impact each of us directly in positive and negative ways on a daily basis. Most county and city officials are elected in **nonpartisan elections**, which will be discussed in greater detail in later chapters.

Counties

Types of Counties

The **county** is responsible for overseeing public services, such as providing education, health and welfare, sheriff and fire departments, courts, roads and park services. The first California Constitution (1849) created 27 counties controlled by an elected **county board of supervisors** for each. For the first 30-years the counties were under the direct control of the state legislature. The Constitutional Revision of 1879 structured the counties to be governed locally, thus creating **general law counties**. As part of the progress era in 1911, another amendment was adopted by the state legislature. The **Home Rule Amendment** allowed for the creation of **charter counties**. Since the State was founded in 1849, the numbers of counties have increased from 27 to present day 58. The counties are very diverse in size, population, geography, and political views.

In addition to the board of supervisors, there are several other offices at the county level. These offices include a Chief Administrative Officer, District Attorney, Public Defender, Assessor, Treasurer, Sheriff, and Voter Registrar.

Functions of the County

Regardless of the type of county, they all have similar responsibilities that they must carryout and each county's board of supervisors ensures that these duties are implemented. These responsibilities include education that is controlled by a County Superintendent of Schools, who is responsible for the overall administration of Kindergarten to Community College education. The County Sheriff is responsible for the areas in the county outside of larger cities. This department in some counties also protects the harbors, airports, and oversees the county jails. The infrastructure is sustained by that county's department of public works. They are required to maintain the roads that lead into the main highways and freeways as well as all county roads that link cities and rural areas. The parks department or a department of recreation controls the county's parks and campgrounds as well as maintains the facilities.

The first day the unemployment office opened its doors in San Francisco, 1936. Courtesy of Library of Congress

County –
large geographic areas initially established to bridge the gap between city governments and the state by providing services.

County Board of Supervisors –
The county legislature that sets policy and budgets. Most boards are elected in a nonpartisan election for staggered, four-year terms.

General Law Counties –
Counties that may establish the number of county officials and their duties, but are required to have the approval of the state legislature.

Home Rule Amendment –
The idea that local people are better equipped to solve their own problems because they are the most familiar with them.

Charter County –
Has its own charter or constitution that allows for flexibility in collecting revenue-producing taxes, electing and appointing officials, and, running and controlling the programs of the county.

County Revenue –
Money that the county receives from all sources.

Proposition 13 –
Placed limits on the amount of annual property taxes to a maximum of 1 % of the March 1, 1975 market value or selling price of the property, whichever is higher, with a limited increase of 2% each year thereafter.

A Local Agency Formation Commission (LAFCO), created by the county board of supervisors, determines the boundaries of any proposed incorporated city within that county's area. While this function is generally not known to the public, it plays an important part in regulating growth in areas. Lastly the County Tax collector collects taxes in order for the county to have an operating budget to perform the above responsibilities. These are only of few of the many departments that are funded at the county level. The amount of services that are required for the public is paid for by the taxes collected for an expansive county government.

County Revenues

Most counties receive funds or revenues from various sources, such as the federal government, the state government, property taxes, sales taxes, and other fees. The state and federal government contribute nearly 50% of the revenues to the counties' budgets. As noted above, these funds usually come with strings attached or matching requirements so the counties are required to add funds for health and welfare programs, to name a few.

Checks on Property Tax

When counties experienced budget defects, they would raise property taxes. In order to place a check on the local governments, the citizens of the state passed **Proposition 13**, also known as the Jarvis-Gann property tax initiative. Proposition 13 placed limits on the amount of property tax a county could collect. When Proposition 13 went into effect in 1978, California counties lost huge amounts of revenues, which forced a cutback in numerous services and programs in the schools.[11] Despite the state's efforts to send monies to the counties, it was never enough to replace the missing funds. As a result, the services that were provided by the counties have never returned to the level that they once were prior to implementation of Prop 13. In addition, with the counties now being dependent upon the state for money, most of them have been weakened even further, shifting power back to the state.

County Expenditures

The funds that are received from the various revenue sources are disbursed to each department within the county government. Each division creates a budget and submits its requests to the board of supervisors. In accordance with state law and review, the budgets are approved and sent to the Auditor/Controller to transfer funds to the departments.[12] The budget requests come from social services such as county hospitals and public health departments, the sheriff's and county fire department. After Proposition 13 went into effect, there was little room left in the county budgets to provide for extra service. In recent years, counties in California have felt the effect of unfunded mandates from the federal government, which in turn increases the states' expenses for protection against terrorism, the west Nile virus, earthquakes and other natural disasters. Between the years of 2001 and 2004, California spent over 12 billion dollars in security for the harbors, bridges, dams, airports, and other vital county improvements. When Governor Schwarzenegger assumed office, one of his first visits was to President Bush to see if the federal government would cover part of the additional expense of national security. Of the 12 billion dollars spent, the federal government only repaid 2-3 billion, leaving California and its counties to absorb the majority of the costs.[13] In order to make up for these shortcomings, politicians in California have decided to borrow funds from investors rather than raise taxes. This quick fix is more expensive in the long run because the next generation is left paying the high interest rates of the previous generations' band-aids.

Cities

Incorporation

The California State Legislature created the Municipal Corporations Act (1883) that originally established cities based on population. The act also established the requirements for towns to be incorporated as a city. By definition, an incorporated area is referring to a city. For an unincorporated area to become incorporated, it must petition the County Board of Supervisors. The Board will review the application and will request the appropriate departments to submit their recommendations. Once that process is complete the Board will request the Local Agency Formation Commission (LAFCO) to notify the public regarding the request and to hold hearings on the matter thus gaining public input. Once the hearings are complete, the LAFCO will propose the borders of the new city and the commission submits their approval to the Board of Supervisors. At this time an election is called and the citizens of the impacted areas vote. If approved by the voters, the unincorporated area becomes a city.

General and Charter (Home Rule) Cities

After the city becomes incorporated, they begin as a general law city. A general law city consists of the elected officials such as the mayor, city council but other officers (the treasure and city clerk) are also elected. The mayor and city council hire or appoint other city officials, such as the chief of the police, fire department, and city manager to name a few.

A City may create a charter after being a general law city. Most cities elect to become charter cities. There are a number of advantages to transition to a charter city, one of the most important is the power is shifted to the city away control of the county and state. With this freedom to address issues as they arise, the citizens and city officials can discuss how best to resolve them.

City Administration

There are two main types of city government. A strong mayor system is one where the mayor is in control of the daily operations of the city and the other is a weak mayor system who is a figure-head; the day-to-day operations are controlled by the city manager who reports to the mayor and city council during their schedule sessions. Regardless of the mayoral system, the city has many responsibilities that require additional professionals to administer the various divisions. This is why cities hire chiefs of Police, Fire, Financial Officers, public works, and planning and community development officials, who in turn hire the necessary staff to fulfill the duties of the office. In addition, some cities have citizen councils to help advise the city council on local block issues such as redevelopment, crime, and other improvements.

City Revenues

Cities, like the federal, state, and county systems, get most of their funds via taxes (sales, hotels, utilities, business, and property). In addition to taxes, cities also collect funds from issuing permits, fines, and other violations.

City Expenditures

In order to meet the needs of the citizens, the city spends it funds providing services for the public, including police and fire protection, education, public works such as water, sewer, trash, and roads, and general government services like collecting taxes. With the budget cuts from Proposition 13 on the counties, cities and counties have had to increase their cooperation in order to get the most for

---

Strong Mayor System – The mayor has some veto power over the council and power to appoint and remove certain city officials.

Weak Mayor System – The mayor is more a ceremonial position, with the mayor being selected from among the city council members.

City Manager– A professional manager who implements the city council's programs.

City Council– A nonpartisan board that is elected to handle the executive business of the city.

their money. However, some of the services that are provided by the county are paid for by the city; services such as jails, property and sales tax collection, and road and water maintenance fees.

Districts

Districts –
Units designated for a specific governmental purpose, usually to provide a public service, such as education.

A **district** provides a specific set of services such as schools, water, air quality, and other municipal services. Within the state of California, there are over 1000 school districts ranging from K-12 schools to community colleges. And, like the counties and cities, the laws governing the creation of a district were established by the state legislature. In order for a district to be formed, a petition must be approved by the voters in the proposed area. Once approved, it is sent to the board of supervisors where a majority must approve it in order for the district to be created.

School Districts

With over 1000 school districts in the state, they are by far the largest category. These districts cover the entire state and are divided into 630 elementary districts (K-6), 285 unified districts (K-12), 115 union districts (high school district which includes several elementary school districts), and 72 community college districts. Each unified and union school district is governed by a board of education. The board is elected in nonpartisan elections that are held within each district. The board is responsible for hiring the administrators, teachers, and staff; furthermore, they evaluate curriculum requirements, create and maintain the budget, and they approve budget expenditures. The board is accountable to the state board of education that is appointed by the governor and managed by the Superintendent of Public Instruction. Community colleges are governed by their own boards and have more power over within their districts, as compared to K-12 institutions, which have very little control. The boards report to the State Board of Governors of the Community Colleges.

A large part of funding for public schools came from property tax and Prop 13 had a significantly negative impact on the quality of education. It should be noted that prior to Proposition 13, California schools were some of the best in the nation; but within the last few decades, surveys and polls say they have dropped to some of the worst in the nation. The lack of funds contributed to an increased student-teacher ratio, poor facility maintenance, and lack of new technology in the classroom. Now, most of the funding for public education comes from state sales and income taxes (60%) with only about 10% coming from the federal government.[14]

Water Districts

In some areas of California, especially southern California, water is more precious than gold. If the supply is compromised even in the slightest way, most of the state's industrial and agriculture base would feel the hardship within a very short amount of time. Water districts were created to provide water in a fair way for each and plan for the times when the resources are scarce. The Metropolitan Water District of Southern California (MWD) covers six counties (San Diego, San Bernardino, Riverside, Orange, Ventura, and Los Angeles), which is most of Southern California. It is by far the largest water district, running from the Pacific Ocean for more than 70 miles inland and between Oxnard and the U.S./Mexican Border.

The issue of fighting for water extends beyond the political arm-twisting between the rural and large urban centers and between counties. It impacts all of the western states and Mexico. As the states continue to grow, so does the demand for water. Much political arguing has gone on behind the scenes as the debate continues to heat up. Colorado wants to dam more water from the Colorado River to meet the needs of its growing population and industry. At the same time, the southwestern states require more water for their population and industrial base. As more water is dispersed among the states, the amount of water reaching Mexico has decreased dramatically causing tension and violation of international treaties. While experts are trying to resolve this very serious problem, they can only agree on one thing – everyone needs to conserve more and waste less; for if the public doesn't learn to use resources more wisely, it's going to get worse before it gets better, something that is already indicative in the many debates over global warming.

Regional Issues

If you live in California, especially in the Southern California **region**, it is often hard to distinguish where one city begins and another ends. Given the similar and share problems that impact neighboring cities, some **regional governance** has been established to help coordinate efforts. By combining their limited resources (funds, staff, etc), cities are able to be more effective in dealing with water shortages, air pollution, road repairs, traffic flow, and emergency services.

Councils of Government

The Councils of Government (COGs) are a group of city and county leaders from neighboring cities and counties from a specific region who come together to solve problems that impact most communities within those regions. Some examples of these COGs are the Southern California Association of Government (SCAG), which covers six counties and 180 cities; the Association of Bay Area Governments (ABAG) coordinates with nine other counties and over 100 cities; and the Sacramento Area Council of Governments (SACOG) manages four counties and a segment of a fifth. The issues these organizations cover a wide range of public and environmental concerns, such as transportation needs, coastal issues, maintenance of clean air, impact of pollution, and refuse disposal, to name a few. These are just a few of the functions that COGs carry out to serve Californians throughout the state.

Region –
A geographic area that contains a number of cities and counties and covers a large portion of the state.

Regional Governance –
The process of planning and policy making with the help of cities, counties, and businesses with regional issues.

Council of Government (COGs) –
An association of city and county government officials, within a given region, whose purpose is to provide solutions to the regions' problems.

How Do We Compare?

Germany and the United States

The study of modern German politics provides an excellent opportunity to learn about some of the basic complications that can arise during both nation-building and democracy-building. It is not just the socio-cultural, economic, and international context of German politics that has undergone fundamental change since 1945, but also, there are a number of institutional developments that have

Grand Coalition – A coalition of two or more large parties that previously opposed one another.

Bundestag – lower house of German parliament.

Arch in Berlin, Capital of Germany
Courtesy of Jupiter Images

played a major role in the consolidation and relatively smooth performance of the West German political system - now the German political system - since its conception.[15]

Like the United States, Germany has a federal system, with many powers distributed to its sixteen Länder (states). The Federal Republic of Germany consists of ten West German Länder, five in East Germany and five in Berlin. In some cases, German Länder have more powers than states do in the United States. For instance, in Germany, the states control the education, welfare, and the police to name a few.

The German constitution, known as the Federal Republic's Basic Law (Grundgesetz), maintains these divisions. In addition, their constitution has some very important guarantees of basic human rights, including some obvious reactions against the terror practices of the Nazi regime. For example, there is a constitutional guarantee of political asylum, the prohibition of capital punishment, and the emphasis on the dignity of human life and protection of it. Again, as a reaction to the Nazi era, there has been an emphasis on strong separation of power. In addition, their constitution outlines the powers of each branch of government and their relation to the Länder. The main style of government is the parliamentary model (see chapter one). Germany has a president, which is largely a ceremonial post, and a chancellor or prime minister, who is the real leader of the government. In 2005, Angela Merkel became chancellor of Germany. In order for her party to govern, she needed to form a **grand coalition** with other parties.

Germany has a bicameral legislature with a roughly 660 member **Bundestag**, which has less power than the chancellor. Similar to Britain's House of Commons, the Bundestag selects the chancellor, who is usually the leader of the largest party. In 2005, Chancellor Merkel's cabinet was comprised of a partnership of two parties seated in the Bundestag. Contributing to Germany's stability is a vote of no confidence. One caveat is that the only condition in which the chancellor can be voted out is if the Bundestag holds an election to vote a new chancellor in. The Bundestag normally follows the recommendations made by the cabinet. Germany prides itself on good party discipline – therefore, bills are generally passed after some deliberation amongst the committees. The committees of the Bundestag are analogous to the ministries (or departments), which creates an intimate interaction between the executive and legislative committees. Many deputies within the Bundestag consist of civil servants who are on leave as well as members from interest groups.

Since 1945, a much greater emphasis on federal checks and balances, the **Bundesrat**, also called the upper house, consists of 69 members that come from Land governments; its power is equivalent to the power of the Bundestag on issues that affect the states. Over other matters, it only has the power to impose a weak veto. The Constitutional Court holds the power of judicial review and has been very active when it comes to overturning legislation that it feels violates the laws. The Court operates through two separate court chambers, each with its own area of jurisdiction: One basically deals with issues of "rights", while the other deals basically with "powers". There are other important differences from the U.S. model, including the largely non-controversial manner of appointments (one-half by the Bundestag, one-half by the Bundesrat), the limited terms (twelve years on a rotating basis), and the even number of judges in each chamber.

Bundesrat (Federal Council) – Upper house of German parliament made up of representatives from the 16 Länder.

Germany has had a "two-plus" party system, but over the years, it has splintered into a system with many parties. Led by Angela Merkel, the Christian Democratic Union (CDU) has dominated the position of being the largest party in Germany. Its Bavarian sister, the Christian Social Union (CSU) stands side-by-side with the CDU as part of the largest political party in Germany. The Social Democratic Party (its acronym, SPD, represents the German title, Sozialdemokratische Partei Deutschlands) the only German party dating back to the days of the Kaiser, has gradually become less radical. It was not until the SPD formed a functional government did it finally come to power in 1969. The Free Democratic Party (FDP) hovers around centrist views, which offers citizens an alternative to the CDU/CSU and the SPD; however, it narrowly meets the 5-percent threshold. The Greens and the former Communist Party, the Democratic Socialism Party, are now winning seats, which puts them in prime positions to compete for cabinet positions. The largest nationalist party, the Republicans, has yet to win any seats.

Several countries have copied the German electoral system, which combines proportional representation with single member districts. Unlike the United States, a German citizen is allowed two votes on the same ballot - individual and party list. The party list determines the number of seats for the Bundestag party and some are held by members who are individually elected. In order to insure that Germany does not fall prey to small radical parties, a threshold clause of 5 per cent has been established to bar these radical parties from infiltrating the Bundestag.

Chapter Summary

This chapter provides an introduction to the concept of federalism. An understanding of federalism arises when we scrutinize the complex relationship that exists between the national and state governments. In reviewing the issue of public schools (No Child Left Behind Act), we took a brief look at a policy that illustrates the concept of federalism. The concept was then defined and reviewed in the context of the Constitution and the numerous Articles and Amendments. Afterwards, we examined how the national government has expanded through rulings made by the Supreme Court and policies created by the national government. We saw how federalism evolved through many stages, such as dual federalism (layer cake) and the stages within cooperative federalism (marble cake). After looking at cooperative federalism, the discussion turned to recent changes within federalism, such as new federalism and devolution. The golden state of California provides us with a clear view of how the states and the federal government are similar, how they differ, and how they cooperate with each other. Concluding the chapter is a comparison between Germany and the United States. This comparison provides another example of how federalism is applied in other countries, further enhancing the effectiveness of federalism.

Key Terms:

Standardized Test

Federalism

Unitary Government

Confederation

Dual Federalism

Cooperative Federalism

Concurrent Powers

Matching Funds

Writ of Mandamus

Creative Federalism

New Federalism

General Revenue Sharing (GRS)

Special Revenue Sharing (SRS)

Police Powers

Redistricting

Gerrymander

Nonpartisan Elections

County

County Board of Supervisors

General Law Counties

Home Rule

Charter County

County Revenue

Proposition 13

Strong Mayor System

Weak Mayor System

City Manager

City Council

Districts

Region

Regional Governance

Council of Government (COGs)

Grand Coalition

Bundestag

Bundesrat

Websites:

Federal & State Sites

Assessing the New Federalism
www.urban.org/Content/Research/NewFederalism/

National Center for State Courts
www.ncsconline.org

National Conference of State Legislatures
http://www.ncsl.org

State Constitutions
www.findlaw.com/

California Sites

Southern California Association of Governments (SCAG)
www.scg.ca.gov

League of California Cities
www.cacities.org

California State Association of Counties
www.scac.counties.org

This page left blank intentionally.

President Bush Speaking at an Event.
The media and the president have a love-hate relationship. Dan Rather,
news journalist commented that in today's climate, reporters are more concerned with
access than their responsibility of questioning government officials objectively.

CHAPTER 4

THE MEDIA

CHAPTER OUTLINE

Democracy and Action –
The News Source of Choice

Do you need your daily "Moment of Zen?"

If you're under 55 years old, you have probably heard of Jon Stewart or *The Daily Show*. If you are under 45, you most likely have seen the show at least once. If you are under 25, *The Daily Show* may very well be your main source of news - so goes the burgeoning effect of the satirical nightly news show.

© *Getty Images/Peter Kramer.*

Though *The Daily Show* has been on for some ten years, it wasn't until Jon Stewart took on the anchor chair in 1999 did the show's popularity and respect skyrocket. With its sharp and biting political wit, *The Daily Show* has morphed into one of cable television's biggest hits. According to the Pew Institute, some 21 percent of adults aged 18 to 34 get the bulk of their news from *The Daily Show*. On September 18, 2006, when former President Bill Clinton appeared on the "*Daily Show*" to promote his Global Initiative to solve the world's "pressing challenges", he paid Jon a compliment saying that his daughter Chelsea said that *The Daily Show* is <u>the</u> news source of choice for discerning young adults.

The previous statistic has worried some in politics and journalism who assume that receiving most of your news from a comedy show cannot possibly lead to responsible citizenship, or worse, it may fuel an already strong cynical attitude in young people and trivialize politics. Not true studies according to the non-partisan National Annenberg Election Survey in 2004. Viewers of *The Daily Show* tend to be better informed on issues than people who access their news from traditional outlets, such as network news and daily newspapers. Furthermore, Nielson Research Statistics show that Daily Show viewers are 78 percent more likely to have four or more years of a college education than the average adult. Despite the fact that it is coined as that "fake news" show, *The Daily Show* has acquired a very discerning and savvy set of viewers. One could say that the success of the show is perhaps due to the probing and intelligent questions Stewart raises on each show. Many of his guests are authors of best-selling books that boast a wide range of topics – from doctors on the frontline in Iraq to string theory quantum physics – Stewart reads them all. Perhaps Stewart's expert comedic timing opens up an avenue of dialogue for its viewers and guests that would never normally be afforded to so-called serious news shows.

The Daily Show and its successful mock conservative spin-off, *The Colbert Report* (the 't' is silent in both words, a pun on the host's name, Stephen Colbert), has apparently had a huge impact on young adults. *The Daily Show* has attracted some impressive guests, among them two presidents (Carter and Clinton), a vice president (Gore), several cabinet secretaries, and a host of senators and representatives. In 2006, guests have included the sitting president of Pakistan and 2006 Nobel Peace Prize winner, Muhammad Yunus.

Many politicians have wanted a piece of the action, that 18 – 34 demographic. Numerous government office holders and politicians in Washington now make it a point to be a guest on the show, and quite a few have made frequent appearances. Presidential hopefuls such as Senator John Kerry (D-MA) and Governor Bill Richardson (D-NM) have appeared on the show to supposedly gain the youth vote. Making good on a promise that he made on *The Daily Show* on October 28, 2002, Senator John Edwards (D-NC) announced his run for the 2004 presidential election, live via satellite, on *The Daily Show*, September 15, 2003. The show has also caught the attention of some viewers in Congress with several of members complimenting *The Daily Show*, saying that the show helps them laugh at themselves, it is more insightful than much of the main stream media, and it tends to point out the inconsistencies and absurdities in politics. Even conservatives have slowly begun to realize the impact *The Daily Show* has had on contemporary political issues. Despite his liberal leanings, Stewart has interviewed such conservatives as former Secretary of State Colin Powell, former House Speaker Newt Gingrich, former Attorney General John Ashcroft, and John Bolton, former United States Ambassador to the United Nations. It is not Stewart's goal to belittle and chastise these conservative guests, quite the opposite – by all accounts, he asks tough and challenging questions but he does so with respect and even humility and always with humor and non-aggressive honesty.

So if you find your day incomplete without hearing Jon Stewart's "Moment of Zen" or Stephen Colbert's "The Word," you are not alone and you are also likely to belong to one of the more intelligent and politically informed group of citizens in the United States.[1]

Watch Dog – In this context, a watchdog is the agency or group, such as the media, that holds those in power accountable.

Investigative Journalism – Press coverage whose chief goal is to uncover corruption, scandal, conspiracy, and abuses of power in government and business; more intensive in both depth and time spent than standard press coverage.

The Media

> *"All of us who professionally use the mass media are the shapers of society.*
> *We can vulgarize that society. We can brutalize it.*
> *Or we can help lift it onto a higher level."*
> – *William Bernbach*

In the information age, it's becoming harder to discern what information is true and accurate. People today have more data thrown at them at any one time than at any other point in history. Those who provide the news are assigned the difficult task of serving not only their editors and shareholders but more importantly, the national interest. Because of this, the news is somewhat filtered. This is why one of the roles of the media in a democracy is to act as a **watchdog**. It's the duty of the press to keep watch over the government and inform the voters when issues arise. The importance of this kind of **investigative journalism** was demonstrated in the movie, "All the President's Men," starring Robert Redford and Dustin Hoffman as the writing team Woodward and Bernstein, whose series of articles eventually exposed Nixon and the Watergate scandal in the early 1970's. Above all else, the job of the media is to provide accurate information so voters can make educated decisions. If the media fail in this task and provide inaccurate information, then it will lead voters to make poor decisions and unfair judgments on citizens. The First Amendment states that "Congress shall make no law...abridging the freedom ... of the press". This clause ensures that the government cannot intimidate, prosecute, or censor the media while in pursuit of notifying the public on the actions of government officials. This is somewhat unique to America. There are many other countries which commonly close offices or incarcerate members of the press because of their reports (see Profile in Politics, Anna Stepanovna Politkovskaya, this chapter). When we hear this we tend to think of dictatorships and tyrants, but this is not always the case. Even democratic countries place limits on what the media can report. An example of these limitations can be found in the United Kingdom, which has strict secrecy laws that restrict what the press can and cannot say about the government and its activities. Also, in Italy, the communications mogul Silvio Berlusconi owns virtually all companies havng to do with any mode of communication – telephone, television, radio, newspaper, satellite – you name it, he owns it. In light of the media control in other countries, it may appear that the American media is still granted greater liberties than their foreign colleagues.

Here in the United States, information is delivered via radio and print media as well as through faxes, electronic mail, and online information sources. At the local level, people read the newspaper or watch television for local, regional, national, and international news. During the heyday of the information age, during the 1980's and 1990's people were beginning to watch twenty-four-hour news stations such as the popular Cable News Network (CNN), to gain additional insights to events happening around the globe. Now with satellite and the Internet, those that are technologically savvy receive their news via cell phones, PDAs, Ipods, and of course, the Web. The impact technology has had on politics is, simply put, amazing. Political campaign managers have had to become more creative in their methods of reaching younger voters. In general, politicians must be more watchful of what they say or do for fear that it will be taken out of context, recorded, and uploaded onto Blog pages on the Internet within a matter of minutes.

The Role of the Media in Democracy

Media provides a "window to the world" of people, places, and events that we cannot observe firsthand ourselves. The role of media in a democracy is to perform three basic functions: (1) it observes events, (2) it interprets these events, and (3) it provides information to individuals about other cultures.

Media as Observer

In their role as observer, the media should provide us with non-biased information on world events, cultural issues, and national and local concerns. Through these observations, the media have helped make the world a smaller place. Unfortunately, because the events the media observes are often too complex for a sixty-second report, reporters often skip over salient background details, perhaps in an attempt to control the focus on a specific aspect of an event. The end result is a story that can lead to misconceptions about an individual or a group of people and their culture, creating confusion instead of enhancing understanding. In addition, even though a reporter may find a story that s/he deems important, the editors may not feel that it is **newsworthy** or perhaps not as important as other news events, depending on the intended audience of the paper. As a result, some stories never see the light of day.

Another way to interpret the role of media as an observer is that in a democracy the citizens are supposed to govern and the media is "free" to report on the actions of the government - however, there are artificial filters put in place. These filters run counter to the role of the media as a non-biased observer.

Media as Interpreter

The media, in addition to being an observer, also interpret events by attaching meaning and context to them. In so doing, the media often shape public opinion. Under the informal rules of **objective journalism**, explicit interpretations by reporters are to be avoided, except in the cases of commentary or opinion editorials. Even if a

Issues For You
What role do you think media plays in a democracy? Do you disagree or agree with the concepts in this chapter regarding media? Why or why not?

Newsworthy –
Worth printing or broadcasting as news, according to editors' judgments.

Objective Journalism -
News reported with no evaluative language; contains opinions that are not attributed to a specific source.

journalist knows an official is lying, they cannot simply come out and state this. They must find an alternative way to call them out, for example, s/he can interview or quote someone close to that official. One major news network that does not seem to do this is Fox News. They tend to push or bend the rules of objective journalism. In order to insert their own opinions in the guise of facts, many of their reporters use the phrase "some people say…" without verifying who these people are or if they are legitimate sources. This also applies to the public officials who stage press events, such as news conferences on a beach to announce a bill that protects the environment when in reality the proposed legislation could be increasing the amount of pollution going into the ocean. For cases such as this sometimes reporters find an expert or **pundits** to point out the problems with the setting and announcement.

Media as Informer

The media play an important role as agents of **socialization**, through which people learn to adhere to their society's norms and values. As you'll learn in the following chapter, most children acquire their views and information about their world from the media, either directly or indirectly through media influence on parents, teachers, or friends. In addition, the media play an important role in helping teenagers and young adults to develop their own opinions. As you read in the opening vignette, most 18-34-year olds receive their news from late night television shows, like *The Daily Show* with Jon Stewart, or *Late Night* with Jay Leno. Despite the fact that these are comedy shows, young people find the style of delivery much more appealing than regular prime time news broadcasts who are often construed as agents of sensationalism and fear mongers. For teens and young adults, studies have also indicated that more of them are receiving their information over the Internet and other types of electronic media such as cell phones and PDA's. While these sources have great appeal to younger generation, the quality of the information and those providing it are not always reliable.

Types of Media

Media is plural for medium. A medium is an intervening agency, means, or instrument by which something is conveyed or accomplished. The phrase **mass media** refers to the method in which a medium is delivered, such as newspapers, magazines, radio, television, and the Internet. The media is then made accessible to people all over the globe.

As far back as Caesar's time in Rome, the public has required of their leaders to provide some way of staying informed of the goings on in local politics and how the latest trends may affect their own communities. To quote King Arthur in the musical *Camelot* when he explains to the fair maiden Guinivere what the commoners do in their spare time, he says that they sit around saying, "I wonder what the King is doing tonight." Originally, news was spread by word of mouth by individual conversations, religious officials such as priests, or by using heralds, which were public officials that announced news to the cities as well as took care of any civic functions. This method can be compared to a children's game of telephone. If you grew up in America, chances are you played the game of telephone or password. In this game, the players sit in a circle and a simple message such as, "He won't eat green eggs and ham," is said to the person next to you and is then passed on to the next person and the next, until the last person and then that person says out loud what was told to h/er. Invariably the last person has a completely different message than the one the first person launched. Needless to say, the accuracy of information in the pre-print era was extremely unreliable.

Pundit –
Somewhat derogatory term for print, broadcast, and radio commentators on political news.

Socialization –
The process by which people learn to conform to their society's norms, beliefs, culture, and values.

Mass Media –
The various ways in which information is delivered from its original source to the general public.

With the invention of the printing press in Germany by Johannes Gutenberg in 1440, the reliability of information was tremendously improved. In addition, the genius of the printing press provided a record of events and correspondence beyond just personal letters, not to mention the first mass printing of the Bible, which later became known as the Gutenberg bible, one of which is currently housed in the Huntington Library in Pasadena, California. Despite the profundity of this invention, there were two main problems with the printing press in terms of delivering the news to the people: first, the trustworthiness of reporters was still in question and second, most people were illiterate and still dependent on word of mouth for information. If you remember from the previous chapters, these are some of the reasons the framers like Alexander Hamilton felt that the commoners should not govern. Regardless of these drawbacks, the printing press was a revolution unto itself not only because it transformed communication across Europe, but it also ignited in both men - and women - a desire to read and think on their own.

Newspapers

By the 1500's, printing presses could be found all over Europe; nearly 2,500 print shops had been created. These shops produced over fifteen million books.[2] As books became more available, the number of educated readers increased, which in turn caused "radical ideas" to circulate. In reaction to this, governments and the Catholic Church made many attempts to control what was being printed. Authors and reporters were arrested, labeled as heretics, and were even charged with crimes against the state. Print shops were closed and the presses were destroyed. By the time of the American Revolution, the importance of newspapers was directly apparent when used as a tool to influence public opinion. Newspapers were the platform on which the debate over ratification of the Constitution stood. The *Federalist Papers* written by Alexander Hamilton, James Madison, and John Jay, were originally published as articles in the *New York Independent Journal*.

Courtesy of Jupiter Images

Early political leaders such as Thomas Jefferson saw the press as the key to a thriving deliberative democracy. He believed that the printed word would allow the framers to educate the public about the new political system, which would then help the common man make informed decisions: "Give them full information of their affairs through the channel of the public papers...those papers should penetrate the whole mass of the people."[3]   After the Constitution was ratified, both the Federalists and the Democratic Republicans published newspapers to inform the public about their parties' positions and plans of action. The mass media revolution was in full swing by 1850. Between 1850 and 1900, the number of daily papers increased from 250 to over 2,200. By 1898, the competition to increase circulation was vigorous. William Randolph Hearst's New York Journal and Joseph Pulitzer's New York World published thrilling and melodramatic stories about the Cuban Insurrection. These stories pushed the limits of objective journalism and helped strengthen anti-Spanish sentiment in the United States. This growing disdain for the Spaniards was reinforced when the papers published biased accounts of the sinking of the USS Maine in Havana Harbor, Cuba. These events would mark the beginning of the era of **yellow journalism** and muckraking, the latter of which will be covered later in the California section of this chapter.

This is an example of yellow journalism that distorted the true events that occurred during the Maine incident
Courtesy of the Library of Congress

The term yellow journalism was based on the comic strip, "Yellow Kid." The comic strip was about a kid who wore a yellow gown. Unfortunately, the color presses of the 1890's were not perfect and this created problems with the finished product. The colors for the Yellow Kid's costume often smeared. People began calling the World and the Journal, "the yellow press". Some readers commented of the papers that "they colored the funnies, but they colored the news as well."[4]

During the late nineteenth and early twentieth centuries, journalism changed significantly both in the language used and in the types of events the editors considered newsworthy. The quality of journalism declined in that it tended to move away from objective journalism and more towards sensationalism, going so far as to print outright lies in order to increase profits. The battle between Hearst and Pulitzer used weapons of innuendo, rhetoric, and lies – the reporting of actual facts had become boring and tedious. In order to capture the imagination and attention of the general public, the writing style became more casual and conversational and the stories became overly dramatic with a bent toward the sordid with an emphasis on sex and violence. In the case of the USS Maine and other fabricated stories, the lack of truth was not an issue. Due to weak enforcement of slander (false spoken words) and **libel** (false written words) laws, the papers did not have to fear lawsuits from those the papers vilified. To cover the war and the story on the USS Maine, Hearst sent one of his reporters, Fredrick Remington. Shortly after arriving, Remington cabled Hearst saying, "There is no war. Request to be recalled." Hearst responded with his now infamous quote, "Please remain. You furnish the pictures, I'll furnish the war" – Hearst all too

Yellow Journalism – Gaudy and sensational news reporting, written to boost sales and titillate the public; usually consists of dramatic pictures, half-truths, sometimes outright lies.

Libel – Published material that damages a person's reputation or good name in an untruthful and malicious way. Libelous material is not protected by the First Amendment.

The U.S.S. Maine in the Havana harbor, Cuba.
Courtesy of the Library of Congress

eagerly followed through with gusto. For weeks after the Maine sunk, Hearst's paper ran pages of stories and editorials accusing Spanish agents of planting explosives on the ship and demanded that the Maine be avenged. Other papers followed suit and the rally cry "Remember the Maine!" was heard throughout the country. In reality, Spain had nothing to do with the sinking of the Maine and in fact did their best to rescue crewmen. The accident was a result of simple human error. Gun powder was on the opposite side of the wall, near the boilers that generated the power to propel the ship. The heat from the boilers caused the powder to explode, causing the ship to sink. Captain Sigsbee of the Maine wrote how lifeboats from other ships in the harbor came to help rescue survivors, "Chief among them were the boats from the *Alfonso XII*. The Spanish officers and crews did all that humanity and gallantry could encompass."[5]

This type of journalism still exists today in such tabloids as *The National Enquirer* and the *Globe*, which mainly focused on scrutinizing celebrity hairstyles and love interests, reminiscent of the subjects of King Arthur in *Camelot*. The negative impact of this type of shoddy and non-factual reporting has spread to major network news broadcasts on television, radio, and the Internet. Ultimately, these tactics have damaged the collective social conscience, creating a culture of mistrust and cynicism.

Radio

The next big evolution in the media was radio. Unlike print media that, at the time, took a few days to reach individuals, radio allowed for all people to hear about events within hours. Radio was developed at the beginning of the twentieth century and then spread across the country from 1910 to the 1930s. Within twenty years, radios could be found in most homes and cars, allowing greater access to a diverse population, regardless of their level of education and ability to read. At the beginning of the radio era, a lot of print journalists crossed over to become on-air personalities. The skills they acquired as print reporters were applied to the spoken word as well. One of the best news reporters of this era was Edward R. Murrow. Mr. Murrow established an intellectual and straight-forward style of delivering the news, interviews, and opinion editorials. Murrow was able to combine his investigative skills with a succinct writing style, a persuasive speaking voice, and sense of dramatic flare. His legacy was often thought of as the catalyst for the transition from radio to television.

Franklin D. Roosevelt, 32nd President of the United States, during one of his fireside chats. © AP

Radio provided something that a newspaper could not. When someone reads a paper, they are removed from the event and delayed from receiving the story for a day or so whereas with radio, the listener could observe the event as it unfolded. The listener could be drawn into a story or event. Politicians could now reach out to listeners across the country and make them feel as if they are being addressed directly. President Franklin Roosevelt represents perhaps the best example of how to reach out to the American public and have them respond in kind. His infamous "fireside chats" proved to be an effective medium to convey a sense of security to the public during the troubled times of the Great Depression and World War II.

As we saw with the effects of yellow journalism on print media, we can see a similar phenomenon emerge with radio. In 1926 Father Coughlin was a supporter of Roosevelt and his policies but by the 1930s, he turned arch conservative and used his program that reached millions of Americans weekly to attack President Roosevelt, communists and Jews. At times Father Coughlin's fervor was so intense that he seemed to support the Nazi movement. Coughlin used a "fire and brimstone" method to deliver his message saying, *"The great betrayer and liar, Franklin D. Roosevelt, who promised to drive the money changers from the temple, had succeeded [only] in driving the farmers from their homesteads and the citizens from their homes in the cities … I ask you to purge the man who claims to be a Democrat, from the Democratic Party, and I mean Franklin Double-Crossing Roosevelt."* By the 1940's, Father Coughlin's show was so controversial, the Catholic Church forced him to focus on his parish duties.[6]

By 1948, radio began to see a decline in listeners as television took off. While television has added a new dynamic to the media game, radio is still a formidable force in American politics and culture. Some of the stars that have impacted the airwaves today can be found at the liberal end of the dial - Al Franken, Amy Goodman, Sonali Kolhatkar, to name a few and on the conservative side, Rush Limbaugh, Chuck Colson, and Sean Hannity. Radio has also moved into the realm of satellite media, which operates in what is deemed 'international space.' Satellite programs that feature risqué personalities like Howard Stern can broadcast his lurid escapades and elude the grasp of the FCC by orbiting the earth, just out of reach. However, there still appears to be limits to what the public will allow 'shock-jocks' to say on the air, in light of the firing of controversial and ethnocentric radio personality, Don Imus.

Boob Tube – Term that came about around 1965–70 that implies that television programming is foolish, induces foolishness, or is watched by foolish people.

Television

Television is perhaps equally the most powerful medium of communication and the most damaging. Virtually every home in the United States has at least one television (sometimes called the '**boob tube**') but most have two or three. On average, the TV is watched for about seven hours a day. Television, unlike newspapers and radio, gives viewers vivid images in addition to an audio narrative, the latter making TV accessible for the blind and the technology of closed captioning assists the hearing impaired. The impact TV has had on politics is beyond what anyone could have possibly imagined in 1948. As you'll see in chapter 10, politicians have found ways to use television to their advantage. Early on, politicians learned that people believe

Television is the main medium from which people receive information.
Courtesy of Jupiter Images

Issues For You
Discuss the impact television has had on modern politics. Do you think this is good or bad? Why or why not?

what they see over what they hear. For example, the John F. Kennedy and Richard Nixon appeared on televisions first live debate. Kennedy appeared to be more 'camera-friendly' – good-looking, photogenic, and at ease - while Nixon was sweating profusely due to a high fever. He was also apparently not aware that he was blinking rapidly and his eyes seemed to shift back and forth, perhaps due to his illness. Since that time, visual images are paired with catch phrases that run counter to the message being delivered and they are run over and over, day and night. On February 14, 2002, President George W. Bush announced his "Clear Skies & Global Climate Change Initiatives" during a speech at the National Oceanic and Atmospheric Administration. President Bush announced a drastic change in the 1972 Clean Air Act. Behind him on the stage was a blue backdrop with an eagle soaring over a canyon with the phrases, "Clean Air" and "Bright Future" all over the backdrop. While Mr. Bush's lips were delivering the message that: "The Clean Skies legislation I propose is structured on this approach because it works. It will replace a confusing, ineffective maze of regulations for power plants that has created an endless cycle of litigation. Today, hundreds of millions of dollars are spent on lawyers, rather than on environmental protection. The result is painfully slow, uncertain and expensive programs on clean air,"[7] - his actions were thought by many environmentalists, to be "gutting" the 1972 Clean Air Act by removing specific regulations that allowed businesses to trade credits. This is a prime example of how politicians can use visual images to distract the people from hearing the true meaning behind the message.

Most people get their local news and weather from three main local news networks, ABC, NBC, and CBS affiliates stations. For more national and international coverage, most adult Americans turn to cable news programs like *CNN, Fox News, CNBC,* and *MSNBC.* In times of national crises, Americans become more dependent on television news for their information than any other media outlet. In a Pew Research Center Study, when subjects were asked where they would go first to get information during a crisis, 66% of those surveyed said they would turn on the TV.[8] While television is still the main media leader, new technologies are beginning to edge TV out. These new technologies will be discussed in later chapters.

New Technologies

Efficient use of technology has long been the driving force behind the media. As we have seen, the inventions of the printing press, radio, and television, have all had an impact on the public and politicians. Advances in satellite technology have enabled mainstream and cable networks to broadcast news events as they are happening, which has had a huge impact on not only the number of news stations but also the way in which politicians make use of television. Computers are no different in this regard. Differences amongst the numerous types of media can be distinguished by the degree of immediacy that each has. Things that happen on the other side of the world are reported within a matter of minutes. People who have instant messaging can receive updates on world or political events by accessing email on their cell phones and PDA's. As stated earlier, students today have more access to information than any other generation before them.

Those of you reading this text probably know better than most the role and impact the Internet has had in providing political information. News agencies have their own home pages that are constantly being updated. In the 2004 presidential nomination election, every Republican and Democratic challenger in the primaries had their own website that discussed their platforms and provided information to voters around the clock. In addition, all of the websites made it possible for donors to make online contributions to the candidates of their choice. The Democratic and Republican National Committees, along with nearly every governmental agency and lobbying or interest groups, provide websites that offer voters valuable information. Within this textbook and the companion website, you'll have access to numerous websites and simulations that help provide greater insight into the relationship between the Internet and politics. The companion website for chapter one provides students with the tools to become active in the political process. The Internet is one way in which citizens are encouraged to participate and possibly shape the government into the kind of democracy they want. A recent Pew study on the 2004 presidential election revealed how much the Internet made a difference, especially for younger Americans. The Internet is part of the younger generations' culture. Children start using a keyboard at a much younger age than when baby boomers or Gen-xers started using it to surf the Web. Like most powerful tools, however, it can be used for good or evil - a quick search for neo-Nazism will reveal how free the Internet market is to all walks of life. However, the Internet can also be a tool that empowers and educates young people in a format with which they are comfortable. It can further aid them in exercising their political rights to challenge and question authority and ideas in a civil and educated way. Currently for Americans, television is still the most widely used source for information, but the Internet is not that far behind.[9]

How the Media Works

The media perform a wide variety of tasks. As you have seen, the media provides the public with information and in turn, the public develops opinions. Since the media has continuously increased its influence over the American public, it is vital that you have an understanding as to how the media works and how it is organized. First off, unlike other countries, most of the media in the United States are privately owned businesses. To add to this, most media partner with very large corporate conglomerates, such as Time Warner.

Media Ownership

Some would argue to avoid making too much of a big deal regarding the ownership and control of mass media outlets and the "liberal bias" that is tossed around. There are a number of studies that suggest that the mass media's overwhelming bias is not liberal or conservative but corporate, a category unto itself. The issue of who is providing the information is tantamount to knowing who is running the country. With the media in the hands of the few, some argue that there is no real way for alternative voices to be heard, therefore weakening the public discourse. Case in point, Eric Alterman, author of *What Liberal Media?* points out that Rupert Murdoch owns:

– Fox Broadcasting Network;

– Fox Television Stations, including over twenty U.S. television stations, the largest U.S. station group, covering more than 40 percent of U.S. TV households;

– Fox News Channel; A major stake in several U.S. and global cable networks, including fx, fxM and Fox Sports Net, National Geographic Channel, Fox Kids Worldwide, and Fox Family Channel;

– Ownership or major interests in satellite services reaching Europe, the United States, Asia, and Latin America, often under the Sky Broadcasting brand;

– 20th Century Fox, with its library of over 2,000 films; 20th Century Fox International, 20th Century Fox Television, 20th Century Fox Home Entertainment, Fox Searchlight Pictures, Fox Television Studios;

– Over 130 English-language newspapers (including the *London Times* and the *New York Post*), making Murdoch's one of the three largest newspaper groups in the world;

– At least twenty-five magazines, including *TV Guide* and the *Weekly Standard*;

– HarperCollins, Regan Books, Zondervan Publishers;

– Fox Interactive, News Interactive, www.foxnews.com;

– Festival Records;[10] [and]

– consider acquiring the Wall Street Journal

This is further enhanced by deregulation, which is supposed to open various outlets to new investors, thus increasing competition even more - unfortunately, this has had the opposite effect. Instead, small networks and private ownerships have been bought out by larger corporations wanting to increase their market shares in order to create monopolies. For example, in the newspaper industry, large groups like Gannett, Thomson, and Knight-Ridder control more than 80 percent of daily circulation of all newspapers. Within the last two decades, cross-ownership of media has increased as well. It's long and winding history reads something like the American children's nursery song, "There Was and Old Lady" (do an Internet search if you're curious, and type in "nursery rhymes" or the title of the song). Newspapers, television, publishers, and Internet service providers (ISPs) are all owned by conglomerates. For instance, Time merged with Warner Brothers to create Time Warner. They in turn purchased Turner Broadcasting, which owned CNN, Headline News, and TNT cable networks. With the "dot com" boom, Time Warner was then acquired by America Online. At the same time, Disney acquired Capital Cities, who owned ABC. ABC owned numerous cable stations, including ESPN. By 1990, Capital Cities/ABC owned the ABC television network, which is affiliated with nearly 30 radio and television stations, ten daily newspapers, and a variety of other publications. NBC is owned by General Electric, which is also in the business of GE Capital credit services and electronics, which includes appliances and defense contractors and CBS is owned by Westinghouse, who also owns credit services, nuclear power, and other manufacturing businesses. Given the complexities of the parent companies, it is difficult to imagine that media outlets would ever condemn their owners' policies or report any major negative publicity. With the ownership being controlled by the hands of a few, ultimately it will be difficult for citizens to obtain accurate and unbiased information.

Another area that needs to be examined is the source from which the media obtains its information. Years ago, many newspapers and television networks had bureaus in all major metropolitan cities, state capitals, Washington D.C., and other prominent locations all over the world. As more media corporations emerged, more emphasis was placed on the profit margin. News directors and editors had to become creative in order to stay competitive. In many areas, foreign bureaus and non-major cities were closed down. In order to fill that void, agencies like the Associated Press (AP) and Reuters news services were contracted to fill the void. This system is based on a network of reporters, which is oftentimes independent from any major news service that reports or writes the story. AP or Reuters would purchase the stories and then would notify the subscribers. The various media outlets determine the news worthiness of the stories and whether or not to use them. While this is cost effective for the profit margins, it presents a dilemma for the consumer. Think of the number of times, you have changed the channel on the television or radio only to hear the same reports but with slightly different interpretations, channel after channel – did you ever wonder why this is? By having the same stories cycling repeatedly throughout the nation, the voters end up less informed. If the information is inaccurate, incomplete, or just plain wrong, the public is bound to make poor decisions about issues that affect how they vote or think.

In light of dilemma, technology and specialty publications have provided a solution. With camcorders, cell phones, and the Internet, individuals have become unofficial vigilante reporters. The Rodney King beating by a small group of Los Angeles Police officers in 1992 and the sounds of gunshots at the tragic shootings of 32 students and faculty by a disturbed student, Seung-Hui Cho, at Virginia Tech University in 2007, were both captured by bystanders who were quick to draw their simple recording devices. In the case of Virginia Tech, the media was told to withhold the names of the deceased until all the families could be notified. Even though the families were notified as quickly as humanly possible, it still wasn't fast enough for some – concerned students on campus quickly set up chat rooms and Blog pages to receive and exchange more expedient news of their loved ones' whereabouts. Receiving news from around the world is delivered with equal speed. Images and details of the terrorist bombings in the tube (subway) system during rush hour traffic in London on July 7, 2005, or the oil spill of the Prestige on the northwest coast of Spain were quickly uploaded and compiled into 'jpg's', and sent across the continents to America, soliciting prayers and donations.

Infotainment – The merging of hard news and entertainment in news presentations.

In addition, individuals who are especially interested in politics or other topics can find specialized publications that grant greater insight on the world we live in. These publications are designed to appeal to specific groups of people. *The Weekly Standard* and the *National Review* appeal to conservatives; *The Nation* and *The American Prospect* appeal to liberals; *Commentary* is designed for neoconservative readers; *Mother Jones* is progressive; and lastly, the *New York Review of Books* and *The New Yorker* caters to intellectual and critical readers. Other reputable pop culture magazines whose focus is not political still provide political articles and interviews with influential people who contribute to the political debate. Magazines such as *Rolling Stone*, *Playboy*, and dozens of others fall into this category. The "Web" also provides a wealth of information on government and corporations. Internet political magazines such as *Slate* and *Salon* are beginning to appear. Ethnic, foreign language, and gay, lesbian, bisexual, and transgender periodicals and Websites are steadily increasing readership, which in turn, opens up the political debate to a more diverse population. The presumably thoughtful and politically-minded audiences of these publications have shown a special interest into the inner-workings of the government and the American corporations that drive them. This further aids the public in holding the government accountable when it comes to addressing the grass-roots issues that are often overlooked by the mainstream media.

The almighty dollar is placed on a higher pedestal than the quest for responsible and informative journalism. This means that the corporations are more than happy to broadcast stories that titillate and hold the viewers' attention. So, instead of putting money into controversial or overly-cerebral news, such as those having to do with politics or election fraud, the media executives would rather appeal to the largest audience possible. Many shows such as *Entertainment Tonight* have sets and broadcasters similar to traditional news stations. The major difference is lack of substance since the stories are mostly devoted to covering human interest, lifestyles of the rich and famous, or the latest trends in pop culture. Just to maintain the guise of a news show that offers real information, perhaps a very quick report on the latest sound bite some politician uttered might be thrown in. These types of shows have come to be known as **infotainment**. Advertisers pay exorbitant amounts of money to advertise in these major media publications and infotainment shows. Try counting how many times the camera shots change within a one-minute commercial on television – what the viewer experiences is a lot of flash in a very short amount of time. So it goes with the type of evening news that most of America watches after a long day or night away from home – nothing too challenging – each story 30 seconds or less, coverage of local crimes, warm and fuzzy anecdotal spots, and perhaps a few scandals for good measure – something that is more exciting than the average person's daily ho-hum existence. All of these stories are delivered by pleasant beautiful people speaking 'standard' American English. Not to discredit those who are skilled journalists, however, by all appearances, one needn't have an advanced degree in journalism or a brilliant reporting record to land one of these host jobs. You merely need to be able to toss about playful banter and cackle hysterically when the weather forecaster makes a funny.

Impact on Politics

When discussing the media, one must not overlook the impact it has had on politics. The media impacts politics in two main ways: the first is the coverage the media gives to politics and the second is the role it plays in shaping public opinion.

Press Coverage

Media coverage has impacted politics in that the amount of coverage media devotes to politics plays a significant role during election years. As the race progresses toward the primaries and caucuses, the media often focus on reporting candidates' standings in the race, limiting coverage to those in the lead, which consequently strengthens their positions in the eyes of the public. Over the years the use of public opinion polls has expanded dramatically. Organizations such as Gallup, Harris, and Roper, along with newspapers and television networks have increased their use of polls. Large newspapers and magazine publishers, including the *New York Times*, the *Washington Post*, *USA Today*, and *Newsweek*, as well as CNN and major television networks often conduct public opinion surveys on a wide variety of national issues; in fact, much of their news coverage focuses on the polls. We know that actions of the media have impacted politics – the question is to what degree? There isn't conclusive evidence saying that public opinion is influenced by media polling; but, what does seem to be clear is the impact media coverage has on candidates' ability to raise campaign funds. Often times if a candidate is not considered to be in the top three spots, donors will often withhold funds from them for fear of wasting their money on a lost cause. Paul Wellstone's campaign for the U.S. Senate is a good example of this. Wellstone was a college professor teaching political science at Carlton College in Minnesota. During the caucuses, Wellstone made a good showing and raised a substantial amount of money. However, being the Democratic nominee, he had to face Rudy Boschwitz, the incumbent candidate for the Republican Party. As a sitting Senator, Boschwitz was well financed and had developed an extensive network of contributors and fundraisers. Given his low polling numbers against the incumbent candidate, Wellstone did not receive financial support from the Democratic Party or other high profile contributors. It was not until the very end of his campaign, when it appeared in the polls that he stood a chance of defeating Rudy Boschwitz did Wellstone finally acquire some substantial monetary backing.[11]

Live Televised Fireside Chat with Jimmy Carter
Courtesy of the Library of Congress

Just as the general public is influenced by polling trends, so are elected officials. They utilize polls in their respective districts and states to take note of what their constituencies think. For example, after 9/11, when President George W. Bush's approval numbers were over 60%, the President and other leading administration officials proclaimed that those who do not support the war do not support the troops. After the 2006 midterm elections, when only a little over 30% of Americans approved of the war in Iraq, the President and his administration appeared to do a complete 'flip-flop' from their previous criticisms, saying that people are allowed to disagree with the President regarding the war and they would not be considered unpatriotic.[12]

There are growing numbers of voters who tend to watch exit polling to see if their vote will actually make a difference. This sentiment has serious implications on the process of democracy and it has caused a negative rippling effect of voter apathy across the Midwest and West Coast of the United States. In the 1980 elections, for example, many of President Jimmy Carter's supporters complained that the networks that began discussing early exit polls may have discouraged voters on the West Coast from voting because many of the projected polls showed Ronald Reagan winning by a large margin. The 2000 election exit polls created a great embarrassment for the major news networks when they announced prematurely that Al Gore had won Florida. Today exit polls are still inaccurate and are still surrounded by controversy further causing voters to question their value.

Equal Time Provision – The former requirement that television stations give or sell the same amount of time to all competing candidates.

Talk Shows

Candidates running for office appear on talk shows more often as election time draws near. Jay Leno spent time working on his good friend, Arnold Schwarzenegger's campaign during his first bid for Governor of California.

In California's 2006 gubernatorial race between incumbent Governor Arnold Schwarzenegger and State Treasurer Phil Angelides, Angelides' campaign charged that Governor Schwarzenegger's numerous appearances on "*The Tonight Show with Jay Leno*" constituted a violation of the Federal Communications Act's **equal time provision**. To remedy this, Angelides demanded that NBC and "*The Tonight Show*" offer the same amount of airtime to the Treasurer.[13] The amount of television and call-in radio talk shows that are being utilized by candidates presents an interesting dilemma for voters. How do individuals know when they are being entertained and when they are being solicited for their support? Today, there are thousands of radio and television stations across the nation. Nearly all Americans have access to television and radio at home, in their cars, at work – even gas stations have televisions mounted above gas pumps for patrons to gawk at while filling up. A well placed appearance on a popular talk show can give the candidate access to thousands of Americans and, more specifically, to a targeted demographic group. Again, "*The Daily Show with Jon Stewart*" is a prime example of a show that attracts politicians who are trying to reach 18-25 year-old voters. Other examples of trying to reach a specific demographic are Democratic candidate Bill Clinton appearing on *MTV*, Al Gore appearing on *Saturday Night Live*, and Independent gubernatorial candidate Jesse "The Body" Ventura appearing on *Larry King Live*. By the end of the decade, it had become common practice for political figures to use daily talk shows to convey their message to the voters. In 1994, radio talk show hosts like Rush Limbaugh were believed to be a key factor in the Republicans taking control over Congress. Political analysts have acknowledged talk shows as the new vehicle for information. In response, they have resorted to watching talk shows for material to discuss instead of the usual resources such as unions, civic groups, and other mainstream political sources. The talk show route is less controversial and has more accessible language that the average citizen process and discuss casually, whereas the target audiences of *Face the Nation*, *Meet the Press*, and *Washington Week* are reportedly college bachelor's degree holders or higher. These traditional *"Sunday Morning Shows"* used to be the main avenue that politicians would go to market their platforms and get media coverage, but now they go to *Oprah*.

Television

To get the maximum mileage out of their campaigns, presidential hopefuls and their staff skillfully use television commercials and appearances to spread the word. This is done by the use of sound bites. A sound bite is a 10-15 second blurb that is picked up by major news outlets and repeated over and over and over. An example of a sound bite would be when then Vice President George H. Bush said, "Read my lips, no new taxes." In 1992, the sound bite came back to haunt Bush when then Governor Bill Clinton used it against the President after he raised taxes during his term in office. As stated above, the object of campaigns is to provide voters with information on the issues. This raises the question how can 10-15 second sound bites accomplish this task? The simple answer is, not at all. Most of these sound bites do not contain enough information to give voters clear distinctions between candidates. Most campaigns and political parties have conducted polling and surveys to see what interests the voters. The messages that are crafted into short sound bites begin to sound the same regardless of the candidates' positions on the issues, forcing the voters to base their decisions on other factors.

Campaign Commercials

Originally, campaign commercials used to address the issues and introduce the candidate to the public. Over the years the "message" has changed from focusing on the issues to getting the "message of the day" out to the public. The message of the day usually tends to emphasize what the candidate or the campaign wants the public to hear, which may or may not reflect the candidate's position on a specific policy. As you saw above, the use of sound bites is one of the tools used by politicians and their staff in order to achieve their goal. Part of this goal is to present the candidate in a positive light while trying to discredit the opposition. During a political campaign, being labeled and portrayed in a negative light by the opposing side for several news cycles can be very costly, not only kicking a serious dent in the funds but also damaging image. This causes the receiving side to waste precious time and energy on counterattacks and news ways to recreate or "re-spin" a positive image again. If a negative label or accusation, sometimes called an "attack ad" or "smear campaign", is successful, it forces the opposing campaign to deal with the new issues brought up by the ads, which sometimes changes the direction of the entire campaign plan for all candidates. The main tool for running attack ads is campaign commercials. For example the "Daisy Girl" commercial from the 1964 Presidential Election was a powerful image that was very controversial. In the "Daisy Girl" commercial, the Johnson campaign portrayed Senator Barry Goldwater (R-AZ) in a negative light. The commercial showed a little girl sitting in a meadow, counting daisy petals. While she was counting, a man's voice counting down from ten was overlapped with hers, which gradually faded out. When the counting finished, the

FOR YOUR CONSIDERATION
SOUND BITES – MARKETING A WAR

Used by politicians across the nation, sound bites are the short, glib catch phrases that are intended to become a slogan for a campaign or platform. George W. Bush's "No Child Left Behind" sound bite in the 2000 Presidential Campaign is such an example, just as John Kerry's (R-MA) 2004 campaign used "Let America Be America Again." Bush's sound bite was in direct reference to his proposed legislation for national education reform (called the No Child Left Behind Act), whereas, Kerry's slogan was catchy, patriotic, and somewhat persuasive, but could also be construed as slightly ambiguous, which is common with political sound bites. Other campaign slogans have made outlandish promises that were next to impossible to keep, such as Herbert Hoover's 1928 campaign promise to ensure "A chicken in every pot and a car in every garage."

Catch phrases or repeated words that focus on the most prevalent needs on the minds of Americans attract the public's attention and hopefully their vote. During the World Wars, certain "buzz" words used included "peace" "normalcy" and "prosperity". Since the 1970's, following Nixon's resignation, sound bites used were "change" "reform" and "progress." Sound bites are also attached to marketing strategies for wars, such as the military phrases "shock and awe" and the mission's name "Iraqi Freedom." These terms become commonplace first in news broadcasts home from embedded reporters, and then in everyday conversations with the public. Oftentimes, the language of war conjures up over dramatization of the conflict, in order to maintain the focus of the general public on supporting the President's policies, especially when it appears to be waning as the months drag on. Think of the movie *Wag the Dog* that was based on the book American Hero by Larry Beinhart, first published in 1993. The plot of the movie revolves around the pairing of a very skilled spin doctor played by Robert DeNiro and a larger-than-life famous movie producer portrayed by Dustin Hoffman. The fictional president's senior staff called on DeNiro who consorts with Hoffman in order to create a diversion from a scandal involving the president and a "firefly" girl, sort of the equivalent to a Girl Scout. Under the close supervision of DeNiro, Hoffman creates the best work of his producing career, filming a fake war, complete with refugees, a hero nicknamed "Old Shoe" that needs to be rescued, and a theme song written by Willie Nelson designed to play on the emotions of the American public. In an eerie coincidence, the movie *Wag the Dog* was released in 1997, right around the same time the news broke of President Clinton and his alleged extra-marital activities with White House intern, Monica Lewinsky. In fact, one of the first scenes of the movie shows a picture of the back of the fictional president and the firefly girl, proudly wearing her beret and uniform as he is greeting her troop to the Oval Office. The photo bares an uncanny resemblance to the image of Clinton reaching out to hug the beret-topped Lewinsky in a crowd of people during an event outside the White House. Shortly thereafter, President Clinton ordered missile attacks on several key installations (buildings) in Africa and Afghanistan. In a reaction to perhaps the most chilling example of truth being stranger than fiction, many opponents of President Clinton criticized the President by stating that his actions emulated the movie, creating a circus of cynicism rather than focusing on the conflict as a real and actual event. The Republicans successfully rode the propaganda machine and had Clinton impeached but did not have enough votes in the Senate to remove him from office.

Issues For You
Do you agree or disagree with the idea that *Wag the Dog* further fueled Americans' cynicism of politicians. Why or Why not?

In the 2000 Presidential election, one repeated phrase that could be heard about then Governor George W. Bush was that he had a "fresh face in politics", which was later replaced by Bush's own description as a "war president" and a "decider not a divider."

In the 2008 Presidential campaign, the newest "fresh face" is Senator Barack Obama (D-IL), which implies that despite his inexperience, the public has once again been charmed by something new and shiny. This is not to say that he wouldn't make a fine President – the point is image first, political platform later. The power of language and attention-grabbing political lingo has been used time and again to influence voters during election time and public support during war time. The old adage of "it's not what you say, it's the way that you say it" holds true, especially in politics.[14]

picture of the girl in the meadow froze, and the next image was that of a mushroom cloud from a nuclear bomb that had been detonated. The giant mushroom cloud replaced the picture of the little girl with the daisy and a voice announced: "These are the stakes, to make a world in which all God's children can live, or to go into the darkness. Either we must love each other or we must die." While this ad was only aired once by the Johnson campaign, the debate that ensued generated enough negativity to place the Goldwater camp on the defensive for the rest of the campaign. The idea had been placed in the public's mind that it was too dangerous to elect Senator Goldwater for president.[15] While the daisy girl commercial succeeded in weakening the resolve of the Goldwater camp, sometimes campaign commercials can be counter productive, backfiring and turning public opinion against the candidate that launched the attack. If the smear campaign is viewed as too damaging, media consultants will usually advise the candidate to leave it alone. As a result of increased attack ads, candidates must now, by law, appear at the beginning of commercials, stating that they "approve this campaign commercial." In following chapters, the impact of negative campaign commercials will be discussed. For now, it should be noted that these commercials can be a double edged sword.

Government Regulation on the Media

The First Amendment provides freedoms for the press. Over the years, there has been a tug-of-war between the media and the press. Comparative studies have shown that the U.S. government allows the media to have freer reign than other countries. In the comparative section of this chapter, there will be a discussion on how we compare to Russia. For now, the discussion will focus on government controls over the print and electronic media.

Print Media

Prior to our separation from the United Kingdom, the colonists used newspapers and pamphlets to spread the news on the events that were transpiring. After they had won their independence, they took steps to insure that the government would not prevent the press from reporting the news (First Amendment). Within a few years, the first attempt to limit what editors and journalists could publish occurred. The Alien and Sedition Acts of 1798 was a reaction to several Anti-Federalist newspapers criticizing the Presidency and administration of John Adams. Both editors and journalists were arrested for their "attacks" against the state. It wasn't until the 20th century that the Supreme Court began ruling that the Constitution protected the press from governmental interference.

Beginning in the 1920s, the U.S. Supreme Court has ruled that the press has First Amendment protections that prevent the government from passing laws on censorship of newspapers from "abridging freedom of speech, or of press." The main limits on "freedom of the press," according to the Court, are during war time and when it involves national security. In these situations, government can use **prior restraint** and prevent a story from being printed. For example, in 1971, the Supreme Court ruled against President Nixon's restraining the New York Times and the Washington Post from publishing excerpts from the **Pentagon Papers**. In his concurring opinion, Justice Hugo Black stated, "the Government...carries a heavy burden of showing justification for the enforcement of such a restraint... The Government had not met that burden."

Prior Restraint – The government's power to prevent publication of a story, as opposed to punishment afterward.

Pentagon Papers – A secret Defense Department study about the U.S.' involvement in the Vietnam conflict; the report was leaked to the *Washington Post* and the *New York Times*.

FOR YOUR CONSIDERATION
FAIRNESS DOCTRINE

The policy of the U.S. **Federal Communications Commission (FCC)** that became known as the **Fairness Doctrine** is an attempt to ensure that all coverage of controversial issues by a broadcast station be balanced and fair. In 1949 the FCC took an official position that broadcast station licensees are "public trustees", and therefore obligated to provide the public a reasonable opportunity to hear divergent points of view on divisive issues that concern the public.[16] Initially the doctrine was borne out of numerous applications for broadcast frequencies. This raised concerns that the broadcasters would monopolize the airwaves with single-perspective broadcasting. The FCC wanted the stations to take an unbiased role and air as many perspectives possible for the good of the public. The administrative courts had traditionally ruled on what exactly is controversial. However, the FCC has ruled that "two viewpoints" was satisfactory for the licensee. During the 1940's the FCC instituted the "Mayflower Doctrine", prohibiting stations that were purely editorial in nature, a practice that later softened when stations began to allow other viewpoints. This and the Fairness Doctrine were the FCC's parallel act to Section 315 of the Communications Act of 1937, which required stations to offer "equal opportunity" to political candidates running for a public office. The Communications Act was federal law passed by Congress, as opposed to the Fairness Doctrine which was simply FCC policy. But in the 1969 case of Red Lion Broadcasting Co. Inc. v. FCC (395 U.S. 367),[17] the FCC asserted that the station had failed to meet its responsibility to the public by allowing a guest to be "attacked" without opportunity to respond. The U.S. Supreme Court upheld the doctrine, thereby sanctioning the doctrine, which means that the doctrine was approved. This caused controversy among journalists, who considered it a violation of their First Amendment rights. Some reacted in extremes, not only failing to provide "all the view points" of controversial issues, but going so far as to refuse covering the issues all together. Despite its initial contribution to democracy, the FCC's plan for fair broadcasting eventually backfired on them.

Issues For You
Do you think the fairness doctrine should be reinstated? Why or Why not?

Fairness Doctrine –
The now abandoned requirement that television stations present contrasting points of view.

FCC –
A government commission formed to allocate radio and television frequencies and regulate broadcasting procedures.

The 1980's cable television boom changed the need for the doctrine, as many more stations became the "other opinion" the FCC had sought to provide. The Fairness Doctrine began to go by the wayside, and the FCC changed its attitude about many rules, including the Fairness Doctrine. This was even more recognized in the FCC's 1985 report that the doctrine could indeed have been in violation of the First Amendment rights. In August 1987, following another decision in Meredith Corp. v. FCC, the courts declared the FCC did not need to continue enforcing the doctrine because it was not mandated by Congress. Later legislation to pass the doctrine into law was vetoed by President Reagan, in keeping with his deregulation efforts, and later on by President Bush.

The Telecommunications Act of 1996 changed the rules allowing for a single company to increase it's ownership of radio and television stations in the national markets. Take for example that the Act eliminated the entire national ownership cap on commercial radio stations that had been set at 40 stations years before. Now, the law permits one company to own as many as eight stations in the nation's largest local markets, up from a local limit of four stations per market. This gave way to mergers that in turn created larger telecommunication conglomerates. The unintended consequences of this Act was that instead of increasing competition and lowering rates for consumers, competition is only found among the large corporations, resulting in increased phone rates for consumers by 20 percent and cable rates by 50 percent.[18]

Today, the doctrine looms over the media, an occasional threat for when concerns heighten over broadcasting and cable-casting practices. But with the numerous news, radio, and satellite radio stations, the FCC has little concern over a lack of opportunity to express opinion. Some say that this is evident in the attempt by journalists and producers to cover controversial subject matter with contrasting viewpoints, analyst commentary, public opinion polls, viewer email, and so on. However, complacency can sometimes breed familiarity, and history tends to come around again full circle. It is for this reason that the people need to continue to hold broadcast corporations accountable from all angles of the political spectrum.

Since Vietnam, the government has tried to control what the press reports. This forces the reporters to limit what they can say regarding on-going military actions. Think back to when the U.S. invaded Iraq in 2003. Most of the reporters were connected to combat units thus preventing them from saying what was occurring because it could jeopardize the lives of American Service men and women. This action is not new. During World War II, reporters were imbedded with the troops and their reports were subject to strict government censorship. In stark contrast, the lack of censorship and the popularity of television during the Vietnam War produced a negative backlash of public opinion as images of the wounded and dead were aired nightly. As a reaction, nearly every military operation since Vietnam has come with strict censorship stipulations on the press. When the 1991 Persian Gulf War began, CNN was the only news service that was able to report from Baghdad. Bernard Shaw and others were providing audio reports of the U.S. and allied bombings. For the rest of the reporters not in Iraq, they were assigned to press pools and the military limited their access to forward units. The technique of embedding and press pools have worked well for the Department of Defense and will continue to be refined whenever there is conflict.

Electronic Media

The electronic media are more regulated by government than their print media counterparts. However, over the years as technology has developed, governmental controls have begun to erode. With the advent of radio, the federal government began to regulate the use of the airwaves, which are owned by the public. With the passage of the Radio Act of 1927 and the Communications Act of 1934 (which led to the creation of the Federal Communications Commission, or the FCC), the government has given itself the power to regulate licensed radio and television stations and adhere to rules in order to maintain their licenses. The FCC establishes the frequencies radio and television stations are allowed to broadcast on to prevent interference with competing stations. When you listen to your favorite radio station, they identify the radio station by giving the call letters and numbers in order to follow FCC rules. For example, if you're driving through Los Angeles while listening to the radio, some of the longer standing commercial radio stations you may hear are KROQ – FM 106.7 or KIIS FM at 102.7; public (member-supported) stations also have call numbers, such as KPCC FM 89.3 or KCRW FM 89.9. Less known, more liberally-slanted stations also must have identification, such as KPFK FM 90.7 and *AirAmerica* which airs on KTLK – AM 1150.

With the development of cable television, competition for market share and types of programming expanded. With cable television, the government had regulations because of the delivery method. More daring programs were offered and public concerns over the content being aired caused congressional investigations and eventually the FCC tightened controls on cable and network television. The FCC used fines as the main method of controlling networks. Congress aided the FCC by threatening to increase on-air-indecency fines to as much as $3 million a day. As a response, many company cracked down on the show hosts of supposedly risky programs. "Shock Jocks" such as Howard Stern were fined on several occasions and were forced to change venues. Instead of being on network radio, at the time of printing, Stern has found a home on satellite radio, an area yet to be scrutinized by the FCC or by congressional investigations.

"Welcome to PBS" (Public Service Broadcasting)

Congress mandated that the FCC regulates the airwaves for the "...public interest, convenience, or necessity." This led to the development of a public service broadcasting corporation that is responsible for creating programming that keeps the public informed on news, education, global perspectives on humanity, the environment, science, and personal enrichment stories, mainly at the local community level. Some of the programs that have become a staple for PBS television are *Sesame Street*, *The NewsHour with Jim Lehrer*, *Frontline*, *Nova* and *Masterpiece Theater*. The intent of this kind of programming was to provide neutral or unbiased opinions for citizens to receive information so they can make informed decisions. In recent years, PBS has been charged with being too "liberal" or too "elitist" in its programming and Congress has reduced its funds forcing stations to cut some of their programs or seek outside sponsorship to air them. As a result, PBS has been forced to make the same "marketing" decisions as the main networks. If a program is too controversial, the sponsors may not pay for it, so the story goes untold. Many PBS stations hold quarterly fund drives to offset the sponsors due to a lack of federal resources. Despite constant funding challenges and changing trends in television, PBS still offers the best alternative to the mainstream stations.

Internet

Unlike radio and television, the internet has not been met with the same level of regulations. Originally, the Internet was created as a method of communications for the Department of Defense. It was turned over to the public in the early 1990's. The Internet or "World Wide Web" has had a global impact, which is part of the reason why it is difficult for any one government to regulate it. Despite several attempts by congress to censor some content on the web, mainly pornography, the U.S. Supreme Court has ruled the legislation to be an intrusion on free speech and struck the laws down as being unconstitutional. An example of this would be the Child Online Protection Act of 1998 (COPA) in which Congress attempted to limit access to whatever they decided was harmful to children by blocking access to adult Websites. In 2004, COPA was ruled to be a violation of free Speech and was struck down by the Supreme Court. The Internet and electronic mailing remains to be a relatively free system with little known government regulation. The lines of privacy have been somewhat blurred with the 2001 passage of the Patriot Act in the United States, but overall, the public seems to e-mail and publish Websites with relatively little worry of surveillance.

Profiles in Politics
Bill Moyers (1934 -   )

Courtesy of the Library of Congress

Bill Moyers has achieved a unique place in American Journalism. A familiar face on public television, Moyers has demonstrated a commitment to the story that few have the courage to tell. Often the story is political, but he has also been fascinated by issues of human spirituality, how we can die with dignity and compassion, the common mythologies of world culture, modern poetry, the book of Genesis, and the environment. But through all his work runs the common theme of "telling truth to power." This may sound easy, but power has the effect of seducing or paralyzing, and rather than truth, many journalists simply tell the story that the powerful want to be told.

Moyers was born in Oklahoma in 1934, and grew up in Texas. He earned a Bachelor's Degree in Journalism at the University of Texas in Austin, and then went on to earn another Bachelor's Degree, this time in Divinity, from the Southwestern Baptist Theological Seminary in Fort Worth. He was preparing to teach Christian Ethics at Baylor University when he was offered a position as an aide to the powerful Senator from Texas, Lyndon Baines Johnson, for whom he had been a summer employee a few years before.

Moyers ran Johnson's vice-presidential campaign in 1960 and acted as liaison with John F. Kennedy's presidential campaign staff. He left Johnson in 1961 to serve as Associate Director of the new Peace Corp, which had just been created by President Kennedy. After the assassination of President Kennedy, Moyers returned to the White House as a special assistant to President Johnson. He played a key role in the development of the programs known as "The Great Society," Johnson's initiatives to end poverty and discrimination in America. He was a principal architect of Johnson's 1964 Presidential campaign, and then went on to become Johnson's Chief of Staff and was later also assigned the position White House Press Secretary. He performed both jobs until he left the administration in 1967 to become publisher of *Newsday*. In 1970, he became Editor-in-Chief of "Bill Moyers' Journal" on PBS. This was the first of what was to become a long association with Public Television.

Moyers work on PBS and elsewhere has dealt with some of the most profound issues of the human condition. He is very well known for a seminal series of interviews with theologian/mythologist Joseph Campbell, which traced the common roots of modern religions to the early myths of humanity and their origins in the human psyche. He wrote and produced series such as "On Our Own Terms," about the process of death with dignity; and "Genesis: A Living Conversation," which brought thinkers of different religious perspectives to discuss the foundational biblical story and its ramifications. This program encouraged participation by spawning discussion groups all across the country. More recently, "Bill Moyers on Faith and Reason" addressed the issues of the responsible role of faith in the context of the political ascendancy of conservative and fundamentalist Christianity. Throughout all of these series, Moyers explored the issues with thinkers from a wide variety of informed perspectives.

Profiles in Politics
Bill Moyers (1934 -   )

Moyers has also been committed to the story that the "powers that be" didn't want told. "I grew up in the South, where the truth about slavery, race and segregation had been driven from the pulpits, driven from the classrooms and driven from the news rooms. It took a bloody Civil War to bring the truth home, and then it took another hundred years for the truth to make us free."[19] After 9/11, PBS approached Moyers and asked him to start a new weekly series, telling the stories no one else was reporting, and to offer a venue to people who might not otherwise be heard. "NOW" with Bill Moyers became a Friday night staple. It quickly created a backlash in conservative Washington, even though conservative views were given a fair opportunity to be heard on the show as well. According to Moyers, "NOW" didn't play by the rules of conventional Beltway journalism. "Those rules divide the world into democrats and republicans, liberals and conservatives and allow journalists to pretend they have done their job if, instead of reporting the truth behind the news, they merely give each side an opportunity to spin the news."[20]

Moyers presented a post election commentary in 2002, predicting the likely consequences of having all three branches of government controlled by one party dominated by the religious, corporate, and political right, assuming they would use their power the way they had been advocating that they would do so for the next twenty five years. Events since have proved the accuracy of his statements. But friends told him they were hearing mumblings around Washington that PBS funding would be in trouble unless "Moyers was dealt with."

The Corporation for Public Broadcasting (CPB) was created by Congress to act as a "buffer" between the politics of Washington and public television and radio. Its mission (and Moyers was there at its creation) was to shield public broadcasters from the political intimidation of their federal funders. However, Kenneth Tomlinson, appointed by George Bush as Chairman of the CPB Board, felt his mission was to pursue the agenda of his ideological brethren, rather than to protect the opportunity for diverse views to be expressed without fear of political intimidation. Tomlinson had the CPB spend $10,000 to hire a consultant to watch "NOW" and report on its political bias. Moyers notes that Tomlinson could have called Moyers and asked him, or checked the on-line listings for free. Feeling he had become the story, rather than just covering it, Moyers eventually left "NOW." But he has continued to tell the important stories on PBS in series such as "Moyers on America" which covered the corruption scandal of the lobbyist Jack Abramoff along with Congressman Tom Delay of Texas and their objective of directing lobbying dollars to conservative causes; the efforts of major media conglomerates to end "net neutrality" and limit the access of smaller internet content providers; and the debate among conservative Christians on how and if their position on environmental issues has been shaped by conservative political forces. Moyers continues as a weekly presence on PBS, telling the stories that are vital to protect American Democracy.

California and the Media

Just like many other parts of the country, Californians have traditionally received their news from newspapers and later radio and television. Originally, most of the print media was owned by a few families. However, when electronic media was introduced, its popularity helped change the way Californians viewed politics.

Muckraking –
The exposure of scandal, especially of public figures.

Californian Newspapers

The main newspapers in California were founded in the 1800's. The big four papers in the state were the *Los Angeles Times* which was owned by Harrison Gray Otis; the *San Francisco Examiner*, owned by William Randolph Hearst; the *Examiner's* neighbor, the *San Francisco Chronicle*, operated by the de Young Brothers; and the *Sacramento Bee* controlled by James McClatchy. While some of the papers have changed ownership, the original families that owned these papers are still as influential today as they were yesterday.

In their heyday, newspapers and their owners wielded a substantial amount of power. The issues and candidates they supported were given great exposure while those whom they opposed were recipients of bad press. In the case of the *Los Angeles Times*, Harrison Otis supported the party machines lead by the Southern Pacific Railroad and opposed labor unions. Needless to say, the candidates that were supported by the railroad were put into a positive light while those who supported organized labor were commonly portrayed as trouble-makers. At the turn of the 20th century, the progressive movement was well underway in California. As stated in previous chapters, the progressives (also known as the reformers) wanted to end the monopoly the railroads had over California politics. Otis, like most of the newspaper owners, was a staunch conservative and took up the cause against the progressive movement. As a reaction to Otis' activism, Hearst, McClatchy, and the de Young Brothers, along with other journalists began a reform movement whose goal it was to try to counter the editorials from the right. Just like the rest of the country, progressives and reformers were tired of the "old-boys" political network. The opposition wanted to open the political dialogue to any citizen who wished to run for office. It was at this time that the term **muckraking** came about.

The Man with the Muck Rake was a character in John Bunyan's allegorical tale, *Pilgrim's Progress*. This character could only keep his eyes cast downward with his rake in hand. Neither wealth nor spiritual enlightenment could pull the Muck Rake man's attention away from the grimy filth on the floor. President Theodore Roosevelt referenced this same character, saying that while "it is very necessary that we should not flinch from seeing what is vile and debasing…and it must be scraped up…and there are times and places where this service is the most needed of all the services that can be performed. But the man who never does anything else, who never thinks or speaks or writes, save of his feats with the muck rake, speedily becomes, not a help but one of the most potent forces for evil."[21]   The term muckraking was coined for a style of reporting that can be thought of as the predecessor to investigative journalism today - whether the muckraking journalist is a force for evil or the seeker that exposes it can be left to interpretation. Muckraking journalists attempted to expose the graft and corruption that existed in politics and other populist issues, such as living and working conditions that were abused and exploited by the elites. While their reporting did expose how much control the railroad and wealthy individuals like Otis had over California's political process, problems arose when some reporters' credibility was compromised. Some of these muckrakers were manipulated to write stories with a bias toward the upper class, changing the focus of the stories from important social issues to those that increased profit. This was reminiscent of yellow journalism in the style of Hearst and Pulitzer. Despite these drawbacks, the reformers' victory over the newspaper owners was instrumental in shaping the role the print media plays and continues to play in California's politics.

Even after all this, the conservative owners and editors continued to promote their candidates and issues long after the democrats and progressives came to power in the state. This trend continued until the early 1960's. At this time, most of the newspapers were sold to the major media corporations who consequently put a professional face on the news. The career-minded editors made the newspapers more objective in their reporting and even began to promote liberal causes. Much of the state politics were left to the big four newspapers and local papers more typically covered community issues and local politics. As the demographics shifted from the cities to the suburbs, so did the print media. Most daily papers could no longer operate in the smaller markets and were forced to sell to larger media groups, or convert to weekly journals, such as *LA Weekly* and *OC Weekly*. With the domination of electronic media, even the larger daily papers are facing hard times and their future appears to be bleak unless they can adapt to the ever-advancing technology of iPods, cell-phones, and Blackberries.

Beat –
The regularly assigned locations where journalists gather information for articles.

Electronic Media

In addition to mergers and the reformers reinventing print media, television was also a big instigator of change in the Californian landscape of news and information. Many studies by Nielson Ratings and other polling systems show that Californians are glued to at least one or more televisions in one home and use it as their main source of news. Unfortunately, in many local newscasts, state issues and politics receive less than two minutes of air time per broadcast. Infotainment, discussed earlier in this chapter, receives much more time, perhaps in response to what the viewers say they want. Given this limited exposure, most state politicians either hire media consultants to get them exposure or they fly to the "hot spots" of the state to get maximum exposure. For California politicians, the four main hot spots are Sacramento, San Francisco, Los Angeles, and San Diego. These four markets add up to about 90% of the state's population. In stark contrast with print media, very few local stations have news bureaus in the state capital. There are two main explanations for this. First, most viewers are not interested in state politics. The average viewers focus more on national politics and local issues, which also tend to cover the state, in part. Second, broadcast journalists are more general whereas print journalists are more specialized in their "**beats.**" An exception to the rule is Hal Fishman who is a political scientist and anchorman for KTLA news. Mr. Fishman usually includes a segment about his views and on state politics in his broadcast to help inform the public on state related issues. Within the last two decades, with a decline on California Politics on local news, many media consultants have encouraged their candidates to use the 30-second "infomercial" as a way to inform voters. As noted above, these campaign commercials paint the politician in the best possible light by focusing on personal characters, not policy positions. Californians can hear candidates' positions on policy issues during televised debates, which only occurs when it is getting close to election time. Most of the mainstream stations do not carry the state officials' debates because of lack of interest – these are often left up to local PBS stations. During gubernatorial and other high state official campaigns, most mainstream broadcasters will report on the debates or air excerpts on them during their newscasts.

Profiles in Politics
Arnold Schwarzenegger (1947 -   )

From Olympia to California

Few people have become as internationally renowned as Arnold Schwarzenegger. Born July 30, 1947 in Thal Austria, Arnold Alois Schwarzenegger's fame began in the world of body building. Between 1966 and 1981 Schwarzenegger won 4 Mr. Universe titles and 7 Mr. Olympia titles for bodybuilding. He used his success as a world famous weightlifter to spring board right into Hollywood. Mr. Schwarzenegger began his acting career in 1970 with the movie *Hercules in New York*. Despite less than rave reviews, he continued to appear in similar typecast roles. In 1984 Arnold starred in the blockbuster hit *The Terminator* and was catapulted into media stardom. In 1986, he married Maria Shriver, daughter of Sargent Shriver, creator of the Peace Corps and Eunice Kennedy Shriver. Schwarzenegger followed this with a half dozen other blockbuster hits that grossed over 100 million dollars and by 2003, he was a well known movie icon, symbolizing the success that an immigrant can achieve.

On August 6, 2003 Arnold shocked the world with his announcement that he would run for governor of the state of California. He had just finished promoting his most recent film *Terminator 3* when he appeared on *The Late Show with Jay Leno*. By this point the recall election of Governor Gray Davis was in full swing. Arnold had stated that he would make an official announcement about his candidacy on *The Late Show*. However, with only three days left to register as a candidate, and the fact that he would be running against another potential candidate, his friend republican Richard

Riordan, many expected Arnold to bow out. Nevertheless, in front of a live studio audience, Schwarzenegger declared his bid for the governor of the state of California. This marked the beginning of another high-profile Hollywood-style campaign, reminiscent of the actor Ronald Reagan who forever blurred the line that separated celebrity from politician.

Issues For You

What do you think it says about California politics when it was said of Governor Schwarzenegger, "It wasn't his political skills but his ability to 'act' that allowed him to win California's governorship."

Always looking for high ratings, the media was more than eager to pay attention to the boisterous Schwarzenegger. While the other front running candidates tried to engage and challenge him on the issues, Schwarzenegger avoided the early debates and continued to ride the wave of the media frenzy that surrounded him. On September 3, 2003, the top five candidates, except Schwarzenegger, participated in a live televised debate. Opting for a more familiar forum, Arnold appeared on *Oprah*, Howard Stern's radio show, and *Larry King Live*. To further bolster his image Schwarzenegger personally financed a large part of his campaign with the millions of dollars that he had made from acting. When other candidates such as Cruz Bustamante raised finances to combat this through donations from special interest groups, the Schwarzenegger campaign was able to run negative ads that claimed Bustamante was in the pockets of special interest. As the election date approached, another televised debate was held, pitting the five major remaining candidates, Schwarzenegger, Bustamante, Huffington, McClintock, and Camejo against each other on September 24. Unlike earlier debates, this one drew more mainstream attention. As the question of whether Arnold could really win with no prior political experience drew near, correspondents from mainstream news outlets and Hollywood entertainment shows and magazines flocked to cover this debate. By this point, Schwarzenegger led in the polls and it was clear that the other candidates would need a decisive win to effectively challenge him. This did not happen and Arnold came off as a competent candidate. On a special election day, October 7, 2003, 55.4% of voters recalled Governor Gray Davis and elected Arnold Schwarzenegger to replace him. The new governor beat out the 134 other candidates on the ballot with 48.6% of the vote and went on to become the 38th Governor of California.

News Coverage of California

California is the most populous state in the union and the world's sixth largest economy. Despite these important details, news coverage of California politics is largely ignored by television and newspapers usually list state issues deep inside the main sections after the sensational, international, and national issues. In light of the historical context of media in California, the coverage is far better today than it was in the late 19th and early 20th century. Most of the reporters today are professional and are more objective when reporting the news.

The Internet provides citizens with expedient and copious access to information and candidates. Courtesy of Jupiter Images

With the specializations of print reporters, every major paper has a bureau in Sacramento covering the major events. While newspapers still lead in state politics, it should be noted that in recent years, the large media conglomerates who own the "big four" have shifted their attention to profit margins and have forced cut backs in the bureau staff. Take for example the *Los Angeles Times*. The Times has the largest pool of reporters in Sacramento but it has been scaled back because the owner, Tribune Company believed that 25% profit was not enough for its shareholders. In order to maintain the Los Angeles Times' exceptional coverage of state and local issues, a consortium of individuals and businesses offered to purchase the paper from the Tribune Company. Despite this offer, the Tribune Company opted to sell the *Times* to another media conglomerate instead of the Los Angeles based consortium.

Internet

Given all of this, California is still media rich. The state is home to print media, broadcast journalism, major movie studios, and within the last three decades, California has become a major leader in computer manufacturers (HP, Apple, etc), software developers, internet service providers, networking hardware and software (Cisco Systems), and search engines (Google) to name a few. The Internet has also provided an avenue for politics and political observers to discuss issues, raise campaign funds, and post their views on issues.

In the 1980's and early 1990's phone banks and direct mails were the main way to contact voters. Now the system includes emailing lists, websites, and Blog pages (web logs). Unlike its predecessors, websites and email is more cost effective. A staffer only has to post or email the issue of the day and it can reach thousands of people within seconds. Websites are accessible virtually 24 hours a day so supporters and other interest parties can log on and get the latest campaign news. Campaign fund raising has become easier as well. With such web services such as Paypal, individuals can donate money day or night, making it convenient for people in different time zones. Furthermore, the information is automatically recorded for accounting and outreach purposes. There is a downside to using the Internet. While most homes in California have at least one computer with Internet access, there still exists a digital divide. There are people who still don't know how to use the

Internet or "surf" the Web; a campaign must still use phone banks and direct mailers to reach those individuals as well.

While technology has advanced Californian's awareness of politics over the last century and a half, voters still need to be leery of where news is coming from and if there are alternative motives present. This is especially true with Internet information. The Internet provides citizens with a wealth of easily accessible information but with this volume of resources, one must be even more cautious. Take for example the recent media frenzy over the shocking death of celebrity spectacle, Anna Nicole Smith. *Wikipedia*, a publicly maintained online encyclopedia, had posted the news several hours before her death was even announced by the county coroner. In this case, it was speculated that the individual who posted the announcement wanted their "15 minutes of fame".

How Do We Compare?
Russia and the United States

When comparing Russia to the United States, especially in the area of media, one must understand Russia's history, culture, and institutions in order to gain a greater insight on how the country and people have evolved. Unlike the United States, the

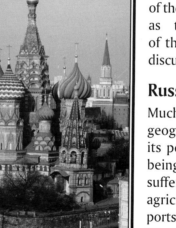
Courtesy of Jupiter Images

media in Russia, even prior to the Soviet Union, experienced oppression at the hands of the Tsars. As stated in chapter one as well as throughout this chapter, freedom of the press is especially important when discussing democratic theory.[22]

Russia: A Brief History

Much like the UK and Germany, Russian geography has played an important role in its political development. Despite Russia being the largest country in the world, it suffers from long, harsh winters, weak agriculture, and only a few warm-water ports. As with most countries of Europe and Western Asia, Christianity has played a major role in developing Russian culture. The difference between European nations and Christian nations of Asia is that Eastern Slavs received Christianity from Constantinople, not Rome. When Constantinople became **Orthodox** in religion, Russia followed suit and developed the Russian Orthodox Church. The Russian Orthodox Church also uses a **Cyrillic** alphabet instead of the Roman alphabet. These factors along with two centuries of control by the Tartars kept Russia isolated from Europe. This has proven to be a major obstacle for Russia. As its neighbors to the west embraced modernity and the resurgence of democratic values via the enlightenment, Russia would be stuck with **feudalism** for several more centuries.

In the 1500s, the same time when the writings of Descartes and Macchiavelli encouraged Europeans to embrace democracy, Tsar Ivan the Terrible of Moscovy removed the Tartars and established the Russian pattern of **autocracy**. Most of Russia accepted autocracy in order to avoid **anarchy**. It wasn't until the early 1700's that Czar Peter the Great forced Russia to modernize. He based his modernization

Orthodox –
Conventional established methods, attitudes, beliefs, conduct, etc.

Cyrillic –
Geek-based alphabet of Eastern Slavic languages.

Tartars –
Tribes of Mongolian origin who ruled Russia for centuries.

Feudalism –
System of power that is dispersed among kings and nobles.

Autocracy –
Absolute rule of one person in a centralized state.

Anarchy –
Absence of any conventional form of government.

of Russia on the European model by creating western industry, clothing, and organization styles. This process of forcing Russia to modernize would develop into a pattern as time progressed.

Despite Tsar Peter the Great's attempt to modernize Russia, it remained far behind its European counter parts. France's invasion in 1812 illustrated how backwards Russia really was. The Russia intelligentsia encouraged the leaders to copy the West but the Slavophiles wanted to maintain Russian Slavic heritage. When individuals get a taste of freedom, especially economic freedom, they want more, such as political freedom. Russians are no different. As the Russian economy began to prosper, they wanted to expand their political freedoms, similar to that of the U.S. (freedom of speech, assembly, press, and association). Unfortunately, the autocracy control by the Tsar didn't change. The failure of the government to respond forced some Russians to look to extreme measures to remedy the situation. Some of the radicals wanted to assassinate the Tsar while others, mainly those who studied Marxism, wanted to have a revolution.

Karl Marx believed the workers or proletarian revolution would begin in an advanced capitalist society. Lenin turned Marx's theory upside down to fit into the Russian model, coined **"Marxism/Leninism"**. According to Lenin, capitalism can be overthrown at its "weakest link," in this case, Russia. Lenin argued that Russia was being exploited by the capitalist nations and therefore could act as the catalyst to start the revolution. Given that most Russians were uneducated, Lenin designed a party of professional revolutionaries known as the **Bolsheviks**. Between the two theories, one can either see them as divergent or as building upon the other. Marx thought the workers would just arise, a natural and inevitable evolution of capitalism. Lenin decided to help it along with the "vanguard of the proletariat!"

After Russia was defeated by Japan in 1905, a revolution began. To end the revolt, Tsar Nicholas initiated reforms and established the **Duma**. Shortly thereafter, Nicholas reneged on his promise to reform and tension escalated. With the onslaught of World War I, came the beginning of the end for Tsarist Russia. As the war dragged on and Russia lost more and more men, there were constant reports of defeats at the frontline. Finally, the Tsarist government collapsed and in March of 1917, the Kerensky regime, a moderate government, became the Provisional Government. The Provisional Government may have had a chance to succeed except that it gave in to the pressure of the Western allies and stayed in the war. Lenin returned to Russia after being in exile in Switzerland and, with the help of the Germans, he and his Bolshevik party took control of Petrograd and Moscow with his slogan, "Bread, Land, Peace." In November 1917 (October in the old Julian calendar), power shifted from the Kerensky regime to the Bolsheviks by way of revolutionaries. These groups of revolutionaries were called councils or "soviets" in Russian. They consisted of peasant and factory workers and military personnel. The Bolsheviks held the power within the party while the Soviets acted as the foundation of the party.

Lenin and the Bolsheviks won the civil war against the White forces (supported by the United States, Britain, and France) and tried to reform the country by creating the institution of war communism. This program was unsuccessful and led to the starvation of many Russians (Soviets). Under increasing pressure of his failed economic policies, Lenin created the New Economic Policy in which individuals could own businesses and sell their produce for money (**privatization**). The only area that was off limits to privatization was the heavy industry. This was controlled by the government. The New Economic Policy (NEP) was in place from 1921 to 1928. Unfortunately for Lenin, he did not see the project through. He died in 1928 and

Marxism / Leninism – Communist ideology combining Marx's economic and historical theories with Lenin's organizational techniques.

Bolsheviks – Translates to "majority" in Russian; early term for Soviet Communist Party.

Duma – Russia's national parliament.

Privatization – Use of private firms to provide public goods and services and/or the selling off of state-owned firmsto private agencies.

Joseph Stalin took control by seizing power from Trotsky and subsequently dominated the communist party. Stalin then implemented the first of many Five-Year Plans which forced unrealistic quotas for agricultural and industrial products for exports. This forced modernization killed millions of Soviets, mainly peasants, through starvation. When Stalin was faced with a dilemma, he reacted to the instability by increasing the oppression. He purged thousand of party members and forced large numbers of Soviets into the prison camps in Siberia, thus further weakening the state. By the time World War II began, Russia was virtually in ruins. The war with Germany caused over 27 million Soviet deaths.

Over the course of the next fifty years, the Soviet Union would raise itself from the ashes of World War II and Stalin's failed policies to become one of the world's most powerful countries. The United States and the Soviet Union were engaged in a "Cold War" from 1948 to 1999. Even though the Soviet people were still oppressed and faced many internal and external problems, such as food shortages, a weak economy, Chernobyl's nuclear accident, and competing with the United States in a weapons race, they still clung to a faint hope for real change. Throughout this time there were many attempts to reform Stalin's system. Some of the reformers were Khrushchev, Gorbachev, and Yeltsin.

Issues For You

Do you think Russia will ever become a "true" democracy? Why or Why not?

Nikita Khrushchev came to power in 1955 after Stalin died in 1953. He attempted to experiment with economic and cultural reform and promised utopia at the end of the journey. Khrushchev was removed from power in 1964 by the party elites who were afraid of change and chaos. After Khrushchev, Leonid Brezhnev took control and returned to some of Stalin's policies. Brezhnev led the Soviet Union from 1964 to 1982. It wasn't until 1985 when Mikhail Gorbachev, who came of age during Khrushchev's hints at liberalization, assumed power. Gorbachev initiated sweeping change and transformed the Soviet system by *glasnost* (media openness) and *perestroika* (economic restructuring). As chaos ensued, Gorbachev caved in to the pressure from the party elites, reversed his policies, and never implemented the complete economic reform that he promised. In 1991, the military attempted a coup but was forced to back down by Boris Yeltsin and the Soviet people. This was the end of the Soviet Union. Yeltsin pushed Gorbachev out of office and ushered in the post-Soviet Russia. Under Yeltsin, Russia's privatization went badly. Corruption was prevalent, giving enormous wealth to a few oligarchs who supported Yeltsin. Yeltsin seized power from the Duma and began naming and removing prime ministers and other officials while the economy declined and crime and corruption continued to increase.

Yeltsin faced a coup in 1993 when he dissolved the Russian parliament. After defeating the coup, Yeltsin became semi-dictatorial until ill health forced him out of power in 1999. Yeltsin's successor was an unknown ex-KGB officer, Vladimir Putin. Putin quickly became popular with his promise to bring an end to the rebellion in Chechnya. In order to regain power over the economic problems spurred on by uncontrollable governors and the Russian Mafia, Putin pushed laws through the Duma, further extending his reach. As the media began to oppose Putin, he began to limit the press by shutting down opposition newspapers and television studios and replacing them with more state run media. Putin began to emerge as an authoritarian and focused on rebuilding a strong Russian state with little concern for democratic values.

Profiles in Politics
Anna Stepanovna Politkovskaya (1958 - 2006)

Tireless. Fearless. Passionate. Independent. Honest journalism. Polemic. Bravest of the brave. Inspirational to journalists both at home and abroad. These are the words that all manner of journalist and government officials alike have used to describe the controversial and outspoken Russian journalist, Anna Stepanovna Politkovskaya, who was brutally assassinated on October 7, 2006. Russian President Vladimir Putin, who was the primary focus of Politkovskaya's vigilant criticism, waited three days after her death to say to the world that Politkovskaya had very minor influence on Russian political life. Her tireless reporting on Putin and the crimes against humanity committed in Chechnya is what many believed eventually put an end to her life. There are different reports as to exactly how Politkovskaya was murdered – three bullets to the body, one to the head, or the other way around, ambushed in the elevator of the apartment building in which she lived in Moscow while she was supposedly on her way to the offices of *Novaya Gazeta*, one of the only national Russian newspapers that took a liberal stance and was consistently critical of the Kremlin. Despite the dodgy details, the general consensus of those that respected and admired Politkovskaya all agree that it was indeed an ordered contract killing. It was not the sort of fate that one would expect for a mother of two and the 2004 joint winner of the Olof Palme Prize for human rights work, and so many other journalism and human rights awards earned since 2000. Sadly, it has become quite commonplace for journalists in Russia to be censored, illegally laid off or arrested, harassed, beaten, or poisoned.

Since Putin the ex-KGB officer came into power, poisoning seems to have made a comeback. "The list is rather long, and since Putin assumed power in Russia, poisoning has been one of the preferred political tools used by the Kremlin," Pavel Felgenhauer, a Russian military analyst, told the Associated Press.[23] The list he speaks of is indeed long: in 2003, Yuri Shchekochikhin, a journalist colleague of Politkovskaya at *Novaya Gazeta* who was also very vocal about government corruption, died from an apparent severe allergic reaction, though fellow staffers believed he too had been poisoned. A year later, while on her way to cover the Beslan school siege in Moscow, Politkovskaya was handed a cup of tea and the next thing she remembered was waking up in a hospital. Anna later told BBC's *Woman's Hour* that she believed she had been drugged. Later still in December 2004, after a political dinner event, Viktor Yushchenko became seriously ill. The head of the Rudolfinerhaus hospital, Dr. Michael Zimpfer reported that the tests revealed "no doubt" that the illness was caused by dioxin poisoning - Yushchenko had 1,000 times the normal amount of dioxin in his bloodstream. Yushchenko felt certain that because he was running against Ukrainian Prime Minister Viktor Yanukovich whom Putin favored, that this was the reason for the attempt on his life. And the list goes on and on. Tragically, Politkovskaya was subjected to a worse fate than surviving being poisoned – the sentence of murder. She was the 13th Russian journalist who had been killed since Putin became president.

It was because of the constant death threats and ransacking of her living space that she chose to live alone, and she chose to continue in her controversial writing style because, in her own simple words, "I am absolutely sure that risk is part of my job as Russian journalist. Doctors give health to patients, singers sing; duty of journalist is to write what journalist sees in reality – it is only one duty". Only months before her assassination, Politkovskaya wrote the first in what was to be a series of detailed accounts of torture by the Chechen rebels. It turned out to be her last article. On October 12, *Novaya Gazeta* decided to print Anna's article posthumously, under the headline "*We Declare You a Terrorist.*" In it, Politkovskaya submitted detailed transcripts of the horrible torture of Beslan Gadayev, a Chechen migrant who had been deported from Ukraine to Chechnya.

Profiles in Politics
Anna Stepanovna Politkovskaya (1958 - 2006)

He had contacted Anna in a letter, describing what the Chechen army had done to him in order to get him to confess to unsolved murders. The article included vivid pictures from videotapes. The article was released the same day that Russia was being held accountable by the European Court of Human Rights for the murders of five Chechen civilians in early 2000. Even in death, Politkovskaya continued to do her one duty as a journalist to the people of Russia and anyone listening in the rest of the free world.

Politkovskaya was not only a committed journalist but was also a respected political negotiator and expert on Chechen matters. She had several opportunities to help with negotiating in October 2002, when Chechen terrorists took an entire Moscow theater, about 900 people, which included cast and audience members, hostage during a performance of a popular Russian musical Nord-Ost. Not only did she help in negotiating the release of hostages, she continued to speak out on the incident, saying that she believed that Putin himself selected a secret poisonous military gas - this was the instrument deployed by Russian special forces that ended the conflict, leaving 129 people dead.[24]

Polikovskaya wrote several books, some in English, entitled *A Dirty War: A Russian Reporter in Chechnya* (2001), and *Putin's Russia* (2004). From her article *In Hell*, July 2000, she writes about the capital of Chechnya, Groznyy: "The city ruins are like a new Caucasus mountain range. African-style famine. Painfully thin children...living streets full of dead eyes. Mad and half-mad people. Streets teeming with weapons. Mines everywhere. Permanent explosions. Despair." In December 2005, at a Reporters Without Borders conference, the theme of which was freedom of the press, Politkovskaya's said in a modest yet foreboding way: "People sometimes pay with their lives for saying aloud what they think. In fact, one can even get killed for giving me information. I am not the only one in danger. I have examples that prove it."

Russian politics continues to struggle with the concept of democracy. Many Russians harbor resentment, blaming the United States for forcing economic shock therapy and privatization that they believe gave power to the **oligarchs**, who were able to gain mass amounts of wealth while most Russians suffered. In trying to find a democratic model that worked for them, the conservative leaders consulted France's semi-presidential system. This hybrid model gave power to the executive and it is what allowed Yelstin and Putin to usurp power away from the Duma during their power struggles. Putin has been able to seize control over all ministries and the Duma. He has also removed power away from the regional governments by appointing the governors directly from Moscow and by only allowing the regional legislatures a straight yes or no vote on his appointments. These new powers have also allowed Putin to demolish the power of the oligarchs by renationalizing their companies and imprisoning them for tax fraud. In examining the case of YUKOS, the second largest oil producers in Russia, Putin's administration charged and arrested the Chairman and Chief Executive Officer Mikhail Khodorkovsky for tax evasion and other illegal activities. All of Khordorkovsky's shares of YUKOS were seized and he was forced to resign.[25] Many skeptics point out that Khodorkovsky was providing funds to political opponents and also owned media outlets that were critical of Putin's policies and actions.

Oligarchs, Oligarchy – Rule by the few; political system in which a small group dominates distribution of resources while also serving their own interests.

The current state of Russia is a quasi-authoritarian government created by President Putin. He was able to alleviate some fears that Russians lived through with the oligarchs and mafia but at the same time, he created new concerns over his style of governance. Nevertheless, there still may be an opportunity for Russia to become more democratic by embracing freedom of the press, free and fair elections, and by giving Russia the powers for which they yearned for several hundred years – popular sovereignty.

Chapter Summary

Through out this chapter we have examined the impact the media has had on politics, both past and present. By examining the role and history of the media in a democracy, we have seen how it has evolved into the "fourth" branch of government. Technology has also played an important role. From the printing press to the internet, each advancement has provided the citizens with the ability to stay informed about the political leaders' actions. While these opportunities have not reached their potential, we can see how the media and technology might move us ever closer to the true democratic ideal. In examining the impact of media in California's politics, we have seen how a state with millions of residents and access to a wide variety of media, is having difficulty providing information on state and local issues because of the large media conglomerates desires to maximize their profits. In the case of Russia, one can develop a greater understanding of how after centuries of control by the Tsar's and later communism, Russians still have continued to struggling with being informed with accurate information. While some individuals have tried, they have met stiff resistance, including jail and even death. In the end, we have developed a greater understanding of the need for a free media – free of government and business interference so the citizens can make informed decisions based on untainted information.

Key Terms:

Watchdog

Investigative Journalism

Newsworthy

Objective Journalism

Pundits

Socialization

Mass Media

Yellow Journalism

Libel

Boob Tube

Infotainment

Equal Time Provision

Sound Bites

Prior Restraint

Pentagon Papers.

Fairness Doctrine

Federal Communications Commission (FCC)

Muckraking

Beats

Orthodox

Cyrillic

Tartars

Feudalism

Autocracy

Anarchy

Marxism/Leninism

Bolsheviks

Duma

Privatization

Oligarchs

Websites:

Polling Websites

Doonesbury
www.doonesbury.com/arcade/strawpoll/index.cfm

Gallup Organization
www.gallup.com/

California Sites

California Research Bureau
www.library.ca.gov

This page left blank intentionally.

U.S. Troops on Patrol in Iraq

© Grant Terry, 2007. Used under License from Shutterstock, Inc

CHAPTER 5

PUBLIC OPINION

CHAPTER OUTLINE

Democracy and Action -
A Cautionary Tale for Governments

Public opinion is an important tool in many areas of society today. Because the United States is a democracy in which all citizens over the age of 18 have the right to vote, public opinion is essential when it comes to government, and especially imperative when it comes to matters of legislation. A vivid illustration of how powerful the court of public opinion can be took place in the state of South Dakota in 2006 regarding the issue of abortion.

In February 2006, the legislature of the state of South Dakota passed the Women's Health and Human Life Protection Act, which prohibited all abortions in the state, including those where the woman's health may be threatened and also those pregnancies resulting from rape or incest.[1] This act was not proposed and passed because it was an important issue to the citizens of the state; instead, the very conservative South Dakota legislature, seeing a more favorable U. S. Supreme Court makeup, passed this legislation in order to directly challenge the 1973 U.S. Supreme Court decision, Roe v Wade, which made abortion legal in the United States. The Governor of South Dakota signed the new Act into law in March 2006.[2]

The U.S. army, post WWII, used public education announcements like this poster to inform Japanese citizens that they should be aware of their new rights.
Courtesy of the Library of Congress

What the South Dakota Legislature and Governor did not prepare for was the collective public uproar from not only many people around the country, but from the people of the normally conservative South Dakota as well. Under South Dakota state law, its citizens can petition, with enough collected signatures, that a newly enacted law be put on hold while the issue is put to the people of South Dakota via election; this is precisely what happened in 2006. In May of that year, a South Dakota based group, the Campaign for Healthy Families, collected enough signatures to delay the law from taking effect in order to put the issue before the voters of South Dakota in the November 2006 election. In that election, South Dakota voters soundly rejected the new law, 56 percent to 44 percent.[3]

The law's defeat serves as a reminder of how crucial the role that public opinion plays in the act of governing. It was a major victory for South Dakotan voters as well as a cautionary tale for all legislatures and government leaders in the United States who decide to proceed with any controversial lawmaking without consulting the court of public opinion.[4] In a democracy, the people will remain supreme.

Public Opinion and Democracy

"The voice of the people?! There is no such thing. You got 240 million voices all yelling for something different. The only thing you all agree on is you don't want higher taxes. The voice of the people, my fanny!"
– Jack Lemmon as President Kramer in the movie "My Fellow Americans"

If you've ever taken a philosophy, sociology, or political science class, you have probably been asked about your views about human nature. Your views often dictate how you might perceive society and the role of government within that society. You may not realize it but by now, you probably have a moral code that you live by. Perhaps it is founded in your parents' upbringing and was then passed on to you; nevertheless, you have developed your own **core beliefs**. Each person's core beliefs make up our political culture. In America, this has come to mean limited government, individualism, a free enterprise economic system, and personal liberties. These terms are the basis for **political attitudes**, which emerge from our core beliefs about government. To get a better idea of how a community or even a region thinks about general political issues, surveys are often administered to a larger group of citizens to collect what is referred to as **public opinion**.

Public opinion is the cornerstone of democracy. Government can not claim to represent the citizens unless they understand and know what the people want. The phrase the "voice of the people" characterizes what leaders consider when developing and implementing public policy. In order to gauge the citizens' views on various issues, politicians will often hire polling organizations to design, administer, and analyze polls. The statistics from these polls can be spun in many different ways but to the astute politician, they offer a sampling of what the constituents, whether politically savvy or not, are thinking. However, as you can see from the above quote, sometimes it is difficult for politicians to discern what it is the people exactly want. Furthermore, some politicians, such as Edmund Burke, political philosopher from the 1790's felt that elected officials should be attentive to the interests of the citizenry, but not necessarily subservient to their will. The idea that the people are ignorant began with the framers and continues to today, but in more subtle ways. Shows such as "Are you smarter than a fifth grader?" hosted by comedian Jeff Foxworthy or Tonight Show host Jay Leno's segment "Jaywalking" expose just how much the public knows – or doesn't know – about politics, history, and popular culture. As discussed in Chapter 4, most of the public gets their information from television, making that medium very powerful but not necessarily accurate.

Core Beliefs –
One's views about human nature, society, and economy; makes up a political culture.

Political Attitudes –
One's views about public policies, political parties, candidates, politicians, and government in general.

Public Opinion –
The collective expression of attitudes about the prominent issues of the day.

Straw Poll –
A non-scientific way that public opinion was measured.

Representative Sample –
A sampling of people that includes all the characteristics of the total population.

How Do We Get the Numbers?

Like many traditions in America, the idea of public opinion and how it is measured finds its roots in farming. The **straw poll** was used to measure public opinion by throwing straws up in the air and judging which way the breeze might carry them, much like the way public opinion is bandied about by the political trends of the time. Obviously, this method of measuring public opinion is tantamount to an old wives' tale (a myth) and it isn't the best way to retrieve an accurate sampling of a representative population. It is not practical to survey all Americans or get everyone's opinion so pollsters use a **representative sample** of the public. An ideal representative sample should be characterized by all the different cultures, ethnicities, languages, beliefs, and so on, that are present in the total population. There are many different strategies to obtaining a sample as well as many factors to consider. We will discuss some key terms that are important to the process of analyzing public opinion.

If a sample does not represent a fair cross-section of the population, and only targets a small demographic, like for example, only middle-class white families, then the public opinion culled from surveying this sample can hardly be called accurate or scientific. George Gallup is one statistician from the 1930's whose name is probably a household name for most when it comes to discussing polls. You can go to www.gallup.com to view up to date polling information. The method he applied utilized statistical techniques after conducting interviews with small representative samples of the voting public. This requires, first of all, at least a few hundred people. The larger the **sample size** (usually 1,500 to 2,000 respondents), the smaller the **margin of error** (down to as little as 3 percent) and the higher the reliability of the findings will be (accurate at least 95 percent of the time). Next, these people must be selected randomly, as in a **random sample**, and there must be no **sampling bias** present. In other words, no one group of people should dominate over another group in the final sample – the samples should be as equally diverse as possible.

Sample Size –
Number of people being surveyed for a poll.

Margin of Error –
The percentage of possible error in a survey will fall within a range of plus or minus several points of the actual number, had the entire population been polled, instead of just as sample.

Random Sample –
A technique employed to obtain truer poll results in which every member of a population has an equal opportunity of being surveyed in a sample.

Sampling Bias –
Can occur when a particular set of people in a population at large appears in a final survey to a lesser or greater degree than other sets of people.

President Jimmy Carter faced strong criticism by the public for the way he handled the Iranian take-over of the U.S. Embassy in Tehran. Courtesy of the Library of Congress

The technology of random digit dialing (RDD) computers is often used to choose phone numbers, hopefully both listed and unlisted, by chance.

Even with all of the above methods in place, there is no way to eliminate all possible variables that may negatively influence the end numbers. For example, there is a small percentage of homes that do not have telephone service. Invariably, these families live in urban areas that are stricken with extreme poverty. Because of the lack of phone service, they are excluded from any polls. Sadly, they are often communities that need to be heard from the most. Additionally, in this day and age of caller-ID and repeated interruptions from advertisers who say that they are conducting important research, the ability to obtain a truly random sample of respondents is becoming increasingly difficult. Variables like these are often accounted for in a margin of error, as was briefly mentioned above. This means that after the data is analyzed and sifted down into numbers, each number can be said to be plus or minus several percentage points if the whole of a population were to be polled, rather than just a representative sample. The margin of error can include human error or susceptibility to conventional wisdom that can sometimes be incorporated during the analytical stage unknowingly by scientists and statisticians. Other aspects of human error can also be found in survey design and research methodology.

As is often found when analyzing statistics, polling results can be manipulated to reflect a specific aspect of the surveys. Similar to research, pollsters may look at numbers with a pre-disposition toward an issue or the way they would like the results to be presented. This means that those who contribute to the writing of these surveys are very attentive to how the questions are worded. Someone may disagree with a policy but answer "yes" depending on which way the question is leading. For example, during wartime there may be many polls regarding the United States' role in that war. The question "Do you agree that the United States should defend itself against terrorism?" would most definitely draw a "yes" answer every time. However, if the goal of the study was to gather meaningful data regarding the complexities and history leading up to that war, the question would, first of all, not be limited to just a yes or no answer; perhaps a Likert-scale might be used to indicate responses (strongly disagree, disagree, neutral, agree, strongly agree, for instance). Secondly, the questions might be more close-ended and the answers are sometimes referred to as forced choices. An example of such a question would be, "What do you think is the main reason the U.S. invaded Iraq?" Forced-choice answers might be oil, terrorism, Saddam Hussein, Osama bin Laden, or revenge. An open-ended question involves direct interviews, usually conducted on the telephone or in "**focus groups**", so the respondent may speak freely on the subject, rather than choose from pre-fabricated answers. This creates a potential problem, however, because interviewers may unknowingly impose their own views and biases in the way that they ask the questions. It is crucial for the interviewer to remain as neutral and open as possible to insure the accuracy of the data. Furthermore, respondents tend to show themselves in the most positive light possible when answering questions, so they may not be completely truthful about their feelings, depending on what they perceive the interviewer wants to hear, even though theoretically there is not a right or wrong answer. In addition, some respondents are very curious and they want to know more about the study. They may ask questions like how will my answers be used, what are you looking for, is it okay if I say so and so… and so on. Of course, the interviewer cannot explain in too much detail the purpose of the survey because it may influence the respondents answers which would in turn, skew the data.

You may wonder - why are these polls so important and who is interested in the results? To answer this question, we can refer back to chapter four, which discussed the media and politicians (namely, presidential or gubernatorial candidates) who use polls to track candidate support or the latest issues that the public cares about. In following chapters, the subject of polling will come up again when we discuss elections and voting, the legislature, and the executive branch.

Agents of Socialization – Who we are

In the United States, political scientists use scientific methods to discuss ideas and mutual knowledge in the political realm. Political scientists also draw information from a foundation in the social sciences, which means that they study group and individual behaviors. Often times, political analysis involves asking questions about cultural dispositions to help explain voter behavior and voting choices. In order to understand how **political socialization** comes about, we examine how people arrive at their beliefs on human nature, the role of government, and their position on policy issues such as same sex marriage or welfare reform. In today's climate, political parties and candidates are always interested in what will garner the most support on the issues. The term "Pastor-in-Chief" became a popular nickname for President Bush among conservative churches and Christian groups during the 2004 Presidential Election. Senator John Kerry was not so lucky as he was threatened by some Catholic priests anticipating his visit, saying that they would not allow him to take communion because of Kerry's pro-choice position on abortion. (See Table 5.1) The manner in which beliefs and attitudes such as these are acquired are due to agents of socialization, which was briefly mentioned in chapter four. These agents can include parents, extended family, teachers, inspirational mentors, religious leaders, major events in history (both past and present), and of course the media. Media covers a multitude of agents such as movies, fashion trends, magazines, celebrity views, and advertising.

Focus Groups – A small group of people selected from a wider population that are questioned together about their opinions about issues, products, activities, etc; used especially in market research or political analysis.

Political Socialization – The process by which we learn about the world of politics and develop our political beliefs.

Issues For You Think about your political party affiliation. Do you remember consciously choosing it or did you inherit it from your parents? Explore the platforms of several parties, not just Democrat and Republican, and look at them objectively as to where you best fit in.

TABLE 5.1 - Presidential Election Percentage and Church Attendance		
	KERRY	BUSH
Several times a week	35	64
At least once a week	41	58
At least once a month	49	50
Several times a year	54	45
Does not attend	62	36

Source: "National Election Pool, November 2004," Trends, 2005, 35.

Religious mentors do play an important role in socialization, but family perhaps even more so. The economic status of a family can greatly influence the attitudes and views of parents and how they raise their children. Family characteristics may have a great deal to do with our perspective and involvement in the political dialogue. Parents' political identity is not something kids are conscious of until perhaps they are old enough to form their own opinions. Generally, during the so-called formative years from birth until around age ten, depending on the family, children subscribe to the same world views as their parents. They receive their parents' opinions and ideas through casual conversations, whether directed at them or overheard, disciplinary actions, community and/or school involvement, reactions to programs and news broadcasts on television, and so on. Whether the opinions are trustworthy or valid is not questioned – children simply see the world through their parents' eyes. Nowadays, children are maturing faster and are seemingly taken in by influences outside the family at an earlier age. Peer pressure on impressionable kids can sway their thoughts and feelings a different direction every day. It has been said that between the ages of 18 to 25, most young adults tend to lean toward a liberal stance due to the sudden acquisition of freedom from the home they grew up in, if they move away for work or school. During the college years is when many twenty-somethings learn to debate about political issues with classmates and they are better able to separate from their inherited views. Some young people that come from sheltered cultural backgrounds may experience a certain amount of culture shock while processing all the new ideologies and lifestyles available to them.

Conversely, between ages 25 to the senior citizen age of 55, career and family responsibilities turn most adults to the other side of the political spectrum, a conservative ideology. This transition into adulthood dictates how we feel about social services, taxation, and government programs in schools, to name a few. From 55 on, because people begin to contemplate their mortality, health related issues, and decreased mobility, they realize that they do want federal support for medical services, prescription drugs, social security, and assisted living for retirement communities.

Issues For You
Think back to when you were growing up – were your parents or guardians living examples of good citizens? What does it mean to be a good citizen today as compared to yesterday?

Family characteristics were included above as a possible determiner of the political views we adopt as young children that affect our views the rest of our lives. If parents raise their kids with a sense of civic duty they are teaching them to be responsible citizens. Patriotism and honor are values that are sometimes taught through songs, folk stories, and historical accounts of the actions of presidents, Washington and Lincoln being the two popular ones for 2nd and 3rd graders. Sometimes parents assume that the schools are responsible for teaching their children about civic values. However, the lessons that kids learn in school are much more effective when there is a partnership with their families. In fact, due to the controversy that can arise for educators regarding any curriculum dealing with morals or political ideas, the home life is hopefully a place where children can make sense of all the messages they receive from all the adults in their lives. The theme of civic participation is a central concept throughout this book. Civic participation is more than just voting. It can encompass volunteerism, contacting elected officials, working on campaigns, or just being involved in the betterment of your community. As the chapters progress, you will see more examples of civic participation and political socialization.

Groups and How They View Politics

If you look around the classroom or in most areas around the country, you'll see differences between race and ethnicity, religions, places of origins, income, education, gender, and so on. Still, given these differences, there are additional variables that impact how an individual views the political world. In the following section, we will examine the environment in which people shape their political attitudes. Some have already been touched on above but now we will take a closer look at some social institutions that play a part in shaping our attitudes and habits. It should be noted that these are very general characterizations and there are of course, exceptions to every generalization. By no means are all individual cultural practices in these groups completely accounted for in this section. It's meant as a way for you to understand and become more aware of these additional variables. Hopefully after reading this section, you will see how much more we all have in common instead of how different we are.

"Race" and Ethnicity

An individual's "racial" and ethnic background impacts how they view the role of government. In fact the concept of "race" as an ideology is a hotly debated topic amongst anthropologists, linguists, sociologists, and biologists. The American Anthropological Association's Official Statement on "Race" purports that "race" is an "out-of-date" and useless concept from the viewpoint of understanding and explaining human biological diversity."[5] The statement also explains that "race" was thought up as a social tool to justify slavery and even worse, to propel and validate the monstrous brutalities of the Holocaust during WWII. Even now in the 21st century, in most

Displaced – Forced out of home and country by war, exile, economic hardship, or natural catastrophe, causing the ruin of shelter.

One way to express public opinion is through protest marches; large groups of Palestinians, shown protesting here, have been displaced for several decades. Courtesy of Corel

countries around the world, minority groups are still being discriminated against simply on the basis of skin pigmentation, perceived cultural superiority, or religion, to name a few reasons. Judging from newspaper headlines over the past twenty years, it seems that the horrors of the Holocaust have been repeated. During both Republican and Democratic residency in the White House, acts of ethnic cleansing were committed in Rwanda, Burundi, Kosovo, Chechnya, Iraq, and Indonesia. Hundreds of thousands of people are murdered in an astonishingly short amount of time, usually in the quest of land, power, and money. The accounts of genocide in the Sudan were filtered into the American media very slowly, and only after high profile athletes, celebrities, and musicians started to speak up specifically for Darfur. In Darfur alone, since 1993, over 200,000 men, women, and children have been murdered and 2.5 million citizens were **displaced**. Ethnic cleansing does not stop with just murder. In fact, death may come as a welcome relief to the hundreds of thousands of women and young girls that have been systematically raped as a method of control and degradation in war. Starvation, illness, and lack of medical supplies are additional killers during and in the aftermath of genocide. Intense ethnic clashes are not exclusive to countries other than the United States. We are still plagued with racial and ethnic violence. Throughout much of our history and even today, we seem unable to get beyond cultural and religious differences, causing extremist groups to rise up. Think back to right after September 11th, when Sikh Indians, Arabs, Iranians, and other Muslim groups were attacked and having their property vandalized or destroyed.

African Americans have a long history of being discriminated against. However, there are few apparent differences between African Americans and other ethnic communities throughout America. Most groups have a strong sense of the "American Ideal" or the "American Dream", which is if you work hard, you can get ahead in life. The main caveat to this dream is whether everyone has equality of opportunity. We as a nation are still struggling with this. During the ordeal of the civil rights era in the 1960's, the Democratic administration stood behind civil rights and took anti-poverty measures. These actions drew African Americans who were alienated by the apparent futility of the political process, into the Democratic platform. This increased membership for the Democratic Party, at least in America. Being that the New Deal generation passed onto their children their Democratic values, most African Americans today tend to support candidates who tout federal assistance for the greater public good for services such as education, housing, and health benefits. However, due to strong roots in revivalist Christianity, they are more inclined to be conservative on social, sexual, and reproduction issues. Statistically speaking, African Americans appear to be less likely to vote than whites. For additional information, please refer back to chapter one.

Asian Americans, while being diverse in their own right, have a tendency to be better off economically and have more education than other minority groups. There are many corporations in Asia that sponsor students to come to America and study in intensive language institutes and continue to obtain university degrees. Because of a gradual increase in economic success over the past few decades, Asian Americans have become more and more conservative, voting Republican. Another factor that can contribute to this conservative leaning could be due to the fact that most "mainland" Asians have fled from "communist" countries such as Vietnam, Cambodia, China, and a smaller number from North Korea to seek refuge and freedom. Economic hardship and corruption in countries like the Philippines and other Pacific islands also cause prospective immigrants to come to America to have a chance at a better life.

Latinos are diverse not only because of their places of origins but also in their political patterns as well. The Central & South American countries and parts of the Caribbean represented in America are so numerous that debate has arisen over the years as to a suitable cultural identity or label that best embodies Latinos as a whole. Despite the many Democratic communities scattered all over the U.S., most Latin Americans identify themselves as Democrat. However, in the case of the Cuban

American community, like Asians, they have specific reasons for belonging to the Republican Party. Cuban Americans prefer Republican values perhaps due to having lived or been raised by a family member who lived under a dictatorship and a dispassionate communist leader for years. Also, Republicans in America were more overtly anti-communist than Democrats, who had a degree of common cause with socialist ideology. Whether Cuban American or not, Latinos in general are largely brought up in the Roman Catholic church, making their basic moral code conservative, similar to African Americans. Despite being the fastest growing ethnic population in the United States, studies have shown that Latinos are the least likely to vote. Low voter turnout amongst Latinos may stem from their distrust of government due to the poor treatment their language and heritage have received in the American media, education system, and the workplace. Another possibility is that their distrust was already in place from their country of origin where there may be an oppressive and corrupt government. On the contrary, due to unsatisfactory changes and debate in immigration law, Hispanics of all backgrounds have come together at protest rallies and walk-outs all across the nation.

As was shown in the 2000 Presidential election, White America (peoples of European descent) seems to be split down the middle when it comes to political beliefs. White Americans (formerly called **Caucasians**) used to be dependent upon their countries of origin and religious beliefs. Most groups such as Irish Americans and Italian Americans have become part of the dominant ethnic community and are socially and politically diverse. However, the **Christian Coalition of America** has unified fundamentalists, causing the left to coin America as "Jesus-land" either in support or disgust for America's increasingly intolerant and religiously conservative extremists. During the last two years of President George W. Bush's term, the divide amongst centrist and liberal leaning Republicans has widened, stirring up controversy to an unprecedented degree, in the party known for its solidarity between cultural conservatives and business/economic conservatives. As with most groups, religious practices play a central role in political socialization, depending on the administration in power and the influence they have over the media.

Religion

Religious differences have created political conflicts globally as well as in the United States. There are two main premises that support political differences. The first is the more religious you are, the more conservative you might be on social and economic issues. The adverse is true as well - the less religious you are the more liberal you tend to be on social and economic issues. While this is true in most countries, America is considered the most religious of countries when compared to other western powers. Those individuals who are less orthodox about religion tend to vote Democrat. The second premise is that the dominant religious group in any country tends to be more conservative. Whether comparing the United Kingdom to the United States, the dominant religion is Protestantism. In both countries, there is a history of oppression and intolerance of other religions. In the United Kingdom, there were several civil conflicts between the Church of England and the Roman Catholic Church. This carried over to the United States for almost two centuries. Protestants didn't trust the loyalties of Catholics to hold the office of President.

Caucasians – Derived from Caucasus, the mountainous region between the Black and Caspian Seas; a somewhat outdated ethnocentric term used to describe people who have light, fair skin.

Christian Coalition of America (CCA) – Founded by Rev. Pat Robertson in 1989. See section on Religion below.

Issues For You
When it comes to moral and social issues do you think people should put more weight on the values set forth in the Constitution or in religion? With so many diverse religious beliefs in America, how can people come up with a universal code of moral conduct?

Jews have fared no better. During the 1200's, Jews were ordered to leave England or convert. Here in the United States, while Jews haven't been displaced, they have been ostracized for their religious and cultural practices in much the same way as Muslims are today. Due to this culture of exclusion, many minority religious groups tend to vote more liberal or Democrat, whereas most Protestants tend to vote more conservative or Republican.

Two grassroots organizations, People for the American Way (PFAW) and the Christian Coalition of America (CCA) both claim to be defenders of a free America. The PFAW, founded in 1981 by Norman Lear, Barbara Jordan, Father Theodore Hesburgh, and Andrew Heiskell, is celebrating its 25th year of "equal rights, freedom of speech, religious liberty, and equal justice under the law for every American".[6] From the perspective of the PFAW, they exist for the greater good of America and to preserve a society that is diverse and democratic, free from oppression from the radical right. The PFAW views the CCA as "best known for the distribution of slanted voter guides and surveys" and that they "urged conservative Christian candidates to conduct stealth campaigns to win elections".[7] The CCA on the other hand feels that they need to protect America from being "bombarded with countless political messages from across the ideological spectrum".[8] They feel that they are the largest grass-roots conservative political organization that can help promote the "pro-family agenda" and help Americans better distinguish between right and wrong. Both try to carry out their missions through voter education, lobbying Congress, and holding information sessions (the CCA calls them "training schools"). The difference between these two groups is that the PFAW bases their mission on the Bill of Rights and the Constitution while the CCA preaches from their modern day interpretation of Judeo-Christian values, two of which are "banning homosexual 'marriage' " and "keeping votes for human embryonic stem cell destruction research bill to a minimum".[9] The CCA proved the power of their convictions when President Bush won the 2004 election.

Region

Depending on what part of the country you grew up in, a skilled political analyst may be able to guess how liberal or conservative you'll be. Take for example, if you are raised in the North East, it is likely that you'll have a strong sense of liberal ideology based on the traditions of that region. The same holds true for people from the South and Midwestern states. Their residents are considered to be some of the most conservative voters, but they may belong to either party, Democrat or Republican. After the Civil War (or the War of Northern Aggression if you're from the South), most Southerners registered as Democrats because President Lincoln was a Republican. This began with the passage of the 1960's Civil Rights Act and continued up through the Republican Revolution of the 1990's when some Southern Democrats switched sides. In addition, in examining the impact of rural and urban centers on politics, the rural areas are predictably conservative (given the long traditions of family and agriculture) whereas the urban centers lean more toward the liberal end, perhaps because of the fast pace of the city and constant influx of new ideas and technology.

Class

The economic class you are born into can have a great impact on your political views. Many Americans believe in the "American Dream" for all, and so, they attribute achieving long-lasting success in life to the level of education one can complete. Those who are able to enroll in higher education institutions tend to make more money and face less hardship than those who are not able to go to a 2-year college or a 4-year university after high school. The view is even bleaker for those who are not able to complete high school. Even more surprising and alarming is the fact that since 2000, the education job market itself has become so competitive and saturated that even those with multiple master's degrees are being edged out by Ph.D. holders. Education and social class distinctions can dictate a person's inclination to participate in the political process. Those who come from a higher income background, or upper strata, tend to be more active in politics than those in the lower-strata. In addition, those who have more total years of schooling tend to have a higher voter turnout than those who don't. Some believe that within the political process, there exists inherent biases toward the rich. If this is so, then there must be a way to trace a trail from those who receive more benefits than others to those that end up paying for them. The question is can this bias toward the wealthy be reversed or overcome? Is it simply a matter of jumping in and becoming politically active, regardless of class and level of schooling or is it a social situation that has become so metastasized that we don't notice it anymore? If the key to a more deliberative democracy is education, then one must scan the history of education in America. Very often, the mentality of teaching "skills for the poor and knowledge for the rich"[10] is systemic and it is a big dilemma in this day and age of standardized testing. Throughout America's history, the privileged few, those with more money and consequently higher education, seem to always have more access and motivation to make an impression on their elected officials than those who are too tired from working multiple jobs to care about being heard.

FOR YOUR CONSIDERATION
THE GENDER GAP

Since the beginning of America's coming of age as a country, women have fought for the right to vote. It wasn't until the passage of the 19th Amendment on August 18, 1920 that their quest was vindicated. As you read in chapter one, the struggle to obtain the right to vote was a difficult fight for everyone except white males who owned property. Despite winning the right to vote in 1920, it wasn't until the late twentieth century that women started to win more representation, becoming a formidable force in Congress. For the first time in history, in 2007, a woman, Nancy Pelosi, was sworn in as Speaker of the House of Representatives.

Gender Gap –
A difference in the political opinions of men and women.

For many decades, women have predominantly voted Democrat because of their positions on issues that are important to them, such as reproductive rights, education, equal pay for equal work, and assistance programs for the poor and elderly. Within the gender gap, there exist differences between male and female voter turnout. Although men and women often agree on a specific issue or prefer a certain candidate, the percentages in voter turnout is of interest. For six decades following the passage of women's suffrage in 1920, women voted at consistently lower rates than men in every election. Perhaps some women were still being strong-armed and discouraged from voting by their husbands; there is always the possibility that the more sheltered women were not convinced that it was a woman's place to vote. Reinforced by representation in Congress, the 1980's and 1990's also brought more women to the voting booths. Since then every election has seen a significant increase in the number of female voters, often exceeding the male vote. A plausible explanation for the increase is that women out number men in the general population. But the percentage of the female population who actively participate in voting and other civic duties has increased, whereas the number of males that vote has remained consistent, with an occasional decrease.

The following statistics were culled from the presidential elections from 1996 – 2004. The 1996 elections saw 56.1 million women vote (55.5% of the female population), as opposed to 48.9 million men (52.8%). In the 2000 elections, 59.3 million (56.2%) of women voted, compared to 51.5 million (53.1%) of men.[11] Although there is only a 3.1% gender gap in the 2000 voter turnout, that percentage represents a difference of 7.8 million more women than men who cast their votes. The 2004 elections showed an even more substantial increase. Women voters numbered 67.3 million (60.1%), up 8 million from the 2000 elections, or a 13.5% increase.[12]

The gender gap has had several implications in recent campaigns and candidates are expected to court the female vote with greater concentration. In fact, during the 2004 presidential campaigns, then Governor George W. Bush used "W stands for Women" to mobilize the female vote, while John Kerry used "Women for Kerry." Generally speaking, there are more undecided female voters who typically wait until the last minute to make their decisions, possibly waiting to see how the candidates' platforms evolve throughout the election process.

In general, more recognition of women in traditionally male-dominated activities like sports, literature, music, military, and so on, is still sought. The purpose in focusing on the female vote does not mean that the male vote carries less significance. However, the candidate who can analyze and respond to the growing political influence of women may very well come out ahead in the polls.

Can the People Rule?

Most political observers have mixed emotions as to whether or not the people are fit to govern. Despite the incredible speed of the Internet highway and the multiple tools to access it, people are still not generally more informed than several decades ago. In fact, the voter turnout in America was higher in the 1920's than it was in the 1990's – granted the population was smaller then – but the ratio of civic involvement to voter apathy was higher during the Great Depression (for other eye-opening statistics on voter-turnout, see chapter 8). Was Alexander Hamilton right in saying that the passions of the people needed to be controlled and that the uneducated were not worthy of voting? What are the characteristics of the average citizen? The very fact that politics is inherently problematic to discuss without tempers flaring makes it difficult to imagine that a civil dialogue can take place between two people from opposite ends of the political spectrum. This next section discusses how savvy the general public is about political ideologies.

Political Involvement

Information is power. The more individuals get involved in the political process the more they'll understand it and the more they'll be able to influence the actions of their elected representative or even be encouraged to run for office. Those on the

Howard Smith and Harry Reasoner, journalists commentating on the Carter-Ford Presidential debate in 1976. Courtesy of the Library of Congress.

inside game of politics tend to take a rather caustic view of the average American. This cynicism has been part of our political culture since the time the framers began their secret meetings. Alexander Hamilton had a very negative view of the people. Some political observers today say things haven't changed in over two hundred years. Their views were simple. The American public is generally poorly informed, which can sometimes lead to irrational opinions or voter apathy, especially when politicians don't do what they want.

As stated earlier, even with the advancements in technology over the last century, Americans' ability to discuss political issues hasn't improved very much. Polls throughout the second half of the twentieth century revealed that Americans didn't exhibit much awareness of the world around them. When asked about their political party, most could not identify the major components of their party's platform or who their elected representatives are. During the Cold War most Americans didn't know who the United States' allies were, nor did they know the ideological difference between the Soviet Union and the United States. A more glaring event in school curriculum was that during the later part of the 20th century, American students stopped learning geography. When asked to locate the United States on a global map, over 40 percent of graduating seniors from college placed it in what was then the Soviet Union. While there is a certain amount of responsibility that we as citizens and parents must accept for these egregious errors, the teachers who plan curriculum, the administrators who say what goes and what doesn't, and the priorities of our elected officials are also extremely instrumental in the education of our future leaders.

Profiles in Politics
Walter Cronkite (1916 -   )

Walter Cronkite was one of the few journalists that the public trusted. He was instrumental in shifting public opinion on the viability of the Vietnam War. Courtesy of the Library of Congress

Arguably the most famous face in the history of television network news, Walter Cronkite was largely seen as one of, if not THE main arbiter of public opinion during his time in the main anchor chair at CBS News, a period of roughly 20 years. Millions of Americans tuned in to his nightly newscasts to listen to "the most trusted man in America."

Walter Leland Cronkite, Jr. was born in St. Joseph, Missouri in 1916 and raised in Missouri and Texas. He began his long career in journalism as a reporter for his high school, then college newspapers and various short stints at small radio stations. In 1937, he received his first major job in professional journalism as a correspondent with United Press.[13]

During his years at United Press, Cronkite covered many of the major battles of World War II, including the landing of Allied troops in North Africa, the battle of the North Atlantic in 1942, the beachhead assaults in Normandy in 1944, and he even took part in the B-17 raids over Germany. After covering the German surrender in 1945, Cronkite opened up United Press bureaus around Europe and became the bureau chief in Brussels; while there, he covered the Nuremburg trials. He was then transferred to Moscow, where he became the United Press's chief correspondent there.

In 1950, Walter Cronkite became a television correspondent for CBS News where he stayed for the next two decades. He was promoted to anchor in 1962. He was one of the pioneers of the 30-minute news broadcast – newscasts previous to this were only 15 minutes long. Because network newscasts in those days covered politics and foreign affairs predominantly, Cronkite became well known and well respected among many politicos in Washington D.C. He opened the very first 30-minute newscast with an interview with President John F. Kennedy.

During Cronkite's time in the anchor chair he covered many of the most historical moments of the mid-20th century, including the fight for civil rights, the Vietnam War, the Apollo moon landings, Watergate, and probably most famously, the assassination of President Kennedy.[14] His conscientious reporting earned him a place of trust and reverence in the hearts of the American public.

Cronkite is partially credited with helping to shape America's reaction to events, providing reliable plain-spoken coverage as seen in his reporting on the space program and Watergate. Cronkite gained substantial respect for his extensive coverage, reporting the story behind the story about the U.S.'s controversial involvement in the Vietnam War. In this latter example, Cronkite's reporting is considered to have had an influence on President Lyndon B. Johnson's willingness to negotiate with the North Vietnamese. According to an aide, Johnson himself remarked, "If I've lost Cronkite, I've lost America."[15]

Since stepping down from the anchor chair in 1981 at age 65, Walter Cronkite could hardly be referred to as retired. He maintains an office at CBS News and has done several programs for the Discovery Channel, as well as for CBS and PBS. In addition, he has authored several books, on topics ranging from reporting and his own life to his love for sailing. In surveys taken by the U.S. News and World Report, Cronkite was the only journalist to be named in the top ten "most influential decision-makers in America" as well as the "most influential person" in broadcasting. Throughout his illustrious career in news broadcast, Walter Cronkite has earned many awards and honors, including a prestigious Peabody Award and an Emmy award.[16] In 1985, he was inducted into the Academy of Television Arts and Sciences Hall of Fame. We end this section with the immortal and concise words that Walter Cronkite said at the close of each broadcast, "…and that's the way it is."

Interest in politics must improve in order for the public to exercise the power of popular sovereignty over their elected representatives. In the past less than one third of the public claimed to be active in the electoral process. Even though political literature has been made readily available in multiple mediums for the citizenry to be in touch, few people actually devote focused time to read, research, and understand the events that lead up to controversial issues. An even smaller number of citizens actually take the time to contact their elected representatives, take part in political activities, or deliberate in a true exchange of ideas and current events with their fellow citizens.

Despite the general conventional wisdom about Americans' waning interest in politics, the author chooses to remain more optimistic, believing that the American people are generally well informed. Their opinions are rational and, when given the opportunity, they do participate. The main variable that seems to dictate civic

Donald Rumsfeld's last day as Secretary of Defense. © Jason Grower, 2007. Used under License from Shutterstock, Inc.

participation is the constant message that people receive from the media, politicians, and other community leaders, which is that the American public at large is apathetic, uninformed, and irrational, reminiscent of Hamilton's sentiments. Sociologists and psychologists alike have shown that if an individual or a group is given a negative message and that message is reinforced by the media and those in powerful positions, the person listening to these notions will eventually believe it and become exactly that - apathetic and ignorant. How can this be remedied? Those who teach and write textbooks may need to change the way lectures and materials are presented. While it is important to review significant political events and engage in the usual controversial social issues, it is hoped the student and anyone who reads this book will be better informed and better yet, inspired to become more active in the political process.

Polling research has shown that most Americans can identify names of their regional leaders (Representative or mayor) and some national leaders (U.S. Senator, President, and some cabinet secretaries); but is this enough to make our republic more democratic? Scholars will continue to debate this in the years to come but for now, the answer is uncertain. Keep in mind that the government is responsible for carrying out the will of the public. However, if the public doesn't do their part, those in power will make decisions that will benefit the few over the many. Citizens can prevent this by focusing on the policy issues, not the image of a candidate. The public must hold their elected representatives accountable when they vote on important issues. Case in point, in the months leading up to the invasion of Iraq in 2003, Senators and Representatives had to vote on

President Reagan, former popular Hollywood actor and radio star, was known for being the "Great Orator". He was able to persuade public opinion through his humour during speeches and press conferences. Courtesy of the Library of Congress.

whether to give the President a "blank check" to fund the war. At that time, President Bush had an 80% approval rating, largely due to his immediate call to action after 9/11. Fast forward to 2007, as both Democrat and Republican candidates began campaigning for the office of the President, the voters demanded that the candidates "come clean" as to whether or not they regretted condoning the war, since at that point Operation Iraqi Freedom had become hugely unpopular. Every press conference and debate from the start of the campaigning season became a high-pressure confessional situation, due to public opinion that the troops should be pulled out of Iraq. As the death toll of American troops increased to over 3,000 since the Operation commenced, the people wanted to know each candidate's exit strategy, if they were to be elected. The media frenzy over the war was just as much a culprit in fueling the war as they are today in forcing candidates to make this the major focus of every debate.

While people do need to be informed and open to deliberating the issues, it is just as important for the media to objectively present the issues in order to present the most accurate information possible, free of bias. But, being a flawed and inherently skewed system, media must also be held accountable by the public. To do this, the public can put pressure or boycott the sponsors that fund television programs. Another option is to simply turn the channel, causing their ratings to plummet. If you still don't think you can make a difference, just skim over the chapters and all the inspirational "Profiles in Politics". We truly are all connected somehow and everything we do – or don't do – affects each one of us in ways seen and unseen.

Do Politicians Listen to Us?

As we have seen from the many examples listed so far, it is fair to surmise that public opinion is an integral part of the political process. It can greatly impact government policy, which in turn may positively or negatively affect the way people coexist. If one of the key concepts in representative democracy is that the power rests with the people, then it would behoove elected representatives to listen to their constituents. When first analyzing the correlation between public opinion and the actions of elected representatives, one might be shocked to see the conspicuous contradictions between the two. If public opinion automatically translated into policy with few obstacles, the country would look much different, in good ways and bad, depending on who you talk to. Congress would be constantly pulled out of their comfort zone, because changes would occur day to day. For example, there would probably be term limits on Congress, limits on campaign finance and access by lobbyists, less foreign aid, and strong restrictions on handguns. As for the effect on our personal lives, affirmative action would be eliminated, the terminally ill would have the right to die, prayer would be allowed in public schools, and you would not be allowed to burn an American flag as a sign of political protest. If the government is supposed to do what the people

Cindy Sheehan, whose son died while serving in the army in Iraq, became an activist. She started or inspired several interest groups (Meet with the Mothers, Camp Casey Peace Institute, and Goldstar Families for Peace) to urge President Bush and Congress to take responsibility for failed policies in Iraq.
© Jeff Goldman, 2007.
Used under License from Shutterstock, Inc.

want, then why don't their policies more accurately reflect public opinion? There are several answers to this question. First, remember that the framers wanted to insulate the representatives from the passions of the people. That's why they developed an elaborate maze of checks and balances, separation of powers, and arduous procedures to complete before a bill becomes a law. If something is able to stay in the public discourse long enough, there is a chance that it will become law someday.

Will there ever be a balance between the will of the people and the actions of the government? Due to the diversity present in the desires of the people and the clashes that arise, probably not. We can move closer to a true democracy but that would require an enormous amount of individual commitment and a concerted effort put forth by those in power. Until then, we must work within the confines of the existing system and make gradual changes. The public must somehow grasp a better understanding of the process and realize that for every action, there is a reaction. This is one of the first lessons our parents and teachers try to get into our soft malleable brains when we are still in grade school. Take for example the desire to have more public services in health care without raising taxes. In order for the government to meet this demand, they have several options. The first option, to do nothing, is probably the least popular action. The second would be to cut other programs to pay for the new services, also unpopular for some of the public. The third would be to tell the public it is unrealistic to offer this program without increasing taxes. Finally, they would have to borrow the money in order to implement the new service, increasing the national debt in the process.

Let's examine these plans a little more closely and consider them on their merits. The first option doesn't work because the **"ostrich" technique** does not make the problem go away. The second option could cause more problems in the long run by provoking an increase in cost for other services. The third, while being the most realistic, could cost the representative votes and career. The last option, borrowing the money, is the one most selected, even though at first, not raising taxes is a promise that candidates often make while courting voters, as in President George H. W. Bush's sound bite, "Read my lips, no new taxes". Simply borrowing the money meets the immediate desires of the public but passes the debt onto future generations. In other words, passing the buck to politicians in the future relieves the current generation of politicians from having to make the tough decisions. Sadly, it still does not solve the problem – in fact, it creates bigger ones later.

Politicians do listen to public opinion but the system is designed to prevent rapid changes, so the public is left feeling insignificant. In this fast paced society, the public expects immediate results, forcing politicians to devote their entire campaigns on getting re-elected, rather than actually implementing policy effectively. They don't have the luxury to hold numerous meetings with focus groups or wait for survey results, revealing the true wants of the public. In order for this to change, the public needs to be more aware of the political process in order to develop a feasible plan of action with realistic expectations.

"Ostrich" Technique – To ignore a problem as if this alone would make it "go away"; derived from the peculiar habits of the ostrich, a large flightless African bird, of whom it has been said to bury it's head in sand if threatened or pursued; however, ostrich farmers say they do this to search for food.

FOR YOUR CONSIDERATION
EXIT POLLS

Nearly every news channel, newspaper, and website discusses and analyzes public polls on everything from who will win the Academy Award for Best Director to whether or not people think California will fall into the ocean in their lifetime. Not to be outdone by Hollywood or the environment, overly eager-pundits have a field day predicting outcomes and possible implications of polls administered during campaigns. These exit polls, taken soon after constituents leave their polling locations, carry a unique significance, especially during national elections.

Exit Poll -
Polls that question voters as they "exit" or leave the voting location for the purpose of predicting the outcome of an election before the polls have closed.

Early indications as to how an election may turn out provide the mass media a tool by which they can "spin", if they are sponsored by a corporation that favors a particular candidate. However, predicting the outcome of an election too early has been known to be extremely problematic and even scandalous, as studies have shown that premature predictions sway voters before they even arrive at the polls, if they do at all. Today exit polls are still inaccurate and are still surrounded by controversy further causing voters to question their value.[17]

California's People and Their Opinions

Most Americans think of the birth of the nation as originating on the east coast, in the colony of Jamestown in 1607. However, as you learned from chapter two, Juan Rodriguez Cabrillo sailed into a supposedly unclaimed sparkling harbor in 1542, a whole 65 years before Jamestown. He christened the area San Miguel, which is now known as San Diego. This kicked off the pioneer spirit that is now deeply ingrained in California culture and history. The mission systems set in place by Father Junipero Serra, the Gold Rush of 1849, and the mobility of the Pacific Railroad system are all examples of the Golden State's exciting qualities that have sparked the imagination of immigrants from all over the world for hundreds of years.

Courtesy of Jupiter Images.

California's expansive population continues to grow exponentially. Major metropolitans areas such as Los Angeles and San Francisco are poster children for the phrase "urban sprawl". Within these pockets of communities, there are many aspects of diversity: ethnically, regionally (urban vs. rural), and culturally. Because of this diversity, California is a microcosm of the nation as a whole. In the same manner that our core beliefs are formulated, these accepted traditions and cultural practices shape and develop public opinion unique to California.

Regional & Ethnic Aspects

Little Saigon (Westminster), Little Seoul (Garden Grove), Little India (Cerritos), Chinatown (Los Angeles) – these are just a few communities in southern California that have attracted so many immigrants to particular regions that they have adopted ethnic-specific names that are registered within the main host city. In Northern California, in downtown San Francisco proper and surrounding urban areas, the style is to name the neighborhood name, followed by the name of a country. For example, there is North Beach's Little Italy, Pacific Heights' Japantown, and simply, Russian Hill. Of course, virtually all major metropolitan areas in California have their own version of a Chinatown or a Little Tijuana. Long Beach (southern California) has the largest concentration of Cambodian residents outside of Cambodia itself. Fresno reportedly has between 30,000 and 41,000 Hmong residents.[18] California basically consists of small pockets of ethnic groups – cohabitating successfully is a veritable necessity, considering that 1,600 people move or are born in California daily. These large concentrations of ethnic groups have come to be well known here and abroad. But one must ask, what's in a name when discussing these quaint nicknames for these little pockets of ethnic communities? Does it instill a sense of pride in the immigrants so much so that it improves their opinions of America and its government? Or does it give off an impression of detachment by isolating themselves from the host country by creating these sub-countries? Even though immigrants and refugees are generally eager to flee their countries of origin, whether it is for better work opportunities or political asylum, assimilating into their new surroundings can bring up positive and negative factors in "native" Californians' views of their role as host to so many immigrants as well as the political landscape in general.

Linguistic & Cultural Aspects

Language Shock – When an ELL experiences feelings of embarrassment, anxiety, or homesickness associated with the stress of learning a new language in a strange country, especially when native speakers laugh or mimic their foreign accents.

Suffice it to say that one cannot separate language from culture and vice versa. How to define what exactly is California culture can be as mind-boggling as the rate of population growth in California, as mentioned above. However culture is defined, each person's traditions and moral code stems from their core beliefs, upbringing, and ancestry. During the mid-1980's the conflict in South and Central America led to the emigration of thousands of refugees to America. A few years earlier, in 1978, linguist John H. Schumann hypothesized about displaced peoples and the adjustment they go through when they come to America. Schumann explained it through observations of adult immigrants who were in the process of acquiring English as a Second Language (ESL), thus proposing an acculturation model. According to Schumann's theory, which is referred to as the Acculturation Model,[19] there are three possible scenarios that can occur for these English Language Learners (ELLs): assimilation, preservation, and acculturation. Assimilation takes place when the new culture or target culture is fully adopted and the originating culture is abandoned. Preservation occurs when the ELL experiences culture and **language shock**, thereby rejecting the target culture and preserving their own. Lastly, acculturation is successful when both cultures are in balance, and the ELL adapts to the new culture while staying in touch with their native culture. While this is just one theory on what struggling ELLs experience, it raises important questions about Californians' ability to acknowledge the experiences of others and whether their instincts are to help or hurt.

Charlie Chaplin, silent film star, was one of the greatest physical humorists' the world has ever known. For two decades, Chaplin resisted the technological march toward "talkies", or films with dialogue. He explained that it alienated people who did not speak English. His silent films conveyed comedy, heart, and the triumph of the human spirit not with words but with compassionate acting and music he himself composed.
Courtesy of the Library of Congress

In most countries it appears that people are bilingual or even multi-lingual. Switzerland for example, has four official national languages (German, French, Italian, and Rumantsch)[20]; Spain also has four (Spanish, Euskara, Catalan, and Galician)[21]; and South Africa has 11! (Afrikaans, English, isiNdebele, isiXhosa, isiZulu, Sepedi, Sesotho, Setswana, siSwati, Tshivenda, and Xitsonga).[22] And so, why hasn't America followed suit and declared a few official languages of its own instead of demanding only English? Is it because some believe that there is a threat of language loss of English? Or is it simply a leftover elitist racist view of "foreign" languages as being inferior to American English. The immigration reform bill proposing that English be declared the national language of the United States passed in the Senate in May of 2006, and by the following year, although there were changes proposed, there are not too many people happy with the proposals, causing many immigrants to hold mass walk-outs and causing a media stir. The bill is waiting to go back to the House of Representatives for the amendment to pass. But, as America's English-speaking, rich, white, land-owning forefathers intended, amendments to the Constitution are rarely passed - only 27 in the past 200 years and the first 10 passed only to ratify the Constitution. Some perceive that this reform bill is rooted in anti-immigrant sentiments, which makes the issue of declaring official languages very controversial in America. This has strong implications of the public's opinion of territorial issues and identity crises. Despite this general unrest, many U.S. territories and states have adopted English as an official language and some are officially bi- or tri-lingual (Hawaii, Northern Mariana Islands). Due to the hundreds of English dialects in existence around the globe, even Americans themselves have trouble defining what exactly is "standard" English? Linguist Walt Wolfram said optimistically (perhaps somewhat naively or idealistically) that the key to dealing with potential discrimination [in teaching Standard English] is to "change society's attitudes toward various dialects, so that all varieties of English would be accepted".[23]

It is interesting to note that California's first Constitution in 1849 recognized both English and Spanish as official languages. However, their second Constitution adopted in 1879 removed Spanish as an official language, perhaps due to new research about the so-called damaging effects of living in two languages. In some cultures, continuing to speak in two languages after being told it was forbidden would sometimes cause you to get your mouth washed out with soap or earn you a cane-beating. Culturally speaking, many linguists and sociologists claim that being bilingual broadens one's outlook on other cultures, thereby increasing an appreciation for other orientations of life. Bilinguals seem to enjoy greater employment opportunities and perhaps are more likely to travel or live in other countries besides their native home land. It has even been proven in the ground-breaking research by Peal & Lambert, that there is a significant and undeniable relationship between intelligence and binguality. Peal & Lambert hypothesized that this was due to bilinguals having a "greater mental flexibility and a greater facility in concept formation". Their findings opened up other possible advantages bilinguals enjoy, such as exceptional ability to compartmentalize and analyze more than one concept at a time, ability to synthesize semantic relations between words, superior skills at correcting ungrammatical sentences, and displaying more genuine creativity when it comes to higher thinking critical skills. So what possible reasons could anyone have to doubt the benefits of becoming bilingual? Again, why is the need to declare one official language so much more important to Californians than other states and even other countries?

California is indeed, the place to be; not many would disagree that California's vast landscapes encompass bits of the entire nation in one state. Woody Guthrie described it best in his heartfelt tribute song to America, *This Land is Your Land* – the redwood forests, sparkling sands, and golden valleys are all present in the golden state. However, to have light, there must also be a dark side. It is revealed in verses five and six of Mr. Guthrie's song and such is the case with public opinion in California's history and America in general.

How Do We Compare?
South Africa and the United States

This section of the chapter will survey the recent developments that have led South Africa from exclusive and repressive white rule toward a form of multiracial democracy. There are clearly some very difficult legacies to overcome, not the least of which is severe socio-economic inequalities between the races. Like the United States, South Africa was a colony first before gaining independence and its citizens faced ethnic strife and oppression from a group of white Europeans who, although small in number at first, grew to be the dominant power.[25]

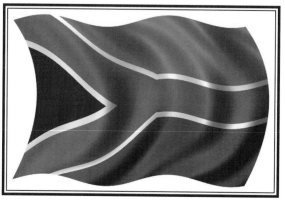

Flag of South Africa.
© *Carsten Reisinger, 2007. Used under License from Shutterstock, Inc.*

South Africa was founded in 1652 as a "refreshment station" at the Cape of Good Hope for the Dutch East India Company. The Dutch encountered the Khoi Khoi natives, with whom they coupled and produced the "Coloured people". Needing more slaves, the Dutch imported them from the Indies and Madagascar. The resulting mixture produced the "Cape Coloureds". Whites quickly developed exclusivist attitudes on race and classified the Coloureds as a different and inferior group. As the Dutch Farmers (Boers) expanded their land, their sense of entitlement became overpowering, believing that the land was exclusively theirs and that the natives were to be either enslaved or exterminated. As the Cape colony grew, French Huguenots and Germans arrived. The English began to arrive in the Cape in 1806. It wasn't until Napoleon occupied the Netherlands that he allowed the British to take control over the Cape and in 1814 the Netherlands officially turned over the Cape to Britain, officially making it a British colony. Many Boers bristled at British rule, especially with the use of the Queen's English and equality before the law. When Britain ended slavery throughout its empire, the Boers became convinced that the English were destroying their language, institutions, way of life, and freedom. Between 1836 and 1838, an estimated 12 thousand Boers loaded oxcarts and moved inland seeking new lands and freedom; this was called the Great Trek. The "voortrekkers" seized lands from the tribes and forced them to relocate or they would be expunged. When the lands were settled, the voortrekkers consolidated their settlements into two small republics, Transvaal and the Orange Free State. It was in these republics that the Boers lived and had a strained but peaceful relationship with the British. This already uneasy tolerance was obliterated when gold and diamonds were discovered.

With the discovery of these precious gems and metals in South Africa, Europeans and even Americans poured into the Cape. To the Boers, it looked as though the English were once again pursuing them, so the Boers made life difficult for them, denying them the right to vote and ignoring their petitions. As a result, disenfranchising became an **Afrikaner** tactic to preserve dominance. The British, hoping to grab the Transvaal and Orange Free State, provoked the Boers into declaring war in 1899.

After a brutal 3-year war, the Boers surrendered; but the British, guilty over the misery they had inflicted, gave their new subjects full political rights. Over time, the Afrikaners used their legal powers to ultimately take over all of South Africa.

The defeated Boer republics were made into British crown colonies but were given internal self-government; the colonies were made into one country in 1910, the Union of South Africa, and the English and the Afrikaners seemed to be coexisting cordially. However, many Afrikaners were unhappy with this alliance for two main reasons. First, it tied them to British policy because South Africa was under British command. Second, Afrikaners were economically inferior and underdogs to the English, who nearly monopolized industry and commerce. Their perceived path to salvation was to organize themselves to promote Afrikaners in business and politics. They built cultural associations, insurance companies, schools and universities and they also founded the National Party, the "Nats". These early forms of racist policies later culminated in the policy of apartheid, officially introduced by Dr. Malan's National Party government in 1948 and later. Under this official policy, the hand of racial segregation stretched even further and was more fiercely extended than in previous years. Opponents of apartheid were brutally suppressed, often with the use of what were presented as "anti-Communist" ordinances and laws. Long prison detention awaited for some, like African National Congress leader Nelson Mandela, who was imprisoned for 27 years before he was elected president. Internationally, South Africa became more and more isolated and eventually, it left both the Commonwealth (1961) and the United Nations.

The selective dismantling of colonial rule began in parts of Africa in the mid-1950s (Ghana). By the 1970s and early 1980s, colonialism and exclusive white domination collapsed in most of the rest of sub-Saharan Africa. This left South Africa increasingly isolated. Two very important events were the Portuguese retreat from their African colonies in 1975 and the abandonment of white rule in former Rhodesia to the north, now Zimbabwe, in 1980. As part of a concerted international effort to make South Africa abandon its racist rule, there came a rapidly growing set of international **sanctions** imposed by in the 1980s. The collapse of the **Soviet bloc** and the end of the Cold War added still more pressure to reform.

It is fair to say that the new leader of the National Party, President F.W. de Klerk, also played an important role in guiding his government and his party on a path toward reform. It would have been possible to pull back the reigns on the march toward reform for a little while longer, but de Klerk evidently concluded that it was better to take charge of an earlier reform than become a victim of later and more drastic reform, imposed by others. The end of apartheid took the form of a negotiated elite settlement or even a "negotiated revolution". Until recently, South African institutions were designed to keep blacks powerless. As you can see, these historical events are extremely parallel to the formation of the American nation.

With the release of Nelson Mandela from jail in 1990, breathtaking changes began to occur, reminiscent of the inspirational leadership of Martin Luther King, Jr. during the civil rights movement, thirty years earlier. In 1993 and 1994, an advisory committee representing the many ethnic groups of South Africa, created an interim constitution that went into effect with the first multiracial elections in 1994. The new parliament completed a permanent constitution in 1996. The constitution can be changed only by a two-thirds majority of parliament, which is similar to the practically impenetrable amendment procedure of the U.S. Constitution. South Africa's president is both the head of state and head of government. The president is elected

Sanctions –
Agreements among a group of states to cease trading with an offending state; the boycotted commodity could be military goods, major building materials, electronics and so on. The effect of sanctions on other countries sometimes endangers the citizens of that state more than it does intimidate its leaders.

Soviet Bloc –
Also known as the Warsaw Pact, a Soviet-led Eastern European military alliance, formed to counter the North American Treaty Organization (NATO) alliance.

Profiles in Politics
Nelson Mandela (1918 -   )

Not many people rise to world renown due to their imprisonment, but Nelson Mandela is most widely known for precisely that reason. Largely seen as an icon of political oppression, Mandela became a cause célèbre for putting an end to apartheid in South Africa.

Nelson Mandela Square.
© Photobar, 2007. Used under License from Shutterstock, Inc.

Nelson Rolihlahla Mandela was born to a tribal chief in Transkei, South Africa in 1918. Though groomed for high tribal office, Mandela decided to become a lawyer after watching the cases that were heard before the tribal court. He entered politics in 1942 by joining the African National Congress (ANC), a political party formed earlier to unite Africans and defend their rights and freedoms. Together with a few other members, Mandela helped found the ANC Youth League in 1944, a younger and more radical offshoot of the party.

The victory of the National Party (Nats), a party that espoused apartheid, in the all-white elections in 1948 prompted the ANC Youth League to subscribe to tactics such as strikes, boycotts, and civil disobedience, among other things, as a way to fight the Nat's policies. The Youth League's goals were to attain full citizenship and direct parliamentary participation for all South Africans.

For his role in organizing the Defiance Campaign, a campaign aimed at organized mass non-cooperation, Mandela was arrested and convicted of violating South Africa's Suppression of Communism Act. He was given a suspended sentence but was still confined to Johannesburg, in spite of the finding by the court that Mandela had consistently urged followers to use peaceful tactics and to avoid violence. [26]

During his containment, he took and passed the attorney's examinations and opened up a law practice with fellow ANC Youth League member Oliver Tambo. After being ordered by authorities to move their law practice to the outskirts of the city, Mandela and his partner decided to send a message of protest to the authorities by defying their orders.

Throughout the 1950s, Nelson Mandela was at the forefront of many resistance movements seeking to empower his brothers in arms; among them were struggles against unfair labor practices and the segregation of universities. For his part in these movements, Mandela was forbidden to engage in political activities, arrested, and even imprisoned. In 1960, the ANC was officially outlawed; most of the movement went underground at that time and Mandela became its most prominent leader. His challenge to the apartheid government was for a national convention to be held in order to design a constitution that created a democracy in which all members of South Africa could participate. If these requests were not met then he was prepared to subject the government to a general strike. The plan was enthusiastically received from Africans, but it evoked animosity from the government.[27] He was forced into hiding to avoid detection by government forces.

Profiles in Politics
Nelson Mandela (1918 -   )

Nelson Mandela illegally traveled abroad and not only spoke in many countries, but also used the time to arrange for guerilla training for his followers. When he returned to South Africa, he was arrested and convicted and began serving a five-year sentence. While serving this sentence, Mandela was further charged with sabotage; upon conviction, he was sentenced to serve a life term in a maximum-security prison. His words at the opening of the sabotage trial sum up Mandela's cause very eloquently and succinctly:

"During my lifetime I have dedicated myself to this struggle of the African people.
I have fought against white domination, and I have fought against black domination.
I have cherished the ideal of a democratic and free society in which all persons live together
in harmony and with equal opportunities. It is an ideal which I hope to live for and to achieve.
But if needs be, it is an ideal for which I am prepared to die."

During the 1980s, while Mandela was imprisoned, much attention began to be drawn to the issue of apartheid and its sad history in South Africa; many countries including the United States began putting economic and trade sanctions on the country. Through the continued actions of many outside countries, the state-sanctioned apartheid practiced in South Africa became a thing of the past and in 1990, Nelson Mandela was finally freed after spending 27 years in prison.

After his release, Mandela was elected president of the ANC, and shortly thereafter, became the first democratically elected State President of South Africa. He has spent his time since being released doggedly working to achieve the goals of full citizenship and participation for everyone in the government of South Africa. He received the Nobel Peace Prize in 1993 in recognition of his life's work against racism and apartheid. Nelson Mandela retired from public life in 1999.[28]

by the National Assembly for a five-year term, and a maximum of two terms. They can be ousted by a parliamentary **vote of no-confidence**; this makes their position more like a prime minister, but the president still has tremendous power. The first President of the new South Africa was Nelson Mandela. In 1999 Mandela was replaced by his deputy president, Thabo Mbeki. Mbeki had spent 28 of his adult years in exile while also serving as an **emissary** of Mandela's African National Congress (ANC) to foreign governments and anti-apartheid organizations abroad. South Africa's capital moves twice a year; the parliament buildings are in Cape Town and the administrative capital is in Pretoria. In response to demands from several groups, South Africa shifted from a unitary to a federal system, consisting of 9 provinces; each has its own legislature concerned with local affairs; each also elects its own premier. The cabinet has 27 ministers. Each party that wins 5 percent of the popular vote is entitled to a share of cabinet ministers roughly proportional to its vote.

Similar to the legislative branch in the U.S., South Africa's bicameral parliament is fairly conventional and has much less power than the president. Elections must come every 5 years by proportional representation. There are two houses - one representing population, the other provinces. The lower house, the National Assembly, has 400 members elected by proportional representation on 2 levels - one national, the other provincial. 200 are chosen from nationwide party lists and the other 200 from the provinces with seats proportional to population. The upper house, the Council of Provinces, has 90 members, 10 from each province, elected by provincial legislatures. This second house has special powers to protect regional interests, including the safeguarding of cultural and linguistic traditions among ethnic minorities. In addition, the courts are independent from both the legislature and the executive branches. There is a special 11-member Constitutional Court with rotating membership.

It should be noted that the decision to strive for a multiracial form of power-sharing is essential to the principle of consociational democracy. This form of shared rule is unlike majoritarian democracy because it seeks to include rather than exclude different groups, including smaller ones, in the governing process. In other words, this is very different from the Westminster (British) model (please refer to chapter 2) of majoritarian government.

South Africa's parties are the African National Congress (ANC), which is splintered amongst itself; the mostly white Liberal Democrats who now also draw Indian and Coloured voters; the zulu-based Inkatha Party, concentrated in KwaZulu/Natal; the largely Afrikaner New Nats; the interracial United Democratic Movement; and the small white conservative Freedom Front. The violent revolutionary black Pan Africanist Congress (PAC) won no seats. The ruling ANC faces bilateral opposition, with forces tugging both left and right. All citizens receive common ballots and may vote for whichever party they wish in the secrecy of the voting booth. The ANC is a broad catch-all party, including everything from Black-power extremists, militant trade-unionists, moderate Africans, black entrepreneurs, conciliatory persons, and Communists. The ANC has to be two-faced: to its black voters it must promise jobs, housing, and education rapidly, no matter what the cost; the other face has to calm and reassure whites, especially white capitalists, who are their only hope for rapid economic growth. The ANC now confers with the great economic engines of South Africa and the dialogue goes both ways. The capitalists explain investment and growth to the former ANC radicals, and the ANC explains that if the capitalists wish to retain their wealth and position in South Africa they must quickly deliver new jobs, boost the economy, and promote blacks to the executive level. The richer,

Vote of No-Confidence –
A vote that is held if the government leaders find the actions of the president or prime minister discordant with their Constitution.

Emissary –
An agent or representative sent on a mission or errand.

English-speaking white liberals of the Democratic party are more likely to understand and accept the ANC argument – they have little worry about their economic and social status. Much of the white working class, however, has had to pay the price of rapid improvement for Africans.

There is some truth to the view that Africans are still very tribal in outlook. Chiefs are still strong; they settle disputes and can deliver much of the rural vote. But, for the many millions who reside in urban areas, many tribes integrate with Africans from other tribes. Industry helped break down tribalism and integrate Africans into a whole. Rapid black urbanization produced greater African education, sophistication, and integration. African political opinion spans the range from mild, even conservative, to violent and radical. During the 19th century, the Boers began to think of themselves as Afrikaners; they had become Africa's white tribe and their attitudes are indeed tribal. Until recently, they frowned upon marriage to white English-speakers. They did not like to share power with other tribes. They treated blacks firmly but (they thought) fairly; although not publicly said, they saw blacks as behind whites in civilization, work habits, and level of organization. They used to consider English liberals hypocrites and cowards, but these views have softened since the end of apartheid. They never saw themselves as oppressors but rather as the aggrieved party.

The total population of South Africa is now estimated at about 45 million. Christianity is the major religion (68 %), but there are others, including some traditional African religions (29 %), also smaller groups practicing Islam (2 %), Hinduism (1.5 %), and Judaism. English-speaking people constitute about 40% of South Africa's whites. There are eleven official languages, including English, Afrikaans, and Zulu (for a more complete list, see the California section, Linguistic and Cultural Aspects). Although called "the English," in terms of ethnic origin, they can be Greek, Irish, Italian, Jewish, Portuguese, German, or even Dutch. They preferred business to politics and as a result lost most political power but continued to dominate commerce and industry. English liberals questioned the form but not the substance of apartheid, and therefore partly earned the scorn of the Afrikaners because at the same time that the English-owned businesses benefited from apartheid, they still found the breath to criticize it.

A vineyard mountain landscape in South Africa.
Courtesy of Jupiter Images.

Perhaps the most worried South Africans are the Indians and the Coloureds. They are neither economically privileged nor have numerical superiority; they are the classic middlemen. There is little feeling of solidarity in either group. The Indians brought with them a strong sense of identity and culture from their native country; the Coloureds have severe identity and culture problems. The bloodiest interaction in South Africa is black against black, namely the turf war between the ANC and the Inkatha Freedom party in its stronghold of KwaZulu/Natal. Inkatha claimed to represent gradual change but engaged in much violence, mostly against ANC members. The real horror is that the violence got worse as the white regime eased its controls; with the legalization of black political parties in 1990, an immoderate struggle for turf and predominance broke out.

For over four decades there was no constructive dialogue between blacks and whites. The regime governed by coercion and repression, banning and jailing were widespread. When some of the worst police-state restrictions eased in 1990, there were still few constructive interactions between blacks and whites. It is still this way today though many whites wish for a constructive dialogue, many blacks are still angry after decades of abuse. This is another situation that echoes the Black American and American Indian experience, to name a few minority groups.

How to carry out a virtual revolution without spilling blood while still retaining the government's legitimacy among all population groups is the difficult task South Africa's government is faced with today. The government is pulled in several different directions; many black militants want "socialism" whereas whites want capitalism. Income inequality in South Africa is high; many blacks are unemployed and below the poverty line while the white minority owns almost all the land and wealth. Nearly all young whites graduate high school; only 1/3rd of young blacks do. In addition to these depressing statistics, black infant mortality is high while white is low.

For many decades, the ANC and its South African Communist Party (SACP) junior partner denounced capitalism and promised a socialist future for South Africa; for blacks, the capitalism practiced by whites looked like brutal exploitation. The release of Mandela and the Legalization of the ANC in 1990 came at a time when socialism simply had no success stories. By 1996, Mandela had come out in favor of privatizing South Africa's extensive state-owned sector. Maybe free markets and private initiative should be given a chance. The real worry is that South Africa could become like Zimbabwe, which started as a multi-party democracy but has been a dominant-party system since 1987 under a president for life. This is a result of a combination of many poor people, a no-grow economy, starvation, and tribe-based politics. South Africa's greatest challenge will be providing education and economic opportunities for all, in the hopes of preventing a totalitarian state that oppresses the weak. Under such circumstances, democracy is likely to fail and power goes to the strongest, a story of much of Africa.

Chapter Summary

Our views of the world can include a moral code, a sense of civic duty, and an idea of how government should work. These views make up our core beliefs. We come by these beliefs through the influence of families, religious leaders, peers, and the media. From these beliefs emerge our political attitudes about government. Politicians desire to understand the political attitudes of their constituents, so they pay attention to public opinion polls. Public opinion is an essential tool in the democratic process. Therefore, these polls have to be formulated without bias and be as open-ended as possible, allowing the subjects to speak freely about their opinions. Political analysts can gather more information about factors, also called agents of socialization that affect our political outlook. Some of these agents can be "race", ethnicity, class, religion, region, and gender. These factors can determine whether a citizen will do all that is possible in order to be better informed about the political process and then, to hopefully vote responsibly. Despite the advances in technology, information alone does not guarantee a more politically savvy public. This brings up the question of whether politicians truly value public opinion enough to implement policy that corresponds to the public's needs. This is the true measure of democracy at its most effective level. States like California possess extremely diverse population, which give rise to cultural and linguistic complexities and clashes amongst ethnic communities that are competing for limited resources. This has brought the debate about immigration law to the forefront of politics in California. In comparison, South Africa and the United States have come from similar beginnings as colonies being oppressed by a dominant ethnic group. Both countries have had to own up to its treatment of its indigenous peoples and must still deal with tense racial relations to this day. In short, what is important to remember about public opinion is that there are no right or wrong answers – it is simply a way to gauge how individuals view the world around them.

Key Terms:

Core Beliefs

Political Attitudes

Public Opinion

Straw Poll

Representative Sample

Sample Size

Margin of Error

Random Sample

Sampling Bias

Focus Groups

Political Socialization

Displaced

Caucasians

Coalition of the Willing

Gender Gap

"Ostrich" Technique

Exit Poll

Language Shock

Afrikaner

Sanctions

Soviet bloc

Vote of No-Confidence

Emissary

Websites:

U.S. Census Bureau
www.census.gov

Slate – Doonesbury @ Slate
www.doonesbury.com/arcade/strawpoll/index.cfm

The Gallup Organization
www.gallup.com/

General Social Survey Codebook
www.icpsr.umich.edu/GSS/index.html

The Pew Research Center for the People and the Press
www.people-press.org

The Political Compass
www.politicalcompass.org

Polling Report
www.pollingreport.com

United States Holocaust Memorial Museum
www.ushmm.org

Stop Genocide Now
www.stopgenocidenow.org

People for the American Way
www.pfaw.org

Christian Coalition of America
www.cc.org

California Sites

Institute of Governmental Studies – UC Berkeley
www.igs.berkeley.edu

Chicana/o Latina/o Net - UCLA
http://clnet.sscnet.ucla.edu/

League of Women Voters
www.ca.lwv.org

Center for Continuing Study of the California Economy
www.ccsce.com

Capitol Hill, Washington D.C.
The capital is home to Congress. Former members of congress retain 'floor privileges'
that allow them access to their former colleagues after they go to work for "lobby shops."
Courtesy of Corel

CHAPTER 6

INTEREST GROUPS

CHAPTER OUTLINE

Democracy and Action - EMILY's List

In the United States, there are numerous special **interest groups**, some of which exercise considerable political power. These groups lobby the members of Congress to pass or prevent legislation favorable to their causes. There are many types of interest groups; among them are **political action committees (PACs)** specially formed for the purpose of electing or defeating certain candidates. One such PAC is EMILY's List.

In 1985, 25 women who were frustrated by the lack of female representation in government formed EMILY's List. These women created the group for the purpose of raising money and providing information to support the election of pro-choice Democratic female candidates for office. EMILY's List is not actually named after a woman; it is an acronym that stands for "Early Money Is Like Yeast". The sentiment behind it is that yeast makes dough rise. These women believed that fundraising early is a key component to making a campaign successful, so they devoted their efforts to raising money early on in a campaign in order to bolster that candidate.

Prior to the founding of EMILY's List, no Democratic woman had ever been elected to the U.S. Senate in her own right, nor elected as governor of any large state.[1] Since its formation in 1985, EMILY's List has been a major factor in the election of dozens of women to Congress, more than a dozen to the Senate and several state governors. Its membership has grown to include more than 100,000 people and one of the largest **grassroots organizations** in the United States. This PAC has also become one of the principal resources for Democratic women running for office.

Every election, EMILY's List selects a list of candidates and promotes them through their website. Instead of donating directly to the group, EMILY's List encourages donors to choose specific candidates from the List and donate directly to their campaigns. EMILY's List hosts convenient links that will connect donors to the candidates' websites. This way, the message is clear that EMILY's List is not necessarily soliciting for personal gains, but that they are committed to grooming candidates early. Being a candidate recommended by EMILY's List gives that candidate access to not only one of the largest pool of donors in politics, but also enables them to be noticed by major individual donors as well.

EMILY's List has expanded to more than just a fundraising and information resource for candidates. They also recruit candidates and train women who are considering running for office. Through their Political Opportunity Program, or POP, EMILY's List actively scours communities seeking pro-choice Democratic women leaders and asks them to run for office.

The List also holds seminars around the country for women who are interested in possibly running for office, and then will train those who decide to make a run.

Interest group –
A group of persons who work to promote their common interest.

Political Action Committees or PACs –
Interest group formed specifically for the purpose of electing or defeating certain candidates that support or don't support their cause.

Grassroots Organization –
A group of ordinary people working toward a common cause; based upon the idea of the power rests with the people.

EMILY's List champions female political candidates like Senator Hillary Clinton (D-NY). © Juliet Kaye, 2007. Used under License from Shutterstock, Inc.

In addition, EMILY's List trains women to be effective activists and campaign professionals as well. They carry out massive "Get Out the Vote" efforts for every election. EMILY's List is an excellent illustration of not only how a good political network gets the job done, but also of the tremendous impact an organized interest group can have on a government and its policies.[2]

The Character of Interest Groups

"If [a] book be false in its facts, disprove them; if false in its reasoning, refute it. But for God's sake, let us freely hear both sides if we choose."
– Thomas Jefferson, 1814

If you've ever waved off somebody trying to get you to sign a petition, hand you a flyer, or ask you if you are a registered voter, you may have just been solicited on behalf of an interest group. In chapter five we discussed public opinion, opinion polls, and whether or not politicians actually listen to the voice of the people. **Interest groups** are organizations that are formed in the hopes of making sure their voices are heard so that they can influence public policy. These groups share a goal or a cause that requires the attention of government. Sometimes also called **pressure groups**, its members confront representatives and elected officials to **lobby** for their cause. The term lobby or lobbyist came about during 18th U.S. President Ulysses S. Grant's visits to the Willard Hotel in Washington, D.C. Those who were privy to his visits would wait in the hotel lobby for him, hoping to gain an audience with him over a smoke and a drink.

Despite voting apathy trends, most people do have concerns about how the government is running things and how it may affect day to day lives. People who participate in interest groups take the extra step to actually be an active instrument of change. Interest groups do not necessarily consist of highly educated scholars, political scientists, or experts on their particular cause. They are everyday people that you come across in your schools, churches, synagogues, places of work, clubs, and sporting events. In short, interest groups are an essential part of a free democratic system.

It is typical at protest rallies for hundreds of smaller groups to demand microphone time, even though the main event of the day may be to protest a campaign to go to war. For example, protests during the first and second Gulf Wars brought together thousands of voices that disagreed with the administrations' decision to perform air strikes. Amongst all the usual "no blood for oil" and "food not bombs" signs, one could see "free Mumia Abu Jamal" or "save our oceans" peppered amongst the crowd as well. While these are valid concerns, it is important for interest groups to remain focused on one mission even when there are so many issues to be addressed. The main goals of an interest group are to influence government, to support those candidates and political figures that are sympathetic to their goals, and to seek out members to perpetuate their mission. In order for a group to be successful, they must have some semblance of organization and appeal in order to acquire a steady membership. They must have a unifying belief or mission that they feel the government is not addressing in a satisfactory manner. There are two types of interest groups, private and public. It is in the strengths of their differences and clarity of their goals that make interest groups stand out and get noticed.

Get Out the Vote – Movement that began by many non-partisan interest groups to increase voter awareness and decrease voter apathy.

Interest, Lobby, and Pressure Groups – Groups that seek to convey its' interests to policy makers; they put pressure on government to implement policies that fit their goals.

Factions and the Pluralist Society

In a democratic society, there will always be divisions between groups. Because resources are always limited, these groups are always competing for the maximum amount of amenities possible. As pointed out in The Federalist No. 10 (see appendix), Madison explained how **factions** are a necessary evil. Factions are basically the concept that we all have different pursuits. These pursuits are embodied in agendas and the groups that act on them are somewhat selfish because they have tunnel vision fixed on their own needs without considering the needs of those around them that may be affected. For example, consider the water from the Colorado River. As the west continues to expand in population, the demands for water begin to exhaust the resources that so many are dependent on. California, Arizona, Nevada, and Colorado itself all rely on the river and each state needs more water day by day. It is the federal government's job to allocate the water and they must do so with the pressure of farmers, urban centers, businesses, and state governments all demanding more. The loser in all this is Mexico. Because of an international treaty with Mexico, the United States is required to insure that they receive their fair share of the water supply as well. However, by the time it reaches the Mexican border, the states have used so much water that it is a mere trickle and this is hurtful for Mexico; but they have little say in the matter.

According to Madison, there are two ways to approach factions. One is to force everyone to think alike and the second is to outlaw them. Neither of these methods is feasible because the first is impossible, especially in a free democratic society, and the second infringes on personal liberties. In both cases, the treatment is worse than the ailment. Therefore, political scientists theorized that American politics are best explained through the concept of **pluralism**.

Pluralism is a system in which groups compete for a specific resource and they try to meet their needs by interacting, negotiating, and reaching compromises. Negotiations between groups can occur on a larger scale through conferences called by the federal government or they can happen at state dinners between governors individually. Let's go back to the example of the Colorado River above. Each state has amenities unique to their geography and industry. California might be able to offer limitations on gambling permits so that Californians continue to make Las Vegas their main gambling destination. Nevada, in turn, might be able to relinquish some of its water rights to California. This way each state is encouraged to discuss with their neighboring states their specific needs and commodities and reach agreeable compromises.

While this may appear to be a fair and efficient system, there are some downsides to pluralism. There can be inequalities among the groups, such as:

• Not every group is equal in power

• Not every group starts out with equal resources

• Not all groups have equal access to representatives

Now let's take a closer look at some of these groups in greater detail.

Factions –
James Madison's term for groups or parties that are out to advance their own agenda at the expense of the greater public.

Pluralism –
The view that American politics are best understood in terms of the interaction, conflict, and bargaining of groups.

FOR YOUR CONSIDERATION
THE ROLE OF RELIGION IN AMERICAN POLITICS

Religion has always been part of the fabric of the United States; most, if not all, of our founding fathers and presidents have been men of faith. Churches have been prominent organizations in their communities since the beginning of our union; and for many citizens, their personal religious beliefs play at least a partial role in how they cast their votes. However, for the most part, the separation of church and state has remained a fairly solid line - that is, until the past few decades.

The presidential election of 1960 was the first election to bring the religion of a candidate up as a big campaign issue. People wanted to know if John F. Kennedy's Catholicism was going to govern a Kennedy presidency. Kennedy managed to allay these fears adequately enough for the public to elect him. In 2000, the fact that Democratic vice presidential candidate, Joe Lieberman was Jewish was largely seen as a non-issue for voters. But in 2008, the specific religion of a presidential candidate has been brought to the forefront again, at least on the Republican side. One of the leading Republican candidates, Mitt Romney, is Mormon; whether Romney can dispel any fears of it affecting his political judgment remains to be seen.

Religion in American politics has by no means been limited to presidential races. During the 1980s, religion began to infiltrate everyday politics. Beginning with the Moral Majority founded by ultra-conservative Pastor Jerry Falwell in 1979, religion, through the vehicle of congregations across the nation, was used as a tool to mobilize conservative voters and issue advocacy. As a direct reaction to the Supreme Court decision of Roe v. Wade, which legalized abortion, and the burgeoning issues of gay rights and prayer in schools, the Moral Majority quickly rose to national prominence. Unfortunately for them, this public stature did not translate into a very solid voting block, at least not at that time. After Falwell disbanded the group in 1989 so that he could focus on the tier 4 law school that he founded, Liberty University, the power of religion has waned a bit in political life. In the 1990's, the mantle was passed to Ralph Reed and the Christian Coalition, and in the 21st century, it is believed that the most influential group is Dobson's Focus on the Family.

That power regained strength in the wake of the 1994 Republican congressional sweep and with the controversial Clinton impeachment; society was seen as rapidly declining in morality and the secular interests (read: Democrats) were to blame. During the presidential campaign of 2000, Republican candidate George W. Bush managed to harness the power of the religious right as a voting bloc and rode that wave to the Oval Office. Bush talked openly and often about his personal faith and the role it played in his decision-making. After assuming office, he banned federal money for stem cell research as well as established an office for faith-based initiatives, both of which helped cement his standing with the religious right. His appointments of conservatives John G. Roberts and Samuel Alito to the Supreme Court bench bolstered this standing even further. Incidentally, in November 2004, Falwell unveiled The Moral Majority Coalition (TMCC), just in time to breathe life into the "evangelical revolution" that was enjoying a rebirth with "Pastor-in-Chief" President Bush and the plethora of pro-life leaders that were recently elected to national standing. Falwell, the ambassador of the religious right political initiative, professed TMMC as a "21st century resurrection of the Moral Majority".[3]

Since the 2000 presidential campaign, religion has been an active topic in politics and elections. Because of the social issues of the day, religion has tended to be a more prominent issue in the Republican Party. The Democrats have struggled to address religion adequately enough to sway the religious community's votes a little more left or at least center. This may be changing during the current election cycle since many of the Democratic presidential candidates seem more at ease discussing their faith this time around. The general electorate, frustrated by many of Bush's policy decisions, appears to be willing to listen.

Who's Special, Who's Not?

As you will see from the example of Enron later on in this chapter, some groups are more "special" than others, meaning that some have more clout, earned not necessarily on honorable reasons but on what contributions they can offer. Although the seemingly feeble voice of the smaller environmental group may not be heard over the loud roar of the huge energy conglomerates, the smaller faction will no doubt rise up and demand to be heard; what may be even more disturbing is the deafening silence of lobbying by foreign nations. This credibility can sometimes be seen in the differences between public and private interest groups.

Private Interest Group –
An interest group that seeks to protector advance the material interests of its members.

Private Interest Groups

Private interest groups benefit a specific group of people or individuals. They usually focus on economic gains from the government, either in terms of protection such as tariffs on trade, or subsidies such as tax credits. In both cases most of the rewards received are meant for the members of this group. Think about oil companies. In a time of record oil profits, oil companies are still seeking tax breaks for future explorations while still protecting their control of the market by limiting alternatives to gasoline or higher fuel standards.

Among many, there are three main categories of private interest groups. They fall under businesses, professions, labor unions. Within businesses, there are several subcategories; however, they all have one thing in common – they are able to influence all levels of government, local, state, and national because of the impact they have on the economy. Because large businesses such as Boeing and Microsoft have production centers located around the world, they are able to influence governments' policies on key issues like trade, research and development, and workers' rights. In the case of trade, Boeing often requests for the United States government to intercede on their behalf when dealing with other countries, especially European countries that belong to the European Union (EU). The EU subsidizes the major airplane manufacturer, Airbus. Boeing does not currently enjoy some of the same subsidies – in fact, they would like to level the playing field by having the U.S. government apply pressure on the EU to eliminate these subsidies. As for Microsoft, they often petition the U.S. to enforce international copyright law in China, where the problem of bootleg copies of software runs rampant, unchecked by the Chinese government, costing Microsoft millions of dollars in revenue.

Professional organizations such as the American Medical Association (AMA) and the American Bar Association (ABA) represent individuals whose profession falls under a higher income bracket. Because of their status in communities, the groups that represent these professionals are able to influence politicians through campaign contributions and local support. Regarding the AMA, they have successfully influenced Congress and state governments to put limits on malpractice suits. Furthermore, they have prevented national healthcare from becoming a reality and they put a stop to any interference with their professional earnings.

Issues For You
In light of the Enron scandal, how can interest groups like the Native American-run casinos, avoid being taken advantage of by corrupt lobbyists?

One of the major scandals that hit Washington in 2005 - 2007 became known as the Jack Abramoff scandal. Jack Abramoff was a lobbyist who arranged private trips (skiing in Vail, CO and golfing in Scotland), campaign contributions, and other questionable activities for powerful members of Congress and their staffers. One of Abramoff's main recipients was his former boss, House Majority Leader Tom Delay (R-TX). As the FBI began to investigate, it became apparent that Abramoff had violated a variety of federal laws. Abramoff was accused of generating a "pay-for-government policy" program, by taking millions of dollars from interest groups, including Native American-run casinos, foreign sources, and then distributing the funds to specific congressional representatives for both their election and personal needs. In return, Abramoff obtained federal aid and legislation passed for his clientele.

The revolving door arrangement was jammed (but not stopped altogether) when top assistant to Abramoff, Michael Scanlon, came clean and pled guilty for his involvement in the scandal. Soon after in January 2006, Abramoff pled guilty to fraud, tax evasion, and conspiracy to bribe federal public officials. The final blow was that up to two dozen more members of Congress, mainly Republicans but also Democrats came under the scrutiny of the FBI. Another key turn in the investigation was when charges were filed against former Christian Coalition leader Ralph Reed. At that time Reed was running for the office of Georgia's lieutenant governor.

Free Rider –
A person who receives benefits without contributing money or participating in the goals of the group.

Despite shrinking membership, labor unions are still a formidable presence within state and national government. They tend to support issues that benefit the greater good of society, such as minimum wage issues, health care, and job security (protection from outsourcing). There are those workers, however, who do not necessarily believe in or support unions, but yet they still reap the benefits of the bargain leaders' hard work. This manner of worker has been called a **free rider**.

Public Interest Group –
An interest group that advocates for a cause or an ideology.

Public Interest Groups

Public interest groups tend to look out for the community as a whole, even if a few individuals disagree with their goals or tactics. Most of these groups are not seeking financial gain for its members; rather they are involved because of a personal belief or ideology. These groups tend to focus on influencing public policy to benefit all members of society. Public groups come in the form of racial or ethnic causes (National Association for the Advancement of Colored People or the NAACP), environmental protection (Sierra Club), rights for citizens (American Civil Liberties Union – ACLU), animals (World Wildlife Fund –WWF), and any other cause for those who feel they are underrepresented. In referring back to the example of the oil companies, there are a number of public interest groups who are upset with them. The environmental groups want to protect areas in which the oil companies want to drill, support measures for alternative energy, and promote higher fuel standards. Advocates for the working poor are accusing the oil companies of price gouging, thus cutting into the already strained budget of the less fortunate.

Both private and public interest groups have varying characteristics. Some groups are very large with offices across the country, like Mothers Against Drunk Driving (MADD) and the American Automobile Association (AAA) while others are smaller and tend to focus on regional issues such as Heal the Bay. Regardless of size or membership, interest groups are a controversial but yet essential component of American politics.

Lobbying for other Countries

Lobbyists have been known to represent international conglomerates. Courtesy of Jupiter Images.

The United States is currently the world's main economic power; this in and of itself shouldn't be surprising. In addition to public and private interest groups, a third category involves foreign companies in other countries hiring private lobbying firms to insure their interests are represented in America as well. This concept is nothing new; in fact it dates back to the very creation of governments when emissaries were sent to other countries, sometimes bearing gifts, to strengthen the ties between governments. Sometimes it was done in public to foster public support and other times it was done behind closed doors and in secret. The main difference between then and now is that back then, one group represents the governments directly, where as now, companies and individuals hire lobbyists on behalf of countries who want to maintain a presence in the U.S. government.

In the mid 1930's, Ivy Lee, a public relations specialist was hired by the German Dye trust to improve the image of Germany in the United States. As it turned out, the German Dye trust was acting on behalf of the German government, which was being led by Adolf Hitler and his Nazi party. When it became known who Lee's client was, Congress created the Foreign Agents Registration Act of 1938 (FARA).[4]

Over the years, FARA has become more of a technicality. Given the power that lobbyists have over Congress, the Act hasn't really been enforced nor any attempts made to update it in the years since it's been enacted. According to the U.S. General Accounting Office, in 1990, it was estimated that "…less than half of the foreign lobbyists who should register under FARA actually do so."[5] One reason for this has been the creation of business interests who lobby on behalf of foreign governments, either with the country's direct knowledge or as a benefactor of the company's actions. Either way, the main focus is gaining money from the U.S. Government or, more directly, from the U.S. tax payer.

In Iraq while Saddam Hussein was still in power he hired Washington Lobby Shops to receive subsidies from the U.S. Government. © Matt Trommer, 2007. Used under License from Shutterstock, Inc.

Beginning in the late 20th century, we have seen countries with atrocious human rights records receive some form of subsidies from the U.S. Government. During the 1990's, China was granted "Most Favored Nation" trade status despite China's arrest and persecution of political, humanitarian, and religious activists. Before President Clinton left office, China was granted the permanent trade status. Since then, lobbyist firms such as APCO Associates, Jefferson Waterman, the Carman Group, Patton Boggs, and Cassidy and Associates, to name a few, continue to be hired by foreign businesses or governments by countries such as Angola, Cameroon, Kazakhstan, Romania, Burma, Iraq, Zaire, Liberia, Nigeria, and Azerbaijan.[6] Most of the countries on this list have, at one point in time, had issues with human rights abuses. In Iraq while Saddam Hussein was still in power, ordering mayhem upon the Kurds in Northern Iraq and on Shia Muslims in Southern Iraq, he hired a "lobby shop" to represent his interests in Washington D.C.[7]   Some lobbying firms argue that the proper precautions and appropriate protocol were followed and that this type of interaction is good for America and her allies. They claim that they are conducting due diligence checks before accepting clients. They also claim that they act with the intention of improving ties between the United States and other nations by way of economic aid and dialogue, thus furthering along the concept of a partnership in democracy in these countries. One can only hope.

Lobbying – Direct and Indirect Tactics

Lobbying can take on the form of direct and indirect tactics. The direct method means exactly that – direct, one-on-one contact between interest group leaders and government officials. The direct method is also referred to as the inside game. As one would correctly guess, the opposite method, the indirect way, is also known as the outside game. The outside game involves securing public opinion, voters, and fundraisers in order to apply pressure on political officials. Discrete tactics are a form of both the inside and outside game. It allows lobbyists to inform government officials and the public as needed with minimal controversy.

Direct Tactics: Inside Game

The inside game implies an exclusivity that reinforces the adage, it's not what you know, it's who you know. The way networks are formed and strengthened is by lobbyists becoming very skilled at building long-term relationships with those in power that are essential to their interests, whether it be individuals or agencies. Also coined "the old boys' network", this large number of former Washington insiders boasts lobbyists that are congressmen and women, members of the executive branch, and high-ranking senior staff. They chose to leave public service to obtain powerful positions on the centrally located K-street, one of the main thoroughfares of the major league hitters in Washington D.C. politics. These connections allow lobbyists to persuade members of Congress to support their programs by illustrating the benefits to their constituents back home.

This game appears to work best on issues that are relatively benign, technical, or highly specialized because they don't seem to cause alarm within the interest groups and they don't draw much attention from either the public or the media (see figure 6.1). There are great benefits to those on the inside able to make minute but important changes to the wording of a bill before it is voted on in committees or subcommittees. Think of the real scenario of oil companies able to pay taxes on the cost of a barrel of oil and not on the profit of oil. It's the difference between paying tax on $20 and that of $70. The change of a word equals billions of dollars in profits for oil companies, while costing the government billions in tax revenue each year.

Lobbying is not exclusive to former Washington D.C. bigwigs. They also have been known to lobby the courts and judicial appointment processes, making their support or lack thereof known for each nominee to the Supreme Court. The interest groups that actively lobby the courts can file an amicus curiae brief (Friend of the Court), in which the group or individual not serving as a party in the case may attempt to sway the judges by filing arguments for or against the issue in support of the side they choose. The courts and processes like these will be covered further in chapter 12.

It should be noted that it's not only business and professional groups who are able to play the inside game. Large public groups, like the Sierra Club also enjoy access to various politicians compared to smaller environmental groups that do not have as much clout. As a result, these larger organizations have much more impact on policy.

Indirect Tactics: Outside Game

Indirect tactics, or the outside game, are mainly used by those groups who do not have direct access to elected officials. In order to gain the attention of the representatives, these groups have to mobilize their base and organize a grassroots movement to get their voices heard. As the divisions between those who have direct access and those who do not continues to widen, the groups that are able to mobilize their members have seen a greater response from those in power. This is the raison d'être of Democracy – it goes hand in hand with action.

The main tactic of the outside game is mobilization of membership. Mobilization includes letters, phone calls, faxes, emails, and even text messages. The Internet and technology have been a major part of leveling the playing field (see figure 6.1). Back in the 1980s, the Republican Party was able to mobilize its members though direct mailing and phone banks. Today, public interest groups like Moveon.org are able to send an email to its members with a link to send a fax or mass email letters and weekly petitions to hundreds of members of the House and Senate, and even the White House. If these tactics aren't enough, some groups are able to raise enough funds to take out ads in newspapers, radio, and even television. Using Moveon.org as an example, they often appeal to their members for small donations ($10 or $20) to run advertising to challenge and hold other interest groups or politicians accountable.

FIGURE 6.1 - LOBBYING FLOW CHART

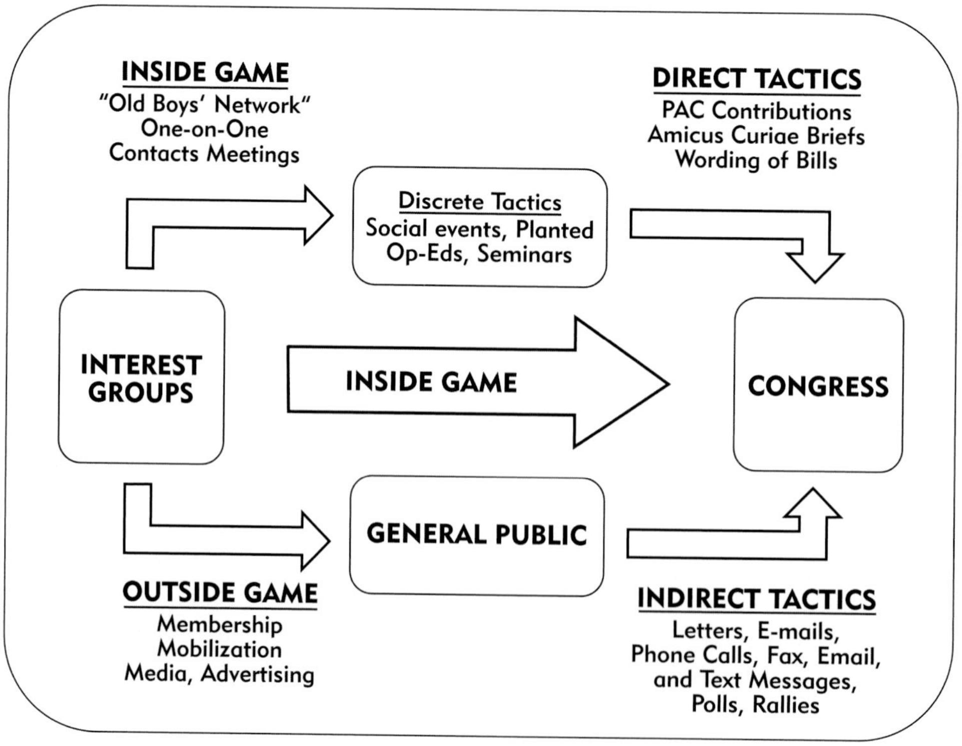

Discrete Tactics

Discrete tactics are those that allow lobbying firms to introduce government officials to groups or individuals. As you learned above, there are firms who lobby for other countries and/or companies who have interests in other countries. Some of the tactics used by representatives, members of the media, or academia to gain support for their client's issues are trips to these countries, social events with guest speakers, "planted" op-ed pieces in newspapers, featured stories in magazines, and holding seminars to name a few. All of these tactics can be used in tandem with other methods of lobbying, such as grassroots organizing.[8]

Grassroots Activity

Grassroots Activity is one of the main tools in the lobbyists' chest. The ability that lobbyists have to mobilize their members in order to sway public opinion towards their cause is a key aspect of their job. Politicians pay attention to protests or other acts that may impact their support for the public. It is interesting to note that not all lobbyists want public attention.

Lobbyists are able to apply grassroots pressure by writing op-ed pieces in newspapers, radio, televisions, rallies, and letter and email campaigns. The main goal of these activities is to show representatives that public opinion supports their cause. A skilled lobbyist knows that one voice can be lost but the roar of the crowd is deafening.

Issues For You

Test your analytical skills. Read the opinion-editorial section in any major newspaper for one week and see if you can distinguish the sincere topics with those that are written with a bias toward a person, country, or issue. Look for repeated themes and track authors who consistently write about one particular issue.

Problems with Factions in a Democracy

As stated above, there are several issues that work against the concept of pluralism. Problems with lack of equality, power, resources, and access to representatives make it difficult for the promise of pluralism to be realized.

Inequality in Power

Not all groups have the same level of power in the state and national capitals; some smaller interest groups aren't represented at all. What does these mean? Simply put, if they don't have a place at the table with the others, they cannot be assured that their issues are being heard. Larger more powerful groups have greater power either in terms of membership, as in the case of the American Association of Retired Persons (AARP), or money, as in the case of the American Medical Association (AMA). This lack of power equates to having to use indirect methods of lobbying, but again, without large numbers, their voices still face a difficult struggle.

Inequality in Resources

Professional groups and corporations have virtually unlimited resources at their disposal. This is mainly because most their members are some of the top income earners in the countries. Recent studies have shown these individuals make anywhere from 6 to 420% more than the average American, depending on their positions. For example, former CEO of the Walt Disney Corporation, Michael Eisner, made over $60,000 an hour, 24 hours a day (including stock options), during the late 1990s. With access to this kind of wealth, politicians are more inclined to hold meetings with the Disney lobbyists than lobbyists from smaller or unknown groups.

Fullerton, California, 1910. Since the turn of the century, oil companies have wielded tremendous influence among politicians.
Courtesy of the Library of Congress

Soft Money –
Campaign funds that are committed to a specific political party or issue rather than a specific candidate.

Independent Expenditures –
Monies distributed, as allowed by a loophole in campaign finance law, by a group or individual not coordinated by a candidate, in the name of a cause.

What Political Action Committees (PACS) Can and Can't Do: Hard Money

Business, professional groups, and trade associations are at the forefront of contributing to politicians and their campaigns. PACs are the product of special interest groups trying to circumvent campaign finance laws. As you can see from Table 6.1 above, most of these groups, both liberal and conservative, raise money for candidates. PACs are able to raise millions of dollars to help finance campaigns. In order to bypass federal campaign financial laws, soft money became the main way to raise funds during the 1990s (see table 6.2). However, after much controversy and public outrage regarding unchecked funding, it was apparent that **soft money** needed regulation. In 2002, the McCain-Feingold Bill, also known as the Bipartisan Campaign Reform Act, was passed and signed into law limiting unregulated soft money and **independent expenditures** or issue campaigns.

TABLE 6.1 - Limtis on PACs, Hard Money
Coporations and Labor Union PACS CAN/have:
• Collect and donate regulated funds to candidates running for Congress or President and political party committees.
• For each election, both primary and general, PACs can contribute up to $5,000 to each candidate and $15,000 per year for each national party committee.
• Give up to $5,000 per year, internally between PACs
• No restrictions on total donations to federal candidates and national party committees
• No restrictions on "issue-campaigns" on media outlets, until the cut-off date before elections
Public interest groups and other private association PACS CAN/have:
• Collect and donate regulated funds to candidates and party committees
• Identical rules for collection and use of regulated funds as for PACs created by corporations and labor unions.

What Political Action Committees (PACS) Can and Can't Do: Soft Money

After several "free speech" challenges by lobbyists that reached the Supreme Court, the Court ruled that the main parts of the McCain-Feingold Bills were constitutional. While this was seen as a first great step toward regulating soft money, there are some issues with the law that need to be addressed. First off, the law allows for more money to be contributed to PACs and from PACs to candidates and political parties. Second, issue campaigns stating the candidates name can be run up to the day of the primary or election. Lastly, there are no limits on the total amount of money that can be spent on media. The impacts of these changes have been an increase in advocacy groups called '527s' named for the federal tax code number. These unregulated groups are allowed to discuss issues and/or candidates' positions, and/or encourage participation and voting. The only limit on the 527 is that they have to stop running ads on television or radio 30 days prior to a primary election and 60 days prior to a general election. The 527 Reform Act was introduced in the Senate in 2005; it proposed that the loophole in campaign finance rules be closed and to curb the influence of 527s. It did not pass the Senate. It later reemerged as the 527 Reform Act of 2007 in the House of Representatives.

TABLE 6.2 - What Political Action Committees (PACS) Can and Can't Do: Soft Money
Coporations and Labor Union PACS CAN/have:
• Make unlimited donations to advocacy groups
Coporations and Labor Union PACS CANNOT/have:
• Use funds from their general accounts to give money to federal candidates or national political party organizations • Use funds from their general accounts to pay for "issue-campaigns" that bring up candidates or office holders on TV or radio 30 days before a primary election or 60 days before a general election
Public interest groups and other private association PACS CAN/have:
• No limits on amount of donations that the group or association accepts or the amount they can accumulate • No limits on "issue-campaigns" before pre-election "blackout" dates • No limits on use of soft money for other issue-campaigning activities including phone calls, specific demographic mailings, e-mail blitzes, door-to-door precinct walks
Public interest groups and other private association PACS CANNOT/have:
• Use unregulated money to pay for "issue campaigns" on TV or radio 30 days before a primary election or 60 days before a general election

FOR YOUR CONSIDERATION
SOFT VS. HARD MONEY

In response to the Watergate scandal, the reforms for campaign financing included establishing limits on party contributions. The funds that candidates receive from a political party, along with

Hard Money –
Regulated money candidates, party committees, and PACs receive for campaigns.

funds received from individual contributors or interest groups, is called **hard money**. This is the money that goes directly to the candidate and can be used how he or she chooses. Limits on hard money are set according to the source from which they are received. Political parties are limited to $10,000 to House candidates and $37,500 for Senate candidates, while individual contributions are limited to $2,000 and interest groups have a $5,000 (per group) maximum

Soft money, on the other hand, are party contributions not handed over directly to the candidate. Although limits are set on monies going directly to the candidate, the post-Watergate reforms of the 1970's did not specify the amount of money a party could use towards party activities. Essentially, parties could receive unlimited amounts of contributions so long as the monies are not channeled to party candidates. Subtle uses of monies for campaigns, rather, are found in advertisements, state and local party organizations, and "Get Out the Vote" drives, which can influence the outcome of an election. In 1996, a $100 million ad campaign funded by the Democratic National Convention (DNC) did not directly urge voters to support Bill Clinton, but his image and references to his accomplishments were used throughout the ad campaign, thus influencing his run for President.

Campaign finance reform became a hot issue since the post-Watergate period, and recently has been the basis of much argument in Congress and the Senate. Senator John McCain (R-AZ) proposed campaign finance reforms in 2000, suggesting a ban on soft money, following the Enron scandal. During a federal investigation into the Enron Corporation, it was revealed the corporation had contributed over $5.9 million to both the DNC and Republican National Convention (RNC) candidates and committees, influencing national energy policy.[9] As a result, Congress placed restrictions on soft money in 2002.

These limits, however, are not the answer to the problem of money and influence in Washington, and nearly every attempt to further regulate the flow of money in the political arena has been thwarted by loopholes or non-support. Either way money finds its way into politics, carrying with it tremendous influence, power, and control.

Inequality of Access to Elected Officials

In addition to the problems described in the sections about hard and soft money, lack of access to elected representatives hinders political equality and popular sovereignty. A main contributing factor to this problem is allowing interest groups to hire former members of congress, the bureaucracy, and the executive branch - it's difficult to decipher who our representatives are really representing. Over the years, Congress at different times has tried to address this problem by mandating time periods on individuals who work in or for the government before being employed by lobbyists. The time frame spans a range from six months to a couple of years. The promise of obtaining a high paying, high profile job after public service makes it quite challenging for government officials to perform their jobs attentively; take for example the idea of the iron triangle. The **iron triangle** illustrates a three-way relationship between an interest group, a bureaucratic agency, and a committee or subcommittee in Congress (see figure 6.2) The goal of this arrangement is to insure that all sides receive equal benefits and that a policy is constructed that aids the government or the targeted group. There will be future discussions on direct lobbying later in this chapter.

Iron Triangle – A long-lasting relationship between an interest group, a congressional committee, and a bureaucratic agency.

FIGURE 6.2 - Iron Triangle System

This is an example of a symbiotic relationship between three agencies. Thousands of troops are returning home from Iraq and Afghanistan showing symptoms of post-traumatic stress disorder (PTSD). The Department of Veterans Affairs (VA), although essential, is ill-equipped to deal with the large influx of veterans. The VA relies on other organizations such as Veterans of Foreign Wars and the American Psychiatric Association to supply information, provide support, and to help solicit funds from Congress.

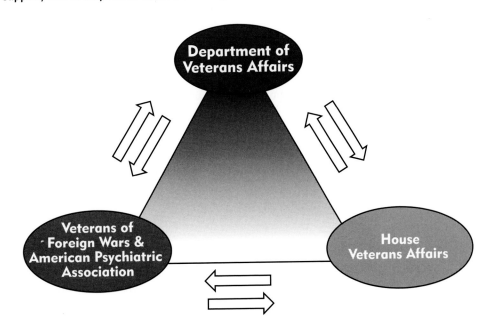

Issues For You
Look at the diagram for the iron triangle. Create one for a public interest group regarding an issue that interests you, such as student fees or healthcare.

While there are some who say that the iron triangle is no longer a real issue, you can see in the following example, that whatever the term, there is a strong relationship between powerful individuals, government officials, and the policies that are created.

Case Study: Problems with Pluralism

The west coast experienced a severe energy shortage that turned out to be a scam instigated by Enron.

A good example of some of the possible flaws that can occur due to pluralism is the story of Enron, an energy company in Texas, lead by CEO Kenneth Lay. Enron had forged a long-standing relationship with Gov. George W. Bush throughout his political career.

During campaigning activities, Enron allowed Bush to use their private jets to travel to various political campaign events. When Gov. Bush became President-elect, Ken Lay was considered for the position of Secretary of Energy. Because of Lay's contributions to the Republican Party and his relationship with Bush, Enron and other major energy corporations were able to work closely with President Bush on energy policies. In 2000, when Vice-President Dick Cheney formed his Energy Task Force, it was privileged individuals and companies like Ken Lay and Enron that were given exclusive access to meetings; whereas environmental, citizen, and alternative energy groups were not afforded the same advantages. When the energy crisis hit California from 2000 to 2001, some individuals criticized the relationship between the Whitehouse and the energy producers, mainly because of the fact that when Governor Gray Davis appealed to the Federal Energy Regulatory Commission for assistance in controlling skyrocketing prices, they refused to take action, thus forcing Californians to pay millions of dollars in additional energy costs.

Placing a Check on Factions

Over the last several hundred years, there have been countless attempts to place a check on factions, but inside and outside the government. More recent attempts to place a check on special interest have been McCain-Feingold, various House and Senate ethics rules, and the Lobby Disclosure Act of 1995. Most of these reforms have not been strictly enforced. In light of this, what is it that can be done? The obvious thing is to get involved and hold government accountable for their actions. There are a number of websites that aid you in registering to vote and informing you of your representatives and their voting history. Vote-smart.org is one of the better sites. It's a very powerful tool to keep up with the happenings in Washington D.C. If you still don't wish to become active in this manner, you should exercise your right to vote. You can also find an organization(s) that represents your interests and supports them. As we've seen in the Jack Abramoff scandal, if factions go unchecked, they tend to gain more power than they should and it's up to the citizens to hold both the elected representatives and the lobbyists accountable. There is still much debate among political scientists' as to which is the best way to counter interest groups. Some have suggested that the key to placing a check on factions is political parties. While this offers some promise, interest groups control

Profiles in Politics
John McCain (1936 -   )

Best known for being a maverick in the United States Senate as well as for his presidential candidacies in 2000 and 2008, John McCain has nevertheless achieved much more in his lifetime. In addition to being a bestselling author and arguably the most famous Vietnamese Prisoner of War (POW), Senator McCain has also been at the forefront of the legislative fight against wasteful government spending.

President Reagan met with McCain and other senators for the purpose of showing constituents that senators have direct access to the President and the White House. Courtesy of the Library of Congress.

John Sidney McCain III was born in the Panama Canal Zone in 1936. Being the son and grandson of distinguished Navy Admirals, his path in life was predestined by a legacy of military service; so naturally, after graduating from the U.S. Naval Academy in 1958, McCain embarked on his career as a Navy pilot. In 1967, during the Vietnam War, North Vietnamese forces shot down his plane and he was taken prisoner. Because of the severe torture that McCain endured, the prison in which he was confined was later coined the "Hanoi Hilton". He was finally released in 1973 after five and a half years of captivity.[10]

Following his retirement from the Navy in 1981, he decided to run for a newly vacant House seat in his current home state of Arizona. In 1982, John McCain became the newest Arizona Representative in the U.S. House. When Senator Barry Goldwater retired from the Senate in 1986, McCain ran for his seat and won. McCain has served as a Senator from Arizona ever since.

His pet causes while in Congress have been putting a stop to wasteful (**pork barrel**) spending and reforming the campaign finance system; McCain has spent most of his government career working to get rid of special interest money from both legislation and elections. As you can imagine, this has won him much support from the general public but not too many friends on K-Street,10 where many lobbyists have offices.

Pork Barrel – Government funding for superfluous projects to benefit a specific district or state; the origins of the term are believed to have begun around 1909; related to "bringing home the bacon", possibly a county fair type of game of catching a greased pig and bringing home the prize – the pig itself.

One of Senator McCain's signature achievements in the Senate was as co-sponsor of the McCain-Feingold Campaign Finance Reform Bill that passed in 2002. The bill, a version of which was first introduced in the Senate in 1995, was geared toward curbing the use of soft money and issue ads, which proliferated during political campaigns, and by design, shut out much of the regular electorate from the election process. The bill was signed into law in March of 2002 and represents a long and hard fight for legislation pursued by very few members of Congress, John McCain being one of the prominent members at the forefront of the fight.

Another fight Senator McCain has taken up is the fight against earmarks, which are pieces of pork barrel spending generally inserted into a bill in the so-called "dead-of-night" and therefore not scrutinized by Congress. He currently supports eliminating all earmarks and should he become president in 2008, he promises to veto "every single pork barrel bill" that Congress sends to him.[11] It will be interesting to watch Senator McCain in these uphill battles against special interests.

both political parties so this may have unintended consequences. Any attempt to increase the power of political parties, without offering extensive reforms on how much access and influence interest groups can have on elected officials and finding ways to increase public oversight would be futile.

California's Special Interest

As stated in the first part of this chapter, most Americans belong to one or more interest group, even if they don't realize it. Californians of all ages also belong to all manners of associations and organizations: labor unions, business associations,

Governor Schwarzenegger appeared to open Pandora's box while trying to reform teachers' tenure and use of union dues for political activities.
© Alan Heison, 2007. Used under License from Shutterstock, Inc.

student, ethnic, and environmental organizations; and boys and girls scouts/clubs, to name a few. The Progressive Movement at the turn of the 20th century played a major part in strengthening interest groups within California. While this is opposite of what the Progressives had in mind, creating weak political parties within the state gave more power to interest groups. Grassroots movements, direct democracy, and increased need

for funds for campaigns, have all contributed to the process. Instead of turning to the political parties, most candidates look to interest groups to help their coffers. One of the largest with over 340,000 members and most powerful interest groups in the state is the California's Teachers Association (CTA). They are able to raise vast amounts of funds for any threat or campaign. Take for example the 2005 Special Election called by Governor Schwarzenegger. Two of the propositions on the ballot had a direct impact on the CTA, Proposition 74 on teacher tenure and Proposition 75 on union dues being used for political campaigns. The CTA spent over $9,000,000 in lobbying during 2005.[12] Their investment paid off because they were successful in defeating Governor Schwarzenegger's propositions, which the CTA believed to be anti-teacher. This proves that interest groups, when organized and focused on a tangible goal, can wield tremendous power in Sacramento and other parts of the state.

Interest Groups on the Rise

Direct democracy was intended to offer the public a way to check the powerful political parties controlled by the "Big Four" (from chapter 2, main players for newspapers and railroads in the late 1800's). Beginning in the 1970's interest groups began using the proposition process as a way to bypass the legislature and have their items written into the state's constitution. Within the last forty years, there have been hundreds of propositions offered, mainly sponsored by interest groups. By having their interest protected by the state's constitution, interest groups are given a guarantee of sorts. If another group tries to amend that part, the original group could run counter ads and or propose a counter amendment. The end result, when Californians go to the polls to vote, many of them are confused over the similarities and the vagueness of the propositions and more often than not, just voting no.

Referring back to chapter three, Proposition 13 provides an excellent example of how this process works. In the early 1970's a group wanted to place a cap on property taxes and proposed a proposition. The passage of this proposition greatly impacted public services in California, such as public school and pest control. The product has been California's becoming 48th in education and a decrease in public health due to the cutback in mosquito and rodent abatements. Since Proposition 13 has become law, there have been several attempts to modify it to address for some of the negative impacts. Each attempt has been defeated forcing additional propositions to be offered, causing further strain on the state's limited resources. In addition, state and local politicians often find themselves acquiescing to interest groups demands in order to raise funds for their campaigns.

TABLE 6.3 - Cumulative spending of 2005 Top five lobbyng organizations	
California Teachers Association	$9,456,813
AT&T and its affiliates	$4,065,146
Western States Petroleum Association	$3,130,034
California Chamber of Commerce	$2,570,516
California State Council of Service Employees	$2,014,715

Types of Interest Groups

As you learned above, interest groups come in all shapes, sizes, and with different agendas. In some cases, groups who seek economic advantages are small in membership but well funded, as in the case of AT&T (see table 6.3). Groups who seek public interest have large memberships but inadequate funds, as is the case with Heal the Bay. Some groups have the best of both worlds - they have a large membership and are well funded. An example of this is the CTA (see table 6.3) with hundreds of thousands of members and millions of dollars at their disposal. Despite the appearance that public organizations have an abundance of money, they have much less than economic groups. The one advantage public groups have over private groups is their membership rosters.

Economic Groups. Given that California by itself ranks in the top seven of the world's economies, every predominant business from around the world either has or employs a lobbyist in Sacramento; banks, oil companies, and the computer industry are just a few of the hundreds of economic groups in the state. The interest groups who represent these companies are the California Bankers Association, the California Council for Environmental and Economic Balance (utilities and oil companies), the California Manufacturers Association, and the

The California Chamber of Commerce is one of the most powerful interest groups in the state. Courtesy of the Library of Congress

California Chamber of Commerce (CCC). It is the job of the associations to protect the interest of their clients. The CCC, like the CTA, has lobbied state and local officials to kill any bill that might hurt business. The CCC has been very successful, they have stopped hundreds of bills from passing that would "hurt the state's economy."

Another major player in California is agribusiness. Agriculture is a major industry in the state. The produce that is generated in California varies. The top ten agricultural commodities are: oranges, almonds, grapes, cotton, strawberries, cattle/calves, milk/cream, flower/foliage, lettuce, and nursery products.[13]

The relationship between agriculture and government is one of dependency. The government needs agribusiness to help keep the economy diversified, exports to other states and countries, and of course campaign contributions. Agribusiness needs the government to secure more

Grapes and all its byproducts are a major crop for California. Courtesy of the Library of Congress

water rights, labor, environmental regulations, and other related issues. To maintain this relationship, there are several farming associations or lobbyists who have offices in Sacramento. One of the most powerful organizations is the California Farm Bureau.

Professional Organizations and Labor Unions. Professional organizations, as stated earlier in the chapter are also located in California. California, like the national government is charged with protecting the public's interests and has the power to shape policy. To that end, interest groups are extremely active in insuring that clients' interests are protected. Earlier in the chapter we saw the example of the AMA. The equivalent to the AMA at the state level is the California Medical Association (CMA). It is very likely that if you are a physician in California, you probably belong to both the AMA and the CMA as well as several others depending on your specialty. The CMA along with the California Association of Realtors (CAR) are two of the most active groups within the state as well as two of the top contributors to political campaigns.

Issues For You

Private interest groups and politicians have complained about the power held by public unions. Discuss whether unions do indeed have special privileges or is it simply private groups crying 'wolf'.

Representing public professionals are organizations such as teacher organizations, the California Association of Highway Patrolmen (CAHP), and the very powerful California Correctional Peace Officers Association (CCPOA). While some of their actions are similar to private professional groups, they are still dependent on their membership dues to raise the needed funds to lobby the state. One of the heavy hitters for state employees is the California State Employees Association (CSEA). The CSEA represents office staff and teachers; essentially anyone who works in education in the state is invited to join. With over 220,000 members and 750 local chapters throughout the state, the CSEA is at the same level at the CTA, CMA, and CAR.[14] Like the CTA, one of the goals of the CSEA is to protect their members' retirement funds. In recent years, when the state has faced a fiscal crisis, they have tried to "raid" the state employees' pensions. The CSEA and CTA along with other state employee unions have been successful in protecting their funds from the political whims of the governor and state assembly.

Other traditional unions, such as the AFL/CIO and Teamsters are active in California. With a large part of the state's economy being based on tourism, the traditional unions have worked to protect the wages of employees in hotels, restaurants, and theme parks. In addition, most supermarkets employees, truck drivers, construction workers, and some agricultural professionals are unionized. Despite the variety of occupations that are covered, less than 20 percent of California's workforce is unionized. Given this, unions are still less powerful, in terms of status and money, than their private sector counter parts. The one main advantage unions have is the size of their memberships.

Minority Groups. Most minority groups have some type of representation in California. Most of these groups rely more on the participation of their members than they do money. Most of these groups are based on ethnicity, gender, and age. There are such organizations the California Chapter of the National Organization for Women (NOW), Migrant farm workers have the United Farm Workers (UFW), and for retirees – the American Association of Retired Persons (AARP), and a whole host of organizations representing gay, lesbian, transsexual, and bisexual causes. While most of these groups are limited in financial contributions, they rely on their abilities to organize their members.

Regulating Groups In California

While there has been much discussion on adding more regulations interest groups, the grip lobbyist have on the legislature and the ability to run counter campaigns has proven to be too powerful for political reform. The one item that passed in 1974 and still holds true today is Proposition 9, the Political Reform Act of 1974. This proposition was sponsored by then Secretary of State Jerry Brown and Common Cause and passed with over 70 percent approval ratings. The Reform Act requires politicians to report their assets, disclose contributions, and state how the campaign funds were spent. Additionally, the Act requires lobbyists to register with the secretary of state. The lobbyist must file quarterly reports on their political activities, and report who received campaign contributions from them.

On February 23, 2007, Assembly Member Martin Garrick (R - San Diego) offered AB 1430, an amendment to sections of the Political Reform Act of 1974 that limits campaign contributions by political parties in local non-partisan elections. Currently, the Reform Act allows counties and cities to enact stronger limitations than those proposed by state law. Assembly Member Garrick proposed modifications would remove the power of local

San Diego was the first city founded in California, originally called San Miguel. It has some of the highest valued properties in the nation. Courtesy of the Library of Congress

governments to enact their measures and force them to comply with existing state law. On May 24, 2007, AB 1430 was voted on in the state assembly, passed with a unanimous vote of 77 to 0, and the bill has been passed on to the state senate. It should be pointed out that both Republicans and Democrats supported this bill.[15]

The annual National Cherry Blossom Festival commemorates the day in 1912 when Mayor Yukio Ozaki of Tokyo gave 3,000 cherry trees to the city of Washington, with the intent of nurturing Japan's relationship with the United States. This gift of giving was reciprocated when cuttings of the original trees went back to Japan after floods destroyed the maternal trees. The most recent exchange occurred in 1999 when a new generation of cuttings from a famous Japanese cherry tree (Gifu province) that was supposedly over 1500 years old, were planted in Washington. Courtesy of Jupiter Images.

How Do We Compare?
Japan and the United States

Japan is important in the study of comparative politics not only because of its economic and demographic size but also because it was the first non-Western country to achieve modernization. It has sometimes been seen as an example of development that has special relevance for the East and South Asian countries - and perhaps the world as well.

The Japanese case of modernization raises the question of the role of cultural, social, and political factors in the development of a country into self-sustaining industrial growth. Max Weber, the German social thinker, concentrated on discovering non-economic preconditions and accompaniments of modernization. His sociological works concentrated on the European examples that were familiar to him. For the field of modernization studies, Weber's specific findings or "answers" are today far less important than the questions he asked, at the beginning of this century, concerning the role of culture and social institutions in economic development. Today social theorists can "stand on the shoulders" of pioneers like Weber and see further across the horizon, so to speak.[16]

Japan is an archipelago of more than 3,000 islands, most of them very small. They stretch some 2,000 miles off the coast of northeast Asia. The four largest make up about 98 percent of the country's land area: Honshu (with Tokyo, the capital), is the largest. The three others are Hokkaido (in the north), Kyushu (in the south), and Shikoku (between Honshu and Kyushu). Japan's land area is about the same as that of California or one and one-half times larger than that of Britain. Japan's population numbers about 127 million, compared to the United States with 300 million. The only large and distinctive ethnic minority consists of about 600,000 Koreans, most of them laborers (or descended from laborers) who were brought to Japan before 1945, when Korea was a Japanese colony. The Japanese are known for having some of the longest life expectancies in the world. It is a rapidly aging population, however, because the low birth rate is not offset by immigration. Dominant religions in Japan are mainly Shinto and Buddhist practices. About 10 percent belong to other faiths, most of them being members of "new" religions that amalgamate elements of several faiths.

With the highly urbanized society and size of Japan's population, only 13 percent of the land is arable and it has very few natural resources. In order to meet the needs of their economy and demands of a growing population, Japan is dependent on imports of raw materials and energy, namely oil. Compared to the United States, Japan is the least self-sufficient among the world's major industrial centers in raw materials and fuels. With only about 2.4 % of the world's population, Japan until only recently accounted for just over 9 % of its gross national product (GNP). This put Japan in second place behind the U.S. in total gross domestic product. It usually ranks as the second largest trading partner of the United States (behind Canada).

Japan's Political History

Japan's modern history began with the Meiji Restoration of 1867-68 that came at the end of two and one-half centuries of the Tokugawa Shogunate (1603 to 1867). The shogunate had established a form of effective rule after a long period of civil violence on the islands. It has been called "centralized feudalism" - a carefully balanced system in which a shogun or military governor shared power with more than 250 feudal lords, who together controlled most of Japan. The system did not survive in its original form, but it left a centralized and hierarchical tradition that influenced and helped shape the rapid modernization that followed.

For centuries, Japan had closed itself off to much of the outside world. The external pressure on Japan to end its centuries-long isolation dates back to the end of the 18th century. But it was the American Commodore Perry's naval visit in 1853-54 that triggered the decision to "open up" the country to international trade and diplomacy. The "Meiji Restoration" began in 1868. It was not really a "restoration" of rule by an absolute emperor. Instead, it was the beginning of a new political era in which a powerful new ruling group (oligarchy) took over and deliberately guided the country toward modernization. The consequence was in many ways a societal transformation, which destroyed much of the feudal structure of Japan, created new centralized decision-making structures, introduced mass public education and modern technology, and established a professional bureaucracy.

Japan's modernization strategy of the 1870s and 1880s (and later) was based on a study of relevant American and European experience, with particular attention to the German example. However, the strategy produced a special Japanese hybrid, taking foreign concepts and incorporating them into the country's own traditions making them uniquely Japanese. Many observers stress the apparent ease with which the Japanese have engaged in the selective adoption and adaptation of foreign cultural elements, managing to infuse them into Japanese culture. This process appears to have begun long before the encounter with the West, for Japan had a long previous history of borrowing a great deal of its high culture and technical skills from China.

The rapid modernization that occurred during the 1860s resulted in an industrial economy, a modern legal and educational infrastructure, and a modern military. Having avoided domination by the European powers, Japan turned to imperial ventures against its neighbors. There were successful wars against China (1894-95) and Russia (1904-05), followed by the annexation of Taiwan, domination of Manchuria, and colonization of Korea (1905).

Issues For You
Artist's and musicians such as painter Vincent Van Gogh (*Japonaiserie: Oiran - after Kesaï Eisen*), musician/composers Gilbert & Sullivan (The Mikado), and later architect Frank Lloyd Wright (Hollyhock House in Los Angeles, CA and many other art media) were all influenced by the opening of international trade with Japan in the 1850's. Visit a museum and see how many different media you can spot that has a Japanese influence.[17]

The Meiji Constitution of 1889-1890 was the legal basis and framework of government and politics in Japan until 1945. It was not particularly conservative by the standards of the time, but it did contain a good many pre-democratic features. It reflected a balance of power between the imperial system and constitutional forces, partly inspired by Germany. The overriding motive was to establish a more effective central control and leadership rather than the introduction of democracy. Nevertheless, the system developed in an increasingly democratic direction until the early 1930s.

Diet –
Names for parliament in Japan and Finland.

Some observers have pointed to similarities with Imperial Germany, which had united in 1871. Thorstein Veblen analyzed Imperial Germany as an "industrialized feudal society," and Barrington Moore would later compare Imperial Germany with Imperial Japan in terms of their shared experience of what he examined as a top-down "conservative modernization."

The traditional-conservative nature of the Meiji Constitution may be seen in the limitations placed on the legal powers of the **Diet**, the almost total lack of local autonomy; the provisions for strong executive rule in emergency situations; and the failure to deal with a reliance on traditional loyalties in the Japanese social and political system.

On the other hand, the Meiji Constitution contained considerable concessions to democratic and liberal norms in the area of popular rights, representation, and greater civil freedoms. The lower house of parliament (the Diet) was elected (the House of Peers was appointed), and this lower house turned out to be more assertive than at first expected. It exercised considerable power over the budget, and it could initiate and pass legislation, levy taxes, and subject ministers to questioning. Once again, the similarities to pre-1914 Germany are indeed striking.

Altogether, the new political system contributed to larger changes in the social and political landscape of Japan. In the years that followed, the traditional clan loyalties decreased, making social hierarchy less rigid. The electorate expanded considerably, reaching universal male suffrage by 1925. The political process became more complex as well as more liberalized -- rather than remaining just a framework for the perpetuation of authoritarian rule in modern form.

The years after the adoption of the Meiji Constitution were ones of intense struggles for power between the ruling government leaders and the party leaders in the Diet. The parliamentary elite wanted to make the government more responsible to the Diet -- but the struggle can also be seen as part of a much broader struggle between the authoritarian and liberal elements in Japanese society. Although there were some outstanding liberal thinkers in Japan, there was no thorough liberal breakthrough in the socio-political realm. Instead, Imperial Japan (like Germany) experienced a major authoritarian resurgence in the early 1930s.

During the 1930s, Japan faced economic problems at home and abroad. Corruption irresponsibility in the Diet, plus the threat of a decline in its international standing caused Japan to turn away from its initial steps in a democratic direction. Military and ultranationalist forces rose, using terror and intimidation to drive the liberal forces back. The democratic institutions were fragile, and they now failed to survive the country's crisis - marked by plots, assassinations, revolts, and attacks on leading statesmen. The military became dominant and replaced the parliamentary form of rule in the early 1930s.

In 1937, Japan used military aggression against China in the pursuit of an East Asian empire several years before World War II. Its decision to enter Word War II in 1941 (by its attack on Pearl Harbor) turned out to be disastrous, bringing an enormous toll in human life, material goods, international respect, and civic rights and liberties. At the end of the war, Japan's authoritarian system was dismantled by the US occupation authorities, headed by General Douglas MacArthur. In 1947, they imposed a democratic constitutional reform.

The development of democracy in postwar Japan cannot be explained solely in terms of the imposition of a formal democratic framework by the U.S. after World War II. As in Germany, there was an indigenous Japanese tradition of legal rights and obligations on which to build. The postwar constitutional system appears to have worked quite well. Some possible reasons:

(1) While foreign-inspired, the constitution did build on previous Japanese practices. By redesigning the Meiji Constitution and preserving the institution of the emperor, the postwar constitution suggested some form of continuity, despite the sharp rupture with the immediate authoritarian past. Japanologists have pointed out that the new political institutions were in any case flexible enough to permit the continuation of Japanese emphasis on seniority, personal ties, clientelism, and even long-term dominance by one party within an overall setting that remains formally democratic.

(2) The new political system won broad support as it became linked to the rapid economic recovery of a country devastated by the war. In other words, the system seemed to pass the "pragmatic test" (it was seen to "work").

(3) Once again, the political system seems to reflect the skill of Japanese reformers who identify desirable features in other countries, "borrow" selectively from them, and then adapt the borrowings to the Japanese setting.

The 1947 Constitution introduced a parliamentary form of democracy. The Diet or Parliament is "highest organ of state power". In the first two decades, the Diet was dominated by a conservative majority, consisting of factions that tended to carry out the decisions reached by the cabinet or dominant party leaders. They united to become the Liberal Democratic Party in the mid-1950s, but the LDP retained a composite character as a factionally divided governing "party." The opposition parties had little chance to be effective and frequently resorted to rhetorical criticism without much hope (in contrast to Britain's adversarial parliamentary opposition) of eventually gaining power for themselves.

Japan's Political Institutions

The Japanese Parliament is bicameral, with both chambers directly elected. As is common outside the United States, one of the two chambers in the bicameral legislature is more powerful. That is, we are dealing with yet another case of asymmetrical bicameralism (unlike the U.S. with its "coequal" legislative chambers or symmetrical bicameralism). The House of Representatives, now 480 members, is both larger and more influential. The deputies are elected for four year terms. One of the institutional rules is that the House of Representatives can be dissolved; on average, the diet is dissolved every 2.5 years and it usually is averaging 30 month. The House of Councillors is smaller and less powerful. Its 252 members serve for six year terms, with half of them elected every three years. It cannot be dissolved early.

Factoid:
Acting as a global connection to Africa, Japan is one of the world's largest importers of ivory because of its value as a status symbol. This encourages illegal poaching in several African countries.

Issues For You
Compare Germany's experience with Japan's "economic miracle."

Observers report that it tends to have a somewhat longer view of things and shows more political independence than the House but, once again, the upper house exercises less influence.

The House of Representatives is given the final, decisive word on some important matters such as:

- it alone decides who will be prime minister;

- it alone can censure or terminate the current administration;

- it has the final word on non-financial legislation. When there are differences between the two houses, it can pass its own resolution a second time and if it receives a 2/3 majority then it becomes law;

- it also has the final word on budget measures and treaties - where the House of Representative's decision leads to automatic passage after 30 days.

- Finally, the government always has a great majority of its ministers from the House of Representatives - only about 3 of 20 cabinet seats are held by Councillors.

The Electoral System: The House of Representatives

The notorious old electoral system was based on the election of 512 members through a unique system of individual-candidate elections in 130 small multi-member districts. Each district had from 2 to 5 members. Voters had one vote and would choose among the individual party candidates, rather than follow a party list. That contributed to the already existing factional competition within the larger parties. A large party could be disadvantaged if it had a very strong candidate who attracted so many votes that it diluted the vote for the party's other candidates. Very small parties were unlikely to win representation in proportion to their electoral strength (as they would have under a proportional representation system), but they and medium-sized parties could hope to win some seats through skillful strategies. For example, a small party would normally present only one candidate in a multi-member district, and all its supporters would be encouraged to vote for that candidate. By contrast, a larger party could hope to win 2 or 3 seats and would therefore present more candidates. In addition, the electoral system showed a very strong bias in favor of rural district in lower house races.

Since 1996 the House of Representatives has been reduced to 480 members. It is now chosen by a combination of plurality elections (winner-take-all) in 300 single-member districts and a PR system that allocates 180 additional seats among the parties based on their relative strength among the voters. Reformers had hoped that the new system would produce a simpler, more cohesive party system. Until now, the multiparty system has persisted, partly because of the introduction of a PR element on the ballot that gives small parties a chance to win some seats and partly because some of the smaller parties are favored by a territorial concentration of their strength that makes it possible for them to win in some single-member districts as well.

The House of Councillors (Upper House) also uses a two-ballot system that combines proportional representation with party lists and single-member district plurality elections. There is some resemblance to the German system here, but the German system is more clearly shaped by the PR part of the ballot that determines the total number of seats a party will win.

FOR YOUR CONSIDERATION
JAPAN'S MINISTRY OF INTERNATIONAL TRADE AND INDUSTRY (1949 - 2001)

At the end of World War II, the Japanese economy was in the tank; more than half a century later, the Japanese economy is one of the strongest in the world. During the first 20 years following World War II, the Japanese economy made a rapid turnaround and began growing at staggering rates. What caused this Japanese "post-war economic miracle?"[18]

One of the major causes of this sensational turn of economic circumstances was the creation in 1949 of the Japanese Ministry of International Trade and Industry, or MITI. MITI had control over most of Japan's industry and also managed trade and tariffs, environment, and energy. This literally put MITI in control of Japan economically during its roughest period; MITI was seen as a sort of "invisible hand" guiding the Japanese economy.

As the agency in charge of restoring Japan's economy, MITI developed and implemented a wide variety of policies governing nearly every aspect of the economy, both domestically and internationally. Most of its policies were intended to foster domestic industrial growth while warding off international competition as long as possible; and indeed for many years, MITI was wildly successful in its efforts.

MITI helped coordinate information and technology sharing amongst Japanese companies, assuring that the companies would all flourish as well as having access to each other's innovations. While this would seem to be contradictory, for Japan it was not, as exemplified in their electronic technology sector (Sony and Toshiba for example) and in their automotive sector (Toyota and Honda, and many more).[19] In fact, this sharing has instead been beneficial to both the Japanese economy as well as for Japanese companies, and many of these companies remain at the forefront of technology and innovation worldwide today.

During the latter part of the 20th century, MITI was forced to incorporate open markets into its policies and also lost some of its control due to limitations imposed upon it by both the Japanese legislature (the National Diet) and the Japanese Prime Minister. Even with these limitations, MITI remained a guiding economic force in Japan until 2001. MITI formally died in 2001 and was reincarnated as METI, the Japanese Ministry of Economy, Trade, and Industry. Though METI is considered a government entity somewhat different from MITI, it is by and large just a product of reorganization; METI remains very similar to its predecessor in both scope and duty.

Economic and Social Changes in Japan

It is necessary to touch upon some social and economic changes that lie behind the formal political dislocations. The following account draws from a perceptive analysis written by William Dawkin for the Financial Times. Dawkin linked the recent political upheavals to Japan's longest economic downturn since the second world war. Like other observers, he stressed that although there are signs of recovery, the long and continuing recession has overturned several traditional assumptions about Japan's economic strength.

Unlike some shorter previous recessions, this one was at least partly caused by internal structural weakness rather than just external blows (like the rise in oil prices in the 1970s). The recovery will be weaker and slower than in the past. -- The long recession has uncovered a heavy over-capacity in what had been the leading sectors of economic growth in Japan, the auto and electronic industries. This constitutes a drag on the economy that may take years to correct. There are no obvious candidates to replace these industries as economic leaders in the new decade. Moreover, what had been a powerful financial system has also come under strain, as banks have been hit by a mountain of bad debt resulting from the unsustainable rise in asset prices in the late 1980s. In previous recessions, banks could be counted on to tide their customers through hard times and provide the funds needed to finance a recovery. This time, banks are letting shaky corporate customers go under in record numbers rather than risk additional bad loans.[20]

But there have also been external shocks to the Japanese economy. The overcapacity in some leading industries, puts the economy under enormous pressure to continue to restructure even as it suffers from recession. Until now, Japanese industry lags far behind its US competitors in restructuring, and even some European competitors have gone further. Moreover, the growing outward shift of production capacity to cheaper locations in south-east Asia has given rise to fears that the industrial base of Japan may be eroded.

Chapter Summary

In a perfect world, the way a government operates would not be dependent on who has the loudest voice, the most members, the most money, the best friends, or the most access. However, due to the nature of the game, the rulebook was slanted from the beginning when an interest group wrote up the nation's Constitution with only their own interests in mind. Ever since then, the public has been trying in various ways to find balance within the system. Interest groups use direct lobbying, or inside game tactics and indirect lobbying, or outside game activities. Grassroots activities and mobilization play important roles in calling attention to the causes of lesser-known or smaller interest groups. All interest groups raise funds or solicit donations from their members in order to support those candidates who believe in that particular interest groups' mission. As with most matters concerning money and candidates, regulation became necessary. Hard money is regulated while soft money is unregulated. Campaign finance reform issues are a thorn in the side of interest groups and politicians because they wish to maintain the power they have cultivated while public opinion shifts every time there is a scandal involving corrupt business practices.

In a democratic society, there will always be divisions between groups. Because resources are always limited, these groups are constantly competing for the maximum amount of amenities possible. In *The Federalist* No. 10, James Madison explained how factions are a necessary evil. Factions are basically the concept that we all have different pursuits. Building on this hypothesis gives cause for pluralism, a system in which groups compete for resources and try to meet their needs by interacting, negotiating, and reaching compromises. The problem with pluralism is that since the groups do not have the same access to representatives or financial resources, they are not always willing to negotiate for fear of weakening their position further. The only way to prevent interest groups from abusing their privileges is the call to action by citizens to hold their elected officials and the groups that support them accountable. This is the theme of this book; this is the essence of deliberative democracy. In the next chapter, we will evaluate the nations' first interest groups, political parties.

Key Terms:

Interest Group

Political Action Committees or PACs

Grassroots Organization

Get Out the Vote

Interest, Lobby, and Pressure Groups

Factions

Pluralism

Private Interest Group

Free Rider

Public Interest Group

Soft Money

Independent Expenditures

Hard Money

Iron Triangle

Pork Barrel

Diet

Websites:

Center for Responsive Politics (tracking money in campaigns):
www.opensecrets.org

Center for Responsive Politics
www.opensecrets.org/

EMILY's List
http://www.emilyslist.org/about/

Global Security
http://www.globalsecurity.org/intell/world/japan/miti.htm

Eventful – Life is short… make it Eventful!
http://eventful.com/performers/P0-001-000016098-5

U.S. Senator John McCain
http://mccain.senate.gov/about/index.cfm?ID=10

The Pew Forum on Religion & Public Life
http://pewforum.org/religion-politics/

Friends of Hollyhock House
http://www.hollyhockhouse.net/index.htm

The Japanese Economy (student project for "East Asia: An Introduction,"
an Indiana University undergraduate survey)
http://www.indiana.edu/~ealc100/Group8/miti/miti.html

John McCain
http://www.johnmccain.com/About/johnmccain.htm

Introduction to METI
http://www.meti.go.jp/english/aboutmeti/data/a320001e.html

The Moral Majority Coalition
http://www.moralmajority.us

Center for Media and Democracy
http://www.sourcewatch.org/index.php?title=Moral_Majority

The Vincent Van Gogh Gallery
http://www.vggallery.com/misc/search_frame.htm

WCSH Portland
http://www.wcsh6.com/news/article.aspx?storyid=57977

National Organization for Women
www.now.org

National Rifle Association
http://www.nra.org/

Project VoteSmart
www.vote-smart.org/

California Sites

California Chamber of Commerce
www.calchamber.com

California State Legislature – Bill Information
http://www.legislature.ca.gov/the_state_legislature/bill_information/bill_information.html

Chicano/Latino Net
www.clnet.ucr.edu

Humboldt State University, interactive atlas of California
http://humboldt.edu/~cga/calatlas

California Schools Employee Association
http://pub.csea.com/cseahome/

KCET – local Public Broadcasting System station
http://www.pbs.org/newshour/bb/politics/july-dec04/religion_10-25.html

News Release – California Secretary of State Bruce McPherson
http://www.sos.ca.gov/executive/press_releases/2006/06_088.pdf

League of Women Voters of California
www.ca.lwv.org

This page left blank intentionally.

Get It On!
(1971) This old-fashioned poster was an advertisement
for the College Republican National Committee.

Courtesy of the Library of Congress

CHAPTER 7

POLITICAL PARTIES

CHAPTER OUTLINE

- DEMOCRACY AND ACTION –
  HAS THE RELIGIOUS RIGHT TAKEN
  OVER THE REPUBLICAN PARTY?

- WHAT ARE POLITICAL PARTIES?

- THE ROLE OF POLITICAL PARTIES

- THE HISTORY OF THE
  TWO-PARTY SYSTEM IN AMERICA
  ALIGNMENTS AND REALIGNMENTS

- AMERICAN THIRD PARTIES

- PARTY ORGANIZATION

- CALIFORNIA'S POLITICAL PARTIES –

- PAST AND PRESENT

- HOW DO WE COMPARE?
  MEXICO AND THE UNITED STATES

Democracy and Action - Has the Religious Right taken over the Republican Party?

Evangelicals –
Christians who emphasize salvation by faith in the atoning death and resurrection of Jesus Christ through "choosing Jesus as personal Lord and Savior"; also professes to the authority of Scripture and the importance of preaching the Gospel of Christ and converting others to repent and believe as they do.

Sprinkled throughout American history, there are references to religion and faith, such as the inclusion of "In God We Trust" on our paper money and notably the adding of "Under God" to our Pledge of Allegiance in 1954 after lobbying by traditional Christian groups. Such groups, like the Knights of Columbus, were not originally meant to be political groups. Nevertheless, political religious groups came about in the late 1970s.

The very first political Christian group to come on the scene was the Christian Voice. It was founded in 1978; among its goals was to cultivate influence in federal and state governments in order to promote a like-minded moral and value-based agenda. Because the group consisted of mainly **evangelical** voters who tended to vote conservative and therefore Republican, this was the beginning of the rise of the Religious Right to political prominence in the Republican Party.[1]

Over the past few decades, several right wing Christian groups have been created; among the most notable are the Moral Majority and the Christian Coalition of America, introduced in chapter 6. Besides recruiting voters and mounting extensive Get-Out-The-Vote efforts on election days, these groups have massive lobbying operations around the country. Among the core issues they advocate are: achieving the overturn of the 1973 Roe v Wade decision that federally legalized abortion; prevention of laws giving traditional rights such as marriage to homosexuals; encouragement of public support for traditional family values and the curbing of media that is at odds with that vision; and the appointment of conservative judges to arbitrate challenges to any such laws that make it into the books.

President Ronald Reagan in the Oval Office, speaking with Republican Senator Alfonse D'Amato (R-NY). Courtesy of the Library of Congress

Beginning with the presidency of Ronald Reagan, conservative Christian groups established a special relationship with the Republican Party.[2] Jerry Falwell, one of the nation's leading evangelicals, credits Reagan for opening doors to Christian groups after having been shut out by previous administrations. Reagan helped the Christian right realize one of their main goals; the conservatism of the Supreme Court today began with Reagan's appointments of conservative justices during the 1980s.[3]

The Republican Party hit a roadblock during the 1990s with the election and reelection of then Governor of Arkansas, Bill Clinton, a Democrat. But with news of the Monica Lewinsky affair and the subsequent talk of impeachment hearings, the Christian right, now a large and formidable voice within the Republican Party, emitted a sharp rallying cry. They were able to help cement the Republican Party's control of both houses of Congress; that hold would continue but for one small aberration, for another eight years.

In the year 2000, the Religious right found in Republican candidate George W. Bush a champion being that he is a self-avowed born again Christian. Believing that he was the key to fulfilling their long hoped for goals, they mobilized a notable voter turnout effort; a whopping 56 percent of voters in November 2000 who stated that they were regular churchgoers voted for him; in November 2004, that number increased to 63 percent.

Bush indeed was a proponent for their causes. In the first years of his presidency, he banned almost all stem-cell research (considered a right-to-life issue for the right); he also enacted a faith-based initiative in which religious outfits, normally forbidden to receive tax dollars, began to receive government money to support their charitable work. Bush's two Supreme Court appointments also pleased the Christian right, and made the Court the furthest right it has ever been. But even the level of support the Christian right received from Bush was not enough to be the sustaining lifeblood of the Republican Party.[4]

Support from within the Republican Party began showing strain in early 2006. In spite of the ascendance of Samuel Alito, Jr. – a very conservative justice - to the Supreme Court, 2006 was shaping up to be a bell weather election year. One of the problems came with the lack of general public support for the platform of the Christian right; many in the general public now viewed stem-cell research as cutting edge science necessary to find cures for many diseases. Furthermore, most of the mainstream public was not terribly interested in the topics of gay marriage and indecency in the media. These things were duly noted by Republicans, many of whom were going to be up for reelection in November 2006 and who were already bogged down with the issue of the war in Iraq.

Support for the Republican Party amongst members of the Christian right also had begun to wane by this time. Several of Bush's seemingly religious based initiatives had begun coming under fire with no end in sight. And even though two conservative justices were appointed to the Supreme Court, Roe v Wade was still the law of the land and the Court had ruled in favor of the separation of church and state within one vote, a couple of times. So when many Republican politicians began backing away from the Christian right's bread and butter issues, many among the Christian right rank-and-file became disenchanted with the Party. They illustrated this disappointment by largely staying home in November 2006, an election in which the Democratic Party took control of both houses of Congress.

So is this the death knell of the special relationship between the Religious right and the Republican Party? It may be, in that many issues that directly affect the general populace seem to be drowning out concern for the monotonous morality issues supported by the Christian right. Also, the Democratic Party has made some inroads into breaking up the monopoly the Republican Party enjoyed with Christian groups for more than 20 years. In addition, the Republican Party is undergoing an examination of what their priorities truly are: are they more religiously conservative or more traditionally conservative? Whether or not the Religious right retains its special place in the Republican Party will play out with each changing of the guard at the White House.

What Are Political Parties?

*"There are many men of principle in both parties in America,
but there is no party of priniciple – Alexis de Tocqueville*

Many Americans don't feel the need to vote because they believe that their votes don't count. In a roundabout way, since our votes are applied toward an electoral college and not directly to the candidate, this can be construed as truth. However, for the most part, every vote is ultimately needed. In local elections the difference between winning and losing could be that handful of people who decided not to vote. Think back to the Presidential Election of 2000. There were a number of citizens who were upset with Ralph Nader, the Green Party candidate, and there were other issues with the ballots. But this begs the question - how many people who stayed home on Election Day would have preferred Vice-President Al Gore over Governor George Bush? Statistics suggest at least 400. This would have been enough to change the course of humanitarian movements, rising environmental concerns, medical research, and domestic and foreign policy from 2000 - 2004. In 2004, the voter turnout of evangelical Christians illustrated the power of voting for their cause. This is a prime example of the power of political parties and how they resemble factions. Just like interest groups, political parties show support for their candidates by raising money and organizing events. Organizing their membership to "Get Out the Vote" is one way to insure popular sovereignty and majority rule works.

Over the years, political parties have come and gone but the Republicans and Democrats have been the two dominant parties for over a century and a half. This shows how they have been able to adapt to the demands of the public during changing times. Because of the support from their members, political parties are able to gain control of government and pursue the policies they wish to see implemented. Today, with the high availability of information coupled with a growing distrust of government, both parties are facing difficulties in maintaining their base. Within the last few decades, both Democrats and Republicans have seen major alignment shifts. The Democrats during the 1990s tried to move toward the center. In doing so they alienated their more liberal flank. The Republicans moving towards the Christian right lost most of their more moderate and fiscal conservatives. Some political observers have stated that in addition to alienating the base of their parties, they are also losing touch with the American people. Within this chapter we will look at the ever-changing spectrum of political parties and their rise to significance - from the perspective of their elite beginnings to their role in the future of American politics. After developing an understanding of political parties at the national level, we'll look at the parties at the state and local levels by shifting the focus to California. We will then conclude the chapter by heading "south of the border, down Mexico way"[5] and examine the unique history of Mexican political parties.

The Role of Political Parties

Simply put, **political parties** are organizations that try to win control of government by electing their representatives to office. In representative democracies, like the United States, parties organize and recruit candidates; they then run their candidates for office in elections. Once their candidates are in office, the parties continue to invest time organizing and coordinating activities, further refining the **party platform**.

Here is a breakdown of the role of political parties in the United States:

To help people understand politics. Party identification helps individuals understand the main position of their parties. Their party's views on important issues help people make sense of the political process. Many individuals may not have the time or access to all of the resources they may need to make informed decisions when voting. But, by identifying with a political party, individuals may agree with the majority of the party's positions and rely on them for voting information.

To create a functional government. The framers intentionally created a maze to prevent rapid change. Although the system of checks and balances and separation of powers holds tyranny at bay, it adds to endless bureaucratic red tape, even today. If a single party is able to gain control of one of both houses in Congress and the executive branch, they could, theoretically, coordinate their efforts to pass legislation that benefits the public.

To insure representatives' response. Political parties can recruit candidates who will listen to their constituents during their time in office. This will allow government to identify the people's needs. In addition, the election process can enable voters to hold their representatives accountable for their job performance.

To be as inclusive as possible. Political parties can add balance to representative democracy by including as many groups of people as possible; the more inclusive they are the stronger the voice of democracy is. They can also form small coalitions to safeguard the smaller groups' place in the political process. When candidates run for office they must speak to the needs of all of the groups and once in office they must do their best to fulfill the needs of the voters. By attracting more diverse groups, parties can prevent majority tyranny by adding universally worded sections into the party platform to accommodate all groups and later implement these additions when their candidates are elected into office.

As one can surmise, political parties can secure democratic values by being inclusive, holding representatives accountable, and reaching out to the voters. In turn, popular sovereignty is maintained through elections, political equality fostered through cultivation of relationships with minority groups, and political liberty achieved through strengthening individual weaker voices, and nurturing opportunities to speak.

Political Parties –
Organizations that exist to allow like-minded members of the population to group together and strengthen their individual voices into a common cause or political ideology; their main goals include promoting individual candidates and influencing government policy.

Party Platform –
A party's statement of its positions on the issues of the day.

FOR YOUR CONSIDERATION
MULTIPARTY SYSTEMS VERSUS TWO-PARTY SYSTEMS

There are several political parties in the United States, which may make it seem like a multiparty system. In reality, however, it is not - the U.S. is considered a two-party system. Multiparty systems, the most common form of political party systems, exist throughout the world and are mostly known for their coalition-style governments. Systems where three or more parties have the possibility of gaining power in an election are considered multiparty systems. These systems are usually found in parliamentary governments, where proportional representation is the norm. Seats tend to be divided among several parties differing in size, forcing parties to create coalition governments. Because of the nature of multiparty systems, proponents tout its ability to provide for a wider variation of political beliefs.

In two-party systems like the United States, power shifts back and forth between the two major parties. The strength of a two-party system lay in its ability to avoid a fate where there are too many parties causing too much fragmentation, each party with lesser and lesser influence over governmental affairs. The weaknesses of two-party systems lay in the fact that with only two dominant parties, lack of diversity creates limitations in the political process.

Because the founding fathers set up our government with separate branches, often, one party has control of one branch of government while the other party controls another. This may cause partisan gridlock, if neither side wants to compromise and government may come to a standstill. However, the two-party system has worked fairly well for us for some 200 years.

So, as you can see, each type of party system has its benefits and its problems. Recently, some third party options have gained a bit of traction here in the United States. The thing to watch for is whether the two-party system will maintain its traditional structure or will a multiparty system possibly serve us better in the future?[6]

Senator Joe McCarthy (R-WI) portrayed in an internal brawl with
the Eisenhower administration, while the Democrats egg them on.
Courtesy of the Library of Congress.

The History of the Two-Party System in America Alignments and Realignments

When examining the history of political parties in the United States, one begins to see the dominance of two parties with smaller third parties sprinkled about. Why is this? Simply put, it's the rules of the game that dictate it. Most democratic governments, with the exception of the United Kingdom, have a multiparty system because their rule book is framed by a parliamentary system, which encourages third party activity and coalition building, as in the case of Germany. The United States has seen the two major parties, Democrat and Republican, since 1836. Minor third parties, such as the Green Party (also called the "Greens"), tend to be single issue parties that do better at the state and local levels. In 2007, the highest ranking office holder from the Green's is Daniel Brezenoff, U.S. Representative from California. Greens also are successful in the local elections for city council or school boards.[7]

Within the two major parties in the U.S., constant evolution is quite evident. The system has had six major periods of two-party stability since our founding. Each period has lasted on average 40 years. In between these six periods, we can identify periods of **realignment**. Political observers have identified two major periods of realignment in American politics: 1896 and 1932. Some have stated that we may be at the dawning of another important era.

Realignment – The process by which one party takes the place of another as the dominant party in a political system.

Election of 1800 – The first election in world history in which one party (the Federalist Party of John Adams) willingly gave up power because of a lost election to another party (the Republican party of Thomas Jefferson) without bloodshed.

The First Party System: 1790's-1820

From the very beginning, political parties were part of the process. The very first party created was the Federalist Party by Alexander Hamilton. After the struggle for ratification of the Constitution, Hamilton wanted to make sure that the government would perform the tasks that were set forth. The opposing side was led by Thomas Jefferson and James Madison. They called their group the Republicans but the Federalists referred to them as the Democratic Republicans. The two groups were divided on domestic issues, such as the national bank and foreign policy. Today, the Democratic Party is the direct descendant of the Democratic Republicans, making it the oldest political party in the world.

The supporters of the Federalists were the same groups who supported the ratification of the Constitution, mainly wealthy urban individuals. The same holds true for the Democratic Republicans. Their support came from rural areas, as well as those individuals that preferred stronger states' rights. The elections of 1789 and 1792 went according to the rules. George Washington became the first president of the United States selected by the electoral college. When Washington decided not to seek a third term in office, political tension emerged.

The Federalists and John Adams, stood off against Thomas Jefferson of the Democratic Republicans in the elections of 1796 and 1800. The **election of 1800** was the first time in modern history that power shifted between two opposing forces without bloodshed or violence. This election was also important because of the impact these fledgling political parties played. All of the electors in the electoral college who supported Jefferson followed their instructions and voted for both Jefferson and Aaron Burr. This caused a tie in the electoral college, which meant that the decision would have to be sent to the House of Representatives, as required by the Constitution. The problems that ensued gave way to the adoption of the Twelfth Amendment, which requires separate votes by the electors for the President and Vice President.

By 1804, it became apparent that the Federalists were losing support and the conflict came to a head with the War of 1812 when they showed sympathies for Britain and became alienated from the middle and lower classes. By 1816, the Federalist Party had come to an end, giving rise to the "Era of Good Feelings" and a one party system.

Factoid:
The term Whigs is possibly derived from *whiggamore*, which is a member of a body of 17th century Scottish Presbyterian rebels.

The Second Party System: 1820-1865

The Era of Good Feelings ended in the early 1820s and a new two-party system began with the disputed presidential election of 1824. In the presidential election of 1824, Andrew Jackson won a plurality of both the electoral college and popular votes but did not receive the majority. Just like the election of 1800, the election went to the House of Representatives who selected John Quincy Adams as President. Those who supported Jackson formed a new opposition party called the Democratic Party. Adams and House Speaker Henry Clay created the Whig Party.

After the election of 1824 was supposedly robbed from Jackson, he and his supporters began a grassroots movement to prepare for the next election. Jackson's popular movement secured his presidential victory in 1828. With their victory, the Jacksonian Democrats had a renewed verve to restore the egalitarian principles of Jefferson. The Democrats drew their support from urban workers from the western states and non-slaveholders from the south. Keeping with democratic principles, in 1832 the party selected Jackson to run for a second-term at a national convention. The delegates were chosen by local party members who, in turn, selected the candidate by a two-thirds vote. In addition, they adopted a statement of party principles, or a party platform, which helped engender a feeling of solidarity and excitement amongst party members. After President Jackson won a second term, one of his first actions was an attempt to take down the national bank. His rationale was that the bank served as a mechanism for protecting the wealthy instead of the general good of the public. Business interests along with slave owners in the south joined forces and created the Whig party and, just like the Federalists before them, supported an active federal government. This spawned an intense competition between the two parties.

Within a few years, the Whig party dissolved over the issue of slavery. The Supreme Court's Dred Scott ruling along with denying African Americans the rights of citizenship added to the tension. In 1854, those who opposed slavery decided to unite and form the Republican Party. The new party attracted former Whigs, anti-slavery Democrats, and other groups, such as the Free-Soilers, who opposed the expansion of slavery into California and other western territories. The new Republican Party's first presidential candidate was John Frémont, in 1856. The Democrats sponsored James Buchanan and won. But in 1860, the Democrats could not agree on whom to run against Republican Abraham Lincoln. In the end, the Democrats split their ticket by having each wing of the party nominate their own candidate. The Civil War created a divided nation and ushered in a new generation of political parties.

The Third Party System: 1865-1896

After the Civil War and Reconstruction, southern states were allowed to rejoin the Union. The two dominant parties, the Republicans and the Democrats, were in balance at the national level from 1876 to 1896. The Democratic Party, despite being weakened from supporting the Confederacy, was able to win the presidency for 8 of 20 years, the Senate for 6 years, and the House for 14 years. Each party controlled different parts of the nation. The Democrats held their base in the South and Midwest, primarily among agricultural rural voters. The Republicans moved from a popular party to become the party of business, the middle class, and African-Americans.

The Fourth Party System: 1896-1932

Primary System – The system of nominating candidates in which voters in the state make the choice by casting ballots.

With the onset of the industrial revolution in the late nineteenth century came much social and political turmoil. Third parties grew out of protest movements against the social injustices they were witnessing. The Populist Party was one of the better

The charismatic speaker Bryan at a campaign rally, October 3, 1896. Courtesy of the Library of Congress.

known third parties of the time. At the height of its political power the Populist Party won 8.5 percent of the total vote in the election of 1892, four states in the electoral college, 8 governorships and 8 state legislatures. In 1896, the Populist Party joined with the Democratic Party and nominated the charismatic orator William Jennings Bryan for president. With his appeals to aid debtors with cheaper currency, Bryan's encouragement of blacks and whites, farmers, and labor unionists to participate proved too much for many businesses. Many conservatives, fearing a populist victory, began supporting the Republican candidate, William McKinley. McKinley's victory brought the Populist Party to its demise. In doing so, it unified the long-term shift in Democratic and Republican bases. The Republicans secured the North and West, while Democrats maintained their influence in the South.

Progressives and reformers argued that the process of nominating candidates should be shifted from the leaders, or party bosses, to the voters through a **primary system**. Between 1896 and 1932, Woodrow Wilson was the only Democrat to win the presidency most likely because Theodore Roosevelt split the Republican vote. With the industrial revolution in full swing, the United States was well on its way to becoming a major world power. Republican victories were consistent for the first part of the twentieth century. This came to an end with the Great Depression of 1932, which brought on the next shift in political power and realignment in party identification.

FOR YOUR CONSIDERATION
FROM O TO Z

First published in 1900, the book *The Wonderful Wizard of Oz* by Lyman Frank Baum (1856-1919) has become a well-loved children's classic for generations of families. The subsequent hit movie of the same name produced nearly 40 years later featuring the young Judy Garland, is more than just a poppy-induced fantasy. Many books and articles have been written analyzing the allegory in a political and economical context over the years. The first to do so was high school history teacher, Henry Littlefield, in 1964. The main gist of Littlefield's claims suggest that Baum's *Oz* is a tale that embodies the plight of farmers and their pleas to the government to coin more silver in order to provide debt relief. After the Civil War, the American economy was in turmoil, especially for farmers who had been enduring deflation (falling prices) for several decades.

Courtesy of the Library of Congress.

Consider the yellow brick road (gold), Dorothy's silver shoes, and the Emerald City, the political nucleus of *Oz*. Incidentally, in the original story, Dorothy's shoes were actually silver, which turns out to be an important facet to these analogies. The movie featured "ruby red slippers" instead of silver because silver does not show up very well on film. Extending the symbolism further, the story begins on a farm where Dorothy lives with her aunt and uncle, suggesting that she is there without her parents. So, she is staying with them as they eke out a modest living and homestead during hard times. The dusty sepia tones of the first few minutes of the film swirl into the main agent that propels the story, the cyclone. Cyclones were referred to as an icon of the "free-silver" movement, which was led by the "silver-tongued orator", William Jennings Bryan. The following characters that Dorothy encounters have been interpreted in the following manner. The scarecrow represents the dull-minded farmer. He wishes to have a brain, which implies that farmers were viewed as slow and responsible for their own ruin. The man made of tin whose joints became rusty and stiff represents industrial workers. He wanted a heart, embodying the idea that industrialization

FOR YOUR CONSIDERATION
FROM O TO Z

isolates humans and desensitizes them. A cowardly lion jumps out at them, trying to scare them, but alas, he has no courage. This cowardice paralleled the same criticism that William Jennings Bryan received because of his opposition to the so-called sensationalized Spanish-American War (see 'yellow journalism' in chapter 4).

The symbolic analysis does not stop at explaining the main characters alone. Dorothy accidentally kills the Wicked Witch of the East, who represents Wall Street and business conglomerates. Once the troop encounters the wizard, he charges Dorothy to hand the same fate to the Wicked Witch of the West, the sister of the East Witch. The West Witch is thought to personify catastrophic acts of nature, such as drought. The topography of the west is such that drought is a common challenge of the climate and the only way to tame this is with water – hence the fatal bucket full of water that leads to the Wicked Witch of the West's melting demise.[8] This act of defeating the leader of the evil forces in *Oz* causes the flight of her Winged Monkeys, namely, Native Americans. The idea behind this is that once tamed or civilized the Plains Indians will be set free from their savage ways. This was an acerbic commentary on the horrendous treatment that the Native Americans received at Wounded Knee and on the reservations.

Factoid:
When L. Frank Baum was pondering a title for his first published children's story, his eyes searched around the room and they finally fell upon his filing cabinets. On the first drawer, "A to M"; on the second, "O to Z". The second file won out and a legendary fantasy land came to life

Finally, Glinda the Good Witch grants Dorothy's transport home, symbolizing Bryan's supporters, the dependable southern Democrats. While all of the above is one man's astute interpretation, it is just that – just an interpretation that may or may not have been Baum's intent. On the final leg of her unwanted excursion, Dorothy is seen clicking her magic slippers together and repeating the mantra, "There's no place like home," suggesting that we needn't look far for the solutions to life's challenges. The story ends with Dorothy back home, alive and safe and surrounded by the characters that joined her on her journey 'into the woods' (that's another story); they were actually people she already knew and loved. Unlike the fate of the struggling farmers and the free-silver movement, for Dorothy and her dog Toto it was all just a terrible dream.

The Fifth Party System: 1932-1968

By the middle of 1932, it was apparent that the Depression was going to hit Americans hard. It left millions of people without work and desolate, with no

Some southern Democrats felt that it was difficult to find common ground with the liberal wing of the Democratic party at the Democratic National Convention held in Chicago, in 1956. Copyright © 1955 by Art Wood. Reprinted with permission.

promise of economic relief from the states. President Herbert Hoover tried to comfort Americans, saying that prosperity was within reach – they simply had to trust him. But, Hoover's staunch subscription to the status quo meant that balancing the budget and offering no government handouts won out. While Hoover's hand was being played out, New York Governor Franklin Delano Roosevelt enthusiastically accepted the presidential nomination of the Democratic Party. He said, "I pledge you, I pledge myself, to a new deal for the American people"; on November 8, 1932, Governor Roosevelt was given the opportunity to honor that pledge. Roosevelt accomplished a landslide victory, winning a 472 to 59 electoral college majority and the popular vote of 22,809,638 to 15,758,901.

New Deal Coalition –
Brought together by Franklin Roosevelt in 1932, the informal electoral alliance of working-class ethnic groups (Catholics, Jews, urban dwellers, racial minorities, and the South) that was the basis of the Democratic party dominance of American politics from the New Deal to the early 1970s.

New Deal –
The programs of the administration of President Franklin D. Roosevelt.

Largely responsible for Roosevelt's successful campaign, the **New Deal Coalition** was an alliance of laborers, Catholics, Jews, unionists, farmers, urbanites, whites, southerners, and blacks. The New Deal coalition supported an expansion of federal government powers and responsibilities in social security, welfare, agricultural subsidies, and regulation for businesses. The **New Deal** allowed the Democrats to dominate national politics from 1932 to 1968. Just like years before, only one Republican became president during this period, Dwight Eisenhower. Every Democratic President expanded on the New Deal. President Truman desegregated the military, President Kennedy expanded federal programs such as NASA, and President Johnson implemented the "Great Society." With the war in Vietnam going poorly, the election of 1968 heralded in a new epoch led by conservative Richard Nixon. Nixon had beat Vice President Hubert H. Humphrey, because of a split in the Democratic Party allowing the Republicans to take control of the White House.

The Sixth Party System: 1968-Present

With the presidential election of 1968 came the end of the New Deal Coalition and Republican domination of presidential elections, in which they have won seven out of the last ten. The two Democratic presidents were southerners and were brought in from the right wing of the party. Despite this dominance, scholars have been unwilling to call this period a realignment. Regardless of the attempts to deconstruct the programs of the New Deal and Great Society, all of the Republican presidents have failed to do so. They have been able to make adjustments but still have had to deal with a Democratic Congress. The Democrats retained majority control of the U.S. House of Representatives from January 1955 to January 1995. Previous realignments have been with the opposition party taking control of Congress, the presidency, and the majority of state governments. Republicans remained the minority party in state and local elections throughout the 1960s and 1970s; however, there are signs that partisanship was fluctuating. After losing the presidency in 1992, a couple years later, the Republicans took control of both houses of Congress for the first time in forty years. They held control in both houses until 2001 when Senator Jim Jeffords (R-VT) was adamantly opposed to some of the changes being proposed by the Bush administration in education and other domestic policies. Changing his party affiliation from Republican to Independent, Jeffords began voting with the Democrats, blocking Republican control of the Senate until the election in 2002. At the state level, the elections of 1998 and 2000 were varied. Moderate Republicans won the governorships of twenty-three of the thirty-four races in 2000. In 2002, the Democratic Party took three governorships, in Pennsylvania, Michigan, and Illinois. The 2004 gubernatorial races maintained the two-party rivalry with the Democrats winning six races and Republicans winning five. The Republicans also gained four additional seats in the Senate, increasing their dominance to a 55–44 margin over the Democrats. The 2006 midterm elections saw another major change. The Democrats took control of Congress and gave the country its first female Speaker of the House, Nancy Pelosi (D-CA).

Profiles in Politics
Barry Goldwater (1909-1998)

Leader of the modern conservative movement and Presidential candidate in 1964, Barry Goldwater.
Courtesy of the Library of Congress

Long considered the "father of modern-day conservatism," the legacy of Barry Goldwater's political career still has an immense impact on the Republican Party and conservatism in general.

Barry Morris Goldwater, born in Phoenix, Arizona in 1909, was meant for a life of public service. After working for a little more than a decade in his family's business, he enlisted in the service with America's entry into World War II and ended up serving almost three decades in various branches of the military. He retired from the service in 1967 after achieving the rank of major general in the Air Force.[9]

In addition to spending a career in the military, Goldwater also served an entire career's worth of time in Congress as well. He was elected to the Senate in 1952, in an almost unbelievable victory over the then Senate Majority Leader. In his first years in the Senate, Goldwater became well known for his conservative values; he believed in a strong national defense policy and an economy unregulated by government.

In 1964, he decided not to seek reelection and instead decided to run for president. This national platform gave rise to a new conservative movement, and Goldwater's Republican supporters became forever known as "Goldwater Republicans."[10] The difference between a Goldwater Republican and a Republican of the 2000s is best described with the words of Goldwater himself. In 1964, he predicted that his conservative values would be considered very liberal in the not too distant future. His position on same-sex relationships, abortion, and the role of religion in politics is reflected in his main modus operandi - that government should not interfere in the personal lives of its citizens. Because of his staunch advocacy of strict, secular conservative values, he is considered the father of that movement; a movement that is credited for changing the face of the Republican Party. Even though Goldwater was instrumental in guiding the Republican Party, he was not happy with the flirting that presidential candidate Ronald Reagan, who considered himself to be a Goldwater conservative, carried on with the religious right majority. This irked the Senator to no end. Despite Goldwater's aversion to Reagan's strong feelings about mixing his religion with politics, Reagan still won the presidency in 1980.

Profiles in Politics
Barry Goldwater (1909-1998)

Senator Goldwater lost the presidential election in 1964 by a large margin to Lyndon Johnson, in spite of the new movement. The now infamous "Daisy" ad is credited with giving Johnson the boost he needed to win (first discussed in chapter 4 on the Media). To review, the ad played upon Goldwater's call for an aggressive defense policy and the fear that such aggressiveness would lead to nuclear war. The ad featured a little girl picking off and counting the petals of a daisy, which then segues into a military countdown; as the camera moves in close to the girls face, a mushroom cloud is seen reflected in her eye. This ad will forever be associated with Goldwater's presidential election loss.[11]

Though his run for the presidency was not successful, in 1968 Goldwater again ran for the Senate and after winning, he served in that body until he retired in 1987. He was viewed as a very open, honest, and decent man who earned the respect of his party as well as that of his colleagues. The conservative movement Goldwater is credited with started fading with the rise of the religious right. In light of the "Pastor-in-Chief'", President Bush's ratings plummeting with the popularity of the Iraq war, there is a renewed push by the moderate members of the Republican Party to return to its conservative roots that Barry Goldwater so passionately advocated.

American Third Parties

Sometimes called minor parties, third parties are exactly as the label describes – having a minor role in policy-making, less of a role in the United States than in any other democratic country. The only minor party to replace a majority party has been the Republicans. Third parties usually don't win more than 10 percent of the popular vote during a presidential election and they are also usually single issue parties. These offshoots of parties may not seem influential at first glance but they are still large enough to be noticed at protests, in state and local elections, and in drawing debate on issues that the major parties wouldn't touch without being pushed to, especially during a presidential election year.

Issues For You

Can you think of several reasons why voters would split their votes for opposing parties?

President Clinton was able to draw voters from third parties because of his ability to incorporate their concerns into his policy positions.
© Jose Gil, 2007.
Used under License from Shutterstock, Inc.

Third parties share some of the following characteristics:

They are protest parties. When the two dominant parties aren't paying attention to the issues that are important to the voters, there is an increase in third parties, such as the Populist Party, the Bull Moose, the Green Party, and in the 1990s, the Reform Party.

Third parties have ideological differences with the major parties. There is a wide variety of ideological parties in the United States. Two examples are the Socialists who prefer a more egalitarian society than the Democrats or Republicans, and the Libertarian Party, which wants to maximize their freedoms in all aspects with no interference from the government.

Third parties aid our political process. By bringing up issues that tend to be ignored by the Democrats and Republicans, they are able to generate some public awareness to the point that their issues are co-opted by the major parties. Take for example the eccentric Ross Perot and his demands for a balanced budget in his 1992 presidential campaign. He was able to force the Presidential candidates to address this issue and make it part of their party platform and campaign strategy. Third parties can also change the outcome of a presidential election. Some examples of split-ticket situations are Theodore Roosevelt's split with the Republicans which allowed for Woodrow Wilson to win in 1912; Ross Perot did the same in 1992, allowing Bill Clinton to defeat President George H. Bush; and Ralph Nader split the Democratic vote in Florida giving George W. Bush Florida's electoral votes in 2000.

Party Organization

Even though political parties are national organizations they are still somewhat decentralized institutions. Power is from the bottom up beginning at the local level and up through the state political structure and finally to the national level with the committees and conventions. In addition, parties act as grassroots organizers at the local, county, and state levels. The local party organization is the point of entry for citizens who wish to participate in the political process by being a volunteer, lead contact, or in some cases, even run for office. Each local party is dependent on the community for its membership. In areas where the party is strong there is an abundance of faithful constituents who are willing to act as precinct captains, coordinators, administrative assistants, and attendees at state conventions. In areas where political involvement is low, the party structures are skeletal in nature, with many vacant posts or the same small bunch of the party faithful trying to keep the organization alive. On occasion, the state parties will send activists into the area to try and revitalize the membership but mainly they depend on the local members for this.

Machine Politics – An organizational style of local politics in which party bosses traded jobs, money, and favors for votes and campaign support.

Local parties can energize the base unlike the national party. Local parties have a higher interaction with members and their platforms are founded on important local issues. Local parties are also highly cost effective; they can accomplish their jobs without seeking huge donations because they have greater access to volunteers. Political activists are a key component in a democracy. They influence the party platform and the politician's actions. It should be noted that party activists are different from the rest of the population. They tend to be wealthier, more educated, and usually come from families that are politically connected or active. Despite that party activists are different from the rest of the population; reform within the party structure has produced a more demographically representative group. Given that the parties operate at the local and state level, the state organizations differ greatly from each other. All party organizations have several jobs: facilitate and provide electoral college votes, raise funds, recruit candidates, and develop campaign strategies. State parties work closely with their state governments to coordinate primaries or caucuses for presidential candidates.

History of Modern Political Parties

From the nineteenth century to the middle of the twentieth century, political parties were considered to be the **machine politics**. The machines were in control of politics in many of the Midwest and East Coast cities such as New York City, Chicago, and Philadelphia. At the center of the machines were the party bosses, who traded jobs, money, and favors for votes. Once elected, the party bosses placed their supporters in city and county jobs and gave handouts and other favors as a method of payment for their continuing support. In addition, the bosses would use public funds for personal purposes and party activities. The party machine was an employment agency and welfare agency. Through these actions the party bosses were able to acquire power, wealth, and privileges.

FOR YOUR CONSIDERATION
PARTISAN POLITICS

To anyone viewing American government today, our politics will seem overtly and profoundly partisan; however, it was not always this way in the United States.

Our founding fathers purposefully gave no official recognition to political parties in the Constitution; in fact, they were worried that parties would corrupt the new republic and threaten democracy. But, shortly after the founding of our country, these men found themselves aligning along loosely ideological lines, and in effect, founding the first parties in American politics. Even with their party associations though, these men still saw the necessity of governmental cooperation.

So, while there were political parties during the early years of the republic, partisan politics did not truly take virulent form until the mid 1800s as the divide between the north and the south widened. Even though there was much name-calling, and partisan attacks became commonplace, when Abraham Lincoln was elected in 1860, he struck a conciliatory tone by appointing members of both parties to his cabinet. The Civil War put a halt to this newfound bipartisanship.[12]

Since the Civil War, politics has remained fairly strongly partisan; but even with the partisan bickering that went on in Congress, its members still saw the virtue in remaining gentlemen and congenial colleagues. They achieved many things due to this spirit of cooperation. Partisanship did not escalate into an all out war until the 1990s.

Frustrated by near Democratic Party dominance of government throughout the majority of the 20th century, the Republican Party was swept into power on the basis of their "Contract with America" in what is now known as the Republican Revolution of 1994.[13] Though the new congress did achieve some of its goals, bitter partisanship skyrocketed during this time. The prime symbol of this rabid partisanship was the impeachment of then sitting president, Bill Clinton, who was impeached for perjury and obstruction of justice, stemming from a civil lawsuit regarding an extramarital affair. The impeachment was largely seen as a partisan-driven circus; since then, partisan feuding has grown rapidly and has seemingly cemented itself into the national political psyche. Many members of Congress seem unwilling to work together. Those that dare cross party lines to negotiate compromises with the other side often become scorned and/or punished by their fellow party members and party leadership. As long as this bitter partisanship continues, it will remain difficult for government to accomplish anything with the people in mind.

With all of the corruption and weakening services for the general public, a backlash from the voter ended the reign of the party bosses. During the twentieth century, there were some attempts to revive the old party bosses but failed due to the change of the American electorate. Most Americans today are more educated and are better off; they aren't in need of political favors as much as previous generations.

In addition, there were four main changes in the system that prevented this type of corruption from occurring again. The first were new regulations on civil service positions, such as testing for qualified applicants. Second, the creation of the modern welfare system that provides for the lower economic strata. Third, the changes made by the progressives and reformers such as primary elections, which shifted more control to the rank and file voters. Lastly, the creation of the secret ballot encouraged voters to vote their conscience over those that the party may want. Today, political parties have changed their focus to more social movements such as voter registration and Get Out the Vote campaigns over the old **graft** and corruption methods.

National Party Organizations

The power of the national parties is most visible in presidential elections. With the shift toward a more democratic election process, **national party organizations** still coordinate, support, and fund the national candidates. But given this, the national party organizations are still weak compared to their state and local counter parts.

The main functions of the national party are to organize the national convention every four years. Along with this comes, from each state, the coordination of delegates, the presidential candidates and their running mates, and composing the party's platform. The platform states the goals of the party, their ideology, the programs they want to implement when elected, and future plans for the next convention.

The daily operations of the national party fall to the national chairman, who is selected by the presidential nominee of the party. The chairman is in charge of hiring personnel for key posts, campaign fund raising, scheduling appearances to convey the party's message to the voters, and conferring with the state party leaders to discuss ways of strengthening support where needed.

Technology has provided a key advantage to fund-raising in the modern era. Websites can collect funds around the clock, computers are able to generate mailing lists and emails for specific needs, software such as geographic information software (GIS) allows the party to target specific groups of voters based on geography, demographics, precinct location, and unique characteristics of each community.

All of these are elements of the national party organization's responsibility to its members and candidates to insure that the party is preparing for the next presidential election the day after the polls close.

Graft –
The acquisition of money, gain, or advantage by dishonest, unfair, or illegal means, especially through the abuse of one's position or influence in politics and business.

National Party Organization –
Party organization at the national level whose primary tasks include fund raising, distribution of information, and recruitment.

National Party Convention –
The national meeting of the parties every four years to choose the ticket for the presidential election and write the party platform.

Similarities and Differences within the Parties

Party organizations are very similar in their structures and in their goals. The differences are mainly in their ideologies and their supporters. The Republicans are more bureaucratic in nature. They focus on administrative duties - raising and distributing funds to candidates and state parties. Because of the Republican focus on administration, they are better at raising funds compared to the Democrats. Democrats encourage voter participation through mobilization and activism, and deliberation among the members.

Ideologies are mixed within the parties. There are **liberals** and **conservatives** in both the Democratic and Republican parties. Some may say that conservative Democrats only appear conservative because of the 'left flank' of their party. However, during the 1990's, many southern Democrats changed their party affiliation and became Republican. In addition, by nominating Gov. Bill Clinton as the presidential candidate in 1992, the Democrats created a "new Democrat". Clinton's new Democrats moved toward the center of the political spectrum, alienating their liberal base, which allowed the Greens to gain support. Simultaneously, the Republicans moved toward the conservative and religious right end of the political range. Similarly, they have alienated the more moderate and liberal members of their party, causing them to turn Independent.

Liberal –
The political position that believes that the federal government has a substantial role to play in economic regulation, social welfare, and overcoming racial inequality.

Conservative –
The political position that believes that the federal government ought to play a very small role in economic regulation, social welfare, and in overcoming racial inequality.

California's Political Parties – Past and Present

Whether they like it or not, Californians have had to dispel their easy-going earthy image and replace it with one that is concerned with every issue from education to neighborhood nuisances. The phrase, "this isn't your grandmother's PTA (Parent Teacher Association)" comes to mind. As we discussed in chapter 6, interest groups like the PTA, Neighborhood Watch, homeowner associations, and the like are requiring more of their participants than just baking cookies or attending one or two meetings; they are expected to be informed, ready, willing, and able to take up their causes. Not only are they expected to be active in a specific political capacity, but they are also expected to know enough about California politics and its budget process to make informed decisions and to be considered a worthy advocate. One of the simplest ways that Californians become active is to collect signatures or lobby elected representatives for specific issues that directly affect their day to day lives. Another way is through political parties.

The most evident sign that a constituent is committed to a particular cause or the very idea of democracy is whether or not that person is a registered active voter. Like most of the country, Californians register as Democrat or Republican. However, Californians are becoming more and more dissatisfied with either party so the trend is to shop for other parties. Voters in California seem to be declining to state or claim a party affiliation at a higher rate; either that or they are registering with other minor parties such as the Greens or the Libertarians. This is not to say that Californians are fickle or have adverse reactions to politics; quite the contrary, there are many grassroots organizations like the ones listed above with which citizens of the Golden State are quite involved. However sincere a voter's attitude is, the real proof of their convictions is conveyed through voter registration patterns.

Enter the Progressives

For almost a hundred years since the turn of the 20th century, the state of California has had a weak party system. Parties throughout U.S. history have groomed themselves to be the vital connection between the constituents and the government. However, due to the dominance of the railroad and other major industries run by powerful individuals, the function of the party affiliation has had a somewhat anemic evolution. Enter the Progressives, who were reformers that were gleaned from both the Democratic and Republican parties for the purpose of empowering the voters.

The Progressives turned their attention mainly toward dissipating the Southern Pacific Railroad's monopoly of party conventions. Using their strong motivation to secure enough delegates at state party conventions, the Progressives were able to nominate many candidates who were anti-railroad. By 1909, the reformers were able to replace the conventions with the primary election, in which each representative from each party had the ability to choose their nominee. With their eyes on the general election in November, the system the reformers set up was the organization they needed to break the dominance the railroads had enjoyed for so long.

The Progressives were responsible for introducing the power of direct democracy. Through the use of tools like the initiative, referendum, and recall (see chapter one), the voters were directly involved in influencing and even creating policy. They were also successful in eliminating the party column ballot, introducing **cross-filing** during the nomination proceedings, and doing away with party labels for the election of judges, the school board, and local officials in order to uphold nonpartisanship.

But for every action there is a reaction, whether positive or negative, and in the case of the Progressives, their tunnel-vision on the voter as an individual gave rise to the necessity for candidates to create a polished and appealing image, not to mention a financially stable one. All the reforms the Progressives worked so hard to make a reality seemed to give the voters too much flexibility and the parties and leaders not enough. For example, the absence of the party column ballot made it easier for voters to cast votes for parties and offices other than their own, resulting in **split-ticket voting**. Also, nonpartisan local elections further weakened the parties' ability to organize as grassroots entities. Even though their intent of direct democracy was virtuous, a side effect of the reformers' plans were that they ultimately weakened the political parties' effectiveness on the nomination process.

The parties attempted to salvage some semblance of control over the nominations process by making their candidate choices known well before the primaries. Again, it wasn't necessarily the large parties that were handling this but it was the unofficial offshoots that spearheaded these strategies. But, like most groups that begin to gain confidence and power, they often abuse their new-found influence. To counter attack this, legislature prohibited any candidate endorsements before the primaries and enacted burdensome rules that made choosing leaders extremely tedious.

You will read more about the primaries in chapter 8, but for a little background, we will introduce the topic briefly here. The California primaries had been held in June since the late 1990's. By this late stage in the campaigning cycle, many candidates during presidential elections would have dropped out by June. Therefore, the front-runners would see no reason to spend anything but minimal time pressing the flesh and holding babies in California. This was unfortunate for Californians who wanted

Cross-filing – The manner in which voters can register when party column ballots were eliminated, allowing voters to file for more than just their own party.

Split-ticket Voting – Instead of voting for just the party line, voters choose candidates from another party, sometimes causing strife amongst the major parties.

to get a better sense of who these candidates were and whether or not they would be able to address their concerns. Beginning in 1996, California's primary was moved to March in the hopes of being courted earlier by the prospective candidates. A few other states followed suit, competing for attention by also moving their primaries to March or earlier. Nevertheless, California marked the pace by setting early debates in motion with the earlier primaries, forcing candidates to come to California with a little more fervor and interest.

Party Structure

Although California's party system has a long-standing reputation of being weak, there are pockets of strong partisan loyalty throughout the state. At the very least, citizens vote their party line when in doubt of any candidate, whether they represent their party affiliation or not. After the 2000 elections, the confusion over the

The State Capitol of California is in Sacramento.
© Mark, 2007.
Used under License from Shutterstock, Inc.

electoral college winner and the popular vote winner caused some voters to feel frustrated and dejected. Depending on the party you belonged to, some changed their party membership from Democrat to smaller minority parties, such as the Greens, who were often accused of splitting the ticket in the past with 'radical' outspoken candidates like Ralph Nader. By 2004, however, in a rally of support, some disillusioned voters changed back to one of the two major parties in order to assure an attitude of commitment. The swing voters are usually the group that parties try to focus on to hopefully win them over to make up the fairly evenly split red and blue states across the nation. California is similar in this regard, but the number of blue voters is somewhat more definitive in the northern parts of the state. Throughout the southern parts of the state, the mix of Democratic, Republican and independent parties is fairly diverse. As mentioned earlier, minor parties such as the Greens, Natural Law, and the Libertarian parties would like to see people vote their "conscience" with no fear of judgment or reprisal from the major parties. Whatever party it is whether major or minor, the procedure to be placed on the ballot is open to any party and is determined by the California State Elections Code.

Political parties are put on the ballot by mobilizing enough members to equal 1 percent of the state vote, according to the last gubernatorial election; or, the potential party may collect enough signatures to equal 10 percent of the same vote. After the party gets put on the ballot and at least one of their candidates wins 2 percent of the votes counted, then they will represent the winning party at the next election. Being placed on the ballot at first appearances seems fairly simple; the real challenge for the smaller parties is to make a dent in the stronghold of the Democratic and Republican voter base. Despite the efforts of all parties concerned, Californians perpetuate that free spirit ideal; not seemingly pressed to identify with a party label, feeling comfortable not claiming a party at all, making up their minds once they get to nonpartisan polling booths or voting via absentee ballot. From the 1930's to the 2000's, California, like the rest of the country, was predominantly Republican. But, as parties began to realign, many lower income and minority voters began to shift toward the Democratic party. Since the Great Depression, most voters have registered as Democrats. While there is still a Republican presence in some regions, the state is largely Democratic.

Elections, voter registration, and party organizations are all governed by state law. As you learned above; all of the parties are similar in structure at the national level. The same is true at the state level. Each party has a state central committee with approximately one thousand members, consisting of all candidates and office holders, and the 58 county chairpersons. The exception is for the Democrats who also have elected representatives from each assembly district. Each state central committee has elected a state chair whose position is rotated between northern and southern California every two years. Under the chair are the state central committees who are also the 58 county central committees. The registered voters of each party elect the committee members every two years during the primary election. Current officeholders are also members of the county committees. This overlap¬ping structure of elected officials, candidates, and county chairs provides institutional memory and acts as a conduit between the county and state levels of the party. Despite the reforms of the Progressives who weakened the party systems, the county central committees still have intense conflicts. The left of the Democratic county central committees usually dominates the political agenda, frustrating the more moderate or conservative members. In contrast, the Republican committees are embroiled in conflict between the moderates and the Christian conservatives who tend to control many of the state's Republican central committees; they require a form of "litmus" tests for candidates on issues important to them. In both situations, the voters have been increasingly upset with the parties because they have become detached from the true needs of the state. Democratic Liberals and Republican Conservatives have stretched the parties to extremes whereas the public tends to be more moderate on many issues, such as immigration, abortion, and welfare reform.

Primary Reforms for the New Century

Since the turn of the previous century, reformers have constantly tried to change the political process in the state. A wide variety of laws and referendums have been passed.

Prior to 1996, California used a closed primary system that allowed only members of that political party to vote for their party's candidate. With the passing of Proposition 198, voters were allowed vote in what is known as an "open" or "blanket" primary in which all voters can vote for any candidate, regardless of their party association. Opponents of the open primary argued that the new system would allow voters of one party to pick the weak candidates of the other party, thus locking in their party's victory in the general election.[14]

On June 26, 2000, the United States Supreme Court overturned Proposition 198 in the case of California Democratic Party, et. al. v. Jones; it asserted that the "open primary system", created by Proposition 198, was unconstitutional because it violated the political party's First Amendment right of association.[15]

The system changed again in 2001 to the "modified closed primary system." The modified closed primary allows for voters to "decline to state" their party affiliation when participating in the primary election.[16]

How Do We Compare?
Mexico and the United States

Mestizo –
From Old Spanish and Latin, to mix; a person of mixed ancestry, esp., in Latin America, of mixed American Indian and European, usually Spanish or Portuguese, ancestry, or, in the Philippines, of mixed native and foreign ancestry; most cultures have a term equivalent to this one.

Mexico, our southern neighbor in North America, offers a fascinating study in economic and political development, and its present experimentation could have a pivotal impact on the rest of Latin America. Moreover, a variety of important issues link the United States closely to Mexico, such as trade, labor, water supplies, environment, and, unfortunately, illegal drug trafficking and immigration.[17]

Mayan Ruins, Yucatan, Mexico.
Courtesy of Jupiter Images.

Mexico has a relatively long, 2000-mile border that it shares with the United States. However, unlike our northern neighbor, Canada, Mexico's population is not concentrated along the U.S. border. It is much more widely spread and includes some huge urban epicenters, such as, Mexico City.

In area, Mexico is almost three times the size of Texas, or 737,000 square miles. It is about one-fifth the size of the United States or Canada but far larger than any single country in Europe except Russia. Its population of approximately 100 million people also places it well ahead of any West or Central European country, but somewhat less than Japan.

Like Canada, Mexico must be placed in the historical and geopolitical context reserved for a former European colony bordering directly on the United States. The struggle for independence from Spain began in 1810 and ended successfully in 1822, followed by a politically ruptured history that saw the country go from empire to monarchy to republic. Externally, Mexico first lost its Central American counties, which seceded in the early 1820s. Then, in the late 1840s, Mexico either lost militarily or sold under pressure, huge territories in the north to the United States (including Texas, California, Nevada, Utah, much of Arizona and parts of New Mexico, Colorado and Wyoming).

The U.S. is an inescapable geopolitical and socioeconomic "older sibling" that looms large over Mexico. There is an adage that describes Mexico's relationship with the U.S. that says, "so far from God, and so near the United States." This mirrors a Canadian saying about the dangers of sleeping next to an elephant. But Mexico also has a very different geopolitical dimension, as a northern arm of the huge Latino or Hispanic presence in the Americas. Moreover, in contrast to Canada and the United States, Mexico has or superimposed its dual Hispanic and Native American heritages.

More than 90 percent of the Mexican population is Catholic in religion. The great majority is **mestizo** (about 60 percent), while about one-third is Native American. Members of this latter group are often poorer and politically more marginalized than the mestizos, but officially, Mexico has at least recognized their important contributions to the country's culture and traditions.

In recent years, the country has endured important economic and political changes. Abandoning its previous economic orientation in the global market, Mexico has moved toward a neo-liberal (deregulated, free market) economy and has become a partner with Canada and the United States in the North American Free Trade Agreement (NAFTA). Currently, Mexico is in a state of very uneven economic development, with great contrasts in wealth and poverty, but it increasingly shows signs of becoming a newly industrializing country. The economy has been expanding rapidly since the late 1990s. The middle class has been growing, in terms of income, education, and occupation. The economy has slowed down as jobs have left Mexico for cheaper labor market in Asia. Another negative impact of NAFTA on Mexico has been its increased dependence on food imports from the United States and China. As individuals left the rural farming areas to seek better jobs in **maquiladoras** along the U.S.-Mexican border, Mexico's agricultural output decreased, causing increased food shortages and forcing Mexico to purchase more raw and processed foods from abroad.

The recent political developments in Mexico are noteworthy. The country is moving from an **authoritarian regime** under one-party rule to a more competitive pluralist democracy, in which there has now been a first-time alternation of the ruling party as the result of an election. Mexico's presidential election of 2000 is comparable in this respect to our U.S. presidential election of 1800, where for the first time in modern history an opposition party defeated an incumbent party and replaced it in office. This was a potentially very important moment in Mexican political development.

Political Background: The Revolution and Civil War, 1910-17

Prior to the Revolution, Porfirio Díaz (1877-1911) presided over a long period of economic development by way of foreign capital investment in mining and industrial development. There was considerable economic expansion, spurred by generous incentives that attracted foreign investments and allowed considerable foreign, mainly American, control of large segments of the economy. Mexican wage earners did not benefit from this arrangement. The middle class wanted democracy. Some wealthy individuals desired to open up more economic opportunities for themselves and reduce the power and influence of the foreign capitalists. It was possible for several different leaders to mobilize these diverse sources of social and political discontent into a loose, heterogeneous and very unstable coalition, producing the Mexican revolution. One of Mexico's outstanding leaders at that time was Francisco Madero. Madero was a presidential candidate who was jailed by Díaz in 1910. This sparked a rebellion using the slogan, "Effective Suffrage, No Reelection!" After being released, Madero was elected president in 1911. Unfortunately he failed to carry through promised reforms that might have won him the support of the peasants. In 1913 he was murdered in a U.S.-sponsored coup, led by Victoriano Huerta.

After the death of Madero, the rebellion continued. It was now directed against the brutal and corrupt regime of Huerta. Three of the competing leaders and groups were Emiliano Zapata, the great peasant leader of the revolution in the southern state of Morelos, "Land and Liberty!"; Francisco "Pancho" Villa who led an army of workers and cattlemen in the north (Chihuahua). His slogan was "Social Equality through Education!"; and Venustiano Carranza who led a group of ranchers and businessmen with the phrase, "Mexico for the Mexicans!"

Maquiladoras –
From Spanish, maquila, measure; also Arabic; assembly plant in Mexico utilizing cheap labor, especially one located on the border between the U.S. and Mexico; imports foreign materials and parts and exports finished product to original market.

Authoritarian Regime –
An oppressive system of government in which basic freedoms to speak, write, associate, and participate in political activities without fear of reprimand.

Great Political Instability, 1917-1928

After the revolution ended in 1917, Carranza served as president from 1917 to 1920, when he was deposed and assassinated. The other two leaders, Villa and Zapata, were also assassinated. The new constitution was drawn up in 1917 and is still the basic framework of Mexican government. It included many of the same formal elements as the U.S. Constitution, including separation of powers, federalism, and a Bill of Rights. The constitution also contained distinctive socialist elements. It gave the state control over all natural resources, gave the federal government the right to redistribute land, and gave workers greater formal rights than they had in the United States at that time. It also contained a strong nationalist tone.

Under this constitution, Mexico has in fact enjoyed more freedom of expression, more tolerance of opposition, and more open criticism of the government than many other countries that have had socialist-oriented revolutions, such as Russia or China. However, these fairly liberal accomplishments have been offset by relatively small progress in achieving the proclaimed social goals of overcoming poverty, raising the status of women, and redistributing the land.

Attempts to Consolidate the Revolution, 1928 - 1940

In 1929, former president Plutarco Elías Calles (the former president) founded the National Revolutionary Party. This was later reorganized by Lazaro Cárdenas, and in 1946 was renamed the Institutional Revolutionary Party or PRI (Partido Revolucionario Institucional). PRI would ultimately come to dominate Mexican politics. Between 1934 - 1940 President Lázaro Cárdenas, the last and greatest of the revolutionary leaders of Mexico, tried to make good on the promises of social justice. His promises, which were linked to the revolution, initiated his extensive land reform and called workers together into a union, the CTM or Confederation of Mexican Workers. The ruling party was reorganized into four constituencies: peasants, labor, the military, and the popular sector (middle class and professionals). Education, and especially rural education, was given a new emphasis. Lastly, he nationalized the oil industry, largely owned until then by U.S. and other foreign companies. This led to the creation of the state oil corporation called Petroleos Mexicanos (Pemex). This step created a period of U.S. boycotts of Mexican oil. After Cárdenas, Mexican presidential politics moved away from its peasant and labor constituencies toward business and the popular sector.

A Period of State-Promoted Economic Growth, 1940 to 1970

This was a period of considerable economic transformation through a form of economic development promoted by the Mexican government. The average rate of yearly economic growth was 6 percent. At the time, there was talk about a "Mexican miracle." The Mexican government had adopted a macro-economic strategy of what became known as "Import Substitution Industrialization (ISI)." Before that, the pattern established under the Spanish colonialists had persisted. The emphasis was the exportation of raw materials and the importation of manufactured goods. Under ISI, Mexican industries were created to produce goods that had previously been imported. The new economic strategy resulted in part from WW II restrictions on trade. Some of it came earlier, during the Great Depression. The results were so positive that the government decided to retain this strategy after WWII. This was done by creating tariff barriers and other import restrictions, so that there would be little or no competition for Mexican goods; keeping both taxes and wages low to promote profits for reinvestments was another tactic.

There were important socioeconomic changes that accompanied ISI. Gradually, government encouraged some limited foreign investment. In agricultural policy, it reversed the previous emphasis on small landowners and instead favored large commercial producers in agriculture. In time, a new business sector developed along with an industrial working class.

Oil Boom and Bust, 1970-1988:
From Economic Expansion to Austerity Programs

In the 1970s, Mexico's economic prospects appeared unusually bright as the result of the discovery of new rich oil deposits and the simultaneous sharp rise in world-wide oil prices. At this time, Mexico borrowed heavily from foreign creditors on the false assumption that oil prices would remain high. A new Export-Led Industrialization policy was adopted

This policy emphasized exports, especially oil, to pay for imports to modernize the economy. The foreign debt grew dramatically in these years, and the interest payments eventually had a crippling impact on the economy. In June 1981, the price of oil collapsed when OPEC came apart.[18] Foreign investors got scared and there followed capital and human flight out of the country. This produced another economic crisis and nearly caused the PRI's downfall.

Unpopular "austerity" measures followed during the 1980s, as a condition of financial support from the International Monetary Fund. These measures, intended to reduce Mexico's foreign debt, including cutbacks on wages, in some cases as much as 40 percent. A natural catastrophe added to the problems in 1985, when Mexico City suffered a devastating earthquake causing over 10,000 deaths and vast physical destruction.

By 1987, there was the beginning of a major political and strategic split in the PRI. One group wanted to go back to the old nationalist economic program of Cárdenas rather than follow the IMF's (International Monetary Fund) strategy of austerity. In other words, they wanted to make greater use of the government to promote development. In addition, this "left wing" wanted to democratize the PRI. One of the reformers was Cuauhtémoc Cárdenas (named after an Aztec chief), a son of the popular former president, who eventually left the PRI and ran as the candidate of a leftist coalition in 1988.

Neo-liberal Reform and Tentative Democratization, 1988-2000

In 1988, the PRI faced the most serious challenge to its continued rule. Mexican critics, like Prof. Jorge Castañeda, pointed to electoral tampering. They suggested that the PRI candidate, Carlos Salinas de Gortari, may have won only because of electoral fraud by his party.

The opposition's main problem, in addition to the entrenched position and incumbent advantages of the PRI, was that the challengers were themselves split between two major candidates of the right and left. Among the main three rivals, Salinas de Gortari and the PRI were thus able to occupy a centrist position. But the candidate of the left-oriented Party of the Democratic Revolution (PRD, Partido de la Revolución Democrática), Lázaro Cárdenas, won a third of the vote and (in the view of many critical observers) possibly quite a bit more. PRI ran Carlos Salinas de Gortari, who ended up with almost 51 percent of the vote. On the

OPEC – Organization of the Petroleum Exporting Countries; a permanent, intergovernmental organization, created at the Baghdad Conference on September 10–14, 1960. Its main purpose is to stabilise the oil market and to help oil producers achieve a reasonable rate of return on their investments. This policy is also designed to ensure that oil consumers continue to receive stable supplies of oil.

"left," he faced Cárdenas, who officially got almost 31 percent but in the eyes of many "really" won; and on the "right," the somewhat conservative, business-oriented National Action Party (PAN, Partido Acción Nacional) ran Manuel Cloutier, who ended up with 17 percent.

President Salinas (1988-1994) was relatively young, in his early forties, when he began the presidency. An economist with a Ph.D. from Harvard, he represented the more technocratic training of recent Mexican presidents. His program was based on a Neo-Liberal Model or Strategy, which has been adopted almost everywhere in Latin America, with the exception of Cuba. Basically it emphasizes getting government out of the economy in several ways: privatization of state-run industries, which often were held to be inefficient. He reduced state-owned industries from 1155 to about 300, according to one estimate; solicitation of foreign capital investments, by removing many restrictions; promotion of free trade, ultimately leading to NAFTA; deregulation of business and industry; and reduction of government spending.

The results were mixed. Some early indicators seemed very promising. There was a marked increase in economic growth rates in the first years. Inflation was reduced significantly. Government spending went down. Moreover, a reduction in Mexico's staggering debt was negotiated with the IMF. For a while, Salinas became quite popular and was celebrated as a wise and forward-looking leader.

During his term in office, Salinas enjoyed a "good press" in the United States and elsewhere. He was identified with efforts to modernize the Mexican economy, remove some of its stultifying state regulations, introduce greater competition, and, of course, support a continental free trade area through the North American Free Trade Agreement (NAFTA).

The very day NAFTA went into effect, however, a guerilla group of poor Indians calling themselves the Zapatista Army of National Liberation declared war against the government and began fighting government troops in the southern state of Chiapas, under the leadership of "Sub-commandant Marcos."

Before the Salinas presidency ended, there were strong signs that the Mexican economy was again in a crisis, related to his failure to devalue the highly overvalued peso. Soon after his term ended, Salinas was charged with improprieties and corruption in office.

The 1994 presidential election campaign was marred by the assassination of the PRI presidential candidate at a campaign stop in Tijuana. This led Salinas to appoint the campaign manager, Ernesto Zedillo as the presidential candidate. There were objections from the "old guard" in the PRI, for Zedillo belonged to the reform wing of the party. PRI won the election against a divided opposition, but only with the lowest official result ever received by a PRI candidate.

President Zedillo (1994-2000) acted quickly to drastically devalue the peso, a step that Salinas had failed to take. The overvalued peso had led to higher imports into Mexico, and this had to be corrected. The devaluation made imports more expensive and exports cheaper. In exchange for severe austerity measures, the IMF and the United States offered an enormous bail-out package for the Mexican economy, accepting Mexican oil revenues as collateral. Less than two years later, Mexico managed the early repayment of $ 4.7 billion to the U.S. by privately refinancing the debt.

Zedillo continued the Neo-Liberal Program, including the policy of privatization and a continuation of the austerity program that cut government spending. The immediate impact was devastating for many Mexicans, especially those living on low incomes, but in later years there were signs of improvement.

Zedillo managed to arrange peace talks with the rebels in Chiapas that led to a temporary end in hostilities and more autonomy for the Indians there. But there was later unrest there and in another province (Guerrero), indicating that the fundamental issue had not been resolved.

The End of PRI Hegemony: 1997 to Present

In 1997, after seven decades of PRI hegemony, the first signs of political realignment appeared. For over a decade, opposition parties had been nibbling at the PRI's power. However, in July 1997, 4 different opposition parties won a majority of 261 of the 500 seats in the lower house of the Mexican Congress and thus took control from the PRI of control for the first time. PAN carried 7 of the 31 state governor's races. The PRD candidate, Cárdenas, triumphed in Mexico City's first mayoralty race ever. It was a sign of political change that there was almost no fraud reported. In the aftermath, the opposition parties used their newly won powers to challenge the government's tight money economic policies, review the budget, and investigate corruption. In 2000, the hitherto "unthinkable" finally happened; Mexico held a presidential election in which the PRI candidate lost!

Basic Political Institutions

You'll find that the basic structure of Mexico's government are quite similar to some of our own, but they clearly operate in a very different historical, cultural, international, and socio-economic context, resulting in very different governing styles and policy outcomes.

Mexico adopted a codified constitution in 1917, which established the formal structure of the national government. It includes extensive guarantees of civil and social rights, a federal system, with 33 states and one federal district. Each state has an elected governor and a unicameral state legislature. Local government is based on the municipio (similar to our townships or a consolidated city-county government), with an elected mayor and council. As in the U.S., the constitution provides for separation of powers. The judiciary normally plays a relatively insignificant role in Mexican politics, however. In practice, the system has been executive-centered, but that may change with the erosion of the PRI's dominant position.

The constitution calls for a bicameral national legislature. The lower house (called the Chamber of Deputies) is elected on a three-year cycle, along with one-half of the upper house, or, Senate. The Senate is comprised of two senators elected from each state who serve a term of six-year. Re-election is possible only after skipping terms (i.e., no consecutive terms in the same office are possible, but it is possible to alternate between the two chambers for several periods).

The Presidency

Mexico has a popularly elected president, who serves a six year term with no re-election. The decree-making powers of the president are considerable. For example, these important rule-making powers make it possible for him to control the manner in which legislation passed by Congress is to be enforced.

The PRI

As Martin Needler has pointed out, the "keystone" of the political system is clearly the presidency. The constitution gives the president an unusual degree of authority, and the incumbent's power was for a long time further augmented through his position as leader of the Institutional Revolutionary Party (PRI), which dominated Mexico's politics between the late 1920s and the year 2000.

The PRI is not just a major party in Mexico. For over 70 years, it was the dominant or hegemonial party. Its top members constituted a distinctive ruling group or political class. Over the years, most of its leading members increasingly came to be a professionally educated group, with a technocratic outlook on society and economics. They were thus very different from the ruling generals in the early post-revolutionary years (between 1920 and 1940, the elected presidents of Mexico were all generals) or, for that matter, the later middle class ones.

Needler also points out that cabinet members in the Mexican government were increasingly likely to have advanced university training in subjects other than law, such as engineering, administration, or fiscal management. Moreover, they were also far less likely to come from the provinces than from Mexico City. He concludes plausibly that the shift in skills and career backgrounds reflected the adaptation of the dominant party to a changing socio-economic and political reality in Mexico.

Voting

Voting in Mexico is legally compulsory. For various dealings with government agencies, it is necessary to have among one's papers a voting credential that has been stamped to indicate that one has fulfilled one's civic duty. Not surprisingly, voter turnout is quite high (although not higher than in some West European countries where voting is a voluntary act): In Mexico, it's generally reported to be over 80 percent.

The electoral system for Mexico's lower house or Chamber of Deputies was originally based on the single-member district with plurality winning ("winner-takes-all") familiar from the United States and Britain. More recently, however, Mexico has used an interesting combination of the old single-member district with plurality election for 300 seats in the lower house, and the multi-member district with proportional representation for the 200 remaining seats.

More Recent Events

Things are beginning to change for Fox and Calderón when PAN won the presidency. They won a huge victory in 2000 and narrowly won again in 2006. The leftist PRD grew and the PRI continued to decline and is still riddled with corruption and crime. Unemployment and poverty run rampant, leading to miles of shantytowns and a flight to the United States for jobs, increasing political tension between the two nations. The guerrilla war that appeared in 1994 still continues in the mountains of Chiapas after the guerrillas were removed from villages and towns by the Mexican Army. In 2006, a strike by teachers in Oaxaca caused an embarrassment to the political establishment as the ruling governor has gone underground, further emphasizing the need for the rule of law in Mexico that all must adhere too. Latin America has only received a small benefit from globalization. NAFTA and other trade agreements have not brought the wealth the politicians have promised. The problems of drugs and illegal immigrants are partly the U.S.'s fault. If we did not buy the drugs and employ the illegal immigrants to do the work that most Americans refuse to do, the flow of both would stop.

An Ongoing Relationship

Mexico and the United States are going to remain neighbors, and will have to continue to work through the difficult issues that characterize their relationship. The issues of trade, economic growth, drug trafficking, and illegal immigration will be of concern for the foreseeable future. Many in the U.S. perceive Mexico as nothing more than a source of problems – illegal immigrants and drugs. Of course, this ignores the culpability of U.S. employers and consumers who have come to depend on the cheap labor of the Mexican workers, or the buyers of illicit drugs who create the market for the drug traffickers. North of the border, the American political system will struggle with these issues, using the mechanisms and institutions which we will continue to examine through the rest of this book.

Chapter Summary

Sprinkled throughout American history, there are references to religion and faith, such as the inclusion of "In God We Trust" on our paper money. Beginning with the presidency of Ronald Reagan, conservative Christian groups established a special relationship with the Republican Party. The Republican Party hit a roadblock during the 1990s with the election and reelection of then Governor of Arkansas, Bill Clinton, a Democrat. In the year 2000, the Religious right found in Republican candidate George W. Bush a champion being that he is a self-avowed born again Christian. Believing that he was the key to fulfilling their long hoped for goals, they mobilized a notable voter turnout effort. Support from within the Republican Party began showing strain in early 2006. One of the problems came with the lack of general public support for the platform of the Christian right; many in the general public now viewed stem-cell research as cutting edge science necessary to find cures for many diseases.

The Democratic Party has made some inroads into breaking up the monopoly the Republican Party enjoyed with Christian groups for more than 20 years. In addition, the Republican Party is undergoing an examination of what their priorities truly are. Simply put, political parties are organizations that try to win control of government by electing their representatives to office. The role of political parties in the United States is to help people understand politics, to create a functional government, to insure representatives' response, to be as inclusive as possible. One begins to see the dominance of two parties and with smaller third parties sprinkled about. Within the two major parties in the U.S., their constant evolution is quite evident.

There have been six major periods of stability since the beginning of the country. Each period has lasted, on average, 40 years. In between these six periods, we can identify periods of realignment. Political observers have identified two major dates of realignment in American politics: 1896 and 1932. From the nineteenth century to the middle of the twentieth century, political parties were considered to be the machine politics. At the center of the machines the party bosses, who traded jobs, money, and favors for votes. Through these actions the party bosses were able to acquire power, wealth, and privileges.

The power of the national parties is most visible in presidential elections. With the shift toward a more democratic election process, national party organizations still coordinate, support, and fund the national candidates. The main functions of the national party are to organize the national convention every four years. Party organizations are very similar in their structures and in their goals. The differences are mainly in their ideologies, usually somewhere on a range from liberal to conservative.

One of the simplest ways that Californians become active is to collect signatures or lobby elected representatives for specific issues that directly affect their day to day lives. Another way is through political parties. For almost a hundred years since the turn of the 20th century, the state of California has had a weak party system. The Progressives were reformers that were gleaned from both the Democratic and Republican parties for the purpose of empowering the voters. Despite their good intentions, all the reforms the Progressives worked so hard to make a reality seemed to give the voters too much flexibility and the parties and leaders not enough. Although California's party system has a long-standing reputation of being weak, there are pockets of strong partisan loyalty throughout the state. Significant events throughout California's history both politically and economically are reflected in voter registration patterns. In the next chapter, we will evaluate the effectiveness of parties at election time as well as take a look at how people vote.

Key Terms:

Evangelicals

Party Platform

Political Parties

Realignment

Election of 1800

Primary System

New Deal Coalition

New Deal

Machine Politics

National Party Organization

National Party Convention

Graft

Conservative

Liberal

Cross-filing

Split-ticket Voting

Mestizo

Maquiladoras

Authoritarian Regime

OPEC

Websites:

Democratic National Committee
www.democrats.org/

The Green Party
www.greenpartyus.org

The Green Party Election Results
http://www.greens.org/elections/

Republican National Committee
http://www.rnc.org/

The Reform Party
www.reformparty.org/

California Sites

The California Democratic Party
www.cadem.org

California Green Party
www.cagreen.org

California American Independent Party
www.aipca.org

California Republican Party
www.cagop.org

California Secretary of State Debra Bowen
http://www.sos.ca.gov/elections/elections_decline.htm

Socialist Party of California
www.sp-usa.org/spca

This page left blank intentionally.

July 12, 1964

Due to Presidential Candidate Barry Goldwater's' views that the federal government should not be involved with imposing civil rights on the states, members of the Ku Klux Klan interpreted this as being in line with their racist sentiments, which is far from Goldwater's intent. They are shown here at the Republican National Convention in San Francisco, California, while an African American man tries to restrain the crowd.

Courtesy of the Library of Congress

CHAPTER 8

ELECTIONS AND VOTING

CHAPTER OUTLINE

- DEMOCRACY AND ACTION –
  THE LETTER – ORANGE COUNTY, CALIFORNIA
- ELECTIONS IN AMERICA
- THE CRITERIA FOR WINNING
- THE ELECTORAL COLLEGE
- VOTING – WHAT & WHY
- WHO VOTES?
- ELECTIONS AND VOTING IN CALIFORNIA
- HOW DO WE COMPARE?
  IRAN AND THE UNITED STATES

Democracy and Action –
The Letter –
Orange County, California

Naturalized Citizens –
An immigrant who pledges to uphold their adopted country's laws after meeting specific requirements; after this, they retain all rights and privileges that are afforded to native citizens in that country.

The right to vote is a much-cherished right in our democracy; it is the way we, the people have a voice in our government. It is a right that was vigorously fought for

by many groups of citizens in this country, among them, working-class white men who didn't own land, women, and people of color. This is why when Americans hear of acts of voter intimidation in developing countries, it is especially deplorable to us. However, one such instance of voter intimidation occurred just prior to the November 2006 Mid-Term Elections, not in some faraway land but in Orange County (O.C.), California, an area with a history of ethnocentric and inter-"racial" tension.

On the morning of October 20, 2006, protesters, and other regional candidates gathered outside of Tan Nguyen's campaign office to voice their displeasure. Several news crews, a few shown here, eagerly filmed the excitement as it was rumored that Nguyen would appear to hold a press conference. © Moonrock Media

Orange County, like most other areas of Southern California, has a large Latino population. In late October 2006, in north Orange County, a letter written in Spanish was received by thousands of registered voters with Latino surnames, most of whom were naturalized citizens, lawfully registered to vote. This letter was sent under the banner of the California Coalition for Immigration Reform (CCIR), a well-known ultra-conservative anti-illegal immigration group. The letter was sent to newly registered Latino voters and it warned that if the recipients were in the country illegally or were simply immigrants, then they were not allowed to vote; if they did they could receive jail time and/or be deported. The letter also stated that the government was keeping a searchable database that tracks votes cast. As it turns out, the mailer was not only incorrect, but fraudulent as well. First, the letter falsely grouped naturalized citizens and illegal/legal immigrants together, saying that all immigrants were not allowed to vote. This country has many legal immigrants, including Gov. Schwarzenegger, who are sometimes more passionate about politics and are more consistent voters than many American born citizens. As a matter of fact, the letter violated several federal and state election laws put into place to expressly prevent such intimidation. Second, the letter was specifically sent to voters with Latino surnames, which qualifies as voter intimidation, which is against federal law. Third, it was discovered that the letterhead was a fake and the CCIR, led by O.C. resident and founder, Barbara Coe, disavowed any knowledge of the letter at all.

Upon investigation, the incident was traced to the campaign office of 47th District Republican candidate, Tan D. Nguyen. Nguyen has had a history of odd behavior, first running as a Democrat in the 46th District in 2004 to unseat Rep. Dana Rohrabacher (R-CA.) and then switching loyalties to run as a Republican in the 47th against Rep. Loretta Sanchez (D-CA.). Nguyen's confused party identity only earned him suspicion and concerns about his true intentions from O.C. Republican Party Chairman Scott

Baugh.[1] Adding even more strangeness to the nature of the allegations, Nguyen's entire platform focuses on immigration issues, but not what you might expect from an immigrant from Vietnam – it boasts ultra-conservative staunch support of anti-illegal immigration measures, support of the **Minuteman Project**, and his opposition to Bush's guest-worker programs.

The scandal was all over local newspapers and all the major news networks ran the story continuously throughout the week; even major newspapers like the Washington Post picked up the story. Sanchez requested that a federal investigation be launched to investigate the possibility of any violations of the Voting Rights Act. "We would like to find who did this and have them prosecuted," said.[2] The Orange County GOP publicly denounced Nguyen and urged him to immediately withdraw his candidacy. Nguyen refused to withdraw; he appeared at several press conferences to steadfastly deny any knowledge of the letter. Nguyen stated that he had fired a campaign worker who was pinned as the one responsible for the mailing. The State's remedy, in light of the fast approaching election, was to send out another letter to all 14, 000 recipients of the fraudulent letter, this time written in both English and Spanish. It was marked "urgent" right below the State Seal and office of the sender, the California Secretary of State. The letter explained that voters should ignore the intimidation letter, that its claims were inaccurate, and that it was not authorized by any legitimate organization. The letter also clarified that it is legal for naturalized immigrants to register and vote and those who are eligible are encouraged to do so.

In the end, Sanchez, the ostensible target of the letter, beat Nguyen easily in the November 2006 election, for a seat that is not always guaranteed a Democratic win. Curiously, talk of the investigation into the origins of the letter tapered off quickly post-election with the announcement of the Attorney General clearing Nguyen of any wrong-doing.[3] The U.S. Department of Justice continues to lead a quieter investigation, employing its voting rights branch to look into issues of translation of the original Spanish letter; specifically with the way the word emigrado was interpreted. As any speaker of multiple languages can tell you, the claim that something got 'lost in translation' is sometimes used as a coping mechanism to buy time to search for the real meaning behind the words. Such is the case of this infamous letter.

The California Department of Justice raided Candidate Tan Nguyen's campaign office in Garden Grove, California. They kept the glass doors shut as onlookers and media watched them dismantle and confiscate several computers for evidence in the pending investigation. © Moonrock Media

It was not the first act of voter intimidation to take place in Orange County, California, nor will it be the last, in light of the current intense partisan environment. In some ways, it is a shame that immigrants who do take the proper measures to become citizens have to be subjected to the mean-spirited tactics of xenophobes; even worse, those who hold elected official positions. Instead of inspiring good-natured debate and voter participation, immigrant minority groups are reduced to intimidating one another, a characteristic that America shouldn't be eager to pass on to new citizens.[4]

Minuteman Project – Founded by Vietnam veteran and former CPA Jim Gilchrist on Oct. 1, 2004, in response to controversial debates over immigration laws; the group's claim is that the federal government is not enforcing existing immigration laws, so Gilchrist recruited volunteers to physically patrol the California-Mexico border, mobilize membership, solicit donations to build fences, and lobby Congress for stricter immigration laws.

Elections in America

Hell, I never vote for anybody, I always vote against. – W.C. Fields

A vote is like a rifle; its usefulness depends upon the character of the user.
– Theodore Roosevelt

Plurality –
More votes than any other candidate but less than a majority of all votes cast.

Voting in elections is the most basic and vital act of participation in a democratic government. However, it's not the only one. As you've learned in previous chapters, voter participation can involve working on campaigns, contacting political parties for information, walking in political protests, signing petitions, or something as simple as sporting a bumper sticker. All of these are connected to elections and voting. Before discussing elections, we will briefly review the major characteristics that make democracy in the United States unique.

The U.S. tends to have more elections than other western style democracies. This is largely due to the many election reforms that have been passed over the centuries, all in an effort to make the country more democratic. Furthermore, elections in the U.S. are generally not held at the same time. The Constitution established when elections should be held for the president and congress. It does not, however, say when the state and local elections should be held. On average, Americans vote every six months. These may include special elections such as school boards, water districts, and so on. Additionally, unlike countries with a parliamentary system (see chapter one) that can dissolve government with a vote of no confidence, the United States has fixed terms in office. Congress holds elections every two years for the entire House of Representatives and one-third of the Senate; the President is elected every four years. Each state tends to emulate the federal system in terms of the legislative and executive branches. For example, most state legislatures are bi-cameral, with an upper and lower house - the executive branch has a governor, which is similar to the President but at a state level. Lieutenant governors parallel the duties of a Vice President. Lastly, the American election is based on a "single member district" which is also known as "First Past the Post." In most cases, when a candidate runs for office, they don't have to receive the majority of the votes (50%+1); they just have to receive a **plurality** of votes. Meaning, whoever crosses the finish line or passes the post first, wins. This can be confusing because the definition of what the plurality entails can vary. In most multiparty systems, parties receive votes for their party and/or for a single candidate. This is known as proportional representation where, generally speaking, the district receives representation based on their party affiliation.

Despite the fact that the framers wanted to put a check on the early movements towards democracy and the passions of the people, American history has shown that the election process has become more democratic since the first stroke of quill to scroll in the Constitution. Take for example the election of the president. Since the election of 1800, the president has been elected by the electoral college. The electors have gradually been selected by the voters of their state. Around the 1840s, parties began nominating their presidential candidates in national conventions instead of congressional caucuses. By the turn of the twentieth century, the national convention delegates were chosen at the state party conventions or through primary elections. This system is still in place today. Originally the U.S. Senators were selected by their state assemblies but with the passage of the Seventeenth Amendment in 1913, the Senate is now popularly elected. In examining these two examples, one can see how the country has become more democratic. The road towards democracy was begun over 200 years ago by those who were willing to take action. While the system has evolved into what most would consider comfortably democratic, the people can still afford to become more involved in the political process.

Congressional Elections

As stated above, every two years the entire House and one-third of the Senate are up for reelection as prescribed by the Constitution. Congressional candidates are not generally household names so the general public is not necessarily familiar with them until they run a campaign. There are a few exceptions such as actors, athletes, astronauts, or individuals from famous families like the political Kennedy dynasty or the wealthy Rockefellers. Most Senators have some advantages if they are former state governors, state senators, or other high ranking state officials. On the other side, members of the House could benefit from all of the above factors but typically, candidates running for congressional seats are unknown, even to their local constituents. The voters often have no idea where some of these individuals stand on the issues, anything about their character or how well they will perform if elected. Instead, most candidates belong to the same social groups and the same level of education as their counterparts in other states. This does not bode well for democracy. If those in Congress are supposed to be representing the people of the districts or states, then what does this tell us about where their interests lie?

On election day, the congressional election, whether midterm or presidential, usually shows a lower voter turnout and less media coverage unless they are important races that may tip the balance of power. Usually the voter turnout is approximately one third of the registered voters. This fractional group is usually considered to be the party faithful from both parties. Even though midterm elections tend to be less attractive to voters and the media, there are times when there could be some surprises, such as the **midterm elections** of 1994 when the Republicans took control of both houses of congress and the election of 2006, when the Democrats took back both houses from the Republicans.

Midterm Elections – Elections in which Americans elect members of Congress but not presidents; 2002, 2006, and 2010 are midterm election years.

Presidential Elections

As mandated by the Constitution, every four years is a presidential election. A century ago, the average campaign cycle, including the party conventions, was

"Cheer up, perhaps we'll find you an ERA job, or something!"
Courtesy of the Library of Congress

less than a year. In recent years, because of the hundreds of millions of dollars needed to get elected, the campaign season is averaging between eighteen and twenty four months. The idea is for the candidate to get noticed early on in order to get ahead; this requires spending more money which will hopefully result in receiving it back by being ahead in the polls. During the primary season, the candidate's focus is on getting the votes of the party and gaining more momentum to obtain the parties nominations. Once they receive their party's nomination, select a running mate, and unite the party, their focus shifts to the general election and on the opposition party's candidates. Once the primary

FOR YOUR CONSIDERATION
MIDTERM ELECTIONS

Midterm elections are the elections that take place two years after a presidential election and in the middle of the president's term – hence, the expression "midterm." While these elections tend to have lower voter turnout and do not garner as much attention as the more visible presidential elections, they are nonetheless, very important.

First, all 435 members of the House of Representatives must be elected every two years, which means they are all elected during both types of election cycles.[5] This creates an accentuated accountability factor for members of the House and gives the electorate of each state a chance to change course every two years if they see fit. The main criticism of this short duration term is that it generates an almost unending election cycle; as soon as the last election is over, the campaign for the next one begins.

Midterm elections also see the election of one third of the members of the Senate, whose terms are staggered at 6-year intervals and many states elect important local and state officials as well. More than half of the states elect their governors during midterm elections.[6] In addition, midterms provide a chance for ballot initiatives to be put before the voters while they are prominent issues instead of having to wait four years.

Midterm elections also serve as an important indicator of how a president is performing; if the president is seen as doing a good job, in theory h/is party will gain seats during a midterm; if s/he is performing poorly, the party will lose seats. In actuality, most of the time the president's party loses seats during a midterm. There have been exceptions to this "rule"; the most recent being the midterm election of 2002, when the Republicans – the president's party - gained seats, but there was a return to the status quo during the 2006 midterm election, with the Democrats mounting a sweeping comeback and putting an end to 12 years of a Republican congressional majority.[7]

campaign is over, the campaign for the general election takes on a new strategy. The campaign moves from appealing to the party faithful to courting the under decided and independent voters by addressing the issues that "Joe Q Public" wants taken care of. Campaigns prepare themselves to respond to any surprises and change the course if the strategy isn't working as intended. One concern during October and November is to avoid any "October surprises" which may give your opponent the winning edge through the election; however, the main task is still convincing people to vote for you. In addition, the campaign managers may decide to formulate campaign commercials that paint the opponent in a negative light; hopefully, this will not end up backfiring on the initiator of the ad. If all the pieces fall into place the way the candidate wants, they may find themselves celebrating on election day.

The Criteria for Winning

When the polls close on election day, anywhere from one-third to one-half of the voters will have made their decision, not because of their party affiliation but on what they learned about the candidates during the campaign. This numbers tell candidates that how the campaign is run can make the difference between winning and losing. In the modern age, the campaign staff is highly trained and headed by political operatives who know the rules of the game. Highly skilled operatives like James Carville, Mary Matalin, George Stephanopoulos, can enhance an already dynamic candidate. Operatives like Karl Rove are credited with creating the Bush electoral juggernaut. This type of savvy campaign consulting is essential to politicians who need to win a national election. Some candidates need more grooming than others.

With the weak political parties of today, candidates and their campaigns must assume many responsibilities that were formerly handled by the parties. In addition to the professional political operatives, campaign managers must hire a professional staff of public relations specialists, media consultants, and expert fund-raisers. Each person on the campaign staff is an essential cog in producing a fine product, which is the candidate; while their duties and responsibilities may vary, they all have one mission – to present their candidate in the best possible light.

It should not be assumed that a professional staff and tremendous fund-raising capabilities can win elections alone (for more discussion about campaign financing and candidate traits, see chapters 7 and 4, respectively). If the campaign does not have a clear mission and a unified plan of attack, then this affects the clarity of the candidates' party platform. This in turn will weaken the candidates' ability to win the hearts and minds of the voters. A sterling example of the kind of steady long-term campaigning is found in the work of 2004 Democratic presidential candidate, Gov. Howard Dean. Dean came upon the campaign scene with just the right balance of enthusiasm, experience, and a down-to-earth appeal. As his campaign gained momentum like the growing waves at high tide, he founded Democracy for America (DFA), a national grassroots organization that is now lead by his brother, James H. Dean.[8] The founding of DFA and its main mission was inspired by Gov. Dean's ideas of rebuilding the Democratic party from the ground up. Their remarkable success was due largely to efficient e-mailing, web links, and a youthful energy, not to mention Dean's "50 State Strategy". Although Gov. Dean did not win the nomination at the 2004 elections, many party officials credit this strategy for the great victories the Democratic Party enjoyed at every level during the 2006 Mid-term Elections. Gov. Dean explains their strategy best: "Election by election, state by state, precinct by precinct, door by door, vote by vote...we're going to lift our Party up and take this country back for the people who built it."[9] The DFA seeks out community leaders and volunteers for every precinct, with the goal of having a "trained, effective organization of Democrats dedicated to winning votes for Democrats." Gov. Dean was elected in February 2005 to the post of chairman for the Democratic National Committee (DNC) and he continues to appeal to the voters whose values reflect the Democratic Party platform.

The Electoral College

Electoral College – Group of 538 electors who meet separately in their respective states and the District of Columbia on the first Monday after the second Wednesday in December following a national presidential election; responsible for officially electing the president and vice president of the U.S.

Electors – Representatives who are elected in the states to formally choose the U.S. president.

Contingency Election – The election held in the House if no candidate wins the required majority in the electoral college.

Most Americans had a refresher course on the function of the **electoral college** during the 2000 Presidential Elections. For weeks people heard and read about dimpled chads, hanging chads, and butter fly ballots (see chapter 4, Media). Since 1888, political observers predicted that Congress would eventually be forced to amend the Constitution if a split between the electoral college and the popular vote were to occur again. It happened in 1876 and 1888, causing the public to question the legitimacy of the electoral process. There are some third party groups and grass-roots organizations, such as the Green Party and Black Box Voting,[10] that have petitioned for official investigations into voting irregularities since the 2000 election. For a few brief months following the fiasco in 2000, it appeared that the predictions would come to pass; but, other issues took over and the focus on the problems with the electoral college shifted out of the political spotlight.

So how does the system work? When Americans go to their assigned polling places to vote for president, they are exercising their right to vote but it is cast indirectly for the candidate they want. In actuality, the votes are for a slate of electors from that candidate's party, who, in turn, have promised to vote for that candidate. Each state's slate of electors is equal to its representation in Congress (all the members of the house plus the two senators). According to the Constitution, the electors can vote for whomever they wish but it is virtually unheard of for an elector to go against their party's candidate at the last minute. In most states, whichever candidate wins the popular vote also receives all of the electoral votes for that state. This is known as the "winner-take-all" system. The two exceptions to this system, Nebraska and Maine, base the "winner-take-all" on each congressional district instead of the overall state's popular vote. It should be noted that the electoral college doesn't actually meet together in one place. Instead, the electors meet in their state capitals and send their list of recorded votes to Washington D.C. as per the Twelfth Amendment. The candidate who receives the majority (271) of electoral votes becomes the president-elect. If there is no clear winner, then the House of Representatives holds a contingency election, at which they will choose among the top three front runners and each state will cast a single vote. This process will be further illustrated in the section on California.

For decades, the electoral college vote mirrored the popular vote. Below are some problems that are inherent within this system.

Distorts the popular vote for the winner. It is possible for the candidate to win the majority of the electoral college vote but not the popular vote. For example, in 1996, President Clinton won 379 electoral votes but only 49% of the popular vote.

May Allow Less Popular Candidates to Win. This is the great disparity that is the cause of much debate over this, some say, antiquated system. As mentioned earlier, the Gore-Bush debacle in 2000 wasn't the first time the candidate with fewer popular votes won (Bush won the electoral, Gore won the popular). In 1876, Rutherford B.

Hayes (Republican) won the electoral vote but Samuel J. Tilden (Democrat) won the popular vote. One last example, in 1888, Benjamin Harrison (Republican) won the electoral vote while Grover Cleveland (Democrat) received the popular vote.

Hinders Third Party Candidates. This may or may not be seen as a bad thing by some, depending on your perspective, but the electoral college system makes it difficult for third party candidates to break into the arena of the two-party monopoly of the Democrats and Republicans. In 1992, even though Ross Perot won an almost unheard of 19% of the popular vote nationwide for a third party candidate, it did not win him any of the electoral college votes because he did not win in any state. Because of the current rules of the winner-take-all system rather than a proportional representation, Perot essentially won him nothing.

Issues For You
Can you think of any other benefits to the electoral college system? Do you feel that it is still an appropriate system for the 21st century?

The debates over the electoral college will continue; those who oppose it will continue to denounce its absurd undemocratic structure and the biased elitist views of the framers that the people were unfit to vote for themselves. Those who support it will maintain that it gives the presidential electoral process legitimacy. It will be up to future generations to take action, especially if the situation like the 2000 Presidential Election repeats itself.

Despite this list of concerns over the validity of the electoral college, some feel that there are some advantages. One advantage is that this system assists the smaller states such as South Dakota, which has only three electoral college votes. In a very close presidential election, three votes could make all the difference.

Even though the electoral college may seem like an antiquated concept in the 21st century, the framers were considered the progressives of their time. In the context of the Constitutional Convention, they were thinking also in terms of the States being the primary actors in National government decision-making, hence a system that afforded influence to smaller states, namely the electoral college and the Senate.

Voting – What & Why

Toward the end of the campaign season, the candidates are thrown into the final last-ditch frenzy: media blitzes, last-push mailers, TV appearances, town hall meetings, rallies on the tarmac, and automated phone messages, in the hopes of nabbing those last few undecided voters. What happens in the calm before the storm, when the voters go home and sift through all the candidates' statements? Do the voters really weigh all of the information objectively or have they already made all of their decisions, shutting out any conflicting feelings along the way? If one were to analyze the character dossier of each person before they stepped into a voting booth, then one might be able to predict the way that person would vote. As discussed in earlier chapters, the agents of socialization that influence the way we vote include religious mentors, ethnicity, parental guidance, economic status, and everyday interactions with co-workers and colleagues. Some political scientists specialize in elections and voting and make it their life's work to analyze the reasons people vote and why.

Civic Duty

The following was conveyed to the author during class one day. Class happened to fall on an election night and the student asked to leave class early. When asked why since there was plenty of time to stay for class and still make it to the polls, the African-American student explained that the matriarch of the family, her grandmother, made it a big family outing and required that they all register to vote together and go to the polls together so she could make sure everyone voted. This is why she needed extra time to get home. The grandmother took it upon herself to bring along even the little ones - her immediate children, her grandchildren, and her great grandchildren, who were not old enough to vote. The student said her grandmother is so proud of the right to vote that she says, "Women have waited over a hundred and fifty years and 'Coloureds' almost a hundred. Others have fought to give us this right and it's our civic duty to make sure we do it!" Truer words have never been said and proclaimed so succinctly.

Party Identification – The core beliefs that a person upholds and votes for in association with a political party.

Very few people think of voting as a civic duty, nor do they possess the insight this dedicated grandmother has about this hard-won right. However, those that do realize the importance of voting remember that in a democracy, voting is the one basic element that guarantees popular sovereignty over their government. It is the voters' duty to safeguard our democracy by holding elected officials accountable to do what they are hired to do. If the elected officials fail, then the only way they can be removed is by the voters voting them out of office. There are other reasons that discourage people from voting no matter how strong the sense of civic duty. This will be discussed later in voter turnout.

Party Affiliation

Decades of research has shown that some Americans vote based on influence from their party affiliation. Voters feel that their **party identification** symbolizes their political beliefs, interests, and way of life. Most people acquire their party affiliation from their parents; evidence has shown that if their families are politically active, the individual will be more inclined to be as well. This accounts for about 25% of the electorate and political parties can count on them to vote for their specific parties and issues, whereas other "undecideds" are pulled outward toward third parties or no party at all. The parties aid voters indirectly, even if they switch parties several times over the course of their lifetime. Despite this, there are some voters who do not have strong party affiliations and over the years, there has been an increase in people registering as Independents or engaging in split-ticket voting. On rare occasions, the 'party faithful' have been known to break ranks with their party, meaning that under extreme circumstances, such as a crucial issue or a personal interest in the candidate, these voters may deviate from the party line.

There are other factors besides just party affiliation that may influence people in the voting booth. Nonpartisan elections, especially local ones, may not have the same predictability as elections for higher ranking offices. However, the scads of political mailers that summarize issues and candidates' platforms in convenient checklists are sent with the intent of advocating a specific party or interest group. In the higher elections such as state office, the ballots identify party affiliation, making it easier for voters. The future of party affiliation is becoming uncertain as more Americans are detaching from the two major parties.

Electability

Even before the genesis of the TV era and televised political debates, the personality, stage presence, and even looks of a candidate greatly influenced voters. The speaking style, charm, and panache of a candidate ultimately connect with voters much more effectively than the actual words being said – at least at first. Great examples of dynamic personalities throughout America's presidential history include George Washington and Abraham Lincoln, who were far from the stiff bewigged stern looking likenesses portrayed on the one and five dollar bill. Other charismatic individuals include Woodrow Wilson, Franklin Roosevelt, and Ronald Reagan. It's not always looks that captivate the general voting public but also perhaps a respected military record, and this goes not just for presidential figures but also Senators and local representatives. Dwight Eisenhower and John F. Kennedy were respected for their military accomplishments; this aided them in winning the Presidency. Sen. John McCain (R-AZ) and General Wesley Clark, both presidential hopefuls in 2004 and 2008, have also referred to their military experience during their campaigns. In America, depending on the region and party affiliation, sometimes people are swayed by an accent, such as the practical minded Harry S. Truman, the folksy drawl of President George W. Bush, or the southern charm of former President Bill Clinton. Linguists have a term to describe the tone, pitch, pace and expression an individual speaks with, which is called pragmatics. A candidates' pragmatic style can sometimes help or hinder the candidate's ability to communicate effectively. For example, the plain spoken Rep. Ron Paul (R-TX) or the on-fire preaching style of Al Sharpton have very distinct and divergent campaigns that appeals to some voters. Even height, girth, physical characteristics, fashion sense, and hairstyle enter into the public's idea of candidate appeal. The diminutive Congressman Dennis Kucinich and the broad-eared shrill-voiced Ross Perot were often the butt of late-night show hosts' jokes on a nightly basis. Whether or not the candidate has that certain *je ne sais quois*, that 'electability' that satisfies the sensibilities of constituents can be tracked in the polls many months before the elections occur. The phenomenal popularity of shiny inexperienced new candidates (Sen. Barack Obama, D-IL) or eccentric ones (Mayor of NY, Rudy Giuliani, Republican) reflects poorly perhaps on those that, when asked why they like a certain candidate, the answer most often heard is, "Well, they seem like a fresh face and a nice guy," or "He was there for us after 9/11 and that's good enough for me!", with no bearing on details of their party platforms. One of the main reasons that should propel citizens to vote is the candidates' policies and issues, rather than pre-conceived notions about their personalities or popularity.

Factoid:
Now Hear This –
Like most candidates running for President in 2008, Sen. Barack Obama's crew had down-loadable ring-tones and Pod casts set up in an attempt to catch the ears of the technologically savvy.

Profiles in Politics
Harry S. Truman (1884 - 1972)

Harry S. Truman, the 33rd President of the United States, is known for being an honest, plain spoken, no-nonsense man. During his tenure as President, he was known for having some fight in him and making some very tough decisions – the toughest a president can make.

President Truman, April 19, 1945, days after being sworn in after the unexpected death of President Roosevelt. Courtesy of the Library of Congress

Harry Truman was born in May 1884 in Lamar, Missouri. After graduating from high school and working at a couple of banks, Truman returned to help his family run their farm. After dogged pursuit, he married his sweetheart Bess in 1919, and his letters as well as his devotion to her became legendary.[11]

A strong sense of patriotism prompted him to serve in the Missouri National Guard. When World War I broke out, he fought in France, remained in the reserves after the War, and attained the rank of colonel. When the U.S. entered World War II, Truman attempted to return to active duty, but was turned down.

In 1922, Truman, backed by the ethically challenged Pendergast political machine in Missouri, was elected to the Jackson County Court – a mostly administrative job. In this position, Truman became known for his honesty and efficiency. In 1934, again backed by Pendergast, in what was generally considered a rigged vote, Truman was elected to the Senate. Again, Truman proved himself worthy of his seat through his honesty and hard work.

In 1944, Truman was nominated to be the vice president for Franklin D. Roosevelt's fourth presidential term. After serving a mere 82 days as vice president, Harry Truman was sworn in as the 33rd President after Roosevelt's unexpected death in April 1945.[12] Thrust into office in the middle of World War II, Truman had his hands full, but as always, through his hard work and straightforwardness, excelled at his tasks.

During the remainder of Roosevelt's term, Truman oversaw the surrender of the Germans and the Japanese. Considered his most controversial decision, Truman agonized over using the newly developed atomic bomb on Japan. While he wanted an end to the War, he was intensely bothered by the high levels of civilian casualties the bomb was expected to produce. In the end, he made the decision to use the bomb, which secured Japan's hasty surrender immediately following the two attacks on Hiroshima and Nagasaki.

Also during that term in office, Truman witnessed the creation of the United Nations (UN), and created his foreign policy, named the "Truman Doctrine," to deal with the increasing threat of the Soviet Union by aiding countries that opposed the Soviets. Truman also promoted the Marshall Plan, named after his Secretary of State, which aided the rebuilding of Europe after the War. He also was a proponent of continuing FDR's New Deal policies and worked hard for the cause of civil rights, which included the desegregation of the military and fighting against segregation through his Justice Department.

Profiles in Politics
Harry S. Truman (1884 - 1972)

In 1948, Truman embarked on his re-election campaign. His opponent was the very popular Republican Governor of New York, Thomas Dewey. Truly a populist president, Truman gave many stern speeches decrying the Republicans as wanting to create a nation governed by the rich for the rich; his supporters began calling out "Give 'em hell, Harry!" which became his unofficial campaign slogan.

Even after inventing what is now known as "whistle-stop" campaigning, in which Truman rode a train cross-country and made a short visit at every train stop (which drew crowds), he was still the underdog. Everyone, including the press, the polls, and even his wife expected him to lose the election. In what is still considered to be the greatest upset in election history, Harry Truman won. One newspaper, the Chicago Tribune, on the evening of the election but before the results were known in this very tight race, printed in large, bold print "Dewey Defeats Truman." One of the most famous political photographs ever printed shows Harry Truman, triumphantly holding up a copy of that newspaper.

During his second term as President, Truman took part in the development of the North Atlantic Treaty Organization (NATO) and committed U.S. troops to defend South Korea against the Communist invasion by North Korea.[13] But in 1952, after eight years of tirelessly fighting both international wars as well as wars with Congress, Truman decided against a re-election run and instead retired to private life. His tremendous impact on both domestic and foreign affairs still reverberates in U.S. policy today.

Policies From the Booth

Deciding on the best candidate is a little like deciding on the best life partner. The initial 'dates' reveal a group of possible suitors who hold press conferences to announce their candidacy. Then we listen, watch, and wait to see how many items of appealing characteristics, and more importantly, how many policies we support, that we can tick off of our lists. Finding one candidate that has supports all the policies and issues we believe in is near impossible. One candidate may seem to have it all but go the opposite way that we want on one major issue, like abortion for example. Another may only have one issue, such as terrorism, that s/he builds h/er whole campaign around. Finally, there may be two candidates from the same party that look really good but you're not which one can beat the other party's seemingly unbeatable candidate, and you're torn. For the voters on extreme ends of the political spectrum, the courting process may be quite frustrating, since most candidates start out catering to their party base and then gravitate toward the middle to appeal to the rest of the nation. They then clarify their intentions if they survive the primaries. This is part of the game that becomes complicated for both campaign advisors and voters; the policies and issues need to be well-defined so that the voters can make clear distinctions between the candidates and their positions. However, most of their policies are compressed down into who has the catchiest sound bite, which doesn't really do anyone any favors. The 30-second (or less; see chapter 4 on The Media) sound bite tends to be value-neutral, easy to digest, and said in the least controversial way possible; in short, it doesn't say much. Again, the 'date' is when people tend to present their best face, which doesn't tend to be an entirely truthful reflection of the imperfections and shortcomings that everyone has.

Issues and Voting

One way that voters narrow down their choices come election time is by focusing on specific issues. This is known as issue voting. In order for issue voting to take place, several situations must be in place simultaneously.

Voter initiative and motivation. The issues that are of great importance to a voter inspire them to take time to become informed as to how each candidate stands on each issue.

Issue Differences. Each front running candidate must have distinguishable policies that are clearly conveyed to the voters, whether it is in person, online, or on television.

Many issues, one candidate. The issues should drive a voter toward one candidate, rather than split their attention among many candidates.

Focus on the issues. The issues should remain the primary focus for the voter, regardless of a candidates personality traits or even the party to which the candidate belongs.

It is true that all of these factors rarely unite during elections, so it is difficult for voters to turn all of their attention to just the issues. They usually must rely on the parties to inform them of the policies and issues that are in line with their core values and beliefs. So, the voter is reasonably assured that voting the party line is very close to an issue vote.

As election time draws near, voters begin to review the issues that have been important to them over the past few terms. They evaluate whether or not the incumbent or party in power has met up to their expectations. This method of issue voting is referred to as **retrospective voting**. It can be a very strong indicator of how the voters feel about the economic state of things under the incumbents' watch.

It's the Economy, Stupid

Retrospective Voting – When voters evaluate the past performance of an incumbent or party in power.

The Clinton Campaign for President in 1992 had a saying that served as a constant reminder to the candidate and staff what was important to the electorate, and consequently what had to be the basis of their message: "It's the Economy, Stupid!" This articulated a well knows campaign truism – the state of the economy has a significant effect on the outcome of presidential campaigns. This is especially true if the economy is on a downturn. The irony of this truism is that the President has relatively limited impact on the economy. However, voters will often hold an incumbent accountable for their own sense of economic insecurity in lean times, and will often give him credit in good times, even if he had little to do with the current economic environment. Hence Clinton's slogan of "It's the economy, stupid." The economy in 1992 was on the downturn, and Clinton's strategy was to highlight how the incumbent president's policies were inadequate, and how Clinton's economic proposals were superior. Ronald Reagan used this to his advantage in his re-election campaign in 1984, with his slogan of "Are you better off than you were four years ago?" This reminded voters that the economy in 1984 was much better than when he was elected in 1980, and sent the message that he was responsible for the turnaround. This particular slogan became popular with subsequent candidates and presidential elections. Economic slogans and sayings, such as "tax and spend liberals" or "voodoo economics" are common in campaigns, and sometimes elections serve as a forum for debate of significant changes in economic policy, as did the 1980 campaign and the debate over supply side economics (or "reaganomics.") Campaigns use these slogans to remind voters of their fundamental concerns of job security, health care, and general prosperity, and how the candidate will ease their fears and make them feel secure.

Foreign Affairs

Voters are not generally interested in foreign policy, except in specific instances that appeal to groups of voters, such as Cuban Americans in Florida who are concerned with the communist regime in their homeland. This also applies during times of war. Like his predecessors before him and their conflicts, President Bush's war in Iraq has proven to be a divisive issue with the voters. Many elected representatives have fallen prey to what the public perceived as handling foreign affairs inadequately. Wars such as those that took place in Korea and Vietnam should have served as a warning to politicians who are eager to engage in conflict. While the public generally views Republicans as better equipped to handle foreign issues, the Democrats have been able to turn this advantage into a weakness. Failure in Iraq cost the Republicans seats in Congress during the 2006 mid-term elections; so foreign affairs can have profound impact. After 9/11, one of the primary concerns being pumped into the media was, how will America handle the threat of terrorism at home and abroad? The importance of choosing a President who exercises diplomacy and who has experience with foreign policy has become more prevalent in the minds of voters since 9/11. A candidate who has what it takes to cultivate an atmosphere of respect and strength among the leaders of other countries has an advantage over one who devotes a disproportionate amount of time focusing on domestic affairs over foreign affairs, and vice versa. With the rise of industrial and technical globalization and free trade, war is but one facet of foreign affairs that a future President has to worry about.

Campaigns

A candidate's past is a large part of the whole campaign. In conjunction with the candidates' political experience, the campaign itself is responsible for painting the candidate in the best possible light. The campaign marketing staff must sell the candidate, sometimes to the point of distorting certain details about their past, in order to promote a likable product. Since primaries are moved up earlier in the year, the race to the presidential elections moves up in tandem. This forces candidates' to extend their campaign tours to last over the summer in the hopes that the early publicity will pay off in the later leg of the run. In fact, by the time the true campaigning season is in full swing in the fall, the candidates' chances of winning the favor of more substantially sized groups dwindles. So, while all of the above factors, electability, civic duty, party affiliation, and economy, do influence voting trends, the campaign itself plays a powerful role in shaping how the voters think and feel in the waning days of the campaign. Swaying those last few swing voters that are undecided, almost up until the first minute the polls open, is the final push that candidates focus on. Over the last few decades, most elections are won by a five percent margin, meaning that if campaigns can reach last minute voters, they may be able to pull off an upset.

Who Votes?

From the beginnings of democracy in Athens, participation in the political process not only thrived but was expected of citizens. Nowadays, the hard-won privilege of voting is often taken for granted and sometimes there are obstacles in place that prevent or discourage people from voting. The percentage of eligible voters that make it to the polls for elections is called voter turnout. Voter turnout is a strong indicator of how citizens' view their role in a representative democracy. There are statistics that point out that those who are financially stable, maybe even wealthy, and better educated tend to be more politically active than those in the lower-income strata. The group that doesn't make it to the polls on a consistent basis may include minorities and those that live in rural areas. Additionally, the more connected constituents are with their community, the more motivated they are to be politically active. Interestingly, married people or lifetime partners are more likely to vote than single people. Similarly, older generations are more likely to see the value in voting than younger generations. In this section, we will discuss a brief overview of voter turnout history in America and other countries, as well as the many reasons for low voter turnout.

A Brief Review

In 1870, the 15th amendment guaranteed men of color, whether previously a slave or not, the right to vote. Even though it was ratified into law, carrying this out in deed was not immediate. African-Americans were threatened, intimidated, beaten, and lynched with minimal hope of legal protection. Besides this, strong measures such as poll taxes, literacy tests, and good character tests were enforced by white election officials. The disenfranchisement was not remedied until nearly a century later, in 1964 and 1965, when the Civil Rights Act, the Voting Rights Act, and the 24th Amendment, which basically did away with any tax, poll or otherwise, as a voting constraint, passed.

African-Americans waiting to vote for the first time.
Courtesy of the Library of Congress

Despite the hardships blacks faced with upholding their right to vote, they at least had the 15th amendment; women had even less rights. To backtrack a bit, during the Constitutional Convention, Abigail Adams, wife of John Adams, reinforced the fact that women played a significant role in America's independence and they should be afforded the same rights and privileges as the men. It was not until courageous women such as Susan B. Anthony and Alice Paul spoke out and led the women's suffrage movement in the late 1800's. These brave women also became active in the abolition movement and the temperance movement (see chapter one). Finally, after more than 150 years, the Nineteenth Amendment was passed in 1920, giving women across the nation the right to vote. Later milestones in America's developing democracy were the 23rd Amendment, which gave constituents of the District of Columbia the right to vote in presidential elections; and the 26th Amendment, which extended suffrage to 18-year-olds.

Voter Turnout – Early Days & Other Countries

During the time of Thomas Jefferson and Andrew Jackson, (the late 1700's and mid-1800's), voter turnout gradually rose from approximately 11 percent of white males all the way to an impressive 80 percent.[17]   Sadly, the same cannot be said about voter turnout in the twentieth century. The percentage of voter turnout has remained fairly constant at 50 – 60 % during presidential elections and even lower during non-presidential election years. Many people may register to vote but when the actual numbers are calculated, the percentage of eligible voters that actually show up to vote is mediocre. This was evident in 1996, when 11 million citizens registered to vote, one of the highest increases at one point in history, due to the Motor-Voter Law. Despite concentrated efforts to make voting as accessible as possible (see For Your Consideration, Motor-Voter Law, chapter one), it doesn't necessarily translate into actual votes. It seems absurd for a country founded on

Profiles in Politics
Lyndon Baines Johnson (1908 - 1973)

Lyndon Baines Johnson, the 36th President of the United States, is probably best known for becoming president in the wake of the assassination of John F. Kennedy. The image of Johnson being sworn in as president while standing next to Jackie Kennedy that day in November 1963 is one of that is burned into the minds of all present and who witnessed the shooting on television. Lyndon Johnson, however, did accomplish much as president in his own right.

Lyndon Johnson was born in 1908 in rural Stonewall, Texas. His father held his father's former seat in the Texas legislature, and young Lyndon would travel with his father on the campaign trail, where

President Johnson signing the Civil Rights Bill in 1964.
© Bettmann/Corbis

he learned the ways of a politician and the art of good deal making. Johnson began his formal political life during 1931 in Washington D.C. as a secretary to a Democratic congressman. He first ran for Congress in 1937 after the death of the incumbent; he ran on a New Deal platform and bested his more experienced opponents.   In 1941, he lost his first race for a Senate seat because of ballot box stuffing by his opponent, although it was never proven. In 1948, Johnson beat his opponent, a popular governor; following his victory there were rumors of Johnson rigging the election.

Johnson became the Senate Majority Leader in 1955 and, using the skills he had learned from his father on the campaign trail as a youngster, he achieved many legislative victories, the biggest being the Civil Rights Act of 1957.[14] In order to get the bill passed, Johnson had to deflect criticisms from competing factions in the Democratic Party, which, at the time, included a significant segregationist wing.

In 1960, Johnson became the Democratic Vice Presidential candidate and along with John F. Kennedy, won the election with one of the narrowest margins of victory in history. When Kennedy was assassinated in 1963 and Johnson became president, he supported the implementation of Kennedy's plans, which included the continuance of the space program and a new civil rights bill. The Civil Rights Act of 1964, Kennedy's bill, was shepherded through a very divided congress. However, with the legislative expertise Johnson had honed during his time in Congress, it was the most ground-breaking civil rights legislation implemented in U.S. history.

Profiles in Politics
Lyndon Baines Johnson (1908 - 1973)

In 1964, Johnson also ran for re-election with his vision of a "Great Society;" a society that "rests on abundance and liberty for all." That platform, combined with the running of the "Daisy" ad, which played into fears that Republican candidate Barry Goldwater's aggressive defense policy might very well lead to nuclear war, are credited with helping Johnson win the presidency with one of the largest margins of victory in election history.

Another victory for Johnson was the space program, which, under his guardianship, was well on its way to achieving Kennedy's (and Johnson's) dream of landing a man on the moon.[15] Though this watershed event would occur after Johnson's presidency, it was Johnson who had the will to vigorously promote it; were it not for Johnson's commitment to the program, it may very well not have survived.

One of Johnson's signature victories came in 1967, when he appointed African-American Thurgood Marshall to the Supreme Court. This appointment was an enormous stride forward for the civil rights movement as well as a great credit to Johnson's commitment to that cause.

Lyndon Johnson's presidency was not without its pitfalls. Ongoing unrest in the inner cities where programs of the New Society were too slowly taking effect was causing massive riots in the streets of cities like Detroit, Harlem, and Watts. Rioters attacked white business owners, which led to a backlash against many of Johnson's New Society programs. Also, in 1964, he received congressional approval to escalate U.S. involvement in Vietnam via the Gulf of Tonkin Resolution. By the end of his presidency, Vietnam had escalated into a quagmire and was largely viewed as Johnson's War, in spite of the groundwork that had been laid by the previous three presidents. Vietnam was going so poorly that in 1968 Johnson decided against seeking re-election.[16]

In January 1973, Lyndon Baines Johnson passed away on his Texas Ranch. He will be forever known for his artful deal-making, forward thinking policies, and also, unfortunately, for the Vietnam War.

democratic principles to have such poor voter turnout numbers, even in comparison to other countries with the same basic principles. A number of countries, such as Australia and Denmark, who have held approximately the same number of elections as the United States since 1945 score in the 90 percentile while the U.S. scores only 48 percent.[18] Other democracies that have held approximately 13 elections, such as Germany and Israel, score in the mid 80s on a regular basis. Canada, our sister nation to the north, scores in the mid- 70's. Even countries with fledgling democratic governments, such as the Republic of the Congo (Zaire) and Malawi manage to turnout higher numbers than the U.S. Globally, voter turnout is generally beginning to come together over time, in both well-developed and newly developing democracies.

Explaining Low Voter Turnout

There are many reasons that may explain why large groups of people may not be inclined to vote. They may:

• Feel happy with the status quo (the way things are).

• Feel estranged or out of touch with the whole political system

• Feel that their vote doesn't count or they are simply apathetic about voting

• Have a strong distrust for the government

• Simply not want to take the time to vote

• Be too overwhelmed with the issues and do not feel educated on them

• Not be happy with the candidate choices and so they don't bother

The right to vote doesn't always guarantee that citizens will be motivated to do it. This cartoon emulates the fable of the Turtle and the Hare except that nobody wins the race because neither cared enough to win.
Courtesy of the Library of Congress

Incidentally, while literacy is not a conclusive indicator of higher or lower voter turnout, countries with higher literacy levels do have higher voter turnout in general.

It is interesting to note that in this day and age, with endless opportunities for people to become more politically active and informed, it doesn't necessarily improve voter turnout numbers. However, some elections may see a higher turnout of issue-voters because of hot debate topics such as same-sex marriage, healthcare, stem-cell research, immigration law reform, or our dwindling rights to privacy.

Voter Affective Filter

There is a theory in education regarding classroom participation; the theory goes that students have what is called an affective filter. The *affective filter* is a term used to describe the factors that may explain why students are slow or reluctant to participate in class; factors such as shyness, fear of judgment, intimidation by peers or by the teacher, or lack of interest in the subject. Voting can be thought of as having similar barriers that hinder voter participation. Some countries in Europe use specific tactics to ensure higher voter turnout, such as requiring citizens to vote and fining them if they don't. Furthermore, election days are holidays, lowering the barriers to vote significantly; although this may at first tempt Americans to just enjoy a day off without voting, the prospect of more polling place volunteers and making voting a positive low stress experience, it is worth a try.

Another effective way that other countries, mostly European ones, show a more successful voter turnout is through strong party unity and involvement. Efficient voter mobilization is spurred on by party rallies, block or community gatherings that celebrate election day activities, and going so far as party representatives showing up at doorsteps to drive the citizenry individually to the polling locations (see For Your Consideration, chapter one, *Democracy's March*).

Past & Future Solutions

One would surmise that starting at the very beginning, voter registration, would be an essential key to higher voter turnout. Some governments, again, mainly in Europe, actually register eligible voters automatically; higher voter registration equating higher voter turnout is also true in the United States, but not to the degree as it is in Europe.

In the ever-changing economy, people may have to move around more often than in past generations, which may also be problematic since voters must re-register with every move. There have been innovative approaches to motivating voters to register – registration through motor vehicle bureaus (Motor-Voter Law), slipping registration forms into class schedules on college campus, and utilizing public libraries and post office to deposit stacks of blank registration forms, available 24/7.

Factoid:
Our traditional understanding of the word *idiot* is generally an uneducated, ignorant person who is lacking in professional skill. However, *idiot* from the Greek, also originally described a private person, or one who was considered selfish because they chose not to participate in public affairs. The Greeks did not look kindly on idiots; in fact it was dishonorable to be so mentally inefficient that one could not discuss reason and logic.

FOR YOUR CONSIDERATION
FEDERAL ELECTION CAMPAIGN ACT

The Federal Election Campaign Act (FECA) was passed in 1971 to prompt disclosure of campaign financing and spending in federal elections. In 1974, it was amended to legally limit campaign contributions as well as create an independent regulatory commission – the Federal Election Commission - to oversee federal elections. It was again amended in 1976 and 1979 to allow unlimited candidate contributions to their own campaigns, and to expand the amount of hard money as well as soft money that parties could spend on party-building activities (see chapter 6, Interest Groups, for a review of hard and soft money).

Created by the 1974 amendment, the Federal Election Commission's duties are to oversee elections and enforce the rules created by FECA. They keep track of all campaign contributions and donors, as well as campaign spending. During election cycles, each candidate, party, and political action committee (PAC) are required to report all contributions and spending each quarter to the FEC, which then compiles a database that is released to the public via the FEC website at www.fec.gov.[19]

FECA and its subsequent amendments allowed large amounts of unregulated hard money and soft money to enter the election cycle, which in turn was viewed by many as an attempt to improperly influence election outcomes. The increasingly hefty amounts of soft money raised and spent by campaigns and parties on activities such as issue advocacy, which seemed to tread a fine line between being strict, straight advocacy and electioneering, convinced Congress to act again in 2002 with the Bipartisan Campaign Reform Act (BCRA, aka McCain-Feingold,) which put heavy regulations on soft money and placed clear limits on campaign and election spending.[20] With the issue of soft money and the public financing of campaigns, whether the FECA and the BRCA laws continue as currently written remains to be seen. In chapter 12, we will discuss the new court rulings, as of 2007, to McCain-Feingold.

Perhaps America can take some risks and try making election day synonymous with a holiday, like the Europeans do. Or, maybe we could extend polling times from one day to two days or even weeks, as has been tried in Texas; a longer period of absentee voting, or voting by mail ahead of time, has been implemented in places like California and Oregon. Another solution may be to allow same-day registration if someone's name doesn't appear on the rolls for whatever reason; some precincts have already implemented this. Taking a cue from early childhood conventional wisdom, Minnesota plants the seeds of democracy very early on by having little polling booths for children, so they too can experience the thrill of democracy and action when they accompany their parents on election day. Despite all of these creative and earnest attempts, the people are the ones ultimately responsible for showing up and taking initiative. It seems apparent that there are many groups of Americans that are more politically active in organizations and the campaign itself. However, the essence of the democratic process is for the citizen to feel a deeper more direct connection to their role in shaping their government; so much so that it motivates them to have full confidence in the power of their vote, a sentiment which is, unfortunately, becoming more and more elusive.

Elections and Voting in California

"Let us never forget that government is ourselves and not an alien power over us. The ultimate rulers of our democracy are not a President and Senators and Congressman and government officials, but the voters of this country."
– John F. Kennedy

It makes sense that in the late 1990's California led the nation in absentee voting, or, voting by mail, because Californians truly are always on the move. Perhaps due to the busy commuter lives of Californians, they prefer to review their ballots at their leisure. Overall, California's voter turnout record mimics the rest of the country which is high registration numbers but mid to low voter turnout in the 50 – 60 percent range. Nevertheless, as we mentioned earlier in explaining low voter turnout, an astronomical volume of eligible voters registering via the Motor-Voter Law does not necessarily translate into actual votes. In California, an eligible voter is someone who is at least 18 years of age and who has lived in California at least 29 days in advance of an election, with the exception of convicted felons or mentally institutionalized patients. Felons lose the right to vote while they are in prison but once they complete their probationary requirements, they are allowed to re-register and vote in the next election.

The reasons so many Californians fail to vote are not unlike the reasons the rest of the nation – apathy, uninformed, too young, non-citizens, and distrust or cynicism of the process; mainly, the most common reason given is that people are just too busy. However, with the highly charged debates regarding immigration law reform, voter turnout amongst those immigrants affected by this in southern California is on the rise, particularly with the large Latino population. Since it appears that the Republican Party is the most outspoken against immigration issues and affirmative action, this has resulted in substantial wins for the Democratic camp.

California is fairly liberal. Most of the state, especially the northern part, is left-leaning or at least centrist. Most of southern California, with the exception of Los Angeles County tends to be more conservative. The ratio of Asians, Latinos, and other non-whites to whites is growing; this makes it necessary for politicians to rethink how they address the hot topics that may be of importance to such a wide cross-section of ethnic backgrounds.

Candidates – Name Recognition & the Power of Family

Like many public professions, sometimes it's not what you know but who you know. High profile relationships, such as Maria Shriver of the Kennedy clan and Gov. Schwarzenegger, can sometimes determine the electability of a candidate in California politics. Celebrities like actor, producer, and jazz musician, Clint Eastwood, ran for mayor in his hometown of Carmel, because of frustration over the bureaucratic red-tape he experienced when trying to erect buildings and other city improvement projects. Having a bit of a popularity advantage, Eastwood won over 70% of the vote in 1986. Another celebrity with money to spend on personal projects was Sonny Bono of the 1960's famous husband and wife musical duo, *Sonny and Cher*. Bono also ran and won as the Republican candidate for mayor of Palm Springs in 1988 and he later won the GOP Congressional seat in the 44th district in 1994. Similar to Eastwood's establishment dilemmas, Bono's initial reasons for running were reportedly over red-tape that was slowing down his remodeling plans for his Italian restaurant. Due to a skiing accident in 1998, Bono's term was cut short, and his wife, Mary Bono (R-Palm Springs) was voted in to complete his Congressional term. She went on to be reelected on her own accord, showing that sometimes being a widow of an elected official is at first an initial boost but is not the focal point of strength for the politically minded family.

Family power definitely came into play when Democrats, Loretta Sanchez and Linda Sánchez made Congressional history in 2002 by being the first sisters and the first women in any familial context to serve in the U.S. House of Representatives at the same time.[21] As of the 2007 election, Loretta is going on her 6th term as Representative in the 47th district in Orange County, California. The 42-year-old Loretta is the more experienced politician of the two, while Linda, 33, won the Congressional seat in the 39th district in the southeast area of Los Angeles County and as of 2007, was serving her third term.[22] Some say that Linda's election to the 108th Congress was helped by big sister Loretta's notoriety. However, since she has been re-elected to her third term, Linda has more than proven herself worthy of her holding her own. One can see the differences between the two, even by looking at how they spell their names, with Linda preferring to use the Spanish accent in hers. Linda is the more liberal of the two and Loretta is slightly more conservative; these differences are evident in other aspects of their lives – music, decorating sense, fashion tastes, and website styles.[23] Nevertheless, they champion each others' careers and ultimately must get along since taking up residence, both literally and figuratively, on the Hill.

Career politicians are sometimes established on the basis of a parent's prior success, such as the Hahn family in Los Angeles. The tremendous accomplishments of Kenny Hahn, elected a record-breaking 10 times as county supervisor, paved the way for his son, Jim Hahn, to win the Los Angeles mayoral election in 2001. Jim went on to set a few records of his own (youngest city controller, record 16 years as city attorney). The Hahn family is a family rooted in politics for the people, with the most recent evidence being the 2005 re-election of Jim's sister Janice to the 15th district in Los Angeles.

Campaign Finance

Compared to the rest of the nation, the party system in California is extremely weak. Because of this, prospective candidates in California must have a strong staff and support system in place in order to compensate for the lack of support from the parties. Some candidates may even hire high-priced consultants to evaluate the strategy, marketing, and fund-raising activities of their campaign. Besides this self-reliance, candidates must also pay close attention to the image they project. It is very much like a salesperson, doing h/er best to present an appealing product; in this case, it is the candidate himself that is the product. Because of the cost involved with TV time, which is needed to market the candidate and campaign message, expenses can reach up to millions of dollars. As a result, the candidate relies much more on interest groups and political action committees (PACs) who can get around campaign spending reform laws. Candidates must also spend a fair amount of their funds on focused mailings to potential donors.

The lives of the candidates and their families are taken over by social gatherings. Unless you happen to be wealthy enough to fund your own events, most candidates must appear at as many public functions as humanly possible, in order to solicit much needed funds and be seen in the community. On a related note, Californians tend to be quite cynical of the political process, making the distraction of a candidate's wealth fleeting. Even though a candidate may be wealthy enough to buy more media time than the grassroots candidate, they still have to work at creating a substantial platform that doesn't involve their money power.

As is usually the case with the influence of money, the astronomical costs of running a campaign can undermine those that do not have the same financial advantages as the incumbent. Proposition 208, co-created by Common Cause and the League of Women Voters, passed in 1996; it was designed to place a check on campaign spending in California. For a short time the measure stipulated that contributions for legislative candidates were limited to $250 and for statewide candidates, $500. Furthermore, fund-raising was not allowed until six months prior to an election. The proposition was short-lived, however, when courts deemed it invalid. By 1998, the absence of limits on campaign spending was evident, when the most expensive election to date was held. Because the incumbent usually has a financial advantage, some see term limits as an indirect way to control excessive spending. Open elections in which there is no incumbent, perhaps due to retirement or death, automatically evens out the competition, "leveling the playing field," so to speak.

Direct Democracy and the Initiative Process

The main goal of direct democracy is to remove power from the elected officials and place it in the hands of the voters. At first glance, California elections are not extremely different from federal elections. As we discussed in several previous chapters, California's unique forms of direct democracy are carried out through the initiative, referendum, and recall. One example of direct democracy is the proposition. In order to place a proposition on the ballot, the number of voter signatures required must be equal to 5% of the votes cast in the last gubernatorial election; to amend the state constitution, the law requires 8% of the votes. Once the paperwork to circulate a petition is processed, the proponents of the issue have 150 days to obtain the required number of signatures. Then, the secretary of state receives the completed petition and verifies the signatures. If there are enough valid signatures, then the proposition is placed on the next election ballot. There is one caveat to this

A poster for candidate Olson, running for governor of California in 1938. After he was elected, there was alleged corrupt activity, but it was never confirmed because of WWII.[24]
Courtesy of the Library of Congress

process – they must obtain twice as many signatures as are required since many signatures are deemed invalid for various reasons; this is done for practical measures, and is not a legal prerequisite. This requires the special interest groups to spend more money advertising the propositions; to hire more solicitors to collect signatures; and we are back at square one, with exorbitant amounts of money being spent either way. The efficiency of California's style of direct democracy teeters between giving the voters complete control and/or calling upon legal counsel to review the validity of propositions before signatures are ever collected.

The money mêlée is probably the biggest threat to the democratic process in California than any other scandal; when the biggest spenders - not the best candidates – win the race. Nevertheless, California's strengths lie in the fact that it was one of the first states to implement the initiative process and now it is a common practice throughout the country. This illustrates that California tends to lead the nation on pertinent issues and innovative solutions on matters of democracy.

How Do We Compare?
Iran and the United States

Iran, or Persia, as it has been known for thousands of years, has been in a constant state of evolution. Their proximity to the Middle East, Europe, and Asia has allowed

them to develop into one of the world's most culturally diverse nations. In Ancient times, Persia was the world's first empire to challenge the Greeks in the west and Afghan tribes and Massagetae (Indus region) of Asia in the east. The trade routes between the Mediterranean and Asia allowed Persia to gain a wealth of knowledge and rare treasures, making them the envy of those around them who sought to gain the same fortune. This has been the story of Iran up to today; a nation of great wealth and beauty, but seen as a hostile force in the region. Iran and its main religion, Islam, is the first of several countries with which the United States has had a complex relationship; we will journey into Iran's tumultuous history in this section.[25]

Both Shia and Sunni Muslims worship in mosques like this one in Iran. Courtesy of the Library of Congress

Ancient Persia, Geography, and Religion

Iranians are believed to be descendants of **Aryans** from Central Asia. This is further supported by their language of Farsi, which is of Indo-European origin. This is important to note because it provides us with a starting point for comparison with nearby nations in the region. It is believed that the first group of Iranians migrated from Asia into the plateau around 1100 BCE and became the dominant group. Around 1600 BCE, the Persians, led by Hakamanish (Achaemenes, in Greek), began consolidating the group in the region under his control. By 550 BCE, Cyrus II (also known as Cyrus the Great or Cyrus the Elder), conquered the entire region and established the Achaemenid Empire, one of the first empires in the ancient world. Geographically, Iran is a high plateau surrounded by mountains, which is an ideal location; it is a natural causeway for half of the world in terms of trade and invasions between the Middle East, Europe, Asia, and Africa. From 550 BCE to the 1940's, Iran has conquered or been conquered by the surrounding countries or other world powers.[26]

Islam, which literally translated means submission to God, was introduced in Iran in 637 CE by Arabs and reinforced by centuries of Ottoman rule. In 632, the prophet Muhammad died, causing a deep division within Islam over who was the rightful successor. The two groups that emerged from these factions were the Sunnis and Shias. The groups that claimed Muhammad's successor should be Ali, his cousin and son-in-law became known as Shia, meaning followers. Ali was assassinated in 661 CE and became known to Shias as the first **imam** (religious leader). Hussein, Ali's son, tried to claim the title. His army was beaten and he was captured, tortured, and killed in Karbala (Iraq), which is now one of Shias holy shrines. Hussein's death introduced the concept of martyrdom for Shias. In all, Shias have 12 imams, the last having disappeared in 873 CE. Some Shias believe that the twelfth imam will return and create a world full of justice.[27] Currently, Islam is the world's fastest growing major religion. Of the two groups, the Sunnis are larger, consisting of about 80% of all Muslims. Shia are the remaining 20%, approximately 100 million people mainly located in southern Iraq, parts of Lebanon, eastern Arabia, and Iran.[28] It should be noted that just like all religions, there are factions within Islam who interpret the Quran to fit their needs. The Quran states that you should not fight against people of the book, which refers to all Jews, Christians, and Muslims (all three religions believe in the same God). Contrary to its simplistic common usage, the term jihad does not translate into holy war; a more accurate description of the term would be the struggle of Muslims either as a group or individually, to live right and defend the community. While the Quran does permit Muslims to defend themselves and their religion, it is considered to be a peaceful religion, like Judaism and Christianity; also similar to Judaism and Christianity, there are those within the faith that twist the scriptures to extremes.

Aryan –
Old Persian name for Iran; also associated with a group of nomad warriors from the Caucus Mountains; used by Nazis in Germany in the 1930's as a label for their supposed superior white race.

Imam –
Saintly religious leader; when capitalized, refers to descendants of Ali, who are regarded by Shia Muslims as the rightful successors to Muhammad.

Introduction of Western Political Thought

Throughout the next thousand years, Iran encountered many trials, such as conflicts with the Ottoman Empire, other Arab states, and its northern and eastern neighbors. It also suffered through weak leadership and financial ruin. Take for example Nasr al-Din Shah who ruled Iran for most of the 1800s. In order to gain support from European countries to unite against the Ottoman Empire, the Uzbeks, the Afghans, and other regional powers, the Shah made countless concessions to European leaders and businesses in order to modernize the country and military. He signed military contracts for Officers from Russia's Cossacks crop to create and train an elite military unit called the Persian Cossacks Brigade. Part of Iran's modernization involved officials appointed by the Shah; their duties were to run the new bureaucracy. In an attempt to strengthen the monarchy, the new Prime Minster began to assert control over the countries' provinces and Islamic leaders by updating the tax system, encouraging trade and industry with foreign powers, and introducing western education. In 1851, the Shah opened the first Polytechnic College with European instructors who taught military and technical subjects. At the same time both Russia and Britain began to claim Iranian territory in Asia. After several conflicts, the Shah was forced to concede all land in Afghanistan to Britain and in Central Asia to Russia. In the process, he pushed the treasury close to bankruptcy. With the influence of Europe came western liberal values, which conflicted with the teachings of the **Mullahs**; as a result, these religious clerics would often lead protests against the Shah.[29] By the 1890's, Iran was financially desolate and contracts with European powers had weakened its' economy. The tremendous wealth acquired by the Shah, his family, and corrupt bureaucrats caused increased taxation, which intensified public unrest; unfortunately, their protests fell on deaf ears. In addition, in 1890, the Shah had given a British company a monopoly over the tobacco trade. In response, the Mullahs issued a **fatwa** forbidding the use of tobacco. The ban was observed by many Iranians forcing the Shah to cancel the contract. This again, set the monarchy up on a collision course with the stringent practices of the religious leaders. With the introduction of liberalism, radical ideas began to emerge and calls for political change began to surface. Finally in 1896, Nasr al-Din Shah was assassinated, allowing for his son, Mozzafar al-Din Shah to become his successor.

Ancient Persian artwork sculpted into a city wall.
Courtesy of Jupiter Images

Mullah –
Title of respect given to a teacher (usually male) who is educated in theology and sacred law, and who usually holds an official post.

Fatwa –
An official ruling or legal opinion issued by a Muslim religious scholar/jurist.

Movement towards a Constitutional Monarchy

Having grown up with an opulent lifestyle, Mozzafar did not alter his habits. Within several years, he had borrowed and spent several large loans from Russia on trips to Europe and ostentatious luxuries. Unable to pay the loans due to lack of taxes, he granted more concessions to European powers, especially Russia, as a form of repayment. Again, the Mullahs used the eminent power of foreign companies to provoke the public into holding protests and to demand a check on the Shah's power.

The Shah ignored the call for political and economic reforms, which further fueled the public's anger. Their dissatisfaction finally erupted when, in January of 1906, religious leaders and merchants took to the streets in mass demonstrations. The Shah agreed to create a "house of justice" in order to end the protests. Shortly thereafter, the Shah went back on his promise. By June, the demonstrations were once again carried out, and 10,000 Iranians overtook the British compound in Tehran. In August the Shah once again promised political reforms by creating a constitutional monarchy. Elections were held in October to choose an assembly who would draft a constitution. In this constitution, it provided limitations on royal power; it also allowed for a cabinet to be approved by the newly created and elected parliament (Majlis). Popular sovereignty and limited political liberties would be granted (freedom of speech, press, association, and security of life and personal property). On December 30, 1906, the Shah signed Iran's first constitution into law. Within five days of creating a constitutional monarchy, however, the Mozzafar al-Din Shah died.[30]

When Mohammed Ali became Shah he wanted to remove the constitution and all of its provisions. The new Shah was met with stiff opposition from the Majlis and the merchant class. After several run-ins with the Majlis, the Shah ordered his Persian Cossacks Brigade to destroy the Majlis and arrest most of the representatives. News of the event spread to the countryside until July of 1909, when the Shah was deposed in a revolution by the combined forces that supported the Majlis. The Shah fled to Russia and was forced into exile.

Despite this victory, the Majlis had several serious problems to overcome. The first was the demise of trade with foreign powers. Without foreign trade, the economy continued to suffer, causing additional discontent with the Iranian people. They were hoping for a better life under the new constitutional government. Second was the threat from the former Shah; with the support of the Russian military, Mohammed Ali Shah launched an invasion in July of 1910. The war would further weaken the fragile power of the Majlis. The third and most dangerous threat was the Anglo-Russian Agreement of 1907. The agreement divided Iran into two parts, the northern part, which would be controlled by Russia and the southern part, which was controlled by Britain. The central part of Iran would be the neutral territory where Britain and Russia would use their influence to gain whatever economic and political advantages they could. Finally, in December of 1911, the Majlis clashed with Russia over the collection of taxes in the neutral zone. When Russia threatened to invade, the Bakhtiari chiefs took control of the Majlis by force, closed the assembly, and once again, delayed the implementation of the Iranian constitution. From this point on, Iran was a semi-colony of both Britain and Russia until after World War I. After the war ended, Britain became the dominant power in the region while Russia was preoccupied with its own civil war. After several years of Iran's uncertain future, in February of 1921, Reza Khan, an officer of the Persian Cossacks Brigade, seized power. In 1925, he began the Pahlavi dynasty and along with it, a new chapter in Iranian history.[31]

The Pahlavi Era

In April of 1926, Reza Khan was crowned as Reza Shah Pahlavi. With the help of army officers and bureaucrats, most of whom were trained in Europe, Reza Shah Pahlavi began to centralize the government and revisit the modernization of Iran. Originally, he pondered the creation of a republic but the idea was met with opposition from the Mullahs, so he abandoned it. Over the next decade, the Shah continued to westernize the country and usurp power from the regional governments as well as the tribes. He created a secular educational system, including a new European style University in Tehran. The primary schools and Universities would encourage this new, more nationalistic thinking. Furthermore, the Shah began to expand the economy by creating public works projects, such as road improvements, railroads, and state owned factories that produced consumer goods, adding to Iran's growing wealth. In addition, by manufacturing products themselves, Iran was becoming self-reliant instead of seeking foreign trade.

Given the conflicts with the Mullahs in the past, the Shah's modernization plan was also designed to weaken the power of the religious clerics. He was systematic in his affront on the Mullahs' power: he created a secular state with secular education; codified laws, both civil and criminal; formulated a legal system which was under the scrutiny of an independent judiciary, free of religious leaders; and required that legal and civil documents be notarized by the bureaucracy, not the clerics. All of these steps transferred tremendous power from the Mullahs to the State. The Shah also took measures to emancipate women. He opened schools to them and allowed them into the work force. He also advocated changing the style of dress from the **chador** to a more modern European style. These were all attempts to inspire secular and nationalistic trends; all of this change came at a cost, especially for those steeped in the traditional teachings of the Mullahs.

Part of his economic policies didn't filter down to the lower class. Foreclosures on property increased because people couldn't pay the taxes. Instead of having the property auctioned off, the Shah added it to his personal assets, thus acquiring large tracts of land. In order to accomplish his centralization of power and insure conformity, the Shah not only cracked down on the religious leaders' powers but also those of the Majlis, the press, and any opposition to his policies. As time progressed, dissatisfaction among the population grew.

In the foreign policy arena, Reza Shah terminated the majority of contracts with Britain and Russia. In 1932, he canceled the Anglo-Persian Oil agreement that produced and exported Iran's oil to Britain. In order to offset these losses, the Shah sought commercial contracts with Germany; by the beginning of World War II, Germany was Iran's largest trading partner.

When the war began, Iran declared itself neutral but on August 26, 1941, it was invaded by both Britain and Russia. The strategic location of Iran allowed supplies to flow from Africa and the Middle East into the Soviet Union. This life line became even more critical when Hitler invaded the Soviet Union in 1941. Knowing that the British would not allow him to keep his throne, Reza Shah abdicated his title on September 16 to his son, Mohammed Reza Shah Pahlavi. Reza Shah was taken to Johannesburg, South Africa by the British. He died in Johannesburg in July 1944.

Chador –
The full-body cloak Muslim women in Iran are expected to wear outdoors; depending on design and how the woman holds it, the chador may or may not cover the face.

President Truman with Prime Minister Josef Stalin at the Berlin Conference in 1945. Courtesy of the Library of Congress

One key development to aid Iran from foreign intervention occurred in January 1942 when Iran entered into a treaty with Britain and the Soviet Union that allowed them to use Iran's territory in exchange for their withdrawal after the war. In September 1943, Iran declared war on Germany entering the war on the side of the allies. Later in November at the Tehran Conference, President Franklin D. Roosevelt, Prime Minister Winston Churchill, and Prime Minister Josef Stalin reaffirmed their promise to aid Iran in its independence and help maintain their territorial integrity; furthermore, they promised to provide economic assistance when needed. These promises were short-lived. Within the next year, Iran's economy was in shambles. Immigrants fleeing the war in Europe and Asia began to take refuge within Iran's boundaries. Xenophobia began to emerge. By 1944, Russia and the United States began competing for Iranian oil contracts. In order to curtail a conflict, the Majlis forbid any discussion of Iran's oil until the war had ended. When the war did end, British and American forces began withdrawing from Iran as promised, whereas the Soviet Union began to amass troops along its borders, remaining in Iran after the war. Under pressure, Iran agreed to provide the Soviet Union with oil in exchange for removing its troops from Iran's territory. It should be noted that Iran became a member of the UN for the purpose of joining forces with the allies during the war. As tensions between the United States and the Soviet Union began to surface, the U.S., Britain, and the UN also applied pressure on the Soviets to withdraw their forces as well.

In addition to this, Iran faced problems within its own government. Tudeh, the communist party, started gaining more power within Iran. With tensions increasing, the internal factions of the Majlis began to fight causing the government to collapse. A new leader came forth, Mohammed Mossadegh, from the National Front Party. One of the first acts his government performed was taking the oil back from foreign control. The Majlis passed a law requiring that the government, not a foreign company, was to produce and export the oil. As the cold war heated up, the Soviet influence over Iran began to shrink while the United States' influence grew. In 1947, the U.S. and Iran signed an agreement for military aid and military advisors.

Mossadegh and Nationalism

Around 1949, Mossadegh and his National Front Party began pushing for nationalist policies such as comprehensive agricultural and industrial expansion; however, the focus was oil. After months of unfruitful negotiations with Britain over oil profit sharing, on March 15th the Majlis voted to nationalize the oil industry. Shortly thereafter in April 1951, Mohammed Reza Shah named Mossadegh, Prime Minister of Iran. When British workers left Iran, as a reaction, Britain imposed an embargo on Iranian oil. In September of the same year, Britain froze Iran's assets, expanded the ban to exporting of goods to Iran, and filed a claim at the International Court at The Hague against Iran as well. After losing the case at The Hague, Britain was forced by the United States to offer more favorable terms; but, Mossadegh found this as an unacceptable position of weakness and rejected their offer. He was assured by his party that all of his demands could be met if they continued to hold out. As Mossadegh's popularity grew, so did his demands - not only of foreign governments but also of the Shah. Eventually, Mossadegh become more powerful and attempted to seize complete power. He defied the Shah's authority by dissolving the Majlis on August 3, 1953. Mossadegh, in response to Britain's embargo, secretly ordered currency to be printed, again without the Shah's consent. His intent was to pay Iran's debts without the hard currency to back it up. In a clear attempt to usurp power from the Shah, Mossadegh had overstepped his position as Prime Minister and, as a result was discharged from office.[32] Mossadegh refused to relinquish power, which was a bold act of insubordination. By this time, unbeknownst to Mossadegh, the United States and Britain had approved Operation Ajax to oust him from power. Kermit Roosevelt (President Roosevelt's cousin), who was an operative for the Central Intelligence Agency (CIA), traveled to Iran and coordinated the military coup with the Shah and loyalist military units. The operation began on August 13 by naming a new Prime Minister; when Mossadegh resisted, the military was sent in to arrest him. Over the next six days, it appeared that Mossadegh's forces would prevail; but, by August 19, the Shah units triumphed. Mossadegh was sentenced to three years in prison but was allowed to live under house arrest until his death in 1967.[33]

The Shah's White Revolution

During the Cold War, Iran and the United States became allies against the Soviet Union. By entering into several agreements the US provided Iran with military assistance and Iran provided the United States with oil. During this time, the Shah began the second development from 1959 to 1962. This development was spurred on by rising oil prices. While the reforms seemed to be working, the populace became discontent with the slow progress, as they had in years past. In August 1953, after an attempted coup, martial law was imposed until 1957.[36] During this time, political dissent was treated as treason against the monarchy; this included contradictory acts of religious leaders.

Beginning in the 1960's, Iran was fraught with the same problems as before. The economy did not turn under the second economic plan as the Shah had hoped. This brought civil unrest among the lower classes. The third economic plan was initiated in 1962 along with political reforms. Under this new plan, freedoms such as the press and association were loosened to release some political tension; despite this, the single-most important component of the Shah's economic plan was land distribution. By redistributing large areas of land held by the wealthy, including land owned by the royal family and the Mullahs, one of the major desired impacts of this reform was to increase wealth at the poorest levels of the population. The purpose was to move the lower strata up the economic ladder, giving them better opportunities. The initial shock to the economy was the recession, which was further along with higher unemployment. Building on the land reform, the government instated six new measures, which included profit-sharing for workers in the private sector, creation of national forests and other public lands, electoral law reform giving more representation to the farmers and workers, the sale of government factories to finance added land reforms, and the creation of the Literacy Corp and Health Corp. The Literacy Corp and Health Corp allowed for men to fulfill their required military service by becoming teachers or administering basic health needs in impoverished areas. The Health Corp made Iran the first country in the Middle East to provide universal vaccinations.[37] At the same time, the Shah announced that he would extend the voting franchise to include women.

These reforms did not directly impact the core issues of the poor or give them money for their immediate needs. The reforms, mainly the land reform and women's suffrage, generated a backlash from the religious establishment. In June of 1963, Ayatollah Ruhollah Khomeini, a religious leader in Qom, gave a speech that directly attacked the Shah; Khomeini was consequently arrested. The arrest sparked riots in the streets, to which the Shah responded with force.

Khomeini was released from house arrest in April 1964 but resumed his criticism of the government and the Shah. By November the authorities could no longer ignore his criticisms and Khomeini was forced into exile; first to Turkey and then relocated to An Najaf, Iraq, for thirteen years, just as Saddam Hussein was coming into power. Over the next few years, the government extended the educational reform programs by creating technical schools and community colleges for the lower classes. Eventually, the reforms began to work, which appeased those that were active in the protests and political unrest. Unfortunately, this did not carry over to the religious establishment.

At the beginning of the 1970's, the Iranians celebrated 2,500 years of uninterrupted rule by the monarchy, dating back to Cyrus the Great. Two events connected to this celebration placed the Shah squarely in opposition to everything the Mullahs stood for. The first event was when the Majlis granted the Shah the title of Arya-Mehr, or "Light of the Aryans." This, according to the Mullahs, put the Shah on par with God and it was absurd and unacceptable. To add insult to injury, the event was more like a Hollywood event, with foreign heads of states and celebrities, not a traditional Iranian ceremony, so it was therefore undignified and too westernized. The next event of conflict occurred in 1975 over the changing of the calendar to coincide with the first year of Cyrus' reign. The Mullah's viewed this deviation of the traditional Islamic calendar as highly disrespectful to their religion. While in exile in Iraq, from what would turn into a most strategic standpoint, Khomeini continued his attack on the Shah. He published a book titled Velayat-e-Faqih which translated basically means *The Vice Regency of the Islamic Jurist*; in it he promoted the creation of an Islamic state headed by the faqih (Islamic Jurist). As more modernization took place under the Shah, Khomeini was able to increase his discipleship of those who had been disillusioned by the perceived disregard for traditional values. Encouraged by the guerrilla tactics used in Vietnam, Cuba, and earlier in China, the youth of Iran began to form rebel groups.[38] Most of the groups were dissolved by security forces but two groups that were able to survive were the Fadayan (Cherikha-ye Fada-yan-e Khalq, or People's Guerrillas), and the Mojahedin (Mojahedin-e Khalq, or People's Struggle). The latter of the two turned to Islam for their political ideology. Coincidentally with the formation of these groups, attacks on police states, foreign businesses, government leaders, including diplomatic personnel became a common occurrence.

The Islamic Revolution

In early 1977 it was apparent that the Iranian economy was faltering. Corruption was wide spread amongst government officials. The differences between the classes were becoming more incongruent, especially amid the wealthy and the poor. This, in addition to the growing western influence on Iranian culture only reinforced Khomeini's position on the monarchy. The government also alienated the businesses and industrial base of the economy. In order to manage the price of rent, the government took over empty apartments and housing and managed them for the owners. As resentment grew among the general public, so did the repression by the government. Human rights groups, such as Amnesty International, began to call attention to the human rights abuses that were taking place. To offset the criticisms, the Shah released political prisoners and announced new regulations protecting legal rights. Many groups who were extremely upset with the Shah's rule took advantage of these reforms and began to openly protest the government.

January 1978 brought negative change for the government. Protests against the government broke out in Qom, over an article that accused Khomeini of being a British agent. The government responded to the protests by confronting

Ramadan –
Occurring during the ninth month of the Islamic calendar (usually around January), this Muslim holiday lasts for one full month. The Holy Quran spells out the attitude and practices that Muslims should observe. During this time, all Muslims fast from dawn until dusk, with the exception of the sick, elderly, those on pilgrimage, and pregnant or nursing women; they must make up the days they cannot fast later on in the year, or they must feed a needy person for every day missed). This practice begins at puberty and continues through adulthood. They fast not just from food but also from sex, smoking, speaking ill-words of anyone, greed, telling lies, and so on. This is done not only for health reasons but primarily as a time of self-purification, reflection, and a closer walk with Allah. It is believed that by refraining from worldly comforts, one can gain true sympathy with the poor and hungry.[39]

Lt. Gen. Katoozian, first from the left, along with other cabinet members, greets His Imperial Majesty, Mohammed Reza Shah Pahlavi, in the royal palace in late 1978. Courtesy of ABT.

demonstrators and amidst the chaos, several were killed. This stoked the turbulent fires of those who held the Shah responsible. By the summertime, large protests were common in a number of cities across Iran, which resulted in more deaths. Khomeini played on the protesters' passions, continuing to call for civil protests and removal of the Shah from power. In August of 1978, a fire broke out in the Rex Cinema in Abadan, killing over 400 people. While evidence suggests that the fire was started by religious students inspired by Khomeini's rhetoric, with the intent of further eroding the support for the Shah, the convenient scapegoat were the Shah's own secret police. In an attempt to reduce tension, the government released religious clerics and other prisoners from jail. But, any attempt to turn back the tide of revolution proved to be too late. On the 4th of September, over 100,000 people took part in a massive public prayer ceremony, which marked the final day of **Ramadan**; this two-day event usually turned into a convenient time to show anti-government sentiments rather than focusing on the holiday itself. In 1978, Ramadan was no different – except this time, the protest rallies became unruly, requiring the deployment of troops. As a result, the eighty-seven deaths that took place between September 7th and 8th forever became known as "Black Friday." Martial law was declared in Tehran and eleven other Iranian cities. These events gave further credence to Khomeini's criticisms. In October the Iraqi government expelled Khomeini from the country due to his inflammatory discourse. Khomeini established new headquarters in Paris and was able to continue his call for an Islamic revolution. While in Iraq, Khomeini was unable to directly communicate with his followers in Tehran, but now that he was in France, he was able to assume direct control over the movement; strikes and civil unrest continued, causing more clashes with the Iranian government. The strikes shut down the fragile economy, which is perhaps the most efficient way to break a government down in the eyes of its citizenry. The Shah made a public appeal for calm only to be met with more objections. Finally, on January 16, 1979 the Shah and his family traveled to wherever it was safe - Panama, Egypt, and so on; the short holiday from the chaos turned into exile, and they were never to return to their homeland again.

Khomeini Returns

Despite the government's attempts to keep Khomeini at bay during the transition period, they were unable to. On February 1, 1979, Khomeini returned to Iran with a hero's welcome, greeted by millions. By February 5th, komitehs (revolutionary committees) had appeared to take control of the day to day operations in the urban areas, which undermined the already weakened government. By February 12th, some military units had defected to Khomeini's side and seized munitions and arms from military armories and police stations, disbursing them to the crowds outside. That afternoon, with the military deciding that it would remain neutral, this aided Khomeini's final evolution into power; the Pahlavi monarchy and government had ended.

Like with most revolutions, death became part of every day life for the next year. As the government faltered, revolutionary committees began to take over. All claimed legitimacy but none had real power. Each group proclaimed the superiority of their own agendas. Khomeini and his new government tried to gain control over these groups but had internal issues to deal with first. As the revolutionary courts began to pass sentences on former government officials, the local committees carried out illegal arrests and executions. Throughout the country, former police and loyalists to the monarchy were being arrested and/or executed. By the end of summer, the central revolution committee had dissolved or combined many of the smaller neighborhood committees. Even though a working government was put in place, Khomeini saw himself as above them and therefore did not have to adhere to their policies; he became what was referred to as the Supreme Legal Guide. So, in response to the rogue committees, Khomeini and his clerics formed the Revolutionary Council to act as the supreme ruling governance. Once established, they were able to disband the collection of smaller committees, and over time, more and more administrative duties assumed by the Revolutionary Council. Because the exiting government did not have the funds or the ability to provide security, the Council created its own security forces. All in all, by the end of summer, the Council had passed a number of reforms, most of which were designed to shift power and wealth away from the individuals to the state, reversing the establishment the Shah had created. Banks, insurance, major industries such as oil, expansive patches of land, and wealth were seized.[40]

On April 1, 1979, Iran became an Islamic Republic or a theocracy. In order to support this new government, Khomeini drafted a new constitution. Overall the new constitution did not veer from the original 1906 constitution; the main difference was that instead of a monarchy, it touted a semi-presidential system, similar to France. Various factions who basically held the same platform as Khomeini were allowed to review the new constitution before it came to a vote. They were surprised to find that Khomeini did not grant religious leaders added jurisdiction and power. In order to appease the conservative clerics, Khomeini decided to let them amend the new constitution. After much deliberation, an amended version was presented that championed a clerical domination over the state. Internal power struggles ensued but the Revolutionary Council would hold its position.

During this time, Khomeini and the splinter groups' spoke out continuously against the ideas and influence of the west. Ironically, the new Islamic Republic still had to deal with the contracts that had been previously set up by the Shah with the U.S. Furthermore, Iran needed military materials and updated intelligence about the Soviet Union and Iraq. Now just a shadow of the royal figurehead he once was, on November 1st, the Shah was allowed to enter the United States for medical treatment. Fearing a U.S. supported coup, hundreds of thousands of Iranians marched in the streets of Tehran, demanding the Shah's extradition. On November 4th, men who called themselves the "students of Imam's line"[41] took over the United States Embassy in Tehran

Pres. Carter appeared on television to notify the nation of the 52 Americans that were taken hostage in Iran. Courtesy of the Library of Congress

and seized over 52 American hostages. This crisis lasted over a year and within that time frame, the United States froze Iranian assets and led an attempted but failed rescue mission. After realizing that the hostages could no longer aid them, Iran opened negations with the United States for the hostages' release; the talks took place in West Germany, allies to the U.S. On January 20, 1981, Iran released the hostages the very same day that then former governor Ronald Reagan was taking the Presidential oath of office. In return, the United States released over $11 billion of Iran's money that had been seized during the revolution. As part of the deal, Iran agreed to pay over $6 billion for loans and other restitutions to other foreign nationals. Iran desperately needed the money for its war with Iraq that began the following year, in September 1980. The Iraq-Iran conflict would continue for nearly a decade.

In addition to the conflict with Iraq that would eventually devastate the economy and eliminate an entire generation of Iranian males, internally, Iran had a number of clashes of their own. Power struggles between the Mullahs, the military, and the Majlis were constant, only to end with bloodshed. With each incident, more power was shifted to the religious factions. An Islamic legal system and Islamic code of social and moral behavior came to be imposed. Any opposition to the new government or its policies was met with severe penalties. On average, an estimated seventy-five people were executed a day by each faction. **Amnesty International** documented a very conservative number of close to 3,000 executions that were conducted within a 12-month period; thousands more were imprisoned. At the same time, councils were created to scrutinize each citizen, to insure that their Islamic beliefs were intact; in order to work in the civil service, attend university, or run for political office, this type of interview was required. If one was found to be deficient in faith and Islamic values, one could not advance. The Council of Guardians, still a functioning entity today, is a panel of senior clerics that verifies that all legislation meets the criteria established under Islamic law. Strict Islamic moral codes were enforced and women were forced to wear chador and single women of any age were required to be escorted by a male relative at all times. These moral police were empowered to arrest or detain anyone who did not adhere to the strict Islamic dress code or conduct. The country began to fade into a repressed state.

With the U.S. imposed **embargo** and **sanctions**, permitted by the United Nations, Iran's economy began to decline again. Unlike previous forays into democracy under the Shah, protests were not allowed. Anyone who criticized the theocratic government faced severe penalties. Iran tried to gain some favor with the United States during the late 1980's by acting as a liaison between the U.S. and Lebanese groups who took American hostages. When Ayatollah Khomeini died in 1989, Iran, in some ways had become the nation that he dreamed of, a theocracy exclusively governed by Islamic law.

Iran after Khomeini

The death of the Ayatollah created a power vacuum that, if not dealt with in time, would have thrown the country into further disarray. As Supreme Legal Guide, Khomeini had governed the country for nearly a decade; the question now was who was going to replace him. The Assembly of Theological Experts that was comprised of senior theologians and other religious jurists, selected President Ali Khamenei to be the new Supreme Legal Guide. Khamenei had served as president from October 1981. As president, it was Khamenei who imposed the strict enforcement of Islamic code that led to the oppression of many Iranians. This served as an indication of how things were going to be under Khamenei's watch. As Supreme Legal Guide, Khamenei had the power to overrule all laws and elections.[42]

Elections to replace Khamenei post as president were held in August of 1989. The winning candidate was the Speaker of the Majlis, Ali Akbar Hashemi Rafsanjani. Compared to Khamenei, Rafsanjani was more moderate in his domestic and foreign policies. He relaxed the social restrictions on women's dress, interactions between the sexes, and usage of social vices. By 1992, Khamenei had overturned these policies and sent the moral police to reinstate the strict codes. Rafsanjani won reelection in 1993 but his margin of victory narrowed and his policies were less controversial. Rafsanjani was replaced in 1997 by Mohammed Khatami who was also viewed as a reformer. Khatami gained support from women and the younger generation of Iran because of his more liberal policies, which tried to include "all Iranians in the electoral process." Even though most of Khatami's plans for reform were approved by the Majlis, they were blocked by the Council of Guardians. By the end of his second term, Khatami was unable to gain approval of any key reforms.[43]

Amnesty International (AI) – A humanitarian grass-roots organization founded in London in 1961; AI is a Nobel Prize-winning activist organization with over 1.8 million members worldwide. One of their functions is to undertake research that focuses on the prevention and termination of egregious abuses of the rights to physical and mental integrity, freedom of conscience and expression, and freedom from discrimination. AI stands alone and neither condemns nor condones any ideologies; not even the views of the victims whose rights they are protecting. It exists simply to carry out, with impartiality, their mission to protect human rights of all citizens of the world.

Embargo – A government order to prohibit merchant ships from moving in or out of its ports, thus banning trade with other countries.

Sanctions – Actions imposed by one or more states on another to force compliance with a former legal contract or agreement.

The presidential election of 2005 saw a return to the old steadfast conservative ways. Hundreds of candidates were prevented from running for office by the Council of Guardians because they were considered too liberal. The former President Rafsanjani ran again but lost to a virtual unknown, Mahmoud Ahmadinejad, the Mayor of Tehran. Ahmadinejad was a student during the revolution and being a hard-line conservative. wanted to put the country back on his version of the correct course.[44]

After all that it had experienced, Iran is still trying to find its footing. It can be viewed as a young adult trying to show its independence, defying the world while all the while, facing an internal struggle. Ahmadinejad had put Iran on a surefire collision course with the west and the UN. His pursuit of uranium enrichment programs has forced the UN to impose sanctions. The capture of 12 British sailors[45] and Marines in April of 2007 illustrated Iran's internal power struggles between the various factions as well as its desire to challenge the United States and Britain in the region. These events may be part of a larger systemic problem, the business of oil. Ahmadinejad has promised to use the oil revenues to aid the poor. The problem is that Iran has to import and subsidize petroleum because it lacks the refining capability. These subsidies have cost the Iranian trade industry to lose billions of dollars, resulting in a downward economic spiral. The government has also begun rationing gas, which provoked civil discontent and riots. In this 21st century, the dilemmas in Iran can be seen as characteristic of most Middle Eastern countries. With resentment building against the west, continued attempts to modernize are met with religious backlash generated by Islamic fundamentalists. This combination of religion, nationalism, managed economies, and strict social norms has forced many counties like Iran to placate their intellectual and business endeavors while catering to the demands of the extremists.[46] In the end, none of the groups in Iran are pleased with the situation, placing the government at odds with its population.

Chapter Summary

Voting in elections is the most basic and vital act of participation in a democratic government. The President and Vice President are elected every four years; Congress holds elections every two years for the entire House of Representatives and one-third of the Senate; and mid-term elections are held two years after a presidential election and in the middle of the president's term. The electoral college, a "winner-take-all" system is responsible for officially electing the President and Vice President. People must cast their votes so that the electoral votes from their state will be counted. Two exceptions to the electoral college system, Nebraska and Maine; these states base the "winner-take-all" on each congressional district instead of the overall states popular vote. Many problems have been cited with the electoral college. While the U.S. tends to have more elections than any other western style democracies, its produces some of the lowest voter turnouts in the world. There are as many reasons explaining why people vote as there are for why they don't. The actual number of people who not only register but who actually submit their votes, either in person or by mail-in ballot is called voter turnout. The reasons why people vote include civic duty, party affiliation, electability of the candidates, and/or specific issues about which the voter feels passionate. There have been ideas to help raise voter interest such as the Motor-Voter Law, same-day registration, and absentee ballot voting, which have all resulted in higher numbers in voter registration, but not in voter turnout numbers, with the exception of California, who is one of the leaders in high absentee ballot voter turnout. Poor voter turnout in California is a reflection on their weak party system. A common reason that many Californians do not vote is simply that they are too busy. Candidates and public servants often emerge from families or marriages that are deeply immersed in the political process. Due to the weak party system, candidates sometimes rely on highly skilled consultants, interest groups, and PACs to handle campaign finance issues. As a result, the candidate who can raise the most money is often the front runner, which is a threat to the concept of direct democracy. For the next four chapters, we will move on to a new section that discusses the institutions that had its beginnings in the Constitution.

Key Terms:

Naturalized Citizens

Minuteman Project

Plurality

Midterm Elections

Electoral College

Electors

Contingency Election

Issues For You

Party Identification

Retrospective Voting

Aryan

Imam

Mullah

Fatwa

Chador

Ramadan

Amnesty International (AI)

Embargo

Sanctions

Websites:

Amnesty International
http://www.amnestyusa.org/index.html

Democratic National Committee
www.democrats.org/

Federal Election Commission
www.fec.gov

The National Archives Electoral College Site
www.archives.gov/federal_register/electoral_college/index.html

Project Votesmart
www.vote-smart.org/

Republican National Committee
www.rnc.org/

California Sites

California Voter Foundation
www.calvoter.org

Congresswoman Loretta Sanchez
www.lorettasanchez.house.gov

Congresswoman Linda Sánchez
http://lindasanchez.house.gov

League of Women Voters of California
www.ca.lwv.org

September 18, 1978
President Jimmy Carter addresses a Joint Session of Congress to announce the peace agreement between Egypt and Israel, also known as the Camp David Accords.
Courtesy of the Library of Congress

CHAPTER 9

THE LEGISLATURE

CHAPTER OUTLINE

Democracy and Action –
Nancy Pelosi –
First Woman Speaker of the House.

On January 4th 2007, a major crack appeared in the so-called **glass ceiling**, when Nancy Pelosi, Congresswomen from California, was elected to be the first female. It was a momentous occasion for women everywhere in the United States, given how hard they've worked throughout the country's history for equal treatment and rights.[1]

The importance of the position has added to the achievement; the Speaker of the House is one of the most powerful positions in government. As the highest-ranking officer in the House of Representatives, the Speaker is the chairman of the Committee on Rules, the most powerful committee in the House, which is responsible for establishing the rules under which any bill

Representative Nancy Pelosi is the female Speaker of the House of Representatives in the history of the United States.
Courtesy of Speaker Nancy Pelosi.

may come to the floor for debate and a vote. The Speaker also chooses the members of all of the **select and conference committees** as well as deciding which bills go to which committees. In addition, the Speaker of the House is the second in line for the presidency (behind the Vice-President), should the President become unable to fulfill his or her duties; this is the closest any woman has ever been to the presidency.

Nancy Pelosi was born in Baltimore, Maryland in 1940. The daughter of a U.S. Congressman, politics played a role in her life from the very beginning. As a young woman, she participated in an internship in the U.S. Senate, and after she married and relocated to San Francisco, California, she became very active in regional politics, working her way up to becoming the Democratic Party chairwoman for Northern California.[2]

In 1987, through a **special election** to fill a vacant seat for California's 8th district in the U.S. House of Representatives, Pelosi began her career in Congress. Since that time, she has been re-elected ten times (at the time of printing), garnering a whopping 75-percent of the vote or better each time. In 2001, she became the first woman to be elected to a party leadership position in Congress when she became the House Minority **Whip** – the party's second-in-command. In 2002, she was elected House Minority Leader, again becoming the first woman to hold a major party's most powerful position in Congress in either house.

Since she was first elected in 1987, Pelosi has become a force of nature in Congress, serving on many influential committees, including Intelligence and Appropriations. She has been a powerful voice in Congress for working families, the environment, health care, better national security, and human rights.

Speaker Pelosi set in motion several ambitious and exciting votes right from the first day of the new House. In a very public proclamation, Speaker Pelosi pledged to venture across party lines and, within the first 100 hours, pass legislature that helps:[3]

Americans feel safer here in the United States. The very first vote dealt with the implementation of recommendations for national security, specifically, an independent, bipartisan 9/11 Commission.

Insure an equitable economy. The new House, for the first time in ten years, voted to gradually increase the minimum wage from $5.15 per hour to $7.25 per hour. Approximately four months after Speaker Pelosi took the House, President Bush signed the wage increase measure into law. On Speaker Pelosi's website, there is a countdown clock that is marking down to the second, the days for the first increase to go into effect, which is $5.85 on July 24, 2007.[4]

Make college available for all Americans. By voting to cut student loan interest fees in half, receiving a college education with a lower bill overall at the end is more of a possibility for more people.

Fight global warming and find more independent energy sources for America. They voted to cut back billions of dollars in taxpayer subsidies for Big Oil; also, they voted to turn more attention to investing in renewable energy and energy efficiency in Middle America, rather than in the usual regions of the Middle East.

Expand research for cures to debilitating diseases. They voted to continue the fight to relieve human suffering because of diseases, by focusing on stem cell research.

Reform Washington's fiscal bad habits. They vowed to put Americans' interests above special interest groups by exercising steadfastness on Congressional ethics reform and keeping a more watchful eye on spending earmarks.

This was just a brief overview of the first 100 hours; within the first 100 days, the House was able to pass some legislation on their agenda (but not all), such as:

Strengthening national security. Secured a firm withdrawal date from Iraq, August 31st, 2008.

Reinvigorate the economy. Cut deficit and balance budget over next five years, create more jobs by moving America toward in renewable and independent energy sources.

These are only a few of the many bills that have been passed by the House but some have yet to be signed into law.

It is through Nancy Pelosi's hard work and astute leadership that she has commanded the respect of her colleagues, who, in the wake of the Democratic sweep in the November 2006 election, chose to elect her as the very first female Speaker of the House in United States history.

Theories of Representation

"Suppose you were an idiot. And suppose you were a member of Congress. But I repeat myself." – Mark Twain, a Biography

As discussed in chapter one, most democracies have a representative democracy, also known as indirect democracy. A representative democracy is one in which the people rule indirectly through representatives who they elected to govern in their stead. There are two main forms of representative democracy. The first is the steward or delegate theory, in which the elected representative votes the way the constituency would like. The second theory is the trustee theory, in which the representative votes the way they feel is best. In the United States, representatives often carry out the latter of the two theories. Edmund Burke (1729 - 1797), British parliamentarian and political philosopher, described these theories in a letter to his constituents, written in 1774. Burke felt very strongly that the trustee theory was better for the public and that it held the representatives accountable to the people without surrendering their own expertise and judgment. His constituents took this to mean that he did not take into account

May 20, 1934 Ceremony in the House of Representatives honoring the centennial anniversary of the death of Lafayette, a French officer who assisted Americans during the Revolutionary War. Courtesy of the Library of Congress.

public opinion, which did not set well with them; they ousted him from Parliament. There have been others such as President Lincoln who favored the delegate theory, saying that the representative should take all cues from the public's feelings on issues. In examining Congress, one can see how most Representatives and Senators use a blend of the trustee and the delegate theory in their decision making process. When asked, some members of Congress have said it is too difficult to reach a consensus between the various factions within their district or states. This way, members of Congress can follow the wishes of their constituency when their preferences are clear and when they are not, Congress can use their own best judgment. While a balance between the two theories is always desired, it is difficult to obtain given that there are national issues and issues that concern only a particular constituency.

Who is Eligible to be a Member of Congress?

The Constitution specifies several requirements to be a member of Congress. In order to be a member of the House of Representatives, you must be at least twenty-five years old, be a U.S. citizen for 7 years, and reside in the state you want to represent, according to Article I Section 2 of the Constitution. In Article I Section 3, it states that in order to be a U.S. Senator, you must be thirty years old, a U.S. citizen for 9 years, and reside in the state you wish to represent. Once these requirements are met, you are eligible to run for office.

Is Congress Representative of the Population?

The House and Senate websites have profiles of all the members who represent the public in Congress. While perusing these sites, it is interesting to note that most of the elected officials are white upper class males. The theory behind representation is that the members should reflect the population of the districts, states, or national demographic; this is called descriptive representation. However, judging by the representatives currently in place, it is palpable that women and other minority groups are underrepresented. This raises the question that if the role of government is to provide for us based on our needs, then how does it work if the representative process is slanted towards one group?

In 1789, the First Congress had sixty-five Representatives and twenty-six Senators, all white males from the upper strata - wealthy, educated, land owners whose occupations included bankers, lawyers, and businessmen. Now, over two hundred years later, some things have changed but some things have stayed the same. There are now 435 Representatives and 100 Senators but most are still white males from the upper strata and extremely wealthy; over 60 members of Congress are millionaires. They are highly educated and once again, they have careers in law, banking, and business. Nevertheless, there are those in Congress who, regardless of their wealth, make every effort to hear and represent the needs of minority groups and the poor. Given this, is it unreasonable to want in a Republican Democracy, more representation that is similar to the demographics of the nation?

Before we can answer this question, let us take another look at what exactly are the demographics of the nation and how it evolved. All over the country, there was a significant influx of immigrants from around the world. The population swelled during the Great Depression when more people gravitated from the east coast to the west. With the help of several movements (women's suffrage, Progressives, Civil Rights movements), minority representation in Congress began to increase during the twentieth century. By the turn of the twenty-first century, the number of women and other racial minority groups increased. In the 110th Congress in 2007, there are 89 women (including delegates) as compared to 55 years ago when there were only 11 women serving in Congress. Because women make up close to 51% of the population in the U.S., these impressive statistics are still not a satisfactory and proportionate representation; nevertheless the actions taken by a committed group of citizens has resulted in a Congress that is more reflective of the nation.

In reviewing the growing diversity of Congress, one can see how the political agenda can change as the population changes. When the number of female representatives increased, the focus on women's issues, such as equal pay, was brought to the forefront. Increased African American representation emphasized civil rights and affirmative action in a similar fashion. It is safe to surmise that the more that Congress represents the diversity of the general population, the more diverse and ethnically oriented the issues become; it will be even more challenging to address the interests of each group.

Factoid:
Two of the best known advocates for representing the lower strata are Senators Ted Kennedy (D-MA) and Jay Rockefeller (D-WV).

Congressional Districts

The ongoing changes in representation of Congress are reflected by the changing demographics of the districts. New districts can allow opportunities for new representation by the location, shape, and size of a group as determined by a state's legislature or subsequent court rulings. The process of defining the boundaries of these districts can become quite political.

Reapportionment –
The reallocation of House seats among the states; applied after each national census, to guarantee that seats are held by the states in proportion to the size of their populations.

Redistricting –
The redrawing of congressional district lines within a state to ensure roughly equal populations within each district.

Originally, Article I, Section 2, of the Constitution established the size of the House of Representatives at sixty-five. When the census of 1790 was conducted the number of Representatives increased to 105 with approximately 33,000 constituents per district. Early in the twentieth century the House had 435 Representatives and each district was approximately 200,000 constituents. In 1929, the Reapportionment Act was passed, permanently setting the number of Representatives at 435. Now the nation's population is over 300,000,000 making the number of constituents per district at approximately 690,000 and growing. In order to accommodate the number of members of the House and keeping the district somewhat equal in population size required the districts to be redrawn by the state legislatures or judicial panels or other special committees with the approval of the Department of Justice after each census. The procedure of **reapportionment** adjusts each states number of Representatives based on the change in population. This takes place every ten years after the national census is administered. As people move from the northeast to the south and southwest, the latter gain more representatives from the former. States like California, Texas, and Florida have seen an increase in their congressional delegations whereas states such as Ohio, New York, and Pennsylvania had lost seats. As you'll be reading in the section on California, the party that controls the state legislature can have a big influence on the political make-up of Congress.

Each of the 435 districts has their own character, so to speak. There is no real model that emulates the nation. The cultural, economical, and political make-up of all 435 districts is different. Each district can be liberal or conservative, rich or poor, and urban or rural; they can also differ on education levels, religious views, and cultural backgrounds. Every ten years even before the census is completed, state parties analyze the numbers to see where their possible gains or losses are on the map. The job of redrawing the districts begins with these steps. At all levels of the state party system, party members meet to discuss the change of population in their areas. **Redistricting** is the process in which districts are reshaped to accommodate those gains or losses while still keeping a balance in the number of constituents.

FOR YOUR CONSIDERATION
GERRYMANDERING

Gerrymandering is the term given to the redrawing of a state's political districts to gain a favorable partisan outcome. The term was coined when Elbridge Gerry, the Governor of Massachusetts, signed into law the redrawing of a district that resembled a salamander, prompting the creation of the term "gerrymander."

Every ten years, after the U.S. national census is taken, each state's legislature redraws its districts to reflect the changing geography of that state's citizens; each district is required to have an equal number of citizens represented. This redrawing is typically a very partisan exercise designed to maximize the number of districts favorable for the party that controls that state's representatives. The increasing partisanship is creating districts that appear to be almost infallible for incumbents, therefore all but insuring the retention of power and the silencing by dilution of those critics residing in those districts.

This redistricting has also resulted in some pretty wild looking districts (as seen with the original salamander) and has prompted some legal challenges as well. In earlier days, representatives made attempts to redraw their districts to dilute racial influence, a practice that was challenged in the courts. Due to the Voting Rights Act, which protected minorities during redistricting, the outcome of the ruling was that a challenge to the redistricting must show discriminatory intent and effect.

Most recently was a more blatant (and humorous) attempt by the predominantly Republican legislature of the state of Texas, aided by House Representative Tom DeLay (R-TX), to redraw Texas districts in 2003, not a census year. This gerrymandering plans had to pass through the Texas House and Senate before being signed by the governor, so each time it would be called for a vote the Democrats on the state legislature would flee the state en masse, in which case there would not be a quorum and they could not be called back for the vote. The Supreme Court ended up ruling that a state could redraw its boundaries as often as it saw fit, but struck down the drawing of one specific district because it appeared to violate the Voting Rights Act.

In the end, gerrymandering just begets more solidly and extremely partisan districts, but it looks as though there is no real way to prevent the practice at this point.

The practice of manipulating districts to favor one political party over another is not new. To **gerrymander** refers back to 1812, when the governor of Massachusetts, Eldridge Gerry approved a redistricting bill that favored his party; most noticeable in this bill were the odd shapes of the districts, including one that looked like a salamander. People combined the governor's name with the second half of salamander, and the term gerrymander was created. These days gerrymandering is used when state legislatures create safe seats for their party by looking at the number of registered voters in the area to safeguard their candidate winning the election. As discussed in previous chapters, the most recent example of this is the case in Texas where the state assembly carved out three "bacon strips" shapes. Justice Steven Breyer, during oral arguments, likened it to a "long walking stick" district that benefited Republicans. In one of the remaining districts that was created, gerrymandering placed four incumbent Democrats against each other. As was intended with the design, the Republicans were able to gain six new seats in the House. The Supreme Court ruled on June 28, 2006 that most of Texas' redistricting would stay in place but part would have to change because two of the congressional districts unfairly weakened the Latino vote in the western part of the state.[5]

Gerrymandering – Redrawing electoral district lines to give an advantage to a particular party or candidate.

Majority-Minority Districts – Districts drawn to ensure that a racial minority makes up the majority of voters.

Majority-Minority Districts

As illustrated in the Texas example, it is illegal to create or break a **majority-minority** district. After the 1990 census, states were mandated to redraw districts in areas that had faced issues with racial discrimination. States throughout the south and southwest created majority-minority districts for the benefit of ethnic minorities; this provided them with opportunities to increase representation in Congress. Like most things in politics, the debates surrounding majority-minority districts were conflict-ridden. Those who were opposed to the plan considered this "racial gerrymandering" while those who agreed with the majority-minority districts saw this as a way to make Congress more representative of the nation as a whole.

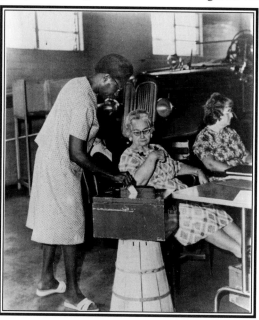

June 7, 1996. African American woman voting in a Congressional primary election in Jackson, MI, one of the key battle ground states for the Voting Rights and Civil Rights Acts Courtesy of the Library of Congress.

In 1995, majority-minority district found their fate put in the hands of the United States Supreme Court. The Court stuck down the Department of Justice redistricting in Georgia because the creation of racial districts violated the equal protection rights of the white voters in those districts. The Court's position was that race can be considered in redistricting, but it can not be the main consideration. In 1996, the Supreme Court reviewed another redistricting plan from Georgia; they allowed the district court to form one black majority district for the elections that year. They felt that this created a good balance (compared to the three the year before) because it did not violate the Voting Rights Act nor the standard established in Reynolds v. Sims (one person, one vote) as outlined in Article I, Section 2, of the Constitution.

As the twentieth century came to a close, the issue of majority-minority districts is still in question. Since the Courts' rulings, some of the Representatives that were elected during the 1990's have been reelected in new districts that are not based solely on racial factors. While some see this as a positive indicator that "racial gerrymandering" is no longer needed, others disagree, saying that the Representatives were re-elected due to the incumbent advantage, not because of any concerted effort to remedy racial inequality. In 2007, the Voting Rights Act of 1965 was up for reauthorization. Some southern members of Congress tried to block it over the issue of election materials being printed in other languages besides English. A compromise was reached and the Act was reauthorized for a few more years. Should there be another legal conflict over majority-minority districts, the two new conservative justices on the Supreme Court may have some influence over a new opinion on the issue.

The Incumbent Edge

Franking Privilege – Public subsidization of mail from the members of Congress to their constituents.

Pork – Also called pork barreling; projects designed to bring jobs and public money to the constituency, for which members of Congress can claim credit.

On average over 90% of Congress is reelected. This means that the incumbent (current officeholder) is able to retain their seat with a minimal threat of being replaced by the opposition party. There are several factors that play a part; one of which we just discussed, redistricting. By creating districts that are "safe seats" the concept of popular sovereignty is removed from the voters. There are other factors that help the incumbent candidate such as campaign contributions, **franking privileges**, and the "**pork**" they bring home to their district. These privileges allow members of Congress to mail letters and updates on their accomplishments for the district, free of charge. In addition, Congress has travel budgets so they can stay "in touch" with their districts and states. The majority of legislative business is scheduled to take place Tuesday through Thursday, allowing for Representatives and Senators to use weekends to attend functions. At these functions (fund raisers and high profile charity events), the Congress member schedules media coverage to make announcements or speeches that will give them free media coverage on important projects or issues for their constituents.

On big advantage incumbents have over their competitors is a sizeable amount of money for campaigning. The campaign contributions that incumbents receive usually come with implied strings attached. As discussed in the chapter on interest groups, when a contributor gives money to a candidate they usually want something in return. Generally, it is easier for the incumbent to raise more money because they already have established contacts with interest groups. On the other hand, not all contributions are corrupt in motive; some groups and individuals donate money because they have believed in the candidate from their first campaign, as all incumbents were once first time candidates.

Another reason for building a large war chest is that the incumbent wants to show members in their party who may wish to challenge the seat and opponents that they would have to raise and spend a tremendous amount of money to win the seat. While campaign contributions are a key component in being reelected, the "perks" a member of Congress has also helps increase their chances of victory. Being a member of Congress provides the incumbents with a number of "free" assets that challengers would have to pay for or wouldn't normally have access to.

One final advantage that incumbents have over most of their challengers is the ability to respond to their constituents needs by having dual offices, one in the home district and state and the other in Washington, D.C. The dual offices allows for the Representative and Senator to address specific requests, such as at the local level, a constituent who is concerned about their social security paperwork would visit the district office; or in the capital office, the incumbents staff could follow up on federal funds for a local park-n-ride parking location. By managing their **casework** in this way, incumbents are able to show the voters how they are always available to discuss their requests and needs. As discussed in previous chapters, an incumbent can also show the voters and supporter how hard they are working for them by bringing home the bacon in pork projects. This can be done in several ways but one area that seems to please most constituents is infrastructure. Representatives and Senators are constantly working to gain federal funds for improvements to roads, bridges, and highways. Take for example the recent expansion of Disneyland's California Adventures. In order to accommodate the increased traffic in the area around the park, federal funds were acquired to expand Interstate 5. When the ground was broken on the project, representatives from all levels of government, federal, state, and local had an opportunity to have a "photo op" for the local media, news letters, and campaign materials.

Casework –
Services performed by members of Congress for constituents.

Public Opinion and Congress

All members of Congress are influenced by public opinion. A large part of the work that is performed by Congress is either swayed by public opinion or they are trying to be the agent that influences public opinion. As discussed earlier, the issue of "red tape" and how the government is designed to be slow in the legislative process have been discussed. There are three ways in which Congress responds to public opinion: they can expedite legislation, stall legislation due to differences in public opinion, or contradict public opinion.

While this is true most of the time, when public opinion calls for action, Congress has been known to expedite the legislative process. Think back to the period immediately following September 11th; within months of the attacks on the World Trade Center and the Pentagon, Congress created the country's third largest bureaucracy (Office of Homeland Security), authorized the Patriot Act, and gave the President funding for the war in Afghanistan. Under normal circumstances, these items would have taken years to implement but because the public supported it, it was accomplished in a very short amount of time.

There are times when public opinion is mixed and depending on the views of their districts and states, Representative and Senators are at usually at odds. The process is temporarily delayed as compromises are worked out so everyone can claim a win of sorts. Take for example the debate over immigration. Over 2004 – 2007, members have introduced legislation in both houses to reform the immigration process. Members in areas that are liberal or heavily dependent upon migrant laborers want practical assurances on work visas or excessive fines or punishments. Those members who have conservative areas or represent Border States want stronger enforcement and preventative measures. The attempted legislation in the Spring of 2007 did not pass despite the President's support of the Bill. Some members on both sides of Congress found parts of the bill insurmountable and voted against it.

Lastly, there are times when Congress defies public opinion and takes a course of action that may cause a public backlash. The impeachment of President Bill Clinton in 1998 is a good illustration of this. Most Americans agreed that the President was guilty of perjury; however, they felt it did not warrant impeachment. Disregarding public opinion, the House, headed by conservative Speaker Newt Gingrich, impeached the President. The Senate chose not to remove him from office. Many Americans wanted to punish Congress' actions by voting some of the members out of office. But because most Representatives are in safe seats, only a few members lost their seats. As stated before, by creating safe seats, the check the voters have on their representatives is virtually removed.

House and Senate Responsibilities and Powers

Congress in the United States is not like its counterparts in other democracies. The members of Congress in America are more independent then members in the parliamentary system or semi-presidential system (see chapter one). This can be explained for the following reasons. First, congressional leadership does not have the power to terminate its members if they do not comply with the leadership agenda. In the U.S., our system focuses on the representatives and senators, not the institutions. The party leadership in each house negotiates, persuades, or coerces members of their parties in order to influence votes for certain proposed legislation. Former Majority Leader of the Senate, Lyndon B. Johnson (D-TX) was known to cross over into intimidation, fearlessly intruding upon personal space to make his point. A more

A session in the House of Representatives. Courtesy of the Library of Congress

recent example is former Majority House Leader, Republican Tom Delay (D-TX), who was also known as "the hammer"; Delay also used intimidation tactics and subtle threats to move his party's agenda through the House.

A second reason that members are more independent is because the House and Senate are different institutions governed by different modes of elections, rules and procedures, and responsibilities (see table 9.1). The members of the House benefit from safe seats, whereas the members in the Senate are subject to more competition, especially those in the House that are looking for more stability with a job in the Senate. Although senators don't have "safe" seats, they do share many incumbent advantages

TABLE 9.1 - Differences Between House and Senate		
	HOUSE	SENATE
MEMBERS	435	100
TERMS	2 - Years	6 - Years
POPULATION OF CONSTITUENCY	–	+
RELIANCE OF STAFF	–	+
REPRESENTATION	Proportional to population	States are represented
RULES	Less Flexible	More Flexible
DEBATE	Limited	Practically unlimited
POLICY SPECIALISTS	+	–
MEDIA COVERAGE	–	+
PRESTIGE	–	+
COMMITTEE LEADERS' POWER	+	Equal Distribution
PARTISAN	+	–
+ = more; – = less		

Party Caucus –
An organization of the members of a political party in the House or Senate.

Pro Tempore –
An official who is second in command, in charge in the event that the head officer cannot govern or facilitate; Latin is literally, "for a time."

A final difference between our Congress and a parliamentary system is that the two dominant political parties, despite being in control of Congress, are weak when compared to parties in the parliamentary system. In most parliamentary governments the candidates are selected and financed by the party. They are then assigned which office to run for and what region they will represent. Here in the United States, the candidates are free to select their own party affiliation, the office their going to run for, and are responsible for raising the majority of their campaign funds. This level of independence sometimes complicates party loyalty. A good example of this is when Senator Joe Lieberman (D-CT) broke off from his party after losing the Democratic primary in his state in the 2006 mid-term elections. He ran as what he called an "Independent Democrat" in the general election and successfully retained his seat in the Senate by defeating both major parties.[6]

The Role of Political Parties in Congress

At the beginning of each new session of Congress, the parties hold their **party caucus** to elect their party and committee and subcommittee leaderships and to distribute committee assignments amongst the other members. In addition, the majority party determines the number of committee members on each committee from each party. The majority in the House elects one of their members to be Speaker of the House and the majority party in the Senate elects one if its members to be the president **pro tempore** (usually abbreviated to "pro tem") and the other leadership positions.

Party Control of Congress

It shouldn't be a surprise to see that the Democrats and Republicans have dominated Congress since before the Civil War. With the party realignment at the turn of the twentieth century, more specifically during the Great Depression, the Democrats gained control of Congress. From 1932 until 1994, the Democrats had maintained control of both houses for all except for 10 years. What is notable about this is that during this time, there were several Republican landslides for the Presidency during the 1980's that did not lead to victories in Congress. During his first term in office, Democrat President Bill Clinton experienced a shift in 1994, when the Republicans gained control during the midterm elections. At that time, many political observers saw this as the beginning of a new era of conservatism in the country. In order to oblige this new trend, President Clinton moved the Democratic Party to the right of center on the political spectrum and subsequently won in 1992. This move toward conservatism was aided by the Republicans gaining and maintaining control of both

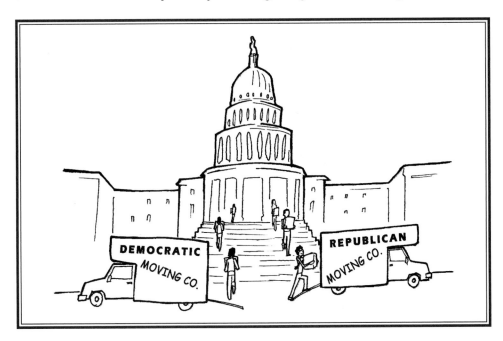

houses in 1994, with the exception of 2001-2002 in the Senate; the final confirmation of this was the election of George W. Bush to the office of the Presidency in 2000. During this time, the Democrats in Congress had difficulty holding the old coalition together. The Republicans did lose some seats but held on until the midterm elections of 2006. In November of 2006, the Democrats regained control of both houses of Congress.

Breakdown of Powers of Congress

Listed here are several key powers that Congress has at its disposal. After reading the list, one may begin to understand why parties compete so passionately for seats in Congress. Congress has the power to:

- Confirm and penalize piracies, felonies on the high seas, and to declare war

- Create rules for naturalization and bankruptcy

- Distribute patents and copyrights

- Establish courts of below the Supreme Court

- Monitor trade with foreign countries and states

- Organize and support an army and navy and set up rules of governance

- Oversee the coinage of money, establish value, and prosecute counterfeiting

- Place and collect taxes and borrow money

Issues For You
What is your
opinion about
how much power
Congress has?
Too little?
Too much?
How would
you change
the distribution
of power?

- Provide for a national guard

- Set guidelines for weights and measures

- Set up post offices and roads to their locations

- Use exclusive legislative powers over the District of Columbia and other federally purchased facilities

- "…make all Laws which shall be necessary and proper for carrying into Execution the foregoing Powers, and all other powers vested by this Constitution in the Government of the United States"[7]

Partisan –
A committed member of a party; seeing issues from the point of view of the interests of a single party.

Voting along party lines

Over the years, voting in Congress has become more **partisan**. This is to say that the members of both parties are voting more along party lines than they have in the past. This became increasingly apparent when the Republicans gained control in 1994 under the guidance of Newt Gingrich. Speaker Gingrich was able to hold his party members accountable by increasing his control over the committee and subcommittee assignments. Prior to 1994, the traditional committee assignments were based on seniority but Gingrich changed this to placing party loyalists in key committees and in leadership posts. Even though many senior members of his party were upset by this action, they received the message load and clear, do what the leadership tells you to do and you can keep your position; don't and you run the risk of losing your committee assignment. Examples of how Speaker Gingrich was able to move his agenda forward in the face of opposition in his own party and public opinion can be found in his implementation of the "Contract with America" and the impeachment of President Bill Clinton. In 2000, partisan politics increased when President George W. Bush took office. His political advisor, Karl Rove enforced party loyalty in the executive branch as well as in Congress, despite the President's campaign statements of him being "…a uniter, not a divider." After the attacks on September 11th, there was a break in partisan politics but this was short lived. As the opposition to the President's agenda on the War on Terrorism began to emerge, so did the partisan rhetoric. One of the key phrases at this time was, "If you don't support the war, you're supporting terrorism."

With the Democrats taking control of both houses again, there hasn't been any improvement with the intensity of partisan politics in Washington, D.C. Party affiliation and the constituent base may also help to explain the increase in partisan voting in Congress. As the Democrats began to see a shift in their ranks in the south they also experienced a number of southern Democrats retiring or changing party affiliation to better represent their district and states. During the 1980's the Republican Party began to court the religious right, most of who were in the south and Midwest. The introduction of the religious right in the Republican Party equated to votes. Enough that an incumbent could lose their seats to someone with more appeal on social issues made more moderate members of the party vote along with their constituents' positions over their own.

There were several phenomena that contributed to partisan voting in Congress. The shift at the district and state levels from Democrat to Republican, the increased debate on social issues, such as gay rights and abortion, and the control of the party leadership are all examples of this. Whether or not this will continue is uncertain but one can project that as the nation becomes more polarized so does Congress.

Profiles in Politics
THOMAS P. (TIP) O'NEILL, JR. (1912 - 1994)

Thomas P. O'Neill Jr., or "Tip," was born into an Irish Catholic working class family in Cambridge, Massachusetts in 1912. The son of a City Councilman, politics was always a part of his life; and though he lost his first political race, his father gave him a valuable piece of political advice that young Tip never forgot: "All politics is local." Building on that advice, O'Neill was elected to the Massachusetts State Legislature in 1936 and never lost an election again.[8]

During his first 40 years in politics, O'Neill steadily moved up through the ranks to leadership in the U.S. House of Representatives.[9] He did not always take the safe position; he was opposed to the

Speaker Tip O'Neill shares a moment Rep. Nancy Pelosi.
Courtesy of Speaker Nancy Pelosi

Vietnam War as early as 1967 – not the most popular position for a Democrat. O'Neill told President Johnson that he believed that Vietnam had become a civil war and that it was morally wrong for the U.S. to continue their involvement in the conflict. He also led the fight against President Nixon throughout the Watergate scandal; he was a leader in advocating for Nixon's impeachment.

He was elected Speaker of the House in 1976 and even though the incoming president was a fellow Democrat – Jimmy Carter - they did not always see eye to eye; O'Neill definitely marched to his own drumbeat. In the end, Carter and O'Neill learned to work with each other and were responsible, together, for some solid legislation. They became friends, and O'Neill was viewed as a sort of political "tutor" to Carter, coaching him in the "art" of good legislating.

O'Neill did not get along with President Reagan quite as well. Although there were some similarities, their political philosophies were entirely at odds. This led to a rather brusque relationship between Speaker O'Neill and President Reagan; Tip was a New Deal Democrat, which made confrontation with Reagan necessary regarding policy. In fact, Tip O'Neill has been described as having three religions: Roman Catholicism, the Democratic tradition, and the Boston Red Sox; he remained true to all three during his entire time in Congress.

Tip O'Neill retired from Congress in 1987 and died in 1994. He was eulogized as having been a "Congressman's Congressman" by Senator Bob Dole and also by President Bill Clinton for O'Neill's love of government because he could truly make a difference in people's lives; in short, Tip O'Neill was a true champion of regular people.[10] It's also quite possible that with the end of the Tip O'Neil era came the end of the gentlemanly camaraderie that used to be able to unify all members of Congress, before the current era of rampant bipartisanship began. Thomas P (Tip) O'Neil Jr. will be remembered as one of the greatest political leaders in United States history.

The Organization of Congress – Leadership and Discipline

The party leadership and discipline in Congress are an essential part of the legislative process. Without the party structure in Congress there would be complete gridlock and competition amongst hundreds of factions. This is not to say that the factions are nonexistent; they do exist but just more under control.

Leadership in the House of Representatives

Issues For You

What can be done to curtail revolts against the Speaker of the House? Or, do you think it is a good thing for the Speaker to be alert and avoid getting too comfortable?

The Constitution states that the leader of the House of Representatives is the Speaker of the House, who is also the third person in line of presidential succession. Prior to the twentieth century, the Speaker was the most powerful person in the House. The Speaker made all of the committee assignments and was the chairperson of the powerful Rules Committee. After a revolt against the Speaker by the other members in 1910, the position was weakened by removing them from the position of chairperson of the Rules Committee and from assigning committees. From 1910 until 1974, the Speaker had to compete with chairpersons from other powerful committees for control over the entire house. In 1974, the Democratic Caucus staged another revolt and placed the power to of committee assignments back to the Speaker. Most speakers kept with the tradition of seniority for committee assignments. Some Speakers, such as Thomas "Tip" O'Neil (D-MA) were able to use the combination of committee assignments along with tact and negation to exert control over the House. As stated earlier, in 1994 Speaker Newt Gingrich assumed even more power, thus making his position almost on par with the power the Speaker had prior to 1910. After the Republican losses during the midterm elections in 1998, Gingrich relinquished his position to Dennis Hastert (R-IL). Speaker Hastert returned some of the power to committee chairs and made some of the assignments based on seniority instead of loyalty. With the Democrats taking control in 2006, the minority leader, Nancy Pelosi (D-CA), was elected.

The party in power elects a majority leader and a whip. Their jobs are to aid the Speaker with scheduling legislation for the House floor; build a strong house Party; and work to get the party's message out. In November of 2006, Congressman Steny Hoyer (D-MD) became the majority leader for the 110th Congress.[11] Speaker Pelosi and Majority Leader Hoyer receive support from the Majority Whip Congressman James E. Clyburn (D-SC). It should be noted that this was the second time in the history of the House of Representatives that an African American ascended to the third ranking position in the House.[12] On the other side of the aisle, the minority party elected their Minority Leader and Minority Whip. The minority leaders' job is to not only work to keep his members on task but also to try to sway members of the majority party to vote with the opposition on key issues. In 2006 after the Republicans lost control of the House, John Boehner (R-OH) was elected minority leader. To aid the minority leader, the minority whip's job is similar to that of the majority whip – to keep members voting the party line. The current minority whip is Roy Blunt (R-MO).

FOR YOUR CONSIDERATION
ROLE OF THE SPEAKER OF THE HOUSE

While the Senate may appear to be the most powerful body in our government, the leader in the House of Representatives – the Speaker of the House – is the most powerful individual in Congress.

First and foremost, the Speaker of the House, although generally a member of the majority party, has four constituencies: his or her district, his or her party, the entire House of Representatives, and the general public. This means leadership may be a tough balancing act, considering that at times there may be competing interests at play.

The Speaker is tasked with setting the legislative agenda in the House; he or she assigns each bill to the appropriate committees and can decide when to bring a bill to the floor if it is marked-up. This means that if the Speaker is favorable to certain legislation, that legislation may receive priority status. This also means that if legislation does not receive the attention a constituency expects or if it does not pass, the Speaker is usually the one to shoulder the blame. Seeing that the Speaker serves several constituencies, balancing everyone's demands is tantamount to a juggling act on a tightrope wire.[13]

The Speaker also plays a key role in committee assignments; he or she facilitates the committee appointment process and directly appoints members to select and conference committees. The Speaker also presides over floor debate; he or she is the person who recognizes members to speak on the House floor. In short, he or she is a good person to be in good graces with and can effectively punish members who go astray from the direction set by the Speaker; he or she is a powerful advocate or a powerful enemy.

Normally, the Speaker does not officially sit on any committees nor does he or she tend to vote or participate in floor debate; he or she generally just presides over the debate and keeps order. Among other duties, the Speaker administers the oath of office to House members as well as signs all legislation passed by the House. He or she is also second in line for the presidency (behind the vice president) if something were to happen to the president.[14]

Leadership in the U.S. Senate

The leadership in the Senate is much different than the House. Unlike the Speaker of the House, the Senate does not have a post with the same powers. The head office is President of the Senate, which is held by the Vice President of the United States. The Vice President's main function according to the Constitution is to cast the tie breaking vote. After the Vice President, the majority party elects the president pro tempore who runs the day to day operations of the Senate. The majority leader in the Senate is the closest position to that of the Speakers. The majority leader is responsible for overseeing some committee and office space assignments, scheduling floor votes, and serving as the point person for the media and other party issues in the Senate. The current majority leader in the Senate is Harry Reid (D-NV) who came to power after the Democrats took control of the Senate in 2006. On the other side of the aisle is the minority leader whose job is the same as his counterpart in the House. The current minority leader as of 2007 is Mitch McConnell (R-KY).

The Committee Structure

Most of the legislative process occurs in the committee and subcommittees. This is where most bills are discussed and modified; it is also where conflicts within the executive branch are aired.

The Purpose of Committees

There are several reasons for having the committee structure in place. Every legislative session turns up thousands of bills on a whole host of subjects. This is the first reason a committee structure is necessary – to act as a filter which prevents the majority of bills from coming to the floor.

It is virtually impossible to know something about everything. The committees allow members to exercise their expertise and gain additional information on the specific subject matter from specialists in the field. In addition, committees are often designed to act as a counter balance to the executive branch. Take for example the powerful Judiciary committees. If Congress has questions regarding a specific issue from the Attorney General's office, the committee can issue a subpoena on the Attorney General or his staff to come testify.

Members of Congress use their positions on committees to help the constituents back home. It is beneficial for a Congress member to be assigned to a key committee to aid him come reelection time. Take for example a representative whose constituents are rural farmers. It would serve his political career well to acquire a position on one of the many committees that oversees agriculture.

The Right Committee Assignment

The right committee assignment can make or break a freshman Representative or Senator. Committee assignments are handled differently, not only between houses but also between the parties. For instance, the House Democrats work with a Steering Committee which is chaired by the floor leader and is usually assigned by seniority. In contrast, House Republicans use a Steering Committee but the Speaker has control of a quarter of the votes and makes the direct assignments to the Ways and Means Committees and as well as the Rules Committee. Both parties in the Senate use smaller steering committees consisting of senior party members and leadership to apply committee assignments.

Types of Committees

The structure of government is complex; in order for 535 individuals to manage the process successfully, several different types of committees have emerged over the years to meet this need. **Standing committees** are those that are permanently established. Members of a standing committee can play a role in the process of writing a bill. Before the bill can be sent to the appropriate committee, it has to be reviewed by the Rules Committee to ensure it is complete. This is the first step in the long process to become a law. Other examples of standing committees in the House are Ways and Means and Rules while in the Senate, there is a committee on Foreign Affairs and Budget and Finance. The makeup of these committees is usually negotiated between the majority and minority party with the understanding that each committee who has the most seats has the majority and serves as the chair. Most committees have several subcommittees that specialize in specific issues. At this level, it is in these subcommittees that most of the **hearings**, negotiations, and **markup sessions** take place. Once all of these issues are worked out, the bill is then submitted to the full committee.

Some committees are temporary and are created for a specific study or investigation of a particular issue. These committees are called **select committees**. Select committees have no power to submit bills for approval to the House or Senate. There are times when serving on a high profile select committee can give the members access to a fair amount of free media. Investigations that have drawn media attention have been the Warren Commission which investigated the assassination of John F. Kennedy; corruption in the Nixon Administration, which was coined Watergate, and the 9/11 Commission which investigated faulty intelligence and how the Bush administration handled the tragedy.

Joint committees are committees on which members from both the House and Senate serve at the same time. These committees are usually created for large cumbersome issues, such as the federal budget. The budget process is an ongoing task. Once the budget is approved, the committee begins work on the next fiscal year, processing budget requests from the various departments. One of the most important joint committees is the **conference committee**. Before a bill is sent to the President, the bills from the House and Senate must be identical. If there is a conflict between the two, the committee can amend them to their liking. The combined bill is then sent to both the House and Senate where they are only allowed to approve it or reject it, no amendments can be added. The hotly contested Immigration Bills in 2007 are a good example of this. The Senate passed their version of the bill and the House passed their version. There was tremendous debate in the conference committee and the final product was not satisfactory to either side, which resulted in both houses causing the bill to "die."

Standing Committees –
Permanent congressional committees that determine whether proposed legislations should be sent to the entire chamber for consideration.

Hearings –
Formal proceedings in which a variety of people testify on the pros and cons of a bill.

Markup Session –
A subcommittee meeting to revise a bill.

Select Committee –
Temporary congressional committees that conduct investigations or study specific problems or crises.

Joint Committees –
Group of members from both chambers, House and Senate, who study wide areas that are of interest to Congress as a whole.

Conference Committees –
Committees that reconcile differences between versions of a bill passed by the House and the Senate.

Congressional Rules

Just like the rest of society, Congress has formal and informal rules about how business should and should not be conducted; standards on civility; and following a hierarchical structure. As stated earlier in this chapter, members of Congress serve on committees in which they become experts. Because it is impossible to know everything, members must defer to one another's knowledge in their areas of expertise, which is called **reciprocity**, a part of the political process, has begun to wane in the house over the years, especially for committee chairs. One explanation for this could be a result of the shift in power from the chairs back to the Speaker over the last three decides. Senators have always been more contemptuous towards each other than their counterparts in the House. Generally the Senate prides itself on a collegial atmosphere. This could be accounted by the fact that the Senate is smaller numerically than the House and have to be more knowledgeable in more areas. In addition, being that a Senator doesn't benefit from the safe seat element, they have to be more independent to show their states how prestigious and powerful they are, assuring them that they can win reelection. Another factor is that the Senate has proven to be the grooming stop for those politicians who wish to advance to the presidency. Just compare the number of Senators running for the office of president as compared to members of the House. Still, whatever the reason, members are expected to act civil towards one another regardless of their political opinions.

Reciprocity – Deferral by members of Congress to the judgment of subject-matter specialists, mainly on minor technical bills.

The Capital building at dusk.
Courtesy of Corel.

In the past, a level of civility was expected during public hearings, in the chambers of both houses, and during the committee session. Even during floor debate in the exchanges between members who were at opposite ends ideologically, would still address each other as the "honorable gentleman from..." In recent years times have changed with Congress being more partisan; contemptuous exchanges are becoming more common place.

In June 2004, there was an exchange between Vice-President Dick Cheney and Senator Patrick Leahy (D-VT) when the Vice-President told the Senator to "Go fuck yourself."[15] In an interview on CNN, Senator Chuck Hegel (R-NEB) said, "I don't think anybody is shocked at that kind of language being used, but let's kind of clean this mess up."[16]

In comparing the two houses, the House of Representatives has more rules governing members' actions than the Senate. In the House, majority leadership controls the legislative agenda. Individual members are less able to gain visibility until they have served several terms in the house. In contrast, the Senate is less rule-bound. Senators are more individualistic and cross party lines more often then their house counter parts.

An example of how the two House are different would be how their floor debates are conducted. In the House, the leaders schedule the bill and allow for each member to make a brief statement about the bill. In addition, amendments to the bill are restricted. On the other side of the building, the Senate conducts business differently. Bills are scheduled by **unanimous consent**. Any one Senator can block a bill if they so wish by voting against it – there are very few limits to an individual Senator killing a bill. In addition, a Senator can place an anonymous hold on any bill for an indefinite period. The rules of the Senate provide the minority party great flexibility in preventing passage of a bill. There are several ways to "kill" a bill in the Senate. One is to add an amendment that no one would dare let pass or adding so many amendments that the bill now longer serves the purpose it was intended for. The final tool in the toolbox is the **filibuster**. Senators who oppose a bill can talk for as long as they want on anything they want. The only requirement is they must not stop talking. They have been known to read books, novels, and or the bible, tell stories about their hometown or their state. Often times, the minority party will work in shifts to stop the legislative process. This is done when the Senator who is talking yields for a question. The next Senator begins their question and continues to hold the floor until they yield for a question. If there is legislation that the majority party would like passed, they can stop the debate by attempting to implement **cloture**. Cloture is a procedure that allows for three-fifths of the Senate (60) to stop a filibuster. This is hardly ever used for several reasons, two of the main reasons are: the minority party could threaten to filibuster more legislation, bringing the Senate to a complete halt; and the post-cloture filibuster, which could continue for an additional thirty hours. Some political observers argue that the filibuster and cloture gives too much power to the minority and obstructs the will of the majority. In 2005, with partisan conflict increasing, the Republican lead Senate vote on the so-called "nuclear option" ended the filibuster for President Bush's judicial nominations. This was narrowly averted after moderate and maverick senators from both parties (14 total), negotiated an agreement to avoid the vote. This allowed for the minority party, the Democrats, to retain the right to filibuster nominations in only the most "extreme circumstances;" opening a window for several of the nominations to be voted on. It just goes to show that partisanship is an ongoing problem with not much improvement in sight.

Unanimous Consent –
Legislative action taken "without objection" as a way to move business along; used to conduct the business of the Senate.

Filibuster –
A parliamentary device used in the Senate to prevent a bill from coming to a vote by "talking it to death", made possible by the norm of unlimited debate.

Cloture –
A vote to end a filibuster or a debate; requires the votes of three-fifths of the membership of the Senate.

How a Bill Becomes a Law

The process of making a bill into a law is extremely complex. On average only approximately 6 percent of the bills that are introduced become law. This means the 94 percent "die" somewhere in the legislative process. Just from examining the numbers, one can see that for a bill to become a law, those who support it must be extremely skilled. In contrast, it is very easy to stop a bill from moving on.

Hopper –
The box in the House of Representatives in which proposed bills are placed.

There are several types of bills, major, minor, and those that deal with the budget and other appropriations. This section is a general description of how the bulk of major bills work through the legislative process. Each house has special rules on how to pass minor bills, so for example the House of Representatives allots for time on their calendars for deliberation on these proposals. The bills concerning the federal budget and other appropriations have their own set of rules governing them.

Introducing a Bill

A bill can only be introduced by a member of Congress. However, the bulk of them are written in by the various departments in the executive branch and special interest groups.

Most bills, except tax bills which originate in the House, may be introduced in both houses. In the House of Representatives the process is very informal. A member or "sponsor" puts the bill in the **hopper** which is presided over by one of the House clerks and is assigned a number that begins with the prefix *H.R.* The process in the Senate is very proper, meaning that the Senator who announces the bill is first recognized by the presiding officer; the Senator may then announce the bill. Senate bills are assigned the prefix S. One technique that helps a bill pass is garnering support by adding cosponsors, especially from both parties.

The Role of Committees

Bills are assigned to committees by the Speaker in the House and the presiding officer in the Senate. In most cases the assigned are routine because the subject matter of the bill dictates the appropriate committee assignment. Tax or Revenue bills are automatically assigned to the Finance Committee in the Senate and Ways and Means Committee in the House. In the remaining cases, bill of a complex nature may have multiple committee authorities. In these cases, the Speaker of the presiding officer may distribute the various components of the bill to the appropriate committees.

In the committees, the Committee chairs will usually assign the bill to the appropriate subcommittee for hearings and other actions. It is here where most bills die. Either the full committee or the subcommittee decides not to take additional action of the bill.

If the bill is accepted, the subcommittee will hold hearings to obtain information from both supporters and opponents and the pros and cons of the proposed legislation. Given the workload of the Senators or Representatives their Congressional staff has the responsibility to prepare summaries, notes, and additional pertinent information for them. In some cases, when the members are not available, senior staff will conduct the hearing in their stead. In most cases the bill, if accepted, will not reflect the original draft. The committee and subcommittee have the authority to rewrite the bill also known as *markup*. During this process the members subject knowledge and negotiation skills are shown. It the new draft, the bill is rewritten to gain the most votes when put to the floor vote. Often times, the subcommittee will also bring in key committee members of the chair for their expertise which also adds additional power to the bill for it to be approved.

Sending the Bill to the Floor

In the House, before a bill can be sent to the floor for debate and the vote, it must first be approved by the Rules Committee. The Rules Committee has the authority whether or not to put the bill on the legislative calendar and decides the rules for the debate (time for the members to talk and the over all time debate is allowed), to allow amendments and what type of amendments if any, or the committee can apply the "closed rule" which means the floor vote will only be yes or no without amendments. The latter is rarely used except for in the cases of tax legislation.

Pocket Veto – When the President refuses to sign or veto a bill that Congress passes in the last ten days of its session, rendering the bill dead when Congress adjourns.

The Senate is different then the house. First off, the committees in the Senate are not as influential as their counterparts in the House. Most Senators will discuss the merits of the bill will the bill is still in committee in order to gain more support for it. This informal approach allows for Senators to gain more information about the bill as well as other nuances. When the bill goes to the floor for debate, there is no time limit and last minute adjustments can be made to bill before the vote. Because the Senate is has more deliberation, their version of the bill may be either more comprehensive or convoluted in trying to appease the most number of Senators.

Once the debate closes the amended bill is put to a vote in the full House or Senate. If the bill passes, it is sent to the other chamber for the process to begin again. If the bill was introduced in both houses simultaneously, the completed bill will have to wait for its counter in the other chamber to be passed as well before proceeding to the next level.

Conference Committee

More often than not, there will be two different versions of the bill when it arrives from both houses. Before the bill can proceed, the conference committee, consisting of members from both houses and traditionally made up of members from the respective committees, must be combined into one bill. Sometimes the difference between the two bills are minor and are merged with very little problem or they can vary greatly and more time is needed to work thru the differences.

Once the bill is completed it is returned to both houses for a straight yes or no vote. No other changes or amendments are allowed. If approved by both houses, the bill is then sent to the president for his approval or rejection.

The President's Role in the Approval Process

The president's role is stated in the Constitution. Before the bill is sent to the president, he received a number of reports while the bill was still in the legislative process from his staff and other advisors. If the president approves the bill, it can he signed into law. If the president agrees with a controversial bill but does not want to go on the official record approving it, he can simply sit on the bill, or in other words, not say no and not say yes; after 10 days it automatically becomes law. If the president disagrees with the bill he can veto it and return it to Congress where they will most likely vote to override the president's veto. This requires a two-thirds vote in both houses. Another way the president can veto a bill is called a **pocket veto** where the president doesn't take any action and Congress is going to adjourn within ten days. This section will be explained in greater detail in the following chapter.

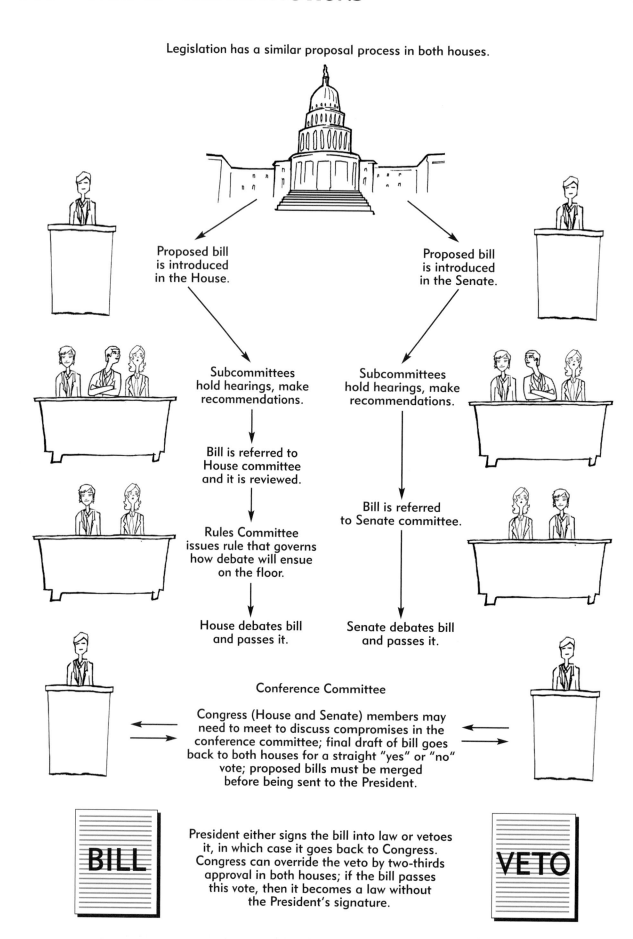

Legislation has a similar proposal process in both houses.

Proposed bill is introduced in the House.

Proposed bill is introduced in the Senate.

Subcommittees hold hearings, make recommendations.

Subcommittees hold hearings, make recommendations.

Bill is referred to House committee and it is reviewed.

Bill is referred to Senate committee.

Rules Committee issues rule that governs how debate will ensue on the floor.

House debates bill and passes it.

Senate debates bill and passes it.

Conference Committee

Congress (House and Senate) members may need to meet to discuss compromises in the conference committee; final draft of bill goes back to both houses for a straight "yes" or "no" vote; proposed bills must be merged before being sent to the President.

BILL

VETO

President either signs the bill into law or vetoes it, in which case it goes back to Congress. Congress can override the veto by two-thirds approval in both houses; if the bill passes this vote, then it becomes a law without the President's signature.

FOR YOUR CONSIDERATION
THE POCKET VETO

There are two types of veto a president can use on a bill that was sent to him from congress for approval. The most traditional type is a regular veto; the lesser-known type is called a pocket veto.

This indirect form of vetoing a bill was laid out in Article I, Section 7 of the Constitution, albeit not termed as a "**pocket veto**."[17] The section states that when presented by Congress with a passed bill, the president basically has ten days to act upon it. If the president chooses to ignore it and Congress remains in session during those ten days, the bill will automatically become law. If however, the president chooses to ignore the bill and the congress adjourns before the ten days are over, the president's neglect to address the bill effectively acts as a veto. The term "pocket veto" alludes to the fact that by ignoring the bill when he knows that Congress will be adjourning is akin to sticking the bill in his pocket and forgetting about it.

Congress and Executive Branch

One of Congress' responsibilities is that of overseeing the Executive Branch; in this context the term "oversight" of the branch is used. This is the area that implements the law as instructed by Congress, who must see to it that the Executive Branch is not abusing their powers.

Oversight of the Executive Branch is generally conducted through the use of committees and subcommittees in Congress. In extreme cases, Congress uses the media when they feel it is important to keep the American public, such as in the case of Watergate during the 1970s, the Iran-Contra affairs in the 1980's, and Whitewater in the 1990's. In the 110th Congress, since 2007, there have been several major investigations on the failures of the wars in Afghanistan and Iraq, and the firing of 8 U.S. Attorneys for alleged political crimes and agendas.[18]

Issues For You

Compare the impeachment hearings of President Nixon and President Clinton. Do you think the punishment fit the crime in both cases?

Hearings are important not only because of the oversight process but also to show the public some issues they should be concerned about. Committee members hold hearings to obtain testimony from experts in the field who can provide additional information instead of just relying on the information from the executive agency being questioned. In addition, most of the testimony becomes part of the public record. Some political observers say that these types of interactions serve as a message to the administration that they need to curtail some of their activities. Looking at the recent example of the Justice Departments termination of 8 U.S. Attorneys, Attorney General Gonzales told the Senate Judiciary Committee that he had very little if any involvement or knowledge about the dismissal of the attorneys. A short time later, Gonzales' former Chief of Staff, Kyle Sampson testified that the Attorney General attended several meetings, received memos and emails, and had other communications with the White House regarding these issues. When the Attorney General returned to the Committee, he acknowledged that he did know about this information but it was in a "different role" as Attorney General.[19] Simultaneously at the time of this text being composed, the issue was still unresolved. President Bush invoked "executive privilege" to prevent other current and former White House officials from testifying before the Senate Judiciary Committee. Furthermore, the Committee began considerations to hold former White House counsel, Harriet Miers in contempt of Congress in a 7-5 vote along party lines.[20] This example further illustrates the level of partisanship that exists in Washington, D.C.; Democrats are frustrated by the White House's perceived indignant toward them and Republicans who feel embattled and resentment towards what they considers cheap political antics to score votes.

The most powerful weapon in Congress' arsenal is the power to impeach high level officials from the executive branch, including the president. An impeachment process is where the House acts as the grand jury that looks for enough information to indict the official. The trial takes place in the Senate and is presided over by the Chief Justice of the U.S. Supreme Court. In the history of the United States, only seven officials have been removed from office by the impeachment process. It should be noted that impeachments are rare but are also highly partisan in nature. Referring back to the above example of Attorney General Gonzales, there were calls by some Democrats to impeach him from office. To date, no official action has been taken.

FOR YOUR CONSIDERATION
WATERGATE

The scandal called "Watergate" was nicknamed this when burglars broke into the Democratic Party's National Committee offices at the Watergate Hotel and stole tapes of telephone conversations and other communications. The astute security guard, Frank Wills alerted police of the break in and a tape found. These events were meticulously scrawled in a log book, which Wills' wrote in to document the movements of his routine rounds around the hotel. The log book has since been made available due to the Freedom of Information Act.

It is hard to believe but one lone security guard was basically responsible for the take-down of five former CIA operatives or associates, who were eventually charged of the burglary and arrested on June 17, 1972. The burglars had been hired by officials in President Richard M. Nixon's administration to spy and sabotage the offices, in order to guarantee the reelection of Nixon. These burglars were not just common hired thugs. Four out of the five were from Miami, Florida; three were heavily involved in the anti-Castro movement; and one was a refugee from Cuba. Nixon's strong anti-communist sentiments seemed to be accented by the hiring of these operatives. It was later revealed that Nixon wanted to keep a constant surveillance on anything the Democrats might have been planning for the upcoming election.

These events, which took place between 1972 and 1974, were responsible for the disillusionment and cynicism of an entire generation. A brief timeline of events illustrates the tumultuous times that made Watergate seem almost predictable. In 1968, in one of the tightest presidential races in U.S. history, Nixon was elected. In 1971, the Pentagon Papers, published in the New York Times, revealed the Defense Department's illegal involvement in the Vietnam War. In June of 1972, the burglars were caught and later on in the fall, a cashier's check for $25,000, supposedly earmarked for the Nixon campaign, was found deposited in one of the burglar's bank accounts. Despite the breaking news of these events, Nixon is reelected, this time a landslide victory. In 1973, G. Gordon Liddy, a former Nixon aide, and James W. McCord, coordinator of the Republican National Committee (RNC) and the Committee for the Reelection of the President (CREEP) are convicted of their part in the espionage and conspiracy of Watergate. McCord was immediately excused from these positions only one day after the break-in.

1973 was hotly peppered with one scandalous event after another: top White House staffers resigned or were fired; memos turned up that described the Watergate burglary plans; testimonials all pointing to Nixon's intricate involvement in the conspiracy were subpoenaed; more officials were axed or forced to resign; and finally, tapes are subpoenaed but 18 ½ minutes are missing in one of the tapes. The Supreme Court rejects Nixon's executive privilege and impeachment hearings commenced. In the midst of the House Judiciary Committee passing the first of three articles of impeachment, Nixon makes history once again by becoming the first U.S. president to resign. Vice President Gerald R. Ford assumes the office without needing to be elected; he later pardons Nixon of charges of his involvement with Watergate.

Despite the corruption and scandal associated with the name, the Watergate Hotel, which is located in Washington D.C., is known to be one of the cities' most elegant hotels, home to many high profile politicians. Now a part of the political lexicon, the term (fill-in-the-blank + "gate" – such as "Monica-gate", in reference to Bill Clinton's impeachment in 1998) is immediately assigned to any event involving any behavior by a politician that is considered to be a disgrace or deceitful toward the American. Call it an atmosphere of secrecy, call it human nature gone amuck; whatever you call political corruption, events like these have left the American public feeling a lot less trusting and naïve and a lot more politically savvy.[21]

California's Legislature

Quorum –
The minimal number of officers and members of a committee or organization, usually a majority, who must be present for valid transaction of business.

Name any public concern; for example, congested highways or whether to use sand or wood chips at the state recreation center playground. Chances are an interest group has lobbied for a bill to be passed in the legislature to address these issues, big or small. Some of the more pressing issues that the legislature handles are more funding for education, affordable housing, and employment. The legislative branch has to review thousands of proposed bills every year, all year round, making it a powerful component of California's government. Most citizens don't pay much attention to the state legislature, despite how important it is; furthermore, most don't know who their state senator is or their Assembly person for that matter. Instead, the focus is primarily on the federal government. This is a problem because in order for the citizenry to become effective in state concerns, they would have to know to whom they can voice them.

State Capital of California in Sacramento.
© Mark Or, 2007.
Used under License from Shutterstock, Inc.

Muddy Beginnings and Early Legislature

Contrary to what many may believe about California, it does have a rainy season. In fact, from late in the month of October to mid-December in 1849, it rained enough to submerge a 3 foot tall tree, if the rain was collected and measured all at once. Needless to say, the roads were quite muddy in rural and rugged California, making it extremely tedious or impossible to travel. This was not the best omen for the First California Constitutional Legislature, which was to meet for the first time in San Jose on December 15, 1849.

Similar to the U.S. Congress, the California legislature consisted of 16 Senators and 36 Assemblymen. But, due to the weather that first rainy night, only six Senators and 14 Assemblymen were able to attend the first session. A **quorum** eventually forged through and the Legislature was able to officially begin its opening day session. This was not, however, the first time a quorum would be slow to come together for California. Attendance was spotty or non-existent for one; furthermore, several Senators and Members of the Assembly resigned, including the Speaker of the Assembly. These weak beginnings may have been indicative of the low priority that politics held for the first legislators and even more telling, a foreshadowing of the lack of public support that was to come in the next hundred years. This was quite understandable in some respects, since many members had literally just become residents of California. Ironically, in this climate of debate over immigration reform in the 2000s, only two members of the first Senate were "native" Californians and there were none in the first Assembly. The ethno-geographic makeup of the first Assembly were mostly from northern states, then southern, then five of unknown origin, and two were born presumably overseas. The first Senate had a similar distribution. One common thread was the influence of the gold rush on California's population, being that one-half of both the Senate and Assembly represented Sacramento and San Joaquin mining districts. It is safe to assume that their interests did not lie with politics but with panning for more gold.

When the Constitution was first written, it started out with sixteen senators who were elected every other year, and thirty-six Assembly members elected annually. After the first revision of the Constitution in1879, the membership of both the Senate and the Assembly augmented; the Senate to 40 members that serve a maximum of two terms of four years each, with half elected every two years; and the Assembly to 80 members elected every two years. Each Senate district must have as close to the same number of constituents as possible and the same is true for Assembly districts. The ratio of districts of Senate to Assembly is 2 to 1; in other words, each Senate district has two times as many residents as each Assembly district.

One of the earliest challenges the First Legislature of California faced was splitting up the state into counties. Assigned to oversee this task was the Senate Committee on County Boundaries. The Committee suggested that California could be sectioned off into 18 counties. The individualism that is characteristic in California was evident even then, since some of the areas preferred to set up their own counties, rather than be assigned a county by the Committee. Nevertheless, in mid February in the year 1850, the legislature passed a bill that divided California up into 27 counties (see chapter three for map of California's county subdivisions).

As discussed in chapter two's California section on Constitutions, the first constitution drawn up in California declared Spanish and English as official languages. In fact, an act was passed to create an office for a State Translator whose primary job was to translate laws and important documents into Spanish, which by today's standards doesn't seem like a very significant high paying job, but actually back then, it was a very relevant and respected position. This was one of many acts that were passed for the good of the state. Other acts led to the creation of numerous offices that were responsible for incorporating cities, collecting property and poll taxes, enforcing the acts as soon as they were passed, abolishing all current laws except the ones passed by the First Legislature.

Factoid:
The First California Legislature adopted 19 joint resolutions, and at the first session, 146 passed and were approved by the Governor.

Leadership in the Assembly

The California legislative branch of the 21st century is still a bi-cameral entity with an "upper" house (state Senate) and a "lower" house (Assembly). Similarities between the two are that both contribute to making public policy and members from either house can propose any bill; a majority of both houses is necessary to pass most bills into law. In contrast with the U.S. Congress, which has exclusive legislative control in the national government, California's legislature shares its authority to make laws with its voters through the referendum and initiative as discussed in previous chapters. Most state laws, however, are settled on in the state's capital, Sacramento.

The Assembly has a speaker who facilitates the process of legislation through committees and its assignments at their discretion, in addition to being responsible for campaign monies. The speaker is chosen, in a caucus or closed meeting, by the party with a majority in the Assembly directly after the November general election. The full Assembly then votes, but this is just a formality as traditionally, they have already made their choice known. The minority party chooses its leader in much the same way as the majority leader is selected. Both majority and minority floor leaders are assisted by their whips during the legislative process, which includes levying taxes and designating money for the many state agencies that handle the affairs of the state. Currying favor with the speaker is a valuable tactic for a legislator when it comes to committee assignments and scheduling legislation, similar to how the House of Representatives operates. In fact, the political strength of the speaker's office has been thought of as almost as influential as the governor's office.

The Democrats enjoyed being the majority party from 1959 to 1995, when the Republicans were successful in passing term limits as law through the initiative process. This was a reaction to the Democrat monopoly of the state Assembly; case in point, San Franciscan Willie Brown held an astonishing 15 year-tenure as speaker from 1980 – 1995, a record. Another first in history was the choice of Democrat Cruz Bustamante from Fresno, the state's first Latino speaker in 1996.

The legislature sessions in lasts two years and any bill proposed within the first year can continue to be reviewed in the second year without needing to be reintroduced. This is a good thing because once introduced, the journey of the bill is a slow complex process that winds through a maze of committee hearings before reaching the floor of the house from whence it came. Basically, the committee organization and chairs are the same as in the Congress, as explained above; one difference, however, is that committee chairs serving in the state legislature are not assigned by seniority.

Leadership in the Senate

In the Senate, the lieutenant governor, similar to the Vice President, is called the presiding officer (president) of the Senate. This is not the most powerful position in the Senate, being that the lieutenant governor can only vote in the event of a tie. The president pro tem, or president "for a time", is the most influential office in the Senate. Similar to the speaker, the office of the president pro tem is a elected by the whole of the Senate and has automatically at its disposal the Senate Rules Committee, which is basically the seat of the pro tem's power. Usually, the party with the majority of senators wins the office of the pro tem. In turn, the minority caucus is allowed to select a minority leader, which balances out the power of the pro tem.

Prior to Proposition 140, which we will discuss in a moment, the speaker of the Assembly was one of the most powerful offices in the state. Some considered it to be on par with the governor. With the passage of term limits, the position has been greatly weakened. Now the speaker delegates some tasks of the office to the Assembly pro tem.

Term Limits

The power that is won by any member in either house in California legislature is short-lived, due to term limits. Term limits became law in 1990 with the passage of Proposition 140. Under Proposition 140 limits elected officials terms in the following way: executive branch officers and state senators may serve two four-year terms and Assembly members may serve three two-year terms. Other limitations hit the legislature in the purse-strings by cutting down the operating budget 38%, making it necessary to lay people off. These changes were brought on by voters who were frustrated with the complacency they felt incumbents had since they seemed to have unfair advantages over anyone new who was running for office.

Proponents of term limits had hoped that it would safeguard against an incumbent becoming too stale or acquiring too much influence because of money. On the other hand however, being that elections are held every two years, candidates are required to campaign, costing the candidates and their parties to shell out more and more money as time goes by. As far as opening up more possibilities for fresh leadership, the jury is still out. Some claim that term limits weed out poor decision makers and others, especially when discussing leaders that are respected by all parties concerned, say that new leaders do not have enough time to surpass the learning curve period and cut to the real meat of the position, let alone hope for any longevity in this career. Incidentally, because bureaucrats and lobbyists are "employees" and "business professionals", they are not accountable to the voters, which has basically shifted power away from the elected officials and given more control to non-elected entities.

The phenomenon of term limits is like a problem that is so close and large that one can no longer focus on what is very obvious. The "turnstile" effect of too many politicians coming and going has engendered a feeling of dissatisfaction among the voters, that nothing is really accomplished. This is because there is no institutional memory for the next group of representatives to use as a point of reference. Because incoming representatives do not always have the knowledge of procedures, topics, or issues, their reliance on special interests and the bureaucrats becomes greater, which isn't always ideal. What was once thought of as a solution has actually become the root of a larger problem. Periodically, further attempts to limit officials' time in office have been proposed, despite the negative ramifications of term limits that have become common knowledge. Term limits are the temporary band-aid covering the real issue, which is much needed campaign finance reform.

Redistricting and Gerrymandering

Building up support in the California legislature can be difficult. However, the constant changes that are present with population growth and mobility also present a challenge for each district. Every ten years, district boundaries are redrawn or realigned after the national census, as specified by the state constitution. The process and timing of this realignment are the same as it is for Congressional districts and California has 53 of them to manage in legislature. This process, explained earlier in this chapter, is referred to as reapportionment or redistricting. Gerrymandering refers to the manipulation of boundaries sometimes in odd shapes to maintain the constituency for the parties involved. It is especially controversial and political in California. The reason for the politically charged climate of redistricting is because legislators have as their base numbered districts, 80 in the Assembly and 40 in the Senate. Voter registration numbers in these districts predicts which party will be the one with the legislative power. Therefore, legislators from both houses, assisted by political scientists and demography experts, draw the lines for these districts to benefit their party. This practice has been the object of partisan criticism and the reason some say for the divide between the two parties' ideologies to widen, pushing Democrats further to the left and Republicans to conservative extremes. Furthermore, it restricts any flexibility for members of either party; a worse scenario as a result of gerrymandering is that by the time the June primaries roll around, the process garners no middle ground since the candidates who tend to win deal with extreme platforms. Finally, possibly the worst side effect of manipulating boundaries too much is that it divides entire areas demographically, causing concern for voter turnout in any given area, depending on where the candidates reach out.

Still Debatable While there is deep animosity between parties due to term limits and gerrymandering in California, some positive changes that have come of these two factors are that the face of legislature has transformed into one that reflects a better-educated, more ethnically diverse Assembly. In 1999, there were more women, African Americans, Latinos, Asians and blacks serving at one time in the

Assembly than any other time in history. Once again, however, the saying the more things change the more they stay the same is appropriate with the legislature as well. Since the legislature is attracting members who are more highly educated, most all candidates have some kind of business background, which in and of itself is not a problem; however, in the latter part of the 20th century, the all business all candidate all the time has edged out other careers in the legislative, making the vocational background of members too narrow. This limits the voters' choices as far as their legislative having a wide breadth of expertise on many administrative areas.

Representative of the nation as a whole, Californians tend to be apathetic and ignore politics, which is typical at the state and local level; and yet, teaching citizens to be more civic-minded seems to be a simple, perhaps naïve, solution. Instead of blaming the candidates, the process, or the institutions, Californians need to take it upon themselves to be more interested and more aware of the power and weight of their actions or inaction. However, as life races by, legislation continues to be passed whether Californians are paying attention or not; and California's political history is rife with propositions that have controlled or restricted various budget policies. It is up to each individual to care about how politics affects their lives and the lives of those around them.

How Do We Compare?
Iraq and the United States

Similar to Iran in the previous chapter, Iraq has served as part of the causeway between Europe, Asia, and Africa, inciting invasions by various groups, vying for control of the region. Looking at Iraq today many see nothing more than a land drowning in violent turmoil. Contentious warfare consumes the nation; just breaths after it had been freed from a tyrannical ruler who had brutalized its own citizens for over two decades. Iraq finds its liberated country amidst perpetual savagery

The new flag of Iraq after the fall of Saddam Hussein.
© Rui Vale de Sousa, 2007. Used under License from Shutterstock, Inc.

and destruction. Religious sects divided with animosity amongst themselves are nevertheless, united in hatred toward western countries, which provokes violence in the form of terrorism. No doubt the Iraqi people watch in horror as the chaos indiscriminately takes the lives of innocent loved ones, making their everyday life an omnipresent state of apprehension and fear.

As unfortunate as it may be, the Iraqi nation has had a long history of despot rulers, violent rebellions, and has been a bitter religious battle ground long before it was called Iraq, a name not used officially until 1921. The land formally known as Mesopotamia has been one of tremendous religious significance for thousands of years, and which still plays a salient role in the histories of the Muslim, Christian, and Jewish faithful. This ancient land has been studied extensively by historians for centuries. Many religious stories from the Torah, Bible, and Quran are accepted as the historical understanding of the region. But, in spite of the spiritual mayhem, Iraq is a region that introduced many of the first accounts of modern art, writings, scientific discoveries, and works of astrology. It was in Mesopotamia where the innovative building blocks for our 24-hour day and 60 minute hour evolved; and where the first traces of governmental law were practiced.[22] In studying Iraq's rich history, individuals gain a full perspective of its ancient civilizations, political makeup, and what it all means with respect to the 21st century nation.

Geography and Impacts of the Past

The name Mesopotamia is derived from the Greek language and means the "land between the two rivers." Since Iraq is located between the Tigris and Euphrates rivers, and water is a priceless commodity, throughout the ages there have been countless attempts to conquer the land and its inhabitants in hopes of setting up residence and livelihood within the territory. One of the earliest of these peoples was the Sumerians which ruled a group of city-states from around 3000 to 2400 BC.[23] A lasting contribution of the Sumerians was a writing system called cuneiform. Cuneiform was "written" by pressing shaped characters into clay wedges; this writing system was later borrowed by neighboring peoples in Iran and Turkey.[24] Around 1750 BCE, King Hammurabi established the world's first empire which came to be known as the Babylonian Empire. Hammurabi's empire was centered in the city of Babylon and his prolific rule extended into the area now known as western Iran. His kingdom would beget the early foundations of a structured legal system, later called the Hammurabi Code. The Hammurabi Code was a systematic legal code which encompassed all areas of societal functioning and represented the beginnings of the modern legal system in existence today.

Babylon was a precarious kingdom, constantly caught in a whirlwind of wars and invasions. In 538, Babylon fell to the armies of Persia. The Persian warriors freed the Israeli people who had been previously captured and brought to the Babylonian region by King Nebuchadnezzar in 586 BCE[25] Further contributions left by this first great empire include advances in math, astronomy, and science.

By the end of the 4th century BC, Mesopotamia was descending into a dire economic and governmental breakdown. Then, in 331 BCE, Alexander the Great shocked the declining nation out of its idleness with his trumpeted conquer of Babylon. Alexander attempted to unify the Mediterranean and Middle Eastern peoples but, nine years later, died prematurely.[26]

Throughout the centuries Mesopotamia saw kingdoms rise and fall, cities destroyed then rebuilt, all the while uncertainty and volatility never ceasing, depriving inhabitants of any lasting sense of peace or security. During the following years, there was a drastic theological transformation with the era of the prophet Muhammad in the 7th century AD. For centuries Mesopotamia had been a polytheistic country, most people worshiping many gods, some of which were closely associated with a reverence for nature, resulting in pious treatment of the environment. After being conquered by surrounding Islamic Arab tribes, the country converted to Islam. This changed the religious focus to one of monotheism. This religion would influence political, societal, and international events in Mesopotamia for centuries to come. Another lasting change for Mesopotamia was the governance of the Ottomans from 1534-1915 AD.[27]

The Opulent Ottomans

Ottoman Sulaiman the Magnificent, fueled by vengeance for the assassination of one of his **emirs**, conquered Baghdad in 1534. The following 300 years of Ottoman rule brought sectarian violence and bloodshed amongst Shia and Sunni. In 1869, Midhat Pasana was appointed to govern Baghdad and he greatly modernized the country, raising the standard of living through a renaissance of educational systems, rule of law, and hospitals.[28] Unfortunately his governance was short lived and with his 1871 departure, Iraq once again crumbled into chaotic disarray. In 1908 a sentiment of Arab nationalism was born through the leadership of the **Young Turks**, a political organization with the goal of "Turkifying" of minorities.[29] However, it would only be a few years until the next major upheaval destabilized the region once again. In 1914 the British would launch a military invasion and Iraq would become a permanent international nation of importance.

The Key Institutions

The 43rd President of the United States, George W. Bush, has been outspoken about his goal of establishing the state of Iraq into a recognizable democracy. If history proves this aim successful it will be a commendable accomplishment of the most spectacular of scales. However, a stable democracy in Iraq appears at the moment to be a visionary wish with all the aggravation of an intangible mirage.

There was a great wave of triumph amongst U.S. government administrators in late January 2005 as Iraqis proudly waved purple fingers for photographers, a symbol of westernization; it meant that they had voted in a free election for an Iraqi National Assembly. This election was supposed to be a landmark occasion, the beginning of a free established democratic Iraqi government. Perhaps there was genuine cause for celebration; after all, many Iraqi's risked, life, limb, and security in an open manifestation for their support of a democratically elected government. But whatever the benevolent intentions, the new Iraqi Assembly did not secure the free and prosperous democratic Iraq that had been hoped for. However, in all fairness, there were virtually insurmountable odds that faced the Assembly, making it almost impossible for them to carry out these wishes. In light of the country's volatile and troubled history with rulers, power, and government, there is little optimism of any long lasting free democratic solutions, or if the westernized democratic ideal is even appropriate or wanted from the region and its people.

The rule of the British-appointed Faisal in 1921 lasted until his death in 1933. During this first government under the newly established British mandate, 3 distinct classes of Iraqi people, the Kurds, Shiite, and Sunni, were brought together under a singular authority. Faisal turned out to be a weak leader, letting portions of monarchal authority slip into the hands of political and military leaders.[30] In 1932 Iraq was granted formal independence and was admitted into the League of Nations. With its newfound autonomy the country began building up a powerful military force. After Faisal's death, his son Ghazi I inherited the kingdom, but had strong anti-British sentiments. With its independence and new found wealth of oil exports, the numerous political factions wanted a piece of the pie and were willing to fight each other over it. Political upheavals, coups, battles and general instability once again marked the next several years.[31]

Emir –
A prince, chieftain, or governor, especially in the Middle East, sometimes a descendant of Muhammad.

Young Turk –
A member of a Turkish reformist and nationalist party that was founded in the latter part of the 19th century and was the dominant political party in Turkey in the period 1908–18.

The onset of World War II altered the political climate throughout the world, and this did not preclude Iraq. In 1941 the mood in Iraq was apprehensive as lucrative oil supplies promised great wealth to many desiring nations. Savvy Arab nationalists recognized the inability of Britain to enforce strict colonial control while preoccupied with fighting axis forces. Iraq was on the brink of another era of mayhem, and it began with the Iraqi Prime Minister Rashid Ali Gailani.

Baath –
Literally means "rebirth" or "renaissance" in Arabic.

Pro German Gailani overthrew British-supporting emir Abdullah and then used his forces to attack a British air base located on the outskirts of Baghdad.[32] Gailani's coup attempt ultimately failed and the British placed the loyal Nur al-Said into power. Nur al-Said did away with all remaining established political vestiges from the former regime and called for fresh parliamentary elections in 1954.[33] Over the next few years, led by western friendly al-Said, Iraq signs an allying agreement with Britain, Turkey, Pakistan, and Iran known as the Baghdad Pact. Iraq receives military aid from the U.S. and forms the Arab Union with Jordan. Predictably, in what may seem like a twilight pattern of institutional calamity, Iraq would once again be pulled into a hurricane of political unrest.[34]

In 1958 a military coup by an Iraqi group known as the Free Officers executes Nur al-Said and his family; shortly afterward, they declared Iraq a republic. Iraq is turned upside down as it distances itself from the west and befriends the Soviets. A new political party called **Baath** is on the rise to prominence.

The Baathist Party originated in Syria under the control of Salah al-Din al Bir and Michel Aflaq. The party spread to Iraq and played a small role in a 1958 coup.[35] Aflaq was Secretary General of the Baathists and remained so until his death in 1989 when he was succeeded by the infamous Saddam Hussein. Although not the official authoritarian leader of the Baathist's until 1989, Hussein was an active Baathist participant as early as 1958. The rising of the Baathist party began an era of terror and chaos to Iraqi politics: decades buried in corruption, murder, mayhem, coups, and genocide. Meanwhile, Iraqi oil prices propelled upward exponentially, granting Saddam fantastic economic prowess by the time he came to rule a dictatorship of the country in 1979.

Saddam Hussein became notorious as one of the most ruthless tyrants in history. He executed thousands of his own people, showing no mercy for the innocents, women, children, or the elderly included. One of his most hellish acts was the 1988 genocidal extermination of thousands of Kurdish, men, women, and children. The leadership of Hussein may have been loathsome, but for once Iraq would have a stable government. This changed in 2003 when the U.S. led invasion attempted to overthrow Hussein.

Political Culture – Iraq's Fight

In the ever-reaching religious right culture of the United States, the line separating church and state is becoming more and more blurry; nevertheless, where there is a constitutional provision for the separation of church and state, it is difficult to imagine a nation's political culture defined completely by religious beliefs. However, Iraq is a country of theocratic roots and the dividing lines between religion and politics have a tendency to coalesce into intangible denominators. Before the birth of Islam, Mesopotamia was a largely polytheistic region, worshiping multiple gods, many of whom represented elements of nature. These gods played an intricate role in political life, as it was accepted among kings that control over religious affairs would grant them enormous political sway over their people. Traditionally, gods would grant authority of kings through the sanctioning of priests. This legitimized the king's rule, making him a sacred ascendancy to be revered by the common people.[36]

Figure on an ancient Mesopotamian wall.
© John Said, 2007.
Used under License from Shutterstock, Inc.

Currently Iraq is approximately 60% Shiite Muslim and 30% Sunni Muslim, in a nation with a population of 25,374,691.[37] The split among the Muslim population goes back to Islam's origins during the 7th century AD. When the prophet Muhammad died in 632 AD, there was a division among Muslims as to who was the proper successor. The controversy escalated to the point of a sectarian partition within the faith, most notably Shiite and Sunni. Shiite believe the leaders of Muslim faith must be family descendents from Muhammad. Sunni Muslim's do not adhere to this belief and are therefore considered inferior by many Shiite.[38] Although Shiite are a majority in Iraq (and Iran), Sunni Muslims make up 85 percent of the worldwide Muslim populous. Shiite and Sunni share much of the same religious beliefs and foster harmonious relationships throughout parts of the Muslim world. But resentment between the extremes of the sects exists over perceived historical animosities; disagreement turn deadly amongst radical factions of the faith. Nowhere is this more transparent then in present day Iraq.

Saddam Hussein was a Sunni Muslim and carried out genocidal attacks against his own Shiite majority people. Since the overthrow of Saddam, the majority of Shiite populous is in the position to carry out revenge, which many choose to do. Sunni fight back with vehemence. The religious chasm between Shiite and Sunni sects leaves a battered and bleeding nation grasping for political and governmental control. Besides the difficulties inherent when two antithetical religious sects attempt to form a unified government, there is the challenge of creating a free democratic society when many believe in a system of traditional Shari law. Shari, or Islamic, law is the traditional religious law that many Iraqi Muslims believe should be aligned with governmental law and authority. Particular interpretations of Shari law may call for the execution of Christians and other non-believers who refuse to convert to the Islamic faith. In searching for a solution to the present day Iraq debacle, suggestions have been made to splinter the nation into three autonomous regions, one Shiite, one Sunni, and one Kurdish.

Around 30 million Kurds makeup the largest distinct ethnic group of people without a homeland; the Kurdish people reside not only in Iraq, but also Turkey, Iran, and Syria. Although Iraqi Kurds are Sunni, they are moderate in their practice than most Arab Sunni.[39] There are approximately 4 to 6 million Kurds in Iraq who inhabit the northern region; the Kurds have their own language and customs. The Iraqi Kurds have existed in a vacillating identity, having autonomous rule being sporadically given and taken away from their people. In the Iran-Iraq war the Kurdish movement sided with the Iranian forces, a move that tyrant Saddam Hussein would not forget. As previously mentioned Hussein carried out genocidal attacks killing thousands of the Kurdish people.

Patterns of Interaction

Iraq became an international country of concern in November 1914 when the British expeditionary corps trounced upon southern Iraqi territory.[40] The British easily conquered the southern most entities but were met with Turkish opposition as they moved toward Baghdad. In 1916 the British surrendered to warriors of the Ottoman dynasty. As the Great War waged on throughout Europe, the Iraqi Arabs revolted against the Ottoman control, bribed by British promises of an Arab kingdom.[41] The British sent troops in support of the movement but would abandon any promises of an Arab nation. Britain accepted the mandate of Iraq at the San Remo Conference in San Remo, Italy, in April 1920.[42]

Although Iraq has been a nation bombarded with conflicts throughout time in memorial, the most memorable and magnificent of 20th century interactions was the Iran-Iraq war. The eight-year battle began on September 23rd, 1980 when Saddam Hussein ordered a military invasion of neighboring Iran.[43] The hostilities between the Iranians and Sunni had been fermenting between Shiite Iranians and Sunni controlled Iraqi regime, and tensions continued to escalate. In addition Saddam hoped to gain control of Iranian waterways and petroleum fields.[44] The prolonged war took an estimated 1.5 million lives, bankrupted both countries' economies, and debilitated oil fields. The Untied Nations succeeded in negotiations of a cease-fire In July 1988.[45] The devastation of the Iran-Iraq war did not dampen the ambitions of an oil lusting Saddam Hussein who soon set his eyes on the lucrative oil fields of next door neighbor Kuwait. Only two years after the Iran-Iraq war settlement, Hussein ordered troops into Kuwait, and led an expedient conquering of the defenseless nation. The United States joined allies in the fight against Hussein with support from Britain, NATO, Japan, Syria, Egypt, Afghanistan, Morocco and Pakistan, and then demanded a precipitous withdrawal from Kuwaiti territory by Jan 15, 1991.[47] Saddam did not withdraw. Operation Desert Storm was immediately underway as U.S. and British aircraft made their way toward Baghdad. Allied forces defeated the Iraqis in an unusually efficient fashion. But the ease of the Gulf War success would belie the precarious animosities brewing between Iraq and the west. Saddam Hussein remained in power and would continue to rule with malevolent despotism until March 2003.

In George W Bush's 2002 State of the Union address he warned of Iraq's support of terror and declared Iraq a part of the "Axis of Evil".[47] For years Saddam Hussein had been vexing the United States with evasive attitudes toward UN weapon inspectors, leading many western nations to suspect the regime was harboring weapons of mass destruction. It was the fear of such weapons which gave reason for the President Bush to order, with overwhelming congressional support, a U.S. led invasion into Iraq to oust Saddam Hussein from power. The United States military and its allies might have done just that, but the regime collapsed less then a month after the first arrival of forces. Unfortunately, after that high point of moral triumph in the fall of a tortuous tyrant, social chaos and anarchy would soon overwhelm the liberated nation. Reports were released that there were actually no weapons of mass destruction; despite this fact, the Bush Administration dismisses the allegations that they launched an illegal war.

After Saddam's capture and confinement to custody, a shock wave spread across the Iraqi political and social atmosphere. Hussein was a dark villain but he managed to maintain political stability. His ousting further aggravated the deep seeded religious hatred already felt amongst Iraqi Shiite and Sunni Muslims, who were no longer silenced by his iron rule. Terrorist attacks began in the form of suicide missions and continued after the freely elected government took office. The provisional government was established in 2005 but lacks legitimacy and is unable to enforce the rule of law. Murder and mayhem flourish daily throughout the nation and arbitrarily takes the lives of Iraqi women and children, not to mention thousands of military casualties from both sides. The United States and its allies seem unable to cease the bloodshed and the war has become increasingly unpopular throughout the world and within the U.S. Rumors of a precipitous American withdrawal and an Iraqi vote of no confidence for their own parliament suggest that political unrest is likely to deteriorate further.

Chapter Summary

Most democracies have a representative democracy, which is also known as indirect democracy. A representative democracy is one in which the people rule indirectly through representatives who they elected to govern in their stead. There are two main forms of representative democracy, the steward or delegate theory and the trustee theory. Many political leaders throughout history subscribe to one theory or another or a balance of both; the key to success is that the public's wishes are being heard. One can see by examining the demographics of the elected officials in Congress (mostly upper class, highly educated, white males) that true representation is difficult to achieve. There have been several movements of immigration and citizen's rights that have helped to improve the representation problem. In the 110th Congress, 2007, there are now 89 women as opposed to only 11, fifty-five years ago. This is an improvement but there is still a ways to go, since women make up close to 51% of the population in the U.S. Elections are the main vehicle in which the people can exercise their control over Congress. However, with gerrymandering and safe seats in the House, it has become increasingly difficult to defeat incumbents. The Senate on the other hand, tends to be more competitive and independent. In evaluating the institutions of each chamber, the strengths and weaknesses of both parties the committee structure, and the influence of special interests. The Constitution initiates a system that requires checks and balances, not only on Congress and the Executive Branch, but also between chambers. This process makes it extremely difficult for bills to become laws. The California section of this chapter shows how the state and federal legislatures are very similar in structure and organization. Institutions, culture, and the history of a country are key elements that point to whether or not a country can or should become a democratic state; it is not always the case as we have seen with Iraq. In the next chapter, we will study another aspect of American institutions, the Executive branch. We will evaluate the state and federal levels, as well compare the Presidential system with the semi-presidential system in France.

Key Terms:

Glass Ceiling

Speaker of the House

Select Committee

Conference Committee

Special Election

Whip

Reapportionment

Redistricting

Gerrymandering

Majority-Minority Districts

Franking Privilege

Pork

Casework

Party Caucus

Pro Tempore

Partisan

Standing Committees

Hearings

Markup Session

Select Committee

Joint Committees

Conference Committees

Reciprocity

Unanimous Consent

Filibuster

Cloture

Hopper

Pocket Veto

Quorum

Emir

Young Turk

Baath

Websites:

CongressLink at the Dirksen Center
www.congresslink.org

U.S. House of Representatives Home Page
www.house.gov

U.S. Senate Home Page
www.senate.gov

California Sites

California State Home Page
www.ca.gov

California State Senate
www.senate.ca.gov

California State Assembly
www.assembly.ca.gov

California Law References
www.leginfo.ca.gov/calaw.html

Search Bills in the California Legislature
www.sen.ca.gov/www/leginfo/SearchText.html

The White House is the center of power of the Executive Branch.
Courtesy of Corel

CHAPTER 10

THE EXECUTIVE

CHAPTER OUTLINE

Democracy and Action – Victoria Woodhull – An Unconventional Woman in a Conventional Time

The Communist Manifesto –
The writings of Karl Marx and Friedrich Engels that discusses class struggles, and how the merchant class and the working class can overthrow capitalists and create a socialist state.

Way before there was Hillary Clinton, even decades before women were given the right to vote in 1920, there was Victoria Woodhull, the very first female candidate for President of the United States. An unconventional woman in a time when women just weren't, Victoria Claflin Woodhull was born in the state of Ohio in 1838. Married at just 15 years old to Canning Woodhull, a doctor almost twice her age,

January 11, 1871. The Judiciary Committee of the House of Representatives receives a group of female suffragists, led by Victoria Woodhull. The women are presenting their position that women have a right to vote, based on the 14th and 15th Amendments. Courtesy of the Library of Congress.

she soon found him to be an alcoholic, and realized that she would be responsible for the support of her family. An innovator at an early age, Victoria and her sister Tennessee became the first female stock brokers; in 1870 they opened Woodhull, Claflin, and Company, the first female owned brokerage house on Wall Street. Also in 1870, with earnings from the brokerage, the sisters founded a newspaper,

Woodhull & Claflin's Weekly, which became famous for its very controversial opinions and was also the first to publish an English version of **The Communist Manifesto**. Through her newspaper, Woodhull became known in the women's suffrage movement. In 1870, she announced her plans to run for the U.S. Presidency. In 1871, she became the first woman to deliver a speech before Congress, specifically the House Judiciary Committee; her speech was in support of women's suffrage. And in 1872, the newly formed Equal Rights Party nominated her to be their presidential candidate for the 1872 election. Frederick Douglass, the American abolitionist and former slave was nominated as her vice presidential candidate, though he never campaigned nor acknowledged it. It was quite a ticket though, for that day and age.[1]

Woodhull's candidacy drew the support of an unusual variety of people, including laborers, suffragists, and communists, all who agreed that there needed to be a change in government. Though few people believed in her ability to win, her supporters knew that her candidacy in itself would send a message; it was time for a woman in the White House.

Woodhull ran into many obstacles during her campaign. First and foremost, women had not attained the right to vote, an obvious shortcoming. Another major roadblock was campaign funding; though she drew on her money from the brokerage house and the newspaper, she was soon running low and fundraising did not bring in enough to mount a substantial campaign. An even bigger obstacle that eventually ended her campaign was criticism from her opponents; they did not focus their attacks on the issues, rather they concentrated on personal attacks instead. She was branded as everything from a prostitute to a witch during her campaign. At first she did not respond to these attacks. When she finally pled with those she supposed were behind the attacks to stop (she suspected the Beecher family), she received the cold shoulder. In frustration, Woodhull published an attack piece in her newspaper with the hopes that they would finally

February 17, 1872. Get Thee Behind Me, Mrs. Satan!
Negative propaganda sought to slander
Victoria Woodhull, during her campaign for president.
Courtesy of the Library of Congress.

leave her alone. This article landed Victoria and her second husband, as well as her sister, in jail for publishing it. In another historic turn of events, she became the first female presidential candidate to spend Election Day in jail on charges of sending obscene literature through the mail. The story she published was about the Reverend Beecher's affair with a married woman, very obscene in those days. The resulting uproar set in motion not only a debate over free speech, but also one of the most notorious trials of its time, pitting the famous Reverend Beecher against his best friend, the scorned husband. Eventually, Woodhull and the others were acquitted of any crimes. Unfortunately, they had spent virtually everything they'd had on the resulting lawsuits and bail. Shortly after acquittal, Victoria divorced her husband and moved to England where she spent the rest of her years.

Still today, some 135 years later, there has yet to be a female U.S. President. And though there have been other female presidential candidates throughout our country's history, most people have not heard of Victoria Woodhull, an unconventional woman in a very conventional time. She was a trailblazer in many ways, but the most profound way was as the very first official female candidate for the Presidency of the United States.[2]

The Presidency Throughout History

A typical vice of American politics is the avoidance of saying anything real on real issues. – Theodore Roosevelt

The Framers of the Constitution had a vision of the role for the president in American politics. But, judging from the day that George Washington was sworn in up until today, the presidency has become much different than the framers intended.

Comparison – Then and Now

When George Washington took office in 1789 the federal government was extremely small. The federal budget was a little over $4 million and there were only 5 cabinet posts: a secretary of State, War, and Treasury, an attorney general, and a post master general. The military consisted of 700 regulars who were charged with protecting the 13 states were under-trained and ill-equipped for conflicts along the western frontier and any possible invasion from France or Britain. The population was less than four million and most of them were rural farmers.

Over two hundred years and 42 presidents later, the federal budget is approximately $2 trillion a year. There are 15 cabinet posts and over 1.5 million serving in the armed forces that are stationed around the world protecting U.S. interests. The nation has a population of over 300 million residents who live in fifty states; 48 are contiguous from the Atlantic Ocean to the Pacific Ocean. The county has changed not only in size and population but also how we govern ourselves. In order to accommodate these changes, the powers of the president have evolved as well.

How the Framers Envisioned the Presidency

The framers wanted a president who would preside over the nation but with limited powers. As discussed in Chapter 2, the Constitution in Article II created a single executive with subordinates to aid him in making and implementing public policy. Unfortunately, the framers had no way to predict the needs of the future so planning the appropriate powers was difficult. Throughout American history the executive powers have gradually expanded in order meet the challenges of a growing nation. Take for example the separation of power with regards to the military. The president is the commander-in-chief and Congress has the power to declare war. In reviewing American history, we can see that the United States has engaged in over two hundred conflicts but only declared war five times. Where did the president get the authority to send the military into action without a declaration of war? A person's interpretation of the Constitution can differ greatly from what the framers intended. For example, the fact that the president is the commander and chief of the military with a standing army implies that he has the power to use it as he deems necessary. George Washington, who was an attendee at the Constitutional Convention, used the army along the western frontier against indigenous tribes without a declaration of war from Congress. The vague language of the Constitution allows for presidents to expand their powers beyond what the framers had envisioned.

From the time the Constitution was adopted in 1789 until the late 1800's, the presidency tended to follow the framer's design. The president executed the policies that were created by Congress; however, throughout this time, certain presidents responded to situations by adding powers to the president. This would occur sometimes without Congressional approval but most of the time, Congress was willing to grant these powers if it was clearly warranted.

Early Presidents 1789-1901

Within the first 110 years of the Unites States, there were 25 presidents. Each left their mark on the office, but some more than others. Regardless of what each did individually, each president undoubtedly helped shape the institution of the presidency to what it is today.

George Washington established the standard for the role of the president. After the revolution, many Americans did not trust the government, especially with regards to the executive. Washington alleviated those fears but working closely with Congress to shape domestic policy. In addition, Washington's experience as a military leader allowed him to establish firm control over military issues both at home and abroad. Thomas Jefferson, who originally opposed a single executive, used his powers to double the size of the nation with the acquisition of the Louisiana territory from France, despite objections from Congress. This set the nation on a course of expansionism across North America. Andrew Jackson, another war hero, made the presidency a popular institution by his magnetism and broad support shown by popular vote; he was also seen as a spokesperson for the average American by opposing the national bank, which was largely seen as a tool for the elites of the nation.

James Polk helped to secure the nation from the Atlantic to the Pacific Oceans by provoking the Mexican-American War, in which the southwest was won, including California. Abraham Lincoln was one of the most activist presidents the nation saw during the 1800s. During the Civil War he raised money for the cause to supplement the funds from Congress. In addition to this, Lincoln took an active role in directing military action and replacing commanders who he deemed unqualified. Lincoln unilaterally issued the Emancipation Proclamation freeing the slaves in the southern states, and he suspended the right of habeas corpus. Furthermore, he had civilians tried by military tribunals, ignoring the Supreme Court's order to reinstate the right. The actions of these past presidents established a blueprint pattern that presidents still use today.

Evolution in the Twentieth-Century (1902-2001)

As the calendar rolled over to the new century, new challenges were presented to the presidency that required additional powers given and created by the men in office.

Theodore Roosevelt. Before becoming president, Theodore (Teddy) Roosevelt had experienced many things that would help him redefine the presidency for the new century. He traveled the world as a big game hunter; sent the **"Great White Fleet"** around the world as Secretary of the Navy to illustrate the nations' military strength; and he led the **"Rough Riders"** during the Spanish-American War in Cuba. As president, he would continue to show the world the growing military power

Great White Fleet –
A U.S. Navy task force that circumnavigated the world from December 1907 to February 1909. This fleet was formed to show the world the growing virility of the U.S. military.

Rough Riders –
The common name given to the First United States volunteer cavalry regiment, led by Teddy Roosevelt during the Spanish-American War.

of the U.S., developed and protected U.S. economic interests, such as pursuing the building of the Panama Canal, and aggressively went after the American "Aristocracy" by imposing regulations and breaking monopolies and unfair business practices. Teddy Roosevelt did more than any other president since Lincoln to expand the presidency. This would aid the nation in the next crisis.

Col. Teddy Roosevelt with officers of the Rough Riders on horse-back during the Spanish American War, 1899. Courtesy of the Library Congress.

Woodrow Wilson. When Woodrow Wilson took office, he began to lay the foundation to shape America into a world power domestically, militarily, bureaucratically and economically. On the domestic front, President Wilson expanded on the framework of Teddy Roosevelt. The anti-trust and Progressive measures included the creation of the Federal Reserve Board in 1913 and the Federal Trade Commission in 1914. With the onslaught of America's involvement, Wilson began to build the military, in terms of personnel and weapons and armament. In order to support this industrious build up of men and machines, a new level of bureaucracy was added to oversee the distribution and production of war supplies. After the war, the President implemented programs to encourage trade to prevent future wars and a forum to discuss conflicts between nations. By using encouraging trade, countries would be able to build their economies on peaceful means instead of destroying their economies, countries, and people through war. The League of Nations was designed to be the conduit for diplomats to work out their issues peacefully. While the League failed, it proved to be ahead of its time and was the predecessor to the United Nations.

Franklin D. Roosevelt. It was under Franklin Roosevelt that the presidency moved to the more modern executive that Americans are used to seeing. In response to the Great Depression and World War II, the expansion of powers that occurred during President Roosevelt's term surpassed anything the nations had ever seen before or since.

The Great Depression made the President accountable for the economy. While the office had always played a role in economic development, this was the first time that power began to emanate from the states to the federal government. As discussed in chapter 3, the very concept of federalism changed. No longer would there be a clear division between the states and federal government powers but a melding of the two. The New Deal created a series of laws that evolved into comprehensive federal programs such as farm assistance programs, public works projects, and loans for business. In addition, the federal government expanded its oversight of corporations and the stock market by introducing more regulations to guarantee the public would not have to endure such a crisis in the future. Benefits for the people were also enacted. Unemployment insurance for those out of work and Social Security to encourage older workers to retire in order to open jobs for younger employees. To protect employees, the Wagner Act was passed to help workers unionize.

The majority of the changes occurred as a result of World War II. The entire nation was mobilized for war. Men were drafted, women joined the work force in record numbers filling the jobs that men had vacated, and plants that produced cars were converted to produce war materials such as jeeps, tanks, and troop transports. The long term impact of the war would secure America's place as a superpower both in its economy and its military forces. Every president since Roosevelt had access to a large standing military, a global base structure to exert American power and influence, and an arsenal of nuclear weapons.

The improvements in the economy developed in several ways. With the government taking control of most production of goods and resources, it created a level of micromanagement to the economy that had never existed before. In order to oversee this new economic structure, the government would hire returning vets who were well trained and eager to continue to do their part. While many of these agencies no longer exist, they left behind many able-bodied governmental activists and officials. This new generation of agencies continues to influence domestic and foreign policy at the president's bidding, as they have done since World War II.

John F. Kennedy. Even though his term was short, Kennedy's charisma electrified the nation. His use of television allowed his passion, youth, and good looks to be seen around the world. Early in his term he had to face off with the Soviet Union over the Cuban Missile Crisis, a hot war between the United States and the Soviet Union was diverted through diplomatic channels. Divided Berliners and all of Europe were moved when he said, "Ich bin ein Berliner," in an attempt to convey U.S. support and empathy for West Berlin during the Cold War.

His encouragement to the new generation to seek a "new frontier" not only on familiar terrain but also in uncharted outer space inspired millions to serve

John F. Kennedy signing the proclamation enacting the U.S. arms quarantine against Cuba. © Bettmann/Corbis

their country. When Kennedy said, "Ask not what your country can do for you – ask what you can do for your country," the response by college graduates willing to volunteer was tremendous.

While still a Senator campaigning for the presidential election in 1960, he spoke to the students of the University of Michigan Union in the wee hours of the morning, asking them not only for their support of his campaign, but also to challenge them to work and live for peace in developing countries around the world. This eventually became the basis and mission of the Peace Corps, whose goals are not only to help train men and women as needed but also to promote peace, friendship, and cultivate an exchange of understanding between the Americas and other countries.[3]

There were several projects that President Kennedy would begin but never see come into fruition; a man on the moon and the Civil Rights Act to name a couple. Kennedy's speeches, ideas, and commitment to the country inspired Americans during his term and subsequently, caused great pain and loss after he was assassinated less than a thousand days into his presidency.

The Importance of Individual Presidents

Does the event make the man or is it the man who masters the event? History has tracked the rise and fall of presidents who have been presented with challenges that seemed insurmountable; but with the proper advice, skills, and personal tenacity, they have been able to persevere and brought the nation through the turmoil and made it better for it. Individuals like Lincoln, Wilson, Roosevelt, and Kennedy were such presidents who were able to make choices based on what was right for the entire country and not just a few individuals.

Other presidents have been known to use political force to achieve a means to an end. While history has a mixed perspective on their actions, some of the tasks benefited the country in other ways. Andrew Jackson, Teddy Roosevelt, Harry Truman, and Lyndon Johnson are all presidents who, to paraphrase Teddy Roosevelt, were able to walk softly and carry a big stick; sometimes for show and sometimes to use. Their actions, while controversial in nature, have proven to benefit the nation as a whole. History has not shown the same kindness on other presidents, yet. More modern presidents, such as Richard Nixon, Jimmy Carter, Ronald Reagan, George H. Bush, and Bill Clinton are still beloved but are still waiting for history's final report.

Profiles in Politics
Franklin Delano Roosevelt (1882 - 1945)

Franklin D. Roosevelt, the 32nd President of the United States, is arguably one of the greatest presidents in our nation's history. He lifted the country out of the Great Depression and set us on a course toward economic recovery as well as shepherded the country through one of its most major international crises, World War II.

Pres. Roosevelt signs a declaration of war against Japan in December, 1941. Courtesy of the Library Congress.

Franklin Delano Roosevelt was born in Hyde Park, New York in 1882. A distant cousin to Theodore Roosevelt and part of a prominent family, FDR attended Harvard University and then the Columbia University of Law. He practiced law in New York for a few years and then entered politics in 1910 with his election to the New York Senate. In 1913, President Woodrow Wilson appointed FDR as Assistant Secretary of the Navy, which he remained until 1920. In 1928, he became Governor of New York, and in 1932 was elected President of the United States.[4]

Between his public service stints, Roosevelt contracted polio in 1921 and lost the use of his legs; though he tried and would even appear on crutches occasionally, he never regained use of them. Later on, as President, he established the March of Dimes to help combat polio.

Elected president at the height of the Great Depression, Roosevelt set out to enact major changes to save the citizens from the mires of despair. During his first 100 days, with the assistance of Congress, Roosevelt put his plan for relief and recovery, which he called the New Deal, into effect. It involved setting up several agencies designed to help various businesses and interests recover as well as assist the people, many of whom were by this time long unemployed and starving. When all was said and done, Roosevelt's first 100 days were remarkable and remain to this day the bar by which all presidents are measured.[5]

The New Deal also involved setting up government programs to assist the welfare of the citizens. These programs included Social Security and unemployment compensation. Roosevelt also put into effect a huge government labor program that got folks back to work; he was also a proponent of organized labor and fair employment practices. Roosevelt was overwhelmingly reelected in 1936.

Profiles in Politics
Franklin Delano Roosevelt (1882 - 1945)

Frustrated by the Supreme Court overruling several of his policies, Roosevelt made his biggest and quite possibly his only) mistake. He introduced a proposal for judicial reform which included enlarging the Supreme Court. This move created a public outcry and Roosevelt was accused of attempting to "pack" the Supreme Court with justices favorable to his policies. Needless to say, his proposal failed, but Roosevelt managed to recover; in the end, due to his long presidency, he was able to appoint seven justices anyway.[6]

Though FDR knew that economic recovery and relief would go far with the American people, he also realized that psychologically, they needed comfort and reassurance. To provide this measure of hope and confidence, Roosevelt harnessed the relatively new power of radio and began having periodical "fireside chats" with the American people. During these informal addresses, he spoke reassuringly, encouraging the public that if they all worked together, they could help lift the country out of the depression. He continued these chats throughout his entire presidency, more than 12 years. By combining the actions of government policy and personal reassurance, Roosevelt was a successful steward of the country during a rough period. For his leadership, the country reelected him again in 1940.

The country's problems would not remain primarily domestic for long however. As war broke out across Europe, Roosevelt instituted a policy to provide assistance to Great Britain and France in every way except with military troops as the Germans marched through Europe. Everything changed on December 7th 1941, when the Japanese attacked Pearl Harbor. During the days immediately following the attack, both Germany and Italy also declared war on the United States, leaving Roosevelt no choice but to answer with force. Working closely with his commanders in the field, FDR oversaw a successful wartime strategy where the Allies eventually triumphed over the Axis powers, though Roosevelt did not live to enjoy the victory.

After being elected for an astounding fourth term in 1944, Roosevelt died unexpectedly shortly into that term, in April 1945, while the world was still at war. The length of Roosevelt's presidency did however prompt Congress to introduce a constitutional amendment in 1947 to limit a president to serving two terms. After Roosevelt's four consecutive elections there was a concern that a president, popular as he or she may be, could in effect become a sort of benevolent dictator that could serve for his or her entire lifetime, and thus possibly consolidate enough power to undermine the separation of powers set up by the founding fathers. That amendment, the 22nd, was ratified in 1951.[7]

His legacy looms large; his first 100 days are legendary; his policy initiatives revived the country's ailing economy and steered it toward a spectacular recovery. He instituted social welfare programs to create a safety net for all citizens. He boosted the morale of the American people and successfully guided the country through the perils of a World War. Because of his leadership in the face of extraordinary challenges, Franklin Delano Roosevelt will forever be seen as one of this nation's greatest presidents.

Constitutional Powers of the President

As stated in the previous chapter, the president and Congress have overlapping and sometime conflicting powers. This was done intentionally by the Framers. The design of checks and balances were created as a firewall, if you will, to block tyranny from developing by either of the two branches.

Who is Eligible to be President of the United States?

One area that sets the president apart from Congress is the eligibility requirements. The Constitution states in Article II Section 4 states three requirements, the president must be at least thirty-five years old, reside in the nation for a minimum of 14 years, and be a natural born citizen. This was part of the framers design to guarantee that the executive was mature enough to hold office and did not have a conflict with loyalties to other nations, such as England after the revolution.

The President and Congress

There are several areas in which the design of the Constitution gives the power to both branches of government. Congress has the power to originate and modify legislation but before it can become law, it must be sent to the president to sign it into law or veto it. If he elects to veto it, then Congress can vote to override the president's veto, thus making it a law. The president has the power to nominate Judges, Supreme Court Justices, ambassadors, and other high ranking administrators in the executive branch. After the president makes his nominations, they must first receive approval from the Senate before being sworn in. The president has the power to negotiate treaties with other nations but again, he must submit these plans to the Senate to be ratified.

Congress controls federal funding and defines how the funds must be used through the legislative process. The president is in charge of the executive branch but the moneys that are used to run it are appropriated by Congress. Congress has the power of oversight to guarantee the funds are being used as directed.

With great power comes great responsibility. This sentiment is not just a fact for superheroes but also for the great office of the U.S. presidency. We look to the president to make difficult military decisions and to represent us as a nation when dealing with foreign affairs. This can be extremely demanding since everyone has a different interpretation of the image they want America to project. Despite the differing opinions that are bandied about in Congress, the president is ultimately the one authority that has the responsibility and power to declare war. Case in point, an area of conflict that exists between the president and Congress is domestic and foreign policy. The president may lose support of Congress or even from his own party if public opinion turns against his policies, as in the case of the Iraq War and President Bush. Congress may feel that the president has usurped too much power; for example, the U.S.A Patriot Act. For example, with the U.S.A Patriot Act, President Bush was given wide authorization to combat terrorism. However, as time progressed, it became apparent that this power was being misused and overextended into American lives by illegal wire-tapping, surveillance of library and computer usage, and so on.

Profiles in Politics
Barack Obama (1961 -   )

The presidential campaign of 2008 is breaking new ground on many fronts; among them, we have our first truly viable African American contender, Senator Barack Obama (D-IL).

Obama's parents met while studying at the University of Hawaii, where his grandparents lived. They bought a house and studied by way of the G.I. Bill, since his grandfather served in World War II just after Pearl Harbor. Also, his mother worked on a bomber assembly line in support of the war effort. Barack was born in Hawaii in 1961. His parents split up when he was still very young. His father returned to his native Kenya while young Barack remained with his mother in Hawaii and a few years in Indonesia with his stepfather.

Sen. Barack Obama (D-IL) is considered to be the first viable African-American presidential candidate.
© Russell Shively, 2007.
Used under License from Shutterstock, Inc.

Following high school, Obama continued his education at Columbia University in New York. He graduated in 1983, and in 1985, he moved to Chicago and worked as a community organizer for a local church group. After working in poor communities for a few years, Obama decided to pursue a law degree at Harvard University. He had come to believe that he could better serve the community by influencing legislation. While at Harvard, Obama became the first African American president of the prestigious Harvard Law Review in 1991.[8]

After earning his law degree in 1991, Obama returned to Chicago and began practice as a civil rights attorney. He also taught constitutional law at the University of Chicago. In 1996, Obama took the plunge into politics and was elected to the Illinois State Senate. In 2004, after serving 8 years in state government he continued to pursue higher ground by running for the United States Senate. During the campaign, he was chosen to be a keynote speaker at the Democratic National Convention in Boston. Barely known outside of his state, Obama gave one of the most electrifying speeches in front of an awestruck audience, an impressive national political debut. In November 2004, he was overwhelmingly elected to the Senate, garnering a whopping 70 percent of the vote. It was a landmark event and Obama became only the third African American ever elected to the Senate since Reconstruction.[9]

Frustrated with national politics as usual, after months of speculation on the part of the media, Obama finally threw his hat in the ring for the 2008 presidency in early 2007. Riding a wave of media infatuation and public excitement, he has raised a record amount of money for his candidacy and showed robust poll numbers right from the start.EN Questions of his inexperience and platform (besides an exit plan for troops in Iraq) crept in only after the initial media frenzy died down. Now the American public, with many strong frontrunners to choose from thus far, want to know just what Obama is all about. All of this, however, has not deterred the appeal of the freshman senator's charm and potential greatness. At the time of this writing, Obama was in the top three of the Democratic hopefuls, next to Sen. Hillary Clinton (D-NY), and Sen. John Edwards (D-SC). Time will tell whether he can win the Democratic nomination. Regardless of the results, Obama has firmly cemented his place in American politics.[10]

Elections

In the United States, the elections are staggered, as we discussed in the chapter on elections and voting. There are many difference reasons for this but one of the main points is that there is always a line of continuity. Every two years the entire House

of Representatives and one-third of the Senate are up for reelection. Every four years there is a presidential election. Midterm elections are held in years when there isn't a presidential election. Midterm elections are usually dramatic when there is a shift in the majority party in one or both houses of Congress. This is usually depending on the popularity of the president. In 1986, the Democrats took back the Senate under President Reagan; in 1994 the Republicans gained control of Congress with President Clinton at the helm; and more recently, the Democrats regained control of Congress during the midterm elections of 2006, making President George W. Bush's second half of his second term

Attendees at the 1956 Republican National Convention in San Francisco, CA. Courtesy of the Library of Congress. extremely challenging.

Navigating the Agenda through Congress

As you already know, the Framers built in to the Constitution a system of checks, preventing one branch of government becoming more powerful over another. However, other factors come into play as well. If the president has difficulty with his policies or has a conflict with the opposition party, or even his own, in Congress, gridlock could ensue, effectively shutting down the government. Ever since the institutions were created, presidents have sought ways to succeed in getting their agendas enacted by Congress. Many political operatives have examined the facets that make some presidents succeed where others have failed.

Political Parties and Ideologies

This may seem obvious but if the president's party controls one or both houses of Congress and the members agree with his ideology, the president's agenda has a much greater chance of passage. However, there are times in which the president's party doesn't agree with his policies, further complicating his relationship with Congress. Take for example the division between many Congressional Republicans and the President's policies regarding "aggressive interrogation techniques." The Republican led Congress passed legislation limiting the use of torture against detainees from Iraq and Afghanistan. The President signed the legislation into law with one caveat. President Bush added a signing statement allowing the use of techniques that may violate international law if it might gain information to aid the U.S. in the war on terrorism.

Vetoes

Sometimes a president can influence the wording and or the passage of a bill if they threaten to veto. The problem is if the bill passes despite the threat of a veto, this essentially forces the president to do exactly that – veto the bill. Presidents are somewhat assured that their veto won't be overturned. This was the case in July of

"Wool Bill" rams leaping over Presidential Veto banner, held by House Leader Oscar Wilder Underwood and Speaker James Beauchamp Clark dressed as clowns in the "Democratic House of Representatives" arena. Courtesy of the Library of Congress.

2006 when President George W. Bush threatened to veto a stem cell research bill and after it passed both houses of Congress he was forced to veto the legislaton.[11] In reviewing the Congressional records, one would find that on average less than five percent of presidential vetoes are overturned. Throughout history there have been some presidents who haven't experienced a problem vetoing legislation. Presidents Franklin Roosevelt, Harry Truman, and Gerald Ford were individuals who used the power of the veto to send clear messages to Congress about the legislation that was being sent to them. President Clinton didn't use the veto during his first two years in office but did after the Republicans gained control of both houses. In 1995, during the budget

impasse with the Republican controlled Congress, he used the veto 11 times. During his first six years in office, President Bush used his power to veto twice; the first time was on the stem cell research bill in July 2006 and the second was in April 2007 on legislation that required the Withdrawal of U.S. Troops from Iraq.[12]

Foreign Policy

One area that the presidents tend to have more influence over is foreign policy. During the Cold War, Congress gave deference to the president on issues that dealt with the Soviet Union. On occasion, Congress has held hearings on specific events such as the Gulf of Tonkin or the Iran-Contra Affair to name a few. After the Cold War ended, Congress continued to allow the President to maintain control over foreign policy. In January of 1991, Congress passed a resolution giving President George H. Bush the funds to deploy troops to free Kuwait from Iraq's control and later to aid United Nations peace keepers in Somalia. In the late 1990s, even though the Republicans controlled both houses of Congress, they provided funding for President Clinton's peace keeping missions and U.S. intervention in Haiti, Bosnia, and Kosovo.

Former Pres. Clinton speaks at his daughter Chelsea's college graduation at Stanford University.
© Jose Gil, 2007.
Used under License from Shutterstock, Inc.

After the attacks of September 11, 2001, both parties in Congress gave President George W. Bush board authority to go to war in Afghanistan, Iraq, and other key areas around the globe.

Popularity

Many political operatives feel that the popularity of a president is an advantage when negotiating with Congress. The rationale behind this is because members of Congress are concerned with challenging a popular president. Take the above example of 9/11. President Bush's first eight months in office showed his approval ratings around fifty percent. In the months following the attacks, President Bush's approval ratings surged to an unprecedented ninety percent and stayed in that range for the next six months. It wasn't until 2006 when the President's approval ratings began hovering around thirty percent did the majority of the members of Congress, from both parties, begin to criticize the President's strategies in Iraq.

Broadening the Executive Powers

Article II of the Constitution opens with the statement, "The executive Power shall be vested in a President of the United States of America." Aside from that, the framers did not stipulate on what "executive power" is. With each president there has been a redefining of what that statement means. For some, like Teddy and Franklin Roosevelt, it meant the power to use the office to regulate business and protect America's interests abroad. For others like Jimmy Carter, it meant the job of stewardship, and to pursue options other than force to protect the nation's interests. Either way, the narrow statement has been used as a spring board to advance individual president's political philosophy and agendas.

Presidential War Powers

As we mentioned earlier in the section on the president and Congress, the president has unique and forceful authority when it comes to foreign policy-making. The Constitutional powers granted to the president encompass influence over Court and Congress as well as establish the president as the commander-in-chief of America's armed forces. Some Presidents have first hand military strategy experience and others must rely more heavily on its appointed military leaders, who may just as well prefer it this way.

At times the privileges and power of the commander-in-chief produce some unpreventable side effects. This is to say that because the power is so absolute, the president may use them to take action against a perceived threat in the name of his or her military command. For example, Franklin Roosevelt used his authority to order the internment of thousands of Japanese Americans in retaliation of the Japanese bombing of Pearl Harbor; Lyndon Johnson used vague congressional resolutions to put troops on the ground during the Vietnam conflict, when it turned out to be a war that was engaged for illegal reasons. It is true that the president has the power to move war through Congress and present convincing arguments to do so; but having these powers does not make the president immune to checks, such as through the process of impeachment hearings. Nevertheless, whether the above presidents' reactions to complex situations during war-time accurately reflect fair and balanced usage of their power remains to be seen.

The War Powers Act

In order for Congress to monitor presidents' military actions, they were successful in passing the War Powers Act in 1973, despite President Nixon's veto. The resolution stipulates that the president must make every effort to confer and report to Congress within 48 hours of ordering U.S. troops into hostile territory if no declaration of war has been made. The troops must be withdrawn within 60 - 90 days if Congress disagrees with the president's actions. Congress does not have the power to halt the president's military order if a resolution passes in both houses, which is called a concurrent resolution.

Essentially, this means that the president does not need to wait for a congressional declaration of war before sending American troops into live combat. This is where the line between "declaring war" and "making war" become blurry. As we have seen with President Bush's actions in Iraqi Freedom, it is difficult for Congress to go against the president's decisions for fear of leaving troops without the funding needed for the proper gear and tactical equipment. This leaves Congress no choice but to support the president's decisions even though may not agree with the way the president handles war; furthermore, Congress itself has the power to declare war themselves. However, it is more accepted common practice for Congress to allow the president to justify the conditions that warrant going to war, making Congress, in some situations, just as negligent as the president.

The quagmire of a "war on terror" is that there is no identifiable face that can place a definitive opponent. How does a war on terror look when it is won? For this reason, a president may introduce a bill that is worded in such a way that Congress is obligated to grant the power needed to use military force. Continuing on the example of President Bush's war on Iraq, Bush presented a bill to Congress saying that he needed more power to purge Iraq of all chemical and biological weapons, including nuclear weapons. Congress would be hard-pressed to not support the removal of such a threat; however, the justification for this war turned out to be false and to some degree unfounded. At this point, the situation is between a rock and a hard place – leaving the troops in Iraq is reminiscent of Vietnam and a conflict we can no longer tame; on the other hand, pulling out doesn't finish what was started.

Informing the Public

The president is a product of generational pressures and social norms, just like anyone of us. A common complaint among the citizenry from generation to generation is that politicians cannot be trusted, they have hidden agendas, or they do not take responsibility for their actions. The more savvy the people become, the harder it is for political officials, especially as high up as the president, to rely on positive media spin to appear in the best possible light.

This is not to say that there are not "true believers" in the political science universe. The American president is a model to any other developing countries who aspire to have a democratic republic as long-lived as ours, still on our original Constitution. The person who holds the highest office in the land, the president,

Issues For You

What is your opinion on a "war on terror"? Does it always need to involve sending troops abroad?

John Q. Public – Illustration of FDR and his use of radio broadcasts to inform the public. He hoped to sway public opinion during his battles with Congress over his New Deal programs. Courtesy of the Library of Congress.

FOR YOUR CONSIDERATION
EXECUTIVE PRIVILEGE

Executive privilege is the claim of implied power inherent of the office of the president which enables him or her to withhold information. Though not expressly laid out in the Constitution, presidents have used variations of this argument since the beginning of the country. One of the primary explanations for invoking executive privilege have been claims that the requested information falls into the category of matters of national security and to release said information could in fact harm the security of the country or even the ability of the president to carry out his or her

April 13, 1973. A satirical look at Nixon clones bullying Congress by overusing presidential powers. Courtesy of the Library of Congress.

duties. This reason has been used many times in the past (President Eisenhower used this privilege forty times within two terms!) and has been again invoked by the Bush Administration.

Another prime reason administrations invoke executive privilege is their claim that for proper functioning of the executive branch, the need for an administration to receive honest and unfettered advice trumps the other branches' need for information. This argument has been used repeatedly, though President Nixon's attempt to use it to prevent releasing the Watergate Tapes failed. Vice President Cheney's use of it to prevent releasing information on his Energy Task Force was successful.

The current administration is under fire for allegedly abusing executive privilege. The scope of executive privilege has not truly been under the microscope of the courts as of late but when it is, it will no doubt be a hotly debated topic within each branch of government.[13]

must focus on conveying to the public that his or her administration is truly in touch with the American public. This connection between the president and the people is maintained through media, public appearances, televised interviews, charity events, and newspaper articles. With today's technology, websites, Ipods, PDA's, video clip websites, and so on, the repertoire of communication available to the public and to politicians is astounding. All of this can be reviewed by going back to the chapters on media and public opinion.

The People's President

The public's demands for a more transparent and accessible federal government was not always the case in America's quest for democracy. As we have discussed at the beginning of this book, the framers believed in a democratic republic but within certain limitations. The delegates that wrote the Constitution were mostly aristocrats, so it follows that they felt the president should also maintain elitist standards in order to properly lead. They expected the president to be aware of the public by addressing them in speeches a few times a year, but ultimately, to remain separate and immune to any passionate whims. Continuing this leadership style throughout the nineteenth century, the president mainly interacted with Congress. This indirect access to electing the president is evident in the Electoral College system (see For Your Consideration below).

Nowadays, presidential candidates need to have a certain star quality that captivates the public while also offering substance and integrity. Most people expect this from a president, even though such a complete package in a president has been hit and miss, over the years.

Two important goals a president must continually pursue are to make their priorities clear to the public and to win approval for these proposed policies from the public. Sometimes a president will try to curry favor with the American public before trying to negotiate with Congress. Occasionally, presidents will take the risk of going public on certain issues, even though it means compromising the already shaky communication that goes back and forth between Capitol Hill and the White House. This strategy may backfire on the president, however, as it sometimes leaves the members in Congress feeling put off or manipulated. Nevertheless, the president relies on public approval ratings to gauge the public's morale on her or his watch.

FOR YOUR CONSIDERATION
THE ELECTORAL COLLEGE

The Electoral College was established in Article II, Section 1 of the United States Constitution.[14] Essentially, the creation of the College represented a compromise of sorts; some of the founding fathers preferred an executive elected by the members of Congress, others preferred that the winner be determined by popular vote.

The compromise created a special group of electors that would come from each state and whose number would be equal to the amount of that state's members of Congress. Each state would be able to decide how to choose its electors, and in turn, the electors would meet following a presidential election and cast their vote to elect the president. The operating theory was that the people's elected representatives in the state would decide how to select their state's electors, therefore indirectly making the electors representative of the state's populace.[15]

Over the years, the process of the electors casting the votes for president has become nothing more than a formal ritual; almost every state awards its entire slate of electors on a winner-take-all basis therefore taking any true vote-casting out of the electors' hands. This seemingly empty tradition has raised the issue of whether the Electoral College should be abolished.

George W. Bush won the presidency in 2000 after the Florida recount.
© Jason Grower, 2007. Used under License from Shutterstock, Inc.

The presidential election of 2000 brought the issue to the forefront of public discourse. Then Vice President Al Gore was running neck and neck in the state of Florida against then Texas Governor George W. Bush. There were issues with the ballot count and recounts were ordered, the criteria of which was contested in the courts. After being ruled against by the Florida State Supreme Court, Governor Bush then appealed to the U.S. Supreme Court, which took the case. Due to time constraints and Florida State's wish to have their electors appointed by the federal "safe harbor" deadline that was fast approaching, the Court ruled that due to timeliness there was no way to develop a fair, uniform, and constitutional recount process. This halted the recounts and allowed the state's earlier certification to stand, effectively awarding the state's electors to Bush. The abolition of the Electoral College was the topic of much discussion because Gore had decisively won the popular vote in the nation; but due to the Florida controversy, he did not end up winning the electoral vote. Thus the president that was sworn in the following January was not the one the American people had popularly chosen to be their leader.[16]

Since the 2000 election, calls for changing the Electoral College system have quieted down and it looks as though no change will occur at least in the near future. Likely the next time the issue will come to the forefront will be the next time we have a highly controversial election.

A President of Many Hats

The many hats of the President

Like any person in a leadership position, the president is expected to be all things to all people. This includes playing multiple roles, sometimes simultaneously, in the democratic process. With each role come expectations, implied and literal. In this section, we will discuss the many hats the president must wear while in office.

Chief of State. The office of the president is just as much ceremonial as it is functional. The president must learn the customs and practices of other countries in order to interact with the proper decorum. Whether greeting kings, heroes, foreign ambassadors, athletes, or babies, the chief of state must be able to carry the office with the same elegance as royalty. It is also appropriate for the president to conduct him or herself with grace and levity, depending on the situation. Ceremony and traditions are a vital part of all cultures, regardless of religion ethnic backgrounds. The president acts as a symbol of the United States and all we hold dear.

Chief Diplomat. This role goes hand in hand with Chief of State, except that this role deals specifically with allies and enemies. The president must be able to communicate with both in a diplomatic manner. Meeting with world leaders requires the president to know when it is appropriate to be a mediator or a leader. Much of the presidents' interactions with leaders of other countries come directly from the Oval Office, rather than through the confines of the State Department. Therefore, the president must be able to negotiate skillfully in the face of complex historical and cultural relationships with presidents from other countries.

Commander in Chief. As described earlier, expansive war powers designate the president as the Commander in Chief of all our military forces. In United States, the military shall always be governed by a civilian. One cannot sit as Commander in Chief and hold a military rank at the same time. This prevents conflict of interest as well as reaffirms the chain of command. In fact, if a presidential candidate happens to be in the military reserves, they must resign their commission or be discharged of their position (depending on their rank) should they be elected. This must take place before they are sworn in to office.

The president takes an oath to uphold the Constitution, which may entail committing troops to combat. It is up to the Commander in Chief, with the help of the Joint Chiefs of Staff, to interpret a military situation and respond swiftly, or else risk being seen as indecisive or fragile. Some past presidents have wanted to take more time to try peaceful negotiating tactics and put off forceful action as long as possible. However, the American public is fairly unforgiving when it comes to variations in leadership style. The bottom line is they want their Commander in Chief to portray the full authority of a decorated high-ranking military officer, whether or not that president has served in the military at that level or not.

Crisis Control. Hurricanes, wildfires, earthquakes, shooting tragedies, racial clashes and rioting, 9/11, war – all of these situations cause the American public to look to the president for guidance, reassurance, and hope. The president is even expected to respond in some way to crises that occur abroad. In times of national crisis, Congress and the president generally put aside differences and work together to support the citizenry in a nonpartisan manner. Sometimes these crises can provoke a "rally 'round the flag" effect on people, meaning that the presidents' popularity tends to rise during war time. Critics of the president during times of crisis may have their opinions but it is somewhat taboo to voice them too loudly until a more appropriate time. This is usually when the media starts to analyze the president's response or the events leading up to the disaster or war in the first place.

Chief Legislator. On the other side of the president's duties with foreign affairs lay responsibilities with domestic policies. The president works closely with Congress to propose and review legislation with the American public's best interests in mind. Depending on the president's agenda, he or she can hinder (veto) or lobby legislation (see How a Bill Becomes a Law, chapter nine). Although there are many committees and interest groups that influence proposed legislation, it is the president who must ultimately decipher urgent domestic needs.

Chief Executive. The president sets the mood and atmosphere for the character she or he wishes the administration to convey to the bureaucracy. Thousands of executive branch members and officials answer to the president. Interest groups keep a close watch on the executive branch to see if legislation is satisfactory, depending on the group. The president may sign executive orders to secure assets or act on behalf of American interests. For example, the president has at his or her disposal the National Security Agency and the Department of Defense. The president can also create agencies to conduct operations for specific purposes, such as the Department of Homeland Security, formed under President Bush after 9/11.

Chief Model Citizen. There is an interesting phenomenon that happens with the American public when it comes to how they view prominent leaders and celebrities. They seem to hold them to a higher moral code on so many levels, even though some of the greatest leaders have embarrassing skeletons. Presidents are supposed to be pure of character, financial gurus, economic geniuses, committed to family, prominent scholars, talented in many past-times, well-traveled, cultural connoisseurs, and even better looking than the average citizen. Indeed, some of America's past presidents have possessed many of these characteristics. However, there are just as many that have fallen from grace due to poor judgment and so-called "immoral" behavior, despite the good they have accomplished in their professional capacity. For example, in the Judeo-Christian bible (King James Version), Micah 4:3, it clearly states that "nation shall not lift up a sword against nation, neither shall they learn war anymore." Furthermore, one of the 10 commandments is "Thou shalt not murder". And yet, when it comes to the question of a justifiable war in a region where American troops are not wanted, morals are very rarely in question.

The task of playing all these roles and donning all these hats is tantamount to Atlas shouldering the whole world upon his shoulders while still ruling as king of Arcadia – it simply isn't possible to do it all. Few presidents are able to carry out all of their responsibilities, bring all cultures of the nation together, and still remain loyal to their own party. Regardless of whether they are successful, the presidency is expected to try to juggle all of these roles and keep all the balls in the air at all costs. Many rise to the challenge but most fall short because of a shift in integrity or a change in agenda.

The Institutional Presidency

Back in the days of George Washington's presidency, the idea of an entire White House staff that works closely with the president did not exist. In fact, Washington had one assistant whom he paid out of his own income. It wasn't until seventy years later during the presidency of Andrew Jackson that Congress appropriated money for one clerk. Even then, Jackson's assistant was limited to specific tasks. The president was still responsible for writing his own correspondence and his own speeches. In 1857, amidst growing tensions between the North and the South that eventually led to the Civil War, Congress budgeted for a proper White House Staff, complete with a private secretary, a mansion steward, couriers, and a contingency account. By the time Roosevelt's New Deal agencies burst onto the American public, it became clear that the presidency needed an expanded solid White House Staff. Roosevelt commissioned an advisory board, the Committee on Administrative Management, also known as the Brownlow Commission, to address his needs, both personal and institutional.

The White House Staff

It was the astute foresight of the Brownlow Commission that set the foundation for what the White House Staff has come to be. They stipulated that the aides to the president held privileged and honorable roles as the president's closest advisors. This permanent staff was to have a heightened sense of duty, loyalty, and wisdom and yet be willing to never be called out for special recognition; a staff of "true believers" if you will. They were required to be top-notch scholars, able to be effective in crises, but also very careful to not abuse their indirect power or influence on the president.

Although there have been many portrayals of the White House Staff in the movies in the past thirty years or so, the television show *The West Wing*, created by writer Aaron Sorkin, has probably depicted the truest reflection of what a White House Staff goes through on a daily basis. The show has done thorough research of the layout of the White House as well as interviewed actual former White House Press Secretary, Dee Dee Myers.

The president sometimes chooses for his staff past operatives from a prior office held or from campaigning days. Pending approval from the Senate, the chief lieutenant staff conducts their business in the East and West Wings of the White House. The president's main office is the West Wing Oval Office. Besides the Oval Office, the staff works with the president in the Situation Room and the Cabinet Room. Other offices and staff present in the West Wing are the National Security Council Staff, the office of the Vice President's, and additional administrative assistants that "serve at the pleasure of the president." All of these units collectively make up the Executive Office of the President (EOP). Each director and each organization, descriptions of which will follow, is put into place ideally because they all possess the rigorous tenacity and insight that is essential to each position on the President's staff.

Chief of Staff. The chief of staff is by far the closest advisor to the president. Not only does this official serve as the top counselor to the president, but she or he also supervises a number as well as and delegates tasks to the other supporting White House Staff. This includes the press secretary, communications director, political advisor, the legislative affairs director, and hundreds more. In this regard, the chief of staff may dictate to the staff everything from dress code to proper ways to address the president. The chief of staff builds a rapport that allows the president to confide in her or him as a sounding board before discussing issues with the rest of the staff. The president determines the extent of power she or he wishes to grant to the chief of staff. Past presidents may give full advising authority to the chief of staff or they may have that person share the responsibilities with another top assistant. The chief of staff works long hours and sometimes gains prestige for being an extension of the president's power, often being melded into one with the president in the eyes of those privy to the goings on of the executive branch.

National Security Advisor. The national security advisor chairs the National Security Council (NSC), which was established in 1947. Also falling under the NSC umbrella are the State and Defense Departments and the Central Intelligence Agency (CIA). The NSC advisor meets with the president daily to review the day's events and give recommendations. Some advisors stay close to the president and act as flanking team members, efficiently carrying out the president's bidding to the letter; such as Bush's advisor, Condoleezza Rice. However, past presidents have appointed advisors that were a trifle more controversial or outspoken when it came to foreign policy, such as Henry Kissinger, who served under Nixon; Zbigniew "Zbig" Brzezinski under Carter; and Sandy Berger under Clinton. These types of personalities can sometimes offer the president the "devil's advocate" perspective needed to balance out options and reactions to situations.

Office of Management of Budget (OMB). The OMB is the organization that makes budget proposals regarding the flow of money for each program the government funds. This makes the OMB very powerful within the Executive Office. The OMB has the power to push the president's agenda and also halt proposed legislation if it believes it is not within the parameters of the budget. Although their primary responsibility is to prepare and put the budget into operation, the OMB acts as the nucleus of all tentacles of the president's plans. This is to say, the OMB reaches into the operating processes of all departments within the federal government.

Council of Economic Advisors (CEA). The CEA provides reports predicting the activity of the economy based on national trends. The CEA, together with the secretary of the treasury and the OMB, offers economic counsel to the president.

Other peripheral EOP departments that have gained prominence are the Council of Environmental Quality, the Office of Homeland Security, and the Office of Science and Technology Policy. These offices came about due to threats to national security or whatever issue the president deems needs immediate action.

The Vice Presidency

The vice president is like the supporting understudy cast who rehearses and rehearses but who may never get to play the starring role. This was not the case for many vice-presidents however, such as Lyndon Johnson and Gerald Ford, both of whom were called to duty because of the death or resignation of their Commander-in-Chief. Except for the very important duty of being next in the line of command after the president (see table 10.1), the office of the vice presidency is sometimes misunderstood or even disrespected. Mainly a figurehead who takes on ceremonial duties that the president does not have time for, the vice president him or herself can easily develop an inferiority complex. One important role the vice president plays is serving as a liaison between the president and Congress. The vice president serves as the president of the Senate and may cast the deciding vote in a deadlock. Aside from this, however, the vice president is the main go-to official for errands of the state.

TABLE 10.1 - Presidential Line of Succession	
OFFICE	INTERESTING NOTES
1. Vice President	Moved into presidency due to death or resignation – Calvin Coolidge, Lyndon B. Johnson, Gerald R. Ford
2. Speaker of the House of Representatives	Nancy Pelosi, 2007 - First Woman Speaker
3. Senate President Pro Tempore	
4. Secretary of State	
5. Secretary of the Treasury	
6. Secretary of Defense	
7. Attorney General	
8. Secretary of the Interior	Secretary Gale Norton, 2001-2006, first woman to head this 153-year-old department
9. Secretary of Agriculture	
10. Secretary of Commerce	
11. Secretary of Labor	
12. Secretary of Health and Human Services	
13. Secretary of Housing and Urban Development	
14. Secretary of Transportation	
15. Secretary of Energy	
16. Secretary of Education	
17. Secretary of Veterans Affairs	

Every presidential candidate who has ended up being considered for a running mate has to put aside greater aspirations of leading the country in a more significant role. Nevertheless, there have been vice presidents who have brought meaning to their position, thereby making valuable contributions to the American people and sometimes the global community. Some presidents have chosen to make more use of their vice presidents for specific policy issues. For example Al Gore was slated for vice president because of his work on environmental issues and knowledge of the inter-workings of the federal government after serving as a U.S. Senator for a number of years.

The Cabinet

With such a large political system, there must be separate executive departments to handle all the areas that fall under federal government obligations to the American public. The president occasionally meets with the leaders of these departments along with the vice president. Like most officials and organization leaders in the federal government, the cabinet must be approved by the Senate. For this reason, members of the cabinet may be called upon during congressional hearings. The cabinet consists of the secretaries of all the departments that make up the bureaucracy. They advise the president but they also have a constituency to monitor. Some examples of these departments of the bureaucracy (see table 10.2). Some departments are so highly specialized that it seems counter-productive to have all heads meet at one time. Discussing matters of foreign policy with the postmaster general, for instance, seems a colossal waste of time.

Each president may choose to meet with the cabinet as little or as much as they see fit. It really depends on the innovations of the president and how she or he plans to use the cabinet. Some presidents use the cabinet as merely a sounding board, even shunning advice; however, there are presidents who have actually given more clout to the cabinet's usefulness within the EOP. Case in point, President Eisenhower appointed a cabinet **secretariat** to help with smoother communications between him and the cabinet. That said, the fact remains that each cabinet is highly specialized so most cabinet leaders meet with the president individually, so as to not waste the president's or the rest of the cabinet's time.

Secretariat – The officials or office entrusted with administrative duties, maintaining records, and overseeing or performing secretarial duties, especially for an international or governmental organization.

TABLE 10.2 - Cabinet Posts 2000 - 2007[17]	
Department of Agriculture	Secretary Mike Johanns
Department of Commerce	Secretary Carlos Gutierrez
Department of Defense	Secretary Robert M. Gates
Department of Education	Secretary Margaret Spellings
Department of Energy	Secretary Samuel W. Bodman
Department of Health & Human Services	Secretary Michael O. Leavitt
Department of Homeland Security	Secretary Michael Chertoff
Department of Housing & Urban Development	Secretary Alphonso Jackson
Department of the Interior	Secretary Dirk Kempthorne
Department of Justice	Attorney General Alberto Gonzales
Department of Labor	Secretary Elaine Chao
Department of State	Secretary Condoleezza Rice
Department of Transportation	Secretary Mary E. Peters
Department of the Treasury	Secretary Henry M. Paulson, Jr.
Department of Veterans Affairs	Secretary Jim Nicholson

Cabinet Rank Members – Vice President - Richard B. Cheney
White House Chief of Staff - Joshua B. Bolten
Office of Management and Budget - Rob Portman
United States Trade Representative - Ambassador Susan Schwab
Environmental Protection Agency - Stephen Johnson
Office of National Drug Control Policy - John Walters

Overseeing the Bureaucracy

Even though the president is the head of the Executive Branch of the federal government, there are still specific protocols in place that the president must follow in order to enact a formal directive to the **bureaucracy**. The president can sign an **executive order** to provoke action from a bureaucrat. Situations in which the president may want to apply pressure on the executive officials usually concern an urgent military action. In the next chapter, we will discuss the bureaucracy in more detail but for now, here is a list of departments appointed by President George W. Bush. Usually these posts are filled with officers who belong to the same party as the president.

Bureaucracy – Administration of a government through bureaus or departments staffed with non-elected officials. This term can also have negative overtones, meaning any organization in which any action is bogged down by excessive and unnecessary procedures or red tape.

Executive Order – An order that carries the full weight of the law as issued by the U.S. President to military forces or any other parts of the executive branch of government.

California's Executive Branch

Although the governor is the most powerful publicly appointed official in California, she or he shares this power with seven other executive officers: the lieutenant governor, attorney general, the controller, the secretary, the treasurer, the insurance commissioner, and the superintendent of public instruction. The majority of the governor's authority as head of this executive branch is derived from formal powers that were written into the state constitution and laws. There are also informal powers that come from the notoriety gained with the electorate during the term. He, along with the other officers, figures the state budget, organizes policymakers to work in the executive and judicial branches, gets involved in the reapportionment of the legislature and congressional delegation, and addresses the public's concerns by attempting to make it clear where it is he stands on highly debated issues. Just as they do with the president, members of the other branches may find themselves at a stand-off with the governor when it comes to controversial issues, since they are elected independently. This means that partisanship can become quite volatile and public. This dissipation of executive authority sometimes leads to a short stay for California governors, even before Proposition 140 made term limits a law.

The Seven

The duties of the seven executive officers who work with the governor are described below.

1. *The Lieutenant Governor.* The lieutenant governor resembles the Vice President of the United States in that, although the position has few official responsibilities, the position is nonetheless very important since it is second in line after the governor. This may be necessary if the governor is appointed to a higher office, such as when Earl Warren became chief justice of the U.S. Supreme Court in 1953. He was succeeded by Goodwin Knight. The lieutenant governor to Gov. Schwarzenegger is Democrat John Garamendi. The lieutenant governor heads certain committees such as the State Lands Commission which oversees 4 million acres of public land. Similar to the Vice President's position with the federal Senate, the lieutenant governor sits as the president of the state senate. He or she may vote to break ties but that is the extent of the responsibilities.

2. *The Attorney General.* Although the lieutenant governor would be next in line for the position of governor, the attorney general is considered more powerful in terms of duties and activities. The attorney general is the head of the Department of Justice, which entails a wide spectrum of responsibilities, including over

seeing law enforcement, acting as legal counsel to state agencies, interpreting and proposing laws, and representing the state in significant cases. This position benefits from being somewhat autonomous, which allows the attorney general to formulate a separate course of action than the governor on important state issues.

3. *The Secretary of State.* The duties of the state secretary are not as crucial as the U.S. cabinet position. The secretary of state has responsibilities that are more traditional such as keeping records, supervising elections, validating signatures for initiative, referenda, and recall petitions. While this position may seem fairly innocuous, the accomplishments achieved in this position can sometimes boost that person's career as it did for Democrat Jerry Brown, who later became Governor.

4. *The Superintendent of Public Instruction.* The main job of this position is to head the Department of Education. It is the only position that is selected without the influence of a party label. The way the public learns anything about these candidates is through educational entities such as teachers' unions and interested administrators. Because funding is dependent on the budget, the superintendent's actions and powers are highly scrutinized by the state board of education and other legislative committees.

5. *The Controller.* In the same way the secretary of state's position can act as a stepping off point to higher positions, so goes the controller's position. The controller deals with government finance. She or he audits expenditures, supervises financial limits for local governments, and, as a member of the Board of Equalization, the controller can influence tax collections. In addition, as a member of the State Lands Commission, the controller has substantial leverage when it comes to appointing inheritance tax appraisers.

6. *The State Treasurer.* The main focus of this office is to facilitate custody over tax collections implemented by several state agencies; the treasurer also maintains deposits, sells bonds, and manipulates stock investments.

7. *The Insurance Commissioner.* As the title suggests, the job of the insurance commissioner is to maintain an eye on the insurance companies and all the types of insurance they sell throughout the state. This position was once appointed by the governor but a ballot initiative changed it to an elected office beginning in 1990.

Budgetary Responsibilities

While the rest of the state is celebrating during the holiday season from December to the beginning of the year, the governor is down to the last days left to prepare his recommendations for a balanced budget. The constitution decrees that a plan for a balanced budget must be presented to the legislature within the first ten days of the calendar year. Budgetary responsibilities dominate the governor's schedule, along with the schedule of the director of finance, who is appointed by the governor. Together the director and the governor work on a rough draft of the budget right from the beginning of the fiscal year, July 1st. After the budget is signed by the governor about a year later, it is sent to the legislature, who must respond no later than June 15, in time for the budget to take effect on July 1st. The task of reviewing the budget is daunting as the document is usually several inches thick. While they do have the option of ignoring any part of the budget and can pass their own version, this is rarely done; what they end up passing is fairly identical to the governor's plans. Although this is an accepted professional courtesy to the governor, in modern politics, this kind of deference is a rare commodity. Legislative budgetary discretion is limited by initiates, which have amended the constitution in order to mandate various types of budget decisions. As a result, these decisions are taken out of legislative control. In all honesty, the legislature's willingness to acquiesce is probably more due to pragmatic reasons than any gesture of being dutifully subordinate. The governor ultimately has the final say, within reason; she or he may not add money, but they do have the option of reducing or eliminating expenditures through the line item veto privilege before he or she signs the budget into law.

In order to reverse the Governor's **line item vetoes**, the legislature needs two-thirds of the vote, which is all but impossible to obtain. Rather than go through all of these steps, further delaying the passage of the budget and putting thousands of state employees' paychecks and other related services on hold, the legislators would rather negotiate with the governor beforehand. While the item veto is only for appropriations measures, the general veto makes it possible for the governor to reject any other bills passed by legislature; the legislature again, may overturn this action by obtaining from both houses an absolute two-thirds vote. Some governors, such as Republican Governor Pete Wilson, used this power in excess, which infuriated the Democrats. At that time, even though the Democrats had the majority in both houses they were not able to gather enough votes to overturn even one veto. The veto is a powerful tool for the executive, especially when the legislature is controlled by one party and the governorship is controlled by the other. This is similar to the federal government in that there have been several periods in history when the legislature was controlled by the Democrats and the governor's offices were controlled by the Republicans.

Usually, the governor has twelve days to act on a bill that has been passed by the legislature. If there are large stacks of bills passed by the legislature at the close of the session, which is quite often the case, then the governor has thirty days to act. Similar to the journey of a bill becoming a law in the federal system, any unsigned or unvetoed bill becomes law after the governor has surpassed the time limit. If the governor is not satisfied with the legislation that has been passed, she or he may call a special session. This is a grandiose act on the part of the governor, but it is a procedure they are allowed to call upon. In this special session, the policymakers discuss only the specific concerns the governor has regarding what they feel the law is lacking. There are certain circumstances, such as natural catastrophes, when special sessions are called; in California, earthquake country, this is something that is unfortunately a periodic occurrence.

Governorships

California has a rich history of grooming governors that have gone on to shape the nation. For example, Republican Earl Warren (Governor 1943-1953), who was nominated by both the Democrats and Republicans, was the driving force behind desegregating the state in the 1940's and less than a decade later, he desegregated the nation. From 1959 – 1967, Democrat (Edmund) Pat Brown created the nation's largest higher education system and developed volumes of infrastructure projects, such as the genesis of the freeway systems and the California Aqueduct. Then Republican Ronald Reagan cut his political teeth, first as the president of the Screen Actors' Guild and after that as Governor of California (1967-1975). From 1975 to 1983, Pat's son, (Edmund) Jerry Brown served as one of California's more eccentric bohemian governors. He tried to convey to the public that he was a simple everyday guy; he declined to live in the Governor's mansion and opted to drive a state-issued Plymouth instead of being driven around in the Governor's limousine. Furthermore,

Issues For You

Why do they call special sessions for natural disasters? Does it tie into sessions to review legislation not yet ratified by the governor?

Line Item Vetoes –
The power of the executive to veto specific items of a bill without having to veto the entire bill.

he was a single fellow in his 30's, making him one of the most eligible high profile bachelors in the state. As an idealist, he was an instrumental force in developing policies on energy efficiency and he set a record by being the first to champion and sign labor laws that protected farm workers in the United States.

Arnold Schwarzenegger being sworn into office by the Chief Justice of the California Supreme Court, with wife Maria Shriver looking on.
© Karin Lau, 2007. Used under License from Shutterstock, Inc.

Republican Pete Wilson (1991-1998) challenged the status quo by clashing with the democratically controlled legislature over the state's budget, thus creating an impasse that lasted for 61 days. This standstill forced state employees and creditors to be paid by vouchers (IOUs) instead of checks. He also became a proponent of anti-illegal immigration legislation. Wilson's successor was democrat Gray Davis (1999-2003). Even though Davis argued for improvements in education and protecting the state's environment, what he will be remembered for is being the first governor in the history of the state to be recalled due to the energy shortages orchestrated by Enron. Davis was followed by Republican Arnold Schwarzenegger, the current Republican Governor (2003 – present as of this publication). Voters were convinced by Schwarzenegger's projected campaign image that he was a moderate. However, within the first few months of Schwarzenegger being sworn into office, disillusioned Californians observed him pandering to his party base. The self-professed "Govenator" has pursued aggressive policies in promoting health, improving education, attacking public unions, and limiting workman's compensation. After losing several propositions in a special election (see list below), it appears the Governor has moved back to the center of his party, attempting to work with the legislature on all the promises he made while campaigning.

The following table (10.3) of the propositions that Governor Schwarzenegger pushed during the Special Statewide Election held on November 8, 2005 illustrates how he moved to the right soon after taking office. The positions he supported were all highly ideological "hot button" conservative issues.

TABLE 10.3 - Proposition Results, Special Statewide Election November 8, 2005[18]	
NUMBER ON BALLOT / RESULT	BALLOT TITLE
73 / NO	Waiting Period and Parental Notification Before Termination of Minor's pregnancy. Initiative Constitutional Amendment.
74 / NO	Public School Teachers. Waiting Period for Permanent Status. Dismissal. Initiative Statute.
75 / NO	Public Employee Union Dues. Restrictions on Political Contributions. Employee Consent Requirement. Initiative Statute.
76 / NO	State Spending and School Funding Limits. Initiative Constitutional Amendment.
77 / NO	Redistricting. Initiative Constitutional Amendment.

Gubernatorial Appointments

Besides being responsible for the state budget, the governor is also responsible for appointing hundreds of administrative personnel to approximately fifty departments, which can be categorized under business, transportation, housing, health and human welfare resources, state and consumer services, and young adult correctional systems. Also serving on the governor's cabinet (pending Senate confirmation) are the directors of various departments: Child Development and Education, Food and Agriculture, Finance, Industrial Relations, and Information Technology to name a few. As many as 656 posts have been filled within a period of eight years, as was the case during Pete Wilson's time in office. Some boards require members in an advisory capacity, such as fine arts councils. Others are influential in policy making, outside of the governor's realm of control, like the California Occupational Health and Safety Administration (Cal-OSHA). While this seems like a tremendous amount of power over who works where, the governor is actually only responsible for appointing 1 percent of the total workforce in the state. The rest of the state appointees are civil servants.

One of the governor's most important and long-lasting decisions is appointing judgeships. The governor must fill any vacancies plus any judgeships that are created by the legislature. The judges that are chosen will most likely still be serving long after the governor who chose them has left office. The governor is free to appoint whomever he or she wishes, but a check is in placed on these appointments by an assortment of judicial commissions and by the voters in elections held later on.

Charging members to serve on administrative boards is also a power the governor holds. They too are made in conjunction with the state Senate's supervision. These appointees are most likely in favor with the governor's political agenda. Examples of administrative boards (in these cases, related to education) include:

- The Board of Regents – responsible for governing the nine campuses of the University of California system of colleges; consists of 18 members who serve twelve-year terms; seven of the members are ex-officio and one is a student of a UC college, who serves for one year.

- The Board of Trustees – responsible for governing the twenty campuses of the California State University system of colleges; also consists of eighteen members who serve eight-year terms; five of these members are ex-officio.

- The Board of the Governors of the California Community Colleges – responsible for coordinating the seventy-two community college districts; each district has local control over it's administration; consists of sixteen members, which includes one faculty and one student member; each serves for four-year terms.

- The State Board of Education – responsible for making policies regarding curriculum and textbook adoption for all public schools throughout the state of California.

Other administrative boards that the governor appoints are the Personnel Board that oversees the vast civil service bureaucracy; the Public Utilities Commission, which licenses thousands of private utility businesses; the Energy Commission, the Fair Employment and Housing Commission, and so on. Should a position become vacant due to death or resignation, the governor is allowed to appoint replacements.

Informal and Other Powers

Unexpected qualities, such as popularity, can be an informal and useful asset for the governor. For example, Governor Schwarzenegger already had high visibility as a bodybuilder, actor, and restaurant proprietor of the flashy Planet Hollywood chains. Being elected to the governorship seemed to be a natural albeit unconventional career move. He has been able to use this high profile image to boost his platform both during his campaign and also in overpowering opponents. Other governors have used this notoriety to publicize their pet programs, such as Jerry Brown's "era of limits" and George Deukmejian's support of capital punishment and his opposition to state taxes.

Other powers include the governor's ability to call special sessions in order to suggest new legislation into the political forum. The governor may plant seeds regarding the new legislation during the yearly State of the State and budget proposal. These are then introduced by members of the state Assembly or Senate who are supportive of the governor's proposals.

The governor also wears the hat of commander-in-chief of the California National Guard, which she or he may call to active duty for emergencies within the state. The Guard usually does not get called into national service abroad but this is exactly what has happened with President Bush's war in Iraq. In the case of a smaller emergency, the governor may utilize the local police force to intervene. Both the local police and the National Guard may assist Californians in the event of devastation caused by earthquakes, flash floods, wildfires, or riots, all of which has been part of California's repertoire of emergencies.

Controversial Power

One of the governor's more challenging powers is that of executive clemency. This can consist of the power to grant official pardons, postponement or reduction of sentences for convicts, or commuting an execution to a life sentence; the latter of these powers sometimes causes local protests or international media attention. The governor has the final say in whether a convict will live or die, regardless of any penance, reform, or celebrity status acquired by the convict. Such was the case for Stanley "Tookie" Williams, the well-known co-founder of the L.A. based gang, the Crips. Since being convicted in 1981 for a crime Williams says he did not commit, the ex-Crip had written several books that warned children of the peril of gang life. Williams' plight to be forgiven for past sins caught the sympathies of protest folksinger songwriter, Joan Baez; the Reverend Jesse Jackson, former Crip turned rap star, Snoop Dogg, and Sister Helen Prejean. Prejean was portrayed in the movie "Dead Man Walking", a movie that reawakened the debate of capital punishment nationwide. Williams had even inspired college professors and a Swiss legislator to nominate him for the Nobel prize in both literature and peace. Despite all of his efforts and that of his supporters, Williams' case was not reopened by the Supreme Court and he was not successful in winning Gov. Schwarzenegger's compassion. The governor did not grant clemency to Williams and he died on December 13, 2005 by lethal injection in San Quentin, California.[19]

California's executive branch has a dynamic history. For years, it was controlled by special interest groups (Southern Pacific Railroads, newspapers, for example). At the turn of the twentieth century the progressive movement, made up of both Republicans and Democrats, returned the executive branch to carry out the will of the people, making California a republic with a developing sense of direct democracy. If a governor does manage to endure the many challenges that go along with this office, they have at their disposal extraordinary power and political prospects.

How Do We Compare?
France, Great Britain, Germany and the United States

For this section, we are returning to some concepts of democratic structures that were introduced in chapter one. We will compare the French semi-presidential system created in the 5th republic to the United States' presidential system, the same system we have had since 1789.[20] For further illustration and developing comparative skills, we will also compare facets of the German government discussed in chapter 3, and Britain's government in chapter 2.

Introduction to France

In France, there is a tradition of political discontinuity, instability and "immobilism" or paralysis. Before 1958, France went through many metamorphoses: the "Bonapartist" or "savior" regimes in the late 1700's to the early 1800's; and the constitutional engineering performed by Charles de Gaulle and Michel Debré in 1958, when they created the Fifth Republic. Since then, institutional adaptations associated with the peculiar presidential-parliamentary system of the 5th Republic have been numerous.

Out of 700 submissions, Gustav Eiffel's design was chosen to celebrate the French Revolution centenary in 1889. It was unveiled at the International Exhibition of Paris the same year. Courtesy of Jupiter Images.

France is a large country, at least by European standards. Shaped like a hexagon, with three sides bounded by sea and three by land, France is by far the largest territorial state in Western Europe. There is a "north-south" divide in French regional culture and politics, but it is not nearly as marked as the east-west divide in Germany (see chapter 3) or in Canada (see chapter 11). In Germany, the old "north-south" divide, which goes back to the religious wars of the 17th century, has now been complicated by the far more recent and politically more sensitive "east-west" divide after the national reunification. Within England (see chapter 2), there is curiously a "north-south" divide in economic development, with the south enjoying greater economic prosperity, the opposite of the situation in Italy.

France has long been regarded as something like an experiment in a kind of political laboratory; but it would be a mistake to see it simply as a prototype of modern politics. Like each of our other countries of study, it illustrates some widely shared traits as well as some exceptional features. The country can be seen as the result of a long process of centrally led state- and (later) nation-building, promoted by French kings from the Paris region. This produced a strong legacy of political centralization and bureaucratization.

Many Americans view the American Revolution as the turning point of modern political development but in reality it was the French Revolution that has left a permanent mark upon French (and European) politics. It is the origin of modern politicized nationalism as well as much of the vocabulary and some major ideas and symbols in modern political ideologies. In addition, such political terms as "revolution" or "ideology" as well as our understanding of conservative, socialist, and liberal positions on the political spectrum have their origins in the French Revolution or its aftermath. The writings of such important political thinkers as Edmund Burke, Alexis de Tocqueville, and Karl Marx & Friedrich Engels can be read against the political backdrop of France after 1789.

Throughout France's political history, one can try to look for some long-term patterns or thematic developments during the French political experience since 1789. This will provide a greater understanding of how the Fifth Republic came into being. The institutional focus will be on the Fifth Republic's hybrid form of presidential-parliamentary government, which has recently been imitated by some post-communist constitution-makers in Central and Eastern Europe, and the political responses to the new institutional infrastructure, including the adaptation of the formerly somewhat chaotic political party system and the emergence of a new form of power-sharing, called cohabitation. The Fifth Republic can be seen in part as a response by constitutional engineers to what they saw as fatal weaknesses in the French political traditions - political instability and paralysis during the 3rd Republic (1870 to 1940) and the 4th Republic (1946 to 1958). At any time while reading this section, it may benefit your understanding if you return to chapter one and review the section on democratic structures of governments comparing the parliamentary system, the presidential system, and the semi-presidential system.

Absolutism –
The principle or theory that complete power in the government or one single ruler is absolute, unchangeable and not confined to context; sometimes enforced through threats of punishment or violence.

The French Tradition of Political Discontinuity: 1788 to 1958

In marked contrast to Britain, the modern French political experience has been one shaped by considerable political and constitutional discontinuity with a resultant weak constitutional legitimacy. One can also compare this to the long U.S. experience of what some have called "constitutionalism". There have been between 13 and 17 different constitutional arrangements since the Revolution of 1789, depending upon which of the sometimes short-lived, successive regimes are counted. If you contrast the French series of political ruptures with the British experience of gradual, evolutionary constitutional development, one will see Tony Blair's approach to constitutional reform was conducted in a remarkably piecemeal, almost ad hoc fashion.

France is a nation of great wealth and beauty but throughout its history is one that has been subjected to invasion. The invasions of the Romans, Normans, English, along with the German conquests in the 1890s, 1910s, and 1930s have all contributed to the rise of **absolutism** in France. France was conquered by the Roman Empire and was hence forced to assimilate into Roman culture, an effect that is still felt today linguistically, since French is considered to be a "romance" language or being of Rome. Based on their Roman predecessors, French kings developed a system of building a city progressively from the center out, rippling like water in rings of development. If one were to examine a map of Paris, it would be evident that the core areas of power are in the nuclei of the cylindrical structure of the city. This urbanization leads to regional power becoming the hub of all activities in the area, such as the concept of unifying the nation through a national language. Teachers were trained in Paris and sent to the various provinces of the country so everyone would speak a uniform dialect of French regardless of regional dialects.

Thus making France "…a nation of Frenchmen." Compared to German and Russian structural centers at their core, the development is not as clear.

In the fifteenth century feudalism began to transform into absolutism under Louis XI. With the coronation of Louis XIII came further control of the provinces by Paris. This was orchestrated by Cardinal Richelieu, who was considered to be an organizational genius. The provinces were governed by **intendants** who were appointed by Paris. By the seventeenth century, Louis XIV, who was called "the Sun King", brought absolutism to a climax. Ruling for an astounding 72 years (he took over the throne from his father at age four), his pursuit of policies of "war and magnificence" along with mercantilist economic policies of his minister Colbert, especially helping the American colonies' revolt against Britain, nearly bankrupted the country. Increasing taxes and lack of compassion from the King caused discontent among intellectuals who criticized the system and the government. They also complained of the lack of structure for wider political participation by the people.

Change came slowly but by the time Louis XVI convened the **États généraux**, the more the Third Estate (**bourgeoisie**) seized control over the other two (nobles and clergy) and made it not a stamp of the monarch but a challenge to his power. Finally, on July 14, 1789, a mob stormed the **Bastille** and eventually seized the palace of the king. As often happens when toppling a tyrant, despite the unjust rule, the period following the revolution was more traumatic than living under the king. The First Republic began with extremist Jacobins taking control and establishing revolutionary counsels. The leader was Robespierre who ruled through the **Reign of Terror**, guillotining more than 20,000 people, including the monarchy; eventually he also met the same fate.

The Reign of Terror ended and with a **coup d'état** in 1799, when Napoleon became the First Consul and later crowned himself emperor in 1804. Encouraging nationalism, Napoleon led France to conquer most of Europe until he was removed from power. It should be noted that with Napoleon came another French political tendency, the act of seeking a "savior." Whenever France has problems, they tend to seek out an individual to "save" them rather than working through their own problems.

The Second Republic, which began with a new democratic style of government, was ushered in with the **Bourbons** coming to power. The division within French society from the revolution ran deep. The antirevolutionary side supported the monarch, the Catholic Church, and eventually evolved into the more conservative right-wing party. The revolutionary side consisted of individuals who believed in a republican form of government that was also anticlerical; a very radical entity emerged as the more liberal left party; both are still visible today in French politics.

After the Franco-Prussian War of 1870, the Third Republic was born along with the Paris Commune. The Third Republic lasted until the German invasion and subsequent control of France. The Vichy government (1940-44), named because of its location in the city of Vichy, was formed by the conservative political elements that began to collaborate with the Germans. After World War II, the Fourth Republic was created but was plagued with **immobilisme** due to a weak executive; small factions of political parties controlling the National Assembly; and a weak executive with an unstable cabinet. The problems and costs of the colonial wars in Vietnam (1946-1954) and Algeria only further illustrated the weakness in the existing system. As a way to thwart another coup by the military, the government

Intendant –
French provincial administrators, answerable only to Paris; early version of prefects, or an administrator of department.

États généraux or the States General –
A legislative assembly of representatives from the estates of the nation instead of a provincial assembly.

Bourgeoisie –
French term describing the Middle Class; the term has been adopted into the American lexicon but it is used in a derogatory manner, as in something being common or pedantic, bourgeois.

Bastille –
Paris jail that is no longer used; Bastille Day is now a national holiday, celebrated in France every year on July 14.

Reign of Terror –
Robespierre's rule by threat of the guillotine (decapitating contraption used for executions) from 1793 – 1794.

Coup d'état –
An uprising led by the military, with the intent of overthrowing the current government.

Bourbons –
French dynasty before the Revolution.

Immobilisme –
Government inability to solve big problems.

sought and empowered a new savior, General Charles de Gaulle, to fix the paralysis of the government. De Gaulle's solution was to institutionalize a strong executive in the Fifth Republic.

In 1958 de Gaulle became the last prime minister of the Fourth Republic. His price for taking over was to demand the authority to draft a new governmental system for the Fifth Republic in France. He was not given a blank check in this respect; it was understood that the new system should retain a parliamentary framework, but within the confines de Gaulle and his loyal follower, Michel Debré, devised. This framework was actually a hybrid semi-parliamentary and semi-presidential system of government that provides for a "dual executive" and combines crucial features of both. In addition, the changes instituted a leaner parliamentary system, in which the legislature was considerably weakened and the prime minister was strengthened (in his dealing with the parliament); a presidential system, in which the president was given considerable political power also over the prime minister.

It surprised no one when the first (indirectly elected) president of the Fifth Republic turned out to be de Gaulle. Equally expected, de Gaulle named the loyal Debré as his first prime minister. One of de Gaulle's powers was the referendum process. In 1962, a referendum was used to change the presidential election from an indirect method, using a huge electoral college consisting of thousands of local government officeholders, to a direct election (with a run-off between the two top contenders, if no one gains an absolute majority of the popular vote in the first round). This was a major and very controversial change that strengthened the position of the president, who would henceforth be able to present himself as the only elected official with a national, democratic mandate in the country.

One of the tradeoffs caused de Gaulle a great disappointment. He lost some of his most adamant right-wing supporters when he settled the Algerian question by granting independence to the region. The move was approved in a national referendum in 1962. As a result, de Gaulle became the target of several almost successful assassination attempts, planned by a secret counter-revolutionary organization of reactionary military and political figures (the so-called OAS).

Factoid –
Nicolas Sarkozy, the president of France as of June 17, 2007, surprised the French people when he went against the long-time Bastille Day tradition of erasing parking ticket violations and granting mass pardons to French prisoners who had been convicted of non-violent crimes. Sarkozy, a young conservative, has fast made a reputation for himself and his agenda as a no nonsense "law and order" regime.[21]

Profiles in Politics
Charles de Gaulle (1890 - 1970)

You may recognize the name - if you've traveled in France, there is a good chance you may have flown into the Charles de Gaulle International Airport, the main airport in Paris and one of the world's most well known. But how much do you know about its namesake?

Charles de Gaulle was born in 1890 in Lille, France. After a primarily Catholic education, he chose to enter the military and became a lieutenant in the infantry division. He saw action during World War I and was a prisoner of war from 1916-1918, when he was released following the armistice.

During the 1920s and first half of the 1930s, de Gaulle rose through the military ranks and became known as an independent thinker with new (and sometimes radical) ideas. He published many papers and lectured on his ideas, which largely involved reshaping the military and rethinking military strategy. In the beginning of World War II, de Gaulle saw action again and in 1940 he was appointed to the position of Under Secretary of State for National Defense and War. He was tasked with coordinating war strategy with Britain, but upon return from one of his meetings with Churchill, he found that he had been replaced and was therefore no longer a part of the government.

A picture of Charles deGaulle around the time of World War II. Courtesy of the Library of Congress.

In response to being replaced as well as to a newly announced armistice agreement, de Gaulle broadcast a call for a French resistance movement; for this, the Vichy government condemned him to death. Shortly after his call for resistance, Churchill officially recognized de Gaulle as the leader of the Free French, and de Gaulle set up a sort of de facto shadow government that operated throughout World War II. Upon the liberation of Paris in 1944, he reclaimed the French government and helped to set up democratic elections; due to differences with the newly elected National Assembly, de Gaulle stepped down as Chairman of the Assembly in 1946.

After the War, de Gaulle pushed for a constitution similar to the United States with its separation of powers and with a strong executive. When that was rejected, he decided to fight the party system, and ultimately ended up traveling around the country speaking about his ideas. During the mid 1950s, he took a break from public life for a while, but in 1958, he was back.

In May of 1958, he was requested to return to public service and formed a government that was then elected to the National Assembly. He set into motion the constitutional reform he had advocated before and was elected President of the French Republic.

Profiles in Politics
Charles de Gaulle (1890 - 1970)

As President, he had to deal with some longtime and nagging issues, such as what to do about Algeria; his proposal that eventually bore fruit was independence for the country. Also during his presidency, he helped guide France into an era of modernization. One of the key things de Gaulle advocated for was to return France to the world stage as a power. He also pushed for the president to be elected by the popular vote as opposed to the members of the National Assembly.

1968 was a tough year around the globe; in France, there were massive student protests that led to a general strike and paralyzed the workforce. De Gaulle work out a deal with the unions and employers and dissolved the National Assembly, which in turn set in motion an election cycle; parties began focusing on the upcoming elections, while regular people increasingly returned to work.

When the elections failed to foster the change de Gaulle had been hoping for, he held a referendum on regionalization and Senate reform. When this measure failed to pass, de Gaulle announced that he was stepping down from his position a president. He retired in 1968 after a life spent serving his country in one capacity or another and shepherding it through some of its darkest hours. Charles de Gaulle died just two years later in 1970.[22]

A Long Tradition of a Strong, Centralized State -- Now Modified

Like Britain, France has a unitary system of government, in which power is concentrated at the center, whereas Britain can look back upon a centuries-long tradition of fairly strong local authorities, resting on power devolved to the counties and towns from the national level of government, France has traditionally had a system in which significant political direction and oversight came almost exclusively from the center.

As noted in chapter 2, there was a shift towards reducing the power of British local governments in the 1980s, under Margaret Thatcher. This change in the balance of power between the national and local governments in Britain resulted from the prime

British Parliament. Courtesy of Jupiter Images.

minister's determination to weaken political opposition to her policies that often came from Labour-dominated local councils. Previous governments in Britain, beginning in the early 1970s, had already reasserted national control over Northern Ireland, in response to the civil strife in Ulster and the breakdown of the regional government there. In addition, Tony Blair's government had decided to strengthen local governments considerably, going beyond a restoration of the status quo ante (a restoration of the previous status quo). For the first time London had an elected mayor, and its council had important powers restored.   In addition, Blair's government had established up new regional assemblies in Scotland and Wales and had passed power to an elected regional government in Northern Ireland, which was based on a "consociational" form of power-sharing between the two major groups (Protestants and Catholics).

It is interesting that France has also, in its own way, sought to shift the balance of power away from the center in favor of subordinate governments. Basically, the old system of centralized government, reaching back to the autocratic kings and strengthened by the Revolution and by Napoleon, was rejected in the early 1980s as both undemocratic and highly inefficient. In should be noted, the French tradition of highly centralized government goes back at least to Louis XI, who in the fifteenth century greatly increased the size of France, weakened the feudal system with its traditional checks on the monarch, and established an early system of national bureaucracy to increase the center's ability to control and tax.

In the early seventeenth century, while England was steering toward a civil war that greatly reduced the power of its monarch, France headed still further in the other direction. Cardinal Richelieu - acting as Louis XIII's chief minister - installed a system of intendants that controlled the provinces on behalf of the national government. Later in the same century, under Louis XIV and his chief minister Colbert, royal absolutism in France reached its height. It was backed by a mercantilist economic system in which the government supervised the economy, laying the foundation for a long tradition of economic protectionism (through tariffs and other controls, grants of monopoly, special subsidies, and government economic plans) rather than promoting market forces. To this day, economic protectionism finds more support in France than in Britain or Germany.

Administrative centralisation increased further under Napoleon, who abolished the historic provinces, and instead created a system of fairly small administrative units, or départements, overseen by a prefect (similar to the system of intendants), who acted as an agent of the national government. Today there are 96 mainland and 5 overseas départements, each administered by a prefect, appointed by and acting as an official of the national interior ministry.

In 1969, the conservative President de Gaulle tried unsuccessfully to initiate some devolution of power from Paris. In 1982, socialist President

Built in 1788, the Brandenburg Gate in Berlin is a symbol of how the city was divided during the Cold War. It is the last gate around the city still standing. Courtesy of Jupiter Images

François Mitterrand was successful and went farther than de Gaulle had intended in decentralizing the French system of government. Under a law passed by the national legislature, local and regional governments were given more authority:

1. Currently, there are elected councils in both the 96 départements and the 22 newly created regions (each of the latter is based on two or more départements). They have some policy-making and taxation powers in such matters as education, local and regional economic development, housing, and job training.

2. Decentralization has made local and regional government somewhat more important and innovative than under the earlier highly centralized system. By American standards, the system is still remarkably centralized.

3. As a result, there are still frequent complaints of over-centralization in France. Apparently, it is not easy to change a style of governing and administering that has centuries of tradition behind it. Moreover, there is a "mandarin-like" class of highly trained top civil servants, who have an institutionalized interest in and knowledge about this form of top-down controls.

4. Finally, the devolution of a unitary system, as practiced in France or Britain, differs from a constitutionally delineated federal division of power, as it exists in the United States or Germany. Even in the U.S., of course, there can be shifts in the balance of power within the federal system, as when we speak of shifts from more nation-centered to more state-centered federalism (and back again) in our history. But our basic governmental pattern is much less centralized than that of France.

De Gaulle's Institutionalization of a Strong Executive

Like Britain, France has a bicameral national legislature. The upper house or Senate is elected indirectly, by a huge electoral college consisting of elected local officials. It cannot censure the government, but it does vote on all legislation. The term is very long - 9 years with staggered elections, so that there is never a complete turnover of the upper house.

Before the Fifth Republic, France had a legislature-dominated form of government in the Fourth (and Third) Republic. Before 1959, the lower house or National Assembly often appeared to be the center of French politics. It made and changed laws, made and unmade governments. The press reported on its lively debates. Lobbyists centered much of their attention on the elected deputies, itself a clear indication of the location of power, since interest groups will normally concentrate their activities on those officeholders who have the power to affect any interests represented by the lobbyists. However, the National Assembly usually lacked a clear and consistent governing majority and often played an obstructionist role vis-à-vis the government rather than that of providing a consistent flow of majority support, or toleration, for the cabinet as its executive committee.

In the Fifth Republic, the powers of the National Assembly have been enormously reduced, and it attracts far less attention from the press or lobbyists. As noted earlier, de Gaulle's constitution strengthened the position of the government (and prime minister) primarily at the cost of the National Assembly. The National Assembly's powers were pruned back in the 1958 constitution. For example, these include provisions that allow the executive branch to act by decree on many matters or on the basis of decree powers given to it by specific acts of parliament, such as restricting parliament's power of the purse. To clarify, its power to increase expenditures or decrease revenues without the consent of the executive weakens the powers of the legislative committees; thus making them larger in size, and reducing them in number as compared to the past.

As noted earlier, the Fifth Republic also strengthened the political executive in another and quite different way, by superimposing on the parliamentary system, with its prime minister and cabinet, a strong presidential executive with a fixed term in office. In the constitution, the president's role is described as someone above day-to-day politics. He/she is someone who will function as an arbiter, who seems to stand above partisan politics and ensures the "regular functioning" of the government and the "continuity of the state." In political reality, the president soon came to play a central role in the Fifth Republic's governments. One American specialist concluded that the system had become much more presidential than it was parliamentary.

The Term

The term of office for the office of the president in France was very long - seven years - until it was reduced in a national referendum in the fall of 2001 to five years, with the possibility of reelection. Furthermore, the president added political weight to his office by becoming directly elected in a national vote as a result of the constitutional referendum which addressed this question in 1962. The president has the power to appoint the prime minister, and he or she can dissolve the National Assembly and call new elections at his discretion (a limit of once per year). He or she can propose a referendum and thereby bypass the Parliament. If the "institutions of the Republic are threatened in a grave and immediate manner" then, by decree, the president has the power to declare a state of national emergency and rule.

Whenever the president has a supportive majority in the National Assembly, as was the case from 1959 to 1986, this adds to the presidential leverage within the system. For example, it gives him the additional ability to dismiss prime ministers and cabinet ministers at will (this power is not granted by the constitution). There are other institutional innovations, such as the nine-member Constitutional Council.

Party and Electoral Politics in the Fifth Republic

The political party system in France used to be highly fragmented, with relatively little internal party unity, discipline, or cohesiveness, outside the traditional left. The latter was divided between democratic Socialists and Soviet-oriented Communists.

In the 3rd Republic (until 1940) and again in the 4th Republic (1946-1958), the result was a high degree of government paralysis and instability (not unlike the problems of the Italian Republic after 1945). De Gaulle despaired over this multiparty system and resolved to institutionalize a strong executive-led political system to replace it. He got his opportunity in 1958, when he and Michel Debré (later his first prime minister) oversaw the construction of a "duplex" or hybrid presidential-parliamentary system, the Fifth Republic. It was, in effect, designed to provide strong political leadership and largely neutralize what de Gaulle saw as a debilitating political effects of a multiparty system with little party discipline in the Fourth (and Third) Republic.

In the Fifth Republic (since 1958), the French party system changed considerably, partly in response to the new political architecture and its strong executive leadership, partly because of other societal developments. The party system has become much simpler, with fewer and more disciplined parties in the National Assembly. There also appears to have been a decline in ideological polarization. While the centrist groupings have become weaker, the ideological division between most of the Left and Right - once very deep - has in recent years become less important, both in political rhetoric and practice. This development towards a depolarization and consolidation of the party system is important, but it should not be exaggerated.

France currently has five political parties, three large and two small. Going from the far right to the far left, the parties line up as follows. The National Front is the furthest right party in France. It's mainly concerned with immigration and often pursues anti-immigrant policies. To the left of the National front are the two right of center parties, the neo-Gaullists (UMP) and closer to the center, the Union for French Democracy (UDF). On the left side of the political spectrum are the Socialists and to the left of the Socialists are the Communists. Over the years, the Communists have lost members to the socialists, whereas the National Front has actually gained some of the UDF and UMP members.

France and the United States

France's Fifth Republic sheds some light on how the presidential system of the United States works and the role of political culture. While the two countries started their republics around the same time, the United States is still on its first Constitution, amended only 27 times whereas France is on its fifth republic and has had 13 constitutions.

The Statue of Liberty was a gift from the people of France as a symbol of friendship in 1886. Courtesy of Jupiter Images.

The presidential powers that were created with the Fifth Republic were curtailed in 1986 with Socialist President Mitterrand. During Mitterrand's fifth year of his seven year term, he lost the majority in parliament to the conservative party. The French constitution did not stipulate what was to be done in this situation so Mitterrand appointed neo Gaullist Jacques Chirac as premier; Chirac oversaw domestic issues and Mitterrand would remain head of state and focus on foreign policy. This division of powers between two opposing parties is known as cohabitation, and it has occurred three times since 1986. Mitterrand had to cohabitate with the neo-Gaullists in 1986 and again in 1993. Chirac was elected president in 1995 but lost the majority in parliament to the Socialist in 1997 and cohabitated with Socialist Premier Jospin. French cohabitation is similar to the early presidential elections (see above in this chapter). Today it would be similar to presidential-congressional "deadlock." French presidential terms are now five years.

French cabinet ministers change depending on the president's program. Typically there are twenty ministries and tend to be restructured every few years with the approval of parliament. Here in the United States the departments tend to be somewhat stable. Most changes occur after a new president takes office or is reelected.

Most Americans were embarrassed about the presidential election in 2000 and the numerous recounts conducted in Florida. France had a similar experience in their 2002 presidential election. As stated earlier in this section, France has a runner-off between the top two candidates. It was predicted that the Socialist Jospin would face Chirac in the second round. Many voters who felt mislead by Jospin voted for several leftist candidates in protest. This resulted in moving the anti-immigrant extremist Le Pen ahead of Jospin; the second round went to Chirac and Le Pen. Realizing the problem they created, voters on the left were forced to vote for the more moderate of the two candidates, giving Chirac his second term.

The French are very proud of their culture and history. Many of their intellectuals often placed themselves in the liberal camp, effectively aligning them with the French Socialist and Communist parties. But as problems with the Soviet Union escalated along with the failures of communism, they began to criticize the left. However, the intellectuals were still somewhat anti-American because of U.S. led capitalism and the infiltration of western ways into the French culture. Despite the intellectual's criticisms of the U.S., the French, especially the younger generation, are not completely averse to McDonalds, Levi jeans, Hollywood, and American music.

All French leaders want to create jobs but are opposed to U.S.-style capitalism, which they consider to be "savage." French conservatives do not necessarily like a free market economy but do prefer it over a state sponsored economy. In 2006, the Conservatives called for a measure to expand jobs by making it easier to terminate first-time employees. This was a personal affront to French students, who reacted by participating in massive protests, which forced the measure to be revised and ultimately it failed.

France, like most countries has issues with immigrants. Almost 9 percent of France's population is Muslim, mainly black and North Africans from former French colonies. Just like in the United States, Britain, and Germany, immigrants in France take the lowest, dirtiest work that most citizens won't do. Recent civil unrest in the Muslim immigrant community has highlighted the issue of whether these groups can effectively assimilate into French society, so much so that French politicians were forced to enact tough new legislation that limited the number of incoming immigrants. Some French, like their American counterparts, want the immigrants sent home. These sentiments aided the rise of the National Front (the anti-immigrant party). Many immigrants want to assimilate into French life, but some resent this process because it dismisses the importance of their own cultural values. In some cases, minority Arab groups have become isolated by keeping within their own communities. Over the last two years, there have been instances of angry Arab youths clashing with French police, who have met them with harsh treatment. This came to a head in 2005 when nationwide riots occurred.

As in the United States, many French want to increase understanding of other cultures through education and view this as the key to improve racial tension. But to implement programs to aid this project requires a substantial amount of money, and many French municipalities, like states in the U.S. complain the burden on them is unfair. In addition, many schools in France face the same problems as schools in the United States. Many "bacs" (equivalent to U.S. High Schools) have expanded their technical and vocational programs. The French lycée and university systems are overcrowded and are badly in need of repair. Unlike students in the U.S., French students hold mass political protests demanding improvements at the poorest of schools. Health care is another area where the U.S. can learn something from France. While many Americans criticize socialized medicine, the World Health Organization conducted a study in which France's system was ranked the world's best in medical care, and at a lower cost than U.S. healthcare.

By looking at the French semi-presidential system and comparing it to the United States presidential system, one can see the strengths and weaknesses in both. Although there exists some animosity between the U.S. and the French in regards to clashes in culture, it appears that both countries share an equal amount of fascination with each other. We in the U.S., like the French, are very proud of our customs and values; and, as we discovered with the U.S. election in 2000 and France's elections in 2002, both countries had to struggle to save face to the rest of the world.

Chapter Summary

When Washington became the first President of the United States, his job was easy compared to modern presidents. By the third president, Thomas Jefferson, the job began to change, as it did under Andrew Jackson, and Abraham Lincoln. With the turn of the twentieth-century came an even greater evolution of the office. Events such as World War I, the Great Depression, and World War II all played vital roles in shaping the men in Oval Office. With the inauguration of President Franklin Roosevelt, the era of the modern president began. Now with the twenty-first century upon us, the office of the president faces new challenges and new powers will be needed to meet those challenges, both foreign and domestic. With her or his staff, advisors, and bureaucracy at her disposal, the president has the vast experience and support she needs to content with any emergency or day to day decision making. In evaluating California's governor, one can see how the powers and the staff of the governor's office emulate those of the president. With the introduction to France, a comparative approach is used to illustrate how the field of study works. By comparing France's 5th Republic, with the United States, Britain, and Germany, we are able to see the overlapping structures along with the nuances that make France the unique nation it is.

Key Terms:

The Communist Manifesto

Great White Fleet

Rough Riders

Secretariat

Bureaucracy

Executive Order

Line Item Vetoes

Absolutism

Intendant

États généraux or the States General

Bourgeoisie

Bastille

Reign of Terror

Coup d'état

Bourbons

Immobilisme

Websites:

White House Home Page
www.whitehouse.gov/

President's Cabinet Links Page
http://www.whitehouse.gov/government/cabinet.html

The Center for the Study of the Presidency
www.thepresidency.org

Potus
www.potus.com

Watergate Site
www.washingtonpost.com/wpsrv/national/longterm/watergate/front.htm.

California Sites

California State Home Page
www.ca.gov

Office of the Governor
http://gov.ca.gov/

State Office Links Page
http://www.ca.gov/Government/State.html

University of California System
www.ca.gov/s/learning/uc.html

California State University System
www.ca.gov/s/learning/csu.html

This page left blank intentionally.

Gulliver in the land of the Lilliputians – This illustration from the early 1950's characterizes the frustration felt by corporations who wanted to use atomic energy for commercial purposes, but were limited by government controls.

CHAPTER 11

THE BUREAUCRACY

CHAPTER OUTLINE

Democracy and Action – FEMA & Hurricane Katrina: A Heck of a Mess

Though it existed under other names and operated under the purview of several different federal agencies at different points in history, the Federal Emergency Management Agency, or FEMA, was officially formed in 1978 to be the federal

government's arm that coordinates emergency management - to assist citizens, states, and federal interests in case disaster strikes. In 2003, FEMA became a branch of the Department of Homeland Security. Once the President declares a federal state of emergency, FEMA is our federal government's first to respond. Although it sound like a simple plan, for the city of New Orleans, FEMA's response to Katrina was anything but simple.

A satellite picture of the eye of a hurricane, a terrifying view from the quiet of space. Courtesy of Jupiter Images.

On the late afternoon of August 26, 2005, the U. S. National Hurricane Center (USNHC) realized that the major Hurricane named Katrina was on a direct course to hit the city of New Orleans, Louisiana. New Orleans is home to almost a half a million residents who live below sea level. Their main avenue of defense from flooding is a complex and arcane levee system.

Kathleen Babineaux Blanco, governor of Louisiana, realized the possible scope of the coming disaster and declared a State of Emergency. She also requested that President George W. Bush declare a major disaster in the state of Louisiana in order to release federal assistance and deploy federal troops to help coordinate this assistance through FEMA. President Bush obliged her requests on August 27th.

On the morning of the 27th, the USNHC issued a hurricane watch for the city of New Orleans and by that evening, they had upped that watch to a full-blown hurricane warning. By the morning of August 28th, it became clear that Katrina would most likely be a massive category 3 hurricane by the time it made landfall. This declaration prompted a strongly worded bulletin by the National Weather Service about the impending large-scale damage the hurricane would inflict. State and local governments in Louisiana began issuing voluntary evacuation orders (some mandatory) for areas directly in the storm's crosshairs.

On the 28th, Mayor C. Ray Nagin of New Orleans changed the voluntary evacuation order to mandatory for the entire city, and requested that all residents who could not or did not have a way out of the city take refuge at the Superdome, the large stadium downtown, as a last resort refuge. More than 26, 000 people took the Mayor up on this offer.

Katrina made landfall the morning of Monday August 29th, slamming into the Louisiana coastline, and, as expected was a large and powerful category 3 hurricane. It quickly made it's descent upon New Orleans. By early afternoon, there was confirmation that at-least three levees had been compromised and massive flooding was underway. By late afternoon, much of New Orleans was under approximately ten feet of

After a hurricane, a barbed wire fence that once corralled in cattle and other livestock now protrudes out of floodwaters like cattails in a pond. Courtesy of Jupiter Images.

water and homes were completely submerged in some areas with only rooftops visible in others.

The local rescue effort began that afternoon as small boat patrols began evacuating people that were stranded on rooftops. But, fire and rescue teams outside of the disaster area were urged by FEMA director Michael Brown not to go into the disaster areas without specific requests for help from the state and local governments, possibly compounding the chaos that was unraveling the area. Brown did however request on the afternoon of the 29th that 1,000 Homeland Security workers be dispatched to the region, though he acknowledged that this process would take two days.

By August 30th, most major media outlets had cameras and reporters in New Orleans. Images of floating debris were broadcast all over the world and the nation began to grasp the scope of the devastation. Overcrowding and illness further compounded the dire conditions at the Superdome. Reports were beginning to come in about the failure of plumbing and the lack of food and clean water. It also became clear that the levees could not be plugged, so the complete evacuation of New Orleans was ordered, including those stranded at the Superdome. This was especially hard on families who did not have transportation or enough resources to buy gas. Some elderly folks simply had no next of kin and nowhere to go. Local law enforcement had looting and chaos around the city on their hands while tangible presence of FEMA was nowhere to be seen.

Two days later, on September 1st, with thousands of people still stranded in squalid conditions at the Superdome and at Convention Center, the New Orleans Emergency Operations Chief Terry Ebberts was asked about FEMA's seemingly slow and inadequate response. He replied that he had yet to see a "single FEMA guy." Later that day, the National Guard finally began arriving in the city to hand out food, water, and ice. The Red Cross arrived a day later and amazingly was told to hold back for 24 more hours due to ongoing military rescue operations.[1a]

Friday September 2nd, a full four days after Katrina made landfall, President Bush toured a portion of the area hit. It was on this tour that he praised Michael Brown, Director of FEMA, and made that now infamous statement "Brownie, you're doing a heck of a job."[1b] Meanwhile, it had become very clear to the general public that those stranded were mostly the very poor African-American residents of the city, prompting much speculation on whether race or class had been a component to the alarmingly slow and scattered response by FEMA.

The Superdome was finally completely evacuated by Sunday September 4th and an investigation was launched into the mishandling and slow emergency response by FEMA. The investigation found that in some cases, FEMA officials had turned away help when offered immediately following landfall, during the small window of time before the situation reached critical status. It was also discovered that FEMA director Michael Brown had been appointed to the top spot without having any previous experience in emergency management. After being scrutinized by the media, he stepped down as director on September 12th.

In the end, process and public perception had been put above need. FEMA had been massively mismanaged and had become so entangled in its own protocols that many in Louisiana endured terrible conditions for days. The many serious missteps during Katrina not only complicated a devastating situation, but it also cost many people their lives. FEMA's response had been so egregious that some have said that the events leading up to Katrina and its aftermath have become the example of what complete failure by government bureaucracy looks like.[1c]

Bureaucracy –
A large complex organizational system in which tasks, roles, and responsibilities are structured to achieve goals that are relevant to day to day living. The bureaucracy answers to the President and Congress, so their policies are influenced by them as well.

Bureaucrat –
A person who works in a bureaucracy at all levels of government.

Even hurricane evacuation signs could not point people directly to safety, as destruction and debris topple buildings and wash away access roads.
Courtesy of Jupiter Images.

The Federal Bureaucracy

Trust is essential for our social wellbeing. Without trusting the good will of others we retreat into bureaucracy, rules and demands for more law and order. Trust is based on positive experiences with other people and it grows with use. We need to trust that others are going be basically reasonable beings.
– Eva Cox from A Truly Civil Society

How Americans View Bureaucracy

In the United Kingdom, individuals go to schools that train them how to become a professional bureaucrat. The term **bureaucrat** in this context doesn't necessarily have the same negative connotation as it might normally carry. It's simply a different view of how the government should work. Here in the United States, being called a bureaucrat is often tantamount to being called a high class criminal who is wasteful and not to be trusted. Elsewhere, being a bureaucrat is considered an honorable way to serve one's country.

Having a mistrust of the government is practically instinctive in the U.S. since questioning authority is one of America's core values. In addition, as discussed in chapter 3, most Americans do not feel that that the government can perform their duties effectively so they turn to the private sector, believing that they can perform better. But, after the accounting scandals at companies like Enron, these notions have been thrown out with yesterday's shredding, leaving the American public unsure and cynical as to who is worthy of trust.

Despite the sentiments described above, the explanation as to why Americans dislike bureaucrats so much should not be oversimplified. There are several answers to this question. One possibility is that civil servants do not receive the same pay as their counterparts in the private sector. This may explain why a large number of highly skilled individuals are lured away from the grind by private sector opportunities. Furthermore, many bureaucrats are limited in their jobs not by their abilities but how the structure is established. Rules and regulations prevent government workers from being more efficient. In the private sector purchases are generally left up to the purchasing department to find the best price of say a computers. In the government, in order to purchase the same computers, there are a number of requests and justification forms and if the purchase is over a certain dollar amount it must be sent out to bid. After the bids are received, the winning bid is submitted for approval. The entire process can take months. In addition, many citizens and groups that work directly with the government complain that the process is full of red tape. The process of applying for permits or bidding on government contracts go through a similar process as a purchase order for computers.

Bureaucratic Structure

Bureaucratic power is based on the area and level an individual is within the government. In order to gain a better understanding of bureaucratic power, one must have an understanding of how the executive branch is organized; following is a brief review.

Under the president and vice president are the cabinet-level secretaries who are nominated by the president and confirmed by the Senate. The secretariat oversees the departments who in turn provide vital services for the government; departments such as the Department of State, Department of Defense, and Department of Treasury to name a few. As stated in the chapter on the executive, there are fifteen departments in the current administration. Departments can vary in size and shape depending on the duties they need to fulfill. The Department of Defense is the largest of all of the departments with over three million employees located in military bases and installations around the world. Compare this with the Department of the Interior which employees around seventy thousand and has a smaller office throughout the U.S. and its territories. Many departments were created out of necessity, such as the Office of Homeland Security, were created after the attacks of September 11, 2001.

Within these departments are bureaus and agencies. Each department has its own internal structure depending on the duties with which they are charged. Returning to the example of the Department of Defense, each subdivision works in strict conjunction with the directives of the President. The military is based on a **hierarchical** structure which requires strict adherence to the chain of command. In contrast, other agencies may be less formal, like the Department of Agriculture which works more closely with the general population.

Independent agencies are groups that also fall under the archway of the executive branch. These agencies report directly to the president; however, their directive is to work independently from the political process to guarantee the health and welfare of the general public. An example of an independent agency would be the United States Food and Drug Administration (USFDA or just the FDA). The FDA monitors and approves medicines that may not be politically popular such as the "morning after" pill or the RU-486 pill. Federal law prohibits the president or any of

Hierarchy – A clear chain of command and communications going from executive director (top) down to all other levels of employees.

Independent Agencies – Established independent agencies that regulate a sector of the nation's economy in the public interest.

FOR YOUR CONSIDERATION
CIVIL SERVICE

The term "civil service" refers to the occupation of working for a government agency in a non-military capacity. Employees in civil service are often referred to as civil servants. For instance, a person working for the Department of Agriculture or the FBI would be considered a civil servant. There are civil service jobs at every level of government, federal, state, and local.

Maximilian "Max" Weber (1864-1920) was a leading scholar of modern sociology. He promoted organizational theory in government, which can be seen in the hierarchical structures of the civil service. This type of structure helps people build a career in civil service without political retribution. Courtesy of the Library of Congress.

Every country has civilians working for the government as part of their bureaucracy. In some countries, civil service jobs are given based upon knowledge and experience; in others they are given as a reward or favor. Civil servants may work as ambassadors and diplomats, legal counsel and judges, all the way down to clerks and administrative assistants.[2]

One of the largest reformations of civil service in the United States occurred under President Franklin D. Roosevelt. During the Great Depression, with much of the population unemployed and basically staving, Roosevelt put into action his New Deal programs, which created several new government agencies and added numerous jobs in the public sphere. Many people were able to return to the workforce because of this massive job creation.[3]

Civil Service jobs are considered fairly difficult to get, but the benefits that come with a civil service job include good health care and pension plans as well as job stability and union protection. Could a career in civil service be in your future? If you are considering employment in the civil service force, it is best to develop patience and perseverance now – the civil servant must go through many hoops before even being considered to be interviewed. This seems painfully appropriate for a job within the bureaucracy.

his staff to apply pressure on the FDA to withhold approval of this drug, just because of their moral or religious ideologies about the function of this drug, which prevents a pregnancy from occurring if taken a few hours after the risky behavior occurred.

Similar to the independent agency is the independent regulatory commissions (IRC), which regulate parts of the economy to ensure that public interests are protected from illegal practices. Independent regulatory commissions are protected by federal law from interference from both the executive and legislative branches of government. The commissions are overseen by commissioners who have overlapping terms. In order to run smoothly, a balance between Republicans and Democrats serving on the commission is ideal. An example of an IRC is the Securities and Exchange Commission which regulates trading of stocks on the stock market.

Other types of agencies are government corporations. Government corporations are organized in the same manner as the private sector. They were created to provide a vital part of the economy. An example of a government corporation is the U.S. Postal Services (USPS). Although the USPS was one of the original agencies formed back in 1790 (see chapter 10), its status was changed in 1970 in an attempt to make it operate more cost effectively. The jury is still out as to whether this was the actual result.

Foundations are another type of organization that is protected from executive or legislative interference. Their job is to oversee the development of the arts and sciences in the nation. Some of the best known are the National Endowment for the Arts (NEA) and the National Science Foundation. On occasion the NEA has funded art exhibits that have caused great controversy in Congress and some have called for it to be dismantled.

Lastly, there are quasi-governmental organizations. Quasi-governmental organizations are hybrids of public and private organizations which allow the government to provide services without taking control of it. They are usually governed by the board of directors who are appointed by both the federal executive branch as well as the private sector. Examples of these types of organizations are the Federal Reserve Board which regulates monetary policies and the Corporation of Public Broadcasting (CPB) which provides entertainment and information to the public at large (see the chapter on media for additional information).

The Federal Reserve building in Washington D.C. Courtesy of Jupiter Images.

FOR YOUR CONSIDERATION
THE DEPARTMENT OF HOMELAND SECURITY

President George W. Bush first proposed a new addition to the Cabinet, the Department of Homeland Security (DHS), in 2002 with the intent of improving the way various agencies deal with protection of the nation or the homeland from various threats. Following the attacks on September 11, 2001 and the resulting chaos, it was hoped that the DHS would be able to streamline communication and coordinate these agencies more efficiently. The department was officially up and running by March of 2003.

The groupings of agencies fall under various canopies: a Border and Transportation sector, which includes the INS, customs, and the newly formed Transportation Security Administration; the Emergency and Preparedness Response division which oversees agencies like FEMA and the Nuclear Incident Response Team; other divisions include a Science and Technology division and an Information Analysis and Infrastructure Protection division.

In theory, forming the DHS was a good idea, given that communication and coordination between the various agencies was sporadic at best. Unfortunately, all it really did was create another layer of bureaucracy in an already large government. Furthermore, it eventually created more opportunities for exploitation of those who were already predisposed to it.

Some of its more spectacular failures have been the cases of the undercover agents getting past security checkpoints in airports while carrying weapons and explosives.[4] Then there were the findings that some Air Marshals on planes slept and/or imbibed while on the job.[5] And of course, the event that set the bar for departmental ineptitude - the incompetent and bungled response by the government to Hurricane Katrina, which destroyed much of the Gulf Coast and most of the city of New Orleans along with it.[6]

Other criticisms of the DHS were documented reports of lavish spending on frivolities such as banquets[7] a seeming attempt by the government to utilize the DHS for political propaganda purposes.[8] There were also reports that the department was more concerned with appearance than actual security.[9]

Another major worry regarding the DHS was the very real possibility that violations of civil rights and liberties could easily occur, especially considering that a few of the agencies being incorporated into the DHS had been guilty of previous violations.[10] The department attempted to counter this criticism by creating an Office for Civil Rights and Civil Liberties. Despite the addition of this office, the DHS has still come under fire for secretly putting into effect programs that Congress had banned[11] as well as the appointment of Michael Chertoff as DHS Secretary, whose record on civil liberties is questionable according to the ACLU.[12]

FOR YOUR CONSIDERATION
THE DEPARTMENT OF HOMELAND SECURITY

Suffice it to say that the Department of Homeland Security has always been somewhat controversial and as time goes by it has been subject to higher degrees of scrutiny. New questions continually pop up regarding its various functions (or dysfunctions as the case may be). However, Gallup opinion polls indicate, as of August 2005, approximately 49 - 55% of a sample of the American public feel that the actions of the agencies responsible for preventing terrorism have made the country a little safer.[13]

The next largest percentage of the sampling felt that the nation is a lot safer, followed by no difference, then a lot safer, then little less safe and a lot less safe fairly close, and in last place, those who have no opinion on the matter. As more questions go unanswered, the DHS has not been completely let off the hook as to the cause of the very infringements and violations it was meant to prevent. Perhaps those with no opinion are waiting to see what the DHS will do next before offering any true opinions on national security.

Democracy and Bureaucracy

Issues For You
Discuss the connection between your vote during presidential elections and the bureaucracies that we all rely on. Why is it important to vote and also make your opinions known to your local representatives in regards to the bureaucracy?

What is the role of a bureaucracy in a democracy? If the people are to have a say in the government, what is their role in overseeing the bureaucracy? In a democracy there is an air of openness and the right to question your leaders, whereas in a traditional bureaucracy a hierarchical structure is borne out of an organizational loyalty and secrecy to a fault. Furthermore, in a democracy, elections are held so people can vote for the leadership they want, thus having an opportunity to hold the candidates accountable. In contrast, in a bureaucracy the officials are nominated by the president and confirmed by the Senate and they have very little pubic accountability. Even though the federal bureaucracy is often criticized for their lack of responsiveness or transparency, for all intents and purposes is it the "fourth branch" of government. The function of the bureaucracy is to promote the common good through the directives that have been established by the president and authorized and funded by Congress. Without the federal bureaucracy, many Americans would be dire straights if they did not have the services provided by the government.

Who are the Bureaucrats?

In this section we will examine the Federal civilian employee work force. There are millions of other federal employees found in the ranks of the military. There are over fifteen thousand job classifications in the federal bureaucracy. They range from labor intensive "blue collar" jobs such as print-shop workers, carpenters, and mechanics to highly-skilled "white collar" positions such as veterinarians, accountants, and of course, attorneys. Not all federal employees work in Washington D.C. Roughly ninety-percent work in other parts of the nation, territories, and abroad. If one was to compare the number of federal employees in Washington, D.C. to California, they would se that the two nearly have the same numbers of federal employees.

In order to accommodate such a large work force, the federal government owns over 400,000 government buildings domestically and abroad. Federal employees of the 21st century are better educated and trained than their predecessors. In terms of compensation, federal employees are also better paid than those of yesteryear. However, when comparing the federal employees' compensation with their civilian counterparts, they are on average paid significantly less. Even though most bureaucrats are political appointees, research by the Office of Personnel management has shown that the federal workforce is more diverse then the private workforce.

What Do Bureaucrats Do?

It's hard to avoid feelings of animosity toward bureaucrats. All one has to do is turn on the evening news and listen to politicians' endless rhetoric or recall the images of New Orleans under water without food or supplies to bemoan the inefficiency of the bureaucracy. Americans may have ill-feelings toward bureaucrats at all levels of government because they do not understand what it is that bureaucrats do exactly. This is partly because when things are going well in our day-to-day transactions, we tend to not notice or we take it for granted. However, if one little thing goes wrong, the entire system is to blame. Bureaucrats make the trains run, the planes fly, the borders secure, the streets safe and clean, the housing, food, air, and water safe for our consumption. Civil servant jobs may not be exciting but they are a key element to ensuring that the country continues to run efficiently. Think of the person who sits behind a desk day after day processing student loan paperwork or the water

Imagine how many more people would be waiting in line if we were to cut back on bureaucratic organizations?

quality engineer who drives great distances to test the quality of water tables (underground cisterns) and reservoirs. Without these people processing all the proper forms and reports, you, the student would not receive their financial aid checks or we would have a dysentery epidemic on our hands from contaminated water, just to name a couple scenarios.

In recent years, there has been a push to privatize or simply allow the free market to do the work of government. While some of these attempts to privatize have gone awry, leaving the tax payers to pay more money for the same job a civil servant could have done. The up side to this is that the bureaucracy has found ways to improve their performance despite the limitations placed on institutional regulations. Overall, many bureaucrats are specialists in their fields and tend to understand not only the political process but the bureaucratic processes as well. Their expertise in their job performance can be seen in several areas: implementation, regulation, and administration.

Implementation

The main job of the bureaucracy is to implement the rules, regulations, and laws that were established by the legislative and executive branches. In referring to the "For Your Consideration" on the Department of Homeland Security, the new department merge several existing agencies along with several new ones to meet the task they were assigned. The new department employed approximately 200, 000 people, many of whom were civil servants, making it the third largest bureaucracy in the federal government after Department of Defense and Veterans Affairs. All of these changes required individuals with great expertise in their job to implement any regulations that needed to be met. When drafting legislation Congress will usually state a policy directive, provide funding, and occasionally oversight to meet those ends; but, Congress will defer to the expertise of those departments in the field. It is up to the department administrators to use **administrative discretion** to establish the procedures on how to implement the policies.

Most policies are implemented with the best of intentions but even with that, problems can emerge. Go back to the previous example of the Department of Homeland Security. One piece of legislation that was passed after the attacks on September 11th was the Patriot Act, granting the executive branch wide latitude on combating terrorism. In the following years, Congress and the American public began to hear stories about possible abuse of powers by the administration. One such example was the unwarranted wiretaps also known as Terrorist Surveillance Program, "or TSP, which was conducted by the National Security Administration (NSA). The purpose of this program was to monitor telephone calls and e-mails between the United States and overseas without a warrant, if the government determined that one of the parties was linked to al-Qaeda or other terrorist groups. Prior to the Patriot Act, a search warrant issued by a Court was necessary to conduct an investigation that crossed boundaries into private homes. After the act was past, search warrants became secondary and countless numbers of Americans had their communications monitored."[14]

Administrative Discretion – The latitude that an agency or bureaucrat has in interpreting an applying laws.

Regulations

The bureaucracy is responsible for creating, enforcing, and resolving disputes in regards to regulations. Virtually every aspect of life is regulated and maintained by

Originally, an embossing seal was used to notarize official government documents. Courtesy of Jupiter Images.

some form of bureaucracy, which can entail one or more agencies in the executive branch of government for every service needed. From the time you get up to the time you go to bed, you are protected by government regulations. The bed you sleep in, the alarm clock that wakes you up, and the clothes you put on have more than likely been reviewed by the Consumer Product Safety Commission. The Department of Agriculture, U.S. Customs along with food safety inspectors, and the Environmental Protection Agency is side by side with you as soon as you turn on the water for your shower, pour your first cup of coffee, and the first bite of food you eat throughout the course of the day. Some of the strictest regulations are administered by the Environmental Protection Agency (pollution control standards) and the Federal Highway Administration (speed limit on the interstates and seat belt laws). The enforcement of these regulations is left to the individual states and local municipalities. If they fail to enforce the regulations, the Federal Highway Administration can withhold their allocation of federal funds until they comply.

Administration

One of the jobs assigned to bureaucracy is that of administration. This basically means overseeing day to day operations in order to implement policies set forth by Congress and/or the president. Turn once again to the chapter's opening vignette discussing Hurricane Katrina. Before the hurricane hit land, many state and local bureaucracies were implementing their emergency procedures. Before the city was flooded the Army Corps of Engineers was trying to reinforce the levees. After the hurricane had passed, the Environmental Protection Agency, along with the Army Corp of Engineers and Federal Emergency Management Agency (FEMA) went to work trying to rebuild the impacted areas, finding temporary housing for the survivors, and launching search and rescue operations for those who were missing or in need of assistance.

In reviewing these three main components of implementation, regulation, and administration, one is able to see the complex nature assigned to each department and agency. Given these tasks, the bureaucrats need tremendous power to fulfill their duties. The bureaucracy does indeed serve the public in all aspects of life. Despite this, there are those who continue to attack the bureaucracy. Studies have shown that the morale of state and federal bureaucrats is consistently low because of the nature of their work environment. So the question becomes do people really try to appreciate what they have or do they continually need more to be happy? Where is the line between holding the bureaucracy accountable and recognizing how truly fortunate we are? These questions can only be answered on an individual basis.

Governmental Influences

Bureaucrats have to respond to the president, Congress, the courts, special interests, and the public. In this section, we will examine the influences of the president and Congress on the bureaucratic process.

The President

As stated in chapter ten, the president is the chief executive with the burden of overseeing the entire executive branch, including the bureaucracy. However, nearly every president since President Franklin Roosevelt has been astonished at their inability to control or reform the federal bureaucracy. The wall the president runs into is the "institutional memory" of each department. Being that civil servants tend to be specialists in their fields, they expect the president and the political leadership to give them deference when implementing their policies. With every new administration and attempts to "improve" the process, one can hear as they walk down the halls the old adage, "This is the way it has always been done."

President Nixon was beside himself with frustration towards the federal bureaucracy. One of his solutions was the creation of block grants (see chapter three) to bypass the bureaucracy which he considered to be an extension of the Democratic Party. His other plan was to use intimidation tactics on bureaucrats by conducting domestic surveillance on many of the head civil servants. His activities lead to the conflict with the House Judiciary Committee. At the end of this section is a "Profiles in Politics" with additional information on President Nixon and his activities.

In reviewing why presidents feel so frustrated with their inability to reform the bureaucracy, all they have to do is look at the bureaucratic structure to see why. Removing the size and number of employees from the equation, there are several other reasons why a president does not wield absolute power of the bureaucracy. First off, most civil servants are beyond political reproach because of civil service regulations. Unlike the private sector, a president cannot dismiss someone without just cause. In addition, the bureaucracy report not only to the president, but also to Congress, who unlike the president can serve for more than eight years so bureaucrats tend to be more loyal to a powerful Representative or Senator than their political leadership. More over, if you refer back to the iron triangle in the chapter on special interest groups, one can also see the role that special interest plays as well. If there is a powerful special interest connected to a bureaucracy they can always counter the president by using their power to influence his behavior and for Congress to apply their own pressure on the president to change his policies.

The Presidential Toolbox

Even with these limitations, the president still has power at his disposal to influence policy. In times of crisis, the president has tremendous powers to move the bureaucracy. Throughout modern history, one can see how President Franklin Roosevelt was able to get his New Deal legislation implemented and shortly thereafter, the **Lend-Lease Act**, which gave Roosevelt the authority to sell, transfer, exchange, and lend equipment to any country that he considered to be an ally against the Axis powers. President Kennedy was able to get the space program up and running in record time, and President George W. Bush was able to merge several small bureaucracies into the new Department of Homeland Security.

Even in non-crisis times, the president has the power of the microphone and television to sway the bureaucracy. Bureaucrats are ordinary people who can be responsive to the call to action from a popular president. President Roosevelt used his fireside chats to keep the nation's and bureaucracy's morale up; President Kennedy used his charm, appearance, and oratory skills on television to move the nations forward. Even President George W. Bush's popularity after the attacks helped him with his standing in the bureaucracy. Along the same lines, every modern president has, at one time or another criticized the bureaucracy on radio and television which seems to provoke the bureaucrats to respond. President Carter was able to reduce the CIA after criticizing their actions during the Vietnam War; President Reagan criticized the actions of the EPA and the impact they had on the economy. President Bush also attacked public education to encourage implementation of his No Child Left Behind policy (see chapter three).

 The powers of the purse and of appointment are two more tools in the president's tool box. A president calls on each department to complete annual budget requests. If there is a department or agency that is not complying with the presidential agenda, he can reduce their operating budget, forcing drastic cutbacks. President Reagan exercised this power when his budget proposal was below the minimum amount that the EPA needed to maintain its operating level. When the money wasn't there, the department heads couldn't get the materials and supplies they needed. Employees became frustrated and left. Without the ability to fill the vacant positions, the morale and the added stress on the department caused more employees to leave. Eventually, the President didn't have a problem with the EPA because there weren't enough inspectors in the field to conduct inspections.

The ability to appoint his own department heads greatly increases the probability that the president will see successful implementation of his policies. By choosing individuals who share the same political ideology, she or he has the reassurance of some loyalties. For example, regarding the termination of several U.S. Attorneys, an e-mail from Carl Rove suggested that when filling the vacancies, they should be filled with "loyal Bushies."

Profiles in Politics
Richard M. Nixon (1913 - 1994)

Richard Milhous Nixon was born on January 9, 1913 in Yorba Linda to Francis A. and Hannah Milhous Nixon. He died on April 22, 1994 in New York, New York and was buried at his presidential library in Yorba Linda, California. He was participated on the debate team in high school and then served as undergraduate president at Whittier College in California, where he graduated in 1934. He later attended Duke University Law School in North Carolina on a scholarship and graduated third in his class in 1937.

Richard M. Nixon (1913-1994), 37th President who served from 1969 – 1974. Courtesy of the Library of Congress.

In 1937. In 1940, he married Patricia Ryan. They had two daughters, Patricia (Tricia) and Julie. After five years as a lawyer, Richard Nixon joined the navy in August 1942, serving as an air transport officer in the South Pacific and a legal officer stateside before his discharge in 1946 as a lieutenant commander. After the war, he ran for Congress in California as a Republican in the 1946 election in which he defeated Representative Jerry Voorhis. As a member of the House Un-American Activities Committee, he ironically made a name as an investigator of Alger Hiss, a former high State Department official, who was later jailed for perjury.[15]

In 1950, Nixon defeated Representative Helen Gahagan Douglas, a Democrat, for the Senate. His anti-Communism ideals, his Western roots, and his youth figured into his selection in 1952 to run for vice president on the ticket headed by Dwight D. Eisenhower. The ticket won easily in 1952 and again in 1956. In 1959 while visiting Moscow, Richard Nixon won acclaim for his defense of U.S. interests in an impromptu "kitchen debate" with Soviet premier Nikita S. Khrushchev. After losing the 1960 race for the presidency to John F. Kennedy and the 1962 bid for California's governorship, he became a Wall Street lawyer. He kept his old party ties active however, and developed new ones through constant travels with speaking engagements representing the Republicans independently.

In 1968, he won the Republican presidential nomination and selected Governor Spiro T. Agnew of Maryland as vice president. Together, they edged out the Democratic ticket headed by Vice President Hubert H. Humphrey to become the 37th President of the United States. Committed to winding down the U.S. role in the Vietnam War, he pursued "Vietnamization" - training and equipping South Vietnamese to do their own fighting. He improved relations with Moscow and reopened the long-closed door to mainland China with a good-will trip to China in February 1972. That May he visited Moscow; while there he signed agreements on arms limitation, trade expansion, and approved plans for a joint U.S.–Soviet space mission in 1975. On August 15, 1971, with unemployment rising, Nixon abruptly announced a new economic policy, which found favor with the American republic, since he was elected a second time in 1972.[16]

Profiles in Politics
Richard M. Nixon (1913 - 1994)

In January 1973, hints of a cover-up emerged at the trial of six men found guilty of the Watergate burglary. With a Senate investigation under way, he announced on April 30th the resignations of his top aides, H. R. Haldeman and John D. Ehrlichman, and the dismissal of White House counsel John Dean III. John Dean's testimony stunned the nation. He exposed both a White House cover-up of the Watergate Hotel espionage activities and massive illegalities in Republican fund-raising in 1972. Additionally, Dean testified that Nixon routinely tape-recorded White House meetings and telephone conversations. On October 10, 1973, Spiro Agnew resigned as vice president, and then pleaded no-contest to a negotiated federal charge of evading income taxes on alleged bribes. Two days later, Richard Nixon nominated House minority leader, Representative Gerald R. Ford of Michigan, as the new vice president who was confirmed December 6, 1973.

On July 24, 1974, the Supreme Court ordered Richard Nixon to surrender the subpoenaed tapes, which he resisted turning over, resulting in a nasty struggle figuratively back and forth. In July 30, 1974, the Judiciary Committee referred three impeachment articles to the full membership. On August 5, 1974, Richard Nixon released tapes showing that he halted an FBI probe of the Watergate burglary six days after it occurred, in effect an admission of obstruction of justice. He also could not explain 18 minutes of white noise (erased space) on the tape. To avoid being impeached, on August 9, 1974 Richard Nixon became the first president to resign from the Office of the President. One month later, President Ford issued an unconditional pardon for any offenses Nixon might have committed as president, thus forestalling possible prosecution. After President Nixon left office, he returned to Southern California where he resided until he died on April 22, 1994.[17]

Congress

Congress also plays a keep role in influencing the bureaucracy. They accomplish this task through approving presidential appointment, legislation and budgets, and oversight hearings.

Power to Confirm Presidential Nominations

As stated in the Constitution, the Senate has the power of "advice and consent" on the president nominations. Most of the political appointees of the executive branch need to be confirmed by the Senate. If there is an issue with any appointee, the Senate can use it to their advantage to get concessions from the president on other nominations or key legislation.

Control by Legislation and the Budget Process

Every department requires legislation in order to have any staying power. Congress has the power to create the organizational details and design the mission statements to reflect their policies, instead of the presidents' preferences. If the president or a department head deviates too far from Congress' intent, Congress can pass new legislation or they can close the purse for future funding.

Congressional Oversight

Congressional oversight is one tool the Congress has to check if a department or agency has crossed the line. If they have, usually a committee or subcommittee will hold hearings to investigate what went wrong. As discussed at the beginning of this chapter, there were a number of reasons why FEMA and other agencies dropped the ball on Hurricane Katrina. In the aftermath, as horror stories of bureaucratic waste and fraud began to emerge, Congress opened hearings and requested that an audit be preformed on the monies spent for aid to the victims. The audit revealed that a handful of bureaucrats from FEMA purchased speed boats for their own use, and plastic surgery for themselves or family members. Meanwhile, New Orleans and the surrounding area are still short on supplies and housing (see chapter three).

Congress can also hold private organizations as well as federal agencies, accountable for a problem. Within weeks of the energy crisis in California and other western states in 2001, Congressional committees, mainly in the democratically controlled Senate, called for the commissioners of the Federal Energy Regulatory Commission (FERC) and representatives from the energy companies of Enron, Reliant Energy, and Mirant to testify. It was implicated that the FERC was negligent in managing these corporations because when Governor Gray Davis of California requested for the FERC to impose limitations on cost per megawatt, the FERC refused. The FERC claimed the market would correct itself. In response to the crisis and being called to testify, the FERC opened their own investigations in an attempt to uncover whether or not there was price gauging.[18]

Criticisms of Bureaucracy

Truth be told, the criticism of federal bureaucracy is valid on some level. There is indeed excessive waste and lack of accountability; however, one must understand that in the modern state, the bureaucracy acts as the final buffer between special interest, political interest, and the public interest. In comparing the government to the private sector, one can see that there is more fraud and corruption in the private sector than the public sector. The reason for this is in the public sector redundancy is mandatory and if there is fraud or corruption, the perpetrator will be caught. The Whistleblower Protection Act protects **whistleblowers** to ensure that they won't be fired for exposing any wrong-doing against the public interest. In reality, given the sheer size and complexity of the bureaucracy, the level of competence of the federal workforce is astounding. Take for example the Social Security Administration. While they may not meet all of Congress mandates, they have managed to generate hundreds of millions of social security numbers, maintain records of earnings and how much has been contributed to their accounts, and send out annual statements to all taxpayers notifying them of their social security accounts, all on a monthly basis. In 2005, there was an estimated 47.7 million recipients of social security, which equated to 47.7 million checks a month or approximately 572.4 million checks per year (see table 11.1 for specific details).[19]

Whistleblower – A civil servant who reports occurrences of bureaucratic mismanagement, corruption, inefficiency, and financial impropriety.

Table 11.1 - Facts about Social Security 2005	
Sources: Social Security Administration: Facts and Figures about *Social Security 2004*, *Social Security factsheet 2005*; Social Security Trustees Report, 2005	
SOCIAL SECURITY RECIPIENTS	
Total Recipients (in millions)	47.7
Retired workers	30.0
Spouses of retired workers	2.6
Disabled workers	6.2
Children and spouses of disabled workers	1.8
Families of deceased workers	6.7
Other, e.g. grandchildren of retired workers	0.4
AVERAGE MONTHLY BENEFIT	
Retiree/retiree and aged spouse	$955/$1,574
Disabled worker/d.w. & spouse, children	$894/$1496
Widowed parent and 2 or more children	$1905
MAXIMUM BENEFIT AT NORMAL RETIREMENT AGE [65 yrs 6 mo]	$1,939

Even though corporations and citizens always complain about government bureaucracy, there is always a reason why regulations are in place, to protect the public. Think about it like this; in the current affordable housing shortage, developers have found creative ways to make the most money with the least overhead. One such way is turning old abandoned factories and warehouses into condominiums or artist lofts. If you wanted to buy one of these quaint little places, you probably would like to know what was once manufactured there and what exactly was stored in the warehouse. There are reasons why government regulations require businesses to start filling out business applications early, one of which is to have the inspector check the premises for any hazardous materials.

Can This Bureaucracy Be Reformed?

For as long as there has been government, there has been bureaucracy and with that has come attempts to reform the bureaucracy. To coin the phrase, "Can this marriage be saved?" the relationship between the government and the bureaucracy is very much like a partnership in marriage. Here in the United States the major push for reform began around 1880. In all, there have been four stages of development within federal bureaucracy, all of which has achieved some level of reform: the formalistic stage (1883 -1937), the reactionary stage (1937 -1960), the new public administration stage (1960 -1980), and devolution stage (1980 -present). It should be noted that within each of these stages there was also a similar movement within the American society. As times and people changed so did the theoretical approaches.

In a response to all of the graft and corruption, the Pendleton Act was passed in 1883, thus beginning the formalistic stage. The formalistic stage was part of the Good Government movement, which supported the idea of a higher level of professionalism within the bureaucracy. This meant moving away from hiring unqualified political acquaintances, friends, and/or family. The Pendleton Act created strict personnel policies, such as hiring qualified applicants only, awarding promotions to experienced workers only, and the creation of the civil service which was meant to protect bureaucrats from political pressure. In addition, the government tried to implement scientific principles based on the writings of Frederick Taylor's management approach, which promoted the use of science and logic when dealing with the performance of the bureaucracy. Taylor's theories, infused into the formalistic period, can be summarized in a few basic principles. First, politics could and should be separate from the bureaucracy, allowing the bureaucrats to focus on serving the public and not the politicians. Secondly, if the bureaucracy can be run and modeled after scientific principles, then it will possibly run more efficiently. The scientific principle supposes that there may be many ways to do something but there is, theoretically, only one best way to do it. If this one best way can be discovered, then that is how it should be done. If the administration can be improved structurally from within, then it follows that the bureaucracy will also benefit from these improvements.

The Reactionary period 1937-1960 could be defined as the evolution of the social-scientific approach. During this time the focus became the organization along with those who worked inside the organization. Areas such as how people interact with their work environment, how they communicate both formally and informally, and so on, were examined. Procedures were put in place to aid the responsiveness of the bureaucracy.

The next period was the New Public Administration stage (1960 -1980) where the focus became showing the citizens that the government and bureaucracy were responsive to their needs. Theory and applications of making the departments and agencies more open and user friendly were the themes of the time. These could be accomplished through the understanding of how people lived and how the organizations were managed. New management styles, similar to the private sector, were introduced. One feature was pay and bonuses correlated to employee output. Also during this period, the Civil Service Reform Act in 1978 created the Senior Executive Service (SES). The SES was a group of upper-management bureaucrats who were reclassified to match their private sector counterparts, providing them with finance rewards if they succeeded in raising productivity and possible

Issues For You
After reading about all the reform attempts, have noticed any improvements in your day to day dealings with bureaucratic organizations? In what way?

termination if improvements were not evident. The experiment did not yield positive results. In fact, many of the SES managers left their jobs with bitter feelings about it.

Issues For You

Why do you think the government is paying private contractors large amounts of money to protect our military convoys (supply trucks containing food, water, medical supplies, and munitions) when a substantial percentage of enlisted personnel's income is so dismal that they qualify for food stamps and welfare? What does this say about the privatization of the military? How do you think this affects the soldiers' morale? Can you see any problems with conflict of interest between civilian contractors and trained military personnel?

The current period as introduced in chapter three is the devolution stage where government has tried to cut waste and redundancy and shift some responsibilities to the state and local governments. During the 1980s and 1990s a number of commissions were created to examine the problems within the bureaucracy and to make recommendations for solutions. There have been several attempts to privatize some parts of the government but the results have been mixed. When President Bush took office in 2001, one of his top agenda items was to establish private accounts for younger employees instead of having all of their retirement money placed with Social Security. Wall Street was excited about this idea because it meant billions of dollars in commissions for them. Many long term members of Congress and bureaucrats knew that in order to accomplish this there would be two glaring problems. The first was in order to get the accounts established the government would have to borrow billions of dollars which could result in wasting loads of money before one penny could be invested. The second problem was the possibility that the national debt would balloon because most of the social security surplus buys treasury notes, which in essence, acts as a loan to the government so it wouldn't have to borrow from outside sources. If the President had implemented his policy of private accounts, the trickle down effects would cost U.S. tax payers hundreds of billions of dollars in unnecessary start up funds and interest paid to outside investors.

Currently many Americans are displeased with the way the federal bureaucracy operates. While most of their criticisms are valid, there is no one solution to fix the intricate problems of the system. In recent years, the Bush administration has proposed privatization of many parts of the federal government, including the military. As this text is being written there are approximately 150,000 American troops in Iraq, most of which are being paid less than $3,000 a month. There is also approximately the same amount of private security forces that are being paid by the federal government close to $9,000 a month. Privatization has its advantages but currently it has more serious disadvantages as discussed in the examples of Katrina and the war on terrorism, due to lack of accountability.

California's Bureaucracy

Part of the job of bureaucracy, both state and federal, is to protect our national treasures, such as Mt. Shasta in California. Courtesy of the Library of Congress.

The elected officials are the most visible part of the state's administration. State workers are the backbone of the administration or the bureaucracy; without these thousands of workers no programs would be successfully implemented. The governor also relies on the Department of Finance, to help manage the bureaucracy. The governor and other executive officials are responsible for appointing only a small percentage of the bureaucracy. A larger portion is employed through the University of California (UC) and the California State University (CSU) tenure track systems. As of 2005, there were upwards of 250,000 California State employees working in all manner of capacities, under a merit system. The merit system has been a staple for government workers since the 1930's, and it is exactly that – advancement based on merit. It allows CSU workers the opportunity to be promoted and earn salary step-increases based on their experience, education, and specific job skills. It also protects workers from being unjustly fired or from being subjected to the political agendas of their departments or superiors. If the supervisors of CSU workers are meticulous in keeping track of their subordinates' responsibilities, especially if the workers are doing more than what is on their job descriptions, they can petition the personnel or human resources officers to elevate the category of that particular position. This aids the CSU worker in earning what they are worth; if their position is re-categorized to a higher level of skill requirements, this results in the worker earning appropriate pay for the work they are already doing but were not originally hired to do.

An additional note about California's merit system that is worthy of discussion are the collective bargaining agreements or unions that help determine fair wages, benefits, and working conditions. These unions help give a voice to those that do not feel confident speaking to their superiors should a personal problem arise. The California State Employee Association (CSEA) and the California Faculty Association (CFA) are examples of these unions. Even those faculty or state employees that do not support the unions (do not pay dues, attend meetings, consider the activities of unions as unwanted propaganda) enjoy benefits that the collective bargaining agreements have afforded them; benefits such as being able to donate or receive additional sick leave pay should theirs run out due to a long-term illness; and state subsidized tuition for themselves or their families. While there have been cases of unions taking advantage of unsuspecting state workers, for the most part, they are organizations run by the workers for the workers.

The remaining state workers are recruited (hired) and released (fired) through the civil service bureaucracy after going through rigorous testing, evaluations, interviews, and probationary periods; all of which help to confirm their qualifications before they are hired. These machinations of the bureaucracy were the brainchild of the Progressives who had the intent of protecting government employees from being influenced by outside political sources as well as to insure a certain level of professionalism (instead of nepotism or "crony-ism").

The main goal of the bureaucracy, along with a smattering of guiding agencies, is to see that programs that are created by the executive, legislative, and judiciary branch are carried out successfully. The power that comes from holding a permanent position within the bureaucracy is evident in their ability to influence the programs and policies they are meant to oversee. In other words, the bureaucracy may use their full-time long-term offices to lobby for their interests or to operate behind the scenes, working closely with public officials who are a captive audience, subject to the bureaucrats' advice.

Within the bureaucracy there are numerous departments, each of which are headed by governor-appointed administrators, pending senate approval. Civil servants, once appointed, do enjoy permanent status; however, the governor may request their resignation at will and these administrators must heed the governor's bidding. This fact dispels the myth that once a civil servant, always a civil servant – or – they can never be

Gov. Edmund "Pat" Brown, father of Gov. Jerry Brown, left his mark by investing in the state's infrastructure, such as California's natural harbors, like this one in Wilmington, CA. Courtesy of the Library Congress.

fired. This governmental mandate is a built-in check on civil servants, should they become too autonomous, complacent, or overly flamboyant in their debates with the political appointees.

With all of these departments, appointees, branches, and civil servants, it is hard to believe that no one person is actually in charge, not even the governor. This is to say that all the cogs fit together to make one bureaucratic unit, working together, struggling together, in the hopes that they can meet somewhere in the middle to carry out the people's wishes. It might seem that there are too many cooks in the kitchen, which is what some reformers have observed; some have suggested that reducing the number of departments and offices would help streamline the day-to-day operations. Despite these aspirations, instead of eliminating offices, one was actually added – the insurance commissioner.

Despite these complications, innovative governors have been able to leave their mark, (whether positive or negative is up to the observer), on their time in office. For example, as we mentioned in chapter 10, Jerry Brown was an advocate for farmers' rights; Gray Davis worked toward improving education; and Governor Schwarzenegger has strived to refine the state's infrastructure. The governor, along with his army of workers, must endure the scrutiny of the legislative branch, the bureaucracy, other executive members, and, most importantly, the evaluation of the electorate as a whole.

How Do We Compare?
Canada, Britain, and the United States

Comparing Canada and the United States is a unique case study. They are in fact, sister nations, originating from the same parent countries. Many Americans don't have an understanding about Canada beyond the accent or its number one sport of hockey, whereas Canadians cannot escape the looming big-sister presence of its imposing neighbor to the south. However, today there is a Canadian "identity" which is often defined by way of contrasts to the United States. In this section, Canada will be compared to the United States and Britain.[20]

Victoria Government Parliament Building in Vancouver, BC, Canada was constructed in 1893 celebrated Queen Victoria's Diamond Jubilee, 25 years as head of state. Courtesy of Jupiter Images

Population, Territory, Economy

The terrain of Canada covers an enormous amount of land, slightly larger than the United States. Although Canada, in terms of geographical region is the second biggest country in the world, it is the home to only about 35 million people – a little shy of California's 40 million, but absolutely dwarfed by the whole of the United States, with its 300 million people.

The vast majority of Canadians, about 90 percent, live within 100 miles of the 4000 mile-long border, which has often been referred to as the "longest undefended border in the world," with the expansive northland very sparsely populated. Thus the north-south axis in economics and mass culture is relatively short and often draws Canadians close to their nearby neighbors in the United States. By contrast, the east-west dimension of populated Canada is narrow and stretched out; it is clearly the result of political nation-building. Descendants of the indigenous peoples in this part of North America make up about two percent of Canada's population. On April 1, 1999, the Canadian government created a large new Arctic territory called Nunavut, in which the small Inuit tribe (related to the natives called Eskimos in Alaska) exercises local rule.

The first European settlers came from France and settled primarily in the southern part of the territory that now forms the province of Québec. After the British conquest of French Canada in the 1760s, a new flow of immigration came from the British Isles and spilled into adjacent territories of today's Maritime Provinces and Ontario. Additional settlers, often called the Empire Loyalists, fled northward from the United States after 1776, and some of these newcomers (and their descendants) came to play a leading or elite role in the social and political life of British North America.

Factoid –
The term "Canuck" showed up into American slang to describe French Canadians. It was originally used offensively but is now used as an innocuous term to refer to all Canadians. The origins of the word are unconfirmed. Dictionary.com proposes that it is derived from the word "kanaka" from Hawaii to describe French Canadians and islanders employed in the Pacific Northwest fur trade. Etymonline.com offers the possibility that the word is a cross between and the native people in the Columbia River region. Although Canadians are not excessively patriotic, there have been cartoon characters throughout the years that embody a certain nationalist sentiment. In 1869, Johnny Canuck was created as a national superhero and younger relative to America's Uncle Sam or Britain's John Bull. Johnny Canuck reemerged in 1942 as the cartoon defender of Canada against Nazism. A final example came about in 1975, when Captain Canuck and Québec's Capitaine Kébec, in their superhero suits of "electro-thermic underwear," shared one specific characteristic - to avoid conflict whenever possible, perhaps an accurate portrayal of both the Québécois and Canadians in general. Today, Canadians fully embrace the term, even naming a hockey team the Vancouver Canucks.[21]

There was an important westward expansion in the nineteenth century, leading to some territorial disputes with the United States. In 1846 an important border settlement was established in the Pacific Northwest (British Columbia). In the following decades, north-south trade increased enormously.

In the twentieth century, and especially after 1945, the country encouraged a relatively large immigration from continental Europe. In recent years there has been an increasingly large influx of immigrants from Southern and Eastern Asia. A fairly large and continuous southward emigration from Canada into the United States offsets the northward immigration from the U.S. into Canada. There has also been some immigration from the West Indies.

Today Canada remains the most important trade partner of the United States. The reverse is also true and to a much higher degree for Canada. In fact, some would argue that Canada has long been in a relationship of economic dependency to the U.S. that outranks similar situations of some Latin American countries. A Free Trade Agreement between the two countries was negotiated and passed in 1988/89. It was at first highly controversial in Canada, where it divided the country's then-governing party of Conservatives, led by former Prime Minister Brian Mulroney, which was the opposition party of Liberals. After taking over the government, following their electoral victory in 1993, the Liberals under Jean Chrétien became supportive of a slightly modified FTA -- which in 1994 became NAFTA (North American Free Trade Agreement) by including Mexico. In retrospect, it is widely agreed in Canada that the country as a whole has benefited from the free trade arrangement, even though there have been some losers.

Political history

Unlike the United States, Canada has not had a revolution with which it broke away from the "mother country", i.e., Britain, after the conquest of French Canada. Indeed, many "Loyalists" from the American colonies moved to what became eastern Canada. In the twentieth century, Canada gradually loosened its ties with Britain but retained Queen Elizabeth II as formal head of state. She is represented federally by the Governor General, and provincially by the Lieutenant-Governors. The Queen, via the Governor General, maintains certain powers over the prime minister and ministers. In extraordinary circumstances the Queen or Governor General can protect Parliament and the citizens of Canada against the prime minister and ministries from gaining too much power.

One U.S. scholar, Seymour Martin Lipset, in his very important book, *Continental Divide*, argued that Canada has a more conservative-and-statist political tradition as well as a less individualistic culture than the United States (Lipset and his theories were introduced in chapter one). These special traits are exemplified in the stronger presence of government interventions and controls in public life in Canada, including the extensive regulation of fire arms, a comprehensive national health insurance system, some publicly owned corporations (federal and provincial), and so on. So, with that in mind, one possible definition of a Canadian is a North American who is covered by a national health plan and who is not likely to have an unregistered firearm.

Canada is often described by Americans as a "kinder, gentler country" - some would add "and more boring." On a serious note, a widely used "quality of life" index has regularly awarded Canada first place among advanced countries, despite a GDP per capita that is somewhat lower than that of the U.S.

Federalism and Constitutional Independence

Canada gradually gained its independence from Britain in a series of reforms that spanned about three quarters of a century, beginning with the British North America Act (BNA) of 1867.

Francophone –
A French-speaking person, especially in a region where two or more languages are spoken.

Originally, the Canadian founders attempted to set up a federal system with a stronger national government than the one which they observed south of the border. They were, in part, reacting to their observation of the U.S. Civil War. Over the years, however, the interpretation of the BNA by the Privy Council in London (a kind of judicial review of Canada's basic law) came to favor the provinces. As a result, Canada ironically ended up having a federal government that in some ways has become weaker in dealing with the provinces than its counterpart in the U.S. In other words, while the U.S., with some periodic shifts, on the whole moved towards the creation of a stronger federal government, the Canadians on the whole moved in the other direction.

In 1982, Prime Minister Pierre Trudeau (Liberal) was instrumental in finally bringing "home" a reconstructed Canadian Constitution that contained a modern Charter of Rights and a gender equality provision. It also reflects the stronger power gained by the provinces within the federation, in large part a consequence of the special political relationship with **francophone** Québec. The Constitution is now interpreted by a very active Canadian Supreme Court. Like its U.S. counterpart, it has 9 members.

Parliamentary Government

Canada has a system of asymmetrical bicameralism, with popular election of the far more powerful lower house, the House of Commons. The upper house or Canadian Senate is appointed by the federal government, with some attention to a representation that reflects the country's regional, ethnic, and social diversity. There are unicameral legislatures in each of the 10 provinces, similar to the state of Nebraska, which if you'll remember, is the only state in the union that has a single chamber of legislature. Each province has its own cabinet government headed by a premier.

The federal and provincial governments operate on the parliamentary principle that first emerged in Britain: The political executive is in power as long as it enjoys a sustained flow of majority support or at least are politically tolerated in the elected legislature. Like the Westminster Model in the U.K., the relationship between the "ins" and "outs" of the government party and the opposition parties is usually an adversarial one rather than the more consensual system found in some of mainland Western Europe. The U.K. has clearly served as a model here.

Profiles in Politics
Agnes Macphail (1890 - 1954)

Agnes Macphail is probably not a name you recognize, but in politics, she was a trailblazer. She was the first woman ever elected to the House of Commons in Canada, which may not seem all that earth-shattering nowadays, but she was elected way back in 1921.

Agnes Campbell Macphail was born in a rural area of Ontario in 1890. As a young woman, she became a schoolteacher, teaching in rural areas of southwestern Ontario. Originally concerned with agricultural problems, Agnes entered politics by joining the United Farmers of Ontario, where she became an outspoken and active participant. In 1921, the very first election where women could vote in Canada, Macphail ran and became the first woman ever elected to the Canadian Parliament.[22]

First female member of Canadian Parliament, Agnes Macphail.
Courtesy of New Paramount Studio/
Library Archives Canada/PA-127295.

Macphail began with the intention of representing her rural constituents, but she soon became interested in additional areas. One of those areas was the area of disarmament. Because of her strong views on international disarmament, she was appointed to be a Canadian delegate to the League of Nations, where she was a member of the Disarmament Committee. Macphail was the first Canadian woman to ever be sent as a delegate. She also became a member of the Women's International League for Peace and Freedom.

Another area in which Macphail was interested was that of human rights. After learning about the appalling conditions in prisons, she became an outspoken proponent of prison reform. She formed the Elizabeth Fry Society, named after the 19th century British activist, to help advocate for prison reform. She succeeded in 1936 when the government established a commission to investigate the Canadian penal system.[23]

As seen in her advocacy for prison conditions, especially conditions in the women's portions of penitentiaries, she was not only concerned with human rights, but also with women's rights. She helped promote civil rights for women, including legislation ensuring equal pay for equal work, which succeeded in 1951.

In spite of her successes, Macphail was defeated in the elections of 1951 and spent the remainder of her life as a journalist and public speaker until she died in 1954.[24] Throughout her 19 years in the House of Commons and 5 later years in the Ontario Legislature, Agnes Macphail left her mark on Canadian politics and paved the way for other women to follow in her footsteps.

A Major Canadian Issue: Cultural Dualism and Separatism

More than one-fifth of all Canadians are primarily francophone. They are concentrated in the province of Québec, where over 6 million of the province's seven million people use French as their first language. Most of the rest of Canada's population is primarily English-speaking or Anglophone. There has long been an ebb and flow of tension between these two main cultures in Canada. The French-speaking people of Québec were able to remain a major factor in Canadian politics, because of their large number and cohesion -- for a long time, the so-called "battle of the cradle" coined as such because of the relatively high birth rates in Québec, which offset the immigration into English-speaking Canada. Until the early 1960s, Québec was very traditional in its social structure and prevailing culture as far as its French-speaking population was concerned. A major role in maintaining this state of affairs was played by a very traditional Church. At that time, the modern elites in Québec province (business, technical professions, finance, etc.) tended to be English-speaking.

Québécois –
The people Québec.

The so-called "Quiet Revolution" of the 1960s changed Québec dramatically, by way of a politically promoted modernization effort. Educational efforts and affirmative action programs promoted francophone Canadians into modern careers and leadership positions. A new **Québécois** self-confidence and assertiveness began to be felt everywhere. Birth rates dropped dramatically as Québec modernized, but this accelerated a pervasive fear that francophone culture in North America would "die out" unless countermeasures were taken.

Pendulum Swings in the Politics of Québec Separatism

In the late 1960s and early 1970s, a movement for Québec's autonomy, separation or independence from Canada gained headway. A countervailing attempt to stem this nationalism was led by the flamboyant new Liberal Prime Minister of Canada, Pierre Trudeau, himself a Québécois who supported a more bicultural version of Canadian patriotism. His moves for conciliation and cultural guarantees for the Québécois within a strong Canadian federation did not resolve the problem. In 1970, he invoked the War Measure Act to send troops to Québec to put down a wave of separatist terrorism, leaving the province "subdued but sullen" (New York Times).

The PQ in Power, 1976 to 1985

Some form of political independence became the key demand of the Parti Québécois (PQ), although it preferred to speak of "sovereignty-association" for Québec. An electoral victory in 1976 brought the party to power under Premier René Lévesque. In office until 1985, it enacted some far-reaching legislation intended to protect and promote French as the dominant language of Québec and also to establish much greater provincial control over government programs and institutions. It is estimated that about 140,000 English-speakers left Québec, mostly for neighboring Ontario, along with hundreds of businesses. The economic structure of Québec has become more fragile as a result.

Defeat of a First Provincial Referendum in Québec

Lévesque's plan for sovereignty-association was defeated by a strong majority in a provincial referendum in 1980. This was at least partly because it had initiated a major countermove by Trudeau, who pledged to seek complete constitutional independence for Canada and then move on to secure a special constitutional settlement within Canada for Québec. The Parti Québécois was reelected in 1981, however, and stayed in power until 1985. In 1985, the federalist (anti-separatist) Liberal Party defeated the PQ and took over the provincial government for almost a decade.

In the early 1990s, there were two failed attempts to find a federal settlement of the Québec issue. Already in 1994, the Conservatives had replaced the Liberals as the governing party in Ottawa. Prime Minister Brian Mulroney, himself from Québec and bilingual, thereupon led two major attempts to gain the cooperation of the new and much more moderate provincial government in Québec to resolve the issue of that province's relationship to the rest of Canada.

The so-called Meech Lake Accord of 1990 attempted to clarify the federal-provincial relationship within the new Canadian Constitution in such a way that the powers of all the provinces were enhanced. Crucial, however, was the provision intended to further placate Québec through an official recognition of its identity as a "distinct society." The proposed accord met with opposition in parts of Canada and failed to become law when two provinces, Newfoundland and Manitoba, declined to ratify it by a June 1990 deadline. The defeat was widely explained in terms of Anglophone reaction against some unusually determined measures by the Québec government to enforce the primacy of French within Québec, including laws that discriminated against the commercial use of English.

An alternative attempt to resolve the issue took the form of a national, Canada-wide referendum on a tentative agreement to restructure the federal government and, once again, give the provinces considerably more power. This measure was met with initial opposition in Québec for not going "far enough"; nevertheless many Anglophone Canadians came to see it as leading to a possible breakup of their nation. It was defeated decisively in the national referendum of 1992.

Since then, Canada has lived with an awkward national status quo and gotten used to the existential ambiguity it entails. There has been one more attempt by a Québec government to force the issue. In 1994/1995, the PQ returned to power and attempted a second provincial referendum that failed. As a result of the provincial election in September 1994, the separatists or sovereigntists, returned to power in Québec and formed a new government under party leader, Jacques Parizeau. They quickly prepared another referendum on "sovereignty" for Québec, held in the fall of 1995. The PQ government proposed that Québec declare its "sovereignty" and then promptly offer to renegotiate economic and political "association" with Canada, but Ottawa reacted by leaving the public impression that it was not interested in such a deal. Polls indicated that there was considerably more Québécois who favored this "muted form of secession" or limited autonomy where they would have more local rule but would still be part of Canada and its political process.

In the end the proposal was defeated by only about 140,000 votes (less than 1 percent of those voting). Right after the referendum, the charismatic PQ leader in the federal parliament, Lucien Bouchard, replaced Jacques Parizeau as premier of Québec. Parizeau had made a poor impression during the campaign when he seemed to make slurs directed at ethnic minorities that identified with the Anglophone cause.

The PQ government, headed by Bouchard, was re-elected in 1998, although the party won only 42.7 percent of the popular vote, while the pro-federalist Liberals registered a slim plurality with 43.7 percent of the popular vote. Because of the advantageous geographical "spread" of the PQ vote throughout much of the province, the PQ received a majority of 76 seats, while the Liberals won only 48 seats despite their plurality of the popular vote. One seat went to a small third party.

The PQ had hoped to do better in the provincial election of 1998. It still wants to hold another referendum but it has been waiting for a more promising electoral moment. The PQ continues to portray the federal government in Ottawa as obstructing legitimate attempts by Québec to have more control over its "own affairs". There are some parallels to the U.S. issue of "states' rights," but the Québec version of this problem is far more complex because of the linguistic-cultural dimension.

In the meantime, however, the PQ seems to have lost some popular appeal. It has also been weakened by a sharpening division between its more radical and more moderate wings. During an escalation of this factional struggle, Bouchard became identified with the moderates. In a move of protest against what he saw as xenophobic elements in the party, Bouchard stepped down as premier of Québec in late 2000. Seen in connection with the relatively poor performance of the Bloc Québécois in the federal election of November 2000, the move was interpreted as contributing to a further political weakening of the sovereigntist or separatist movement.

Possible Dissolution or Break-up of Canada?

Even if there should one day be an absolute majority in Québec for separation or "sovereign association," which itself doesn't seem as likely today as it did a few years ago, the province could not unilaterally separate from the rest of Canada. In a landmark decision, the country's Supreme Court in 1998 ruled unanimously that there would have to be negotiations with the rest of Canada on the terms of secession, as though it were an amendment to the Canadian Constitution. There were three Francophones among the nine judges who made the ruling. The Court stressed that there is no right to unilateral secession in international law, except for colonies and oppressed people, which it said does not apply to Canada. In effect, the Court said that separation would be extremely difficult, but not impossible: "The devil would be in the details," the justices wrote. Their milestone decision was generally thought to have put a damper on the separatist movement. No one seriously believes that the last word has been spoken, but in recent polls only 25 percent in the province say they want Québec to have "complete separation" from Canada.

Issues For You
Can you think of any regional differences between cultural, social, or religious groups in the U.S that may eventually lead to dissolution or divisions within the country?

Another Canadian Source of Political Division: Regionalism

In addition to the major cleavage of cultural dualism (reinforced by the territorial identity of the Québécois), there is a major center-periphery dimension in Canadian politics. Ottawa, the nation's capital, lies in eastern Ontario, far removed from the provinces on the Atlantic seaboard and, even more, from those located in the West (Manitoba, Saskatchewan, Alberta, and British Columbia). As a consequence, there has long been a strong regionalist element in Canadian politics, especially in the four Western provinces, which were populated later and now have a total of 88 seats in the 301-seat House of Commons, compared to Ontario's 103 seats. The Western regionalism manifests itself in a number of populist ways. First, "voters' revolts" against what is seen as an East-led governing party, whether Liberal or (at times in the past) Conservative. Second, strongly expressed resentment against what is regarded as federal favoritism of the East along with unnecessary federal intrusion into western affairs (including what is regarded as high levels of federal taxation). Lastly, political resistance to what has been condemned as "extortions" or "concessions" to francophone Québec, have angered the western provinces. There are parallels with our U.S. history of conflicts over "states' rights," but the Canadian version of regional alienation has intensity and some other peculiarities (regional parties) of its own.

Elections and Political Parties

Like the United States and the United Kingdom's House of Commons, Canada uses the winner-take-all system of plurality elections in single-member districts. Unlike the U.S., Canada has used a national referendum. Like most other democracies, Canada also has a system of automatic registration of the voters, which has not always equated to a high voter turnout. For example, until the turn of the twenty-first century, the voter turnout stayed around the same level for almost 25 years, approximately 20 percent higher than the U.S. voter turnout rate. In the first two elections of the new millennium, however, Canadian voter turnout had declined to the approximately same levels as the mid 1960s.

The winner-take-all system of elections is often associated with a party system dominated by two major parties, as in the U.S. or, to a lesser extent, Britain. That used to be the case in Canada as well, where the Conservatives and Liberals long exercised a kind of duopoly, with their respective strongholds in Ontario and Québec. The situation has long since changed, as Canada's strong political regionalism has resulted in a complex, more-than-two party system.

The Liberals have a long history as a major party, traditionally based on their electoral stronghold in Québec, before the rise of the PQ. Even today, the Liberals receive considerable support in the francophone province, and they have largely replaced the Conservatives as the main party of the other most populous province, Ontario. Many Liberal Party leaders have been from Québec, including Prime Minister Pierre Trudeau who dominated Canadian politics while the country established its new constitutional identity.

The Progressive Conservatives were for a long time Canada's second major party. Their stronghold was Anglophone Ontario, and they received considerable support in the Atlantic Provinces as well parts of the West. The party was long identified with being more cautious on "concessions" to Québec than were the Liberals. Ironically, however, it was a Conservative government led by Brian Mulroney, himself a bilingual native of Québec, which attempted to promote a far-reaching accommodation by granting Québec a special constitutional status as a "distinct society" within Canada. It ran into strong opposition as did his support of a free trade agreement with the United States. His successor as Conservative Prime Minister, Kim Campbell, was the first woman to head a national government in Canada. She could not save her party from electoral disaster in 1993, resulting from the unpopularity of the economic and constitutional initiatives taken by her predecessor. The Conservatives were almost wiped out. Under Joe Clark, himself an erstwhile prime minister, the old party has regained some regional support, but in much of Canada's west, moderate Progressive Conservatives have been replaced by the more right-wing Reform Party and its successor, the Canadian Alliance.

The New Democrats have long formed a traditional "third" party, which stands for democratic socialist reforms. It has been in power at various times in three of the western provinces (Saskatchewan, Manitoba and British Columbia) as well as Ontario. In recent federal elections, the party has performed less well.

The Parti Québécois (Bloc Québécois at the federal level), advances a separatist agenda and tends to be strongly statist in orientation. Within Québec, it favors more public works programs.

The Canadian Alliance grew out of the Reform Party in an attempt to leave behind the latter's limited appeal as a western-based populist protest party. Both were preceded by a similarly oriented Social Credit Party. Like its populist predecessors, the Alliance takes anti-governmental positions with respect to economic and cultural matters, but it is typically populist in stressing a strong law-and-order agenda. It is internally divided, but it voices some widespread regionalist discontents in the western provinces.

In comparing the two sister countries, one can see how coming from the same origins can produce separate results. The beginnings of both nations were very similar but after the American Revolution in 1776, the two countries took different paths. In the end, Canada started out more conservative but has become more socialist whereas its older sister, the U.S. started off as more liberal but has become more conservative. Watching the evolutions of these two nations should continue to be a unique facet to the study of comparative politics.

Chapter Summary

Despite the dissatisfaction that is widely felt with the American bureaucracy, its many services are an intricate part of our daily lives. Bureaucrats spend their time carrying out the law, regulating it, or playing referee to disputes. Bureaucrats are non-elected officials, some of whom are appointed directly by the president. Institutions that play a part in influencing the bureaucracy are the president, the courts, Congress, interest groups, and public opinion. The size of the bureaucracy has been the target of many calls for reform. Most of the time, the bureaucracy is a smoothly oiled machine – it's the few times when the bureaucracy really falls short, such as with FEMA, when the negative overshadows the positive things that the bureaucracy accomplishes. Changes proposed to improve the executive branch are supposedly expected to reform the bureaucracy as well. As a result, unnecessary personnel cuts and privatization have been introduced into the bureaucracy, causing morale to lower amongst civil servants. Advocates of Fred Taylor's writings propose applying principles of science and logic to help make bureaucracy more efficient. California has the same approximate number of federal employees as Washington D.C. Furthermore, California has the largest state bureaucracy compared to the other 49 states. Just like the rest of the country, California bureaucrats are the favorite scapegoats of politicians and businesses. Canada serves as an excellent example in comparative politics since Canada and America are considered sister countries. We have the same beginnings but we ended up on very different paths as nations. To paraphrase the words of Seymour Martin Lipset, the U.S. is the land of revolutionaries who fought for its independence with a loaded gun and Canada obtained their independence by much more peaceful means through the legislative process.

Key Terms:

Bureaucracy

Bureaucrat

Hierarchy

Independent Agencies

Administrative Discretion

Lend-Lease Act

Whistleblower

Francophone

Québécois

Websites:

The Federal Register
www. archives.gov/federal_register

Fedworld
http://www.fedworld.gov/

The President's Cabinet
www.whitehouse.gov/government/cabinet

California Sites

California State Homepage
www.ca.gov

California Secretary of State
www.ss.ca.gov

California Department of Transportation
www.dot.ca.gov

California Research Bureau
www.library.ca.gov

Border Region Information
www.borderrecoweb.sdsu.edu

This page left blank intentionally.

The U.S. Supreme Court, as of 2006:
(First Row L to R), Justices A. Kennedy, J.P. Stevens, Chief Justice J.G. Roberts, A. Scalia, D.H. Souter,
(Second Row L to R), Justice S. G. Breyer, C. Thomas, R. B. Ginsburg, and S. Alito.
© *Matthew Cavanaugh/epa/Corbis*

CHAPTER 12

THE JUDICIARY, LIBERTIES, AND RIGHTS

CHAPTER OUTLINE

Democracy and Action – Thurgood Marshall – First African American Associate Justice

In 1967, a major threshold was crossed in the United States. In an era known marked by much civil unrest, the very first African-American justice was appointed to the Supreme Court.

Thurgood Marshall was born in Baltimore, Maryland in 1908. His father, the son of a former slave, instilled in Thurgood an intense appreciation for the Constitution of the United States. After graduating from college, Thurgood wanted to apply to the law school at the University of Maryland, but was told that due to their segregation policy, he would not be admitted. Instead, he received his law degree from Howard University, and later devoted himself to fighting for the application of Constitutional rights to all Americans.

Thurgood Marshall, champion of civil rights and the first African American Associate Justice. Courtesy of the Library of Congress.

After setting up his law practice, he began working with the National Association for the Advancement of Colored People (NAACP), arguing cases before court in which a person's civil rights had been violated. At the age of 32, Marshall won his first Supreme Court case and was appointed as Chief Counsel for the NAACP.

Marshall won 29 of the 32 cases he argued before the United States Supreme Court, the most famous being Brown v. The Board of Education of Topeka. This momentous decision overturned the "separate but equal" doctrine that had been in place since 1896. Brown was responsible for making school segregation against the law. It was a giant victory for civil rights and one for which Marshall will always be remembered.

Marshall was appointed to the U.S. Court of Appeals by President John F. Kennedy in 1961, and in 1965, President Lyndon Johnson appointed him Solicitor General, making Marshall responsible for arguing the federal government's cases before the Supreme Court.

On June 13th 1967, upon the retirement of Justice Tom C. Clark, President Johnson made the historic appointment of Thurgood Marshall to the U.S. Supreme Court, with the statement that this was "the right thing to do, the right time to do it, the right man and the right place."

Marshall served on the Court for the next 24 years, compiling a record of strong support for the protection of individual rights, especially in the area of civil rights as well as in the area of criminal procedure. During his years as Supreme Court Justice, as the Court slowly became more conservative in its opinions, Justice Marshall earned himself the nickname the "Great Dissenter." With his eloquently written dissents, Marshall served as a sort of conscience for the Court, constantly siding with the "little" guy, as opposed to government interests.

Justice Marshall retired in 1991 and died of heart failure in 1993 at the age of 84. His legacy will be viewed through his constant championing of equal rights for everyone, first through his work as a civil rights attorney and then through his Supreme Court judicial opinions. Thurgood Marshall was truly an American revolutionary.[1]

Constitutional Powers of the Courts

It is the spirit and not the form of law that keeps justice alive. – Earl Warren

In many ways, the appointments and the rulings made in the Supreme Court impact our lives more than most political decisions. President George W. Bush's appointments of the new Chief Justice John Roberts and Associate Justice Samuel Alito have shown their willingness to move the Court to the right of the political spectrum on issues relating to search and seizure, free speech, campaign finance reform, and the powers of the executive branch. Court decisions that have impacted our society have been Earl Warren's 1954 case of *Brown v. Topeka School Board*, which desegregated schools across the nation; also, his 1965 case of Ernesto Miranda which places limits on police searches and requires a defendant to be told their rights. Warren Burger's opinion reinforced the Brown ruling in James Swann's case that legitimized busing as the method of school integration. In 1973, in the case of *Roe v. Wade*, Harry Blackmun's opinion granted women a right to choose to have an abortion for an unwanted pregnancy if they so desired. These are just a few of the main examples of the role in which the court play in shaping policy and how important the appointment process.

Chief Justice Warren Earl Burger, served under Pres. Nixon from 1969 – 1986. Courtesy of the Library of Congress.

While the Supreme Court has the ability to greatly alter the way we live our lives and how the Constitution is interpreted, the judiciary is the most undemocratic of the three branches of government. Nominated by the president, confirmed by the Senate, lifetime appointments, and deliberations in complete secrecy, this group of nine individuals can dictate the course of the nation for the next century. In the following sections of this chapter, you will see how the Court has evolved over the last two centuries and possibly gain some insight as to how the current, more conservative court will impact the next half century. In addition, we will examine the structure of the lower courts and the role they play in this symphony of Constitutional and legislative music.

In comparing Article III of the Constitution to Article I and II, one of the first comments usually made is how vague it is. In fact, it doesn't elaborate on the power of the court or details on how it should interact with the executive and legislative branches of government. The article creates the federal judiciary, the office of the chief justice, establishes their length of service and the types of cases the high court will hear, and gives power of Congress to create additional federal courts.

Expanding the Powers of the Court

One of the Supreme Court powers is not defined in Article III of the Constitution. The power of **judicial review** is an implied power. Since the first time it was used, the question of its validity has been in question. The concept had already been established in England before the framers in America began their deliberations at the Constitutional Convention. There is evidence that the concept was discussed but the framers intentionally omitted it from the final document.

In reviewing comments by those who attended the convention and others who opposed the Constitution, there was clearly a division on when and how the Constitution should be applied and interpreted. Most Americans at that time believed in the need of a rule of law and a document that conveyed their principles after their conflicts with the absolute power of the monarchy and parliament. Individuals like Jefferson and Madison held the view that the legislature and the executive were fully capable of upholding the Constitution. Others, like Hamilton, as discussed in The Federalist No. 78 (see appendix), felt that the Constitution limited the powers of the government and only the Court can prevent the passions of the legislature from overcoming their sensibilities.

Marbury v. Madison (1803)

This decision was the Court's first exercise of the judicial review. William Marbury had been named Washington D.C.'s justice of the peace by President John Adams and confirmed by the Senate in 1801 just before Thomas Jefferson took office. At the time of the appointment, John Marshall, Adam's Secretary of State, was chosen to serve as Chief Justice to the United States Supreme Courts. It was Marshall's responsibility to convey Marbury's commission. Marshall did not deliver it before

John Marshall, Secretary of State under Pres. Adams, served as Chief Justice of the U.S. Supreme Court, 1801 - 1835. Courtesy of the Library of Congress

turning the position over to Jefferson's secretary of state, James Madison. Marbury, having not received his commission, requested Madison to turn it over to him. Madison refused the demand. Marbury asked the Supreme Court for a **writ of mandamus** via a provision in the Judiciary Act of 1789. Chief Justice Marshall, when writing the Court's majority opinion, stated that Article III, Section 2, in the Constitution, which allows the Court to issue a writ of mandamus only under its jurisdiction as an appellate court.

Therefore, that section of the Judiciary Act of 1789 that allowed for such requests to be fast tracked to the Supreme Court was void. In a case where there is conflict between legislation and the Constitution, the legislation is found to be unconstitutional, based on Articles III and VI's supremacy clause of the Constitution. This case codified the court's power for judicial review and implied powers.

While this act may have looked as an attempt to avoid a showdown with the executive branch, what it actually did was strengthen the power of the court by placing itself in the position as the final arbitrator of what is and is not constitutional. However, they have been reluctant to use this power for fear of reprisal from the legislative and executive branches. It wasn't until a half century later after the case took place before it was used again. Between 1855 and 2000, the Supreme Court has ruled approximately 150 federal acts and laws as

Judicial Review – The power of the Supreme Court established in *Marbury v. Madison* to overturn acts of the president, Congress, and the states if they commit acts that violate the Constitution. Essentially determines the Supreme Court as the final interpreter of the Constitution.

Writ of Mandamus – A court order that forces an official to act.

unconstitutional. However, the Court has proven to be more forceful with the states and local municipalities in ruling their acts and laws to be unconstitutional over 1,000 times within the same time frame.

Additional Powers

In addition to judicial review, the court has two other powers. In adopting the power of **statuary construction**, the Court can discern what state and federal laws are saying. In some laws the intent of the legislature is not clearly stated because the wording is so convoluted. Therefore the Court is forced to decipher what the original intent of the law was, based on their interpretation. Statuary construction is not used very often, instead the Court uses its next power more than any other powers previously stated.

More often than not, the Court uses its power to do nothing at all and allow for the lower courts' ruling to stand. The Supreme Court can do this just by refusing to review a case. There are thousands of petitions sent to the Court asking the Justice to review cases, but only a couple of hundred are selected. Most of the cases are selected not because of individual issues but on an overarching Constitutional question, where the Court can combine several cases into a single issue.

Independent Judiciary

The framers of the Constitution believed in the concept of an independent judiciary. In order to ensure the judiciary would not be penalized by the executive or Congress, the Constitution provided for safeguards for the Judiciary from reprisals. The Justices are nominated by the president and confirmed by the Senate, the Justices are appointed for life, and Congress is prevented from lowering the salaries of the Justices while they are serving on the bench.

While the Court is independent, it can be influenced by the president and Congress. The president can change the direction of the Court by the type of Justice he nominates, as in the case of Chief Justice Roberts and Associate Justice Alito, who were nominated by President George W. Bush and approved by the Republican controlled Senate, thus moving the Court further to the right. The president can refuse to fill any vacancies on the Court. Congress can influence the Court as well. They can pass legislation that overturns Court decisions, increase the number of justices on the Court, or refuse to approve the president's nominees, which hinders nominations from proceeding. This increases the lower courts workload and ultimately slows down the legal process.

Courts – Types & Organizations

As you'll read in the section on California courts, most of the state courts mirror the federal court system. In comparing the federal courts to the state courts, most of the cases are handled at the state and local levels. Most state cases are criminal and civil in nature and on occasion, state constitutional issues. The federal courts focus on federal laws that the U.S. Constitution issues. The two systems are separate but from time to time do overlap. When state issues cross over into federal jurisdiction, such as in cases regarding Constitutional questions, the federal courts take the case over. There are three levels to the federal court system, the lower federal courts, which are the **trial courts**, these are where the case originates, the **appellate courts** or circuit courts, and the U.S. Supreme Court.

Statuary Construction – The power of the Supreme Court to interpret or reinterpret a federal or state law.

Trial Court – The point of original entry in the legal system, with a singly judge and at times a jury deciding matters of both fact and law in a case.

Appellate Courts – The court that reviews an appeal of the trial court proceedings, often with a panel of several judges but without a jury; it considers only matters of law.

Trial Courts

The trial court is the court of original jurisdiction, which is simply where the case begins. A trial court is designed to have a single judge presiding over the case and give instructions to the jury or attorneys. During the course of the trial, the judge discerns what the facts of the case are and how the law should be applied. If there is a jury, the judge provides instructions as to how the jury should behave, what is and is not admissible, and answers any questions the jury may have regarding statutes, sentencing guidelines, or constitutional questions.

The appellate court is designed to review the hearing of the lower court and does not allow for the introduction of new evidence. A panel of judges reviews the trial transcripts to see if the trial judge violated any laws or procedures. After review the appellate court will either require a new hearing or stay with the lower court's decision.

In reviewing how this system works, an illustration would go something like this: a man walks into a liquor store and holds it up. He is caught on the store's video-tape which leads to his arrest and charge. During the trial his attorney tries to have the tape excluded because it was shown on the evening news which created a bias against her client. The trial judge allows the tape to be admitted as evidence and shown to the jury. The accused is found guilty and sentenced to 7 years in prison. The defense attorney submit an appeal to the appellate court restating her objection to the tape being admitted as evidence requests the court to review the trial transcript. The three-judge panel reviews the transcript and the tape and rules that the lower court's ruling stands.

Structure of the Federal Courts

There are three main levels to the structure of the federal courts. The U.S. Supreme Court at the top level, the appellate or circuit courts on the second level, and the district courts on the third level. All three of these courts are called **constitutional courts** because they are brought up in Article III of the Constitution.

The district courts are the original trial courts. On a yearly average, the 94 district courts with at least one in every state have approximately 400,000 cases filed with them. There are approximately 700 jurists who hear and review the legality of the complaints. The cases that are filed with the district courts are not only violations of federal law in terms of civil and criminal, but also reviewing the actions of federal that are filed at the federal level are decided here.

The second level is the federal court of appeals also known as circuit courts (called this because the jurist used to travel or "ride the circuit" tour to hear their cases). There are 13 appellate courts across the nations with 11 of them having multi-state jurisdiction. The Twelfth Circuit

Courtesy of Corel.

court is located in the District of Columbia and is considered to be the second most important court after the U.S. Supreme Court because of the number federal cases it reviews from the federal regulatory commission and other agencies.

Constitutional Courts –
Federal courts created by Congress under the authority of Article III of the Constitution.

Legislative Courts –
Highly specialized federal courts created by Congress under the authority of Article I of the Constitution.

The Thirteenth Circuit is the U.S. Court of Appeals for the Federal Circuit. The cases for the Thirteenth Circuit are focused on appeals regarding patents and contract claims against the federal government. There are approximately 170 jurists who receive and review over 60,000 appeals from lower courts.

The decisions from the appellate courts are diverse in nature, mainly because of political ideology. Conservative jurists have the majority (nine of the courts) with two more teetering in their direction. The Ninth Circuit, which covers the western states of California, Alaska, Hawaii, Montana, Idaho, Oregon, Washington, and Nevada, is the only one that is controlled by liberal jurists. Under the Rehnquist Court, the majority of appeals to the U.S. Supreme Court from the Ninth Circuit were overturned, compared to the more conservative southern Fourth and Fifth Circuits who enjoyed having the majority of their appeals upheld by the Supreme Court.

In addition to the constitutional courts, there are **legislative courts**, which were created from Article I, Section 8, of the Constitution are also considered appellate courts. Legislative courts are designed for a specific area of the law, such as the U.S. Court of Military Appeals, and the U.S. Tax Court. These jurists serve for fixed terms. Any rulings by the legislative courts can automatically be appealed to the constitutional courts.

With the changes in global relations over the last thirty years, the courts have had to change as well. In 1978 the Foreign Intelligence Act (FISA) created a secret court that consisted of eleven federal jurists who were appointed for seven year terms. This court reviews federal intelligence agency requests for search warrants for electronic wiretaps, secret searches, and other issues that relate to national security but can not be disclosed to the public. After September 11th a new court was created, the Alien Terrorist Removal Court, which reviews deportation orders for legal aliens who are suspected of engaging in terrorist acts. The jurists are selected by the chief justice of the U.S. Supreme Court.

How Judges Are Appointed

In a democratic society, the appointment process is extremely important considering that jurists are appointed to serve life terms. The only step that the public is allowed to weigh in on is during the hearing before the Senate Judiciary Committee where citizens can voice their opinions to the respective Senators. Aside from this, the process is almost void of democratic oversight.

Judicial Appointments

Article III of the Constitution does not stipulate any requirements for serving as a justice or a judge in the lower courts. By custom, many of the nominees are attorneys, almost half of whom have never served as a jurist prior to the appointment. Some of the less experienced jurists on the Supreme Court have proven to be some of the most influential, such as John Marshall, Louis Brandeis, and Earl Warren.

Sandra Day O'Connor was the first female associate justice, serving from 1981 to 2006. She was often the deciding vote in controversial decisions, especially regarding women's rights, between liberal and conservative justices. Courtesy of the Library of Congress.

Similar to the other branches of the federal government, the judicial system has been dominated by upper-class, white, Protestant, males. It wasn't until the 1960's that the nation had its first African American justice, Thurgood Marshall (see the opening vignette) and the second African American justice was Clarence Thomas. It wasn't until the 1980s that the first woman justice was appointed to the bench, Sandra Day O'Connor and shortly thereafter the second woman justice, Ruth Bader Ginsburg was also nominated. In terms of religious representation on the high court, there have only been nine Catholics and seven Jews who have served. The lower courts tend to be much better in terms of representation but on the whole, the judicial system is still not nearly as representative of the American public as one would like to see.

Table 12.1 - Chief Justices of the Supreme Court of the United States[2]			
NAME	STATE APPOINTED FROM	APPOINTED BY PRESIDENT	DATES OF SERVICE
John Jay	New York	Washington	1789 - 1795
John Rutledge	South Carolina	Washington	1795 - 1795
Oliver Ellsworth	Connecticut	Washington	1796 - 1800
John Marshall	Virginia	Adams	1801 - 1835
Roger Taney	Maryland	Jackson	1836 - 1864
Salmon Chase	Ohio	Lincoln	1864 - 1873
Morrison Waite	Ohio	Grant	1874 - 1888
William Taft	Connecticut	Cleveland	1888 - 1910
Charles Hughes	New York	Hoover	1910 - 1921
Harlan Stone	New York	F. Roosevelt	1930 - 1941
Fred Vinson	Kentucky	Truman	1946 - 1853
Earl Warren	California	Eisenhower	1953 - 1969
Warren Burger	Virginia	Nixon	1969 - 1986
William Rehnquist	Virginia	Reagan	1986 - 2005
John Roberts, Jr.	Maryland	Bush, G.W.	2005 -

The Process

A president views his judicial appointments as an extension of his policies after he has left office. With that, every possible consideration is given to a nominee.

The president usually weighs all factors before making her or his selection. He will often consult with his advisers, with the ranking members of the Senate, and the Senate Judiciary Committee, for fear of having their nomination rejected or reprisals from the Senate on other parts of his legislative agenda. The Constitution requires the Senate to advice and consent on presidential nominations. Since the founding of the Republic, the Senate has only rejected 29 nominations, 5 within the twentieth century and 1 in 2005. Many long term court watchers were surprised when President George W. Bush went against this semi-tradition and nominated close friends and allies to district and appellate seats. In addition, in nominations to the U.S. Supreme Court, President Bush seemed to place his religious convictions above party loyalty or custom.[3] This has caused the Senate Democrats to filibuster his nominations, as well as one of his Supreme Court nominees, long time friend Harriet Miers to be withdrawn after intense conflicts with the Senate and conservatives over her credentials.[4]

As discussed in chapter 9, partisan politics have increased within the last few decades. This division has carried over into the judicial nomination process. When the Senate was controlled by Republicans under President Bill Clinton, the Judiciary Committee held up a number of his nominations to the lower courts. When President George W. Bush took office, the Senate Democrats filibustered a number of his judicial nominations to the point where the Senate Republicans almost used the "nuclear option" (see chapter 9).

During the selections process, presidents try to match their nominees' political values with their own. John Adams wanted to maintain the Federalist stronghold by packing the courts with his midnight appointment after losing the elections to Thomas Jefferson. President Roosevelt packed the lower courts and threatened to increase the size of the Supreme Court in order for the New Deal to be implemented. President Reagan placed conservative jurists who would remove parts of the New Deal, the Great Society, and affirmative action. This was continued by both George H.W. Bush and George W. Bush.

President Clinton wanted to use his political capital on the passage of NAFTA so he nominated two moderates, Ruth Bader Ginsberg and Stephen Breyer, during his first term. On the lower courts, his nominations reflected his position on creating a diverse federal government. Over half of his nominations to the courts were women and others were minorities.

On occasion, presidents are often disappointed in their selections once the jurist takes oath. President Eisenhower was beside himself when Chief Justice Earl Warren caused the Court to overhaul the nation's civil rights policies. President Nixon was speechless when Chief Justice Burger voted to override his claim of executive privilege with regards to Watergate. President George H.W. Bush was disappointed when Justice Souter refused to overturn a woman's right to choose in *Planned Parenthood v. Casey* in 1992. Aside from these examples, the Justices who are nominated are a fair indicator as to how the high court will rule. Many judicial observers are waiting to see what Chief Justice Roberts will do on issues relating to privacy, and the broadening of the executive powers.

Profiles in Politics
Earl Warren (1891 - 1974)

Earl Warren (1891 – 1974) devoted his life to public service, and profoundly changed the basic tenets of society in the United States and the world. Earl Warren served as Governor of California, ran for President, and as Chief Justice of the Supreme Court wrote the landmark desegregation decision *Brown v. Board of Education*, which changed the direction of civil rights law and the whole debate on racial equality in America.

Earl Warren was born in Los Angeles and grew up in Bakersfield. His father worked for the railroad, as did the younger Warren during the summers. This exposed him to the issues of the working class and racial discrimination, especially the anti-Asian sentiments common in California at the time. He went on to study political science and law at The University of California at Berkeley, graduating in 1914. He practiced law in the San Francisco area, and in 1919 joined the District Attorney's office in Oakland.[5] Warren spent the rest of his professional career serving the public. In 1926, he was elected District Attorney in Oakland and established a reputation as a crime fighter. He established broad bi-partisan support because of his centrist to liberal views, and was elected Attorney General of California in 1938. In 1942, he was elected Governor, and is the only person to be elected to that office for 3 consecutive terms. So broad was his support, he won the election in 1946 unopposed, after winning the primaries for the Democratic, Republican, and Progressive parties.

Chief Justice Earl Warren served from 1953-1969.
Courtesy of the Library of Congress.

One interesting example of his progressive tendencies was his initiative (unsuccessful) for universal health-care. However, he also was vocal in demanding the internment of the Japanese during World War II. Warren always defended that action, stating that it was the correct thing to do at the time. In his memoirs, however, he acknowledged the error.

Warren ran for vice-president as Republican Thomas Dewey's running mate 1948, only to lose in the famous upset to Harry Truman. Four years later, he unsuccessfully ran for the Republican nomination. However, when Dwight Eisenhower won the nomination, he supported his candidacy and was instrumental in his election. Eisenhower rewarded Warren in 1953 with a recess appointment as Chief Justice of the Supreme Court after the death of Justice Fred Vinson.

Warren joined the Court at a point in its history when it was deeply divided between justices who advocated a more active role and justices who believed in judicial restraint. The Court was just about to deliberate on the case of Linda Brown, who was denied admission to her local elementary school in Topeka Kansas because she was African-American. Warren recognized the social and political implications of finding in favor of Brown. It would overturn centuries of racial tradition and over 50 years of legal precedent, including the concept of "separate but equal" from the 1896 decision of *Plessy v. Ferguson*.[6] Warren proved himself an exceptionally skilled jurist, "amassing the court" and securing consensus for a unanimous decision from his divided justices in favor of Brown. This told the nation that the court was of a single, unambiguous voice on the issue of civil rights and racial

Profiles in Politics
Earl Warren (1891 - 1974)

equality. Of course, the country would struggle over the issue of "race" for the next decade and beyond, but it is interesting to speculate how the debate would have been different if opponents had seen an opportunity for reversal in a slim court majority.

Warren's decision in *Brown* is fascinating in that he does appeal to precedent, the 14th amendment, or even an analysis of the Constitution. Instead, (to the disappointment of believers in judicial restraint) there is an emphasis on common sense, justice, fairness and a reliance on social science and psychological research. Warren believed that Government played an important role in society. However, he concluded that the Constitution did not allow it to act unfairly against the individual. This established the Court as a protector of civil rights and civil liberties, a profound change in the role of the government.

The court under Warren would go on to pass a series of important cases in support of the individual over the government. After he retired from the court in 1969, he concluded that his greatest contributions were a series of cases which opened the way to legislative and Congressional reapportionment, in which he reinforced the principle of "one man, one vote."   These cases resulted in a major shift in legislative power from rural areas to the cities. His court also decided cases establishing the right of a defendant to counsel (*Gideon vs. Wainright*, 1963) and protections from police abuses (*Miranda vs. Arizona*, 1966).[7]

In 1963, Warren chaired the commission investigating the assassination of President Kennedy. Warren was reluctant, concerned that his service could tarnish the court's reputation. Nevertheless, President Johnson convinced him to chair the commission.   The commission was given

unrestricted investigatory power, and was directed by the President to evaluate all the evidence. Afterward, he was to present a complete report of the event to the American people. The findings of the Warren Commission were and remain controversial. It firmly refuted rampant speculation that the assassination was the result of a government conspiracy, stating that Lee Harvey Oswald acted alone. Those who were prone to believe in conspiracy discounted the Commission's findings. Never-

Pres. Johnson signing the Civil Rights Bill into law. Courtesy of the Library of Congress.

theless, the Warren Commission addressed painful questions after a shocking national tragedy, and possibly may have helped calm some of the social and political tensions of a very tense decade.

Earl Warren retired as Chief Justice in 1969, after 15 years on the Court and nearly 50 years of public service. He died in 1974, after opening society to a legacy and tradition of the rights of the individual over his government.

The Supreme Court Decides

Once appointed and confirmed, justices must adhere to justice etiquette, which has come to mean how the Court conducts itself. The Court has its own code of cultural and social rules. Justices must maintain a guarded attitude and stay as separate and detached from the public and media as possible. This gives the Courts a certain mystique and respectability which is also expected of the secretaries and clerks who work with the justices. Even with all of this secrecy, humans have their flaws and breaches in security occasionally occur.

Not only are the justices expected to follow the preset attitudes and etiquette of their positions, but they are also expected to rule the same way. This means they are to refer to precedent when making decisions on cases. In this case, the adage, "this is how we always do things" is entirely appropriate and proper. When departures from precedent have taken place, which is allowed but highly irregular, it erodes the ground-breaking accomplishments achieved in landmark cases, such as the near overturning of *Roe v. Wade* or the recent McCain-Feingold upsets that occurred in 2007, under the Court ruled large parts of the law as unconstitutional because it violated corporations and unions free speech by placing limits on when they could air the campaign commercials. Depending which way the political pendulum swings, some changes in precedent may appear to be a change whose time has come or a change that will set justice back a number years, never to be regained for the greater good again.

Setting the Agenda

So as not to get bogged down in non-essential cases, the Court has certain processes in place that sift through lesser cases and retain more significant ones that may address federal or constitutional issues. Just controlling the sheer volume of cases requires the Court to make sure the cases are a genuine disagreement between two parties that cannot resolve the issue in the lower courts to a satisfactory degree. The sincerity of the disputants must be obvious and deliberate, meaning that their "standing" is true and straightforward. Furthermore, the case cannot be hypothetical – the injury must have actually occurred for the Court to even consider taking it. Defining exactly what kinds of guidelines are determined for proper standing is up to the Court; their strictness or laxness may directly affect access for the plaintiff.

The Supreme Court is named as such because it is the highest court in the land. Therefore, once a case reaches the Supreme Court, it must have gone through all the proper protocol and be "ripe" for the picking. This means that all possible appeals have been attempted within the appropriate timeline, all paperwork filed correctly and completely, all fees paid or accounted for through affidavit **in forma pauperis**, and, as stated above, must not be a "what if" dispute – the injury must have actually already taken place.

An important and powerful tool that the Court has at its disposal is the **writ of certiorari**. The grant of "cert" is when the Court decides that a case raises a worthy federal or constitutional issue. The **rule of four** means that favorable votes of at least four justices are needed in order for a petition to be granted cert. This is easier said than done because these types of cases are usually very controversial and challenging to the harmony of the Court, often provoking split decisions. If the Court decides to deny cert then the decisions reached in the lower court stand.

In forma pauperis –
"In the manner of a pauper" – when the filing fee is waived if the petitioner is very poor; this guarantees the right of all defendants to have representation, even in criminal cases.

Writ of Certiorari –
A grant of "cert" is the Courts' decision that an appellate case is a significant federal or constitutional case.

Rule of Four –
The votes needed for justices to vote in favor of granting cert to a petition.

After a case is granted cert, oral arguments must be presented. It is to the attorney's advantage to address issues that the justices are interested in considering. This comes in the form of briefs that are submitted by other interested individuals, interest groups, or other organizations in the federal government that have a vested interest in the case. The official title of these briefs is called amicus curiae briefs, or "friend of the court" brief. Sometimes, even the president may submit an amicus curiae if the case is significant to his or her agenda. See the For Your Consideration on amicus curiae briefs below.

When Court issues a ruling, there are usually three types of opinions explaining their rationale. The **opinion of the Court** is the majority's written opinion. A **concurring opinion** is the opinion by a justice who agrees with the majority but for different legal reasons. The **dissenting opinion** is the rationale by the minority as to why they felt the majority was incorrect in their ruling. History has shown that dissenting opinions can lead to future Court majorities.

After the hearing, the justices will meet in a conference to deliberate on the merits of the case. Once all of the justices state their positions and why, the conference is then opened to questions and answers. Once the session is over, the Chief will assign the opinions to be written. Writing an opinion is one of the powers a Chief Justice uses to influence the other justices. In assigning the writings of opinions, the Chief, if in the majority, has the option to write the opinion themselves or assign it to another member. If the Chief is in the minority, then the most senior ranking member in the majority will get the assignment. Any member of the majority can write a concurring opinion if expressing how they reach the same outcome through a different line of logic.

Once the assignments are given, the author has the ability to work using law clerks and also justices in drafting their opinion. The process usually entails numerous revisions as members often offer suggestions on reasoning and wording. In addition, the author can turn to the logic of an amicus brief as a resource in drafting their opinion.

After the opinions are drafted, they are presented to the other jurists in a conference. The justices may change their earlier vote if they find the majority opinion compelling. If there is a concerning opinion that conveys the majority positions better, it can become the majority opinion and the original majority opinion can become a concurring opinion.

Opinion of the Court – The majority opinion that accompanies a Supreme Court decision.

Concurring Opinion – The opinion of one or more judges who vote with the majority on a case but wish to set out different reasons for their decision.

Dissenting Opinion – The opinion of the judge or judges who are in the minority on a particular case before the Supreme Court.

FOR YOUR CONSIDERATION
AMICUS CURIAE BRIEFS

Courtesy of Jupiter Images

Amicus curiae briefs, or amicus briefs for short, are literally defined as "friend of the court" briefs. These types of briefs are often filed in Supreme Court cases by people and organizations not affiliated with the case at hand, but who believe they may be able to provide the Court with information pertinent to the case.

Advocacy groups such as the ACLU often file amicus briefs for cases where a decision is expected to have ramifications for a number of people or groups. The briefs may contain information on a point of law or the organization's reasoning and a description of the effects a decision would have on the group for which the organization advocates. Sometimes, the group filing an amicus brief is a state that is concerned about possible effects the decisions would have on that state.[8]

Cases are given one hour with 30 minute rebuttal time built in. These arguments are presented in the context of a meeting between the lawyers and justices, or sometimes just between the justices alone.

Cases that tend to attract more amicus briefs are any that deal with First Amendment rights or civil rights. Also, any case that is noteworthy (or notorious) generally attracts many briefs as well. The more amicus briefs filed on behalf of a case, the more likely it is to be heard by the Supreme Court.[9]

The Policy Maker, the Supreme Court

As you will read in the California section, the federal Supreme Court has acted in a political capacity that affects public policy with no real intent of doing so. Controversial issues that stir the American people, such as abortion and the right to privacy have far-reaching effects after the Court lays down its decisions. Despite the powerful role the Court plays in making policy, it does not forget that the case went through scrutiny and judgment in the lower courts, making this a concerted effort in the judicial system.

Constitutional interpretations and opinions of policymaking cases have evolved over time, which is usually evaluated in terms of four eras or stages. Many of these significant events are discussed all over throughout the text. What follows are brief accounts of a few notable accomplishments, milestones (either negative or positive, depending on your point of view) or important cases, and significant individuals' or concepts' "claim to fame."

Laissez-faire –
The political-economic doctrine that holds that government ought not interfere with the operations of the free market.

Structures in the Judiciary

Stage 1 – From the Framers to the Civil War (1700's to 1860's). Obviously, in a nation just finding its legs, much growth and miles are covered in 75 years.

- **Notables:** Chief Justice John Marshall shaped the personality of the Supreme Court and the future greatness of the American Constitution as law from 1801 – 1835, influenced by the robust and outspoken writings of Alexander Hamilton.

- **Important cases:** *Fletcher v. Peck* (1810), *McCulloch v. Maryland* (1819), and *Gibbons v. Ogden* (1824).

- **Claim to Fame for Justice Marshall:** Interpreted Constitution as law to mean that it offers the maximum protection of property and nationalism.

Stage 2 – After the Civil War to the Great Depression (late 19th century to the early 20th century). Mass-production in a new industrial economy determined the role of government to be betwixt the economy and the people.

- **Notables:** Civil War, Industrial Revolution, triggers the rise of the big business corporation. The question was raised of both state and federal governments, to regulate or not to regulate corporations?

- **Important milestones:** the Supreme Court as powerful interpreter of the Constitution and ally to business interests; **laissez-faire** as part of an economical attitude is reflected in actions of the Court to squelch several state and federal governmental efforts: welfare assistance for the poor, regulation of monopolies, income tax, regulation of railroad rates, scholarships for students, regulation of working conditions, wages, and hours, and safety precautions and protection for consumers. The Court went so far as to condone judicial injunctions to cease formation of labor unions and strikes.

- **Claims to Fame for the Constitution and Teddy Roosevelt:** The 14th Amendment, Section 1 passed to guarantee the rights of newly recognized citizens, freed slaves. By the time the Great Depression hit, the expanded responsibilities of the federal government's New Deal demolished the Supreme Courts partnership with big business. The Court passes the Social Security Act, Labor Relations Act, and state minimum wage laws in 1937.

Stage 3 – WWII (1940's) to the mid 1980's. The World War II efforts shifted government's focus to the civil liberties and rights of the individual, discussed later in this chapter.

- **Notables:** The young soldiers, nurses, and Rosie Riveters all roll up their sleeves and join the country in supporting our troops; families all across the nation make sacrifices and live leaner lives; the internment of Japanese-Americans after Pearl Harbor blurs the lines of right and wrong.

- **Important milestones:** Leaps and bounds in equality for minorities because of *Mendez v. Westminster* and *Brown v. Board*, "one person, one vote" (see chapter one).

- **Claims to Fame for Chief Justice Earl Warren:** Many significant triumphs for fair trials, religious expression, and free expression and association during Warren's tenure; the Bill of Rights is applied to the states.

Chief Justice Roy Moore of Alabama Supreme Court installed a 5,000 lb monument to the 10 Commandments. The U.S. 11th Circuit Court ordered him to have it removed because it violates the separation of church and state.
© Jamie Martin/epa/Corbis

Stage 4 – mid-1980's to the present. With the election of President Reagan and George H.W. Bush, the nation gradually turns to a born-again conservatism that in turn, affects the sanctity of former cases dealing with individual rights, liberties, even gun control; a return to laissez-faire style of government.

- **Notables:** The neo-conservatives want to overhaul federalism and reinstate "states rights" and curtail past actions of Congress with the Interstate Commerce Clause; the reign of the conservative Supreme and the swing vote was apparent in the four conservative justices, Rehnquist (Chief Justice), Kennedy, Scalia, Thomas and the four liberals, Ginsberg, Stevens, Souter, and Breyer with the swing vote being O'Connor.

FOR YOUR CONSIDERATION
JUDICIAL ACTIVISM

There has been a lot of discussion and argument about judicial activism in the past few years. Most of this discussion has revolved around the question of what makes an ideal Supreme Court justice. Although both conservatives and liberals claim no affection for judicial activism and conservatives especially tend to describe themselves as "strict constructionists" or "originalists" (both just fancy wording for advocating judicial restraint,) in actuality, both ideological camps are quite fond of so-called judicial activism when it serves their purposes.

The term judicial activism generally infers that the court has broadly interpreted the case before them, and is usually influenced by the "spirit of the times and the needs of the nation."[10] The courts have used this type of constitutional interpretation actively for more than 200 years.

To see where judicial activism began, one must look back to the landmark U.S. Supreme Court case *Marbury v. Madison*. Writing for the majority, then Chief Justice John Marshall writes "It is emphatically the…duty of the judicial department to say what the law is" and "that a law repugnant to the Constitution is void."[11] This historic decision gave the Supreme Court wide latitude to interpret the law in accordance with the Constitution with no limitations.

Since then, there have been many instances of judicial activism. Many times, such as in the case *Griswold v. Connecticut*, the Court ruled that married couples had the right to use contraceptives, inferring that the Fourteenth Amendment includes a right to privacy. In this case, activism was, hands down, the proper and right way to interpret the Constitution. Another example, *Mapp v. Ohio*, where the Court ruled that state courts must "exclude from criminal cases any evidence found during an 'unreasonable' search or seizure,"[12] illustrates the necessity of judicial activism; to not read this broadly would be contradictory to the purpose of the Bill of Rights.

Issues For You
Considering the Constitution was written over 200 years ago, do you think judicial activism is necessary for the modern era? Why or why note?

Of course, conservatives who say that judicial activism is bad will hold that the only proper way to interpret the constitution is through the "original intent" of the Framers. Not only is it next to impossible to ascertain what the original intent of the Framers was, but many of these vocal conservatives fall silent when judicial activism results in an outcome favorable to their causes. One example would be *Kimel v. Florida Board of Regents*, where the Court ruled that citizens had no right to sue their own states, when in fact there is no such prohibition in the Constitution.[13] Another prime example of judicial activism suiting conservative needs can be seen in the case of *Bush v. Gore*, where the Supreme Court used the weak argument of equal protection to stop the Florida recount during the 2000 presidential election. Apparently, judicial activism is not strictly limited to liberals; it also appears to appeal to conservatives just as much.

- **Important milestones (that advanced the conservative agenda):** Court overturns federal law banning guns in neighborhood areas near public schools (1995) and the federal statute that barred age discrimination in the workplace;

- **Claims to Fame for State Sovereign Immunity:** the 11th amendment is used in several instances, giving the Court broad latitude to say that the states have expansive immunity from interference from the national government; this includes any lawsuits by state employees under the Americans with Disabilities Act (ADA) (2001); also, the states are protected from rulings instigated by federal agencies when they take action on complaints regarding private individuals (2002).

Overturning Prior Decisions

Even though deference is given to precedent when ruling on cases, some Courts have not had an issue with overturning prior Courts decisions. The Courts of Warren, Burger, and Rehnquist have shown little restraint when it comes to reversing their positions. The most often cited case for this was under Chief Justice Earl Warren when Brown overturned the long standing precedent of *Plessy v. Ferguson* (1896).

Ruling on "Political" Issues

Many political observers become concerned with the Court venturing too far into the political arena. In recent years, critics of the Court have claimed that the justices are adjudicating too many political issues that should be left up to the other branches of government. Supporters claim that the Court needs to take action when the other branches of government are violating individual freedoms and liberties. The case of *Bush v. Gore* created a firestorm of criticisms when the Court made its ruling only apply to this one case. Critics contend that this shows that the Court knew they had gone too far and yet still proceeded into dangerous waters by stopping the recount, resulting in the House of Representatives taking the final vote, as stipulated in the Constitution.

Part of the debate surrounding judicial activism has to do with the concept of **original intention**. Those who support the original intent and **strict construction** of the framers and the Constitution are concerned with preserving what the framers wanted when drafting the Constitution. The added rights and liberties that have been granted in the twentieth century, such as the right to privacy, are not based on the framer's vision or wording and are therefore not protected by the Constitution. Those who oppose this view complain that the framers were unable to exercise foresight during the drafting of the Constitution. Furthermore, the guidelines are almost draconian and impossible to know their true intent. They claim that the Constitution is in need of a modern evaluation instead of a historical one.

In light of all of the issues facing the nation, the Court in the modern era is more active than its counterparts of yester years. Because of this, the Court will continue to raise important issues about judicial activism and the government's relationship with the Courts will continue to evolve with the times.

Original Intent – The doctrine that the courts must interpret the Constitution in ways consistent with the framers rather than with modern times.

Strict Construction – The doctrine that the provisions of the Constitution have a clear meaning and that judges must adhere to this when rendering decisions.

FOR YOUR CONSIDERATION
THE NAACP

The oldest civil rights organization in the United States, the National Association for the Advancement of Colored People, or NAACP, was formed in 1909 by a small multi-ethnic group of concerned citizens in response to the "race" riots that occurred in Illinois in 1908. In the tradition of the abolitionist movements of the past, it was an organization borne out of a wish to see that "colored folks" are treated equally.[14]

Aug, 28, 1963 - Civil rights march on Washington, D.C. Courtesy of the Library of Congress.

Their first order of business was choosing a launch date. Since it was coming up, it was decided that Lincoln's birthday would be the appropriate date to unveil their group. They posted notices in the paper and were officially launched in February 1909. Their task was to strive for equal rights for everyone, including an assessment of the nation's progress in civil rights since the Emancipation Proclamation. They held their first convention in May 1909 in New York and by the end of their first year of existence, they had a national membership numbering in the hundreds, both black and white. Their sole mission was to work together to assure that the rights and liberties given to citizens in the Constitution be equally and justly applied to *all* citizens, regardless of "color."[15]

Today, the NAACP has chapters around the world and boasts a huge membership. It still holds its national conference every year, and now has units within the organization for legal advocacy, policy advocacy, and youth advocacy, among others. The NAACP has been a driving force in ending the Jim Crow laws of the South, promoting desegregation, and fighting against "racist" organizations such as the Ku Klux Klan. One hundred years later, the NAACP is still at the forefront in the fight for civil rights.[16]

Influences on the Court

As the Court has become more active as a policy maker, it has found itself more open to outside influences than it has in the past.

Competition with the Other Branches

Test Case –
A case brought to force a ruling on the constitutionality of some law or executive action.

In *The Federalist, No. 78* (see appendix), Hamilton states the Court has neither the power of the "purse or sword" to force compliance with its decisions so it must rely on the other branch's respect for the rule of law, the Constitution, and the role of the Court, in the hopes that others will adhere to the rulings. Therefore the Supreme Court should refrain from being too political and base its opinions, not on their political ideology but on what is best for the nation and the public good. If the Court does become too political it risks the possibility of eroding its influence with the other branches, thus weakening its powers. Some political observers are concerned with the recent appointments to the high Court. Their concern is in regards to their conservative political philosophy and loyalty to the executive who put them there. Chief Justice Roberts is keenly aware of the dilemma the Court will be in if it becomes too political. As a legal scholar, he knows the issues prior Courts have faced. Many long time court watchers have noted that the new Chief looks at the merits of a case and sets aside his political ideology.[17]

Outside Influences

Interest Groups. Aside from submitting amicus briefs and lobbying the Senate and president on judicial nominations, they have another tactic to push their agenda. A **test case** is used to challenge the constitutionally of a law. If a group wants to bypass the legislative process, they can file a complaint in a district court challenging the validity of a statute or a previous ruling by the court. Take for example the law passed in South Dakota in 2006 banning all abortions except for when a woman's life was endangered. This case was a test case directed at challenging *Roe v. Wade*.[18]

Class action suits. Class action suits are cases that are filed on behalf of individuals who have experienced a similar problem with the same company or industry. The growing industry of cell phone providers is a complicated and oversaturated business. In 2004, a law firm in California filed for a class action suit against cell phone providers for over charging their customers for nights and weekend minutes. In the following years, other class action suits had been filed against the same providers for billing errors and other related issues. You may not even realize that you were a participant in a class action suit until you get a notice from our judiciary system stating the specifics of the case. You may even receive a check in the mail, albeit usually a very low amount, simply because you purchased the product that is being sued.

Public Opinion. People may think that the Court is free from public opinion because they do not have to run for office and they are appointed for life. While this is true to some degree, the Court has conformed to public opinion on various issues. As noted earlier, the Court changed its position on the New Deal programs after President Roosevelt won a landslide reelection in 1936. The main job of the Court in these situations is to protect an individual's freedoms against the public's passions. In reviewing the Court's ruling on Congress's Flag Protection Act of 1989 in *United State v. Eichman* (1990) where the Court ruled the act as unconstitutional because if violated a persons First Amendment's rights of free speech. As Justice Brennan stated in the majorities opinion:

"While flag desecration -- like virulent ethnic and religious epithets, vulgar repudiations of the draft, and scurrilous caricatures -- is deeply offensive to many, the Government may not prohibit the expression of an idea simply because society finds the idea itself offensive or disagreeable."[19]

Sunset Clause – A provision that terminates or repeals all or portions of a law after a specific date, unless further legislative action is taken to extend it.

Civil Liberties & Civil Rights

A Bill of Rights is what the people are entitled to against every government, and what no just government should refuse, or rest on inference.
– Thomas Jefferson

The Patriot Act -
Necessary to Fight Terror or an Assault on Civil Liberties?

On September 11th 2001, the United States was thrust into a brave new world by force; as the World Trade Center towers toppled under attack by a rogue terrorist group, it became apparent that our country would never be the same.

Since the "war on terrorism" began, there has been increased surveillance across the nation in order to catch or prevent another terrorist attack. Courtesy of Jupiter Images.

During the first few months after the attacks, patriotism was at a level unseen for decades, if ever. The country was on a high, if you will. There was no need to question the actions of our government, especially if it was all done in the interest of our national security. Thus began the "War on Terror". One of the first reactions our government had to the terrorist attacks of

September 11th was to draw up legislation giving the executive branch more tools and expanded authority to conduct investigations and collect information in order to fight terrorism; the result was named the USA Patriot Act. In order to guarantee quick passage through Congress, the Patriot Act was equipped with a **sunset clause**, which ensured that Congress would have to reauthorize it a few years down the road, so that if there were any problems with the Act, they could be dealt with at that time. Both houses of Congress overwhelmingly passed the legislation and President George W. Bush signed it into law on October 26th 2001.[20]

Over the years since its passage, several portions of the Act have become controversial. This includes a couple of its provisions having been ruled unconstitutional by various U.S. Courts. In addition, the ACLU has condemned it as an assault on privacy, and eight states as well as almost 400 cities and counties have passed resolutions condemning the Act for its violations of civil liberties.

The biggest questions the Patriot Act compels us to ask are, how much liberty must we surrender in order to be secure? Is this surrender compatible with a free democracy? Though there is not a direct mention of it in our Constitution, there is a **penumbra** of privacy implied in its body. Much of the Bill of Rights and many Supreme Court rulings seem to back up this sentiment. There are provisions in the Patriot Act that permit the secret surveillance and gathering of material evidence even in the absence of a warrant, including the gathering of library records and the data-mining of phone company records without even having to show **probable cause**. These things would seem to be in direct violation of the privacy enveloped in the Constitution and quite possibly the beginning of the so-called slippery slope toward a more authoritarian government.

It can be argued that the government already has the power to conduct secret surveillance of subjects they believe to be involved in terrorist activities, by obtaining a warrant through the **FISA Court**, the special Court created specifically to issue such classified warrants. It can also be argued that the terrorists are almost certainly aware of the Patriot Act's provisions as well, and will most likely adjust their moves accordingly to avoid detection. So it begs the question, why would our government need to willingly and knowingly violate our civil liberties in this way when the whole point was to insure our continued freedom and American way of life?

In the debate over whether to reauthorize the Patriot Act in late 2005 and early 2006, there was vigorous discussion of civil liberties in both the House and the Senate. At the behest of many members of Congress, 27 civil liberty safeguards were added to the Act's language. Among them was the allowance of judicial challenges to various types of orders issued under the Act; a requirement of annual public disclosure of all records and letters sought after sent under portions of the Act; and the provision for greater congressional oversight of how the executive branch applies the Act.

Both houses of Congress voted in early 2006 to reauthorize the Patriot Act and President Bush signed it in March 2006. However, this congressional reauthorization did not stop debate on the Act. There were additional sunset provisions included in the reauthorization, so Congress will again revisit the Act sometime in 2009. Also, there are still Constitutional challenges to the Act working their way through the court system. In addition, some members of Congress are mulling over the option of additional legislation to help solve some of the problems raised but left unresolved by the Act. So although the USA Patriot Act is still in full effect, the unanswered questions will no doubt resurface once we find out who the next President will be in 2008.[21]

What are Civil Liberties and Civil Rights?

As illustrated by the preceding section on the Patriot Act, in turbulent times the greatness of a nation is defined by how it treats their citizens. American history is fraught with examples of the people turning against each other in a crisis. In times of political and public unrest, the burden falls on the courts to protect the liberties and rights of all citizens and aliens from all parts of the globe who are within their jurisdiction.

Penumbra –
A right held to be guaranteed by implication in a civil constitution.

Probable Cause –
Reasonable grounds for holding that a charge is well-founded.

FISA Court –
A U.S. Federal Court created by the Foreign Intelligence Surveillance Act of 1978; it is a Court whose proceedings are secret, therefore allowing for the ability to issue warrants without compromising classified investigations.

Most Americans think **civil liberties** and **civil rights** are one in the same. They're not. Civil liberties are rights and freedoms that are afforded to all U.S. citizens by the Bill of Rights and the Fourteenth Amendment's due process clause. These liberties are designed to be out of the reach of the government. This is to say that government should not take them away, however there can be restrictions on them. Civil rights are protections against discrimination based on gender, race, religion, age, ethnicity, or disability. These protections are based on the Fourteenth Amendment's equal protection clause. Civil rights are rights that the government gives us and can take away from us, albeit with due process. Take for example the right to vote. Once you are over the age of eighteen and are a legal citizen, you are eligible to register to vote. If you are convicted of a felony after you register to vote, your right to vote is suspended while you are under incarceration and on parole. In California, once you have paid your debt to society, you are eligible to vote again. In other states like Florida, once convicted of a felony, you forfeit your right to vote until you move to another state or the law changes.

There is another way to understand the distinction between liberties and rights. As stated above, liberties are freedom from government interference. They can also be viewed as a negative. The opening of the First Amendment is "Congress shall make no law…" Civil rights can be seen as more of a positive. The role of government is to remove barriers that prevent specific groups from receiving the same rights and privileges as other citizens. Look at the civil rights movement, the issue was equal access to voting, education, housing, and so on.

In civil liberty cases, the conflict is usually between a group or individuals pursuing their rights under the Constitution and the government trying to place limits on those rights. The court has the responsibility of defining the parameters between the rights of individuals and limits the government can place on them. Campus speech codes have been an issue on many campuses since the 1960s. Administrative policies have been modified to reflect the previous court rulings.

African American female protestor being carried away at a non-violent demonstration. Courtesy of the Library of Congress.

A group of students were protesting against abortions outside the campus library. Some of the signs had pictures of aborted fetuses that some students and faculty found to be distasteful and overly dramatic. The campus had created a free speech zone for student protests in a location that they felt would not interfere with classroom instruction. In order to use the area, students needed to complete and submit an application. These students did not complete this task so they decided to demonstrate in another area without permission. After receiving several phone calls, an administrator asked the students to relocate their protest to the appropriate location because the spot they had chosen was disruptive to the classes.

Civil Liberties –
The individual freedoms and rights guaranteed to every citizen in the Bill of Rights and the due process clause of the 14th Amendment, including freedom of speech and religion.

Civil Rights –
Constitutionally guaranteed rights such as the right to vote and equal protection under the law.

Issues For You
How would you have handled this situation as both the student and the administrator. Do you think the students' free speech was being violated? Why or Why Not?

The student leader refused to comply. They were notified that failing to comply would result in their arrests. The students claimed that the arrest would violate their First Amendment right to free speech and assembly. Shortly thereafter, the local police department arrived and arrested the protesters for trespassing.

This is just one of the many cases that can be found on college campuses today. In a college setting students are encouraged to exchange ideas and deliberate on controversial ideas, but to do so in a non-chaotic and safe manner. The trick is to be able to discern when you are imposing on someone else's rights and liberties in the very act of trying to exercise yours. The job of the administration and faculty is to provide a safe environment for the exchange to take place while maintaining the standards established by the Court.

As you read earlier in the chapter, there are judges who are "activists" and others who practice "restraint." Prior to 1995, the Supreme Court overturned congressional acts every two years on average. From 1995 to 2005 the Request Court overturned either partially or entirely thirty-nine congressional acts. The conservative jurists during this time tended to be more "activists" than their liberal counterparts. We have yet to see how the new Court led by Chief Justice Roberts will be. After being approved for the position as Chief Justice, Roberts said he would like to have a Court similar to that of the Marshall period (1801-1835). This is to say that he would like to have a Court that is able to speak with one clarion voice, instead of a 5-4 split along ideological lines. During Roberts' first term he was able to have more unanimous decisions than most of his predecessors witnessed. His second term seemed to be more challenging in this regard.[22]

The Right To Bear Arms

Profiles in Politics
Dr. Martin Luther King, Jr., (1929-1968)

To many people, Dr. Martin Luther King is a historical figure from a long time ago who fought for civil rights and was assassinated for his efforts in 1968. We are probably most familiar with his "I Have a Dream" speech and we know he is honored with a national holiday in January. That's pretty much the extent of what most people know about Dr. Martin Luther King. But there is much to him than that.

Martin Luther King, Jr. was born in January 1929 in Atlanta, Georgia to a pastor and his wife. Being that he was also the grandchild of a pastor, there was not much doubt that Martin would end up a pastor as well. But education had to come first. A very bright student, King finished high school at age 15 and then attended Morehouse College, where he received a Bachelor's Degree in Sociology. King then entered the Crozer Theological Seminary and received a Bachelor's Degree in Divinity in 1951 and proceeded to attain his Doctorate in Systematic Theology from Boston University in 1955.

Already an ordained minister, Dr. King accepted a job as pastor of a Baptist Church in Montgomery, Alabama, a position which he held until 1959. Then, in 1960, he moved back to Atlanta and served as co-pastor of a church with his father. The main reason for moving back was to take the helm of the Southern Christian Leadership Conference, a group that was very active in the civil rights movement.[23]

March 26, 1964. Civil rights leaders, Martin Luther King, Jr. and Malcolm X, waiting for a press conference. Courtesy of the Library of Congress.

Profiles in Politics
Dr. Martin Luther King, Jr., (1929-1968)

Throughout his public life, Dr. King helped organize various civil rights protests including the Montgomery Bus Boycott that ended up being one of the catalysts for the outlawing of segregation in public transportation. He organized and led successful marches around the South, including the famous ones in Birmingham and Selma, Alabama, to bring attention to racial injustice. Over time, he became a revered figure in the civil rights movement. He was an eloquent and inspired speaker who drew crowds everywhere he spoke. More than 200,000 people marched on Washington D.C. with him and heard him give the famous "I Have a Dream" speech. He truly was a legend in his own time.[24]

His philosophy of non-violent protest and uniting the "races" reached into the hearts of many people during that time. But because the words he spoke were controversial in those days and intense discrimination against blacks was accepted all over the South at that time, Dr. King was arrested several times and spent many a day in jail. Like St. Paul in the Bible, writing from jail to his faith communities, some of King's most famous writings were letters written while incarcerated. There were people who saw him as a danger, and for a while, the FBI monitored him. His family was harassed, his house bombed, he was physically attacked, and he received death threats. Despite all this, nothing could stop him in the pursuit of justice and equality. For his tenacity and fearlessness in pursuing his life's calling of civil rights for all through his method of peaceful protests, Dr. King received the Nobel Peace Prize in 1964.[25]

After 13 tireless years of leading the fight for civil rights, he was struck down by an assassin's bullet in Memphis, Tennessee on April 4th 1968. It was such a violent ending for such a peaceful man. His impact on the struggle for civil rights still reverberates today. His form of non-violent action and the stunning advances in civil rights it accomplished, not just for blacks but for anyone different than the mainstream privileged white males, have inspired similar civil rights movements everywhere.[26] Though many people may simply remember him for his "I Have a Dream" speech and a national holiday, Dr. King's influence on society and how to affect change peacefully and yet directly, have forever emblazoned his legacy as a great leader in the hearts and minds of the American people and the world.

Same Sex Marriage – A New Front in the Fight for Civil Rights

On November 18th 2003, the Massachusetts Supreme Judicial Court found, in a landmark ruling, that the denial of the "protections, benefits, and obligations conferred by civil marriage to two individuals of the same sex who wished to marry" was in direct contradiction to the Massachusetts State Constitution and that the State did not have any rational reason to deny gay couples the right to marry.

The Court gave the State Legislature 180 days to change the law to rectify the situation. When asked by the legislature to clarify the ruling, the Court majority responded that "the history of our nation has demonstrated that separate is seldom, if ever, equal"; that nothing short of equal marriage rights was acceptable; anything lesser would result in a discriminatory status for gay couples. After contentious debate, the Massachusetts State Legislature narrowly approved an amendment to their State Constitution banning same sex marriage. However, the State laws on such amendments were complex and the amendment failed during the following session of Congress. The result was that the State of Massachusetts became the first state of the union to allow gay couples to marry. Due to the existing federal Defense of Marriage Act (DOMA) of 1996, Massachusetts marriages were only valid and officially recognized in-state.[27]

This law was greeted by both bitter opposition and in some places, a certain amount of jubilation. Soon afterwards, the city of San Francisco, California began issuing marriage licenses to gay couples, though the California State Supreme Court promptly put an end to the practice. California currently permits domestic partner registration which confers the domestic rights of marriage to registered same-sex couples.

Conservative religious groups meanwhile fired back with outrage, citing their interpretation of a proper and biblical moral code. They threw their support behind an effort to develop a federal Constitutional Amendment preserving marriage in the U.S. as a union between one man and one woman. And in the Midterm Elections of November 2006, some 7 states passed **DOMA laws** and/or amendments, restricting marriage rights for same-sex couples. Many of these laws also prohibited **civil unions** as well. Arizona was the only state where voters rejected a DOMA law.[28]

Currently, Massachusetts is still the only state recognizing gay marriages within its borders, but five other states, including California, have some sort of civil union recognition for same-sex couples, and the issue of civil unions is being debated in three other states as well. In addition, more and more companies are extending their benefits to the same-sex partners of their employees, including more than half of Fortune 500 companies. Hollywood trailblazing sitcoms and talk shows such as *Will & Grace*, *Ellen*, *The Ellen Degeneres Show*, Logo and HBO channels on cable television, have also aided in bringing **LGBT issues** to the forefront of the media. In terms of equality for gay couples, it may not be anywhere close to adequate, but it is definitely a step toward equal rights.

Issues For You
In light of all that you have learned regarding the exclusion of minorities in democracy, what would you recommend to resolve this issue without creating a second tier citizenry?

DOMA law –
A law restricting the right to marry to couples consisting of only one man and one woman.

Civil Union –
The legal status that ensures to same-sex couples specified rights and responsibilities of married couples.

LGBT –
Lesbian, Gay, Bisexual, Transgender; inclusive acronym often used when discussing gay rights.

California's Judicial System

The general public may not realize this but the judiciary interacts with the political process quite heavily. During the 1970's and 1980's, more people realized how important a role the courts play. The courts took a center stage spotlight in the 2000 Presidential election, in overturning controversial initiatives, and recently, in the highly publicized case of Stanley "Tookie" Williams.

Judges must weigh issues very carefully between legislation already in place and the stipulations laid out in the U.S. and state Constitutions. Whenever interpretation of the constitutions is necessary, the margin for debate is like a deep valley gorge, full of rocky and bumpy surfaces. This is because the California constitution is lengthy and complicated – the index by itself is twice as long as the U.S. Constitution!

The California court system is scrutinized by California's eclectic interests, thus making it just as prone to political debate as the executive and legislative branches at the federal and state levels. California courts have four tiers – the municipal court, the superior court, Courts of Appeal, and the highest court, the supreme court. The four levels can then be split into trial courts or reviewing courts. The trial courts, the municipal and superior courts, utilize a judge and or jury while the Courts of Appeal and the supreme court fall under the category of reviewing courts or appellate courts.

The Courts From the Ground Up

The municipal court, said to be in the lower court, is the first course of action for cases dealing with minor crimes or misdemeanors such as traffic violations or civil suits, which usually involve some kind of contractual conflicts with a monetary value totaling $25,000 or less. If you are the one filing a civil suit, you would be called the plaintiff; your opponent would be the defendant. The bulk of all cases land at the municipal level especially small claims cases with damages up to $2,500 without the need for attorneys or $5,000 or less total. The small claims courts tend to be speedier cases that are informal and fairly inexpensive.

The superior court, located in each county, is also in the lower court and like the municipal court, it too deals with criminal and civil cases but it deals with more serious crimes (felonies), family issues (divorce, child custody), and civil suits totaling more than $25,000 (both rural and city areas). While both the family law and felonies take up a considerable amount of time, the felonies can take much longer since they sometimes ask for a jury trial. At both the superior and municipal levels, the judge can declare jail sentences or juvenile hall for a period of one year or more.

The Appellate Courts review the procedures of the original trial and try to determine if the case was treated properly and legally when it was first tried in the lower courts. Cases that are being appealed land in the Courts of Appeal and, depending on the number of appeals, the case may go all the way up to the supreme court level. The reason it is called Courts of Appeal plural is because there are six district courts of appeal. The break down of the districts is as follows:

First District – San Francisco
Second District – Los Angeles & Ventura
Third District – Sacramento
Fourth District – San Diego, Santa Ana, San Bernardino
Fifth District – Fresno
Sixth District – San Jose

The supreme court must maintain state-wise standards in all legal rulings. Being that the supreme court is the highest court in the state, it hears cases as serious as commuting a death sentence to a life in prison sentence, for example. When a case goes up to the supreme court, it is heard by seven justices (one chief justice and six associate justices). Decisions reached at this level are final unless it is a case having to do with the U.S. Constitution or the federal law; in these instances, it becomes a matter for the U.S. Supreme Court. If the U.S. Supreme Court chooses not to accept the appeal then whatever decision the lower court reached still stands.

Seeking to improve the efficiency of the judicial branch, reformers proposed a constitutional amendment in 1998 to combine the municipal and superior courts. It was met with favorable votes and shortly thereafter, most counties throughout the state merged the two courts. Those who do not win in the lower courts may ask for their case to be reviewed one level up. It is rare that municipal court cases are appealed.

How Justices Are Chosen, Challenged, and Removed

The justices at the Federal level are appointed by the President and confirmed by the Senate. They can enjoy a life-time appointment without any further evaluation. Not so with the state supreme court and Courts of Appeal system. The justices at the state level are appointed by the governor after being confirmed by a judicial council. The governor may appoint whomever he wants but will usually go with the commission's suggestions. Once this is complete, the public gets to vote on the governor's choices on nonpartisan ballots, marking simply "yes" or "no" with no opposing candidates listed. Once elected, the justice may serve a 12 year term and may run again for another 12 year term, once the first one concludes. Incidentally, there are about 26 states that choose their judges by election, rather than by gubernatorial appointment. Even though these are not lifetime terms like the Federal court justices, they are still very long terms. It would behoove voters to be sure to vote come election time for the office of the governor so that the justices chosen reflect their ideology.

The judicial council consists of three commissions and one council member. The three commissions are the commission on judicial appointments, on judicial nominees, and on judicial performance. The three members of the first commission, judicial appointments, are the chief justice of the state supreme court, the attorney general, and a senior presiding justice of one of the district court of appeals. The commission on judicial nominees consists of 25 members who are appointed by the board of governors of the State Bar of California. Finally, the commission on judicial performance consists of nine private citizens who act as the check on the judges' behavior both in and out of the courtroom. They have the power to propose the forced retirement of justices or even the removal of a justice, if they so choose and they have good reason.

California's supreme court had mostly been liberal up until 1986, when Chief Justice Rose Bird, serving at her post since 1977 under Governor Jerry Brown, was rejected by voters. Bird was the first woman justice and one of three liberal associates who were also rejected by the voters. Her lack of experience and liberal stances earned her much criticism for siding with the defendant too much, being in favor of desegregation by bussing, and opposing Proposition 13 among other things. Additionally, at 40, she was also considered too young. By 1986, a newly conservative slate of voters had had enough of the liberal majority and they did not renew the twelve-year terms of Bird and two other justices who had been appointed under Gov. Brown. Republicans George Deukmejian and Pete Wilson helped maintain the new conservative monopoly by appointing conservative justices and promoting a previous appointee, Malcolm Lucas, to chief justice. It is interesting to note that although there are a few minorities serving as appointees in the California judiciary, women and minorities are generally underrepresented. The voters scrutinize age, experience, and extreme stances on controversial issues in the appointees, which sometimes greatly affect their percentages negatively. However, all four appointees post-Gov. Brown, the chief justice and Justices Brown, Chin, and Mosk managed to salvage their incumbent retention by a twenty percent margin.

There are actually four ways to remove a judge in California: through the election process, by impeachment and conviction via the state legislature, by recall if 20% of registered voters sign recall petitions, and by recommendation of the commission on judicial performance, as stated above.

Sometimes, in an act of desperation, a citizen may pay private judges to resolve their civil cases. Private arbitration is usually something we agree to without knowing it – it is part of the paperwork we fill out whenever we visit a doctor or fill out forms for any personal service. The employer or insurer purposefully has a client sign a contract saying the employee will forfeit their right to sue the company in a court of law. Should something arise that would require legal counsel, the citizen needs to settle outside of court through a mediator. With mediation, the plaintiff may appeal the case. Private arbitration takes this a step further and says the client must sign a "no-appeals" contract. For this reason, private arbitration judges have been under a microscope. If their decisions are not above appeal, this greatly inflates their power. Only those with bountiful resources would be able to pay for private judge services, making the winner of a case the one with the most money, rather than the one who deserved to win.

How the Courts Run

After a citizen is arrested, the accused one is brought in front of a judge, probably in the municipal court, and prepares for arraignment. Arraignment is a court meeting in which the judge, in an official capacity, tells the parties concerned what they are being charged with, their legal rights, and the date of their hearing. The judge also sets the amount of money that must be paid to the court before a person can be released from jail. The amount determined is called bail. Sometimes if the accused is considered a non-threat to the court and the public, she or he may be released without having to post bail, or what is known as being released "on her or his own recognizance."

Since criminal trials can be very costly and time-consuming, the ideal situation is for the cases to be resolved without a trial. Plea bargaining is the method used for negotiating an outcome that satisfies both the prosecutor and the defense attorney. It basically is an agreement that is reached by the two parties that the accused may plead guilty to a less severe offense than what the defendant was accused of in the first place. Some see this plea bargaining as too lenient while others feel this allows for a chance at reforming criminals before it is too late.

Punitive Guidelines

Clear guidelines for types of crimes have helped to categorize offenses, making it easier to set punitive codes. The three types of crimes are grouped into infractions, misdemeanors, and felonies, listed in order of severity from least to worst. Infractions, such as the traffic violations mentioned earlier, usually call for a fine to be implemented and in rare cases, jail time. Misdemeanors like stealing small items (think Wynona Ryder, the famous celebrity case of shoplifting clothing) and drunk driving (too many celebrities to list – Robert Downey, Jr, Britney Spears, Mel Gibson, Lindsay Lohan, Paris Hilton, and on and on), are also charged fines and less than one year of prison time. Felonies being the most serious crimes, such as grand theft auto, drug trafficking, and even murder, are punishable by jail time of at least a year or more, or sometimes even corporal punishment in the form of execution.

The system allows for those accused an opportunity to be placed on probation. Probation is a period of granted supervised freedom and a postponement of the sentence on the convicted offender. With the dawn of conservatism from the late 1980's and 1990's, justices were less than willing to allow for criminal reform. This is unfortunate because, with an imperfect system, there are bound to be unjust arrests or overly harsh sentences. The "3-strikes" law is a controversial example. Petitions began circulating in 1992 – 1993, in an emotional response to the case of when Polly Klaas, a young girl whose kidnapping sparked a nation-wide search, was found murdered. The intent behind the three strikes law is to stop repeat offenders from endangering the public. The law increases a sentence for a convicted felon who has had previous convictions for serious or violent felonies. The law is laid out like this:

Table 12.2 - Summary of the "3-Strikes" Law	
STRIKE ONE	One serious to violent felony conviction – first offense to justify stiffer prison sentence
STRIKE TWO	A second felony conviction + one prior serious to violent felony convictions; Doubles the base sentence with no probation
STRIKE THREE	A third felony conviction + two serious to violent felony convictions; Triples the base sentence or 25 years to life, whichever is greater, with no probation

While this may seem to be a good example of being "tougher on crime" it has actually complicated the lives of nonviolent offenders and cost the state multibillions of dollars not only because of expensive trial cases but also with overcrowding the prisons. The unfortunate situation of offenders who have committed non-violent misdemeanors like shoplifting, being thrown away in jail for 50 years because their final strike was stealing videos with no prior violent or serious crimes has shown that this law is in need of more careful scrutiny in terms of being inhumane and cruel and unusual punishment.

During the gold rush days, California participated in vigilante justice by holding civilian hearings followed by public lynchings. Courtesy of the Library of Congress.

Justice Sandra Day O'Connor, along with other conservatives Chief Justice Rehnquist, and justices Scalia, Kennedy, and Thomas, in a 5 to 4 ruling in 2002, justified the 3 strikes law in the case of Lockyer v. Andrade, in which the scenario described above actually did occur. One of the votes against came from outspoken liberal Justice Souter who argued in support of California's 9th circuit court that ruled that the punishment was grossly disproportionate. Souter went on record, saying that Andrade: "did not somehow become twice as dangerous to society when he stole the second handful of videotapes…Since the defendant's condition has not changed between the two closely related thefts, the incapacitation penalty is not open to the simple arithmetic of multiplying the punishment by two, without resulting in gross disproportion…I know of no jurisdiction that would add 25 years of imprisonment simply to reflect the fact that the two temporally related thefts took place on two separate occasions…I am not surprised that California has found no such case, not even under its three-strikes law…the argument that repeating a trivial crime justifies doubling a 25-year minimum incapacitation sentence based on a threat to the public does not raise a seriously debatable point on which judgments might reasonably differ."[29]

The 2002 U.S. Supreme Court case is particularly surprising considering that even the California supreme court (conservative justices presided at the time) unanimously ruled in 1996 that the three-strikes law was in violation of the constitutional separation of powers.

Genevieve Cline was the first woman appointed to the U.S. District Court in 1928. Courtesy of the Library of Congress.

Civil Rights in California

During the internment, some Japanese farmers leased their land to other minority groups in California, like the large Latino population. One such Latino person was Gonzalo Mendez. The farm that Mendez leased was in Westminster, CA but his home was in Santa Ana, CA. He later relocated his family to Westminster, only to be met with discrimination – his children were denied enrollment in the local all-white

Japanese-Americans at an internment camp at Fort Douglas. Courtesy of the Library of Congress.

public school. He was instructed that his children would have to attend a Mexican school because California had been segregated since before the 1920's. The good news was that because of the war-productivity, the farm was doing very well. This generated enough revenue for him to challenge several school districts in court. In March of 1945, the case went to a U.S. District court in Los Angeles where Mendez, the plaintiff, was girded with four other individuals who were standing on behalf of the other districts in Orange County.

In February of 1946, Judge McCormick ruled in favor of Mendez, stating that the actions of the school district were considered discrimination based upon the due process clause of the 14th amendment. The school districts appealed to the U.S. 9th Circuit Courts of Appeal. Several other organizations heard of the case and came to Mendez's support, such as the American Jewish Congress and the NAACP. During the trial, an attorney representing the NAACP, who happened to be Thurgood Marshall, wrote an amicus curiae brief to back Mendez up further. In April of 1947, the 9th Circuit upheld the lower courts ruling.

In June of 1947, California governor, Earl Warren signed into law a repeal of the California school code that allowed the discrimination. By desegregating the schools, all other segregated areas followed suit; public entertainment, and restaurant establishments were also desegregated.

What is unique about the Mendez case is the fact that two key players, Gov. Warren and Attorney Thurgood Marshall, would be in a similar position seven years later with the Brown v. Board of Education case. Marshall was the attorney representing the NAACP for Brown and Warren was now Chief Justice of the Supreme Court. Obviously, Marshall did not have any trouble convincing Chief Justice Warren that segregation was unconstitutional based on the ground-breaking achievements that Warren initiated in the Mendez v. Westminster case. If you go back to the Profile on Earl Warren, you may remember that at one point, he reluctantly supported the internment of the Japanese American citizens, an action that was later considered very discriminatory and wrong. But in a truly full-circle phenomenon, the intern-ment of the Japanese-Americans enabled another minority group, the Mexican-Amer-icans, to challenge another form of discrimination in education. Because of this

FOR YOUR CONSIDERATION
CALIFORNIA PROPOSITION 209

In 1996, the state of California put a proposition on its ballot, Proposition 209, which was designed to end affirmative action in state and local government programs, including higher education. The measure passed.[30]

Previous to the measure, all state and local programs were expected to allot a certain percentage of their employment, contracts, and admissions to minorities and women. The proposition formally ended that practice and forbid such preferential treatment based on race, sex, color, or ethnicity, with very limited exception.

During the 1996 election season, there was intense campaigning on both sides of the issue. Proponents of the measure argued that affirmative action was simply "race" quotas and was borderline reverse discrimination.[31] Opponents of the measure argued that it would end many state sponsored programs that were designed to encourage and prepare women and minorities to take advantage of opportunities available to them.

After its passing, California Proposition 209 was challenged in court and upheld. Upon appeal to the U.S. Supreme Court, the Court declined to hear it, effectively meaning that the law, at least for the time being would remain in effect. In the immediate aftermath of its passing, enrollment by minorities plunged in the California college system[32] and now, more than a decade later in the early 2000's, the college system is working on devising a plan to aid in recruitment of minority applicants in order to increase diversity at their campuses while still keeping in line with Proposition 209.[33]

chain of events and the actions of one brave father, all of California became deseg- regated and eventually, the entire country, leading to desegregation policies that are still in place today. The moral of this story might be that the truth will be revealed no matter how closely it is held up to our face; if we would just be brave enough to take a step back and appreciate that we all just want to be treated fairly and justly.

Democracy & The Courts

In many parts of America, a litigious atmosphere seems to go hand in hand with our thirst for the American dream and a life of consumerism. California in particular has, since 1997, earned a reputation of being particularly focused on litigation, keeping quite literally, hundreds of thousands of attorneys very busy. Built in to California's constitution is the right to a jury trial for both civil and criminal cases. The high volume of cases that actually go to trial with a judge and jury, pending approval of both sides concerned, requires the courts to summon regular citizens to serve on jury duty. Twelve jurors (or less), men and women, per trial case are gleaned from the DMV's list of licensed drivers and from the county voter registration rolls.

A mailer is sent to the potential juror asking the person to call in to the assigned court or appear by a certain date in order to find out if they will be serving on a trial. Usually, jury summons notices are not mailed to the same person more than once a year. The extent of the juror's responsibilities could be one phone call to the court and never have to actually show up in person, or the juror could be chosen for a murder trial that could go on for several months. While all workplaces must honor when an employee is summoned for jury duty, not all employers are willing to compensate that worker. Some offer no pay while others offer $5.00 per day. Some courts offer pay for mileage but the workplace that offers the nominal pay may want that check turned in to them, not to be cashed by the juror. For these reasons, many citizens avoid jury duty by filling out the boxes and spaces on the form saying why they are unable to serve at that moment in time.

People of all walks of life are summoned – professionals, homemakers, retirees, highly educated, high school education only, blue collar workers - even college students are not exempt from serving on jury duty, despite final exam schedules, no transportation, or low income. Because the process of attorneys interviewing groups of jurors can be quite time-consuming, some juror waiting areas play movies on big screens or they have a palatable cafeteria right next door. While these creature com- forts are an improvement, they do little to convince someone to look forward to serving their civic duty. One would hope that it helps pass the time and make it more like a day off rather than a day of obligation.

The reviews of being called to jury duty tend to be mixed – there are those that take great pride in our judicial system and feel it is their responsibility as good citizens to serve willingly and cheerfully. Others see the dreaded red and white envelope with the large capital bold letters that say "JURY SUMMONS" and they cringe and moan. While the latter of these two reactions is quite understandable, it is unfor- tunate. The reason being that the more people avoid jury duty, the more those on trial that fall into the lower-income strata or minority groups go underrepresented, perpetuating a catch-22 of bitterness and distrust of the whole judicial system.

How Do We Compare?
American Exceptionalism
Case Studies in Democracy

The purpose of the country sections at the end of each chapter was to introduce the student to the field of comparative politics. The idea was to use the comparative sections as references to illustrate further the unique characteristics of the United States Government, but also of key elements in other democratic style governments also struggling with the democratic ideal. By adopting a country-by-country approach, the strategy acquaints the beginning American Government student with several topics: historical context, prevalent economical issues, values, leaders of that nation, institutional framework, and climate and geography factors, and political process. When Americans begin learning about the United States, we tend to think of ourselves as being exceptional. The term "exceptional" conjures up a vast array of images and feelings that, when taken to an extreme, can have negative impact. When approached from a comparative manner, exceptional can be viewed through other lenses.

What is meant by "American Exceptionalism?"

The concept was first introduced by European travelers that studied the American structure of government and society. Most notable was Alexis de Tocqueville in 1830 (see chapter one). In his book, *Democracy in America*, he was trying to uncover how America's democracy succeeded whereas the efforts of establishing a democracy in France had failed starting after the French revolution. Being exceptional in the arena of comparative politics does not mean "extraordinary" or "the best"; instead, it refers to qualitative differences. The differences that set the United States apart from the events of other nations are described in the following section.

First, the United States was the first nation to separate from its colonial power. Second, most citizens define themselves through a common history or birthright; being an American is an ideology. Take for example the comments by Winston Churchill in 1941, where he said he did not fear the Communist party of Great Britain because it was made up of Englishmen. In contrast, here in the United States, our history is filled with individuals being considered "un-American" for not sharing the same norms and values as middle-America. The "Red" scares in the 1930's and 1950's were extremely oppressive; citizens were charged with supporting, associating with, or being a communist by the "House Committee on Un-American Activities" (HCUA) from 1938 to 1969. In 1969, the House of Representatives changed the committee's name to the Committee on Internal Security after the HCUA had become synonymous with abuse of governmental powers. In 1975, the committee was eliminated and its duties were transferred to the House Judiciary Committee.

A third characteristic that sets the U.S. apart is the American Creed, which can be described in five terms: liberty, egalitarianism, individualism, populism, and laissez-faire. It should be noted that egalitarianism in this context is equality of opportunity, not of division of wealth.

Fourth, unlike most European countries, the U.S. is without a feudal past, such as the United Kingdom (chapter two), Germany (chapter three), France (chapter ten), and other nations like Russia (chapter four) and Japan (chapter six).

Fifth, most nations have placed a greater emphasis on obedience to political authority and on deference to superiors, whereas the Americans pride themselves on questioning and challenging authority. Lastly, when comparing the United States to other democratic nations, the US is more religious despite the fact that we don't have a national church, unlike Britain and Canada. One of the best ways to gain an understanding of the United States is by using comparative terms.[34]

Case Studies in Democracy

The first chapter had a basic overview of democratic theory. There were two main types, direct and indirect democracy. Unlike France, the United States does not practice direct democracy at the national level. Instead some states practice initiatives, or propositions that require voters to sign a petition for the proposition to be placed on the ballot. Another form of direct democracy is the recall, which allows the voters to remove an elected official from office before the end of the term. The second type is indirect democracy or what most democracies have, like the United States, a representative democracy. A representative democracy is one in which the people rule indirectly through representatives who they elect to govern in their stead, as in the case of Britain, Germany, France, Japan, Canada, and South Africa.[35]

Within a representative democracy there are several main components - they are popular sovereignty, political liberty, and political equality. Popular sovereignty has several elements that are necessary: government must implement the will and wishes of the people through its policies; citizens must have access to accurate information in order to make informed decisions; the citizenry must directly participate in the political process; when representatives are elected, elections must be free and fair; and finally, the majority rules. Political liberty is the belief that there are liberties that the government should not touch. Most of these liberties are enumerated in the Bill of Rights, mainly the First Amendment to the Constitution, which entails the freedoms of speech, religion, assembly and association, and press. Most counties we have reviewed, while they may have practice these concepts in principle, only started implementing them within the last century, as in the case of Canada, Mexico, Britain, and Germany to name a few. Political equality is simply that all citizens are equal not only in the eyes of the law but also in the political realm as well. Regardless of one's position or wealth, all eligible voters' votes carry the same political weight, as illustrated in the examples of France and Japan. After examining the strengths of democracy, the discussion of some possible flaws of democracy, mainly those surrounding majority tyranny were evaluated. The importance of protecting the minority opinion is one that must not be forgotten in a true democracy. Developing countries, such as Russia, Iraq, and South Africa, are struggling with ethnic diversity and are having a difficult time finding ways to live together harmoniously.

The Types of Democratic Government

There are three main types of democratic governments - the parliamentary system, the presidential system, and the semi-presidential system.

Parliamentary system. The parliamentary system is the most commonly used of the three. Most of the governments who use the parliamentary system base their designs on the Westminster model created in the United Kingdom. It is the governing entity in many countries around the world, such as Canada, Germany, and South Africa.

In the parliamentary system, the voters elect representatives to the legislature. The party that wins the most seats in the legislature becomes the ruling party. If neither party has a clear majority, they can form a coalition with a minor party in order to proceed with establishing a government. Once there is a ruling government, a prime minister is selected by the ruling party to lead the government. The prime minister fills the cabinet positions with senior party members. The cabinet then oversees the various ministries to insure that the government's policies are being implemented.

As one can see, there is no real separation of powers between the parliament and the prime minister. If the government loses the support of the people because of the prime minister's policies, the parliament can call for a "vote of no confidence" in which the prime minister is forced to step down. In addition, Britain does not have an implicit codified constitution. Instead their constitution is derived from their history of common laws, traditions, and acts by parliament. Because their "virtual" constitution is so fluid, very few actions taken by the prime minister can be ruled unconstitutional. This is not the same for Germany and Canada who have codified constitutions and supreme courts who use judicial review. The prime minister can call for elections at any time as long as they are within five years of the previous elections. Usually, the prime minister will call for elections when there is stronger public support for their policies, thus enabling their party to gain more seats in parliament.

Presidential system. As you have read throughout the text, the presidential system here in the United States is based on three main concepts – separation of powers between the branches, each branch of government is sovereign within its sphere of influence, and each branch acts as a check and balance on the others.

In the presidential system, the voters elect the legislature separate from the president. In some systems, the president is popularly elected, while here in the United States, the Electoral College elects the president. The president selects the cabinet and the cabinet oversees the ministries or agencies.

In contrast to the parliamentary system found in Britain, the president and the legislature have explicit guidelines in the constitution. If the president is implicated in illegal actions to the level of high crimes or treason, then the president can be impeached by the lower house and removed from office by the upper house. If the legislature does not like the policies of the president, they do not have the option of voting for a no-vote of confidence. The president cannot call for early elections to help his party gain more seats in the legislature - the Constitution spells out when elections are to be held. In order for this to change, the Constitution would need to be amended, which is inherently difficult to do.

Semi-Presidential System. The semi-presidential system, also known as the French system, is a combination of the parliamentary system and the presidential system. President Charles de Gaulle created the semi-presidential system (see his profile in chapter 10) after the fourth republic was no longer functioning.

For the semi-presidential system, the voters elect the legislature and president separately. The president selects the premier and the cabinet. The premier and cabinet guide the ministers in carrying out the president's policies. If the government's policies are at odds with each other and are in a deadlock, the premier can be censured by the parliament and be forced to resign. If this occurs, the president can dissolve the parliament and call for new elections.

Unlike the president and the parliamentary systems, the semi-presidential system gives more power to the president than the legislature. It has some checks and balances between the branches but not as much as the presidential system. Because the executive has more power than the other two systems, the governments of Russia and China has elected to use this as a guide for their structures of governments Global Trends towards Regional Democracies.

Global Trends Towards Regional Democracies

Since the end of World War II, there have been global movements in which regions worked together for security. Within the last two decades there have been shifts to the creation of economic zones such as the North American Free Trade zone (NAFTA). The European Union (EU) is an excellent example of countries who have engaged in wars for centuries are able to unite for economic consideration. They have moved into a very loose confederation with a common currency, the Euro, which was introduced in early 2002. Currently the EU has 25 members with more still pending approval. If this trend continues, there is a strong probability that the continent will continue to unite and evolve into a federation.[36]

A Brief History of the European Union

For thousands of years there have been attempts to have a unified Europe. The Roman Empire and Charlemagne promoted the idea but only through military conquest. As Catholicism spread across the Roman Empire and began to dissolve, the Catholic Church was the main loose conduit that hindered unity across Europe, through its relationships with the various monarchy and heads of states. This tie was splintered with the onslaught of the Protestant Reformation, causing religious wars to break out. With the treaty of Westphalia in 1648, Kings determined what the religion of the state would be. Tensions continued for decades to come.

In the early 1800's Napoleon was able to conquer the majority of the main continent but England remained elusive. With Napoleon's Empire came the major infection of nationalism which was instilled across Europe, further intensifying the divisions. Over the course of the next century and a half, European powers engaged in a variety of conflicts with each other.

The European Union Logo has stars representing the original 12 members. © Vasil Vasilev, 2007. Used under License from Shutterstock, Inc.

Two of the most devastating to the people, land, and resources were World War I (1914-1918) and World War II (1939-1945). After World War II Europeans were exhausted with the conflicts and sought a remedy that would prevent such horrific destruction and suffering from occurring again. The answer came from France's Jean Monnet and Robert Schuman. Their solution was to create the Coal and Steel Community in 1952. This led to the Treaty of Rome in 1957, which eventually founded the precursor to the EU, the European Economic Community (EEC) market consisting of six nations.

By 1973, three more countries had joined, including Great Britain. The EEC expanded to a total of nine members. By 1992 it became apparent that the EEC was ready for the next level. The Maastricht Treaty and Schengen agreements in 1994 created a more cohesive union, even giving it a more self-explanatory name, as stated above, the European Union. Currently the EU is 25 members strong and substantial enough to challenge the United States' economic power; with 455 million people and a gross domestic product of $11 trillion, the EU was well on its way to do just that.

Institutions of the European Union

Brussels is Europe's closest representation of a capital. The European Union's governing institutions are not like others that have been discussed. In some ways they are similar to the structure the United States had under the Articles of Confederation. As stated earlier, the EU is more like a confederation with the bulk of power resting with individual member nations. The executive branch is called the European Commission. Each commissioner is selected from that member's country with the consent of the other members for a five-year term. Those selected are not there to represent their individual nations but the Union as a whole. The collective 25-member presidency then selects one individual to serve as its president.

The Council oversees a 24,000 member bureaucracy. The Upper House is the Council of the European Union with 25 members from each country. What makes the Council unique is that the members serve on a rotation basis from each member state. The minister who is selected is based on their expertise on the subject matter. Take for example the issue of transportation. The movement of goods is costly and in the case of perishable produce, time sensitive. When there is a transportation issue that requires attention, the transportation members from the 25 member states will convene to try to resolve the issue. When a decision is reached, the ministers vote on it. Each vote is weighted based on population, so for the large states (Germany, Britain, France, and Italy) all have 29 voters, where as Malta only has three votes. The total number of votes in the Council is 321.

The European Parliament has offices in both Brussels and Strasbourg. For all intents and purposes, it can be viewed as a lower house. The 732 Members of the European Parliament (MEPs) are directly elected by their home country for a five-year term. Similar to the House of Representatives in the U.S., the number of MEPs a country has is proportional to its population (see chapter 8). For example, Germany's population is approximately 82.5 million and it has 99 MEPs compared to Malta's population of 400,000 and has 5 MEPs. Aside from passing legislation, the Parliament can censure the Commission and ask it to resign; to date this has not happened.[37]

The European Court of Justice is located in Luxembourg and is similar to a supreme court. There are 25 Judges who oversee and rule on European Union law. It has the power to rule on issues surrounding the Commission and conflicts between countries.

FOR YOUR CONSIDERATION
THE INTERNATIONAL COURT OF JUSTICE

Though the creation of the International Court of Justice (ICJ) seems fairly recent, it actually has roots that go back to the year 1899. Back then, Tsar Nicholas II of Russia decided to create a Permanent Court of Arbitration. He chose to base this Court in The Hague in the Netherlands. The court was to be used for mediation, a transaction that states could utilize for arbitration in matters that could not be solved diplomatically. Governments that participated in the court selected international law experts that functioned as the arbitrators.[38]

In 1922, the League of Nations combined with the court to create the Permanent Court of International Justice. When the United Nations came into being in 1945, the name of the court was again changed to the International Court of Justice, and the rules of the court were incorporated into the Charter of the United Nations. The ICJ was up and running under its current name in 1946 and is the official court of the United Nations.

In addition to its original purpose, the ICJ also serves as an advisor to the U.N. when questions of law arise. The court is composed of 15 judges, each from a different country. The U.N. General Assembly and the Security Council elect and rotate five judges every three years to keep the number of justices at 15. Each judge serves a term of nine years.[39]

In order to render justice and still respect the sovereignty of nations, both parties in a case must agree to have it heard before the court, and therefore agree to abide by the decision of the court. However, if one of the parties refuses to comply with the decision, neither the court nor the U.N. has any authority to force compliance. Once a decision has been rendered, it is final; there is no appeal.

Some of the types of cases that have come through the ICJ are cases involving, among other things, border disputes, hostage taking, asylum rights, and commercial law. Some of the most famous cases to come through the ICJ were hearings on the Iran-Contra scandal and the war crimes trial of deposed Yugoslavian leader Slobodan Milosevic.

Cautionary Tale for Developing Democracies

In reading about the developing democracies of Iraq, Russia, and South Africa has shown some of the struggles each country had to endure in order to become a democracy. In learning about American government, you have seen how, after two hundred years, we are still working on instilling strong democratic principles into young children. One lesson developing democratic countries can learn from this is to have faith and persevere because the process of democratization is long. It takes not just months, years, or couple of decades but it is an ongoing evolutionary process where each new generation must build upon the improvements of the past.

In addition to the institutional structures described above, there many other factors that play an important role in a successful democracy. South Africa has shown great promise in terms of the democratic ideal. The problems facing South Africa are similar to those throughout the continent. The issues of AIDS, fresh water, and the lack of a division between land and wealth has lead to civil unrest that has undone all the progress that has been made. Comparatively speaking, at the regional level, South Africa has more resources at their disposal than those in surrounding countries, like Zimbabwe.

When looking at the history of Germany, the blind deference granted to the one authority was the cause of their first attempt at a democracy to fall into the fascist state of the 1930s and early 1940s. It wasn't until the division between West and East Germany that those who lived in the west began to show signs of democratic prowess. Those in the east were exposed to the Stalinistic practices that had been endured by the people in the Soviet Union. The authoritarian regimes that controlled these nations left a mark that is still seen and felt today.

After the unification of Germany, East Germans began to assimilate into the western political culture. In contrast, Russians have been politically oppressed for several centuries, the negative effects of which have metastasized, blocking any further democratic development. Currently, Russia could be described as being akin to the tortured souls in a Chekov play - on the verge of returning to the past, not because it is better but because it is familiar.

In the cases of Iraq and Iran, there is great promise. While Iran is currently a theocracy, Iranians have a political culture that is more westernized than it neighbors and it has a history of democratic governments. Iraq has had a similar experience but on a smaller scale and for a shorter amount of time. The problem facing these countries is religious extremism. Extremists take the scriptures of religion to such literal polar opposite ends that any genuine humanitarian concepts of goodness and mercy are distorted and taken way out of context. For this reason, those in the western world who are ignorant of the religion of Islam mistakenly get their ideas of what the religious culture is all about from the more outspoken extremists. This is not to say Islam is more prone to extremism than any other religion – truly, extremism exists in all of the world's religions, especially in Christianity. There are individuals, sometimes the most pious of ministers and preachers, who misinterpret the Bible or focus only on those areas that fit their preconceived moral codes, rather than taking the whole of the book as symbolic. Extremism leads to fanaticism, which leads to intolerance and irrational behavior, all in the name of God.

Political culture and tolerance are necessary components needed for an open exchange of ideas. Here in the United States we are still in the process of strengthening an atmosphere of political tolerance but also of political acceptance. So, just like the rest of the democratic ideal, success may be achieved not when we think it should but in its own time, as change and trust come slowly for many cultures.

Democracy and Action - Tiananmen Square

In the spring of 1989, the world watched as China experienced a deeply divided struggle for democracy against a corrupt communist regime. Beginning April 17th, thousands of students began to assemble in Tiananmen Square, Beijing, the nation's symbolic space created to mourn the death of Hu Yaobang, the former Secretary General of the Communist Party, himself an advocate for anti-corruption and political reform. The students began asking for freedom of press and other reforms and as the rally cry gained momentum, the demonstrations began to escalate, spreading across the nation to other cities and universities. Soon, workers and officials joined the demonstrators to voice their complaints about inflation, salary, and housing.

During the protests in Tiananmen Square, the students erected a statue called "The Goddess of Democracy", which resembled the U.S.' Statue of Liberty. Courtesy of the Associated Press.

Politburo – Executive committee and policy- making body of a Communist party.

Everyone involved with this uprising became more and more infuriated, feeding off of each escalating event. The Party, divided over how to approach the worsening situation, argued over whether the students were attempting to undermine the government or if their patriotism should be affirmed. As Yaobang's funeral approached, Zhao Ziyang, the Party General Secretary, urged officials to be patient and wait, hoping the funeral would de-escalate the situation. Rather, the funeral brought over 100,000 students demonstrating outside China's Great Hall of the People, with a list of reforms presented for review by Premier Li Peng. His refusal to consider them prompted the boycott of classes and the students began organizing unofficial student unions, an illegal act in China. After convincing the **Politburo** that the students planned to overthrow the Communist Party, Li Peng decided that action must be taken. He released to the media an editorial denouncing the students and their actions.

Multitudinous protests and demonstrations took place across China throughout the month of May, attracting international attention and further dividing the government over what action to take: negotiations or control. An upcoming visit by then Soviet President Mikhail Gorbachev made the Party progressively nervous as the situation became more complex, catching the attention of the world media. It appeared that the demonstrations, though passionate, were quite haphazard and severely lacking clear leadership. Smaller factions that had different agendas emerged, causing more chaos. Although most students finally did agree to return to classes, some refused to end the demonstrations and, learning of Gorbachev's visit, planned a hunger strike in the square intended to draw international attention. Gorbachev's visit was impeded by the protests as the students blocked nearly every street in Beijing, causing the Party extreme embarrassment, which is, in most Chinese and Asian cultures, a bona fide offense.

The Great Wall of China served as a barrier to keep out the Mongolian invaders. Courtesy of Jupiter Images.

As the nation became polarized by the protests, the Party remained just as indecisive as were when the protests began. Acting as peacemaker once again, Zhao tried to establish a dialogue between the Party and the students, even suggesting for the Party to be open to some reforms. Nevertheless, Premier Peng continued to insist that the government should not capitulate, lest the students overthrow the government, the Party, and ultimately China. After many unsuccessful attempts by Zhao to convince the students to end their strike, Martial Law was declared. A massive sit-in was scheduled in the square, drawing nearly 1.2 million supporters including many public service workers and members of the police and military. But when the Party called in the Army to occupy Beijing, the protesters and supporters blockaded the streets and effectively trapped the military inside the city.

This further humiliation became one of the final straws for the Party, and fear of losing control and the collapse of communism prompted the Party to plan military action against the "counter-revolutionary riots." While the Party planned their attack, the city was functioning without a recognizable police presence and the press was effectively free, an essential aspect of the events that soon followed.

Once the military was mobilized, the students and citizens attempted to break through the barriers and blockades. Panic and chaos ensued as the soldiers began to fire on unarmed citizens. The press, unmonitored and uncensored, transmitted the captured carnage to the international community. Many were killed and many more were wounded, overwhelming local hospitals.

On June 4th, the following day, the students, who were under orders to clear the square or face the consequences, finally voted to leave in peace. Some eyewitnesses reported that there were actually more stay-votes than go-votes. Determined to make their voices heard, some people decided to return later the same day. When the students did not leave after being ordered, the military opened fire, killing dozens of protestors at a time. Rescue workers trying to help the wounded were also gunned down, some in the back. Although the Chinese Red Cross initially reported as many as 2,600 deaths, the Chinese government quickly knocked down the numbers. The Chinese government released their official numbers at 241 dead (civilians and soldiers) and 7,000 wounded.[40]

In a final act of courage, one lone unarmed young man, carrying only shopping bags, stepped out in front of the tanks that were slowly rolling along Chang'an Boulevard toward Tiananmen Square. The tank tried to move around him several times, only to have the man step peacefully, persistently in the tanks path. Finally, the tank operator shut down the engines and the young man climbed up on top of the tank to speak with the driver, and shortly after jumped down. Although the young man with the shopping bags was subsequently swept away by two people purportedly trying to protect him, the impact and image of his bravery will never be forgotten. No one knows what became of this man as of yet. Many protestors who survived the events either moved to more remote areas, left the country if they were able, or became faceless people to protect their identities.

In a defiant non-violent act of protest, a young unidentified man stands in the way of approaching Chinese Army tanks.
Courtesy of the Associated Press.

In the aftermath, Chinese officials start a huge spin campaign in an attempt to justify the government's forceful tactics to end the "counter-revolutionary rebellion". This and other terms such as "anti-government riot" are injected into the lexicon of the international press. The city's military museum boasted 4,000 exhibits, showing burned buses and soldiers who had been hanged during the uprising. The government went so far as to say that "not one person was killed" that day in Tiananmen Square. They claimed that those who died were in direct combat with the military.

On the 1994 anniversary of the riots, Li Peng, who is still China's Premier, released a new security policy that any political discourse that opposed the Party line would be considered treason. Meanwhile, the far-reaching hand of the Party continued its sweeping search for dissidents, imprisoning tens of thousands of students, sending them to labor camps, or systematically beating and executing them.[41] As recently as 2004, the government produced a five-hour extremely biased documentary of the Tiananmen Square incident and made it country-wide required viewing for all officials. The Chinese government's absurd denial and desperate need to save face continues to this day. With the power of the Internet and software imported from the West, China forges ahead in its silent and efficient march to erase history.[42]

Developing nations like China are beginning to see that economic freedoms are closely tied in to political freedoms. It will be interesting in the coming months and years to see what positions governments take as their citizens yearn for more democratic principles.

Chapter Summary

On the morning of January 1, 2007 at 12:01am, Chief Justice John Roberts released the 2006 Year-End Report on the Federal Judiciary. Aside from the date and time, the leading statement said:

"Between December 19 and January 8 there are 32 college bowl games – but only one Year-End Report on the Federal Judiciary. I once asked my predecessor, Chief Justice William H. Rehnquist, why he released this annual report on the state of the federal courts on New Year's Day. He explained that it was difficult to get people to focus on the needs of the judiciary and January 1 was historically a slow news day – a day on which the concerns of the courts just might get noticed."[43]

This is very telling with regards to the way Americans view the importance of the federal Judiciary. The U.S. Supreme Court shapes the way we live for years after the president who appointed them has left office. As one of the least democratic branches of the federal government, it is important to understand how the vagueness of Article III along with a life-time appointment places such an importance on the selection process and Senate confirmation hearings. The structure of the federal judiciary is staffed with over one thousand jurists whose job it is to interpret the federal laws and Constitution in addition to overseeing the fifty state courts on federal issues.

The California judicial system is an entity of the state comprising of four levels of courts and many bureaucratic organizations, such as the police force, prisons, and state bar associations that work in conjunction within the system. Citizens participate directly in the court systems by serving on jury duty. They participate indirectly by voting during gubernatorial elections, for it is the governor that appoints most of the justices who serve in the Courts of Appeals and the state supreme court. Therefore, in all branches of government, whether state or federal, voting is essential to the concept of *Democracy & Action*.

The last comparative section discusses the concept of American Exceptionalism along with a summary of the democratic principles and case studies in developing democracies. This reinforces that the concept of democracy may have the same basic principle from country to country; however, the way each country goes about exploring it is as unique as the people, the culture, and the history of each of these countries. In each country we have seen astounding acts of bravery amongst impossible oppressive conditions. We have also seen the countries of the European Union, some former enemies who have engaged in wars for centuries, able to unite in an effort to achieve economic security and harmony. It is the hope of all who worked on this textbook that each student will, in any small way, be inspired to apply what they have learned. When in doubt, take action to affect change for a better democracy.

Key Terms:

Segregation

Judicial Review

Writ of Mandamus

Statuary Construction

Trial Court

Appellate Courts

Constitutional Courts

Legislative Courts

In forma pauperis

Writ of Certiorari

Rule of Four

Opinion of the Court

Concurring Opinion

Dissenting Opinion

Laissez-faire

Original Intent

Strict Construction

Test Case

Sunset Clause

Penumbra

Probable Cause

FISA Court

Civil Liberties

Civil Rights

DOMA law

Civil Union

LGBT

Politburo

Websites:

Federal Sites

The Supreme Court
www.supremecourtus.gov/

Federal Courts Home Page
www.uscourts.gov

Legal Information Institute, Cornell University Law School
http://www.law.cornell.edu

Senate Judiciary Committee
www.senate.gov/~judiciary/nominations.cfm

California Sites

California Court System
www.courtinfo.ca.gov

California Law References
www.leginfo.ca.gov/calaw

Legal Services of Northern California
http://www.lsnc.net/cal_courts.html

Additional Sites of Interest

National Center for State Courts
http://www.ncsonline.org/D_KIS/info_court_web_sites.html

European Union
http://www.eurunion.org/infores/euindex.htm

(English Gateway)
http://europa.eu/index_en.htm

APPENDICES

THE DECLARATION OF INDEPENDENCE

When in the Course of human events, it becomes necessary for one people to dissolve the political bands which have connected them with another, and to assume among the Powers of the earth, the separate and equal station to which the Laws of Nature and of Nature's God entitle them, a decent respect to the opinions of mankind requires that they should declare the causes which impel them to the separation.

We hold these truths to be self-evident, that all men are created equal, that they are endowed by their Creator with certain unalienable Rights, that among these are Life, Liberty and the pursuit of Happiness. That to secure these rights, Governments are instituted among Men, deriving their just powers from the consent of the governed, That whenever any Form of Government becomes destructive of these ends, it is the Right of the People to alter or to abolish it, and to institute new Government, laying its foundation on such principles and organizing its powers in such form, as to them shall seem most likely to effect their Safety and Happiness. Prudence, indeed, will dictate that Governments long established should not be changed for light and transient causes; and accordingly all experience hath shown, that mankind are more disposed to suffer, while evils are sufferable, than to right themselves by abolishing the forms to which they are accustomed. But when a long train of abuses and usurpations, pursuing invariably the same Object evinces a design to reduce them under absolute Despotism, it is their right, it is their duty, to throw off such Government, and to provide new Guards for their future security. — Such has been the patient sufferance of these Colonies; and such is now the necessity which constrains them to alter their former Systems of Government. The history of the present King of Great Britain is a history of repeated injuries and usurpations, all having in direct object the establishment of an absolute Tyranny over these States. To prove this, let Facts be submitted to a candid world.

He has refused his Assent to Laws, the most wholesome and necessary for the public good.

He has forbidden his Governors to pass Laws of immediate and pressing importance, unless suspended in their operation till his Assent should be obtained; and when so suspended, he has utterly neglected to attend to them.

He has refused to pass other Laws for the accommodation of large districts of people, unless those people would relinquish the right of Representation in the Legislature, a right inestimable to them and formidable to tyrants only.

He has called together legislative bodies at places unusual, uncomfortable, and distant from the depository of their Public Records, for the sole purpose of fatiguing them into compliance with his measures.

He has dissolved Representative Houses repeatedly, for opposing with manly firmness his invasions on the rights of the people.

He has refused for a long time, after such dissolutions, to cause others to be elected; whereby the Legislative Powers, incapable of Annihilation, have returned to the People at large for their exercise; the State remaining in the mean time exposed to all the dangers of invasion from without, and convulsions within.

He has endeavoured to prevent the population of these States; for that purpose obstructing the Laws of Naturalization of Foreigners; refusing to pass others to encourage their migration hither, and raising the conditions of new Appropriations of Lands.

He has obstructed the Administration of Justice, by refusing his Assent to Laws for establishing Judiciary Powers.

He has made Judges dependent on his Will alone, for the tenure of their offices, and the amount and payment of their salaries.

He has erected a multitude of New Offices, and sent hither swarms of Officers to harass our People, and eat out their substance.

He has kept among us, in times of peace, Standing Armies without the Consent of our legislature.

He has affected to render the Military independent of and superior to the Civil Power.

He has combined with others to subject us to a jurisdiction foreign to our constitution, and unacknowledged by our laws; giving his Assent to their acts of pretended legislation:

For quartering large bodies of armed troops among us:

For protecting them, by a mock Trial, from Punishment for any Murders which they should commit on the Inhabitants of these States:

For cutting off our Trade with all parts of the world:

For imposing taxes on us without our Consent:

For depriving us in many cases, of the benefits of Trial by Jury:

For transporting us beyond Seas to be tried for pretended offences:

For abolishing the free System of English Laws in a neighbouring Province, establishing therein an Arbitrary government, and enlarging its Boundaries so as to render it at once an example and fit instrument for introducing the same absolute rule into these Colonies:

For taking away our Charters, abolishing our most valuable Laws, and altering fundamentally the Forms of our Governments:

For suspending our own Legislature, and declaring themselves invested with Power to legislate for us in all cases whatsoever.

He has abdicated Government here, by declaring us out of his Protection and waging War against us.

He has plundered our seas, ravaged our Coasts, burnt our towns, and destroyed the lives of our people.

He is at this time transporting large armies of foreign mercenaries to compleat the works of death, desolation and tyranny, already begun with circumstances of Cruelty & perfidy scarcely paralleled in the most barbarous ages, and totally unworthy the Head of a civilized nation.

He has constrained our fellow Citizens taken Captive on the high Seas to bear Arms against their Country, to become the executioners of their friends and Brethren, or to fall themselves by their Hands.

He has excited domestic insurrections amongst us, and has endeavoured to bring on the inhabitants of our frontiers, the merciless Indian Savages, whose known rule of warfare, is an undistinguished destruction of all ages, sexes and conditions.

In every stage of these Oppressions We have Petitioned for Redress in the most humble terms: Our repeated Petitions have been answered only by repeated injury. A Prince, whose character is thus marked by every act which may define a Tyrant, is unfit to be the ruler of a free People.

Nor have We been wanting in attention to our British brethren. We have warned them from time to time of attempts by their legislature to extend an unwarrantable jurisdiction over us. We have reminded them of the circumstances of our emigration and settlement here. We have appealed to their native justice and magnanimity, and we have conjured them by the ties of our common kindred to disavow these usurpations, which, would inevitably interrupt our connections and correspondence. They too have been deaf to the voice of justice and of consanguinity. We must, therefore, acquiesce in the necessity, which denounces our Separation, and hold them, as we hold the rest of mankind, Enemies in War, in Peace Friends.

We, therefore, the Representatives of the united States of America, in General Congress, Assembled, appealing to the Supreme Judge of the world for the rectitude of our intentions, do, in the Name, and by Authority of the good People of these Colonies, solemnly publish and declare, That these United Colonies are, and of Right ought to be Free and Independent States; that they are Absolved from all Allegiance to the British Crown, and that all political connection between them and the State of Great Britain, is and ought to be totally dissolved; and that as Free and Independent States, they have full Power to levy War, conclude Peace, contract Alliances, establish Commerce, and to do all other Acts and Things which Independent States may of right do. And for the support of this Declaration, with a firm reliance of the Protection of Divine Providence, we mutually pledge to each other our Lives, our Fortunes and our sacred Honor.

John Hancock,

Josiah Bartlett, Wm Whipple, Saml Adams, John Adams, Robt Treat Paine, Elbridge Gerry, Steph. Hopkins, William Ellery, Roger Sherman, Samel Huntington, Wm Williams, Oliver Wolcott, Matthew Thornton, Wm Floyd, Phil Livingston, Frans Lewis, Lewis Morris, Richd Stockton, Jno Witherspoon, Fras Hopkinson, John Hart, Abra Clark, Robt Morris, Benjamin Rush, Benja Franklin, John Morton, Geo Clymer, Jas Smith, Geo. Taylor, James Wilson, Geo. Ross, Caesar Rodney, Geo Read, Thos M:Kean, Samuel Chase, Wm Paca, Thos Stone, Charles Carroll of Carrollton, George Wythe, Richard Henry Lee, Th. Jefferson, Benja Harrison, Thos Nelson, Jr., Francis Lightfoot Lee, Carter Braxton, Wm Hooper, Joseph Hewes, John Penn, Edward Rutledge, Thos Heyward, Junr., Thomas Lynch, Junor., Arthur Middleton, Button Gwinnett, Lyman Hall, Geo Walton.

THE CONSTITUTION OF THE UNITED STATES

We the people of the United States, in Order to form a more perfect Union, establish Justice, insure domestic Tranquility, provide for the common defence, promote the general Welfare, and secure the Blessings of Liberty to ourselves and our Posterity, do ordain and establish this constitution for the United States of America.

Article I

Section 1 All legislative Powers herein granted shall be vested in a Congress of the United States, which shall consist of a Senate and House of Representatives.

Section 2 The House of Representatives shall be composed of Members chosen every second Year by the People of the several States, and the Electors in each State shall have the Qualifications requisite for Electors of the most numerous Branch of the State Legislature.

No person shall be a Representative who shall not have attained to the Age of twenty-five Years, and been seven Years a Citizen of the United States, and who shall not, when elected, be an Inhabitant of that State in which he shall be chosen.

Representatives and direct Taxes shall be apportioned among the several States which may be included within this Union, according to their respective Numbers, which shall be determined by adding to the whole Number of free Persons, including those bound to Service for a Term of Years, and excluding Indians not taxed, three fifths of all other Persons. The actual Enumeration shall be made within three Years after the first Meeting of the Congress of the United States, and within every subsequent Term of ten Years, in such Manner as they shall by Law direct. The Number of Representatives shall not exceed one for every thirty Thousand, but each State shall have at Least one Representative; and until such enumeration shall be made, the State of New Hampshire shall be entitled to chuse three, Massachusetts eight, Rhode-Island and Providence Plantations one, Connecticut five, New-York six, New Jersey four, Pennsylvania eight, Delaware one, Maryland six, Virginia ten, North Carolina five, South Carolina five, and Georgia three.

When vacancies happen in the Representation from any State, the Executive Authority thereof shall issue Writs of Election to fill such Vacancies.

The House of Representatives shall chuse their Speaker and other Officers; and shall have the sole Power of Impeachment.

Section 3 The Senate of the United States shall be composed of two Senators from each State, chosen by the Legislature thereof, for six Years; and each Senator shall have one Vote.

Immediately after they shall be assembled in Consequence of the first Election, they shall be divided as equally as may be into three Classes. The Seats of the Senators of the first Class shall be vacated at the Expiration of the second Year, of the second Class at the Expiration of the fourth Year, and of the third Class at the Expiration of the sixth Year, so that one-third may be chosen every second Year; and if Vacancies happen by Resignation, or otherwise, during the Recess of the Legislature of any State, the Executive thereof may make temporary Appointments until the next Meeting of the Legislature, which shall then fill such Vacancies.

No Person shall be a Senator who shall not have attained to the Age of thirty Years, and been nine Years a Citizen of the United States, and who shall not, when elected, be an Inhabitant of that State in which he shall be chosen.

The Vice President of the United States shall be President of the Senate, but shall have no vote, unless they be equally divided.

The Senate shall chuse their other Officers, and also a President pro tempore, in the absence of the Vice President, or when he shall exercise the Office of the President of the United States.

The Senate shall have the sole Power to try all Impeachments. When sitting for that purpose, they shall be on Oath or Affirmation. When the President of the United States is tried, the Chief Justice shall preside: And no person shall be convicted without the Concurrence of two thirds of the Members present.

Judgment in Cases of Impeachment shall not extend further than to removal from Office, and disqualification to hold and enjoy any Office of honor, Trust, or Profit under the United States: but the Party convicted shall nevertheless be liable and subject to Indictment, Trial, Judgment, and Punishment, according to Law.

Section 4 The Times, Places and Manner of holding Elections for Senators and Representatives, shall be prescribed in each state by the Legislature thereof; but the Congress may at any time by Law make or alter such Regulations, except as to the Places of Chusing Senators.

The Congress shall assemble at least once in every Year, and such Meeting shall be on the first Monday in December, unless they shall by Law appoint a different Day.

Section 5 Each House shall be the Judge of the Elections, Returns and Qualifications of its own Members, and a Majority of each shall constitute a Quorum to do Business; but a smaller number may adjourn from day to day, and may be authorized to compel the Attendance of absent Members, in such Manner, and under such Penalties, as each House may provide.

Each House may determine the Rules of its Proceedings, punish its Members for disorderly Behavior, and, with the Concurrence of two thirds, expel a Member.

Each House shall keep a Journal of its Proceedings, and from time to time publish the same, excepting such Parts as may in their Judgment require Secrecy; and the Yeas and Nays of the Members of either House on any question shall, at the Desire of one fifth of those Present, be entered on the Journal.

Neither House, during the Session of Congress, shall, without the Consent of the other, adjourn for more than three days, nor to any other Place than that in which the two Houses shall be sitting.

Section 6 The Senators and Representatives shall receive a Compensation for their Services, to be ascertained by Law, and paid out of the Treasury of the United States. They shall in all Cases, except Treason, Felony, and Breach of the Peace, be privileged from arrest during their Attendance at the Session of their respective Houses, and in going to and returning from the same; and for any Speech or Debate in either House, they shall not be questioned in any other Place.

No Senator or Representative shall, during the Time for which he was elected, be appointed to any civil Office under the Authority of the United States, which shall have been created, or the Emoluments whereof shall have been increased, during such time; and no Person holding any Office under the United States shall be a Member of either House during his continuance in Office.

Section 7 All Bills for raising Revenue shall originate in the House of Representatives; but the Senate may propose or concur with Amendments as on other bills.

Every Bill which shall have passed the House of Representatives and the Senate, shall, before it become a Law, be presented to the President of the United States; If he approve he shall sign it, but if not he shall return it, with his Objections, to that House in which it shall have originated, who shall enter the Objections at large on their Journal, and proceed to reconsider it. If after such Reconsideration two thirds of that House shall agree to pass the bill, it shall be sent, together with the objections, to the other House, by which it shall likewise be reconsidered, and if approved by two thirds of that House, it shall become a Law. But in all such Cases the Votes of both Houses shall be determined by Yeas and Nays, and the Names of the Persons voting for and against the Bill shall be entered on the Journal of each House respectively. If any Bill shall not be returned by the President within ten Days (Sundays excepted) after it shall have been presented to him, the Same shall be a Law, in like Manner as if he had signed it, unless the Congress by their Adjournment prevent its Return, in which Case it shall not be a Law.

Every Order, Resolution, or Vote to which the Concurrence of the Senate and House of Representatives may be necessary (except on a question of Adjournment) shall be presented to the President of the United States; and before the Same shall take Effect, shall be approved by him, or being disapproved by him, shall be repassed by two thirds of the Senate and House of Representatives, according to the Rules and Limitations prescribed in the Case of a Bill.

Section 8 The Congress shall have Power

To lay and collect Taxes, Duties, Imposts and Excises, to pay the Debts and provide for the common Defence and general Welfare of the United States; but all Duties, Imposts and Excises shall be uniform throughout the United States;

To borrow money on the credit of the United States;

To regulate Commerce with foreign Nations, and among the several States, and with the Indian Tribes;

To establish a uniform Rule of Naturalization, and uniform Laws on the subject of Bankruptcies throughout the United States;

To coin Money, regulate the Value thereof, and of foreign Coin, and fix the Standard of Weights and Measures;

To provide for the Punishment of counterfeiting the Securities and current Coin of the United States;

To establish Post offices and post Roads;

To promote the Progress of Science and useful Arts, by securing for limited Times to Authors and Inventors the exclusive Right to their respective Writings and Discoveries;

To constitute Tribunals inferior to the Supreme Court;

To define and punish Piracies and Felonies committed on the high Seas, and Offences against the Law of Nations;

To declare War, grant Letters of Marque and Reprisal, and make Rules concerning Captures on Land and Water;

To raise and support Armies, but no Appropriation of Money to that Use shall be for a longer Term than two Years;

To provide and maintain a Navy;

To make Rules for the Government and Regulation of the land and naval forces;

To provide for calling forth the Militia to execute the Laws of the Union, suppress Insurrections and repel Invasions;

To provide for organizing, arming, and disciplining the Militia, and for governing such Part of them as may be employed in the Service of the United States, reserving to the States respectively, the Appointment of the Officers, and the Authority of training the Militia according to the discipline prescribed by Congress;

To exercise exclusive Legislation in all Cases whatsoever, over such District (not exceeding ten Miles square) as may, by Cession of particular States, and the acceptance of Congress, become the Seat of Government of the United States, and to exercise like Authority over all Places purchased by the Consent of the Legislature of the State in which the Same shall be, for the Erection of Forts, Magazines, Arsenals, dock-Yards, and other needful Buildings; — And

To make all Laws which shall be necessary and proper for carrying into Execution the foregoing Powers, and all other Powers vested by this Constitution in the government of the United States, or in any Department or Officer thereof.

Section 9 The Migration or Importation of such Persons as any of the States now existing shall think proper to admit, shall not be prohibited by the Congress prior to the Year one thousand eight hundred and eight, but a tax or duty may be imposed on such Importation, not exceeding ten dollars for each Person.

The privilege of the Writ of Habeas Corpus shall not be suspended, unless when in Cases of Rebellion or Invasion the public Safety may require it.

No Bill of Attainder or ex post facto Law shall be passed.

No capitation, or other direct, Tax shall be laid unless in Proportion to the Census or Enumeration herein before directed to be taken.

No Tax or Duty shall be laid on Articles exported from any State.

No Preference shall be given by any Regulation of Revenue to the Ports of one State over those of another: nor shall Vessels bound to, or from, one state, be obliged to enter, clear, or pay Duties in another.

No Money shall be drawn from the Treasury, but in Consequence of Appropriations made by Law; and a regular Statement and Account of the Receipts and Expenditures of all public Money shall be published from time to time.

No Title of Nobility shall be granted by the United States: And no Person holding any Office of Profit or Trust under them, shall, without the Consent of the Congress, accept of any present, Emolument, Office, or Title, of any kind whatever, from any King, Prince, or Foreign State.

Section 10 No state shall enter into any Treaty, Alliance, or Confederation; grant Letters of Marque and Reprisal; coin Money; emit Bills of Credit; make any Thing but gold and silver Coin a Tender in Payment of Debts; pass any Bill of Attainder, ex post facto Law, or Law impairing the Obligation of Contracts, or grant any Title of Nobility.

No State shall, without the Consent of the Congress, lay any Imposts or Duties on Imports or Exports, except what may be absolutely necessary for executing its inspection Laws: and the net Produce of all Duties and Imposts, laid by any State on Imports or Exports, shall be for the Use of the Treasury of the United States; and all such Laws shall be subject to the Revision and Control of the Congress.

No State shall, without the Consent of Congress, lay any duty of Tonnage, keep Troops, or Ships of War in time of Peace, enter into any Agreement or Compact with another State, or with a foreign Power, or engage in War, unless actually invaded, or in such imminent Danger as will not admit of delay.

Article II

Section 1 The executive Power shall be vested in a President of the United States of America. He shall hold his Office during the Term of four years, and, together with the Vice President, chosen for the same Term, be elected, as follows:

Each State shall appoint, in such Manner as the Legislature thereof may direct, a Number of Electors, equal to the whole Number of Senators and Representatives to which the State may be entitled in the Congress; but no Senator or Representative, or Person holding an Office of Trust or Profit under the United States, shall be appointed an Elector.

The Electors shall meet in their respective States, and vote by Ballot for two persons, of whom one at least shall not be an Inhabitant of the same State with themselves. And they shall make a List of all the Persons voted for, and of the Number of Votes for each; which List they shall sign and certify, and transmit sealed to the Seat of the Government of the United States, directed to the President of the Senate. The President of the Senate shall, in the Presence of the Senate and House of Representatives, open all the Certificates, and the Votes shall then be counted. The Person having the greatest Number of Votes shall be the President, if such Number be a Majority of the whole Number of Electors appointed; and if there be more than one who have such Majority, and have an equal Number of Votes, then the House of Representatives shall immediately chuse by Ballot one of them for President; and if no Person have a Majority, then from the five highest on the List the said House shall in like Manner chuse the President. But in chusing the President, the votes shall be taken by States, the Representation from each State having one Vote; a quorum for this Purpose shall consist of a Member or Members from two-thirds of the States, and a Majority of all the States shall be necessary to a Choice. In every Case, after the Choice of the President, the Person having the greatest Number of Votes of the Electors shall be the Vice President. But if there should remain two or more who have equal votes, the Senate shall chuse from them by Ballot the Vice President.

The Congress may determine the time of chusing the Electors, and the Day on which they shall give their Votes; which Day shall be the same throughout the United States.

No person except a natural-born Citizen, or a Citizen of the United States, at the time of the Adoption of this Constitution, shall be eligible to the Office of President; neither shall any Person be eligible to that Office who shall not have attained to the Age of thirty-five years, and been fourteen Years a Resident within the United States.

In Case of the Removal of the President from Office, or of his Death, Resignation, or Inability to discharge the Powers and Duties of the said Office, the same shall devolve on the Vice President, and the Congress may by

Law provide for the Case of Removal, Death, Resignation, or Inability, both of the President and Vice President, declaring what Officer shall then act as President, and such Officer shall act accordingly, until the disability be removed, or a President shall be elected.

The President shall, at stated Times, receive for his Services a Compensation, which shall neither be increased nor diminished during the Period for which he shall have been elected, and he shall not receive within that Period any other Emolument from the United States, or any of them.

Before he enter on the execution of his Office, he shall take the following Oath or Affirmation:—"I do solemnly swear (or affirm) that I will faithfully execute the Office of President of the United States, and will, to the best of my Ability, preserve, protect, and defend the Constitution of the United States."

Section 2 The President shall be Commander in Chief of the Army and Navy of the United States, and of the Militia of the several States, when called into the actual

Service of the United States; he may require the Opinion, in writing, of the principal Officer in each of the executive Departments, upon any subject relating to the Duties of their respective Offices, and he shall have Power to Grant Reprieves and Pardons for Offences against the United States, except in Cases of Impeachment.

He shall have Power, by and with the Advice and Consent of the Senate, to make Treaties, provided two thirds of the Senators present concur; and he shall nominate, and by and with the Advice and Consent of the Senate, shall appoint Ambassadors, other public Ministers and Consuls, Judges of the supreme Court, and all other Officers of the United States, whose Appointments are not herein otherwise provided for, and which shall be established by Law: but the Congress may by Law vest the Appointment of such inferior Officers, as they think proper, in the President alone, in the Courts of Law, or in the Heads of Departments.

The President shall have Power to fill up all Vacancies that may happen during the Recess of the Senate, by granting Commissions which shall expire at the End of their next Session.

Section 3 He shall from time to time give to the Congress Information of the State of the Union, and recommend to their Consideration such Measures as he shall judge necessary and expedient; he may, on extraordinary occasions, convene both Houses, or either of them, and in Case of Disagreement between them, with respect to the Time of Adjournment, he may adjourn them to such Time as he shall think proper; he shall receive Ambassadors and other public Ministers; he shall take Care that the Laws be faithfully executed, and shall Commission all the Officers of the United States.

Section 4 The President, Vice President and all civil Officers of the United States, shall be removed from Office on Impeachment for, and Conviction of, Treason, Bribery, or other high Crimes and Misdemeanors.

Article III

Section 1 The judicial Power of the United States, shall be vested in one supreme Court, and in such inferior Courts as the Congress may from time to time ordain and establish. The Judges, both of the supreme and inferior Courts, shall hold their Offices during good Behaviour, and shall, at stated Times, receive for their Services, a Compensation, which shall not be diminished during their Continuance in Office.

Section 2 The judicial Power shall extend to all Cases, in Law and Equity, arising under this Constitution, the Laws of the United States, and treaties made, or which shall be made, under their Authority;—to all Cases affecting ambassadors, other public ministers and consuls;—to all cases of admiralty and maritime Jurisdiction;—to Controversies to which the United States shall be a Party;—to Controversies between two or more States;—between a State and Citizens of another State;—between Citizens of different States,—between

Citizens of the same State claiming Lands under Grants of different States, and between a State, or the Citizens thereof, and foreign States, Citizens or Subjects.

In all Cases affecting Ambassadors, other public Ministers and Consuls, and those in which a State shall be Party, the supreme Court shall have original Jurisdiction. In all the other Cases before mentioned, the supreme Court shall have appellate Jurisdiction, both as to Law and Fact, with such Exceptions, and under such Regulations as the Congress shall make.

The trial of all Crimes, except in Cases of Impeachment, shall be by Jury; and such Trial shall be held in the State where the said Crimes shall have been committed; but when not committed within any State, the Trial shall be at such Place or Places as the Congress may by Law have directed.

Section 3 Treason against the United States, shall consist only in levying War against them, or in adhering to their Enemies, giving them Aid and Comfort. No Person shall be convicted of Treason unless on the testimony of two Witnesses to the same overt Act, or on Confession in open Court.

The Congress shall have power to declare the Punishment of Treason, but no Attainder of Treason shall work Corruption of Blood, or Forfeiture except during the Life of the Person attained.

Article IV

Section 1 Full Faith and Credit shall be given in each State to the public Acts, Records, and judicial Proceedings of every other State. And the Congress may by general Laws prescribe the Manner in which such Acts, Records and Proceedings shall be proved, and the Effect thereof.

Section 2 The Citizens of each State shall be entitled to all Privileges and Immunities of Citizens in the several States.

A Person charged in any State with Treason, Felony, or other Crime, who shall flee from Justice, and be found in another State, shall on demand of the executive Authority of the State from which he fled, be delivered up, to be removed to the State having Jurisdiction of the crime.

No Person held to Service or Labour in one State, under the Laws thereof, escaping into another, shall, in Consequence of any Law or Regulation therein, be discharged from such Service or Labour, but shall be delivered up on Claim of the Party to whom such Service or Labour may be due.

Section 3 New States may be admitted by the Congress into this Union; but no new State shall be formed or erected within the Jurisdiction of any other State; nor any State be formed by the Junction of two or more States, or parts of States, without the Consent of the Legislatures of the States concerned as well as of the Congress.

The Congress shall have Power to dispose of and make all needful Rules and Regulations respecting the Territory or other Property belonging to the United States; and nothing in this Constitution shall be so construed as to

Prejudice any Claims of the United States, or of any particular State.

Section 4 The United States shall guarantee to every State in this Union a Republican Form of Government, and shall protect each of them against Invasion; and on Application of the Legislature, or the Executive (when the Legislature cannot be convened) against domestic Violence.

Article V

The Congress, whenever two-thirds of both Houses shall deem it necessary, shall propose Amendments to this Constitution, or, on the Application of the Legislatures of two-thirds of the several States, shall call a Convention for proposing Amendments, which, in either Case, shall be valid to all Intents and Purposes, as part of this Constitution, when ratified by the Legislatures of three-fourths of the several States, or by Conventions in three-fourths thereof, as the one or the other Mode of Ratification may be proposed by the Congress; Provided that no Amendment which may be made prior to the Year One thousand eight hundred and eight shall in any Manner affect the first and fourth Clauses in the Ninth Section of the first Article; and that no State, without its Consent, shall be deprived of its equal Suffrage in the Senate.

Article VI

All Debts contracted and Engagements entered into, before the Adoption of this Constitution, shall be as valid against the United States under this Constitution, as under the Confederation.

This Constitution, and the Laws of the United States which shall be made in Pursuance thereof; and all Treaties made, or which shall be made, under the Authority of the United States, shall be the supreme Law of the Land; and the Judges in every State shall be bound thereby, any Thing in the Constitution or Laws of any State to the Contrary notwithstanding.

The Senators and Representatives before mentioned, and the Members of the several State Legislatures and all executive and judicial Officers, both of the United States and of the several States, shall be bound by Oath or Affirmation to support this Constitution; but no religious Test shall ever be required as a qualification to any Office or public Trust under the United States.

Article VII

The Ratification of the Conventions of nine States shall be sufficient for the Establishment of this Constitution between the States so ratifying the same.

Done in Convention by the Unanimous Consent of the States present the Seventeenth Day of September in the Year of our Lord one thousand seven hundred and Eighty seven, and of the Independence of the United States of America the Twelfth. In Witness whereof We have hereunto subscribed our Names.

Go. Washington, President and deputy from Virginia; Attest William Jackson, Secretary; Delaware: Geo. Read,* Gunning Bedford, Jr., John Dickinson, Richard Basset, Jaco. Broom; Maryland: James McHenry, Daniel of St. Thomas' Jenifer, Danl. Carroll; Virginia: John Blair, James Madison, Jr.; North Carolina: Wm. Blount, Richd. Dobbs Spaight, Hu Williamson; South Carolina: J. Rutledge, Charles Cotesworth Pinckney, Charles Pinckney, Pierce Butler; Georgia: William Few, Abr. Baldwin; New Hampshire: John Langdon, Nicholas Gilman; Massachusetts: Nathaniel Gorham, Rufus King; Connecticut: Wm. Saml. Johnson, Roger Sherman,* New York: Alexander Hamilton; New Jersey: Wil. Livingston, David Brearley, Wm. Paterson, Jona. Dayton; Pennsylvania: B. Franklin,* Thomas Mifflin, Robt. Morris,* Geo. Clymer,* Thos. FitzSimons, Jared Ingersoll, James Wilson, Gouv. Morris.

Articles in Addition to, and Amendment of, the Constitution of the United States of America, Proposed by Congress, and Ratified by the Legislatures of the Several States, Pursuant to the Fifth Article of the Original Constitution.

Amendment I [1791]

Congress shall make no law respecting an establishment of religion, or prohibiting the free exercise thereof; or abridging the freedom of speech, or of the press; or the right of the people peaceably to assemble, and to petition the Government for a redress of grievances.

Amendment II [1791]

A well regulated Militia, being necessary to the security of a free State, the right of the people to keep and bear Arms shall not be infringed.

Amendment III [1791]

No Soldier shall, in time of peace, be quartered in any house, without the consent of the Owner, nor in time of war, but in a manner to be prescribed by law.

Amendment IV [1791]

The right of the people to be secure in their persons, houses, papers, and effects, against unreasonable searches and seizures, shall not be violated, and no Warrants shall issue, but upon probable cause, supported by Oath or affirmation, and particularly describing the place to be searched, and the persons or things to be seized.

Amendment V [1791]

No person shall be held to answer for a capital or otherwise infamous crime, unless on a presentment or indictment of a Grand Jury, except in cases arising in the land or naval forces, or in the Militia, when in actual service in time of War or public danger; nor shall any person be subject for the same offence to be twice put in jeopardy of life or limb; nor shall be compelled in any criminal case to be a witness against himself, nor be deprived of life, liberty, or property, without due process of law; nor shall private property be taken for public use, without just compensation.

Amendment VI [1791]

In all criminal prosecutions, the accused shall enjoy the right to a speedy and public trial, by an impartial jury of the State and district wherein the crime shall have been committed, which district shall have been previously ascertained by law, and to be informed of the nature and cause of the accusation; to be confronted with the witnesses against him; to have compulsory process for obtaining witnesses in his favor, and to have the Assistance of Counsel for his defence.

Amendment VII [1791]

In suits at common law, where the value in controversy shall exceed twenty dollars, the right of trial by jury shall be preserved, and no fact tried by a jury, shall be otherwise reexamined in any Court of the United States, than according to the rules of the common law.

Amendment VIII [1791]

Excessive bail shall not be required, nor excessive fines imposed, nor cruel and unusual punishments inflicted.

Amendment IX [1791]

The enumeration in the Constitution, of certain rights, shall not be construed to deny or disparage others retained by the people.

Amendment X [1791]

The powers not delegated to the United States by the Constitution, nor prohibited by it to the States, are reserved to the States respectively, or to the people.

Amendment XI [1798]

The Judicial power of the United States shall not be construed to extend to any suit in law or equity, commenced or prosecuted against one of the United States by Citizens of another State, or by Citizens or Subjects of any Foreign State.

Amendment XII [1804]

The Electors shall meet in their respective States and vote by ballot for President and Vice President, one of whom, at least, shall not be an inhabitant of the same State with themselves; they shall name in their ballots the person voted for as President, and in distinct ballots the person voted for as Vice President, and they shall make distinct lists of all persons voted for as President, and of all persons voted for as Vice President, and of the number of votes for each, which lists they shall sign and certify, and transmit sealed to the seat of the government of the United States, directed to the President of the Senate;—The President of the Senate shall, in the presence of the Senate and House of Representatives, open all the certificates and the votes shall then be counted;—The person having the greatest number of votes for President, shall be the President, if such number be a majority of the whole number of Electors appointed; and if no person have such majority, then from the persons having the highest numbers not exceeding three on the list of those voted for as President, the House of Representatives shall choose immediately, by ballot, the President. But in choosing the President, the votes shall be taken by states, the representation from each state having one vote; a quorum for this purpose shall consist of a member or members from two-thirds of the states, and a majority of all the states shall be necessary to a choice. And if the House of Representatives shall not choose a President whenever the right of choice shall devolve upon them, before the fourth day of March next following, then the Vice President shall act as President, as in the case of the death or other constitutional disability of the President.—The person having the greatest number of votes as Vice President, shall be the Vice President, if such number be a majority of the whole number of Electors appointed, and if no person have a majority, then from the two highest numbers on the list, the Senate shall choose the Vice President; a quorum for the purpose shall consist of two-thirds of the whole number of Senators, and a majority of the whole number shall be necessary to a choice. But no person constitutionally ineligible to the office of President shall be eligible to that of Vice President of the United States.

Amendment XIII [1865]

Section 1 Neither slavery nor involuntary servitude, except as a punishment for crime whereof the party shall have been duly convicted, shall exist within the United States, or any place subject to their jurisdiction.

Section 2 Congress shall have power to enforce this article by appropriate legislation.

Amendment XIV [1868]

Section 1 All persons born or naturalized in the United States, and subject to the jurisdiction thereof, are citizens of the United States and of the State wherein they reside. No State shall make or enforce any law which shall abridge the privileges or immunities of citizens of the United States; nor shall any State deprive any person of life, liberty, or property, without due process of law; nor deny to any person within its jurisdiction the equal protection of the laws.

Section 2 Representatives shall be apportioned among the several States according to their respective numbers, counting the whole number of persons in each State, excluding Indians not taxed. But when the right to vote at any election for the choice of electors for President and Vice President of the United States, Representatives in

Congress, the Executive and Judicial officers of a State, or the members of the Legislature thereof, is denied to any of the male inhabitants of such State, being twenty-one years of age, and citizens of the United States or in any way abridged, except for participation in rebellion, or other crime, the basis of representation therein shall be reduced in the proportion which the number of such male citizens shall bear to the whole number of male citizens twenty-one years of age in such State.

Section 3 No person shall be a Senator or Representative in Congress, or elector of President and Vice President, or hold any office, civil or military, under the United States, or under any State, who, having previously taken an oath, as a member of Congress, or as an officer of the United States, or as a member of any State legislature, or as an executive or judicial officer of any State, to support the Constitution of the United States, shall have engaged in insurrection or rebellion against the same, or given aid or comfort to the enemies thereof. But Congress may by a vote of two-thirds of each House, remove such disability.

Section 4 The validity of the public debt of the United States, authorized by law, including debts incurred for payment of pensions and bounties for services in suppressing insurrection or rebellion, shall not be questioned. But neither the United States nor any State shall assume or pay any debt or obligation incurred in aid of insurrection or rebellion against the United States, or any claim for the loss or emancipation of any slave; but all such debts, obligations, and claims shall be held illegal and void.

Section 5 The Congress shall have the power to enforce, by appropriate legislation, the provisions of this article.

Amendment XV [1870]

Section 1 The right of citizens of the United States to vote shall not be denied or abridged by the United States or by any State on account of race, color, or previous condition of servitude—

Section 2 The Congress shall have power to enforce this article by appropriate legislation.

Amendment XVI [1913]

The Congress shall have power to lay and collect taxes on incomes, from whatever source derived, without apportionment among the several States, and without regard to any census or enumeration.

Amendment XVII [1913]

The Senate of the United States shall be composed of two Senators from each State, elected by the people thereof, for six years; and each Senator shall have one vote. The electors in each State shall have the qualifications requisite for electors of the most numerous branch of the State legislatures.

When vacancies happen in the representation of any State in the Senate, the executive authority of such State shall issue writs of election to fill such vacancies: Provided, That the legislature of any State may empower the executive thereof to make temporary appointments until the people fill the vacancies by election as the legislature may direct. This amendment shall not be so construed as to affect the election or term of any Senator chosen before it becomes valid as part of the Constitution.

Amendment XVIII [1919]

Section 1 After one year from the ratification of this article the manufacture, sale, or transportation of intoxicating liquors within, the importation thereof into, or the exportation thereof from the United States and all territory subject to the jurisdiction thereof for beverage purposes is hereby prohibited.

Section 2 The Congress and the several States shall have concurrent power to enforce this article by appropriate legislation.

Section 3 This article shall be inoperative unless it shall have been ratified as an amendment to the Constitution by the legislatures of the several States, as provided in the Constitution, within seven years from the date of the submission hereof to the States by the Congress.

Amendment XIX [1920]

The right of citizens of the United States to vote shall not be denied or abridged by the United States or by any State on account of sex.

Congress shall have power to enforce this article by appropriate legislation.

Amendment XX [1933]

Section 1 The terms of the President and Vice President shall end at noon on the 20th day of January, and the terms of Senators and Representatives at noon on the 3d day of January, of the years in which such terms would have ended if this article had not been ratified; and the terms of their successors shall then begin.

Section 2 The Congress shall assemble at least once in every year, and such meeting shall begin at noon on the 3d day of January, unless they shall by law appoint a different day.

Section 3 If, at the time fixed for the beginning of the term of the President, the President elect shall have died, the Vice President elect shall become President. If a President shall not have been chosen before the time fixed for the beginning of his term, or if the President elect shall have failed to qualify, then the Vice President elect shall act as President until a President shall have qualified; and the Congress may by law provide for the case wherein neither a President elect nor a Vice President elect shall have qualified, declaring who shall then act as President, or the manner in which one who is to act shall be selected, and such person shall act accordingly until a President or Vice President shall have qualified.

Section 4 The Congress may by law provide for the case of the death of any of the persons from whom the House of Representatives may choose a President whenever the right of choice shall have devolved upon them, and for the case of the death of any of the persons from whom the Senate may choose a Vice President whenever the right of choice shall have devolved upon them.

Section 5 Sections 1 and 2 shall take effect on the 15th day of October following the ratification of this article.

Section 6 This article shall be inoperative unless it shall have been ratified as an amendment to the Constitution by the legislatures of three-fourths of the several States within seven years from the date of its submission.

Amendment XXI [1933]

Section 1 The eighteenth article of amendment to the Constitution of the United States is hereby repealed.

Section 2 The transportation or importation into any State, Territory, or possession of the United States for delivery or use therein of intoxicating liquors, in violation of the laws thereof, is hereby prohibited.

Section 3 This article shall be inoperative unless it shall have been ratified as an amendment to the Constitution by conventions in the several States, as provided in the Constitution, within seven years from the date of the submission hereof to the States by the Congress.

Amendment XXII [1951]

No person shall be elected to the office of the President more than twice, and no person who has held the office of President, or acted as President, for more than two years of a term to which some other person was elected President shall be elected to the office of the President more than once.

But this Article shall not apply to any person holding the office of President when this Article was proposed by the Congress, and shall not prevent any person who may be holding the office of President or acting as President, during the term within which this Article becomes operative from holding the office of President or acting as President during the remainder of such term.

Amendment XXIII [1961]

Section 1 The District constituting the seat of Government of the United States shall appoint in such manner as the Congress may direct:

A number of electors of President and Vice President equal to the whole number of Senators and Representatives in Congress to which the District would be entitled if it were a State, but in no event more than the least populous State; they shall be in addition to those appointed by the States, but they shall be considered, for the purposes of the election of President and Vice President, to be electors appointed by a State; and they shall meet in the District and perform such duties as provided by the twelfth article of amendment.

Section 2 The Congress shall have power to enforce this article by appropriate legislation.

Amendment XXIV [1964]

Section 1 The right of citizens of the United States to vote in any primary or other election for President or Vice President, for electors for President or Vice President, or for Senator or Representative in Congress, shall not be denied or abridged by the United States or any State by reason of failure to pay any poll tax or other tax.

Section 2 The Congress shall have the power to enforce this article by appropriate legislation.

Amendment XXV [1967]

Section 1 In case of the removal of the President from office or his death or resignation, the Vice President shall become President.

Section 2 Whenever there is a vacancy in the office of the Vice President, the President shall nominate a Vice President who shall take the office upon confirmation by a majority vote of both houses of Congress.

Section 3 Whenever the President transmits to the President pro tempore of the Senate and the Speaker of the House of Representatives his written declaration that he is unable to discharge the powers and duties of his office, and until he transmits to them a written declaration to the contrary, such powers and duties shall be discharged by the Vice President as Acting President.

Section 4 Whenever the Vice President and a majority of either the principal officers of the executive departments, or of such other body as Congress may by law provide, transmit to the President pro tempore of the Senate and the Speaker of the House of Representatives their written declaration that the President is unable to discharge the powers and duties of his office, the Vice President shall immediately assume the powers and duties of the office as Acting President.

Thereafter, when the President transmits to the President pro tempore of the Senate and the Speaker of the House of Representatives his written declaration that no inability exists, he shall resume the powers and duties of his office unless the Vice President and a majority of either the principal officers of the executive departments, or of such other body as Congress may by law provide, transmit within four days to the President pro tempore of the Senate and the Speaker of the House of Representatives their written declaration that the President is unable to discharge the powers and duties of his office. Thereupon Congress shall decide the issue, assembling within 48 hours for that purpose if not in session. If the Congress, within 21 days after receipt of the latter written declaration, or, if Congress is not in session, within 21 days after Congress is required to assemble, determines by two-thirds vote of both houses that the President is unable to discharge the powers and duties of his office, the Vice President shall continue to discharge the same as Acting President; otherwise, the President shall resume the powers and duties of his office.

Amendment XXVI [1971]

Section 1 The right of citizens of the United States, who are 18 years of age or older, to vote shall not be denied or abridged by the United States or any state on account of age.

Section 2 The Congress shall have the power to enforce this article by appropriate legislation.

Amendment XXVII [1992]

No law varying the compensation for the service of Senators and Representatives shall take effect until an election of Representatives shall have intervened.

The Federalist Papers is a collection of 85 essays written by Alexander Hamilton, John Jay, and James Madison under the pen name Publius. They were published in New York newspapers in 1787 and 1788 to support ratification of the Constitution. Excerpts from Federalist Nos. 10, 51, and 78 are reprinted here.

JAMES MADISON: Federalist No. 10

Among the numerous advantages promised by a well constructed Union, none deserves to be more accurately developed than its tendency to break and control the violence of faction. The friend of popular governments never finds himself so much alarmed for their character and fate as when he contemplates their propensity to this dangerous vice. He will not fail, therefore, to set a due value on any plan which, without violating the principles to which he is attached, provides a proper cure for it. The instability, injustice, and confusion, introduced into the public councils, have, in truth been the mortal diseases under which popular governments have everywhere perished; as they continue to be the favorite and fruitful topics from which the adversaries to liberty derive their most specious declamations. The valuable improvements made by the American constitutions on the popular models, both ancient and modern, cannot certainly be too much admired; but it would be an unwarrantable partiality, to contend that they have as effectually obviated the danger on this side, as was wished and expected. Complaints are everywhere heard from our most considerate and virtuous citizens, equally the friends of public and private faith, and of public and personal liberty, that our governments are too unstable; that the public good is disregarded in the conflicts of rival parties; and that measures are too often decided, not according to the rules of justice, and the rights of the minor party, but by the superior force of an interested and overbearing majority. However anxiously we may wish that these complaints had no foundation, the evidence of known facts will not permit us to deny that they are in some degree true. It will be found, indeed, on a candid review of our situation, that some of the distresses under which we labor, have been erroneously charged on the operation of our governments; but it will be found, at the same time, that other causes will not alone account for many of our heaviest misfortunes; and, particularly, for the prevailing and increasing distrust of public engagements, and alarm for private rights, which are echoed from one end of the continent to the other. These must be chiefly, if not wholly, effects of the unsteadiness and injustice, with which a factious spirit has tainted our public administrations.

By a faction, I understand a number of citizens, whether amounting to a majority or minority of the whole, who are united and actuated by some common impulse of passion, or of interest, adverse to the rights of other citizens, or to the permanent and aggregate interests of the community.

There are two methods of curing the mischiefs of faction: The one, by removing its causes; the other, by controlling its effects.

There are again two methods of removing the causes of faction: the one, by destroying the liberty which is essential to its existence; the other, by giving to every citizen the same opinions, the same passions, and the same interests.

It could never be more truly said, than of the first remedy, that it was worse than the disease. Liberty is to faction what air is to fire, an aliment, without which it instantly expires. But it could not be a less folly to abolish liberty, which is essential to political life because it nourishes faction, than it would be to wish the annihilation of air, which is essential to animal life, because it imparts to fire its destructive agency.

The second expedient is as impracticable, as the first would be unwise. As long as the reason of man continues fallible, and he is at liberty to exercise it, different opinions will be formed. As long as the connection subsists between his reason and his self-love, his opinions and his passions will have a reciprocal influence on each other; and the former will be objects to which the latter will attach themselves. The diversity in the faculties of men, from which the rights of property originate, is not less an insuperable obstacle to a uniformity of interests. The protection of those faculties is the first object of government. From the protection of different and unequal faculties of acquiring property, the possession of different degrees and kinds of property immediately results; and from the influence of these on the sentiments and views of the respective proprietors, ensues a division of the society into different interests and parties.

The latent causes of faction are thus sown in the nature of man; and we see them everywhere brought into different degrees of activity, according to the different circumstances of civil society. A zeal for different opinions concerning religion, concerning government, and many other points, as well of speculation as of practice; an attachment to different leaders, ambitiously contending for preeminence and power; or to persons of other descriptions, whose fortunes have been interesting to the human passions, have, in turn, divided mankind into parties, inflamed them with mutual animosity, and rendered them much more disposed to vex and oppress each other, than to cooperate for their common good. So strong is this propensity of mankind, to fall into mutual animosities, that where no substantial occasion presents itself, the most frivolous and fanciful distinctions have been sufficient to kindle their unfriendly passions, and excite their most violent conflicts. But the most common and durable source of factions has been the various and unequal distribution of property. Those who hold, and those who are without property, have ever formed distinct interests in society. Those who are creditors, and those who are debtors, fall under a like discrimination. A landed interest, a manufacturing interest, a mercantile interest, a moneyed interest, with many lesser interests, grow up of necessity in civilized nations, and divide them into different classes, actuated by different sentiments and views. The regulation of these various and interfering interests forms the principle task of modern legislation, and involves the spirit of party and faction in the necessary and ordinary operations of government.

No man is allowed to be a judge in his own cause; because his interest will certainly bias his judgment, and, not improbably, corrupt his integrity. With equal, nay, with greater reason, a body of men are unfit to be both judges and parties at the same time; yet what are many of the most important acts of legislation, but so many judicial determinations, not indeed concerning the rights of single persons, but concerning the rights of large bodies of citizens? And what are the different classes of legislators, but advocates and parties to the cause which they determine? Is a law proposed concerning private debts? It is a question to which the creditors are parties on one side, and the debtors on the other. Justice ought to hold the balance between them. Yet the parties are, and must be, themselves the judges; and the most numerous party, or, in other words, the most powerful faction, must be expected to prevail. Shall domestic manufactures be encouraged, and in what degree, by restrictions on foreign manufactures? are questions which would be differently decided by the landed and the manufacturing classes; and probably by neither with a sole regard to justice and the public good....

It is in vain to say, that enlightened statesmen will be able to adjust these clashing interests, and render them all subservient to the public good. Enlightened statesmen will not always be at the helm; nor, in many cases, can such an adjustment be made at all, without taking into view indirect and remote considerations, which will rarely prevail over the immediate interest which one party may find in disregarding the rights of another, or the good of the whole.

The inference to which we are brought is, that the causes of faction cannot be removed; and that relief is only to be sought in the means of controlling its effects.

If a faction consists of less than a majority, relief is supplied by the republican principle, which enables the majority to defeat its sinister views, by regular vote. It may clog the administration, it may convulse the society; but it will be unable to execute and mask its violence under the forms of the constitution. When a majority is included in a faction, the form of popular government, on the other hand, enables it to sacrifice to its ruling passion or interest, both the public good and the rights of other citizens. To secure the public good, and private rights, against the danger of such a faction, and at the same time to preserve the spirit and the form of popular government, is then the great object to which our inquiries are directed. Let me add, that it is the great desideratum, by which alone this form of government can be rescued from the opprobrium under which it has so long labored, and be recommended to the esteem and adoption of mankind.

By what means is this object attainable? Evidently by one of two only. Either the existence of the same passion or interest in a majority, at the same time must be prevented; or the majority, having such coexistent passion or interest, must be rendered, by their number and local situation, unable to concert and carry into effect schemes of oppression. If the impulse and the opportunity be suffered to coincide, we well know, that neither moral nor religious motives can be relied on as an adequate control. They are not found to be such on the injustice and violence of individuals, and lose their efficacy in proportion to the number combined together; that is in proportion as their efficacy becomes needful.

From this view of the subject, it may be concluded, that a pure democracy, by which I mean a society consisting of a small number of citizens, who assemble and administer the government in person, can admit of no cure from the mischiefs of faction. A common passion or interest will, in almost every case, be felt by a majority of the whole; a communication and concert, results from the form of government itself; and there is nothing to check the inducements to sacrifice the weaker party, or an obnoxious individual. Hence it is, that such democracies have ever been spectacles of turbulence and contention; have ever been found incompatible with personal security, or the rights of property; and have, in general been as short in their lives, as they have been violent in their deaths. Theoretic politicians, who have patronized this species of government, have erroneously supposed that by reducing mankind to a perfect equality in their political rights, they would, at the same time, be perfectly equalized and assimilated in their possessions, their opinions, and their passions.

A republic, by which I mean a government in which the scheme of representation takes place, opens a different prospect, and promises the cure for which we are seeking. Let us examine the points in which it varies from pure democracy, and we shall comprehend both the nature of the cure and the efficacy which it must derive from the union.

The two great points of difference, between a democracy and a republic, are, first, the delegation of the government, in the latter, to a small number of citizens elected by the rest; secondly, the greater number of citizens, and greater sphere of country, over which the latter may be extended.

The effect of the first difference is on the one hand, to refine and enlarge the public views, by passing them hrough the medium of a chosen body of citizens, whose wisdom may best discern the true interest in their country, and whose patriotism and love of justice, will be least likely to sacrifice it to temporary or partial considerations. Under such a regulation, it may well happen, that the public voice, pronounced by the representatives of the people, will be more consonant to the public good, than if pronounced by the people themselves, convened for the purpose. On the other hand, the effect may be inverted. Men of factious tempers, of local prejudices, or of sinister designs, may by intrigue, by corruption, or by other means, first obtain the suffrages, and then betray the interests, of the people. The question resulting is, whether small or extensive republics are most favorable to the election of proper guardians of the public weal; and it is clearly decided in favor of the latter by two obvious considerations.

In the first place, it is to be remarked, that however small the republic may be, the representatives must be raised to a certain number, in order to guard against the cabals of a few; and that however large it may be, they must be limited to a certain number, in order to guard against the confusion of a multitude. Hence, the number of representatives in the two cases not being in proportion to that of the constituents, and being proportionally greatest in the small republic, it follows that if the proportion of fit characters be not less in the large than in the small republic, the former will present a greater option, and consequently a greater probability of a fit choice.

In the next place, as each representative will be chosen by a greater number of citizens in the large than in the small republic, it will be more difficult for unworthy candidates to practice with success the vicious arts, by which elections are too often carried; and the suffrages of the people being more free, will be more likely to center in men who possess the most attractive merit, and the most diffusive and established characters....

The other point of difference is, the greater number of citizens, and extent of territory, which may be brought within the compass of republican, than of democratic government; and it is this circumstance principally which renders factious combinations less to be dreaded in the former, than in the latter. The smaller the society, the fewer probably will be the distinct parties and interests composing it; the fewer the distinct parties and interests, the more frequently will a majority be found of the same party; and the smaller the number of individuals composing a majority, and the smaller the compass within which they are placed, the more easily they will concert and execute their plans of oppression. Extend the sphere, and you take in a greater variety of parties and interests; you make it less probable that a majority of the whole will have a common motive to invade the rights of other citizens; or if such a common motive exists, it will be more difficult for all who feel it to discover their own strength, and to act in unison with each other....

Hence, it clearly appears, that the same advantage, which a republic has over a democracy, in controlling the effects of faction, is enjoyed by a large over a small republic—is enjoyed by the union over the states composing it. Does this advantage consist in the substitution of representatives, whose enlightened views and virtuous sentiments render them superior to local prejudices, and to schemes of injustice? It will not be denied, that the representation of the union will be most likely to possess these requisite endowments. Does it

consist in the greater security afforded by a greater variety of parties, against the event of any one party being able to outnumber and oppress the rest? In an equal degree does the increased variety of parties, comprised within the union, increase this security? Does it, in fine, consist in the greater obstacles opposed to the concert and accomplishment of the secret wishes of an unjust and interested majority? Here, again, the extent of the union gives it the most palpable advantage. The influence of factious leaders may kindle a flame within their particular states, but will be unable to spread a general conflagration through the other states; a religious sect may degenerate into a political faction in a part of the confederacy; but the variety of sects dispersed over the entire face of it, must secure the national councils against any danger from that source; a rage for paper money, for an abolition of debts, for an equal division of property, or for any other improper or wicked project, will be less apt to pervade the whole body of the union, than a particular member of it; in the same proportion as such a malady is more likely to taint a particular country or district, than an entire state.

In the extent and proper structure of the union, therefore, we behold a republican remedy for the diseases most incident to republican government. And according to the degree of pleasure and pride we feel in being republicans, ought to be our zeal in cherishing the spirit, and supporting the character of Federalists.

JAMES MADISON: Federalist No. 51

To what expedient then shall we finally resort, for maintaining in practice the necessary partition of power among the several departments, as laid down in the constitution? The only answer that can be given is, that as all these exterior provisions are found to be inadequate, the defect must be supplied, by so contriving the interior structure of the government, as that its several constituent parts may, by their mutual relations, be the means of keeping each other in their proper places....

In order to lay a due foundation for that separate and distinct exercise of the different powers of government, which, to a certain extent, is admitted on all hands to be essential to the preservation of liberty, it is evident that each department should have a will of its own; and consequently should be so constituted, that the members of each should have as little agency as possible in the appointment of the members of the others....It is equally evident, that the members of each department should be as little dependent as possible on those of the others, for the emoluments annexed to their offices. Were the executive magistrate, or the judges, not independent of the legislature in this particular, their independence in every other would be merely nominal.

But the great security against a gradual concentration of the several powers in the same department, consists in giving to those who administer each department, the necessary constitutional means, and personal motives, to resist encroachments of the others. The provision for defense must in this, as in all other cases, be made commensurate to the danger of attack. Ambition must be made to counteract ambition. The interest of the man must be connected with the constitutional rights of the place. It may be a reflection on human nature, that such devices should be necessary to control the abuses of government. But what is government itself, but the greatest of all reflections on human nature? If men were angels, no government would be necessary. If angels were to govern men, neither external nor internal controls on government would be necessary. In framing a government, which is to be administered by men over men, the great difficulty lies in this: You must first enable the government to control the governed; and in the next place, oblige it to control itself. A dependence on the people is, no doubt, the primary control on the government; but experience has taught mankind the necessity of auxiliary precautions.

This policy of supplying by opposite and rival interests, the defect of better motives, might be traced through the whole system of human affairs, private as well as public. We see it particularly displayed in all the subordinate distributions of power; where the constant aim is, to divide and arrange the several offices in such a manner, as that each may be a check on the other; that the private interest of every individual, may be a sentinel over the public rights. These interventions of prudence cannot be less requisite to the distribution of the supreme powers of the state.

But it is not possible to give to each department an equal power of self-defense. In republican government, the legislative authority necessarily predominates. The remedy for this inconvenience is, to divide the legislature into different branches; and to render them by different modes of election, and different principles of action, as little connected with each other, as the nature of their common functions, and their common dependence on the society will admit. It may even be necessary to guard against dangerous encroachments, by still further precautions. As the weight of the legislative authority requires that it should be thus divided, the weakness of the executive may require, on the other hand, that it should be fortified. An absolute negative on the legislature, appears, at first view, to be the natural defense with which the executive magistrate should be armed. But perhaps it would be neither altogether safe, nor alone sufficient. On ordinary occasions, it might not be exerted with the requisite firmness; and on extraordinary occasions, it might be perfidiously abused. May not this defect of an absolute negative be supplied by some qualified connection between this weaker department, and the weaker branch of the stronger department, by which the latter may be led to support the constitutional rights of the former, without being too much detached from the rights of its own department?

There are, moreover, two considerations particularly applicable to the federal system of America, which place that system in a very interesting point of view.

First. In a single republic, all the power surrendered by the people is submitted to the administration of a single government, and the usurpations are guarded against by a division of the government into distinct and separate departments. In the compound republic of America, the power surrendered by the people is first divided between two distinct governments, and then the portion allotted to each subdivided among distinct and separate departments. Hence a double security arises to the rights of the people. The different governments will control each other, at the same time that each will be controlled by itself.

Second. It is of great importance in a republic not only to guard the society against the oppression of its rulers, but to guard one part of the society against the injustice of the other part. Different interests necessarily exist in different classes of citizens. If a majority be united by a common interest, the rights of the minority will be insecure. There are but two methods of providing against this evil: the one by creating a will in the community independent of the majority—that is, of the society itself; the other, by comprehending in the society so many separate descriptions of citizens as will render an unjust combination of a majority of the whole very probable, if not impracticable. The first method prevails in all governments possessing an hereditary or self-appointed authority. This, at best, is but a precarious security; because a power independent of the society may as well espouse the unjust views of the major, as the rightful interests of the minor party, and may possibly be turned against both parties. The second method will be exemplified in the federal republic of the United States. Whilst all authority in it will be derived from and dependent on the society, the society itself will be broken into so many parts, interests and classes of citizens, that the rights of individuals, or of the minority, will be in little danger from interested combinations of the majority. In a free government the security for civil rights must be the same as that for religious rights. It consists in the one case in the multiplicity of interests, and in the other in the multiplicity of sects. The degree of security in both cases will depend on the number of interests and sects; and this may be presumed to depend on the extent of country and number of people comprehended under the same government. This view of the subject must particularly recommend a proper federal system to all the sincere and considerate friends of republican government, since it shows that in exact proportion as the territory of the Union may be formed into more circumscribed Confederacies, or States, oppressive combinations of a majority will be facilitated; the best security, under the republican forms, for the rights of every class of citizens, will be diminished; and consequently the stability and independence of some member of the government, the only other security, must be proportionately increased. Justice is the end of the government. It is the end of civil society. It ever has been and ever will be pursued until it be obtained, or until liberty be lost in the pursuit. In a society under the forms of which the stronger faction can readily unite and oppress the weaker, anarchy may as truly be said to reign as in a state of nature, where the weaker individual is not secured against the violence of the stronger; and as, in the latter state, even the stronger individuals are prompted, by the uncertainty of their condition, to submit to a government which may protect the weak as well as themselves; so, in the former state, will the more powerful factions or parties be gradually induced, by a like motive, to wish for a government which will protect all parties, the weaker as well as the more powerful. It can be little doubted that if the State of Rhode Island was separated from the Confederacy and left to itself, the insecurity of rights under the popular form of government within such narrow limits would be displayed by such reiterated oppressions of factious majorities that some power altogether independent of the people would soon be called for by the voice of the very factions whose misrule had proved the necessity of it. In the extended republic of the United States, and among the great variety of interests, parties, and sects which it embraces, a coalition of a majority of the whole society could seldom take place on any other principles than those of justice and the general good; whilst there being thus less danger to a minor from the will of a major party, there must be less pretext, also, to provide for the security of the former, by introducing into the government a will not dependent on the latter, or, in other words, a will independent of the society itself. It is no less certain than it is important, notwithstanding the contrary opinions which have been entertained, that the larger the society, provided it lie within a practical sphere, the more duly capable it will be of self-government. And happily for the republican cause, the practicable sphere may be carried to a very great extent, by a judicious modification and mixture of the federal principle.

ALEXANDER HAMILTON: Federalist No. 78

We proceed now to an examination of the judiciary department of the proposed government.

In unfolding the defects of the existing confederation, the utility and necessity of a federal judicature have been clearly pointed out. It is the less necessary to recapitulate the considerations there urged; as the propriety of the institution in the abstract is not disputed; the only questions which have been raised being relative to the manner of constituting it, and to its extent. To these points, therefore, our observations shall be confined.

The manner of constituting it seems to embrace these several objects: 1st. The mode of appointing the judges; 2nd. The tenure by which they are to hold their places; 3rd. The partition of the judiciary authority between courts, and their relations to each other.

First. As to the mode of appointing the judges: This is the same with that of appointing the officers of the union in general, and has been so fully discussed … that nothing can be said here which would not be useless repetition.

Second. As to the tenure by which the judges are to hold their places: This chiefly concerns their duration in office; the provisions for their support; the precautions for their responsibility.

According to the plan of the convention, all the judges who may be appointed by the United States are to hold their offices during good behavior; which is conformable to the most approved of the state constitutions…. The standard of good behavior for the continuance in office of the judicial magistracy is certainly one of the most valuable of the modern improvements in the practice of government. In a monarchy, it is an excellent barrier to the despotism of the prince; in a republic, it is a no less excellent barrier to the encroachments and oppressions of the representative body. And it is the best expedient which can be devised in any government, to secure a steady, upright, and impartial administration of the laws.

Whoever attentively considers the different departments of power must perceive, that, in a government in which they are separated from each other, the judiciary, from the nature of its functions, will always be the least dangerous to the political rights of the constitution; because it will be at least in a capacity to annoy or injure them. The executive not only dispenses the honors, but holds the sword of the community. The legislature not only commands the purse, but prescribes the rules by which the duties and rights of every citizen are to be regulated. The judiciary, on the contrary, has no influence over either the sword or the purse; no direction either of the strength or of the wealth of the society; and can take no active resolution whatever. It may truly be said to have neither force nor will, but merely judgment; and must ultimately depend upon the aid of the executive arm for the efficacious exercise even of this faculty.

This simple view of the matter suggests several important consequences: It proves incontestably, that the judiciary is beyond comparison, the weakest of the three departments of power, that it can never attack with success either of the other two: and that all possible care is requisite to enable it to defend itself against their attacks. It equally proves, that, though individual oppression may now and then proceed from the courts of justice, the general liberty of the people can never be endangered from that quarter; I mean so long as the judiciary remains truly distinct from both the legislature and execu-tive. For I agree, that "there is no liberty, if the power of judging be not separated from the legislative and executive powers." It proves, in the last place, that as liberty can have nothing to fear from the judiciary alone, but would have everything to fear from its union with either of the other departments; that, as all the effects of such a union must ensue from a dependence of the former on the latter, notwithstanding a nominal and apparent separation; that as, from the natural feebleness of the judiciary, it is in continual jeopardy of being overpowered, awed or influenced by its coordinate branches; that, as nothing can contribute so much to its firmness and independence as permanency in office, this quality may therefore be justly regarded as an indispensable ingredient in its constitution; and, in a great measure, as the citadel of the public justice and the public security.

The complete independence of the courts of justice is peculiarly essential in a limited constitution. By a limited constitution, I understand one which contains certain specified exceptions to the legislative authority; such, for instance, as that it shall pass no bills of attainder, no ex post facto laws, and the like. Limitations of this kind can be preserved in practice no other way than through the medium of the courts of justice, whose duty it must be to declare all acts contrary to the manifest tenor of the constitution void. Without this, all the reservations of particular rights or privileges would amount to nothing.

Some perplexity respecting the right of the courts to pronounce legislative acts void, because contrary to the constitution, has arisen from an imagination that the doctrine would imply a superiority of the judiciary to the legislative power. It is urged that the authority which can declare the acts of another void, must necessarily be superior to the one whose acts may be declared void. As this doctrine is of great importance in all the American constitutions, a brief discussion of the grounds on which it rests cannot be unacceptable.

There is no position which depends on clearer principles than that every act of a delegated authority, contrary to the tenor of the commission under which it is exercised, is void. No legislative act, therefore, contrary to the constitution, can be valid. To deny this would be to affirm, that the deputy is greater then his principal; that the servant is above his master; that the representatives of the people are superior to the people themselves; that men, acting by virtue of powers, may do not only what their powers do not authorize, but what they forbid.

If it be said that the legislative body are themselves the constitutional judges of their own powers, and that the construction they put upon them is conclusive upon the other departments, it may be answered, that this cannot be the natural presumption, where it is not to be collected from any particular provisions in the constitution. It is not otherwise to be supposed that the constitution could intend to enable the representatives of the people to substitute their will to that of their con-stituents. It is far more rational to suppose that the courts were designed to be an intermediate body between the people and the legislature, in order, among other things, to keep the latter within the limits assigned to their authority. The interpretation of the laws is the proper and peculiar province of the courts. A constitution is, in fact, and must be, regarded by the judges as a fundamental law. It must therefore belong to them to ascertain its meaning, as well as the meaning of any particular act proceeding from the legislative body. If there should happen to be an irreconcilable variance between the two, that which has the superior obligation and validity ought, of course, to be preferred; in other words, the constitution ought to be preferred to the statute, the intention of the people to the intention of their agents.

Nor does this conclusion by any means suppose a superiority of the judicial to the legislative power. It only supposes that the power of the people is superior to both; and that where the will of the legislature declared in its statutes, stands in opposition to that of the people declared in the constitution, the judges ought to be governed by the latter, rather than the former. They ought to regulate their decisions by the fundamental laws, rather than by those which are not fundamental....

It can be of no weight to say, that the courts, on the pretense of a repugnancy, may substitute their own pleasure to the constitutional intentions of the legislature. This might as well happen in the case of two contradictory statutes; or it might as well happen in every adjudication upon any single statute. The courts must declare the sense of the law; and if they should be disposed to exercise will instead of judgment, the consequence would equally be the substitution of their pleasure to that of the legislative body. The observation, if it proved anything, would prove that there ought to be no judges distinct from the body.

If then the courts of justice are to be considered as the bulwarks of a limited constitution, against legislative encroachments, this consideration will afford a strong argument for the permanent tenure of judicial officers, since nothing will contribute so much as this to that independent spirit in the judges, which must be essential to the faithful performance of so arduous a duty.

This independence of the judges is equally requisite to guard the constitution and the rights of individuals, from the effects of those ill-humors which are the arts of designing men, or the influence of particular conjunctures, sometimes disseminate among the people themselves, and which, though they speedily give place to better information, and more deliberate reflection, have a tendency, in the meantime, to occasion dangerous innovations in the government, and serious oppressions of the minor party in the community.... Until the people have, by some solemn and authoritative act, annulled or changed the established form, it is binding upon themselves collectively, as well as individually; and no presumption, or even knowledge of their sentiments, can warrant their representatives in a departure from it, prior to such an act. But it is easy to see, that it would re-quire an uncommon portion of fortitude in the judges to do their duty as faithful guardians of the constitution, where legislative invasions of it had been instigated by the major voice of the community.

But it is not with a view to infractions of the constitution only, that the independence of the judges may be an essential safeguard against the effects of occasional illhumors in the society. These sometimes extend no farther than to the injury of the private rights of particular classes of citizens, by unjust and partial laws. Here also the firmness of the judicial magistracy is of vast importance in mitigating the severity, and confining the operation of such laws. It not only serves to moderate the immediate mischiefs of those which may have been passed, but it operates as a check upon the legislative body in passing them; who, perceiving that obstacles to the success of an iniquitous intention are to be expected from the scruples of the courts, are in a manner compelled by the very motives of the injustice they meditate, to qualify their attempts....

That inflexible and uniform adherence to the rights of the constitution, and of individuals, which we perceive to be indispensable in the courts of justice, can certainly not be expected from judges who hold their offices by a temporary commission. Periodical appointments, however regulated, or by whomsoever made, would, in some way or other, be fatal to their necessary independence. If the power of making them was committed either to the executive or legislature, there would be danger of an improper compliance to the branch which possessed it; if to both, there would be an unwillingness to hazard the displeasure of either; if to the people, or to persons chosen by them for the special purpose, there would be too great a disposition to consult popularity to justify a reliance that nothing would be consulted but the constitution and the laws.

There is yet a further and a weighty reason for the permanency of judicial offices, which is deducible from the nature of the qualifications they require. It has been frequently remarked, with great propriety, that a voluminous code of laws is one of the inconveniences necessarily connected with the advantages of a free government. To avoid an arbitrary discretion in the courts, it is indispensable that they should be bound down by strict rules and precedents, which serve to define and point out their duty in every particular case that comes before them; and it will readily be conceived, from the variety of controversies which grow out of the folly and wickedness of mankind, that the records of those precedents must unavoidably swell to a very considerable bulk, and must demand long and laborious study to acquire a competent knowledge of them. Hence it is, that there can be but few men in the society, who will have sufficient skill in the laws to qualify them for the stations of judges. And making the proper deductions for the ordinary depravity of human nature, the number must be still smaller, of those who unite the requisite integrity with the requisite knowledge....

This page left blank intentionally.

GLOSSARY

Absolutism – The principle or theory that complete power in the government or one single ruler is absolute, unchangeable and not confined to context; sometimes enforced through threats of punishment or violence.

Administrative Discretion – The latitude that an agency or bureaucrat has in interpreting an applying laws.

Amnesty International (AI) – A humanitarian grassroots organization founded in London in 1961; AI is a Nobel Prize–winning activist organization with over 1.8 million members worldwide. One of their functions is to undertake research that focuses on the prevention and termination of egregious abuses of the rights to physical and mental integrity, freedom of conscience and expression, and freedom from discrimination. AI stands alone and neither condemns nor condones any ideologies; not even the views of the victims whose rights they are protecting. It exists simply to carry out, with impartiality, their mission to protect human rights of all citizens of the world.

Appellate Courts – The court that reviews an appeal of the trial court proceedings, often with a panel of several judges but without a jury; it considers only matters of law.

Aryan – Old Persian name for Iran; also associated with a group of nomad warriors from the Caucus Mountains; used by Nazis in Germany in the 1930's as a label for their supposed superior white race.

Authoritarian Regime – An oppressive system of government in which basic freedoms to speak, write, associate, and participate in political activities without fear of reprimand.

Baath – Literally means "rebirth" or "renaissance" in Arabic.

Barrister – A lawyer who is a member of one of the Inns of Court; s/he has the honor of making appeals in the higher courts.

Bastille – Paris jail that is no longer used; Bastille Day is now a national holiday, celebrated in France every year on July 14.

Bear Flag Revolt – American settlers in California feared the Mexican government would attack them.

Bourbons – French dynasty before the Revolution.

Bourgeoisie – French term describing the Middle Class; the term has been adopted into the American lexicon but it is used in a derogatory manner, as in something being common or pedantic, bourgeois.

Bundesrat (federal council) – Upper house of German parliament made up of representatives from the 16 Länder.

Bundestag – Lower house of German parliament.

Bureaucracy – Administration of a government through bureaus or departments staffed with non–elected officials. This term can also have negative overtones, meaning any organization in which any action is bogged down by excessive and unnecessary procedures or red tape.

Bureaucrat – A person who works in a bureaucracy at all levels of government.

Casework –Services performed by Congress for constituents.

Chador – The full–body cloak Muslim women in Iran are expected to wear outdoors; depending on design and how the woman holds it, the chador may or may not cover the face.

Charter County – Has its own charter or constitution that allows for flexibility in collecting revenue–producing taxes, electing and appointing officials, and, running and controlling the programs of the county.

Checks and Balances – Systems that ensure that every branch in government has an equal and opposite powers in a separate branch to restrain that force.

City Council – a nonpartisan board that is elected to handle the executive business of the city.

City Manager – A professional manager who implements the city council's programs.

Civil Liberties – The individual freedoms and rights guaranteed to every citizen in the Bill of Rights and the due process clause of the 14th Amendment, including freedom of speech and religion.

Civil Rights – Constitutionally guaranteed rights such as the right to vote and equal protection under the law.

Civil Union – The legal status that ensures to same–sex couples specified rights and responsibilities of married couples.

Cloture – A vote to end a filibuster or a debate; requires the votes of three–fifths of the membership of the Senate.

The Communist Manifesto – The writings of Karl Marx and Friedrich Engels that discusses class struggles, and how the merchant class and the working class can overthrow capitalists and create a socialist state.

Concurrent Powers – Those powers shared by both the state and the federal government.

Concurring Opinion – The opinion of one or more judges who vote with the majority on a case but wish to set out different reasons for their decision.

Confederation – An association of sovereign states or communities that delegates powers on selected issues to a central government.

Conference Committee – A committee consisting of members of both houses, specifically created to reconcile differences between the houses on a particular bill once it is passed.

Conservative – The political position that believes that the federal government ought to play a very small role in economic regulation, social welfare, and in overcoming racial inequality.

Constitutional Courts – Federal courts created by Congress under the authority of Article III of the Constitution.

Contingency Election – The election held in the House if no candidate wins the required majority in the electoral college.

Cooperative Federalism – federal and state governments work in tandem to insure that the general welfare of the people is taken care of.

Council of Government (COGs) – An association of city and county government officials, within a given region, whose purpose is to provide solutions to the regions' problems.

Council of Revision – a combined body of judges and members of the executive branch having a limited veto over national legislation and an absolute veto over state legislation.

County Board of Supervisors – The county legislature that sets policy and budgets. Most boards are elected in a nonpartisan election for staggered, four–year terms.

County Revenue – Money that the county receives from all sources.

County – large geographic areas initially established to bridge the gap between city governments and the state by providing services.

Coup d'État – An uprising led by the military, with the intent of over-throwing the current government.

Creative Federalism – an initiative begun in the 1960's under President Johnson that augmented the idea of a partnership between the national government and the states.

Cross–filing – the manner in which voters can register when party column ballots were eliminated, allowing voters to file for more than just their own party.

Democracy – a system of government in which the people rule, either directly or through elected representatives.

Diet – Names for parliament in Japan and Finland.

Direct Democracy – a type of government in which people govern themselves, vote on

Disenfranchisement – Preventing the right to vote to a person or group of people. It may occur explicitly through law, or implicitly through means such as intimidation.

Dissenting Opinion – The opinion of the judge or judges who are in the minority on a particular case before the Supreme Court.

Districts – Units designated for a specific governmental purpose, usually to provide a public service, such as education.

DOMA Law – A law restricting the right to marry to couples consisting of only one man and one woman.

Dual Federalism – a system in which each level of power remains supreme in its own jurisdiction, keeping the states separate and distinct from the national government.

Election of 1800 – The first election in world history in which one party (the Federalist party of John Adams) willingly gave up power because of a lost election to another party (the Republican party of Thomas Jefferson) without bloodshed.

Electoral College – Group of 538 electors who meet separately in their respective states and the District of Columbia on the first Monday after the second Wednesday in December following a national presidential election; responsible for officially electing the president and vice president of the U.S.

Electors – Representatives who are elected in the states to formally choose the U.S. president.

Embargo – A government order to prohibit merchant ships from moving in or out of its ports, thus banning trade with other countries.

Emir – A prince, chieftain, or governor, especially in the Middle East, sometimes a descendant of Muhammad.

États généraux or the States General – A legislative assembly of representatives from the estates of the nation instead of a provincial assembly.

Eureka – "I have found it!"

Evangelicals – Christians who emphasize salvation by faith in the atoning death and resurrection of Jesus Christ through 'choosing Jesus as personal Lord and Savior"; also professes to the authority of Scripture and the importance of preaching the Gospel of Christ and converting others to repent and believe as they do.

Executive Branch – The branch of government that executes laws.

Executive Order – An order that carries the full weight of the law as issued by the U.S. President to military forces or any other parts of the executive branch of government.

Factions – James Madison's term for groups or parties that are out to advance their own agenda at the expense of the greater public.

Fatwa – An official ruling or legal opinion issued by a Muslim religious scholar/jurist.

Federalism – the distribution of power in a government between a central authority and individual state governments

Filibuster – A parliamentary device used in the Senate to prevent a bill from coming to a vote by "talking it to death", made possible by the norm of unlimited debate.

FISA Court – A U.S. Federal Court created by the Foreign Intelligence Surveillance Act of 1978; it is a Court whose proceedings are secret, therefore allowing for the ability to issue warrants without compromising classified investigations.

Francophone – A French–speaking person, especially in a region where two or more languages are spoken.

Franking Privilege – Public subsidization of mail from the members of Congress to their constituents.

Free Rider – A person who receives benefits without contributing money or participating in the goals of the group.

General Law Counties – Counties that may establish the number of county officials and their duties, but are required to have the approval of the state legislature.

General Revenue Sharing (GRS) – a function from the New Federalism program in which funds were given to the states, free of any restrictions on how it could be spent.

Gerrymander – an attempt to create a safe seat for one party during state redistricting of congressional voting boundaries.

Gerrymandering – Redrawing electoral district lines to give an advantage to a particular party or candidate.

Get Out the Vote – Movement that began by many non–partisan interest groups to increase voter awareness and decrease voter apathy.

Glass Ceiling – An intangible barrier that prevents women or minorities from obtaining upper–level positions career–wise.

Graft – The acquisition of money, gain, or advantage by dishonest, unfair, or illegal means, esp. through the abuse of one's position or influence in politics and business.

Grand Coalition – a coalition of two or more large parties that previously opposed one another.

Grandfather clause – a device that allowed whites who had failed the literacy test to vote anyway by extending the franchise to anyone whose ancestors voted prior to 1867.

Grassroots Organization – A group of ordinary people working toward a common cause; based upon the idea of the power rests with the people.

The Great Compromise (also called the Connecticut Compromise) – A plan presented at the Constitutional Convention that upheld the large–state position for the House, its membership based on proportional representation, balanced by the small–state posture of equal representation in the Senate, where each state would have two votes.

Great White Fleet – A U.S. Navy task force that circumnavigated the world from December 1907 to February 1909. This fleet was formed to show the world the growing virility of the U.S. military.

Hard Money – Regulated money candidates, party committees, and PACs receive for campaigns.

Hearings – Formal proceedings in which a variety of people testify on the pro's and con's of a bill.

Hierarchy – A clear chain of command and communications going from executive director (top) down to all other levels of employees.

Home Rule Amendment – The idea that local people are better equipped to solve their own problems because they are the most familiar with them.

Hopper – The box in the House of Representatives in which proposed bills are placed.

Imam – Saintly religious leader; when capitalized, refers to descendants of Ali, who are regarded by Shia Muslims as the rightful successors to Muhammad.

Immobilisme – Government inability to solve big problems.

In Forma Pauperis – "In the manner of a pauper" – when the filing fee is waived if the petitioner is very poor; this guarantees the right of all defendants to have representation, even in criminal cases.

Independent Agencies – Established independent agencies that regulate a sector of the nation's economy in the public interest.

Independent Expenditures – Monies distributed, as allowed by a loophole in campaign finance law, by a group or individual not coordinated by a candidate, in the name of a cause.

Initiative – a proposal submitted by the public and voted upon during elections.

Institutional Pluralism – refers to the creation of a monarchy, two legislative houses, civic governments in the cities, and courts.

Intendant – French provincial administrators, answerable only to Paris; early version of prefects, or an administrator of department.

Interest Group – A group of persons who work to promote their common interest.

Interest, Lobby, and Pressure Groups – Groups that seek to convey its' interests to policy makers; they put pressure on government to implement policies that fit their goals.

Iron Triangle – A long–lasting relationship between an interest group, a congressional committee, and a bureaucratic agency.

Jim Crow Laws – laws passed by southern states that separated the races in public places such as railroads, streetcars, schools, and cemeteries.

Joint Committees – Group opf members from both chambers, House and Senate, who study wide areas that are of interest to Congress as a whole.

Judicial Review – The power of the Supreme Court established in Marbury v. Madison to overturn acts of the president, Congress, and the states if they commit acts that violate the Constitution. Essentially determines the Supreme Court as the final interpreter of the Constitution.

Judiciary – the branch of government that interprets laws.

Laissez–faire – The political–economic doctrine that holds that government ought not interfere with the operations of the free market.

Legislative Branch – The branch of government that makes laws.

Legislative Courts – Highly specialized federal courts created by Congress under the authority of Article I of the Constitution.

Lend–Lease Act – Established March 11, 1941, the Lend–Lease Act was created to defend the U.S. without directly engaging in combat.

LGBT – Lesbian, Gay, Bisexual, Transgender; inclusive acronym often used when discussing gay rights.

Liberal – The political position that believes that the federal government has a substantial role to play in economic regulation, social welfare, and overcoming racial inequality.

Line Item Vetoes – The power of the executive to veto specific items of a bill without having to veto the entire bill.

Literacy Test – a test that required voting applicants to demonstrate an understanding of national and state constitutions. Primarily used to prevent African Americans from voting in the elections.

Machine Politics – An organizational style of local politics in which party bosses traded jobs, money, and favors for votes and campaign support.

Majority Tyranny – Suppression of the rights and liberties of the political minority by the majority.

Majority–Minority Districts – Districts drawn to ensure that a racial minority makes up the majority of voters.

Maquiladoras – From Spanish, maquila, measure; also Arabic, ; assembly plant in Mexico utilizing cheap labor, esp. one located on the border between the U.S. and Mexico; imports foreign materials and parts and exports finished product to original market.

Markup Session – A subcommittee meeting to revise a bill.

Matching Funds – federal funds given to the state or local governments that must be matched, dollar for dollar by the receiving agency, or they will not be granted.

Mestizo – From Old Spanish and Latin, to mix; a person of mixed ancestry, esp. in Latin America, of mixed American Indian and European, usually Spanish or Portuguese, ancestry, or, in the Philippines, of mixed native and foreign ancestry; most cultures have a term equivalent to this one.

Midterm Elections – Elections in which Americans elect members of Congress but not presidents; 2002, 2006, and 2010 are midterm election.

Minister – Head of a major department as in a "ministry of government."

Minuteman Project – Founded by Vietnam veteran and former CPA Jim Gilchrist on Oct. 1, 2004, in response to controversial debates over immigration laws; the group's claim is that the federal government is not enforcing existing immigration laws, so Gilchrist recruited volunteers to physically patrol the California–Mexico border, mobilize membership, solicit donations to build fences, and lobby Congress for stricter immigration laws.

Minutemen – Were called because they were ready to take up arms in a minute's notice.

Mission – Spanish style adobe building with high arches and long corridors with a courtyard.

Mixed Constitution – The republican policy of balancing rule by one, by the few, and by the many in to a single government. This creates a system of checks and balances preventing on branch of government or group of people from gaining control over the others, according to Aristotle.

Mullah – Title of respect given to a teacher (usually male) who is educated in theology and sacred law, and who usually holds an official post.

National Party Convention – The national meeting of the parties every four years to choose the ticket for the presidential election and write the party platform.

National Party Organization – Party organization at the national level whose primary tasks include fund raising, distribution of information, and recruitment.

Natural Rights – S right that everyone has by way of being human – they cannot be granted or taken away by anyone or any political authority.

Naturalized Citizens – An immigrant who pledges to uphold their adopted country's laws after meeting specific requirements; after this, they retain all rights and privileges that are afforded to native citizens in that country.

New Deal – The programs of the administration of President Franklin D. Roosevelt.

New Deal Coalition – Brought together by Franklin Roosevelt in 1932, the informal electoral alliance of working–class ethnic groups (Catholics, Jews, urban dwellers, racial minorities, and the South) that was the basis of the Democratic party dominance of American politics from the New Deal to the early 1970s.

New Federalism – a program that shifted power away from the federal government to the state governments.

The New Jersey Plan – a plan presented to the Constitutional Convention of 1787 designed to create a unicameral legislature with equal representation for all states. Its goal was to protect the interests of the smaller, less populous states.

Nonpartisan Elections – elections where the party identity of the candidate is not discussed to the public. This was done to weaken the party system in California.

OPEC – Organization of the Petroleum Exporting Countries; a permanent, intergovernmental organization, created at the Baghdad Conference on September 10–14, 1960. Its main purpose is to stabilise the oil market and to help oil producers achieve a reasonable rate of return on their investments. This policy is also designed to ensure that oil consumers continue to receive stable supplies of oil.

Opinion of the Court – The majority opinion that accompanies a Supreme Court decision.

Original Intent – The doctrine that the courts must interpret the Constitution in ways consistent with the framers rather than with modern times.

Partisan – A committed member of a party; seeing issues from the point of view of the interests of a single party.

Party Caucus – An organization of the members of a political party in the House or Senate.

Party Identification – The core beliefs that a person upholds and votes for in association with a political party.

Party Platform – A party's statement of its positions on the issues of the day.

Penumbra – A right held to be guaranteed by implication in a civil constitution.

Pluralism – The view that American politics are best understood in terms of the interaction, conflict, and bargaining of groups.

Plurality – More votes than any other candidate but less than a majority of all votes cast.

Pocket Veto – When the President refuses to sign or veto a bill that Congress passes in the last ten days of its session, rendering the bill dead when Congress adjourns.

Police Powers – these powers permit all the states to protect citizens' health, safety, and welfare.

Politburo – Executive committee and policy– making body of a Communist party.

Political Action Committees or PACs – Interest group formed specifically for the purpose of electing or defeating certain candidates that support or don't support their cause.

Political Parties – Organizations that exist to allow like–minded members of the population to group together and strengthen their individual voices into a common cause or political ideology; their main goals include promoting individual candidates and influencing government policy.

Poll Tax – a fee that had to be paid before one could vote; used to prevent African Americans from voting; now unconstitutional.

Pork – Also called pork barreling; projects designed to bring jobs and public money to the constituency, for which members of Congress can claim credit.

Pork Barrel – Government funding for superfluous projects to benefit a specific district or state; the origins of the term are believed to have begun around 1909; related to "bringing home the bacon", possibly a county fair type of game of catching a greased pig and bringing home the prize – the pig itself.

Presidios – Spanish forts along the frontier.

Primary System – The system of nominating candidates in which voters in the state make the choice by casting ballots.

Prime Minister – Chief of government in Parliamentary systems.

Private Interest Group – An interest group that seeks to protect or advance the material interests of its members.

Pro Tempore – An official who is second in command, in charge in the event that the head officer cannot govern or facilitate; Latin is literally, "for a time."

Probable Cause – Reasonable grounds for holding that a charge is well-founded.

Proportional Representation – a system of representation popular in Europe whereby the number of seats in the legislature is based on the proportion of the vote received in the election.

Proposition 13 – Placed limits on the amount of annual property taxes to a maximum of 1 % of the March 1, 1975 market value or selling price of the property, whichever is higher, with a limited increase of 2% each year thereafter.

Public Interest Group – An interest group that advocates for a cause or an ideology.

Pueblos – a group of adobe homes, a church, and small business that created a small town.

Québécois – The people Québec.

Quorum – The minimal number of officers and members of a committee or organization, usually a majority, who must be present for valid transaction of business.

Ramadan – Occurring during the ninth month of the Islamic calendar (usually around January), this Muslim holiday lasts for one full month. The Holy Quran spells out the attitude and practices that Muslims should observe. During this time, all Muslims fast from dawn until dusk, with the exception of the sick, elderly, those on pilgrimage, and pregnant or nursing women; they must make up the days they cannot fast later on in the year, or they must feed a needy person for every day missed). This practice begins at puberty and continues through adulthood. They fast not just from food but also from sex, smoking, speaking ill–words of anyone, greed, telling lies, and so on. This is done not only for health reasons but primarily as a time of self–purification, reflection, and a closer walk with Allah. It is believed that by refraining from worldly comforts, one can gain true sympathy with the poor and hungry.

Ranchos – Large parcels of land given to influential families to raise cattle.

Realignment – The process by which one party takes the place of another as the dominant party in a political system.

Reapportionment – The reallocation of House seats among the states; applied after each national census, to guarantee that seats are held by the states in proportion to the size of their populations.

Recall – progressive reform allowing voters to remove elected officials by petition and majority vote.

Reciprocity – Deferral by members of Congress to the judgment of subject–matter specialists, mainly on minor technical bills.

"Red Coats" – A derogatory name for the British troops by the colonists.

Redistricting – Also known as reapportionment. The process by which the state legislature redraws the district lines for its members of the U.S. House of Representatives, and at the same time, redraws district lines for its own state legislature.

Region – A geographic area that contains a number of cities and counties and covers a large portion of the state.

Regional Governance – The process of planning and policy making with the help of cities, counties, and businesses with regional issues.

Reign of Terror – Robespierre's rule by threat of the guillotine (decapitating contraption used for executions) from 1793 – 1794.

Representative Democracy – A system of government in which the voters select representatives to make decisions for them; sometimes called an indirect democracy.

Retrospective Voting – When voters evaluate the past performance of an incumbent or party in power.

Rough Riders – The common name given to the First United States volunteer cavalry regiment, led by Teddy Roosevelt during the Spanish–American War.

Rule of Four – The votes needed for justices to vote in favor of granting cert to a petition.

Sanctions – Actions imposed by one or more states on another to force compliance with a former legal contract or agreement.

Secretariat – The officials or office entrusted with administrative duties, maintaining records, and overseeing or performing secretarial duties, esp. for an international or governmental organization.

Segregation – The practice of separating people by race, deemed legal by the U.S. Supreme Court in 1896 via the Plessy v. Ferguson decision; also known as the "separate but equal" doctrine.

Select Committee – A committee appointed to perform a special function above and beyond the scope of a regular, or standing, committee.

Separation of Powers – State in which the powers of the government are divided among the three branches: executive, legislative, and judicial.

Signing Statement – Which is an official legal document that gets recorded in the federal register.

Soft Money – Campaign funds that are committed to a specific political party or issue, rather than a specific candidate.

Speaker of the House – The presiding officer of the House of Representatives; second in line to the presidency after the Vice–President.

Special Election – An election held to fill a political office that has become vacant between general elections.

Special Revenue Sharing (SRS) – another facet of the New Federalism program in which clusters of categorical grants–in–aid in like policy areas, such as crime management or health care, were joined into a single block grant.

Split–ticket Voting – Instead of voting for just the party line, voters choose candidates from another party, sometimes causing strife amongst the major parties.

Standardized Test – Test designed to be consistently uniform in questioning, scoring, and application.

Standing Committees – Permanent congressional committees that determine whether proposed legislations should be sent to the entire chamber for consideration.

Statuary Construction – The power of the Supreme Court to interpret or reinterpret a federal or state law.

Steward or Delegate theory – An elected representative acts on the wishes of their constituents.

Strict Construction – The doctrine that the provisions of the Constitution have a clear meaning and that judges must adhere to this when rendering decisions.

Strong Mayor System – The mayor has some veto power over the council and power to appoint and remove certain city officials.

Sunset Clause – A provision that terminates or repeals all or portions of a law after a specific date, unless further legislative action is taken to extend it.

Supremacy Clause – A clause in Article IV of the Constitution holding that in the case of conflict between federal laws and treaties and state laws, the will of the national government always has the last word.

Tenant Farmers – Were farmers who farmed the land of another and paid rent with cash or with a portion of the produce.

Test Case – A case brought to force a ruling on the constitutionality of some law or executive action.

Three–Fifths Compromise – A compromise that stated that the apportionment of representatives by state should be determined "by adding to the whole number of free persons . . .three–fifths of all other persons" (Article I, Section 2), meaning that it would take five slaves to equal three free people when counting the population for representation and taxation purposes.

Trial Court – The point of original entry in the legal system, with a singly judge and at times a jury deciding matters of both fact and law in a case.

Trustee Theory – based on Edmund Burke's philosophy that an elected representative acts under the own volition and takes the constituents input under advisement.

Unanimous Consent – Legislative action taken "without objection" as a way to move business along; used to conduct the business of the Senate.

Unicameral Legislature – a legislative system consisting of one chamber.

Unitary Government or System – locus of power is given to a centralized government.

Universal Suffrage – that everyone must have the right to vote.

Veto Power – the President may either approve and sign the bill or return it to Congress with his objections.

The Virginia Plan – A plan presented to the Constitutional Convention; favored by the delegates from the bigger states.

Weak Mayor System – The mayor is more a ceremonial position, with the mayor being selected from among the city council members.

Whip – In the legislature, the second ranking (assistant) member of a political party, whose job it is to ensure that the other party members attend and vote according to the party leadership's wishes.

Whistleblower – A civil servant who reports occurrences of bureaucratic mismanagement, corruption, inefficiency, and financial impropriety.

Writ of Certiorari – A grant of "cert" is the Courts' decision that an appellate case is a significant federal or constitutional case.

Writ of Mandamus – A court order that forces an official to act.

Young Turk – A member of a Turkish reformist and nationalist party that was founded in the latter part of the 19th century and was the dominant political party in Turkey in the period 1908–18.

Zeitgeist – "Spirit of the Time"

ENDNOTES
AND
FURTHER
REFERENCES

Chapter One Endnotes:

1. Berlin, Isaiah, *Liberty* (Oxford: Oxford University Press, 2002), 55.

2. *The White House,* www.whitehouse.gove/omb/budget/fy2006/pdf/tables.pdf (accessed October 5, 2006).

3. Rawls, John, *Theory of Justice* (USA: Harvard University Press, 1999), 118-123.

4. *Blackbox Voting,* www.blackboxvoting.org (accessed October 12, 2006).

5. Jaffa, H, Accretion; Lincoln scholar, unpublished raw data.

6. Balakian, Peter, *The Burning Tigris: The Armenian Genocide and America's Response* (New York: HarperCollins Publishers, 2003).

7. "Women's Suffrage," *American Memory, Library of Congress,* October, 2003, http://memory.loc.gov/ammem/awhhtml/awmss5/suffrage.html (accessed October 12, 2006).

8. Blackwell, Alice Stone, *Armenian Poems, Rendered into English Verse,* (Boston: Atlantic Printing Company, 1917).

9. *Armenian House, www.*armenianhouse.org; www.mith2.umd.edu (accessed October 13, 2006).

10. Biography Resource Center, "Biographies of Suffragists, Alice Stone Blackwell," (October, 2003), *University of Rochester,* http://www.rochester.edu/SBA/biographies.html (accessed October 13, 2006).

11. This statement is a simplification of major points from Christian beliefs. Not all sects agree with this position but it helps illustrate how people view human nature.

12. This statement is a simplification of major points from Buddhist beliefs. Not all groups agree with this position but it helps illustrate how people view human nature.

13. Robert Dahl, *Democracy and Its Critics* (Conn: Yale University Press, 1989).

14. Roskin, M., *Countries and Concepts, Politics, Geography, Culture* 9th ed., (New Jersey: Prentice Hall, 2006). The illustrations for the Parliamentary and Presidential systems can be found on page 38 and the illustration for the French system or the semi-presidential system is found on page 103.

15. Kekic, Laza, "A Pause in Democracy's March," *The Economist,* 2007 print edition, used by permission.

16. Roskin, Michael, *Countries and Concepts, Politics, Geography, Culture*, 9th ed., New Jersey: Prentice Hall, 2006), 1-3.

17. *Sacred Text,* http://sacred-texts.com/cla/ari/pol/index.htm (accessed October 13, 2006); Jowett, Benjamin, "The Politics of Aristotle" translation, book 4, in Ball & Daggers, *Political Ideologies and the Democratic Ideal,* 5th ed, chapter 2, (New Jersey: Prentice Hall, 2006).

18. Ball & Daggers, *Political Ideologies and the Democratic Ideal,* 5th ed, chapter 2, (New Jersey: Prentice Hall, 2006).

19. Amendment VI: right to a speedy and public trial before an impartial jury, to cross-examine witnesses, and to have counsel; Amendment VII: Right to a trial by jury in civil suits.20. Ball & Daggers, *Political Ideologies and the Democratic Ideal,* 5th ed, chapter 2, (New Jersey: Prentice Hall, 2006).

21. Lexington, "An odd bunch," *The Economist*, January 13, 2007, p. 32.

22. Ibid.

Chapter Two Endnotes:

1. *Congresspedia,* "Presidential Signing Statements," http://www.sourcewatch.org/index.php?title=Presidential_signing_statements (accessed December 30, 2006).

2. *United States Department of Justice*, "The Legal Significance of Presidential Signing Statements," November 3, 1993, http://www.usdoj.gov/olc/signing.htm (accessed December 30, 2006).

3. *The American Bar Association,* "Blue Ribbon Task Force Finds President Bush's Signing Statements Undermine Separation of Powers," July 24, 2006, http://www.abanet.org/media/releases/news072406.html (accessed 4 January 2007).

4. *Washington State University,* http://www.wsu.edu/~dee/GLOSSARY/DIVRIGHT.HTM (accessed October 28, 2006).

5. Matthew 6:20-21, "But store up for yourselves treasures in heaven, where moth and rust do not destroy, and where thieves do not break in and steal. For where your treasure is, there your heart will be also."

6. Author's opinion that *The Prince* was written as Machiavelli's way of venting.

7. Parliament granted freedom of worship to "dissenters" or Protestants.

8. *Boston Massacre Historical Society*, "The Boston Massacre Timeline," http://:www.bostonmassacre.net/timeline.htm (accessed January 23, 2007); Patterson, Thomas, *We the People*, (San Francisco: Von Hoffmann Press, 2004); Davidson, James West, *Nation of Nations*, (San Francisco: McGraw-Hill Company, 2006).

9. Margaret Conrad and Alvin Finkel, *Canada: A National History*, (Toronto: Longman, 2002)

10. Tindall, George Brown, *America: A Narrative History*, (New York: Norton, 1988), 207-208.

11. Evans, Sarah M., *Born for Liberty: A History of Women in America*, (New York: Free Press, 1997); John Hope Franklin and Alfred A. Moss, Jr., *From Slavery to Freedom*, (New York: Knopf, 1967).

12. Gary B Nash and Julie Roy Jeffrey, *The American People, Creating a Nation and a Society*, (Menlo Park: Addison Wesley Longman, Inc, 2000).

13. Smith, Jessie Carney, *Black Firsts: 2,000 Years of Extraordinary Achievement*, (Canton: Visible Ink Press, 2003).

14. Gary B. Nash and Julie Roy Jeffrey, *The American People; Creating a Nation and a Society*, (Menlo Park: Addison Wesley Longman, Inc, 2000).

15. Ibid.

16. Harrigan, John, *Empty Dreams, Empty Pockets: Class and Bias in American Politics*, 2nd ed, chapter 2, (New York: Longman, 2000).

17. Lutz, Donald S., *The Self-Guiding Republic: Popular Consent and Popular Control, 1776-1789*, Introduction, (Oxford: Oxford Journals, 1978).

18. Edward Greenberg and Benjamin Page, *The Struggle for Democracy*, 7th ed, (New York: Longman, 2005).

19. Holton, Woody, "From the Labours of Others, The War Bonds Controversy and the Origins of the Constitution in New England," *The William and Mary Quarterly*, 61. no. 2, April, 2004, http://www.historycooperative.org/cgi-bin/justtop.cgi?act=justtop&url=http://www.historycooperative.org/journals/wm/61.2/holton.html (accessed January 11, 2007).

20. Beard, Charles A. *An Economic Interpretation of The Constitution of The United States*, (New York: The Macmillan Company, 1913, 1935, & 1941).

21. Calliope Film Resources, Shays' Rebellion." Copyright 2000 CFR, www.calliope.org/shays/shays2.html (accessed on January 1, 2007); Minor, G.R., *History of the Insurrections in Massachusetts in the Year 1786, and the Rebellion Consequent Thereon*, (Boston, 1810); Holland, Josiah G., *History of Western Massachusetts*, 2 vols, (Springfield, 1855); Bowen, Catherine Drinker, *Miracle at Philadelphia: The Story of the Constitutional Convention*, May to September 1787, (Boston: Little, Brown & Co., 1966.); Conrad, Randall, *A Captain with the Insurgents': Jason Parmenter of Bernardston*, in Martin Kaufman, ed., *Shays' Rebellion: Selected Essays*, (Westfield: Institute for Massachusetts Studies, 1987); Henritta, James A., *The Evolution of American Society, An Interdisciplinary Analysis*, 1700-1815, (Lexington: Heath & Co., 1973).

22. *Library of Congress*, http://memory.loc.gov/ammem/collections/madison_papers/index.html (accessed October 13, 2006).

23. *The Charters of Freedom, The National Archives*, "America's Founding Father," January, 16, 2007, www.archives.gov (accessed October 23, 2006).

24. *The Federalist Papers*, Numbers 10, 51, & 78 (see appendix).

25. *The Progressive Magazine*, April 1999.

26. This section is based on the research of Dr. Christian Søe; Roskin, Michael, *Countries and Concepts, Politics, Geography, Culture*, 9th ed., (New Jersey: Prentice Hall, 2006).

27. Articles 3 & 4, *Annual Editions Comparative Politics Reader*, 2000/2001.

28. Roskin, Michael, *Countries and Concepts, Politics, Geography, Culture.*, 9th ed., chapter 2, (New Jersey: Prentice Hall, 2006).

29. In late fall of 2006, MSNBC's Matt Lauer was the first to call the war in Iraq a civil war. The Bush administration and other major networks have maintained that it is not a civil war but merely "sectarian violence." The semantics and language of this 'war on terror' has been a subject of controversy in the media and among the American public.

30. Roskin, Michael, *Countries and Concepts, Politics, Geography, Culture*, 9th ed., chapter 3, (New Jersey: Prentice Hall, 2006).

31. W.S. Gilbert and Arthur Sullivan, *The Pirates of Penzance or The Slave of Duty*, (New York, 1879).

Chapter Three Endnotes:

1. Dillon, Sam, "Schools Cut Back Subjects to Push Reading and Math," *New York Times*, March 26, 2006, http://www.nytimes.com/2006/03/26/education/26child.html?ex=1301029200&en=2ac2867806003319&ei=5090&partner=rssuserland&emc=rss (accessed 26 January 2007); National Education Association, "No Child Left Behind: State Legislative Watchlist," April, 2005, http://www.fairtest.org/nattest/NEA_NCLB_leg_watch.pdf (accessed 27 January 2007); Smith, Sam, "Teachers, Parents Lining Up to Dump No Child Left Behind," *Susan Ohanian*, December 20, 2006, http://www.susanohanian.org/show_nclb_outrages.html?id=2502 (accessed 27 January 2007); The U.S. Constitution Online, "Constitutional Topic: Federalism," http://www.usconstitution.net/consttop_fedr.html (accessed January 26, 2007); U.S. Department of Education, "No Child Left Behind,"

January 8, 2002, http://www.ed.gov/nclb/landing.jhtml?src=ln (accessed 26 January 2007).

2. Quoted in the notes of Judge Yates, Speech to the Constitutional Convention concerning the United States Senate, June 18, 1787.

3. Gradzins, Morton, "The Federal System," in *Goals for Americans: The Report of the President's Commission on National Goals* (Englewood Cliffs: Prentice-Hall, 1960), 365-366.

4. Noble, C, *Welfare as We Knew It, A Political History of the American Welfare State*, (New York: Oxford University Press, 1997), 39 – 42, 47 – 49.

5. Walker, David B., *Toward a Functioning Federalism* (Cambridge: Winthrop, 1981), 68, 79.

6. Schulman, Bruce, "The Great Society," in *Lyndon B. Johnson and American Liberalism*, 2 ed, (Boston: Bedford/St. Martin's, 2007), 87-110.

7. *CNN,* http://money.cnn.com/2004/04/07/news/fortune500/walmart_inglewood/ (accessed November 5, 2006).

8. Massachusetts, Division of Health Care Finance and Policy- www.mass.gov/Eeohhs2/docs/dhcfp/pdf/50+_ees_ph_assist.pdf and the accompanying spreadsheet at www.mass.gov/Eeohhs2/docs/dhcfp/pdf/50+_ees_ph_assist_ss.pdf; state employee figures from www.walmartfacts.com, (accessed November 7, 2006).

9. Huber, Walt, "Early History and the Federal Government," in *California State and Local Governments in Crisis*, 4 ed. (Covina: Educational Textbook Company, 2000), 26-31.

10. "High Court Hears Texas Redistricting Case." Interview by Nina Totenberg. *National Public Radio, Morning Edition*, March 1, 2006, www.npr.org, (accessed November 5, 2006).

11. "Howard Jarvis Taxpayers Association," http://www.hjta.org, (accessed November 15, 2006).

12. Budget Process, *Orange County Auditor/Control*, http://www.ac.ocgov.com/cam1_36/a2.asp#1_1 (accessed November 5, 2006).

13. *The White House*, http://www.whitehouse.gov/news/releases/2003/10/images/20031016-3_govelect-515h.html (accessed November 12, 2006).

14. *California Department of Education*, http://www.cde.ca.gov/, (accessed November 15, 2006).

15. Based on the research of Dr. Christian Søe; Roskin, M, (2006). *Countries and Concepts, Politics, Geography, Culture*. 9th ed., (New Jersey: Prentice Hall, 2006), Chapter 13.

Chapter Four Endnotes:

1. "O'Reilly: Young Americans 'have no idea what's going on' because they 'get their news from Jon Stewart," *Media Matters for America*, 25 May 2006, http://mediamatters.org/items/200605250003 (accessed 29 January 2007); Rothstein, Betsy. "Capital Living: Jon Who? The Daily What?" *The Hill*, September 21, 2005, http://www.hillnews.com/thehill/export/TheHill/Features/CapitalLiving/092105.html (accessed January 29, 2007)

2. http://www.ideafinder.com/history/inventions/story039.htm (accessed November 15, 2006).

3. Jefferson, Thomas, *Going Public*, in Samuel Kernell, (Washington: Congressional Quarterly Press, 1993), 94.

4. http://www.smplanet.com/imperialism/remember.html (accessed November 23, 2006).

5. Ibid.

6. http://www.ssa.gov/history/cough.html (accessed November 23, 2006).

7. http://www.whitehouse.gov/news/releases/2002/02/20020214-5.html (accessed November 23, 2006).

8. *Pew Research Center for People and the Press*, http://people-press.org June 2000, (accessed November 25, 2006).

9. "Cable and Internet Loom Large in Fragmented Political News Universe—Perceptions of Partisan Bias Seen as Growing, Especially by Democrats," January 11, 2004, http://people-press.org/reports/display.php3?ReportID=200, (accessed November 25, 2006).

10. Ibid, 234-5.

11. McGrath, D. and Smith, D., *Professor Wellstone Goes to Washington*, (Minneapolis: University of Minnesota Press), 1995.

12. ABC/Gallup Polling, June 2003 and January 2007.

13. Kennedy, J. Michael, "Schwarzenegger Cracks Jokes on Leno Show as Angelides Fumes," *Los Angeles Times, California Metro*, Part B, 5, October 12, 2006.

14. "Presidential Campaign Slogans, U.S. Presidents," http://www.presidentsusa.net/campaignslogans.html (accessed January 28, 2007).

15. Home Box Office (HBO), *Mr. Conservative: Goldwater on Goldwater*, December 2006.

16. Fairness Doctrine, U.S. Broadcasting Policy, "The Museum of Broadcast Communications," *Museum TV,* http://www.museum.tv/archives/etv/F/htmlF/fainessdoct/fairness.htm (accessed January 28, 2007).

17. U.S. Supreme Court Archives, *Red Lion Broadcasting Co. v. FCC, 395 U.S. 367*, (1969).

18. Healy, Jon, "Provisions: Telecommunications Act," *CQ Weekly*, February 17, 1996.

19. New Content, WGBH Educational Foundation, *Public Broadcasting* by *WGBH*, © 2002-2003 PBS/WGBH, PBS Online, WGBH, ©1997-2002, (accessed May 27, 2007). http://www.pbs.org/wgbh/amex/presidents/26_t_roosevelt/psources/ps_muckrake.html.

20. Moyers, Bill, Excerpt From Moyers Address to the National Conference on Media Reform, *Democracy Now!*, St. Louis., May 16, 2005.

21. Ibid.

22. Based on the research of Dr. Christian Søe; Roskin, Michael, *Countries and Concepts, Politics, Geography, Culture*, 9th ed, (New Jersey: Prentice Hall, 2006), chapters 18-22.

23. "Ukraine Opposition Leader Victim Of Poisoning," *Public Broadcasting System PBS*, http://www.pbs.org/newshour/extra/features/july-dec04/ukraine_12-15.html (accessed May 28, 2007).

24. "Another killing in Moscow," October 10, 2006, *The New York Times*, www.researchnavigator.com, (accessed, May 28, 2007).

25. "Theater Honours Hostage Victims,"http://news.bbc.co.uk/1/hi/world/europe/2435149.stm, (accessed May 28, 2007); Gorst, Isabel, "Yukos Cairman Eyes Russian Presidency," *Financial Times*, May 16, 2007, www.financialtimes.com, (accessed February 25, 2007).

Chapter Five Endnotes:

1. *Choice USA*, "South Dakota Abortion Ban Threatens Women," November 2, 2006, http://choiceusa.org/about/press.php?id=219 (accessed 13 January 2007).

2. *CNN*, "America Votes 2006: State Races, South Dakota," http://www.cnn.com/ELECTION/2006//pages/results/states/SD/index.html (accessed 12 January 2007).

3. *Online News Hour*, "South Dakota Abortion Ban," March 3, 2006, http://www.pbs.org/newshour/bb/law/jan-june06/abortion_3-03.html (accessed 13 January 2007).

4. *South Dakota State Legislature*, "HB 1215," http://legis.state.sd.us/sessions/2006/bills/HB1215enr.htm (accessed 15 January 2007).

5. American Anthropological Association, "Official Statement on Race" *Newsletter*, (1997): 38:6.

6. Who We Are, "People For the American Way Foundation Celebrates More Than 25 Years," *People For the American Way*, http://www.pfaw.org/pfaw/general/default.aspx?oid=21156 (accessed 16 June 2007).

7. "Right Wing Watch, Right Wing Organizations, Christian Coalition of America," *People for the American Way*, September, 2006, http://www.pfaw.org/pfaw/general/default.aspx?oid=4307. (accessed 16 June 2007).

8. "About Us, Christian Coalition of America," *Christian Coalition, of America*, http://www.cc.org/about.cfm (accessed 16 June 2007).

9. Christian Coalition of America Legislative Agenda, "Attempting to Get a Vote on a Federal Marriage Amendment," "Keeping Votes for Human Embryonic Stem Cell Destruction Research Bill to a Minimum, " *Christian Coaltion of America*, http://www.cc.org/issues.cfm, (accessed 15 June 2007).

10. Cummins, Jim, "I'm Not Just a Coloring Person: Cognitive Engagement and Identity Investment in Multilingual Classrooms," 38th Annual CATESOL Conference, San Diego, California, 2007.

11. Center for American Women and Politics, "Gender Gap," *Center for American Women in Politics*, www.cawp.rutgers.edu/Facts5.html (accessed 2 February 2007).

12. Ibid.

13. Walter Cronkite School of Journalism and Mass Communication, "Biography of Walter Cronkite," *Arizona State University*, http://cronkite.asu.edu/walter/waltercronkite.html (accessed 15 June 2007).

14. Auster, Albert, "Cronkite, Walter: U.S. Broadcast Journalist," *Museum of Broadcast Communications*, http://www.museum.tv/archives/etv/C/htmlC/cronkitewal/cronkitewal.htm, (accessed 16 June 2007).

15. Clark, Leslie, "American Masters: Walter Cronkite," *Public Broadcasting System*, 2006, http://www.pbs.org/wnet/americanmasters/database/cronkite_w.html (accessed 16 June 2007).

16. *National Public Radio*, "Walter Cronkite, NPR Biography, " http://www.npr.org/templates/story/story.php?storyId=5512510 (accessed 16 June 2007).

17. Exit Polls, *Exit Poll*, http://www.exit-poll.net/election-night/exitpollsystem.htmp, (accessed January 27, 2007).

18. Johnson, Hans, "How Many Californians? A Review of Population Projections for the State," *California Counts*, *Public Policy Institute of California*, Vol. 1, October 1999, 1.

19. Kakihara, S. "Influence of Attitudes and Strategies on English Acquisition by Japanese Women," *The CATESOL Journal*, Vol. 18, no. 1, (2006): 110.

20. *All About Switzerland*, "Switzerland's Four National Languages: which official languages do they speak in Switzerland?" http://www.all-about-switzerland.info/swiss-population-languages.html (accessed May 13, 2007).

21. Erichsen, G., "Spain's Linguistic Diversity, Introduction to Spain's Other Languages," *About, Inc. A part of the New York Times Company*, http://spanish.about.com/library/weekly/aa050701a.htm, . (accessed May 13, 2007).

22. "The Languages of South Africa," *South Africa, Alive with Possibility, the Official Gateway*, http://www.southafrica.info/ess_info/sa_glance/demographics/language.htm (accessed May 13, 2007).

23. Walt Wolfram and Christian D. Adger, "*Oral Language Instruction, Dialects in Schools and Communities*, (Florence: Lawrence Erlbaum Associates, 2007), 113.

24. Guthrie, Woody, "This Land is Your Land," *Scoutsongs*, http://www.scoutsongs.com/lyrics/boyscoutsofamerica.html (accessed 14 June 2007).

25. Based on the research of Dr. Christian Søe; Roskin, Michael, *Countries and Concepts, Politics, Geography, Culture*, 8th ed., (New Jersey: Prentice Hall, 2004), chapter 29.

26. "I am Prepared to Die," *African National Congress*, April 20, 1964, http://www.anc.org.za/ancdocs/history/rivonia.html (accessed 15 June 2007).

27. "Nelson Rolihlahla MANDELA," *African National Congress*, http://www.anc.org.za/people/mandela.html (accessed June 15, 2007).

28. "Nelson Mandela: The Nobel Peace Prize 1993," *Nobel Prize*, http://nobelprize.org/nobel_prizes/peace/laureates/1993/mandela-bio.html (accessed June 15, 2007).

Chapter Six Endnotes:

1. "About EMILY's List," *EMILY's List*, http://www.emilyslist.org/about/ (accessed 14 January 2007).

2. "Sourcewatch: Moral Majority," *Moral Majority*, http://www.moralmajority.us (accessed June 19, 2007);
   The Center for Media and Democracy, "Online NewsHour: Religion and Politics,"
   http://www.sourcewatch.org/index.php?title=Moral_Majority (accessed June 17, 2007);
   Public Broadcasting System, "Issues: Religion and Politics, "
   October 25, 2004, http://www.pbs.org/newshour/bb/politics/july-dec04/religion_10-25.html (accessed 17 June 2007);
   The Pew Forum, http://pewforum.org/religion-politics/ (accessed 17 June 2007).

3. Silverstein, K., "Their Men in Washington, Undercover with D.C.'s Lobbyists for Hire," *Harpers Magazine*, July 2007.

4. Ibid.

5. Ibid.

6. Ibid.

7. Ibid.

8. Bush, Matt, "McCain Criticizes Wasteful Spending in Memphis Speech," WCSH 6 Portland, April 17, 2007, http://www.wcsh6.com/news/article.aspx?storyid=57977 (accessed 17 June 2007).

9. "John McCain," *Eventful*, December 19, 2006, http://eventful.com/performers/P0-001-000016098-5 (accessed 17 June 2007).

10. "A Lifetime of Service," *John McCain 2008 Campaign*, http://www.johnmccain.com/About/johnmccain.htm (accessed 17 June 2007).

11. United States Senate, "U.S. Senator John McCain, Arizona," http://mccain.senate.gov/about/index.cfm?ID=10 (accessed 17 June 2007).

12. *Secretary of State*, http://www.sos.ca.gov/executive/press_releases/2006/06_088.pdf (accessed June 17, 2007).

13. *Humboldt University*, http://humboldt.edu/~cga/calatlas (accessed 17 June 2007).

14. http://pub.csea.com/cseahome/ (accessed 17 June 2007).

15. http://www.sos.ca.gov/executive/press_releases/2006/06_088.pdf (accessed June 17, 2007)

16. Based on the research of Dr. Christian Soe; Roskin, Michael, *Countries and Concepts, Politics, Geography, Culture*, 9th ed., (New Jersey: Prentice Hall, 2006), chapters 23-27; Rolf Theen and Frank Wilson, general introduction to Japan's political system; Christopher, Robert, *The Japanese Mind*; Johnson, Chalmers, *MITI and the Japanese Miracle*; von Wolferen, Karl, *The Enigma of Japanese Power: People and Politics in a Stateless Nation*.

17. *Hollyhock House*, http://www.vggallery.com/misc/search_frame.htm http://www.hollyhockhouse.net/index.htm (accessed 17 June 2007).

18. "Intelligence: Ministry of International Trade and Industry (MITI), *Global Security,*" April 26, 2005, http://www.globalsecurity.org/intell/world/japan/miti.htm (accessed 17 June 2007).

19. Government of Japan, "Introduction to METI." http://www.meti.go.jp/english/aboutmeti/data/a320001e.html (accessed 17 June 2007).

20. "The History of MITI and Conducting International Business in Japan," *University of Indiana,* http://www.indiana.edu/~ealc100/Group8/miti/miti.html (accessed 17 June 2007).

Chapter Seven Endnotes:

1. Merriam-Webster Online, "Evangelical," http://www.m-w.com/dictionary/evangelical (accessed 02 February 2007)

2. Allen, Bob, "Reagan Credited With Ushering In Religious Right," *Ethics Daily.com*, June 8, 2004, http://www.ethicsdaily.com/article_detail.cfm?AID=4282 (accessed February 1, 2007)

3. CNN.com, "Reagan's Supreme Court Choices Steer Conservative Path," June 2004, http://www.cnn.com/2004/LAW/06/07/supreme.court/ (accessed February 2, 2007).

4. "Perspectives: Ronald Reagan and the Religious Right," *Religion and Ethics Newsweekly*, June 11, 2004, http://www.pbs.org/wnet/religionandethics/week741/perspectives.html (accessed February 1, 2007).

5. South of the Border (Down Mexico Way). Words & Music by Jimmy Kennedy & Michael Carr. Recorded by Frank Sinatra, 1953.

6. Microsoft Encarta Encyclopedia Online, "Political Parties," 2007, http://encarta.msn.com/encyclopedia_761580668/Political_Parties.html (accessed June 18, 2007).

7. The Green Party Election Results, http://www.greens.org/elections/ (accessed June 18, 2007).

8. Dighe, Ranjit S., "The Historian's Wizard of Oz: Reading L. Frank Baum's Classic as a Political and Monetary Allegory," (Westport: Praeger Publishers, 2002).

9. CNN Online, "America Says Farewell to Barry Goldwater," *All Politics*, June 3, 1998, http://www.cnn.com/ALLPOLITICS/1998/06/03/goldwater/index.html (accessed June 17, 2007).

10. PBS Online, "Online Focus: Barry Goldwater," *Online NewsHour*, May 29, 1998, http://www.pbs.org/newshour/bb/remember/1998/goldwater_5-29a.html (accessed 17 June 2007).

11. United States Congress. "GOLDWATER, Barry Morris, 1909-1998." Biographical Directory of the United States Congress. http://bioguide.congress.gov/scripts/biodisplay.pl?index=G000267 (accessed 17 June 2007).

12. Microsoft Encarta Encyclopedia Online, "Political Parties in the United States," 2007, http://encarta.msn.com/encyclopedia_761558305/Political_Parties_in_the_United_States.html (accessed 17 June 2007).

13. United States House of Representatives, "Republican Contract with America," 1994, http://www.house.gov/house/Contract/CONTRACT.html (accessed June 17, 2007).

14. page 19, **Primary Reforms for the New Century** "thus locking in their party's victory in the general election...."

15. page 19, Proposition 198, was unconstitutional because it violated the political party's First Amendment right of association...."

16. http://www.sos.ca.gov/elections/elections_decline.htm (accessed June 18, 2007).

17. Based on the research of Dr. Christian Soe; Roskin, M. *Countries and Concepts, Politics, Geography, Culture*. 9th ed., (New Jersey: Prentice Hall, 2006) Chapter 33.

18. Organization of Petroleum Exporting Countries, http://www.opec.org/home/ (accessed June 26, 2007).

Chapter Eight Endnotes:

1. Geis, Sonya, "California Campaign in Turmoil Over Letters, Aide to GOP Candidate Sent Mailing Saying Immigrants Are Barred From Voting," *Washington Post*, October 20, 2006, http://www.washingtonpost.com/wp-dyn/content/article/2006/10/19/AR2006101901721.html (accessed 22 June 2007).

2. Ibid.

3. Wisckol, Martin, "Tan Nguyen Cleared by State Attorney General," *The Orange County Register,* May 17, 2007, http://www.ocregister.com/ocregister/homepage/abox/article_1697421.php. (accessed June 28, 2007).

4. Asian Pacific American Legal Center, "California: Asian American Organizations Condemn Anti-Latino Voter Intimidation in Orange County," *VoteTrustUSA.org*. October 31, 2006, http://www.votetrustusa.org/index.php?option=com_content&task=view&id=1949&Itemid=113 (accessed January 24 2007); California Secretary of State's Office, "California Secretary of State Bruce McPherson and Major Latino Organizations Send Official Election Letter Refuting Orange County Intimidation Letter," October 25, 2006,

http://www.ss.ca.gov/executive/press_releases/2006/06_161.pdf (accessed February 20 2007); Cavala, Bill, "Republican Campaigns Named As Source of Voter Intimidation in Orange County," *California Progress Report Online*, October 19, 2006, http://www.californiaprogressreport.com/2006/10/republican_camp.html (accessed 24 January 2007); MSNBC Online, "California GOP Wants Own Candidate to Withdraw," October 19, 2006. http://www.msnbc.msn.com/id/15329781 (accessed January 28, 2007); NBC4.TV, "Election Information Letter Sent Over Voter Intimidation," October25, 2006. http://www.nbc4.tv/news/10156618/detail.html?subid=10101581 (accessed February 2, 2007); People For the American Way Foundation, "People For the American Way Foundation to McPherson: Tell Naturalized Immigrants Their Votes Count," October 19, 2006, http://www.pfaw.org/pfaw/general/default.aspx?oid=22853 (accessed February 2, 2007); Santana, Norberto Jr., "Immigrant Voter Intimidation in Orange County: Legal or Illegal?," *NSHP.org*, October 18, 2006, http://www.nshp.org/legal/immigrant_voter_intimidation_in_orange_county_legal_or_illegal (accessed January 24, 2007).

5. CNN Online, "Extra! America Votes 2006 – Q & A," Education with Student News, October 25, 2006, http://www.cnn.com/2006/EDUCATION/10/24/extra.midterm.elections/index.html (accessed 02 July 2007);

6. National Governor's Association, "Governors' Political Affiliations & Terms of Office, 2007," February 2007, http://www.nga.org/Files/pdf/GOVLIST2007.PDF (accessed 02 July 2007).

7. U.S. Department of State, "Democracy: Frequently Asked Questions," *International Information Programs*, March 23, 2007, http://usinfo.state.gov/dhr/democracy/elections/elections_faq.html (accessed July 2, 2007).

8. "What is Democracy for America?," *Democracy for America,* http://www.democracyforamerica.com/about (accessed June 30, 2007).

9. "A 50 State Strategy," *The Democratic Party*, http://www.democrats.org/ (accessed June 30, 2007).

10. www.blackboxvoting.org (accessed March 23, 2007).

11. PBS Online, "The Presidents: Harry S. Truman," *American Experience*, http://www.pbs.org/wgbh/amex/presidents/33_truman/index.html (accessed July 1, 2007).

12. The Truman Presidential Museum and Library, "Biographical Sketch," http://www.trumanlibrary.org/hst-bio.htm (accessed July 1, 2007).

13. The White House, "Harry S. Truman," http://www.whitehouse.gov/history/presidents/ht33.html (accessed July 1, 2007).

14. Lyndon Baines Johnson Library and Museum, "President Lyndon B. Johnson's Biography," http://www.lbjlib.utexas.edu/johnson/archives.hom/biographys.hom/lbj_bio.asp (accessed June 1, 2007).

15. PBS Online, "The Presidents: Lyndon B. Johnson," *American Experience*, http://www.pbs.org/wgbh/amex/presidents/36_l_johnson/index.html (accessed June 1, 2007).

16. The White House, "Lyndon B. Johnson," http://www.whitehouse.gov/history/presidents/lj36.html (accessed 30 June 2007).

17. International Institute for Democracy and Electoral Assistance, "Turnout in the World, Country by Country Performance," http://www.idea.int/index.cfm (accessed July 5, 2007.

18. Ibid.

19. The Federal Election Commission, "Administering and Enforcing Federal Campaign Finance Laws," http://www.fec.gov/ (accessed July 2, 2007).

20. Cornell University Law School, "Subchapter I – Disclosure of Federal Campaign Funds." *U.S. Code Collection*, April 10, 2007, http://www4.law.cornell.edu/uscode/html/uscode02/usc_sup_01_2_10_14_20_I.html (accessed July 2, 2007).

21. Curphey, Shauna, "Sanchez Sisters to Make History in the House" *Women's eNews,* November 19, 2002, http://www.womensenews.org/article.cfm?aid=1114 (accessed July 6, 2007).

22. Roberts, Roxanne, "House Mates: Loretta and Linda Sanchez; Are Congress's First Sister Act. They Work Well Together. The Question Is, Can They Live Together?," *Washington Post*, December 12, 2002, http://www.washingtonpost.com/ac2/wp-dyn/A42823-2002Dec11 (accessed July 6, 2007).

23. Ibid.

24. Newton, Jim, *Justice for All*, (New York: Riverhead Books, 2006), Chapters 8 – 9.

25. Spencer, William, *The Middle East,* (Guilford: Dushkin Publishing Group, Inc, 1996), p. 52-61.

26. http://www.parstimes.com/history/historicalsetting.html#ancient_iran. (accessed July 2, 2007).

27. Roskin, Michael, *Countries and Concepts: Politics, Geography, Culture,* 9th ed. (New Jersey: Prentice Hall, 2006) Chapter 35, page 544.

28. Islamic Affairs Department. The Embassy of Saudi Arabia, 1989. *Understanding Islam and the Muslims*. The Embassy of Saudi Arabia, Washington, D.C.

29. http://www.parstimes.com/history/historicalsetting.html#ancient_iran (accessed July 2, 2007).

30. Ibid.

31. Spencer, William, *The Middle East,* (1996), p. 52-61.

32. Ibid.

33. http://www.parstimes.com/history/historicalsetting.html#ancient_iran (accessed July 2, 2007).

34. Seattle Times, Understanding the Conflict – The Region, "Interpreting veils," http://seattletimes.nwsource.com/news/nation-world/crisis/theregion/veils.html (accessed July 6, 2007).

35. Tait, Robert, "Iran's Fashion Police Put on a Show of Chadors to Stem West's Cultural Invasion," *The Guardian,* Iran Focus, July 14, 2006, http://www.iranfocus.com/modules/news/article.php?storyid=7910 (accessed July 6, 2007).

36. Spencer, William, *The Middle East,* (1996), p. 52-61.

37. http://www.parstimes.com/history/historicalsetting.html#ancient_iran (accessed July 2, 2007).

38. Spencer, William, *The Middle East,* (1996), p. 52-61.

39. Islamic Affairs Department. The Embassy of Saudi Arabia, 1989. *Understanding Islam and the Muslims*. The Embassy of Saudi Arabia, Washington, D.C.

40. Spencer, William, *The Middle East,* (1996), p. 52-61.

41. Ibid.

42. Ibid.

43. Ibid.

44. Macleod, Scott, "Iran's War Within." *Time*, March 26, 2007, pp. 44-47.

45. "Sailing into Troubled Waters." *The Economist*, April 7, 2007. pp. 23-25.

46. "Muzzling Dissent and Moving to a War Footing," *The Economist*, June 30, 2007. pp. 53-54.

Chapter Nine Endnotes:

1. *Feminist Majority Foundation*, "Nancy Pelosi Takes the Gavel, Makes Feminist History," January 2007, https://feminist.org/news/newsbyte/uswirestory.asp?id=10080 (accessed January 21, 2007).

2. *United States House of Representatives,* "Congresswoman Nancy Pelosi Biography," http://www.house.gov/pelosi/biography/bio.html (accessed January 21, 2007).

3. Ibid.

4. *Committee on Education and Labor, U.S. House of Representatives,* "Wage Increase is on the Way for Minimum Wage Workers," July 2007, http://edlabor.house.gov/micro/minimumwage.shtml (accessed July 10, 2007).

5. Mears, B., "High Court Upholds Most of Texas Redistricting Map: Districts that Diluted Latino Strength Tossed," June, 2007, *CNN Washington Bureau,* http://www.cnn.com/2006/POLITICS/06/28/scotus.texasredistrict/index.html (accessed July 9, 2007).

6. *Joe Lieberman United States senator,* "Welcome to My On-Line Office," http://lieberman.senate.gov/ (accessed July 12, 2007).

7. *The Constitution of the United States of America,* (1787), Article I.

8. *Medal Of Freedom*, "Presidential Medal of Freedom Recipient Thomas P. "Tip" O'Neill Jr.," http://www.medaloffreedom.com/ThomasONeill.htm (accessed July 3, 2007).

9. *Biographical Directory of the United States Congress*, "O'Neill, Thomas Phillip, Jr. (Tip), 1912-1994," http://bioguide.congress.gov/scripts/biodisplay.pl?index=O000098   (accessed July 3, 2007).

10. Tolchin, M., "Thomas P. O'Neill, Jr., A Democratic Power in the House for Decades, Dies at 81," *The New York Times: On This Day*, July, 1994, http://www.nytimes.com/learning/general/onthisday/bday/1209.html?adxnnl=1&adxnnlx=1183521668-nl0pVICupa29+60vMhnkRw (accessed July 3, 2007).

11. *Office of the Majority Leader Steny Hoyer,*" Steny Hoyer, Biography," http://www.majorityleader.gov/about_the_whip/about_steny_hoyer/bio.cfm (accessed July 11, 2007).

12. *House Majority Whip James E. Clyburn,* "About Majority Whip James E. Clyburn," http://majoritywhip.house.gov/about/ (accessed July 11, 2007).

13. Carr, T.P., "Party leaders in the House: Election, Duties, and Responsibilities," *CRS Report for Congress*, November, 2004 http://www.rules.house.gov/archives/RS20881.pdf (accessed July 13, 2007).

14. *Speaker Nancy Pelosi*, "About Nancy Pelosi. The Role of Speaker of the House," http://speaker.gov/about?id=0003 (accessed July 13, 2007).

15. Associated Press, Washington/Politics, "Frist Won't Criticize Cheney for Cursing in Senate," *USA Today*. June, 2004, http://www.usatoday.com/news/washington/legislative/2004-06-27-frist_x.htm (accessed July 12, 2007).

16. Ibid.

17. *The Constitution of the United States of America*, (1787), Article I., Section 7.

18. "Inquiry into Fired U.S. Attorneys," *National Public Radio*, http://www.npr.org/templates/story/story.php?storyId=7791372 (accessed July 13, 2007).

19. Day to Day, "Embattled Attorney General Gonzales Testifies," *National Public Radio*, April, 2007, http://www.npr.org/templates/story/story.php?storyId=9682539 (accessed July 13, 2007).

20. Associated Press in NPR, "Panel Moves Toward Holding Miers in Contempt," *National Public Radio*, July, 2007, http://www.npr.org/templates/story/story.php?storyId=11868980 (accessed July 13, 2007).

21. "Watergate: The scandal that brought down Richard Nixon," *Watergate*, http://www.watergate.info/ (accessed July 15, 2007.)

22. Munier, G, (2004), *Iraq, An Illustrated History And Guide* Massachusetts: Interlink Publishing Group, Inc.

23. Davis, C. (2003) *The Middle East for Dummies* (p.38). New Jersey: Wiley Publishing, Inc. Ibid. (p.39).

24. Munier, G. (2004). *Iraq An Illustrated History And Guide* (p. 15). Massachusetts: Interlink Publishing Group, Inc.

25. Ibid. (p. 26).

26. Ibid. (p.27).

27. Ibid. (pp. 28-29).

28. Davis, C. (2003) *The Middle East For Dummies* (p.162).

29. Ibid. (p.162).

30. Ibid. (p.163).

31. Ibid. (p. 164).

32. Ibid.

33. Davis, C. (2003) *The Middle East For Dummies* (p.164).

34. Munier, G. (2004). *Iraq An Illustrated History And Guide* (p. 41)..

35. Davis, C. (2003) *The Middle East For Dummies* (p.40).

36. "The Middle East - the History, the Cultures, the Conflicts, the Faiths," *Time, Inc.*, 2006, 50.

37. Clark, M. (2003). *Islam For Dummies* (p. 201). New Jersey: Wiley Publishing, Inc.

38. "The Middle East - the History, the Cultures, the Conflicts, the Faiths," *Time, Inc.*, 2006, 54.

39. Munier, G. (2004), *Iraq An Illustrated History And Guide* (p. 31).

40. Munier, G., *Iraq An Illustrated History And Guide* (p. 34).

41. Ibid. (p. 32).

42. "The Middle East - the History, the Cultures, the Conflicts, the Faiths," *Time, Inc.*, 2006, 98.

43. Davis, C. (2003) *The Middle East For Dummies* (pp.170-171).

44. "The Middle East - the History, the Cultures, the Conflicts, the Faiths," *Time, Inc.*, 2006, 89.

45. Ibid. (p. 98).

46. Ibid. (p. 110).

47. Ibid.

Chapter Ten Endnotes

1. Shearer, Mary L, "Who Is Victoria Woodhull?" *Victoria Woodhull.com*, October 27, 1999, http://victoria-woodhull.com/whoisvw.htm (accessed February 2, 2007).

2. Women in History Online, "Victoria Woodhull Biography," *Lakewood Public Library* http://www.lkwdpl.org/wihohio/wood-vic.htm (accessed February 2, 2007).

3. *Peace Corps*, www.peacecorps.gov (accessed on July 21, 2007).

4. *The Franklin D. Roosevelt Presidential Library and Museum*, http://www.fdrlibrary.marist.edu/fdrbio.html (accessed July 13, 2007).

5. "The Presidents: Franklin Delano Roosevelt," *The American Experience, PBS Online,*
   http://www.pbs.org/wgbh/amex/presidents/32_f_roosevelt/index.html (accessed July 13, 2007).

6. Franklin D. Roosevelt, *The White House,* http://www.whitehouse.gov/history/presidents/fr32.html (accessed July 13, 2007).

7. Deane, A., "US Presidency, Two-Term Limits On," *International Debate Education Association Online*, (May, 2003),
   http://www.idebate.org/debatabase/topic_details.php?topicID=211 (accessed July 14, 2007).

8. Politics: America Votes 2004, "Obama Projected to Gain Seat for Dems," *CNN Online*, November 2, 2004,
   http://www.cnn.com/2004/ALLPOLITICS/11/02/senate.illinois/index.html (accessed July 14, 2007).

9. "Meet Barack," *Obama '08 Online*, http://www.barackobama.com/about/ (accessed July 14, 2007).

10. The United States Senate, "About Barack Obama." *Barack Obama: U.S. Senator for Illinois*,
    http://obama.senate.gov/about/ (accessed July 14, 2007).

11. Feldmann, L., "Bush makes First Veto on Stem Cells," *Christian Science Monitor.* (July, 2006),
    http://www.csmonitor.com/2006/0720/p02s02-uspo.html (accessed July 19, 2007).

12. Office of the Press Secretary, "President Bush makes Remarks on the Emergency supplemental," *The White House,*
    http://www.whitehouse.gov/news/releases/2007/04/20070403.html (accessed July 19, 2007).

13. Dorf, Michael C, "A Brief History of Executive Privilege, From George Washington Through Dick Cheney," *Findlaw Online*, February 6, 2002,
    http://writ.news.findlaw.com/dorf/20020206.html (accessed July 14, 2007).

14. *The Constitution of the United States,* Article II. Section 1, (1787).

15. NARA Online, "What Is the Electoral College?," *U.S. Electoral College*, http://www.archives.gov/federal-register/electoral-college/about.html
    (accessed July 14, 2007).

16. Oyez Online, "Bush v Gore," *U.S. Supreme Court Media*, December 12, 2000, http://www.oyez.org/cases/2000-2009/2000/2000_00_949/
    (accessed July 14, 2007).

17. *The White House,* http://www.whitehouse. gov/government/cabinet.html (accessed May 15, 2007).

18. "2005 Special Statewide Election," *California Secretary of State, Debra Bowen,* November 8, 2005,
    www.sos.ca.gov/elections/sov/2005_special/contents.htm (accessed July 17, 2007).

19. "Crips Co-Founder Williams Put to Death," *National Public Radio*, http://www.npr.org/templates/story/story.php?storyId=5050214
    (accessed July 18, 2007).

20. Based on the research of Dr. Christian Soe; Roskin, Michael, "Countries and Concepts," 9th ed., (New Jersey: Prentice Hall: 2006).
    Chapters 7-11.

21. Associated Press. "French President Says No Mass Bastille Day Pardons Under His Regime," July 2007,
    http://www.iht.com/articles/ap/2007/07/08/europe/EU-GEN-France-Bastille-Pardons.php#top (accessed July 20, 2007).

22. Charles de Gaulle Online, "Biography," http://www.charles-de-gaulle.org/rubrique.php3?id_rubrique=82 (accessed July 16, 2007).

Chapter 11 Endnote

1. a."Hurricane Katrina Reports of Missing and Deceased,"*Louisiana Department of Health and Hospitals*, August 2, 2006,
   http://www.dhh.louisiana.gov/offices/page.asp?ID=192&Detail=5248 (accessed February 10, 2007); b."Katrina Day-by-Day Recap,"
   Palm Beach Post, http://www.palmbeachpost.com/storm/content/storm/2005/atlantic/katrina/day_by_day_archive.html
   (accessed February 9, 2007); c. "President Arrives in Alabama, Briefed on Hurricane Katrina," *The White House*, September 2, 2005,
   http://www.whitehouse.gov/news/releases/2005/09/20050902-2.html (accessed February 9, 2007).

2. "Franklin D. Roosevelt: 32nd President of the United States," *The Franklin D. Roosevelt Presidential Library and Museum*
   http://www.fdrlibrary.marist.edu/fdrbio.html (accessed 13 July 2007).

3. McKay, Dawn Rosenberg, "Civil Service Employment," *About.com, Career Planning*,
   http://careerplanning.about.com/od/occupations/a/civil_service.htm (accessed 15 July 2007).

4. Hall, Mimi, "Ex-Official Tells of Homeland Security Failures," *USA Today*, December 28, 2004,
   http://www.usatoday.com/news/washington/2004-12-27-homeland-usat_x.htm (accessed 15 July 2007).

5. Ibid.

6. Fessler, Pam, "Upcoming House Report on Katrina Details Failures," *National Public Radio,* February 13, 2006, http://www.npr.org/templates/story/story.php?storyId=5203365 (accessed July 17, 2007).

7. Hall, Mimi. "Ex-Official Tells of Homeland Security Failures." USA Today. 28 December 2004. http://www.usatoday.com/news/washington/2004-12-27-homeland-usat_x.htm (accessed 15 July 2007).

8. Higham, Scott and O'Harrow, Robert, Jr., "Homeland Security Disavows Document Touting Successes," *The Washington Post*, October 29, 2004, http://www.washingtonpost.com/wp-dyn/articles/A7445-2004Oct28.html (accessed 15 July 2007).

9. United States House of Representatives, "Hurricane Katrina Document Analysis: The E-Mails of Michael Brown," *Staff Report for Rep. Charles Melancon*, November 2, 2005. http://www.melancon.house.gov/SupportingFiles/Documents/AnalysisofBrownEmails.pdf (accessed 15 July 2007).

10. Safe and Free: Restore Our Constitutional Right, "Coalition Letter to Homeland Security Secretary Ridge Urging the Appointment of an Officer for Civil Rights and Civil Liberties," *American Civic Liberties Unions*, March 12, 2003, http://www.aclu.org/safefree/general/17358leg20030312.html (accessed 15 July 2007).

11. Privacy and Technology, "DHS Acknowledges That Terror Ranking Program Is Already in Effect, ACLU Says Program Violates Congressional Spending Ban and Public Notice Requirements," *American Civic Liberties Unions,* December 7, 2006. http://www.aclu.org/privacy/gen/27642prs20061207.html (accessed 15 July 2007).

12. Lydersen, Kari, "Despite Poor Civil Liberties Record, DHS Nominee Questioned Mildly." *Global Policy Forum*, February 3, 2005. http://www.globalpolicy.org/empire/terrorwar/liberties/2005/0203chertoff.htm (accessed July 15, 2007).

13. Ibid.

14. Eggen, Dan, "Dismissal of Lawsuit Against Warrantless Wiretaps Sought," January 26, 2007; page A05, http://www.washingtonpost.com/wp-dyn/content/article/2007/01/25/AR2007012501434.html (accessed July 21, 2007).

15. *Infoplease,* www.infoplease.com/ipa/A0760621.html (accessed January 1, 2007).

16. *White House,* www.whitehouse.gov/history/presidents/rn37.html (accessed January 1, 2007).

17. Hughes, Ken, ed., Miller Center of Public Affairs, University of Virginia.

18. Gerth, Jeff, "Price Limits Extended on Power," *New York Times,* June 19, 2001, http://www.nytimes.com/2001/06/19/national/19POWE.html?ex=1185508800&en=88be6088ed89f04f&ei=5070 (accessed July 22, 2003).

19. "Social Security Factsheet 2005; Social Security Trustees Report, 2005," *National Jobs for All Coalition*, 2005, http://www.njfac.org (accessed July 7, 2007).

20. This section is based on research by Dr. Christian Søe; Michael Roskin, *Countries and Concepts,* 9 ed., (New Jersey: Prentice Hall, 2006), chapters 2 – 6.

21. "Johnny Canuck." *Collections Canada,* www.collectionscanada.com, (accessed July 21, 2007).

22. Black, Naomi, "Macphail, Agnes Campbell," *The Canadian Encyclopedia*, http://www.thecanadianencyclopedia.com/index.cfm?PgNm=TCE&Params=A1ARTA0005013 (accessed 11 July 2007).

23. Historica Online, "Historica Minutes: Women: Agnes Macphail: Synopsis," History By The Minute, http://www.histori.ca/minutes/minute.do?id=10212 (accessed 11 July 2007).

24. Library and Archives Canada, "Agnes Campbell Macphail." *Celebrating Women's Achievements: Canadian Women in Government,* April 12, 2005, http://www.collectionscanada.ca/femmes/002026-826-e.html (accessed 11 July 2007).

Chapter Twelve Endnotes

1. America's Story from America's Library, "Leaders and Statesmen: Thurgood Marshall: A Career in Law," *The Library of Congress*, http://www.americaslibrary.gov/cgi-bin/page.cgi/aa/leaders/marshallthrgd/law_3 (accessed 10 February 2007); "Thurgood Marshall: Associate Justice, United States Supreme Court: Obituary," *Arlington National Cemetery,* January 25, 1993, http://www.arlingtoncemetery.net/tmarsh.htm (accessed February 9, 2007).

2. "About the Supreme Court," http://www.supremecourtus.gov/about/about.html, *United States Supreme Court*, (accessed July 28, 2007).

3. *Interfaith Alliance,* http://www.interfaithalliance.org/site/pp.asp?c=8dJIIWMCE&b=865787 (accessed July 28, 2007).

4. "Harriet E. Miers Profile," *Washington Post*, October 27, 2005, http://www.washingtonpost.com/wp-dyn/content/article/2005/10/03/AR2005100300305.html (accessed July 28, 2007).

5. "Earl Warren Biography, Jurist/Political Figure," *Infoplease,* www.Infoplease.com (accessed July 27, 2007).

6. "Landmark Supreme Court Cases," *Supreme Court Historical Society,* 2002, www.landmarkcases.org

7. Ibid.

8. "United States – Amicus Curiae Briefs," *American Law Sources,* June 15, 2007, http://www.lawsource.com/also/usa.cgi?usb (accessed July 14, 2007).

9. "Amicus Curiae," *Tech Law Journal*, 2005, http://www.techlawjournal.com/glossary/legal/amicus.htm (accessed July 14, 2007).

10. "Judicial Activism," *WordReference*, http://www.wordreference.com/definition/judicial%20activism.htm (accessed March 19, 2005).

11. Marshall, John, "Marbury v. Madison: 5 U.S. 137," *A Patriot's Handbook,* Ed. Caroline Kennedy, (New York: Hyperion 2003). 145-146.

12. Meese, Edwin III, DeHart, Rhett, "The Imperial Judiciary...and What Congress Can Do About It." *Policy Review 81, Research Library Core. ProQuest*, (1997): 54-60 (accessed 19 March 2005).

13. Dorf, Michael C, "They Are All Activists Now," *FindLaw,* May 1, 2000, http://writ.findlaw.com/dorf/20000501.html (accessed 11 March 2005).

14. "National Association for the Advancement of Colored People or NAACP, an interracial membership organization, founded in 1909, that is devoted to civil rights and racial justice," *Africana Online Black History*, http://www.africanaonline.com/orga_naacp.htm (accessed 14 July 2007).

15. "Timeline, The NAACP IS Today 2006," *NAACP,* http://www.naacp.org/about/history/timeline/index.htm (accessed 14 July 2007).

16. Ovington, Mary White, "How NAACP Began," *NAACP,* 1914, http://www.naacp.org/about/history/howbegan/ (accessed 14 July 2007).

17. Rosen, Jeffrey. "Roberts Rules," *The Atlantic Monthly,* January/February 2007, (accessed July 27, 2007).

18. Nieves, Evelyn, "South Dakota Abortion Bill Takes Aim at *Roe,* Senate Ban Does Not Except Rape, Incest," *Washington Post*, February 23, 2006, A01.

19. "Selected Historic Decisions of the U.S. Supreme Court," *Cornell School of Law,* http://www.law.cornell.edu/supct/html/historics/USSC_CR_0496_0310_ZS.html (accessed July 29, 2007).

20. "The Patriot Act: Where It Stands," *American Civil Liberties Union*,   http://action.aclu.org/reformthepatriotact/whereitstands.html (accessed 10 February 2007).

21. "USA Patriot Act," *American Civil Liberties Union,* November 14, 2003, http://www.aclu.org/safefree/resources/17343res20031114.html (accessed February 10, 2007).

22. Rosen, Jeffrey. "Roberts Rules," *The Atlantic Monthly,* January/February 2007, (accessed July 27, 2007). .

23. "Biographical Outline of Dr. Martin Luther King, Jr.," *The King Center*, 2004, http://www.thekingcenter.com/mlk/bio.html (accessed 15 July 2007).

24. King Encyclopedia Online. "March on Washington for Jobs and Freedom." http://www.stanford.edu/group/King/about_king/encyclopedia/march_washington.html (accessed 15 July 2007).

25. King, Michael L, "Martin Luther, Jr King Biography (1929–68)," *Biography*, http://www.biography.com/search/article.do?id=9365086 (accessed 15 July 2007).

26. White, Jack E, "Martin Luther King: He led a mass struggle for racial equality that doomed segregation and changed America forever." *Time: The Time 100*. April 13, 1998 http://www.time.com/time/time100/leaders/profile/king.html (accessed 15 July 2007).

27. "State of the Workplace 2005-2006," *The Human Rights Campaign Foundation.* June 29, 2006, http://www.hrc.org/Template.cfm?Section=Work_Life (accessed 10 February 2007).

28. "Voters Show Strong Support for Reproductive Rights and Minimum Wage," *The National Organization for Women*, November 9, 2006. http://www.now.org/issues/election/elections2006/ballotmeasures.html (accessed February 10, 2007).

29. The Supreme Court: Are Penalites Required in "Third Strike" Laws Too Cruel?" *Infoplease,* http://www.infoplease.com/cig/supreme-court/penalties-required-third-strike-laws-too-cruel.html (accessed July 27, 2007).

30. Burress, Charles, "Berkeley: Low Minority Admissions Anger UC's Student Recruiters: They Demand That Campus Improve Diversity Programs," *San Francisco Chronicle*, April 23, 2004, http://www.sfgate.com/cgi-bin/article.cgi?file=/chronicle/archive/2004/04/23/BAGJM69TRH1.DTL (accessed July 14, 2007).

31. "209: Prohibition Against Discrimination or Preferential Treatment by State and Other Public Entities. Initiative Constitutional Amendment," *The California Secretary of State,* 1996, http://vote96.sos.ca.gov/Vote96/html/BP/209.htm (accessed July 14, 2007).

32. Focus, "Supreme Court Update: NewsHour Transcript," *Public Broadcast System,* November 3, 1997, http://www.pbs.org/newshour/bb/law/july-dec97/scotus_11-3.html (accessed 14 July 2007).

33. Weiss, Kenneth R. "Applications to UC Hit A Record High: But the number of African Americans and Latinos seeking admission falls for second year in a row," *Los Angeles Times,* (via UCSB AAD project), February 5, 1997, http://aad.english.ucsb.edu/docs/UC-apps.html (accessed July 14, 2007).

34. Based on the research of Dr. Christian Søe.

35. Based on the research of Dr. Christian Søe and Michael Roskin, *Countries and Concepts*, 9 ed., chapter 1.

36. Ibid.

37. *Central Intelligence Agency The World Factbook,* www.cia.gov/library/publicactions/the-world-factbook/index (accessed March 25, 2007).

38. "International Court of Justice," *Answers*, http://www.answers.com/topic/international-court-of-justice?cat=biz-fin (accessed July 15, 2007).

39. "The Case: The International Court of Justice in The Hague," *Liechtenstein-ICJ-Case*, 2004, http://www.liechtenstein-icj-case.de/en_fall/82.html (accessed 15 July 2007).

40. "The Memory of Tiananmen 1989," *Public Broadcasting System,* www.PBS.org, (accessed January 17, 2007).

41. "China From The Inside," *Public Broadcasting System,* 2005, www.PBS.org

42. Research for this timeline was drawn from FRONTLINE's reporting for the "The Tank Man," its previous 1996 program "The Gate of Heavenly Peace," and *The Tiananmen Papers*, published in 2001 and edited by Andrew J. Nathan and Perry Link.

43. "Chief Justice's Year-End Reports on the Federal Judiciary," *Supreme Court of the United States,* http://www.supremecourtus.gov/publicinfo/year-end/year-endreports.html (accessed July 25, 2007).

Further References

Annual Editions: Comparative Politics. ed. Christian Søe, 23, 24 ed. Dubuque: McGraw-Hill/Dushkin, 2005, 2006.

Aristotle,. *Politics*. trans. C.D.D. Reeve, Indianapolis: Hackett, 1998.

Ball, Terence, and Richard Dagger. *Political Ideologies and the Democratic Ideal*. 6 ed. New York: Longman, 2006.

Barber, Benjamin R. *Jihad vs. McWorld*. 2 ed. New York: Ballantine Books, 2001.

Ben-Ami, Shlomo. *Scars of War, Wounds of Peace: The Israeli-Arab Tragedy*. New York: Oxford University Press, 2006.

Berman, Larry, and Bruce Allen Murphy. *Approaching Democracy*. Portfolio ed. New Jersey: Prentice Hall, 2008.

Blainey, Geoffrey. *The Causes of War*. 3 ed. New York: The Free Press, 1988.

Caputi, Mary. *Voluptuous: A Feminist Theory of the Obscene*. Lanham: Rowman and Littlefield, 1994.

Carr, Edward Hallett. *The Twenty Years' Crisis, 1919-1939*. New York: Harper Torchbooks, 1964.

Conrad, David et al. *Germany's New Politics*. Providence: Berghahn Books, 1995.

Danforth, John. *Faith and Politics*. New York: Viking, 2006.

Danziger, James N. *Understanding the Political World*. 8 ed. New York: Longman, 2007.

Dean, John W. *Worse Than Watergate*. New York: Warner Books, 2004.

Dean, John W. *Conservatives Without Conscience*. New York: Viking, 2006.

The Deliberative Democracy Handbook. ed. John Gastil and Peter Levine, San Francisco: Wiley, 2005.

Dewey, John. *Democracy and Education*. New York: Free Press, 1944.

Dyck, Rand. *Canadian Politics*. 3 ed. Canada: Thomson/Nelson, 2006.

Euben, J. Peter. *Corrupting Youth*. New Jersey: Princeton University Press, 1997.

Fishkin, James S. *Democracy and Deliberation*. New Haven: Yale University Press, 1991.

Gardner, David. *The California Oath Controversy*. Berkeley: University of California, 1967.

Gerber, Elisabeth R. et al. *Stealing the Initiative: How State Government Responds to Direct Democracy*. New Jersey: Prentice Hall, 2001.

The Global Resurgence of Democracy. ed. Larry Diamond and Marc F. Plattner, Baltimore: Johns Hopkins University Press, 1993.

Goldstein, Joshua S., and Jon C. Pevehouse. *International Relations*. 7 ed. New York: Longman, 2006.

Green, Duncan. *Faces of Latin America*. London: Latin American Bureau, 1991.

Greenberg, Edward S., and Benjamin I. Page. *The Struggle for Democracy*. 7 ed. New York: Longman, 2005.

Grenberg, Gershom. *The Accidental Empire: Israel and the Birth of Settlements, 1967-1977*. New York: Times Books, 2006.

Gutmann, Amy, and Dennis Thompson. *Why Deliberative Democracy?*. Princeton: Princeton University Press, 2004.

Habermas, Jurgen. *Critic in the Public Sphere*. trans. Robert C. Holub, New York: Routledge, 1991.

Hamada, Louis Bahjat. *Understanding the Arab World*. Nashville: Thomas Nelson, 1990.

Harrigan, John J. *Empty Dreams, Empty Pockets*. 2 ed. New York: Longman, 2000.

Huber, Walt. *California: State and Local Government in Crisis*. 4 ed. Covina: Educational Textbooks, 2000.

Jackson, Robert J. et al. *North American Politics: Canada, USA, and Mexico in a Comparative Perspective*. Toronto: Pearson/Prentice Hall, 2004.

Kuo, David. *Tempting Faith: An Inside Story of Political Seduction*. New York: Free Press, 2006.

Lipset, Seymour Martin. *American Exceptionalism: A Double-Edged Sword*. New York: W. W. Norton, 1996.

Lipset, Seymour Martin. *Continental Divide*. New York: Routledge, 1990.

Marcuse, Herbert. *One-Dimensional Man*. 2 ed. Boston: Beacon Press, 1991.

Markoff, John. *Waves of Democracy*. Thousand Oaks: Pine Forge Press, 1996.

Moyers, Bill. *Moyers on America: A Journalist and His Time*. ed. Julie Leinnger Pycior, New York: Anchor Books, 2005.

Nasr, Vali. *The Shia Revival*. New York: W. W. Norton & Company, 2006.

Newton, Jim. *Justice for All: Earl Warren and the Nation He Made*. New York: Riverhead Books, 2006.

O'Neill, Thomas "Tip", and William Novak. *Man of the House*. New York: St. Martins's Press, 1987.

Parenti, Michael. *Democracy for the Few*. 8 ed. Boston: Thomson/Wadsworth, 2008.

Pateman, Carole. *The Sexual Contract*. Stanford: Stanford University Press, 1988.

Plato,. *The Trial and Death of Socrates*. trans. G.M.A. Grube, 2 ed. Indianapolis: Hackett , 1975.

Plato,. *The Republic*. 2 ed. New York: Penguin Classics, 1987.

Rainey, Hal G. *Understanding & Managing Public Organizations*. 2 ed. San Francisco: Jossey-Bass Publishers, 1997.

Rawls, John. *Political Liberalism*. New York: Columbia University Press, 1993.

Rawls, John. *A Theory of Justice*. Revised ed. Cambridge: Harvard University Press, 1999.

Remington, Thomas F. *Politics in Russia*. 3 ed. New York: Pearson/Longman, 2004.

Roskin, Michael G. *Countries and Concepts: Politics, Geography, Culture*. 8, 9 ed. New Jersey: Prentice Hall, 2004, 2007.

Roskin, Michael G., and James J. Coyle. *Politics of the Middle East: Cultures and Conflicts*. New Jersey: Prentice Hall, 2004.

Savir, Uri. *The Process*. New York: Random House, 1998.

Schelling, Thomas C. *Arms and Influence*. New Heavan: Yale University Press, 1966.

Sloan, Richard P. *Blind Faith: The Unholy Alliance of Religion and Medicine*. New York: St. Martin's Press, 2006.

Taylor, Charles et al. *Multiculturalism*. New Jersey: Princeton University Press, 1994.

Third Wave Agenda: Being Feminist, Doing Feminism. ed. Leslie Heywood & Jennifer Drake, 2 ed. Minneapolis: University of Minnesota Press, 1999.

This page left blank intentionally.